In Their Own Words

In Their Own Words

Criminals on Crime: An Anthology

MICHAEL BIRZER
Wichita State University

PAUL CROMWELL
University of South Florida

SEVENTH EDITION

New York   Oxford

OXFORD UNIVERSITY PRESS

Oxford University Press is a department of the University of Oxford.
It furthers the University's objective of excellence in research,
scholarship, and education by publishing worldwide.

Oxford   New York
Auckland   Cape Town   Dar es Salaam   Hong Kong   Karachi
Kuala Lumpur   Madrid   Melbourne   Mexico City   Nairobi
New Delhi   Shanghai   Taipei   Toronto

With offices in
Argentina   Austria   Brazil   Chile   Czech Republic   France   Greece
Guatemala   Hungary   Italy   Japan   Poland   Portugal   Singapore
South Korea   Switzerland   Thailand   Turkey   Ukraine   Vietnam

© 2017, 2014, 2011 by Oxford University Press
© 2006 by Roxbury Publishing Company

For titles covered by Section 112 of the US Higher Education
Opportunity Act, please visit www.oup.com/us/he for the
latest information about pricing and alternate formats.

Published by Oxford University Press
198 Madison Avenue, New York, New York 10016
http://www.oup.com

Oxford is a registered trademark of Oxford University Press

Library of Congress Cataloging-in-Publication Data
Names: Birzer, Michael L., 1960- editor. | Cromwell, Paul F. editor.
Title: In their own words : criminals on crime : an anthology / Michael
   Birzer, Wichita State University, Paul Cromwell, University of South
   Florida.
Description: Seventh Edition. | New York : Oxford University Press, 2016. |
   Revised edition of In their own words, 2014.
Identifiers: LCCN 2016004415 | ISBN 9780190298272 (alk. paper)
Subjects: LCSH: Criminology--Fieldwork. | Crime--Research. |
   Criminals--Research.
Classification: LCC HV6030 .I488 2016 | DDC 364--dc23 LC record available
at https://lccn.loc.gov/2016004415

Printing number: 9 8 7 6 5 4 3 2 1

Printed in the United States of America
on acid-free paper

To the greatest joys of my life, my wife Gwynne and my son Michael Jr.

Michael Birzer

To my incredibly wonderful wife and best friend for the past 40 years

Paul Cromwell

TABLE OF CONTENTS

PREFACE xiii

ACKNOWLEDGMENTS xvii

ABOUT THE EDITORS xix

ABOUT THE CONTRIBUTORS xxi

SECTION I **DOING FIELDWORK WITH OFFENDERS**
Introduction 1

Chapter 1 **Researching Crack Dealers: Dilemmas and Contradictions** 5
Bruce A. Jacobs
Jacobs points out the inherent dangers associated with studying street criminals.

Chapter 2 **Consenting to Talk: Why Inmates Participate in Prison Research** 20
Heith Copes and Andy Hochstetler
Copes and Hochstetler discuss the motives of incarcerated offenders in their decision to discuss their crimes and behaviors with researchers.

SECTION II   CRIMINAL LIFESTYLES
            AND DECISION MAKING
            Introduction   35

Chapter 3   **Deciding to Commit a Burglary**   37
             Richard T. Wright and Scott H. Decker
             Wright and Decker explore the motives that drive the
             decision to commit a burglary.

Chapter 4   **Opportunities and Decisions: Interactional
             Dynamics in Robbery and Burglary
             Groups**   55
             Andy Hochstetler
             The author analyzes the decision-making process of
             offenders working in groups.

Chapter 5   **Auto Theft and Restrictive Deterrence**   74
             Bruce A. Jacobs and Michael C. Cherbonneau
             The authors analyze the restrictive deterrence
             decision-making strategies of 35 active auto
             thieves.

SECTION III PROPERTY CRIME
             Introduction   89

Chapter 6   **Establishing Connections: Gender,
             Motor Vehicle Theft, and Disposal
             Networks**   93
             Christopher W. Mullins and Michael C. Cherbonneau
             The authors examine the gendered nature of motor
             vehicle theft.

Chapter 7   **"The Devil Made Me Do It": Use
             of Neutralizations by Shoplifters**   114
             Paul Cromwell and Quint Thurman
             Cromwell and Thurman discuss the justifications,
             excuses, and neutralizations used by shoplifters to
             explain their crimes.

Chapter 8   **Identity Theft: Assessing Offenders'
Motivations and Strategies**   124
Heith Copes and Lynne Vieraitis
Copes and Vieraitis shed light on the motives, perceptions
of risk, and strategies involved in identity theft.

SECTION IV   **VIOLENT CRIME**
Introduction   137

Chapter 9   **Gendering Violence: Masculinity and Power
in Men's Accounts of Domestic Violence**   141
Kristin L. Anderson and Debra Umberson
The authors reveal the strategies used by abusing males
in an effort to portray themselves as rational and
nonviolent.

Chapter 10   **Serendipity in Robbery Target Selection**   159
Bruce A. Jacobs
Jacobs argues that robbers select their victims based not
on rational processes, but on serendipity—victims are
simply in the wrong place at the wrong time.

Chapter 11   **Peaceful Warriors: Codes for Violence Among
Adult Male Bar Fighters**   176
Heith Copes, Andy Hochstetler, and Craig J. Forsyth
The authors elaborate on a code of violence as part of a
system of order and honor as articulated by a network of
white, working-class males in a southern U.S. city who
participate in bar fights.

SECTION V   **OCCUPATIONAL AND WHITE-
COLLAR CRIME**
Introduction   197

Chapter 12   **Crime on the Line: Telemarketing and the
Changing Nature of Professional Crime**   199
Neal Shover, Glenn S. Coffey, and Dick Hobbs
Shover and his associates examine the lifestyles and
motivations of individuals engaged in illegal telemarketing.

Chapter 13   **Drugged Druggists: The Convergence of Two Criminal Career Trajectories**   217
Dean A. Dabney and Richard C. Hollinger
Dabney and Hollinger explicate both the onset and progression of illicit prescription drug abuse by pharmacists.

SECTION VI   **ILLEGAL OCCUPATIONS**
Introduction   245

Chapter 14   **The "Myth of Organization" of International Drug Smugglers**   247
Scott H. Decker and Jana S. Benson
The authors examine drug smuggling from the perspective of those most in the know: the individuals whose roles facilitate the trade.

Chapter 15   **Informal Control and Illicit Drug Trade**   260
Scott Jacques and Richard T. Wright
Jacques and Wright use the rational-choice and opportunity perspectives to explore how and why the frequency and seriousness of popular justice affect the prices and rate of drug sales.

Chapter 16   **A Perversion of Choice: Sex Work Offers Just Enough in Chicago's Urban Ghetto**   286
Eva Rosen and Sudhir Alladi Venkatesh
Using in-depth interviews and participant observation Rosen and Venkatesh investigate Chicago's sex work economy.

SECTION VII   **GANGS AND CRIME**
Introduction   301

Chapter 17   **Gang-Related Gun Violence: Socialization, Identity, and Self**   303
Paul B. Stretesky and Mark R. Pogrebin
The authors examine how gang socialization leads to gun-related violence.

Chapter 18   **Gender and Victimization Risk Among Young Women in Gangs**   325

Jody Miller

Miller explores the extent to which being a female member of a youth gang shapes girls' risk of victimization.

Chapter 19   **Voices from the Barrio: Chicano/a Gangs, Families, and Communities**   339

Marjorie S. Zatz and Edwardo L. Portillos

The authors examine gang members and their families to ascertain the impact of gang activity on the community at large.

SECTION VIII   DRUGS AND CRIME

Introduction   359

Chapter 20   **"E" Is for Ecstasy: A Participant-Observation Study of Ecstasy Use**   361

Wilson R. Palacios and Melissa E. Fenwick

Palacios and Fenwick examine the "club" culture and crime.

Chapter 21   **"Cooks Are Like Gods": Hierarchies in Methamphetamine-Producing Groups**   371

Robert Jenkot

Jenkot reports on his study of methamphetamine-producing groups and identifies the various roles statuses involved in the process.

SECTION IX   QUITTING CRIME

Introduction   387

Chapter 22   **Getting Out of the Life: Crime Desistance by Female Street Offenders**   389

Ira Sommers, Deborah R. Baskin, and Jeffery Fagan

The authors examine the process by which women offenders desist from crime.

Chapter 23   **The Victimization–Termination Link**   403

Scott Jacques and Richard T. Wright

Jacques and Wright analyze the process by which middle-class drug dealers desist from their illicit enterprise.

PREFACE

This anthology provides the reader with an opportunity to view the world from the perspective of criminal offenders. *In Their Own Words*, Seventh Edition, is a collection of field studies of crime and criminals derived from a long tradition of field research in criminology. In this new edition, which contains five new chapters, students will encounter a diverse array of criminals, including auto thieves, drug offenders, armed robbers, burglars, and sex workers, all of whom discuss their motives, perceptions, strategies, and rationalization of crime. Readers will note that in many articles, the methods section has been redacted for brevity. Readers are encouraged to go to the original source of the material for a fuller and more complete methodology.

METHODS OF FIELD RESEARCH

Field research is not a single research methodology. Also called *ethnography*, field research provides a way of looking at the complex contexts in which any research problem exists. Good field research results in what Glassner and Carpenter (1985) call thick description—access to the often conflicting and detailed views of the social world held by the subjects being studied.

According to Maxfield and Babbie (1995), field research "encompasses two different methods of obtaining data: direct observation and asking questions." *Asking questions* involves in-depth interviews (also called ethnographic interviews) with research subjects. Field study interviews are much less structured than survey research interviews. At one level, field interviews may be likened to conversations (Maxfield & Babbie, 1995). At a more structured level, researchers ask open-ended questions in which a specific response is elicited but the respondent is allowed and encouraged to explain more completely and clarify responses. The question is simply a guide that structures but does not limit the interviewee's responses. *Observation* takes several forms in field research. These techniques may be categorized on a continuum according to the role played by the researcher (Gold, 1969; Maxfield & Babbie, 1995). At one degree of involvement, the researcher observes an activity or individuals without their knowledge. A researcher watching shoplifters through a one-way mirror in a department store is an example of this technique. Gold (1969) labels this method *the complete observer*. At a more involved level of interaction, the researcher is identified as a researcher and interacts with the participants in the course of their activities but does not actually become a participant (Maxfield & Babbie, 1995). Gold (1969) identifies this technique the *observer-as-participant*.

The *participant-as-observer* (Gold, 1969) technique involves participating with the group under study while making the purpose of the research clear. Wilson Palacios and Melissa Fenwick used a version of this technique in their study of the Ecstasy club scene in southern Florida (Chapter 20 of this book). The most complete involvement of researcher with subject is the complete participant. Gold (1969, p. 33) describes this role as follows:

> The true identity and purpose of the complete participant in field research are not known to those he observes. He interacts with them as naturally as possible in whatever areas of their living interest him and are acceptable to him in situations in which he can play or learn to play requisite day-to-day roles successfully.

A number of ethical, legal, and personal risk considerations are involved in the complete participant role, and the researcher must tread carefully to avoid pitfalls. Because of these problems, complete participation is seldom possible in criminological research.

Field studies are particularly well suited to investigating several important issues in criminology and criminal justice. Only through field research can we observe the everyday activities of offenders: how they interact with others, how they perceive the objects and events in their everyday lives, and how they perceive the sanction threat of the criminal justice system. By understanding offenders' perspectives, decision-making processes, and motivations, field research may inform crime prevention and control strategies. Wright and Decker (1994) point out that criminal justice policymaking is predicated on assumptions about the perceptions of criminals: "The traditional policy of deterrence rests squarely on the notion that offenders are utilitarian persons who carefully weigh the potential costs and rewards of their illegal actions."

However, the studies in this collection offer strong arguments for other, perhaps equally compelling motivations for many crimes, including so-called economic crimes. Even robbery and burglary, crimes assumed to be driven almost entirely by instrumental (economic) motivations, may have expressive roots as well. By contrast, gang membership, which traditionally has been perceived as turf oriented and centered on conflict, is shown to be increasingly about money: drugs and drug sales. Thus, effective crime control strategies must take into account the various factors that drive crime. Field research that allows offenders to "speak for themselves" is ideally suited to these issues. Field studies such as those in this book also have great value in educating criminal justice and criminology students. The field has sometimes suffered from a distance between student and subject of the study. Would anyone argue that it is possible to train a physician without contact with sick people? The essence of medical training is of course the experience of diagnosing and treating the sick. Yet, in our combined 30 years as criminal justice practitioners and administrators, and our 40 years as criminal justice and criminology educators, we have been troubled by the realization that most graduates never encounter an actual criminal during the course of their education. Some universities provide internships or practicums or arrange field trips to prisons or other correctional facilities. Despite these efforts, however, few students ever experience a "real criminal" during their education. By viewing the criminal event from the perspective of the participants, these studies can help us understand an individual's decision to engage in crime on a personal level and supplement the statistical data from other research.

In Their Own Words enriches the reader's understanding of criminal typologies, criminal decision-making processes, criminological theories, and criminal subcultures and lifestyles. The studies in this book vary in terms of their settings, the crimes being studied, and the researcher's involvement and role in the environment. In every case, however, the story is told from the perspective of, and in the words of, the offender. In each case, the researcher places the offender's words in a theoretical context and provides analyses and conclusions.

REFERENCES

Glassner, B., & Carpenter, C. (1985). *The feasibility of an ethnographic study of property offenders: A report prepared for the National Institute of Justice.* Washington, DC: NIJ Mimeo.

Gold, R. (1969). Roles in sociological field observation. In G. J. McCall & J. L. Simmons, eds., *Issues in participant observation.* Reading, MA: Addison-Wesley.

Maxfield, M. G., & Babbie, E. (1995). *Research methods for criminal justice and criminology.* Belmont, CA: Wadsworth.

Wright, R. T., & Decker, S. H. (1994). *Burglars on the job: Street life and residential break-ins.* Boston: Northeastern University Press.

NEW TO THIS EDITION

- This edition has been reduced from 26 chapters to 23 chapters. We believe this will create greater options for professors who use *In Their Own Words* as a supplemental book in order to cover the majority of the readings in a traditional college semester class.
- Five new chapters have been added covering topics such as auto thieves and restrictive deterrence, codes of violence among bar fighters, drug dealers, efforts to desist from crime, and sex work.

- This edition provides coverage of a promising desistence theory under-pinned in life-course criminology and grounded in in-depth interviews of drug dealers.
- Also included in this edition is a chapter on commercial sex work where the authors conducted in-depth interviews and participant observation over an extended time of the commercial sex industry on Chicago's South Side.

ACKNOWLEDGMENTS

A deep appreciation goes out to the researchers and authors of the studies presented here. The credit for an anthology such as this goes to these individuals. Our task was simply to select the best exemplars of contemporary field research in crime and criminal behavior and attempt to bring them together in an integrated and effective manner. We gratefully acknowledge the scholarly efforts of these researchers. It is truly their book.

In the process of preparing this new edition, we have also benefited from the numerous reviewers who commented on the selections, the organization and integration of materials, and the general worth of the project. Special appreciation is extended to Brandy L. Blasko, George Mason University; Richard Clark, John Carroll University; Shawna Cleary, University of Central Oklahoma; Erik D. Fritsvold, University of San Diego; Nancy L. Hogan, Ferris State University; Tristin Kilgallon, Ohio Northern University; Richard R. Loder, Syracuse University; and Gary Sweeten, Arizona State University.

Of special note in developing the Seventh Edition, we must acknowledge the constant attention and assistance from our editor at Oxford, Steve Helba, and his assistant, Claire Benson.

ABOUT THE EDITORS

Michael L. Birzer is Professor of Criminal Justice and Director of the School of Community Affairs at Wichita State University.

Paul Cromwell is Professor of Public Administration at the University of South Florida.

ABOUT THE CONTRIBUTORS

Kristin L. Anderson is Professor of Sociology at Western Washington University.

Deborah R. Baskin is Professor of Criminal Justice and Criminology at Loyola University Chicago.

Jana S. Benson was a doctoral student at Arizona State University at the time of the initial publication.

Michael C. Cherbonneau is Assistant Professor of Criminology and Criminal Justice at University of North Florida.

Glenn S. Coffey is Associate Professor of Criminal Justice, Criminology and Sociology and Lead Professor at the University of Mount Olive-Wilmington.

Heith Copes is Professor of Criminology and Criminal Justice at the University of Alabama at Birmingham.

Paul Cromwell is Professor of Public Administration and Criminology at the University of South Florida.

Dean A. Dabney is Associate Professor of Criminal Justice at Georgia State University.

Scott H. Decker is Foundation Professor of Criminal Justice at Arizona State University.

Jeffery Fagan is the Isidor and Seville Sulzbacher Professor of Law at Columbia Law School.

Melissa E. Fenwick is deceased. She was formerly an Assistant Professor of Criminal Justice at Western Connecticut State University.

Craig J. Forsyth is Professor of Sociology at the University of Louisiana-Lafayette.

Dick Hobbs is Professor in the Institute for Culture and Society at Western Sydney University.

Andy Hochstetler is Professor of Sociology at Iowa State University.

Richard C. Hollinger is Professor of Criminology and Director of the Security Research Project at the University of Florida.

Bruce A. Jacobs is Professor of Crime and Justice Studies in the School of Economic, Political, and Policy Sciences at the University of Texas at Dallas.

Scott Jacques is Associate Professor of Criminal Justice and Criminology at Georgia State University.

Robert Jenkot is Associate Professor of Sociology and Department Chair at Coastal Carolina University.

Jody Miller is Professor of Criminal Justice and Criminology at Rutgers University.

Christopher W. Mullins is Associate Professor of Criminology and Criminal Justice and Director of University Studies at Southern Illinois University at Carbondale.

Wilson R. Palacios is Associate Professor of Criminology at the University of Massachusetts–Lowell.

Mark R. Pogrebin is Professor of Criminal Justice at the University of Colorado at Denver.

Edwardo L. Portillos is Associate Professor of Sociology at the University of Colorado, Colorado Springs.

Eva Rosen is a postdoctoral Fellow in the Department of Sociology at John Hopkins University.

Neal Shover is Professor Emeritus of Sociology at the University of Tennessee-Knoxville.

Ira Sommers is an Instructor and Director of the Minor in Psychology, Crime and Justice at Loyola University of Chicago.

Paul B. Stretesky is Associate Professor of Sociology at Colorado State University.

Quint Thurman is President of the University of the Southwest.

Debra Umberson is Professor of Sociology at the University of Texas at Austin.

Sudhir Alladi Venkatesh is William B. Ransford Professor of Sociology, and the Committee on Global Thought, at Columbia University in the City of New York.

Lynne Vieraitis is Associate Professor of Criminology and Program Head at the University of Texas-Dallas.

Richard T. Wright is a Curator's Professor Emeritus, University Missouri-St. Louis.

Marjorie S. Zatz is professor of Justice and Social Inquiry in the School of Transformation at the University of Arizona.

Doing Fieldwork
with Offenders

Ethnographic fieldwork with active offenders presents a host of challenges. These challenges include but are not limited to developing gatekeepers or key informants, gaining access to research informants, establishing rapport, and identifying personal safety risks to the researcher(s). Despite these challenges, criminological ethnographies have the potential to provide rich and informative data. Ethnographic accounts of active offenders can provide a great deal of information about offenders themselves, as well as backstage accounts of their criminal activities that we would never be able to attain through other methods. Consequently, ethnographic data can be used to develop or enhance theory, and to help shape crime policy.

In the preface of this book, we discuss the issue of distance between students and the object(s) of their study. Most criminology or criminal justice students (and many of their professors) never come into contact with a criminal, except perhaps during a jail or prison tour. One could hardly image a physician going through training without ever making contact with a sick person. Doesn't it make sense that researchers and students of crime and criminals would have contact with the very persons they study?

In this section, we present two approaches to ethnographic research. One position argues that we should focus on studying the criminal in his or her natural environment—the streets. The leading proponent of this position has been Ned Polsky (1967, pp. 122–123), who states:

> We are always going to be in this spot—always slowly fitting together a jigsaw puzzle that is decades out of date and never even knowing if we have all the pieces, or the right pieces—unless we change our research methods.
>
> This means—there is no getting away from it—the study of career criminals *au naturel,* in the field, the study of such criminals as they normally go about their work and play, the study of "uncaught" criminals and the study of others who in the past have been caught but are *not* caught at the time you study them.

The first article in this section, Bruce A. Jacobs' "Researching Crack Dealers: Dilemmas and Contradictions," repeats Polsky's call for criminologists to reach beyond the comfort of their office and the convenience of interviewing offenders in contrived situations and get into the field to work with criminals in their true environment. It is only in the field that the criminologist will see firsthand what these people do and how they do it.

Jacobs takes us on a journey into the world of street-level crack dealers. This article serves as a sobering reminder of the dangers of such studies, recounting Jacobs' own experience of being held and robbed at gunpoint by one of his participants. The article advances the thesis that "the importance of a strong indigenous tie to the research setting at the beginning of field relations . . . cannot be overstated." Jacobs informs us of the importance of balancing the conflicting agendas of the ethnographic audience, which can range from offenders to social control agents such as the police. Maintaining balance and safety is important. But how does the field researcher effectively maintain balance while uncovering the rich context of backstage criminology? Jacobs' article sheds light on this very question, which we hope will inform other researchers in similar field situations.

Maintaining balance requires that researchers remain aware of the consequences that can evolve from their fieldwork and create serious problems as the study progresses. These consequences include problems from not only the offenders under study, but also the police. The very nature of criminological field research will in some cases attract police attention and scrutiny. Many researchers have had to negotiate with the police as their field research evolves. There have been numerous instances in which researchers have been arrested or harassed by the police while collecting data in the field (Humphreys, 1970; Leo, 1995; Scarce, 1994). As Jacobs' study illuminates, as interaction with field participants increases, a researcher is increasingly confronted with the need to compromise (Georges & Jones, 1980). In the end, Jacobs' article provides crucial information on how researchers can maintain balance in collecting field data while effectively negotiating social distance.

In Chapter 2, Heith Copes and Andy Hochstetler provide an alternative approach to the study of criminals in their natural environment. They argue that criminals can and do provide accurate accounts of their behavior when interviewed in prison and investigate why inmates are willing to participate in prison research. Some criminologists argue that when interviews are conducted in prison and jail environments, offenders provide only the information that the criminologist wants to hear, which may result in exaggerated accounts of their criminality. However, Copes and Hochstetler point out that offenders behind bars have offered open and frank accounts of their lives and crimes during interviews. Because researchers usually do not directly observe the criminal event, data about this event depend on the offender's ability to reflectively discern and communicate aspects of his or her offending. Thus, in the interview, the researcher becomes the data collection instrument, facilitating, guiding, and interpreting the criminological construction of the criminal event as told by the inmate.

It is hard to make an argument against direct engagement with those offenders who can provide reflexive descriptions of their criminal experiences and how they make sense of those experiences. However, what would make an offender want to talk to a researcher? More specifically, Copes and Hochstetler ask, "What would make someone who has been incarcerated for behavior that society has defined as immoral and illegal disregard the potential risks and inconveniences to sit down and openly discuss their lives and misdeeds?" In their study, they asked this question of 73 individuals incarcerated in one of two medium-security prisons in Alabama and Louisiana. Their research informs us that incarcerated inmates participate in prison interviews for numerous reasons. These include the desire to satisfy immediate material needs, such as lack of money ($20 goes a long way in prison), and even the altruistic desire to help out a trusted confederate. Inmates also participate to fulfill emotional and psychological needs, and to give back to others.

An interesting centerpiece of this article that is particularly relevant for qualitative researchers is the discussion of the study's implications for institutional review boards (IRBs). If you have done ethnographic work or used another qualitative approach in your studies of offenders, you have likely experienced the huge challenge of getting past the IRB in order to do your research. Getting research approved by an IRB can be an arduous, frustrating process. Copes and Hochstetler offer some advice here. They argue that crafting the language of the IRB application to demonstrate the direct benefits of having inmates tell their stories may go a long way toward ensuring a smoother approval process. Copes and Hochstetler argue that the process of telling their stories and reflecting on their crimes can have emotional impacts on inmates, which can potentially culminate in therapeutic effects. The article presents the idea that understanding how the research process can benefit those directly involved can make the IRB process much easier to negotiate, allowing researchers to go about their important work of studying and making sense of the meaning that offenders ascribe to their criminality. In all, the article represents an important contribution to our understanding of the motivations that underlie an offender's willingness to talk frankly and honestly about his or her crimes with researchers.

REFERENCES

Georges, R. A., & Jones, M. O. (1980). *People studying people: The human element in fieldwork*. Berkeley: University of California Press.

Humphreys, L. (1970). *Tearoom trade: Impersonal sex in public places*. New York: Aldine.

Leo, R. A. (1995). Trial and tribulation: Courts, ethnography, and the need for evidentiary privilege for academic researchers. *American Sociologist, 26*, 86–112.

Polsky, N. (1967). *Hustlers, beats, and others*. New Brunswick, NJ: Aldine.

Scarce, R. (1994). (NO) trial (But) tribulations: When courts and ethnography conflict. *Journal of Contemporary Ethnography, 23*, 123–49.

CHAPTER 1

Researching Crack Dealers:
Dilemmas and Contradictions

Bruce A. Jacobs

Jacobs discusses the difficulties and dangers of associated with studying criminals in the field.

"Yo, Bruce, come on down the set [neighborhood]. Meet where we usually do," Luther said, and hung up the phone.[1] A trusted contact for an ongoing study of street-level crack dealers and a crack dealer himself, I had no reason to question him. "Just another interview," I thought. Notebooks and file folders in hand, I went to the bank, withdrew fifty dollars for subject payments, and drove fifteen minutes to the dope set I was coming to know so well.

Luther flagged me down as I turned the corner. The 17-year-old high school drop-out opened the door and jumped in. "Swerve over there." He pointed to a parking space behind the dilapidated three-story apartment building he called home. "Stop the car—turn it off." Nothing out of the ordinary; over the previous three months, we often would sit and talk for a while before actually going to an interview. This time, though, there was an urgency in his voice I should have detected but did not. He produced a pistol from under a baggy white T-shirt. "Gimme all your fuckin' money or I'll blow your motherfuckin' head off!"

"What the fuck's your problem?" I said, astonished that someone I trusted had suddenly turned on me. The gun was large, a six-shooter, probably a long-barrel .45. It was ugly and old looking. Most of its chrome had been scratched off. Its black handle was pockmarked from years of abuse. Why was he doing this? How did I get myself into this situation? It was the kind of thing you hear about on the evening news but don't expect to confront, even though I knew studying active offenders risked such a possibility.

Source: Jacobs, B. A. (1998). Researching crack dealers: Dilemmas and contradictions. In J. Ferrell & M. S. Hamm, eds., *Ethnography at the edge: Crime, deviance and field research.* Boston: Northeastern University Press, pp. 160–177. Used with permission.

I frantically pondered a course of action as Luther's tone became more and more hostile. He was sweating. "Just calm down, Luther, just calm down—everything's cool," I trembled. "Don't shoot—I'll give you what you want." "Gimme all your fuckin' money!" he repeated. "I ain't fuckin' around—I'll waste you right here!" I reached in my left-hand pocket for the fifty dollars and handed it over. As I did so, I cupped my right hand precariously an inch from the muzzle of his gun, which was pointing directly into my abdomen. I can survive a gunshot, I thought to myself, as long as I slow the bullet down.

He snatched the five, crisp ten-dollar bills and made a quick search of the vehicle's storage areas to see if I was holding out. "OK," he said, satisfied there were no more funds. "Now turn your head around." I gazed at him inquisitively. "Turn your motherfuckin' head around!" For all I knew, he was going to shoot and run; his right hand was poised on the door handle, his left on the trigger. "Just take your money, man, I'm not gonna do anything." "Turn the fuck around!" he snapped. "OK," I implored, "I won't look, just lemme put my hand over my eyes." I left small openings between my fingers to see what he was really going to do. If he were truly going to fire, which he appeared to be intent on doing—the gun was being raised from the down-low position in which it had been during the entire encounter to right below head level—I would smack the gun upward, jump out of the car, and run a half block to the relative safety of a commercial street.

As I pondered escape routes, he jammed the gun into his pants as quickly as he had drawn it, flung open the door, and disappeared behind the tenements. I hit the ignition and drove slowly and methodically from the scene, grateful to have escaped injury, but awestruck by his brazen violation of trust. All I could do was look back and wonder why.

If this were the end of the story, things would have normalized, I would have learned a lesson about field research, and I would have gone about my business. But Luther was not through. Over the next six weeks, he called my apartment five to ten times a day, five days a week, harassing, taunting, irritating, baiting me. Perhaps twice over that six-week period, I actually picked up the phone—only to find out it was him and hang up. Luther would call right back and let the phone ring incessantly, knowing I was there and letting the answering machine do the dirty work. On several occasions, it became so bad that I had to disconnect the line and leave the apartment for several hours.

I'd arrive home to see the answering machine lit up with messages. "I can smell the mousse in your hair—huh, huh, huh," his sinister laugh echoing through the apartment. "I know you're there, pick it up." More often than not, I would hear annoying dial tones. One message, however, caught my undivided attention: "897 Longacre—huh, huh, huh," he laughed as I heard him flipping through the phone book pages and identifying my address. "We'll [he and his homeboys] be over tomorrow." I didn't sleep well that night or for the next six weeks.

What was I to do—report the robbery, and go to court and testify to stop what had become tele-stalking? Some researchers contend that when crimes against fieldworkers occur, staff are to "report them to the police to indicate that such violations will have consequences."[2] I did not feel I had this option. Calling the authorities, no matter how much I wanted to, not only would have endangered future research with Luther's set and those connected to it, but would also have risked retaliation—because Luther's homies knew where I lived and worked.

So I called the phone company and got caller ID, call return, and call block. These devices succeeded in providing his phone number and residence name, which I used to trace his actual address, but I could still do nothing to stop him. Changing my number was the last thing I wanted to do, because those who smell fear often attack. As other researchers have noted, concern about "violence may cause ethnographers to appear afraid or react inappropriately to common street situations and dangers. . . . Fearful behavior is easily inferred by violent persons" and may often lead to violence itself.[3] Thus, Berk and Adams stress the importance of maintaining one's cool when threatened: "The investigator will be constantly watched and tested by the very people he is studying. This is especially true [with] delinquents who . . . value poise in the face of danger."[4] Danger, it must be remembered, is "inherent" in fieldwork with active offenders, "if for no other reason than there is always the possibility of dangerous cultural misunderstandings arising between researchers and subjects."[5] This is especially true of research among active street-corner crack sellers, who routinely use violence or threats of violence to gain complicity.[6]

After enduring six weeks of this postrobbery harassment, and with no end in sight, I had to do something. I called the police and told them the story. An officer came out and listened to messages I had saved. As he listened, the telephone rang, and Luther's number displayed on the caller ID. "Do you want me to talk to him?" the officer asked sternly. "No," I replied, feeling more confident with a cop three feet away. "Lemme see if I can work things out." I picked up the phone and started talking.

"What do you want?"

"Why do you keep hangin' up on me? All I want is to talk."

"What do you expect me to do, *like* you? [sardonically, on the verge of losing it]. You fuckin' robbed me and I trusted you and now you call me and leave these fuckin' messages and you want me to *talk* to you? [incredulous]"

"I only did that 'cause you fucked me over. I only ganked [robbed] you 'cause you *fucked me*."

"What are you talking about?"

He proceeded to explain that without him, none of the 40 interviews I obtained would have been possible. True, Luther was the first field contact to believe that I was a researcher, not a cop. He was my first respondent, and he was responsible for starting a snowball of referrals on his word that I was "cool."[7] But after he could no longer provide referrals, I moved on, using his contacts to find new ones and eliminating him from the chain. My newfound independence was inexplicable to him and a slap in the face. He wanted vengeance; the robbery and taunting were exactly that.[8]

ETHNOGRAPHY AND SOCIAL DISTANCE?

Such are the risks ethnographers take when studying dangerous, unstable offenders. Although "robbery, burglary, and theft from field staff are uncommon, [they] do occur. In fact, many crack distributors are frequent and proficient robbers, burglars, and thieves."[9] Not so ironically, someone I had trusted and considered a "protector"[10] had become someone to be protected from. Such flip-flops are entirely possible in the world of active offenders, who themselves often admit an inability to control or understand their behavior.

All of this merely underscores the changeable, unpredictable nature of fieldwork relations, especially with active offenders. Johnson notes that "[i]t is incumbent on the investigator to assess the influences of these changes."[11] The important point is for researchers to put themselves in a position where they can do this. Unfortunately, the very nature of criminological fieldwork may work against this.

Much of the problem revolves around the dilemma between social distance and immersion in fieldwork, and the difficulty researchers have in resolving it. The notion of "social distance" is thought to be in some ways foreign to the ethnographic enterprise. Wolff, for example, contends that successful fieldwork inevitably requires surrender—psychological, social, and otherwise—to the setting, culture, and respondents one is studying. It requires "total involvement, suspension of received notions, pertinence of everything, identification, and risk of being hurt."[12] Ethnographers are advised to immerse themselves in the native scene,[13] to become a member of what they are studying.[14] They are told to become an actual physical and moral part of the setting.[15] As Berk and Adams put it, "The greater the social distance between the participant observer and the subjects, the greater the difficulty in establishing and maintaining rapport."[16]

Building rapport with active offenders typically becomes more difficult, though, as the "deviantness" of the population one studies increases.[17] With any offender population, trying to become "one of them" too quickly can be downright harmful. Some contend that the most egregious error a fieldworker can make is to assume that the fieldworker can gain the immediate favor of his or her hosts by telling them that he or she wants to "become one of them" or by implying, by word or act, that the fact that they tolerate his [or her] presence means that "he [or she] is one of them."[18] Similarly, Polsky warns that "you damned well better not pretend to be 'one of them,' because they will test this claim out and one of two things will happen. Either the researcher will get drawn into participating in actions one would otherwise not engage in, or the researcher could be exposed as a result of not doing so, the latter having perhaps even greater negative repercussions."[19] The more attached the researcher gets too early in the process, the more vulnerable she or he may be to exploitation. The researcher is still a researcher, no matter how close the researcher thinks she or he is getting. Subjects know this and may also know there will be few if any serious repercussions if they try to pull something, especially at the beginning of research when the fieldworker tends to be the most desperate for acceptance. Problems are only compounded by the fact that researchers tend to be far more streetwise by the end of fieldwork than they are at the beginning. Perhaps the least important time to be streetwise is at the end; both the number and seriousness of threats tend to decline with time. Where threats are often highest—at the beginning, when the researcher may be labeled a narc, a spy, or simply a suspicious character—the researcher may also be least capable of handling them. This only makes the threats that do materialize more threatening.

Researchers who are victimized at this early stage may often be barred from reporting it; doing so threatens to breach promises of confidentiality and anonymity made to subjects. The practical matter of being labeled a narc who "sold someone out" is a separate issue and potentially more problematic: snitching violates a sacred norm of street etiquette, even if the person being snitched on is in the wrong. At best, snitching will terminate future chains of respondents. At worst, it will label the researcher a "rat" and subject him or her to street justice. Both outcomes are of course undesirable and will likely bring an end to one's research.

Being immersed while remaining to some degree objective is the key. Some researchers stress the importance of using "interactional devices and strategies that allow the fieldworker to stay on the edges of unfolding social scenes rather than being drawn into their midst as a central actor."[20] Others recommend engaging in a paradoxical and "peculiar combination of engrossment and distance."[21] Like the Simmelian stranger, researchers are told to be familiar yet not too familiar, involved yet not too involved, all the while making the balance seem natural.[22] Some modicum of social distance is thus critical to the ethnographic enterprise—"as a corrective to bias and overrapport brought on by too strong an identification with those studied."[23]

In some sense, then, social distance between the researcher and the active offenders she or he studies can be beneficial. As Wright and Decker observe, "[T]he secrecy inherent in criminal work means that offenders have few opportunities to discuss their activities with anyone besides associates, a matter which many find frustrating."[24] By definition, criminal respondents will often have "certain knowledge and skills that the researcher does not have."[25] This asymmetry may empower them to open up or to open up sooner than they otherwise would. Offenders may enjoy speaking about their criminal experiences with someone who is "straight." Perhaps it is a satisfaction gained from teaching someone supposedly smarter than they are, at least in terms of academic degrees. The fact that respondents may see something in the research that benefits them, or an opportunity to correct faulty impressions of what it is they actually do,[26] only facilitates these dynamics.

All of it may come down to dramaturgy. Yet, the very nature of criminological fieldwork dictates that the researcher either can't or won't "act" in certain ways at certain times. Acting inappropriately can compromise the research itself, the fieldworker's ability to remain in the setting, or the ability to remain there safely. The moral and practical conundrum between social distance, immersion, and "participant" observation in criminological fieldwork may, in many ways, be unresolvable.

My failure to manage the distance, immersion dialectic with Luther appeared to have more to do with a practical shortfall in managing informant relations—a myopia if you will—than with going native. Clearly, I had lost objectivity in the process of "handling" Luther. Whether this was a function of over-immersion is open to question, but it undoubtedly played some role. Whether it was avoidable is also open to question, particularly when one considers the practical and methodological paradoxes involved in fieldwork with active offenders. Although myopic (mis)management led to my exploitation by Luther, without putting myself in such a position, I would never have been able to collect the data I did. In many ways, the "shortfall" was necessary and, at some level, advantageous.

The bottom line is that no matter how deft the fieldworker is at managing relations, he or she ultimately never gains total control. Criminological fieldworkers exist in a dependent relationship with their subjects.[27] This makes one wonder who is indeed the "subject" and what he or she can be "subject to" at any given moment. Some contend that the hierarchical relationship between interviewer and subject in social research is "morally indefensible"[28] and should be thrown out. Perhaps the hierarchy may be jettisoned as a matter of course, by the very nature of the fieldworker–active offender relationship. Luther's actions toward me stand as an exemplary case.[29]

STUDYING ACTIVE OFFENDERS

Studying active drug dealers is problematic precisely because their activity is criminal. Active offenders are generally "hard to locate because they find it necessary to lead clandestine lives. Once located, they are reluctant, for similar reasons, to give accurate and truthful information about themselves."[30] "Outsiders" are often perceived as narcs seeking to obtain damaging evidence for juridical purposes.[31] Indeed, the most common suspicion that subjects have about fieldworkers is that they are spies of some sort. As Sluka notes, "It is difficult to find an [ethnographer] who has done fieldwork who has not encountered this suspicion."[32]

Collecting data from drug dealers, particularly from active ones, is likely to be difficult and dangerous unless one can construct friendships within a dealing community.[33] Because of this difficulty, some researchers target institutional settings.[34] Such settings afford the chance of obtaining data without the risk of physical harm associated with "street" interviews.[35] Unfortunately, collecting valid and reliable data in such settings may not be entirely possible, as criminologists have "long suspected that offenders do not behave naturally" in them.[36] Sutherland and Cressey argue that "[t]hose who have had intimate contacts with criminals 'in the open' know that criminals are not 'natural' in police stations, courts, and prisons and that they must be studied in their everyday life outside of institutions if they are to be understood."[37] Polsky is more emphatic, commenting that "we can no longer afford the convenient fiction that in studying criminals in their natural habitat, we . . . discover nothing really important that [cannot] be discovered from criminals behind bars. What is true for studying the gorilla of zoology is likely to be even truer for studying the gorilla of criminology."[38] There are fundamental qualitative differences between the two types of offenders. Institutionalized drug dealers, for example, may represent those not sophisticated or skilled enough to prevent apprehension, or those who simply do not care about getting caught and who sell to anyone with money. Studies of incarcerated offenders are thus open to the charge of being based on "unsuccessful criminals, on the supposition that successful criminals are not apprehended or are at least able to avoid incarceration." This weakness is "the most central bogeyman in the criminologist's demonology."[39]

Knowing this, I entered the field and began frequenting a district near a major university that is both prestigious and expensive, yet which borders a dilapidated neighborhood with a concentrated African American population and heavy crack sales. A lively commercial district, with restaurants, quaint cafes, bars, theaters, and stores, splits the two. The area is known for racial and ethnic diversity, making it relatively easy for most anyone to blend in. Over a nine-month period, I frequented the area and made myself familiar to the regular crowd of hangers-out in the dividing commercial district. Some of these individuals were marginally homeless and spent entire days in the district smoking, drinking, playing music, and begging. Although not crack dealers themselves, they knew who the dealers were and where they worked. After gaining their trust, I was shown the dealers' congregation spots and quickly took to the area.

At first, I would simply walk by, not explicitly acknowledging that anything was going on. Sometimes I would be escorted by one of the "vagabonds," but most of the time I went alone. My objective was simply to let dealers see me. Over the days and weeks, I walked or drove through slowly to gain recognition, trying to capitalize on what Goffman has called second seeings: "[U]nder some circumstances if he and they see each other seeing each other, they can use this fact as an excuse for an acquaintanceship greeting upon next seeing . . ."[40] Unfortunately, this did not go as easily as Goffman suggests, as dealers openly yelled "SCAT!"—a term for the police undercover unit—at me.[41] Jump-starting participation was clearly the toughest part of the research because dealers suspected I was the police. Ironically, it was the police who gave me my biggest credibility boost.

POLICE AND CREDIBILITY

Ferrell notes that "a researcher's strict conformity to legal codes can be reconceptualized as less a sign of professional success than a possible portent of methodological failure . . . a willingness to break the law," by contrast, "[opens] a variety of methodological possibilities."[42]

Hanging with offenders on street corners, driving them around in my car, and visiting their homes must have been a curious sight. My appearance is somewhat akin to that of a college student. Shorts, T-shirts, cross-trainers, and ball caps with rounded brims, "just like SCAT wear 'em" (as one respondent put it), make up my typical attire. Further, I am white, clean-cut, and affect a middle-class appearance, traits the relatively poor, African American respondents associated with the police. These traits appeared to make them even more leery that I was SCAT, or that I worked for SCAT in some capacity.

To offenders who hadn't gotten to know me well, or to those waiting to pass judgment, I was on a deep-cover assignment designed to unearth their secrets and put them in jail. To cops on the beat, I was just another college boy driving down to crackville with a user in tow to buy for me. Such relations are commonplace in the street-level drug scene and have generalized subcultural currency: users serve as go-betweens and funnel unfamiliar customers to dealers for a finder's fee, usually in drugs and without the customer's consent, but generally with his or her tacit permission. When cops see a relatively nicely dressed, clean-shaven white boy driving a late-model car (with out-of-state plates, I might add) and a black street person in the passenger seat, they lick their chops.

Several police stops of me in a one-month period lent some credibility to this proposition. I had not obtained, as Wright and Decker had, a "prior agreement with the police"[43] whereby the police knew what I was doing and pledged not to interfere. I chose not to; the last thing I wanted was to let police know what I was doing. As Polsky explains, "Most of the danger for the fieldworker comes not from the cannibals and headhunters but from the colonial officials. The criminologist studying uncaught criminals in the open finds sooner or later that law enforcers try to put him on the spot—because, unless he is a complete fool, he uncovers information that law enforcers would like to know . . ."[44] Because my grant was not a federal one, I could not protect the identity of my respondents with a certificate of confidentiality (which theoretically bars police from obtaining data as it pertains to one's subjects). My work was undercover in a sense and eminently discreditable. However, contrary to admonitions by some to avoid contact with the police while doing research with dangerous populations,[45] my run-ins with police turned out to be the most essential tool for establishing my credibility.

My first run-in came two weeks after making initial contact with offenders. I was driving Luther through a crack-filled neighborhood—a neighborhood which also happened to have the highest murder rate in a city which itself had the fourth-highest murder rate in the nation.[46] We were approaching a group of ten mid-teen youths and were about to stop when a St. Louis city patrol car pulled behind. Should I stop, as I planned on doing, and get out and talk with these youths (some of whom Luther marginally knew), or would that place them in imminent danger of arrest? Or should I continue on as if nothing was really going on, even though I had been driving stop and go, under ten miles an hour, prior to and during the now slow-speed pursuit? I opted for the latter, accelerating slowly in a vain attempt to reassert a "normal appearance."[47]

Sirens went on. I pulled over and reassured Luther there was nothing to worry about since neither of us had contraband (I hoped). As officers approached, I thought about what to tell them. Should I say I was a university professor doing field research on crack dealers (a part I clearly didn't look), lie, or say nothing at all? "Whatcha doin' down here?" one of the officers snapped. "Exit the vehicle, intertwine your fingers behind your heads, and kneel with your ankles crossed," he commanded. The searing June sidewalk was not conducive to clear thinking, but I rattled something off: "We used to work together at _____. I waited tables, he bussed, and we been friends since. I'm a sociology major up at _____ and he said he'd show me around the neighborhood sometime. Here I am." "Yeah right," the cop snapped again while searching for the crack he thought we already had purchased. Three other police cars arrived, as the cop baited Luther and me as to how we really knew each other, what each other's real names were (which neither of us knew at the time), and what we were doing here. Dissatisfied with my answers, a sergeant took over, lecturing me on the evils of crack and how it would destroy a life others in this very neighborhood wished they had. I found no fault with the argument, listened attentively, and said nothing. After a final strip search in the late afternoon sun revealed nothing, they said I was lucky, vowed to take me in if I ever showed my face again, and let us go.

On a second occasion, Luther and his homie Frisco were in my car when we pulled up to a local liquor store. The two became nervous upon seeing two suits in a "tec" (detective) car parked at the phone booth. I told Luther and Frisco to wait, and I went into the store. As I exited, the two men approached and showed their badges. "What you doin' with these guys—do you know 'em?" "Yes," I said, deciding to tell them who I really was and what I was doing. "Mind if we search your car?" one asked. "No problem," I replied. "Go right ahead." As one searched my car (for crack, guns, or whatever else he thought he'd find), his partner cuffed both Luther and Frisco and ran warrants. As I soon learned, both detectives knew the two as repeat violent offenders with long rap sheets. They took Frisco in on an outstanding warrant and let Luther go with me. "I respect what you're doing," the searching officer said as he finished and approached, "but you don't know who you're dealing with. These guys are no good." I told him thanks and promptly left with Luther, feeling remorseful about Frisco being taken in only because he was with me.

On a third occasion, I was sitting on my car making small talk with four or five dealers when a patrol car rolled by. The officers inside gave a stern look and told us to break it up. "All right," I said, not going anywhere. We continued to talk for a few minutes when the officers, clearly agitated, rolled by again and demanded in no uncertain terms, "Break it up and we mean now." I hopped in my car, drove four or five blocks, made a left, and heard sirens. "Here we go again." This time, I was not nearly as nervous as I had been on the other occasions, ready to dispense my professor line, show my consent forms and faculty ID, and see their shocked reaction. "Get out of the car and put your hands on the trunk," the driver predictably ordered as I began my explanation. They searched me anyway, perhaps thinking it was just another mendacious story, but I kept conversing in a relaxed, erudite tone. Cops are known to have perceptual shorthands to render quick and accurate typifications of those with whom they're interacting,[48] and I could tell my conversational style was creating a good impression. I told them that I was doing interviews, that I was paying respondents for their time, and that the research was part of a university grant designed to better understand the everyday lives of urban youth. This was, of course, specious. The study's true purpose was to identify how crack dealers avoid arrest, something I dared not admit, for obvious reasons. "You can do what you want," one of them said, satisfied after a thorough search revealed no contraband, "but if I were you, I'd be real careful. You don't want to mess around with these punks." His words rang all too true several weeks later when Luther pointed the gun at my abdomen.

I did not realize it at the time, but my treatment by police was absolutely essential to my research. Police provided the "vital test"[49] I desperately needed to pass if my study were to be successful. The differential enforcement practices of these police officers (and many others around the country)—in which young, minority males are singled out as "symbolic assailants" and "suspicious characters" deserving of attention[50]—benefitted *me* immensely. Police detained *me* because I was with "them." Driving alone in these same areas at the same time, though suspicious, would not likely have attracted nearly as much attention. I was "guilty by association" and "deserving" of the scrutiny young black males in many urban locales receive consistently. For my research, at least, this differential enforcement was anything but negative.

As Douglas notes, it is often necessary for researchers to convince offenders they are studying that the researchers do not represent the authorities.[51] Sluka adds that subjects "are going to define whose side they think you are on. They will act towards you on the basis of this definition, regardless of your professions."[52] Words may be futile in convincing offenders who or what one really is. Ultimately, "actions speak louder than words. . . . [T]he researcher will have to demonstrate by . . . actions that he is on the side of the deviants, or at least, not on the side of the officials."[53] The police had treated me like just another user, and had done so with offenders present. This treatment provided the "actions" for me, the picture that spoke a thousand words.

Offenders' accounts of my treatment spread rapidly through the grapevine, solidifying my credibility for the remainder of the project and setting up the snowball sampling procedure I would use to recruit additional respondents. Without the actions of *police* I may not have been accepted by *offenders* as readily as I was or, perhaps, never accepted at all. A skillful researcher can use the police—indirectly and without their knowledge or, as in my case, without even the researcher's own intent—to demonstrate to offenders that the researcher is indeed legitimate and not an undercover police officer. Often thought to be a critical barrier to entry, the police may be the key to access. Of course, undercover officers themselves can manipulate this very dynamic to gain credibility with those they target—something savvy law enforcement administrators may exploit by setting up fake arrests in plain view. Such tactics may make a researcher's identity even more precarious; in my case, though, this did not occur.

Why police never attempted to confiscate my notes during these pull-overs I'll never know. Perhaps it was because the notes appeared to be chicken scratch and were indecipherable by anyone but me. Perhaps it was because my notes didn't reveal anything the cops did not already know, or at least thought they knew. Regardless, the law is clearly against ethnographers, who can be held in contempt and sent to jail for protecting sources and withholding information.[54] As Carey points out, "There is no privileged relationship between the … researcher and his subject similar to that enjoyed by the lawyer and client or psychiatrist and patient."[55] This, of course, says nothing about issues of guilty knowledge or guilty observation.[56] Being aware of dealing operations and watching transactions take place makes one an accessory to their commission, a felony whether one participates or not. Fieldworkers are co-conspirators by definition, no matter their motive or intent. As Polsky concludes, "If one is effectively to study adult criminals in their natural settings, he must make the moral decision that in some ways he will break the law himself."[57]

RESEARCHING ACTIVE CRACK SELLERS: IN PERSPECTIVE

By definition, criminological fieldworkers regularly intrude into the lives of individuals engaged in felonies—felonies for which these individuals can receive hard time. The more illegal the behavior, the more offenders as research subjects have to lose if found out. Obviously, this makes it tougher—and more risky—for researchers to gain access.

Street-level crack selling is thus a paradox of sorts: there is perhaps no other behavior so openly visible and so negatively sanctioned by law as crack selling. It must be this way for sellers to be available to their customers. This is particularly true in a declining drug market such as St. Louis[58] where demand is finite and dwindling, while the number of sellers has remained constant or increased. To compete in such conditions, sellers will often stand out longer and in more difficult conditions than they previously would, in greater numbers, and in greater numbers together. Individual sellers also may rush to customers to steal sales from competitors, drawing even more attention. This situation creates ideal conditions for police—or researchers—to identify open-air sellers and infiltrate them.

Access notwithstanding, the importance of a strong indigenous tie to the research setting at the beginning of field relations—as a way of vouching for the researcher—cannot be overstated. Access and safe access are two wholly different notions. In my case, this tie was Luther—or at least so I thought. More generally, it is an indigenous offender or ex-offender turned fieldworker who acts as gatekeeper and protector. Yet, in a twist of sorts, field research with active offenders often requires strong ties in order to generate weak ones—that is, to initiate the methodological snowball. Micro-structurally and methodologically, this is unique; multiple weak ties rather than one or two strong ones are thought to be indispensable for social-network creation.[59] Indeed, one or two strong ties may actually cut off an actor from an entire social network.

In field research, developing strong ties with the wrong person or persons can, at a minimum, bias the sample or, worse, generate no sample at all.[60] Researchers may gain entry, but it may be with the wrong person. As my encounter with Luther attests, the outcome can be far more threatening than obtaining a biased sample or no sample. Perhaps the larger point here is that, no matter how strong or safe one's ties, danger is inherent in fieldwork with active offenders. Nowhere is this truer than among street-corner crack sellers. Although many dangers can be addressed through planning and preparation, more often than not, danger management hinges on a creative process of "trial and blunder"[61] and results from a combination of skill and luck.[62] As Sluka notes, "[G]ood luck can sometimes help overcome a lack of skill, and well-developed skills can go far to help overcome the effects of bad luck. But sometimes no amount of skill will save one from a gross portion of bad luck."[63] Inevitably, criminological fieldwork is unpredictable and less subject to rational planning than we want it to be. How researchers handle this problem ultimately is a personal choice.

Researching active offenders requires one to balance conflicting agendas. Such agendas emanate from specific audiences—whether police or criminals— each with their own biases toward the ethnographic enterprise. Simply taking sides or currying favor with one audience over the other is not the issue, though this may be done at some point. Research strategies must be weighed carefully because their consequences are inevitably dialectical: police can get you "in" with offenders, but offenders can get you "in trouble" with police. Personal security is dependent on offender acceptance, yet security can be compromised by dependency. Police can be researchers' last bastion of hope against volatile offenders, but reliance on authorities may undermine the very purpose for being in the field. Caught among these contradictions stands the researcher, a true one-person "island in the street."[64] In this lonely position, the researcher must decide when to shade the truth and when to be forthright, when to offer and when to omit, when to induce and when to lie back. Such judgments are subjective and context specific, as any ethnographer will tell you. They must be made with the audience in mind, whether that audience is legal or illegal, academic or social. Each choice affects the kinds of data obtained and revealed. And how far an ethnographer is willing to go to get such data intertwines with the results that ethnographer hopes ultimately to obtain—as my encounter with Luther attests.

REFERENCES

1. All names are pseudonyms to protect identities.
2. Terry Williams, Eloise Dunlap, Bruce D. Johnson, and Ansley Hamid, "Personal Safety in Dangerous Places," *Journal of Contemporary Ethnography*, 21 (1992): 365.
3. Williams et al., "Personal Safety," 350.
4. Richard A. Berk and Joseph M. Adams, "Establishing Rapport with Deviant Groups," *Social Problems*, 18 (1970): 110.

5. Jeffrey A. Sluka, "Participant Observation in Violent Social Contexts," *Human Organization,* 49 (1990): 114.

6. Williams et al., "Personal Safety," 347.

7. Patrick Biernacki and Dan Waldorf, "Snowball Sampling," *Sociological Methods and Research,* 10 (1981): 141–163.

8. See Harold Garfinkel, "Conditions of Successful Degradation Ceremonies," *American Journal of Sociology,* 61 (1956): 420–424.

9. Williams et al., "Personal Safety," 364.

10. Williams et al., "Personal Safety," 350.

11. John M. Johnson, "Trust and Personal Involvements in Fieldwork," in *Contemporary Field Research,* ed. Robert M. Emerson (Prospect Heights, IL: Waveland, 1983), 205.

12. Kurt H. Wolff, "Surrender and Community Study: The Study of Loma," in *Reflections on Community Studies,* ed. Arthur J. Vidich, Joseph Bensman, and Maurice R. Stein (New York: Wiley, 1964), 237.

13. Robert H. Lowies, *The History of Ethnological Theory* (New York: Farrar and Rinehart, 1937), 232.

14. Hortense Powdermaker, *Stranger and Friend: The Way of an Anthropologist* (New York: Norton, 1966), 19.

15. E. E. Evans-Pritchard, *Social Anthropology and Other Essays* (New York: Free Press, 1964), 77–79.

16. Berk and Adams, "Establishing Rapport," 103.

17. Berk and Adams, "Establishing Rapport."

18. Rosalie H. Wax, "The Ambiguities of Fieldwork," in *Contemporary Field Research,* ed. Robert M. Emerson (Prospect Heights, IL: Waveland, 1983), 179.

19. Ned Polsky, *Hustlers, Beats, and Others* (Chicago: Aldine, 1967), 124.

20. Robert M. Emerson, ed., *Contemporary Field Research* (Prospect Heights, IL: Waveland, 1983), 179.

21. Ivan Karp and Martha B. Kendall, "Reflexivity in Field Work," in *Explaining Human Behavior: Consciousness, Human Action, and Social Structure,* ed. Paul F. Secord (Beverly Hills, CA: Sage, 1982), 261.

22. Georg Simmel, "The Stranger," in *Georg Simmel,* ed. Donald Levine (Chicago: University of Chicago Press, 1908), 143–149.

23. Emerson, *Contemporary Field Research,* 179.

24. Richard T. Wright and Scott H. Decker, *Burglars on the Job: Streetlife and Residential Break-ins* (Boston: Northeastern University Press, 1994), 26.

25. Berk and Adams, "Establishing Rapport," 107.

26. See Polsky, *Hustlers.*

27. Peter K. Manning, "Observing the Police: Deviance, Respectables, and the Law," in *Research on Deviance,* ed. Jack D. Douglas (New York: Random House, 1972), 213–268.

28. Annie Oakley, "Interviewing Women: A Contradiction in Terms," in *Doing Feminist Research,* ed. Helen Roberts (London: Routledge and Kegan Paul, 1981), 41.

29. Luther's stalking came to an end only because police picked him up on two unrelated counts of armed robbery and armed criminal action. He is now serving 10 years in a Missouri state penitentiary. With the help of colleagues, I moved. My phone number is now unlisted and unpublished, something I recommend to other ethnographers researching active offenders.

30. John Irwin, "Participant Observation of Criminals," in *Research on Deviance*, ed. Jack D. Douglas (New York: Random House, 1972), 117.

31. See Erich Goode, *The Marijuana Smokers* (New York: Basic, 1970).

32. Sluka, "Participant Observation," 115.

33. See Patricia Adler, *Wheeling and Dealing: An Ethnography of an Upper-Level Drug Dealing and Smuggling Community* (New York: Columbia University Press, 1985).

34. Diana Scully, *Understanding Sexual Violence* (Boston: Unwin Inman, 1990).

35. Michael Agar, *Ripping and Running: A Formal Ethnography of Urban Heroin Addicts* (New York: Seminar Press, 1973).

36. Wright and Decker, *Burglars*, 5.

37. Edwin Sutherland and Donald Cressey, *Criminology*, 8th ed. (Philadelphia: Lippincott, 1970), 68.

38. Polsky, *Hustlers*, 123.

39. George McCall, *Observing the Law* (New York: Free Press, 1978), 27.

40. Erving Goffman, *Relations in Public: Micro Studies of the Public Order* (New York: Basic Books, 1971), 323.

41. SCAT is an acronym for "street corner apprehension team." This 15-man undercover team is charged with curbing street-level drug sales by apprehending dealers immediately after sales to one of their "buy" officers. Hiding nearby in unmarked cars, personnel "swoop" down on offenders in an attempt to catch them with marked money just given them by buy officers. This money either has traceable dye or serial numbers previously recorded that link dealers to undercover transactions. SCAT units were highly feared because they were reportedly merciless in their arrest procedures (i.e., they conducted strip searches).

42. Jeff Ferrell and Mark S. Hamm, *Ethnography at the Edge: Crime, Deviance and Field Research* (Boston: Northeastern University Press, 1998).

43. Wright and Decker, *Burglars*, 28.

44. Polsky, *Hustlers*, 147.

45. See Sluka, "Participant Observation."

46. Federal Bureau of Investigation, *Crime in the United States* (Washington, DC: Government Printing Office, 1995).

47. See Erving Goffman, *Stigma: Notes on the Management of Spoiled Identity* (Englewood Cliffs, NJ: Prentice Hall, 1963).

48. See John Van Maanen, "The Asshole," in *Policing: A View from the Streets*, ed. Peter K. Manning and John Van Maanen (Santa Monica: Goodyear, 1978), 221–238.

49. Erving Goffman, *Frame Analysis: An Essay on the Organization of Experience* (Cambridge, MA: Harvard University Press, 1974).

50. See Jerome Skolnick, "A Sketch of the Policeman's 'Working Personality,' " in *Criminal Justice: Law and Politics*, ed. George F. Cole (North Scituate, MA: Duxbury Press, 1980).

51. Jack D. Douglas, "Observing Deviance," in *Research on Deviance*, ed. Jack D. Douglas (New York: Random House, 1972), 3–34.

52. Sluka, "Participant Observation," 123.

53. Douglas, "Observing Deviance," 12.

54. Irving Soloway and James Walters, "Workin' the Corner: The Ethics and Legality of Fieldwork among Active Heroin Addicts," in *Street Ethnography*, ed. Robert S. Weppner (Beverly Hills, CA: Sage, 1977), 175–176.

55. James T. Carey, "Problems of Access and Risk in Observing Drug Scenes," in *Research on Deviance*, ed. Jack D. Douglas (New York: Random House, 1972), 77.

56. See Adler, *Wheeling*, 24.

57. Polsky, *Hustler*, 133–134.

58. Andrew Gollub, Farrukh Hakeem, and Bruce D. Johnson, "Monitoring the Decline in the Crack Epidemic with Data from the Drug Use Forecasting Program," unpublished manuscript (1996).

59. Mark Granovetter, "The Strength of Weak Ties," *American Journal of Sociology*, 78 (1973): 1360–1380.

60. Douglas's research on nudist beach goers, for example, was jeopardized because of his early bond with a marginal and generally disliked participant (something Douglas did not know until later)—a participant with whom he was able to bond precisely because of that person's marginality; see Douglas, "Observing Deviance."

61. See Karp and Kendall, "Reflexivity."

62. Robert F. Ellen, *Ethnographic Research: A Guide to General Conduct* (London: Academic Press, 1984), 97.

63. Sluka, "Participant Observation," 124.

64. Marin Sanchez-Jankowski, *Islands in the Street: Gangs in American Urban Society* (Berkeley: University of California Press, 1991).

CHAPTER 2

Consenting to Talk:
Why Inmates Participate in Prison Research
Heith Copes and Andy Hochstetler

The authors discuss the various motivations of prisoners' willingness to discuss their past criminal activities. They reveal that prisoners may talk about their crimes due to the financial rewards offered by the researchers, due to their desire to "teach" researchers and others about crime, to reduce boredom, and out of curiosity, as well as to provide certain psychological benefits to themselves.

Criminologists have a long history of interviewing inmates to gain insights into the nature of crime and criminality. By posing questions to inmates, researchers offer the incarcerated an opportunity to explain their histories, offenses, and lifestyles from their own perspectives. This is important because those who have engaged in criminal and deviant activities are in the "unique position of being able to describe, in their own words, the motivations and causes of crime, the level and nature of crime calculus, and the perceived effectiveness of crime control activities in deterring crime" (Miethe & McCorkle 2001:17). When the voices of those who have engaged in illegal activity are coupled with researchers' analyses, academics and criminal justice professionals can get a more realistic glimpse into the world of offenders, move closer toward theoretical explanation of criminal lifestyles and decisions, and better design effective crime control policy.

Clearly, posing questions to offenders is important for a full understanding of crime and criminality. But if criminologists are to garner the benefits of offenders' perspectives, they must both locate these individuals and convince them to talk about their misdeeds. Finding people who have direct experience with criminal behavior can be difficult as they often desire to remain hidden, especially from those outside their social worlds; yet finding them is in no way impossible. While there are many places ethnographers can go to locate offenders (e.g., street

Source: Written especially for this volume.

corners, bars, shelters, rehabilitation meetings, jails, or prison), here we are concerned with those confined to prisons and jails.

Undoubtedly, it is easier to locate people who have engaged in criminal behaviors in prisons than on the streets. They are captive populations after all. Even if criminologists do seek out incarcerated offenders, they must still confront the task of convincing them to share their stories. Ethnographic research requires that we intrude into people's lives and have them reveal personal information that they may not have shared with others before—information that could have negative consequences for them. Despite the inconveniences and potential risks of talking to researchers, inmates are often quite willing to discuss their lives and criminal careers in great detail. Many novice interviewers assume inaccurately that inmates will not discuss certain topics with them. They mistakenly believe that they will be met with "hostility and a lack of co-operation" from those they wish to interview (Shover 1985:154). Fortunately, as Berg (2001:95) notes, "once subjects have been persuaded to participate in an interview, they often tell far more details than the interviewers would ever want to know." This willingness to talk has been documented by numerous researchers (Akerstrom 1985; Girshick 1999; Shover 1985, 1996). Indeed, we too have been astounded by inmates' openness and frankness in their descriptions of their lives and crimes.

What would make someone who has been incarcerated for behavior that society has defined as immoral and illegal disregard the potential risks and inconveniences to sit down and openly discuss their lives and misdeeds? Answers to this question have important implications for qualitative researchers when recruiting inmates and uncovering the meaningfulness of their finished work. The motives inmates have for participating in research ultimately affect the nature of the stories they relay and the type of information they withhold. It was for these reasons that during two separate research projects we posed the question, "Why did you agree to talk to us?" In total, we asked this question of 73 individuals. All were incarcerated in medium-security prisons at the time of the interviews. The first project involved inmates in Louisiana who had committed at least one carjacking ($n = 33$). The other project involved inmates in Alabama who were discussing their perceptions of parole revocation ($n = 40$). In what follows, we discuss the various motives inmates discussed for their decisions to consent to an interview. We found much diversity in their answers. The reasons they gave for consenting to the interview included the desire to satisfy immediate material needs, to benefit emotionally and psychologically, and to give back to others; a few participated because of a misunderstanding about the benefits we were capable of providing.

IMMEDIATE REWARDS

Many inmates agreed to be interviewed for altruistic reasons, such as doing their part to keep the next generation from making similar mistakes or helping out a trusted confederate (Shover 1985). A smaller number of inmates consented to interviews for more self-serving and mundane reasons. Inmates said that they were willing to tell their stories to us because they could use the money that we offered, they simply desired to have a conversation with someone from the outside, they were eager to get a change of scenery, or they were curious to see what it was like to be interviewed.

Financial Incentives

Researchers who rely on survey and interview methods often provide small monetary incentives to encourage participants either to complete a questionnaire or to consent to an interview. Financial incentives can be powerful motivators. This is especially true among populations that have little means of earning money, such as those confined in an institution. Even those who are interviewed in the streets, who could conceivably make more money through hustling than researchers can offer, are attracted to the prospect of making quick cash (Wright & Decker 1994). While there are some ethical dilemmas when deciding how much money to offer, most researchers agree that it is appropriate to compensate study participants for their time and knowledge. A survey of ethnographic research appearing in the top criminology and criminal justice journals showed that over 20% offered financial inducements to participants, with an average amount of $41.25 (Copes, Brown, & Tewksbury 2011). We offered the inmates in Louisiana $20 and those in Alabama $15 to encourage them to sit down and talk with us.

Undoubtedly, our financial incentive did encourage participation; however, it was uncommon for inmates to state that their primary reason for participating in the research was for the money. Statements such as, "Twenty dollars about the only thing good you know. That's about it. That's about the only thing good [about doing this]," or "I needed [the money], you know what I'm saying. I needed it. It helped," were uncommon. In fact, only a handful of inmates claimed that money was the sole driving force behind their participation. Doubtless, easy money does intrigue offenders and whet other motives for participating.

It was more common for inmates to acknowledge that money helped but that other reasons for their cooperation were more important. As such, financial compensation was seen as a nice bonus. Gerald stated, "I'm gonna be blessed with twenty dollars and hopefully I can help you with your study, your career, or whatever you are doing." Echoing this, Francis answered:

> To be honest with you, broke. Needed some money. But no, then again it was a chance to see what's really up, different aspects on what someone thinks and the like. [Maybe] I could get some pointers on trying to classify my life. . . . The money was good, but the interview and session was pretty good too.

While participants mentioned money as a benefit, they underplayed its importance by suggesting that altruism or personal growth was the "real" reason for participating (Fry & Dwyer 2001). Regardless of the priority of money as a motivator, it is clear that even small financial gestures helped to generate compliance.

Conversations with Outsiders

The secrecy inherent in criminal participation means that offenders have few opportunities to relate their exploits to those who are not associates. Offenders often find this inability to share their "war stories" frustrating (Letkemann 1973). This is especially the case when audiences who are familiar with and largely uninterested in such stories other than as diversionary banter surround them. This frustration is possibly even greater among captive populations. Deep reflection on or analysis of one's mistakes is discouraged in most informal contexts of the prison. This is expressed by Derrick, who claimed he wanted to participate "just to talk to a stranger for thirty minutes is cool with me cause I'm getting tired of talking to them [other inmates]." Incarcerated individuals have few opportunities to have meaningful conversations with those who are not incarcerated or who are not criminal justice personnel. They have little opportunity to share their stories with people who do not judge them or assume they are being deceptive or hyperbolic. In the words of Bryan, "It's good [talking to you]. It ain't too often that we get to conversate with someone . . . on an intelligent level, you know what I'm saying. [With someone] that's already overcome certain obstacles and is already successful." Similarly Michael explained, "I ain't never got a visit since I been up here. I haven't seen nobody from the streets in seven years. Ain't had a visit, you know. It was just cool talking to you." When cut off from the conventional and ordinary world any taste of it can be rewarding, or at least a relief from routine. Inmates welcomed the chance to talk to someone who was not in some way connected to the institution (Athens 1997:103).

Additionally, some offenders were motivated by the desire to teach those with formal educations something about life in the streets. Many ethnographers have fostered the teaching role of respondents to generate cooperation from them (Berk & Adams 1970). As Miller (2001:30) points out, "providing respondents with the opportunity to act as teachers can afford them with a sense of meaning and importance." Because marginalized individuals seldom have the opportunity to lend their voice to social discourse, the opportunity to do so acts as a lure for their participation. The value of simple conversation with a person whom they need not impress, with whom they have no official or emotional tie, and with whom they can share their expertise cannot be overestimated as a motive for offenders inside and outside of prison walls.

Change of Setting/Pass Time

To effectively manage prison populations prison staff must structure the daily activities of inmates. This creates a predictable, monotonous routine for prisoners, which can make time creep and the days run together. To disrupt this routine, inmates often seek out activities in the hopes of making time go a little faster. Many inmates enroll in church services, educational programs, and self-help classes not because of desire to change their ways, but simply to change their setting. As Rufus stated, "What are we doing in the dorm? Nothing. This right here, this is passing my time." This desire to break the routine of prison life is a motivating factor for many of those who participate in research as it "provides a break from the boredom and monotony of prison life" (Matthews 2002:10). Several stated that they simply enjoyed the pleasure of "getting away and getting out for a while." In responding to our question about why they came to talk to us, participants gave statements such as Michaels's, "I just want a little walk, you know what I'm saying" and Millicent's, "You stay in the dorm. You be cooped up in there 24 hours a day. Ain't nothing else to do back in the dorm except playing cards or something." Warren might have expressed the sentiment most bluntly:

> A dude told me about it and I said shoot I gotta get up there 'cause there ain't nothing to do around here. Absolutely nothing! We don't have nothing but running, exercising, reading, and writing. That's it! I just wanted to get out, to be honest with you . . . I would have sure done it for free.

Certainly, when people spend most of their time in a confined area any opportunity to travel beyond its borders is welcomed. Doubtless, the motivation increases in bleak settings. The novelty of speaking to a person who is not part of the offender's past or institutional life makes the break from monotony all the more enjoyable.

Curiosity

Many of those who are confined in state institutions share an interest in experiencing the unknown. This same trait is what drove several of the participants to consent to the interview (Matthews 2002). Robbie exemplified this curiosity in his response to our question:

> Well, I wanted to see what it was really about. You know, curiosity. Curiosity killed the cat. I just wanted to see what's happening up here, you know. I decided to come down and see.

Several individuals made direct reference to wanting to "come up here and see what it was like." Part of seeing what it is like was to discern whether something is amiss and to exude confidence in the face of what could be a deception. Showing confidence in chaotic or unknown situations is a trait highly valued by many serious street offenders (Katz 1988). Investigators often get the impression when doing research in jails and prisons, as well as on the streets, that some of the first people they interview see themselves as scouts who can speak with authority to others about whether the situation is "cool." If investigators were to press them for names, dates, or other sorts of information that could lead to trouble, early participants would caution friends and associates considering the interview. Having good rapport with early interviewees did encourage others to participate. In referring to a former interviewee, Sidney said, "The guy that I was talking to about it, me and him are cool, and he say, 'Do you want to do the interview?' I said, yeah, that's cool."

PSYCHOLOGICAL BENEFITS TO SELF

Many offenders decided to participate because they have begun to reassess their crimes and related mistakes. They either were engaged in a new way of life or were exploring the possibility of a new approach. In fact, the interview was often viewed as part of a therapeutic process or as evidence of their recovery. Many believed that talking to professionals, even if they are criminologists and not psychiatrists, might "help them come to terms with their personal problems" (Wright & Decker 1997:25). Thus, sharing their stories acts as a catharsis and as evidence that they are on the right path to recovery.

Catharsis

Talking to interviewers allows offenders to "let it all out" without being perceived as weak or vulnerable. For people who have engaged in illegal behavior the simple act of talking about their misdeeds makes them feel better about what they have done. Several of those we spoke with thanked us for allowing them to talk and acknowledged that they felt better about themselves because of the experience (see Shover 1985). When asked if anything good came from the experience, Melvin answered, "The therapeutic value of being able to discuss as many details of my life and to remain honest in those assessments." As Shawn said:

> It makes me feel better by talking about [my past]. I mean, it's like looking back over all the devious shit that I've done and got away with, I figure, you know, if I can come sit down here and talk to you about half the shit I done did then I can sleep better.

Interviewing offenders not only benefits social science, but it also allows those directly involved in the behavior to explain away, both to others and to themselves, the guilt caused by criminal participation. These benefits were likely due to the fact that the interview allowed them to "let it all out" without being perceived as weak or vulnerable. For people in prison, the simple act of talking about their misdeeds can make them feel better about what they have done and may aid in the important process of making sense of and contextualizing past mistakes (Maruna 2001). Indeed, for many research participants, the interview was a genuine, emotional experience.

The Right Track

The interview is a reflective setting. Offenders get the message that they are supposed to be assessing what went wrong for them. Some think that assessments of their prospects for reform should follow the telling of the unfortunate story. After the interview two participants said they were going to go "straight" and do what they could to get back in school (see Wright & Decker 1997:25). In fact, one of these later contacted us about how to apply for school. We are unaware if he followed through with our advice or if he actually went "straight." More important for present purposes, such statements of conventional goals and assessments of prospects conclude many interviews, even when they are not requested.

Additionally, participating in research requires that offenders adapt or respond to a conventional stance. They explain errors and crimes in a way that might be understood by strangers to the street criminal's world (Maruna & Copes 2005). Offenders, especially those on the slippery path to reform, are likely to portray crime as an aberration and, as such, as something interesting and worth exploring. Criminal acts say nothing about who the offenders are deep inside or who they want to be. Loosely structured interviews aid this interpretation and narrative if only by the implicit assumptions that the causes of crime are complex and the choice to offend is worthy of reflection (Presser 2010; Sandberg 2010).

Offenders experience few settings where an honest recounting of their stories might be interpreted as evidence of noble aims. In the interview, their honesty is more important than the ledger that balances their criminal records and other failures against their accomplishments. Interviews, therefore, fit neatly into offenders' self-improvement projects and help them to refine and construct their stories as honest struggling citizens. Many have only had such conversations with themselves and are eager to voice them in a setting where these stories will not be viewed as overly sentimental or a con game. Their enthusiasm for relating their stories of change also should be interpreted in light of treatment program designs that emphasize claiming one's mistakes, confessing, and sharing tales of struggle and redemption. Many have participated in such programs and all are aware of them. Being given a chance to tell their story, or testify, represents an opportunity to take a step, however small, in the right direction. For this reason, inmates commonly responded to questions about participation with answers much more profound and ambitious than researchers, who typically have humble aims, might initially expect. Charles commented, "I don't know, it's like even though I consider myself halfway, I am getting my mind right." Philip reflected on his motives:

> I'm just trying to get right, you know. I want to go out there and do the right thing and make my mom proud. Settle down, have a little family. I'm tired of coming in here. Selling drugs ain't going to take you nowhere.

Participation in the research process indicates to themselves and to outsiders that they are indeed on the right path to getting their lives in order.

SOCIAL BENEFITS TO OTHERS

Many participants choose to take part in research to help others, either specific people (like us) or more abstract ones. In some cases this is part of their project to do the right thing and make amends for past misdeeds. Where this is the case, they often want to teach the moral lessons of their stories to an imagined audience of people confronting similar decisions to the ones that led them astray. In their imaginings, this may occur when someone's life is directly affected, as is hopefully the case when offenders speak to student groups. Most offenders recognize that they are more likely to reach their target audience indirectly. They intend to help a researcher to understand criminal acts in a way that might indirectly benefit those at risk of crime or help others recognize the social problems that might have contributed to their acts.

Helping Abstract Others

Many of those who agreed to talk to us did so because they recognized that they have acted improperly and wished that their testimonies could help deter young people from making similar bad choices. All who conduct qualitative research hear statements such as Anthony's:

> Maybe it might help somebody. Help some young person. Hopefully, they haven't really gotten into [violent crime] yet. Maybe, they might be stealing cars or something like that, you know. Maybe, I might be able to help them or you might be able to help them by hearing what I have to say.

Omar expressed the sentiment, "I just hope whatever I said could help. Like I said, it's too late for me. My day is right around the corner. I hope the information could get help to others . . . and help the next person." Similarly, Kenneth said he hoped that his words could "inspire somebody else not to end up in this place." Such altruistic intentions on the part of the offender have shaped qualitative criminology since its earliest days. The five Martin boys interviewed by Shaw and colleagues claimed that they agreed to give their life histories in the "genuine hope that the documents might be useful in preventing other boys from becoming involved in delinquency and crime" (Shaw, McKay, & McDonald 1938:143).

In a similar vein, some participants look toward improved community understanding and recognition of some of the external sources of crime as the main reason for participating. As Thomas explained:

> I was cool about it because I really want to let people know why people do it. That's the only reason why I participated. You know, just so they can have understanding that it's more than what society would think. Society put a label on them and put them in jail for the rest of their lives. [People should] try to learn something about this person and why he or she did these things. Then, you understand. I mean [understand] why you want to rob, why you want to kill, why you want to jack this or jack that. If you got a good understanding of their background and environment, then you have a better understanding of why people do these things.

Kelvin echoed this optimism:

> If the analysis would help somebody else, man if it would give y'all some kind of idea about how to help people from coming back like this. If me being one of the tools to help guide y'all toward getting a solution for this, then man, that's the reason I really did it. . . . I don't wanna see nobody coming here so if it help one person it's a plus.

Participants with this motivation believe that "their life history would make an entertaining and perhaps useful contribution to understanding crime and those who commit it" (Shover 1996:190).

Helping the Researcher

These varieties of altruism are common, but participation in a research project can also help others who are more proximate and who are more certain to benefit. Researchers are often impressed at how many participants decide to participate in a project primarily because it will help the researcher. This often comes from a practical recognition that completion of a research project benefits academic careers. While the participants have little understanding of how academic careers advance, they do understand that they are being asked to help and are in a position to aid someone in a conventional pursuit. When asked why he agreed to talk to us, Bryan responded:

> Oh, you alright. I just heard you was at school. If it can help you out, by me being in here, I mean by me giving you this . . . I just hope something comes out of this. Maybe, you can get something out of this.

In keeping with the reflective tone of many interviews, the desire to help someone's academic or professional advancement often is accompanied by statements that failure in the workplace and educational advancement is where they went astray. Derrick lamented, "This is helping you, you know. . . . At least you are doing what you should be doing. I should be in college right now." They also want to help students. As "experts" on crime, they desired to give their expertise to those who study it. The fact that students of crime typically are attached to the university gives the offender a way to tap into, if only temporarily and with the loosest connection, this prestigious world and to put experience to good use.

A desire to help us resulted in several participants refusing to take the money for the interview because they believed this money was coming directly from our pockets. Shover (1985) observed a similar reaction from those with whom he spoke. Like Shover, we insisted that these individuals accept the money.

MISUNDERSTANDING

Ethical guidelines require researchers to disclose the nature and possible dangers of the research to participants. When doing research in a prison setting it is important to inform inmates that their participation is completely voluntary and that it will have no effect, either positive or negative, on their status as an inmate. That is, inmates are informed in advance that participation will not affect parole, admittance into work or social programs, or their relations with staff. Despite these acknowledgments, many inmates are motivated to volunteer because they believe they will somehow benefit from cooperation.

Even though we took special care to let inmates know that we neither worked for nor were affiliated with the prison or the department of corrections, several inmates believed that we could help them with their criminal justice status in some indirect manner. The few who thought this way believed that the study was one of the many programs that the prison implemented to help ex-cons get back on their feet. For example, George acknowledged, "[I agreed because] the prison has a lot of programs that are going on. You don't know what you getting yourself into. It could be something good, you know what I'm saying." Upon further probing it became clear that this individual believed that our research was a part of a program set up by the prison to help inmates. He agreed to talk to us because he thought it was a prerequisite for acceptance into the program. Fortunately, we were able to clarify this misunderstanding and the inmate left with the concluding remark, "Well, if nothing else at least I got out of the dorms."

Millicent, who also misinterpreted our solicitation, agreed to come and meet with us because "I didn't know I was coming in here for an interview. I thought I was coming here to sign some papers to go home." After we explained the intent of the interviews she consented. It is possible that some inmates are under the impression that this is a chance for them to tell stories that may help them with their case. This is often because they imagine that interviewers are informants or are operating at the behest of criminal justice officials. However, none expressed this idea explicitly. We believe that inmates participating for this reason are easy to identify by their reluctance to address many questions and their apparent deceptions. By comparing their words with official records, researchers see deception. If we are right, this motivation is exceedingly rare.

DISCUSSION

Offenders have a project when they come to an interview (Presser 2004). To some extent, their narratives are predetermined and independent of the questions that are asked. Offenders' constructions of their stories may have as much to do with the reasons they consent to the interview as the prompts and probing questions from the researcher. Stories of struggle or reform are, for example, fairly consistent across offenders and of a limited number of types. They rear their heads in much of what offenders say about a variety of topics. Interviewers become familiar with certain scripts, such as the addiction tales of heroin users, the born-again stories of penitents, and the hard-knock stories of early life on the streets of large housing projects. This does not deny that the stories are true or diminish the value of what offenders say for understanding crime; these accounts are part of human and lived experience. Nevertheless, the motivations for sharing and the constructions of accounts by offenders should not escape the attention of qualitative researchers or their readers. One reason is that they introduce an angle into the account that might be missed if researchers do not pay attention to what offenders are attempting to accomplish in interviews. Also, they raise some potential methodological biases.

Participation in almost all research projects and data collection efforts is voluntary. Beyond checking to make sure that those who decline to participate do not differ on potentially important variables from those who do, little can be done about selection biases introduced by volunteering. Students of crime must accept that they generally only know the stories of those who choose to tell them and as they choose to tell them. Participating inmates are likely to adopt certain postures. At some times and in some settings these may be very different than the identities and images they send off when committing crimes. Offenders may be insightful and careful where they know that such a stance is appropriate and that every word will be analyzed. Conversely, some will choose to play the role of criminal in hope that researchers will not be disappointed with their stories. This act may resemble over-the-top identities and cool poses that are characteristic of street corners and the decision to offend. In any case, the proportional distribution of accounts is influenced by the decision to participate in a study, the interview setting, the story that is most viable there, and the motives of participants.

Qualitative researchers themselves introduce another source of potential bias. Articulate and interesting respondents are more likely to influence findings at every stage of analysis. These interviews last longer and are drawn from more heavily. To prove this point, one need only recognize how articulate and insightful many participants are whose statements find their way into print. It is the hope of every researcher that an article is interesting, and it is tempting to select colorful statements for inclusion. Participants, especially those whose interviews are heavily relied upon, probably are more reflective, intelligent, and well-spoken than the typical street offender. The bright, self-reflective, and verbose may be more likely to volunteer in the first place because they believe that they have something interesting and worthwhile to say, or suspect that they are capable of saying it well. Their narratives follow a logical plot line and are easy to organize and understand. Despite the selection bias toward articulate volunteers, every qualitative researcher of street crime learns that a good interview that provides insight on more than a few simple points is highly valued. Readers should not forget that ramblings of the intellectually challenged, the hopelessly intoxicated, and mentally ill respondents seldom make it to paper as the data from these interviews are often useless (see Miller 1986:187). This omission is justifiable, but these shortcomings certainly speak to some of the origins and lived experience of crime.

The Value of Talk

For many years, qualitative research was seen as the most appropriate way to gauge criminal motives. Apart from recognition that reasonable offenders would hide a few details and bend the truth on occasion, the offender was viewed as an impartial narrator of events. This is, of course, not the way reconstruction of motives or answers to difficult questions occur for any of us (Presser 2010; Sandberg 2010). Wider academic interest in the formation of accounts and narratives of complex events has turned attention to this fact. For example, those of us who chose to go to college probably cannot really explain accurately the decision-making processes or events that led us to that conclusion, although we do have a story available should anyone ask. Many questions asked of offenders by qualitative researchers require similar narrative construction. Variation in these constructions may be important over and above the facts relayed. In fact, there is increasing and great awareness among criminologists that the way that offenders understand and depict their lives may have significant effects on their prospects for rehabilitation. The story that offenders tell and how they tell it may give indication of their progress toward the end of a criminal career (Maruna 2001).

The decision to participate in a study and the reason given for it might be similarly relevant and important. Some offenders see their participation in a study as a reaffirming or generative exercise. This decision and its motivations represent the front board of the stories they will relate. For some, it is a small gesture at restitution. For others, it is an attempt to elicit some understanding from an impartial and attentive outsider. A few see the decision as yet another sign that they are on the right track or as a chance to explore their motives publicly. Some are simply raconteurs or curiosity seekers who want to see what kind of reaction they will get from their stories or what a research effort is about. There is, for many, nothing better to do and nothing to hide. Unfortunately, for researchers who are looking for more, a few use the unusual venue to fictitiously portray themselves as unremorseful hard men or criminal insiders who occupy a strange and exciting world. Like some rap artists, who posture as pimps and hustlers, almost none of these are as interesting or exceptional as they think and their insights are familiar, predictable, and fairly easy to tune out. Occasionally, a good qualitative researcher can turn around an interview that has this quality or other indications that it is unproductive. This may well be because offenders' motives shift as they proceed in the course of an interview; they can strike on something unexpected and decide to explore it. But if offenders are really there only for the money or to show off, the good that will come of talking to them is reduced (Jacques & Wright 2008).

Implications for Institutional Review Boards
The current findings and discussion of why offenders consent to interviews have important implications for how researchers complete Institutional Review Board (IRB) reports. The IRB is designed to ensure that researchers treat human participants in a way that is consistent with ethical guidelines. When determining if a certain research project using human subjects is ethical, the researcher must demonstrate that the benefits of the study outweigh potential harm to participants. Those who engage in ethnographic research typically point to the abstract benefits that the research addresses, such as how the study can inform criminal justice personnel on how best to thwart the actions of offenders. Thus, the general public benefits from the words of offenders, but little is said of the actual participants. The current research suggests that the telling of their stories can have direct benefits to participants. Interviews can have real emotional impacts on them. An understanding of how the research process can benefit those directly involved in it can go a long way in facilitating the IRB process, making it easier for ethnographic researchers to leave their offices and speak with thieves, hustlers, and heavy drug users, both inside prisons and out in the free world.

CONCLUSIONS

Like offenders' words themselves, their motives for participating in a study are of interest for voyeuristic, theoretical, and practical reasons. There are patterns and subtexts in narratives based on the narrator's purpose and understanding of what is appropriate. These form a significant part of the story and how the facts are related. The same is true of participants in qualitative criminological research.

Their motives tell something about where the offenders have been, where they are, and where they are going.

It is clear that criminologists have much to gain from interviewing inmates. The accounts of offenders have allowed us to understand the meanings they associate with crime, the criminal decision-making process, and the most effective crime control strategies (Decker 2005). What has been less clear is what these participants have to gain in this research. We have provided a list of many, but certainly not all, of the reasons that offenders have for talking with interviewers. It is important to point out that we elicited the cooperation of individuals who were incarcerated for either violent crimes or parole revocations at the time of the interview. Inmates may have different motives than active offenders for agreeing to be a part of academic research. Those who are living outside prison walls obviously do not participate in research to get a look at new scenery, although they may be looking for a novel activity. Nevertheless, we believe that the reasons these incarcerated individuals gave are likely similar to the reasons non-incarcerated individuals give. That is, participants on both sides of prison walls are likely curious, desire the financial compensation, see it as therapeutic, or simply want to help others by relaying their lived experiences.

In addition, one's position in the social structure may affect interpretation of the research event and motivations for being a part of a study. Those who are approaching the end of their criminal careers surely have different reasons than those just embracing crime or those in the midst of their careers. Similarly, those who engage in especially egregious criminal acts, like murder and rape, may not have the same motivations as those whose crimes are more mundane. White-collar offenders are likely to devote a great deal of effort in interviews to defending their character. Penitents are rare among them. But once again we contend that differences among types of offenders are merely in the relative frequency of motives for participation and not in distinct motives. The desire to help others, to get on the right track, or to just share their lives with others is certainly not unique to those in prisons, those considering giving up crime, or those who engage in violent street crimes (see Wright & Decker 1994, 1997).

REFERENCES

Akerstrom, M. (1985). *Crooks and squares: Lifestyles of thieves and addicts in comparison to conventional people.* New Brunswick, NJ: Transaction.

Athens, L. (1997). *Violent criminal acts and actors revisited.* Urbana: University of Illinois Press.

Berg, B. L. (2001). *Qualitative research methods for the social sciences,* 4th ed. Needham Heights, MA: Allyn and Bacon.

Berk, R., & Adams, J. M. (1970). Establishing rapport with deviant groups. *Social Problems, 18,* 102–117.

Copes, H., Brown, A., & Tewksbury, R. (2011). A content analysis of ethnographic research published in top criminology and criminal justice journals from 2000–2009. *Journal of Criminal Justice Education, 22,* 341–59.

Decker, S. (2005). *Using offender interviews to inform police problem solving.* Problem-Solving Tools Series, Guide No. 3. Washington, DC: U.S. Department of Justice.

Fry, C., & Dwyer, R. (2001). For love or money? An exploratory study of why injecting drug users participate in research. *Addiction, 9,* 1319–25.

Girshick, L. (1999). *No safe haven: Stories of women in prison.* Boston: Northeastern University Press.

Jacques, S., & Wright, R. (2008). Intimacy with outlaws: The role of relational distance in recruiting, paying, and interviewing underworld research participants. *Journal of Research in Crime and Delinquency, 46,* 22–38.

Katz, J. (1988). *Seductions of crime: The moral and sensual attractions of doing evil.* New York: Basic Books.

Letkemann, P. (1973). *Crime as work.* Englewood Cliffs, NJ: Prentice-Hall.

Maruna, S. (2001). *Making good: How ex-convicts reform and rebuild their lives.* Washington, D.C.: American Psychological Association.

Maruna, S., & Copes, H. (2005) Excuses, excuses: What have we learned from five decades of neutralization research? *Crime and Justice: An Annual Review of Research, 32,* 221–320.

Matthews, R. (2002). *Armed robbery.* Portland, OR: Willan.

Miethe, T. D., & McCorkle, R. C. (2001). *Crime profiles: The anatomy of dangerous persons, places and situations.* Los Angeles: Roxbury.

Miller, E. M. (1986). *Street women.* Philadelphia: Temple University Press.

Miller, J. (2001). *One of the guys: Girls, gangs, and gender.* Oxford: Oxford University Press.

Presser, L. (2004). Violent offenders, moral selves: Constructing identities and accounts in the research interview. *Social Problems, 51,* 82–102.

Presser, L. (2010). Collecting and analyzing the stories of offenders. *Journal of Criminal Justice Education, 21,* 431–46.

Sandberg, S. (2010). What can "lies" tell us about life? Notes towards a framework of narrative criminology. *Journal of Criminal Justice Education, 21,* 447–65.

Shaw, C. R., McKay, H. D., & McDonald, J. F. (1938). *Brothers in crime.* Chicago: University of Chicago Press.

Shover, N. (1985). *Aging criminals.* Beverly Hills, CA: Sage.

Shover, N. (1996). *Great pretenders: Pursuits and careers of persistent thieves.* Boulder, CO: Westview.

Wright, R. T., & Decker, S. (1994). *Burglars on the job: Streetlife and residential break-ins.* Boston: Northeastern University Press.

Wright, R. T., & Decker, S. (1997). *Armed robbers in action: Stickups and street culture.* Boston: Northeastern University Press.

SECTION II

Criminal Lifestyles and Decision Making

The chapters in Section II explore the lifestyles and decision-making strategies of criminals. These articles are primarily concerned with offenders' views and attitudes about both criminal and conventional activities and their perceptions of the risks and benefits associated with a criminal lifestyle. Furthermore, we examine how those perceptions are formed and how they change over time. We also consider issues centering on how offenders process their environment and the factors that may influence their criminal decision making. Because a criminal lifestyle is largely hidden from public view and open only to the initiated, criminologists continue to investigate this important issue in order to understand it better. These studies represent a step forward in understanding the dynamics of criminal lifestyles and criminal decision making in that context.

In Chapter 3, "Deciding to Commit a Burglary," Richard T. Wright and Scott H. Decker examine the dynamics underlying the decision to commit a burglary. The authors interviewed 105 active residential burglars by taking them to the scenes of their past crimes and asking them to reconstruct the burglary in extensive detail. In this chapter, they examine the factors that motivated the crime—that is, "Why burglary?" The participants of the study tended to be misfits in a world that values punctuality, schedules, and discipline. Crime appealed to some precisely because it allowed them to flaunt their independence from the routine imposed by the world of work. Their crimes were committed primarily because of their perception of an immediate need for money. This need for money largely stemmed from offenders' desire to maintain their lifestyle, which the authors describe as "high living" and "life as party," although some offenders committed burglaries for licit activities such as food, clothing, and shelter and others committed burglaries for revenge, thrills, and other noneconomic reasons.

In Chapter 4, "Opportunities and Decisions: Interactional Dynamics in Robbery and Burglary Groups," Andy Hochstetler analyzes the decision-making processes of criminals working in groups. He argues that although the role of co-offenders has been recognized for decades, it has not been adequately studied.

He finds that interaction among groups of offenders can "reduce the appeal of law abidance" and make criminal opportunities appear to be more attractive. Although the role and influence of co-offenders vary widely, participants mutually influence each other in terms of decisions to offend, target selection, and evaluation of the risk–gain calculus.

In Chapter 5, "Auto Theft and Restrictive Deterrence," Bruce Jacobs and Michael Cherbonneau interview 35 active auto thieves in an effort to discover the manner in which responsiveness can lead to less detectible crime or more overall crime. They argue that restrictive deterrence is a concept that explains this paradox. In their research they found that restrictive deterrent decision-making strategies fell into three broad categories: discretionary target selection, normalcy illusions, and defiance.

CHAPTER 3

Deciding to Commit a Burglary
Richard T. Wright and Scott H. Decker

Why burglary? Based on their study of residential burglary in St. Louis, Wright and Decker discuss the dynamics underlying the decision to commit a burglary. The authors interviewed 105 active residential burglars, taking them to the scenes of their past crimes and asking them to reconstruct the burglary in extensive detail. In this chapter they examine the factors that motivated the crime—that is, "why burglary?" The subjects in their study tended to be misfits in a world that values punctuality, schedules, and discipline. Crime appealed to some of the subjects precisely because it allowed them to flaunt their independence from the routine imposed by the world of work (See Shover and Honaker 1992 and Akerstrom 1993 in this volume). Their crimes were committed primarily based on their perception of an immediate need for money. Their need for money revolved primarily about maintaining their lifestyle, which the authors described as "high living" and which Shover (1992, in this volume) termed "life as party," although some committed burglaries for licit activities such as food, clothing, and shelter and others had committed burglaries for revenge, thrills, and other noneconomic reasons.

The demographic characteristics of residential burglars have been well documented. As Shover (1991) has observed, such offenders are, among other things, disproportionately young, male, and poor. These characteristics serve to identify a segment of the population more prone than others to resort to breaking in to dwellings, but they offer little insight into the actual causes of residential burglary. Many poor, young males, after all, never commit any sort of serious offense, let alone a burglary. And even those who carry out such crimes are not offending most of the time.

This is not, by and large, a continually motivated group of criminals; the motivation for them to offend is closely tied to their assessment of current

Source: Adapted from Wright, R. T., & Decker, S. H. (1994). *Burglars on the job: Streetlife and residential break-ins.* Boston: Northeastern University Press, pp. 35–61. Reprinted with permission.

circumstances and prospects. The direct cause of residential burglary is a perceptual process through which the offense comes to be seen as a means of meeting an immediate need, that is, through which a motive for the crime is formed.

Walker (1984:viii) has pointed out that, in order to develop a convincing explanation for criminal behavior, we must begin by "distinguishing the states of mind in which offenders commit, or contemplate the commission of, their offenses." Similarly, Katz (1988:4), arguing for increased research into what he calls the foreground of criminality, has noted that all of the demographic information on criminals in the world cannot answer the following question: "Why are people who were not determined to commit a crime one moment determined to do so the next?" This is the question to which the present chapter is addressed. The aim is to explore the extent to which the decision to commit a residential burglary is the result of a process of careful calculation and deliberation.

In the overwhelming majority of cases, the decision to commit a residential burglary arises in the face of what offenders perceive to be a pressing need for cash. Previous research consistently has shown this to be so (Bennett and Wright, 1984; Cromwell et al., 1991) and the results of the present study bear out this point. More than nine out of ten of the offenders in our sample—95 of 102—reported that they broke into dwellings primarily when they needed money.

> Well, it's like, the way it clicks into your head is like, you'll be thinking about something and, you know, it's a problem. Then it, like, all relates. "Hey, I need some money! Then how am I going to get money? Well, how do you know how to get money quick and easy?" Then there it is. Next thing you know, you are watching [a house] or calling to see if [the occupants] are home. (Wild Will—No. 010)
>
> Usually when I get in my car and drive around I'm thinking, I don't have any money, so what is my means for gettin' money? All of a sudden I'll just take a glance and say, "There it is! There's the house" . . . Then I get this feelin', that right moment, I'm movin' then. (Larry William—No. 017)

These offenders were not motivated by a desire for money for its own sake. By and large, they were not accumulating the capital needed to achieve a long-range goal. Rather, they regarded money as providing them with the means to solve an immediate problem. In their view, burglary was a matter of day-to-day survival.

> I didn't have the luxury of laying back in no damn pin-striped [suit]. I'm poor and I'm raggedy and I need some food and I need some shoes . . . So I got to have some money some kind of way. If it's got to be the wrong way, then so be it. (Mark Smith—No. 030)
>
> When I first started out, when I was younger, [burglary] was excitement or a high. But now it's to get by, you know, to survive. I don't ask my father for anything. My mother is not able to help. (Larry Harris—No. 035)

Given this view, it is unsurprising that the frequency with which the offenders committed burglaries was governed largely by the amount of money in their pockets. Many of them would not offend so long as they had sufficient cash to meet current expenses.

Usually what I'll do is a burglary, maybe two or three if I have to, and then this will help me get over the rough spot until I can get my skit [sic] straightened out. Once I get it straightened out, I just go with the flow until I hit that rough spot where I need the money again. And then I hit it . . . the only time I would go and commit a burglary is if I needed the money at that point in time. That would be strictly to pay light bill, gas bill, rent. (Dan Whiting—No. 102)

Long as I got some money, I'm cool. If I ain't got no money and I want to get high, then I go for it. (Janet Wilson—No. 060)

You know how they say stretch a dollar? I'll stretch it from here to the parking lot. But I can only stretch it so far and then it breaks. Then I say, "Well, I guess I got to go put on my black clothes. Go on out there like a thief in the night." (Ralph Jones—No. 018)

A few of the offenders sometimes committed a burglary even though they had sufficient cash for their immediate needs. These subjects were not purposely saving money, but they were unwilling to pass up opportunities to make more. They attributed their behavior to having become "greedy" or "addicted" to money.

I have done it out of greed, per se. Just to be doing it and to have more money, you know? Say, for instance, I have two hundred dollars in my pocket now. If I had two more hundreds, then that's four hundred dollars. Go out there and do a burglary. Then I say, "If I have four hundred dollars, then I can have a thousand." Go out there and do a burglary. (No. 018)

It's like when you smoke a cigarette, you know, you want more and more from the nicotine. Well, from my experience, you can get bigger and better stuff the more times that you do it and you can make more money. I'm addicted to money, I love money. So I just keep doing [burglaries]. (Robert Jones—No. 103)

Typically, the offenders did not save the money that they derived through burglary. Instead, they spent it for one or more of the following purposes: (1) to "keep the party going"; (2) to keep up appearances; or (3) to keep themselves and their families fed, clothed, and sheltered.

KEEPING THE PARTY GOING

Although the offenders often stated that they committed residential burglaries to "survive," there is a danger in taking this claim at face value. When asked how they spent the proceeds of their burglaries, nearly three-quarters of them—68 of 95—said they used the money for various forms of (for want of a better term) high-living. Most commonly, this involved the use of illicit drugs. Fifty-nine of the 68 offenders who spent the money obtained from burglary on pleasure-seeking pursuits specifically mentioned the purchase of drugs. For many of these respondents, the decision to break into a dwelling often arose as a result of a heavy session of drug use. The objective was to get the money to keep the party going (Shover and Honaker, 1990). The drug most frequently implicated in these situations was "crack" cocaine.

[Y]ou ever had an urge before? Maybe a cigarette urge or a food urge, where you eat that and you got to have more and more? That's how that crack is. You smoke it and it hits you [in the back of the throat] and you got to have more. I'll smoke that sixteenth up and get through, it's like I never had none. I got to have more. Therefore, I gots to go do another burglary and gets some more money. (Richard Jackson—No. 009)

It's usually, say we'll be doing some coke and then you really want more, so we'll go and do [a burglary] and get some money. (Sasha Williams—No. 094)

I might find somebody with some good crack . . . while I'm high I say, "Damn, I want me some more of this shit!" Go knock a place off, make some more money, go buy some more dope. (Die Leo—No. 079)

Lemert (1953:304) has labelled situations like these "dialectical, self-enclosed systems of behavior" in that they have an internal logic or "false structure" which calls for more of the same. Once locked into such events, he asserts, participants experience considerable pressure to continue, even if this involves breaking the law.

> A man away from home who falls in with a group of persons who have embarked upon a two or three-day or even a week's period of drinking and carousing . . . tends to have the impetus to continue the pattern which gets mutually reinforced by [the] interaction of the participants, and [the pattern] tends to have an accelerated beginning, a climax and a terminus. If midway through a spree a participant runs out of money, the pressures immediately become critical to take such measures as are necessary to preserve the behavior sequence. A similar behavior sequence is [evident] in that of the alcoholic who reaches a "high point" in his drinking and runs out of money. He might go home and get clothes to pawn or go and borrow money from a friend or even apply for public relief, but these alternatives become irrelevant because of the immediacy of his need for alcohol. (Lemert, 1953:303)

Implicit in this explanation is an image of actors who become involved in offending without significant calculation; having embarked voluntarily on one course of action (e.g., crack smoking), they suddenly find themselves being drawn into an unanticipated activity (e.g., residential burglary) as a means of sustaining that action. Their offending is not the result of a thoughtful, carefully reasoned process. Instead, it emerges as part of the natural flow of events, seemingly coming out of nowhere. In other words, it is not so much that these actors consciously choose to commit crimes as that they elect to get involved in situations that drive them toward lawbreaking (Kennedy and Baron, 1993).

Other subjects, though they claimed that a perceived need for drugs typically triggered their decision to do a burglary, were not under the influence of drugs when the decision was reached. Their aim was to get high rather than to stay high. They regarded themselves as having a drug "habit" which compelled them to crime; the urge for drugs seemed beyond their ability to control and had to be satisfied by whatever means necessary. Although some in this group were addicted to narcotics such as heroin, this was not always the case.

> See, sometimes I wake up and don't have no [marijuana]. I have to go do my [burglary] and get me some money and get me some. (Carl Jackson—No. 022)

Getting and using drugs were major preoccupations for a majority of the offenders, not just a small cadre of addicts. Many of them reported committing burglaries *solely* for the purpose of obtaining money to buy drugs. But even some of those who did burglaries for other reasons ended up spending a portion of the profits on drugs.

> Lot of times when I commit burglary I use some of the money to get drugs, but I don't do the burglaries for that purpose. (Larry Washington—No. 013)

For these offenders, indulgence in drug use represented a crucial aspect of their street identity as "hip"; the street-corner culture from which most of them— black and white, male and female—were drawn is oriented largely toward getting high (Anderson, 1990). In the past, this almost exclusively involved the drinking of beer or cheap wine. While drinking remains a feature of street culture—14 offenders, 21 percent of those who spent their money on high-living, mentioned the purchase of alcohol—it is increasingly being accompanied by illicit drug use. The money required to support such use is substantial and this ensured that the offenders were almost perpetually in need of cash (Shover and Honaker, 1992).

Beyond the purchase of illicit drugs and, to a lesser extent, alcohol, 10 of the 68 offenders—15 percent—also used the proceeds from their residential burglaries to pursue sexual conquests. All of these offenders were male. Some liked to flash money about, believing that this was the way to attract women.

> I guess I like to flash [money] a lot, impress the girls and stuff. Go out and spend some money, you know? (Wayne Jones—No. 055)
>
> [I commit burglaries to] splurge money with the women, you know, that's they kick, that's what they like to do. (Jon Monroe—No. 011)
>
> [I use the burglary money for] gifts for young ladies—flowers or negligee or somethin'. Some shoes, "Put them shoes on, them pumps." [Then] watch 'em nude. (Jack Daniel—No. 054)

Like getting high, sexual conquest was a much-prized symbol of hipness through which the male subjects in our sample could accrue status among their peers on the street. The greatest prestige was accorded to those who were granted sexual favors solely on the basis of smooth talk and careful impression management. Nevertheless, a few of the offenders took a more direct approach to obtaining sex by paying a street-corner prostitute (sometimes referred to as a "duck") for it. While this was regarded as less hip than the more subtle approach described above, it had the advantage of being easy and uncomplicated. As such, it appealed to offenders who were wrapped up in partying and therefore reluctant to devote more effort than was necessary to satisfy their immediate sexual desires.

> I spend [the money] on something to drink, . . . then get me some [marijuana]. Then I'm gonna find me a duck. (Ricky Davis—No. 105)

It would be misleading to suggest that any of the offenders we spoke to committed burglaries *specifically* to get money for sex, but a number of them often directed a portion of their earnings toward this goal.

In short, among the major purposes for which the offenders used the money derived from burglary was the maintenance of a lifestyle centered on illicit drugs, but frequently incorporating alcohol and sexual conquests as well. This lifestyle reflects the values of the street culture, a culture characterized by an openness to "illicit action" (Katz, 1988:209–15), to which most of our subjects were strongly committed. Viewed from the perspective of the offenders, then, the oft-heard claim that they broke into dwellings to survive does not seem quite so farfetched. The majority of them saw their fate as inextricably linked to an ability to fulfill the imperatives of life on the street.

KEEPING UP APPEARANCES

Of the 95 offenders who committed residential burglaries primarily for financial reasons, 43 reported that they used the cash to purchase various "status" items. The most popular item was clothing; 39 of the 43 said that they bought clothes with the proceeds of their crimes. At one level, of course, clothing must be regarded as necessary for survival. The responses of most of the offenders, however, left little doubt that they were not buying clothes to protect themselves from the elements, but rather to project a certain image; they were drawn to styles and brand names regarded as chic on the streets.

> See, I go steal money and go buy me some clothes. See, I likes to look good. I likes to dress. All I wear is Stacy Adams, that's all I wear. [I own] only one pair of blue jeans cause I likes to dress. (No. 011)
>
> I buy fashionable clothes or whatever, you know, just spend [the money]. (Mike West—No. 049)
>
> [I] buy Stacy Adams clothes, sweaters. When I grew up, I always had the basic shit. [My parents] were wealthy and I always got [cheap] shoes and shit and I was always in competition with other kids and [my parents] never understood that. So I would go out and buy me Nikes. I'd buy three brand new sixty-dollar pairs of shoes and clothes. (Joe Wilson—No. 099)
>
> A lot of times I'll buy clothes or tennis shoes or some jogging outfits, something like that. Some type of jacket or buy a hat. (Maurice Ross—No. 040)

Wearing appropriate clothing is an important aspect of fitting into any social situation. This is no less true for street culture, which has its own "dress code." As Anderson (1990) has observed, dressing in the latest status symbol clothing is virtually mandatory for those who want to be seen as hip on the street. The subjects in our sample were responding to this fact by using the money that they made from burglary to purchase fashionable outfits.

After clothes, cars and car accessories were the next most popular status items bought by the offenders. Seven of the 43 reported spending at least some of the money they got from burglaries on their cars.

> I spent [the money] on stuff for my car. Like I said, I put a lot of money into my car . . . I had a '79 Grand Prix, you know, a nice car. (Matt Detteman—No. 072)

The attributes of a high-status vehicle varied. Not all of these offenders, for example, would have regarded a 1979 Grand Prix as conferring much prestige on its owner.

Nevertheless, they were agreed that driving a fancy or customized car, like wearing fashionable clothing, was an effective way of enhancing one's street status.

A sizable portion of the offenders therefore used the profits from their offenses to acquire the material trappings of success. In doing so, they sought to create an impression of affluence and hipness so that they would be admired by their peers on the street and by others. A British burglar interviewed by Bennett and Wright (1984:139) made explicit reference to the desire of offenders to be seen as a "better class of person."

> I don't know if you've ever thought about it, but I think every crook likes the life of thieving and then going and being somebody better. Really, you are deceiving people; letting them think that you are well off . . . You've got a nice car, you can go about and do this and do that. It takes money to buy that kind of life.

Shover and Honaker (1990:11) have suggested that the concern of offenders with outward appearances, as with their notorious high-living, grows out of what is typically a strong attachment to the values of street culture; values which place great emphasis on the "ostentatious enjoyment and display of luxury items." In a related vein, Katz (1988) has argued that for those who are committed to streetlife, the reckless spending of cash on luxury goods is an end in itself, demonstrating their disdain for the ordinary citizen's pursuit of financial security. Seen through the eyes of the offenders, therefore, money spent on such goods has not been "blown," but rather represents a cost of raising or maintaining one's status on the street.

KEEPING THINGS TOGETHER

While most of the offenders spent much of the money they earned through residential burglary on drugs and clothes, a substantial number also used some of it for daily living expenses. Of the 95 who committed burglaries to raise money, 50 claimed that they needed the cash for subsistence.

> I do [burglaries] to keep myself together, keep myself up. (James Brown—No. 025)

Necessities mentioned most frequently were food, shelter, and clothing for the children. Thirty-eight of the 50 offenders (76 percent) reported using money from their burglaries to pay for one or all of these needs. Some of them used the money *solely* for such expenses.

> [I spend the money from my burglaries for] needs, not wants, needs—roof over my head, food in my mouth and things for my kids. (Lynn—No. 095)

The majority, however, paid for their immediate subsistence needs and spent the remaining cash on status-enhancing items and high-living.

> [I use burglary money to buy] food, clothing, drugs—in that order. And a place to stay, that's gon come automatic cause I'm a always find a place to stay. (No. 035)

Quite a few of the offenders—13 of 50—said that they paid bills with the money derived from burglary. Here again, however, there is a danger of being misled by such claims. To be sure, these offenders did use some of their burglary money to take care of bills. Often, though, the bills were badly delinquent because the offenders avoided paying them for as long as possible—even when they had the cash—in favor of buying, most typically, drugs. It was not until the threat of serious repercussions created unbearable pressure for the offenders that they relented and settled their accounts.

> [Sometimes I commit burglaries when] things pressuring me, you know? I got to do somethin' about these bills. Bills. I might let it pass that mornin'. Then I start trippin' on it at night and, next thing you know, it's wakin' me up. Yeah, that's when I got to get out and go do a burglary. *I got* to pay this electric bill off, this gas bill, you know? (No. 009)

Similarly, several of the subjects in our sample reported doing burglaries to pay parking or traffic tickets they had long ignored, having preferred to use their money for high-living.

> I started getting tickets and it was, like, I got four tickets for improper registration plates. Then it was like, "Hey, I need some money, this stuff is calculating up." I [needed] some money and I [didn't] want to run and ask Mom. So I just did [a burglary]. (No. 010)

Spontaneity is a prominent feature of street culture (Shover and Honaker, 1992); it is not surprising that many of the offenders displayed a marked tendency to live for the moment. Often they would give every indication of intending to take care of their obligations, financial or otherwise, only to be distracted by more immediate temptations. For instance, a woman in our sample, after being paid for an interview, asked us to drive her to a place where she could buy a pizza for her children's lunch. On the way to the restaurant, however, she changed her mind and asked to be dropped off at a crack house instead. In another case, we persuaded a male subject to allow three consultants on our research to come along on a visit to the scene of his most recent residential burglary in exchange for a larger than usual participation fee. At the agreed time and place, we arrived to find him sitting with friends in a car in an incoherent state; he had used the promised research payment as a means of obtaining cocaine on credit and was in the process of consuming it despite his scheduled meeting with us!

Katz (1988:216) has suggested that, through irresponsible spending, persistent offenders seek to construct "an environment of pressures that guide[s] them back toward crime." Whether offenders spend money in a conscious attempt to create such pressures is arguable; the subjects in our sample gave no indication of doing so, appearing simply to be financially irresponsible. One offender, for example, told us that he never hesitated to spend money, adding, "Why should I? I can always get some more." However, the inclination of offenders to free-spending leaves them with few alternatives but to continue committing crimes. Their next financial crisis is never far around the corner.

The high-living of the offenders, thus, calls into question the extent to which they are driven to crime by genuine financial hardship. At the same time, though, their spendthrift ways ensure that the crimes they commit will be economically motivated (Katz, 1988). The offenders perceive themselves as needing money, and their offenses typically are a response to this perception. Objectively, however, few are doing burglaries to escape impoverishment.

WHY BURGLARY?

The decision to commit a residential burglary, then, is usually prompted by a perceived need for cash. Burglary, however, is not the only means by which offenders could get some money. Why do they choose burglary over legitimate work? Why do they elect to carry out a burglary rather than borrow the money from a friend or relative? Additionally, why do they select burglary rather than some other crime?

Given the street-corner context in which most burglary decisions were made, legitimate work did not represent a viable solution for most of the offenders in our sample. These subjects, with few exceptions, wanted money there and then and, in such circumstances, even day labor was irrelevant because it did not respond to the immediacy of their desire for cash (Lemert, 1953). Moreover, the jobs available to most of the offenders were poorly-paid and could not sustain their desired lifestyles. It is notable that 17 of the 95 offenders who did burglaries primarily to raise money *were* legitimately employed.

> [I have a job, but] I got tired of waiting on that money. I can get money like that. I got talent, I can do me a burg, man, and get me five or six hundred dollars in less than a hour. Working eight hours a day and waiting for a whole week for a check and it ain't even about shit. (No. 022)
>
> [E]ven if I had a job, I betcha I couldn't find a job payin' me over minimum wage. Then they probably want to pay me every two weeks, so I would have to supplement that week that I wouldn't get paid with somethin'. (Mike Jackson—No. 046)

Beyond this, a few of the offenders expressed a strong aversion to legitimate employment, saying that a job would impinge upon their way of life.

> I ain't workin' and too lazy to work and just all that. I like it to where I can just run around. I don't got to get up at no certain time, just whenever I wake up. I ain't gotta go to bed a certain time to get up at a certain time. Go to bed around one o'clock or when I want, get up when I want. Ain't got to go to work and work eight hours. Just go in and do a five minute job, get that money, that's just basically it. (Tony Scott—No. 085)
>
> I done got lazy . . . I don't even want to work eight hours. I figure I can do maybe only one hour and get paid as much as I would if I worked a full day. (Kip Harris—No. 069)

These subjects closely matched the "high-level thieves" described by Shover (1991:92): "Misfits in a world that values precise schedules, punctuality, and disciplined subordination to authority, high-level thieves value the autonomy to structure life and work as they wish." Indeed, crime appealed to some of the subjects precisely because it allowed them to flaunt their independence from the routine imposed by the world of work (Shover and Honaker, 1992). Not taking orders from anyone—be it a girlfriend, a wife, or an employer—is a bedrock value on which male street-corner culture rests; to be regarded as hip one must always do as he pleases. Accordingly, those who defined themselves most strongly in terms of their street reputation found the idea of getting a job to be distasteful because legitimate employment would require them to do as they were told by the boss.

> I guess [burglary is] in my blood. I don't too much want to work with a job and listen to no boss. But I can, like, do two or three burglaries and take money home to my kids. (Roger Brown—No. 058)

Nevertheless, a majority of the offenders reported that they wanted lawful employment; 43 of the 78 unemployed subjects who said that they did burglaries mostly for the money claimed they would stop committing offenses if someone gave them a "good" job.

> I'm definitely going to give it up as soon as I get me a good job. I don't mean making fifteen dollars an hour. Give me a job making five-fifty and I'm happy with it. I don't got to burglarize no more. I'm not doing it because I like doing it, I'm doing it because I need some [drugs]. (No. 079)
>
> Anything like five dollars an hour might slow me down, stop me completely. And the people at the job ain't buggin' me. I'll stay there the rest of my life if the people don't bother me cause I don't take nothing from 'em and therefore I would've went off on one of 'em or either beat 'em up. They don't bother me and I won't bother them and that five dollars is standin' strong. And wouldn't have to steal nothin' cause I'd have my money there. And I might cut down off my drugs—mainly you do drugs cause there's nothing to do. (No. 009)

While such claims may or may not be sincere—some of these subjects had held reasonably high-paying jobs in the past, but lost them owing to dishonesty or drug and alcohol problems—it is unlikely that they will ever be challenged. Decent employment opportunities are limited for inner-city residents (Wilson, 1987) and the offenders, who by and large are poorly educated, unskilled, and heavy illicit drug or alcohol users, are not well placed to compete for the few good jobs available. Most of them realized this and were resigned to being out of work. In their eyes, burglary represented a more realistic means of "earning" some money.

> Look, [there] ain't no job! I been out here lookin' for work, can't find no work. So I do what I do best. (Leroy Robison—No. 045)

Instead of committing burglaries, of course, the offenders perhaps could have borrowed some cash from a friend or relative. But they did not view this as a feasible alternative. Some of them were unwilling to ask for money because they felt that this would damage their status.

> I like to stand on my own two feet as a man, you know what I'm sayin'? I like to pay my way and I don't like to ask nobody for nothin'. Don't want nobody

talkin' about me like I won't pay my way. I ain't freeloadin' off nobody. I'm a man, so I take care of myself. (Jeffery Moore—No. 006)

Others had borrowed money in the past, but were reluctant to ask for more.

> I can't keep askin' my wife, my brothers and sister and my mother. They'll tell me the same thing, "You a grown man, go out there and get you a job!" Or [they'll hand me some money and say], "Here, don't come back too soon." You know, you can only do that for so long. (No. 018)

And still others simply found that it was impossible to borrow money.

> After you ask for a few dollars from people—your loved ones or your grandmother—and they tell you what they ain't got, you lay back down and try to go to sleep. You don't have no cigarettes, no beer, no nothing. Yeah, it builds up, animosity builds up inside you. Seems like that old devil just push you on out the door [to do a burglary]. (No. 069)

In any case, borrowing money offers only a short-term solution to financial needs. There usually is an expectation that loans will be repaid and this can provide the impetus for carrying out a burglary. Indeed, Katz (1988:217) has gone so far as to suggest that this obligation is a major source of the monetary troubles that drive offenders to crime: "Economic pressures toward crime emerge, not as the direct result of particular substantive needs as much as through the pressure of obligations accumulated in social networks. Borrowing and credit relations among offenders form a subtle, elaborate institution." In the course of our interviews we were told of burglaries that had been carried out because the offender owed money or wanted to reclaim a pawned article. We even encountered an offender who recently had broken into the residence of a fellow burglar in order to collect on a bad debt.

When faced with an immediate need for cash, then, the offenders in our sample perceived themselves as having little hope of getting money both quickly *and* legally. Many of the most efficient solutions to financial troubles are against the law (Lofland, 1969). However, this does not explain why the subjects decided specifically on the crime of residential burglary. After all, most of them admitted committing other sorts of offenses in the past, and some still were doing so. Why should they choose burglary?

For some subjects, this question held little relevance because they regarded residential burglary as their "main line" and alternative offenses were seldom considered when the need for money arose.

> I guess the reason why I stick to burglary is because it makes me a lot of money . . . I guess you could say why I just do [burglary] is because I've been doing it for a while and I'm kind of stuck with it. (Carl Watson—No. 032)

> [I do burglary] because it's easy and because I know it. It's kind of getting a speciality or a career. If you're in one line, or one field, and you know it real well, then you don't have any qualms about doing it. But if you try something new, you could really mess up . . . At this point, I've gotten away with so much [that] I just don't want to risk it—it's too much to risk at this point. I feel like I have a

good pattern, clean; go in the house, come back out, under two minutes every time. (Darlene White—No. 100)

[Burglary is] easy for me. People have armed robberies and sell crack or whatever; I do burglaries. That's the easiest thing I do . . . I'm just saying that's what best suits me. (Karl Alverez—No. 081)

I don't know [why I decided on burglary]. I guess I'm good at it . . . I just like burglary, that's it. (No. 013)

When these subjects did commit another kind of offense, it typically was triggered by the chance discovery of a vulnerable target. As noted in the first chapter, most of the burglars we interviewed identified themselves as hustlers, people who were always looking to "get over" by making some fast cash; it would have been out of character for them to pass up any kind of presented opportunity to do so.

If I see another hustle, then I'll do it, but burglary is my pet. (Larry Smith—No. 065)

Burglars usually just stick to burglary. There's only one time that I was in the process of doing a burglary and I did a robbery. I was gettin' ready to do a burglary and a guy walked up and had a money sack. So I forgot all about the burglary and got the money sack. (No. 055)

The immediacy of their need for money, however, drove most of the offenders to look actively for any illicit opportunity to obtain cash rapidly, and they were open to crimes other than residential burglary. As one put it: "When you need money, you're going to do what you have to." These offenders chose to break into a dwelling when that act represented what they perceived to be the "most proximate and performable" (Lofland, 1969:61) crime available to them. Both their subjective state and the objective characteristics of the situation played a part in shaping this perception. For such offenders, making the decision to commit a residential burglary instead of another type of offense involved more than a cool assessment of the potential costs and benefits associated with the various alternatives; emotion, mood, and intuition also had a powerful influence on this process (Scheff, 1992).

[S]ometimes you feel better about one thing than you do another and sometimes you know where the money is at. It depends on what's there at the time, whether there is transportation or you are in the area. It's just what looks good at the time. What's more comfortable for you to do, what feels better. (Earl Martin—No. 083)

[W]hen you high on crack, you want some more crack and you don't want to wait, so you got to do a robbery. Now a burglary, you might be high at three in the morning, now whose house can you go in at three in the morning and they ain't gonna be there? (Diamond Craig—No. 027)

A few offenders typically did not themselves choose to commit residential burglaries, but went along with offenses suggested by someone else. In need of cash, these subjects were especially receptive to presented criminal opportunities, even if they were not particularly enamored of burglary.

I got a friend that do burglaries with me. He usually the one that sets them up. If he ain't got one set up, then I might go off into somethin' else. (Larry Brown—No. 052)

Some of these offenders seemed, when on their own, to lack the stomach for any sort of serious wrongdoing. Others had a preference for a different type of crime, but were tempted to do an occasional burglary when asked to lend a hand. One subject told us that he usually stayed away from burglary in favor of drug selling, explaining that he regarded the former as morally worse than the latter because "the victim comes to you in drug selling, [while] in burglary you go to the victim." Nevertheless, he admitted being willing to commit a break-in when presented with a good opportunity by one of his associates.

The range of moneymaking crimes from which the majority of the offenders could choose was fairly limited. By and large, they did not hold jobs that would allow them to violate even a low-level position of financial trust (Cressey, 1953). Similarly, few had the technical expertise required to disarm the sophisticated security systems protecting lucrative commercial targets or the interpersonal skills needed to commit frauds. It is not surprising, therefore, that, besides residential burglary, almost all of them stuck to a limited number of crimes requiring little skill, such as theft (mostly shoplifting), stealing cars, street-corner drug selling and robbery.

For many of the offenders, the few profitable criminal opportunities objectively available to them were restricted still further by their belief that certain crimes were too risky or were morally unacceptable. A number of them, for instance, had curtailed or severely limited their participation in drug selling because they felt that the risks of apprehension and punishment were too great.

> It's hard right now, man . . . I can go back to selling drugs which I could lose my ass. A burg, I could get away with four years [imprisonment]. If I get caught on burglary, I know I'm guaranteed four years. I get caught with drugs, I'm a do thirty [years]. So see, I got away from drugs and fell with the number one [offense, burglary]. (Charlie—No. 024)
>
> See, right now they harder on druggies than a burglar or auto thief. They tryin' to save the younger generation now. They sayin' drugs is the cause of the crimes now. (Joe Outlaw—No. 056)

Likewise, some regarded robbery, especially armed robbery, as carrying too much risk.

> See, if you rob a person, they can identify you cause you lookin' right at 'em, you know? They lookin' right at you and they can identify you. And armed robbery is what? Five to ten [years]? Or ten to fifteen [years]? (No. 006)
>
> [T]hey givin' too much time for robbin'. After my eight years for robbery, I told myself then I'll never do another robbery because I was locked up with so many guys that was doin' twenty-five to thirty years for robbery and I think that's what made me stick to burglaries, because I had learned that a crime committed with a weapon will get you a lot of time. (No. 013)

One offender decided against committing robberies because he was afraid of being hurt by the victim or witnesses.

> I'm not going to try no strong robberies cause these people could possibly see me out there in the street and I might be full of some alcohol or something and

> they could get me. They could shoot me or stab me or anything and I wouldn't
> know. (No. 040)

A couple of the burglars we worked with believed that it was wrong to threaten or
to use violence to get money and therefore were reluctant to do robberies. Although the offender quoted below does not say that he avoided robbery for moral
reasons, the tone of his voice left no doubt that this was the case.

> I'd never personally rob a human being, like walk up to them and say, "Give me
> you wallet and give me your purse!" No way. (No. 079)

Even those who were willing to do robberies, however, sometimes were
unable to do so because they did not have the "facilitating hardware" (Lofland,
1969:69–72), namely, a firearm.

> Well, lately I haven't did any [robberies]. But when I was doin' it, I robbed every
> Friday . . . I ain't got no pistol, that's the only reason [I haven't been doing
> them], . . . I swear. (No. 011)

Handguns are in great demand on the street. One of the subjects in our sample
claimed that he would rather have a pistol than cash because "a gun is money
with a trigger." Offenders who are in need of immediate cash often are tempted to
sell their weapon instead of resorting to a difficult or risky crime. The result of
this is that they do not always have a pistol at their disposal. In such circumstances residential burglary, which typically requires nothing more than readily
available objects (e.g., a screwdriver, hammer, or small crowbar) for its commission, becomes correspondingly more attractive.

THE SEDUCTIONS OF RESIDENTIAL BURGLARY

For some offenders, the perceived benefits of residential burglary may transcend
the amelioration of financial need. A few of the subjects we interviewed—7 of
102—said that they did not typically commit burglaries as much for the money as
for the psychic rewards. These offenders reported breaking into dwellings primarily because they enjoyed doing so. Most of them did not enjoy burglary per se,
but rather the risks and challenges inherent in the crime.

> [I]t's really because I like [burglaries]. I know that if I get caught I'm a do more
> time than the average person, but still, it's the risk. I like doin' them. (No. 013)
>
> I think [burglary is] fun. It's a challenge. You don't know whether you're
> getting caught or not and I like challenges. If I can get a challenging [burglary,
> I] like that. It's more of the risk that you got to take, you know, to see how good
> you can really be. (No. 103)

These subjects seemingly viewed the successful completion of an offense as "a thrilling demonstration of personal competence" (Katz, 1988:9). Given this, it is not surprising that the catalyst for their crimes often was a mixture of boredom and an acute
sense of frustration born of failure at legitimate activities such as work or school.

> [Burglary] just be something to do. I might not be workin' or not going to school—not doing anything. So I just decide to do a burglary. (No. 017)

The offense provided these offenders with more than something exciting to do; it also offered them the chance to "be somebody" by successfully completing a dangerous act. Similarly, Shover and Honaker (1992:288) have noted that, through crime, offenders seek to demonstrate a sense of control or mastery over their lives and thereby to gain "a measure of respect, if not from others, at least from [themselves]."

The purest example of the psychic rewards of residential burglary was provided by a probationer who, because he denied being currently active, was not included in our sample. Nevertheless, we spoke to him at great length. This man described, with obvious glee, breaking in to places, rearranging the furniture and leaving, often without taking anything. He portrayed himself as a prankster, explaining that he got a great charge out of picturing the victims trying to make a credible-sounding police report. That his motivations were more sinister, however, was suggested when he commented: "I know that [the victims] are still wondering what I took. And I didn't take a thing!" Though the offenses had occurred months earlier, this individual still appeared to derive satisfaction from having desecrated the living space of his victims; he clearly was pleased by the prospect that his actions continued to unsettle their lives. Katz (1988:69) noted a phenomenon closely akin to this among the offenders he surveyed, concluding that nonacquisitive burglaries were experienced as a "black sacrament," a quasi-religious act of defilement through which criminals attempted "to project something negative into the victim's world."

While only a small number of the subjects in our sample said that they were motivated *primarily* by the psychic rewards of burglary, many of them perceived such rewards as a secondary benefit of the offense. Sixteen of the 95 offenders who did burglaries to raise cash also said that they found the crime to be "exciting" or "thrilling."

> Burglary is excitin'. [I do it] mostly for the money, but a lot of times it arouses my suspicion and curiosity. (No. 046)
>
> [Beyond money], it's the thrill. If you get out [of the house], you smile and stand on it, breathe out. (No. 045)
>
> It's just a thrill going in undetected and walking out with all they shit. Man, that shit fucks me up. (No. 022)

Several of those who were motivated predominantly by financial pressures claimed that the offense represented "a challenge" or "an adventure" as well.

> It wasn't just g'tting' money . . . it was just the thing of doing it, the thrill out of going in [the house] and doing it. I guess it was a challenge. (No. 055)
>
> [Burglary] is a challenge . . . like going on a treasure hunt. (Billy Kelly—No. 048)
>
> [After the money, burglary] is adventure to me. (Rodney Price—No. 057)

And a number of the subjects who reported committing burglaries mostly as a way of making money added that breaking into dwellings was "fun" too.

> [I do burglaries] for the money. Sometimes it is kind of fun. (Ed Alverez—No. 082)

Finally, one of the offenders who did burglaries chiefly for monetary reasons alluded to the fact that the crime also provided him with a valued identity.

> My main reason [for committing burglaries] is because of the money . . . and knowin' that you can hustle, knowin' that you a hustler. (No. 054)

Beyond all of this, quite a few of the offenders who *usually* resorted to burglary out of financial need occasionally committed the offense to get even with someone for a real or imagined wrong. A number of then mentioned doing burglaries from time to time for "revenge." In the case below, for example, a black offender broke into the home of a young white man who had called him "a nigger" during an altercation over a scratched car door.

> I was driving my mother's car and [I pulled into the parking lot of a convenience store]. When I opened my door, I hit this guy's car—a gray Cutlass—and he wanted to fight about it . . . So we were going to [settle it there], but the police broke it up. So I was thinking about gettin' even . . . I followed him [home] . . . I just kept him in sight till I seen what house he was staying in . . . It was Wednesday and, uh, I was plannin' on doing it Friday, but I had to learn their routine first. I watched a little bit the rest of Wednesday and then I came back and watched it a little bit Thursday, but, uh, I had to move quick cause I wanted to get even . . . That was a grudge there, a pay back, so it wasn't too much for the money. I broke up more stuff in there than I stole . . . Normally when I break in a house, it's so that I can get me a high, cause I be having the urge to smoke a little coke. But this particular day, they just pissed me off. I just wanted to get even. I just wanted to hit 'em where it hurts—in they pocket—and I think I did pretty good. (John Black—No. 008)

Other offenders described break-ins designed to punish an ex-lover, collect on a bad debt, or "pay back" an unscrupulous drug dealer. Black (1983:34) has suggested that crimes such as these are essentially moralistic and involve "the pursuit of justice." Indeed, he has gone so far as to argue that many burglaries are best thought of as a form of self-help or "secret social control" (Black, 1983:37). This may be overstating the matter, but it is clear that, on occasion, some offenders find burglary an appealing means of righting a perceived wrong. For instance, several burglars in our sample who often worked together reported targeting the homes of homosexuals who were buying up and renovating property on the periphery of their own neighborhood. These offenders explained that they did not like gays and broke into their dwellings as a means of forcing them to move out of the area. From their perspective, such crimes were justifiable in the circumstances; they represented an attempt to keep the neighborhood from being overrun by outsiders whose way of life was different and threatening.

SUMMARY

Offenders typically decided to commit a residential burglary in response to a perceived need. In most cases, this need was financial, calling for the immediate acquisition of money. However, it sometimes involved what was interpreted as a need to repel an attack on the status, identity, or self-esteem of the offenders. Whatever its character, the need almost invariably was regarded by the offenders as pressing, that is, as something that had to be dealt with immediately. Lofland (1969:50) has observed that most people, when under pressure, have a tendency to become fixated on removing the perceived cause of that pressure "as quickly as possible." Those in our sample were no exception. In such a state, the offenders were not predisposed to consider unfamiliar, complicated, or long-term solutions (see Lofland, 1969:50) and instead fell back on residential burglary, which they knew well. This often seemed to happen almost automatically, the crime occurring with minimal calculation as part of a more general path of action (e.g., partying). To the extent that the offense ameliorated their distress, it nurtured a tendency for them to view burglary as a reliable means of dealing with similar pressures in the future. In this way, a foundation was laid for the continuation of their present lifestyle which, by and large, revolve around the street culture. The self-indulgent activities supported by this culture, in turn, precipitated new pressures; and thus a vicious cycle developed.

That the offenders, at the time of actually contemplating offenses, typically perceived themselves to be in a situation of immediate need has at least two important implications. First, it suggests a mindset in which they were seeking less to maximize their gains than to deal with a present crisis. Second, it indicates an element of desperation which might have weakened the influence of threatened sanctions and neutralized any misgivings about the morality of breaking into dwellings (see Shover and Honaker, 1992).

REFERENCES

Anderson, E. (1990), *Street Wise: Race, Class, and Change in an Urban Community,* Chicago: University of Chicago Press.

Bennett, T., and Wright, R. (1983), "Offenders' Perception of Targets," *Home Office Research Bulletin,* 15:18–20, London: Home Office Research and Planning Unit.

Black, D. (1983), "Crime as Social Control," *American Sociological Review,* 48:34–45.

Cressey, D. (1953), *Other People's Money,* Glencoe, IL: Free Press.

Cromwell, P., Olson, J., and Avary, D. (1991), *Breaking and Entering: An Ethnographic Analysis of Burglary,* Newbury Park, CA: Sage.

Katz, J. (1988), *Seductions of Crime: Moral and Sensual Attractions in Doing Evil,* New York: Basic Books.

Kennedy, L., and Baron, S. (1993), "Routine Activities and a Sub-culture of Violence," *Journal of Research in Crime and Delinquency,* 30:88–112.

Lemert, E. (1953), "An Isolation and Closure Theory of Naive Check Forgery," *Journal of Criminal Law, Criminology, and Police Science,* 44:296–307.

Lofland, J. (1969), *Deviance and Identity,* Englewood Cliffs, NJ: Prentice-Hall.

Scheff, T. (1992), "Rationality and Emotion: Homage To Norbert Elias." In Coleman, J., and Fararo, T., *Rational Choice Theory: Advocacy and Critique,* pp. 101–19, Newbury Park, CA: Sage.

Shover, N. (1991), "Burglary." In Tonry, M., *Crime and Justice: A Review of Research,* vol. 14, pp. 73–113, Chicago: University of Chicago Press.

Shover, N., and Honaker, D. (1990), "The Criminal Calculus of Persistent Property Offenders: A Review of Evidence." Paper presented at the Forty-second Annual Meeting of the American Society of Criminology, Baltimore, November.

———. (1992), "The Socially Bounded Decision Making of Persistent Property Offenders," *Howard Journal of Criminal Justice,* 31, no. 4:276–93.

Walker, N. (1984), Foreword. In Bennett, T., and Wright, R., *Burglars on Burglary: Prevention and the Offender,* pp. viii–ix, Aldershot: Gower.

Wilson, W. (1987), *The Truly Disadvantaged: The Inner City, the Underclass, and Public Policy,* Chicago: University of Chicago Press.

CHAPTER 4

Opportunities and Decisions:
Interactional Dynamics in Robbery and Burglary Groups
Andy Hochstetler

Street offenders more often than not are co-offenders. The theoretical importance of understanding how co-offending shapes conduct has been recognized for decades but is often ignored by investigators. Drawing from interviews with 50 male robbers and burglars who committed their crimes with others, this paper examines how interactional dynamics modify both the perception of criminal opportunities and criminal decision making. Offenders construct opportunity by improvising situational interpretations, communicating expectations, and negotiating shared meanings. As opposed to many prevailing notions of criminal decision making, decisions in groups are incremental, contextually situated, and affected significantly by variation in members' influence. The findings, therefore, highlight shortcomings of decision-making investigations that obscure marked variation in choice by focusing narrowly on individual assessments of risks and utilities.

Criminologists generally focus their research either on the correlates of crime in offenders' backgrounds or else on characteristics of situations and environments where crime is likely to occur. The immediate social context in which offenders construct criminal decisions is a rich and largely unexplored area. Only a few investigators focus on mental processes, action, and interactions that link offenders' backgrounds to immediate environments and discrete criminal choices (Short, 1998, p. 25). This empirical neglect results in understandings of crime that emphasize offender characteristics and situational correlates of offending without considering the processes and events through which these

Source: Hochstetler, A. (2001). Opportunities and decisions: Interactional dynamics in robbery and burglary groups. *Criminology, 39*(3), 737–63. Used with permission of the American Society of Criminology.

correlates and characteristics result in criminal agency. It is well known, for example, that most street offenders in the United States choose crime in the presence of co-offenders (Bureau of Justice Statistics, 1999; Reiss, 1988; Zimring, 1981). However, little research into the potential influence of co-offenders on construction of criminal opportunity or on how criminal groups negotiate meaning and align action to offend exists.

The theoretical importance of understanding how co-offending shapes conduct is recognized in many of criminology's classics. However, investigators generally assume that co-offending influences choice without analysis of the interpersonal interactions that create group effects (McCarthy, Hagan, & Cohen, 1998; Reiss, 1988; Reiss & Farrington, 1991; Tremblay, 1993; Warr, 1996). In this paper, I apply an interactionist approach to investigating the processes by which offenders subjectively interpret and define situations in choosing to commit crime (Athens, 1997; Groves & Lynch, 1990; Katz, 1988, 1991). I draw on interviews with 50 robbers and burglars who committed their crimes with others. Analysis of these interviews reveals some common patterns of interpersonal dynamics, rooted in street activities, which contribute to situational construction of criminal opportunity. By incrementally signaling to communicate their emerging preferences, by referring to target characteristics, and by referencing identities and expectations attributed to co-offenders, group thieves negotiate a shared sense of opportunity. Interaction can reduce the appeal of law abidance to group participants and make developing criminal opportunity difficult to refuse. In addition, co-offender interaction can act as a catalyst for crime by increasing access to illicit pathways and easing the pursuit of criminal objectives.

BACKGROUND

Revival of interest in deterrence and control interpretations of crime in the closing decades of the twentieth century gave new impetus to investigations of criminal decision making. The resulting corpus of research reveals two recurrent approaches to examining the decision-making process. One depicts criminal decisions as the outcome of a straightforward cognitive process in which offenders weigh rewards against costs. Investigators informed by this approach typically require subjects to imagine themselves in hypothetical settings and to evaluate the potential rewards and risks of choosing crime (Carrol & Weaver, 1986; Cornish & Clarke, 1986; Nagin & Paternoster, 1993; Piliavin, Gartner, Thorton, & Matsueda, 1986; Piquero & Rengert, 1999; Taylor & Nee, 1988; Wright, Logie, & Decker, 1996). The vignettes presented to subjects typically contain a small number of variables. Investigators consistently find that expected risks and rewards are significant considerations in offending decisions and target selection. However, research designs that utilize artificial criminal scenarios obscure motivational and contextual factors that potentially complicate offenders' opportunity assessments. Moreover, investigators usually proceed as if criminal decisions are made by lone offenders and fail to consider that interactional dynamics produce decision-making contexts that potential offenders cannot fully anticipate through advance calculation of risk and benefits.

The second approach to criminal choice situates offending decisions in the context of offenders' larger lives and lifestyles (Eckland-Olson, Lieb, & Zurcher, 1984; Gibbs & Shelley, 1982; Jacobs & Wright, 1999; McCarthy et al., 1998; Shover, 1996; Tunnell, 1992; Wright & Decker, 1994, 1997). Investigators informed by this approach typically draw from interviews conducted with active or inactive thieves. Their findings show that criminal decisions are embedded in offenders' chaotic lifestyles. The lifestyles and routines of street life place offenders in situations that impede careful choice and that evoke motivations and cultural outlooks that make crime attractive. One observer, for example, notes that "contexts populated almost exclusively by young, drug-using males simply are not the kind in which decision makers pay close attention to threat and virtue" (Shover, 1996, p. 170). However, investigators of criminal decision making and context typically slight the role of situations immediately antecedent to crime and favor analysis of offenders' more entrenched habits and routines (Fleisher, 1995; Jacobs & Wright, 1999; Tunnell, 1992; Wright & Decker, 1994, 1997). This led Hagan and McCarthy (1992, p. 556) to conclude that although the context of street life produces delinquency, "exactly what aspects of life on the street cause delinquency" remain unclear (Hagan & McCarthy, 1992, p. 556). Although many investigators note that offenders share a style of living and often socialize with other offenders, researchers rarely examine how co-offending affects the decision to commit a particular crime (Cordilia, 1986).

Decision making in criminal groups is seldom a focus of investigation, but acceptance of group effects on individual criminal motivation is widespread. Many investigators note that participation and interaction with co-offenders may moderate individuals' fear of punishment and increase chances of offending (Cloward & Ohlin, 1960; Eckland-Olson et al., 1984; Erikson & Jensen, 1977; Short & Strodtbeck, 1965; Shover & Henderson, 1995). There also is reason to suspect that some participants play a much greater part in encouraging criminal decisions in groups than do others. Results of self-report surveys of youthful offenders document reported variation in individual influence on group decisions to commit crime (McCarthy et al., 1998; Warr, 1996). Even experienced thieves often contend that they "got involved primarily because of partners" (Feeney, 1986, p. 58; see also Bennet & Wright, 1984). Despite widespread acceptance of group effects on choice, some observers find evidence for the effects of interpersonal dynamics on crime choice unconvincing. Gottfredson and Hirschi (1990, p. 158) acknowledge that criminal cooperation eases individual effort required to offend, but are skeptical of imprecise assertions that interpersonal dynamics heavily influence offending decisions. Nevertheless, denying the presence of significant group effects is premature given the substantial evidence that interaction significantly affects choice in other types of small groups.

In classic sociological experiments, investigators found that subjects provided with simple estimating tasks modified their estimates to comply with the estimates of copresent others (Asch, 1951; Sherif, 1936). These early experiments on group conformity inspired scores of scholars in diverse disciplines to investigate interaction and decisions in small groups. In studies ranging from experiments on shifts in individual preferences resulting from accommodation of other group members' preferences to *post hoc* interpretations of foreign policy, investigators find that dynamics of small group interaction affect choice (t'Hart, Stern, & Sundelius, 1997; Turner, Wetherall, & Hogg, 1989). One explanation for individual conformity to group preferences is that some participants persuade others to conform, but individuals modify their preferences and behavior to suit expectations even in the absence of communication with other group participants (Kameda & Davis, 1990; Maas, West, & Cialdini, 1987; Shelley, 1998; Turner et al., 1989; Wright & Ayton, 1994). Group effects result not only from communication, but also from individual participants' expectations and attempts to gauge preferences of others in their group. Group participants predict the group's likely course and adjust their actions to suit their expectations.

Failure to examine choice processes in crime groups potentially is a significant oversight. This article contributes to our understanding of criminal choice in three ways. First, it bridges an empirical gap in the literature between offenders' abstract motivations and lifestyles and their choice of a target. Second, it examines how interaction between co-offenders influences assessments of criminal opportunity and subsequently offending decisions. Offenders construct their sense of opportunity incrementally and in accord with expectations derived from the situational context and the actions of others. The discussion emphasizes that offenders do not respond passively to situational opportunity; they create it by selecting and transforming the situations they confront. Third, and relatedly, findings reinforce the importance of continued investigation of the varied processes and interpersonal interactions that contribute to the construction of criminal opportunity and criminal decisions.

STREET ACTIVITIES AS CONTEXT

Street thieves' descriptions of decision making contrast with depictions of crime choice that cast it as calculating and purposeful. Many thieves report that they do not plan their crimes or spend only a few minutes planning (Cromwell, Olson, & Avary, 1991, p. 61; Feeney, 1986; Short, 1998, p. 10; Tracy, 1987). As other investigators have found, thieves often ignore and can put out of mind consequences of being caught while considering a crime (Cromwell et al., 1991; Shover & Honaker, 1992). In this study, several subjects exhibited an extreme lack of concern with consequences by choosing to commit crimes in which they were sure to be suspects. Some pawned goods using accurate identification, loitered or aimlessly drove their cars near the scene of recently completed robberies, robbed victims they knew, or indifferently allowed themselves to be photographed during an offense. To reconcile offenders' descriptions of criminal deliberation with assumptions of calculating actors, decision making is best understood as "socially bounded" (Shover & Honaker, 1992). Offenders construct decisions in accord with conduct norms and during the activities of street life (Feeney, 1986; Jacobs & Wright, 1999; Shover, 1996; Tunnell, 1992; Wright & Decker, 1994, 1997).

The hallmark of street life, as a style of living, is pursuit of pleasure and status through conspicuous leisure and consumption "with minimal concern for obligations and commitments that are external to the immediate social setting" (Shover & Honaker, 1992, p. 283). Street offenders live for the moment (Fleisher, 1995, pp. 213–214). A burglar explains that his attitude prevented due attention to consequences:

> You just don't care, you know. You get the attitude that, hey, whatever happens happens. I'm not gonna worry about that [consequences] until it happens, and that's . . . the frame of mind you are in [when stealing].

Commitment to street life and crime coincides with periods of drug use and related family and economic crises. Many offenders explain that they had temporarily given up on conventional living and devoted themselves fully to partying. Investigators find that a host of problems accompany theft and that it is much more common during offenders' heaviest periods of overindulgence in drugs and drink (Deschenes, Anglin, & Speckhart, 1991; Faupel, 1987; Horney, Osgood, & Marshall, 1995). A burglar recalls that a lengthy period of intoxication and reckless living made stealing a sensible option:

> Things were crazy anyway. I was worried and paranoid all the time. We sat around the apartment and listened to a police scanner, for Christ sakes. Our apartment was full of stolen stuff and crank, and we were living off of hot credit cards [purchased from other thieves and hotel bartenders]. If you're like that anyway, why not do a crime so you got something to really worry about.

Thieves share their chaotic lifestyles and parties with compatible friends and a loose network of associates who live similarly (Cordilia, 1986; Katz, 1988, p. 212; McCarthy et al., 1998). Expensive drug and alcohol habits, fighting, shoplifting, writing bad checks, and amassing debt to drug dealers, lawyers, and other creditors are normal in their circles of friends. Street offenders often sleep in cheap motels or on associates' couches or move from party to party with little idea of where they will rest next (Wright & Decker, 1997, p. 38). Curtis, a heroin addict, explains that a continuous and mobile party allowed him to maintain his drug habit by reciprocal sharing with others. His lifestyle made locating criminal opportunities effortless and led him to his robbery co-offender, a man that he scarcely knew. When I asked Curtis, "were you partying with Willie?" he responded:

> To an extent, you know, because you go from one place to another place. I'd been like that for some time. You have a car, or he has a car and that's the situation. Then this turns into a better situation, and then you get high some more. It's kind of a balance, who's going to do something [crime] last. Who is doing things just kind of shift back and forth . . . I guess most people who have been doing it understand.

During the activities of street life, offenders encounter audiences who admire risk-taking, fearlessness, and the ability to provide money and drugs for the party (Katz, 1988; Miller, 1998; Shover, 1996). As one burglar notes, "you never know how many friends you've got until you got a pocket full of pills." Criminal events provide money and drugs for conspicuous consumption and are ideal venues for displaying courage and familiarity with dangerous situations (Katz, 1988, p. 148). Offenders often purport that one goal of their crimes is "showing off" courage or ability by exhibiting lack of hesitation, willingness to take risks, or exaggerated calm in the face of danger (Katz, 1988, p. 304; Matza, 1964; Shover, 1996, p. 110). Crime is a form of "edgework" or voluntary chance-taking that contains "a serious threat to one's physical or mental well-being or one's sense of an ordered existence" (Lyng, 1990, p. 857). Part of the enjoyment of edgework is that it sets capable risk-takers who can "maintain control over a situation that borders on chaos" apart from others (Lyng, 1990, p. 859; Shover, 1996). A middle-aged thief proudly recalls his group's management of challenging criminal events: "it's bad to say, but we was good at what we done."

All group participants define a range of appropriate action from a broad understanding of the situation and how they expect copresent others to act in it (Fine, 1979). Street crime originates in "permissive environs allowing the performance of various respectable and non-respectable activities" (Luckenbill, 1977, p. 178). Small groups of friends intent on "partying," a word unambiguously meaning drug consumption and action-seeking to offenders, comprise most theft groups (Giordano, Cernkovich, & Pugh, 1986; Katz, 1988, p. 198; Shover, 1996). In this sample, 44 subjects were drinking or under the influence of controlled substances during their crime. Levels of consumption on the day of the crime were extreme even by the standards of men who construct their lives around drug use and drinking. A robber reports: "I drank a lot. After my divorce, I drank a lot. But, on that day I drank more. We was drinking a *whole lot* on that day!" A robber currently serving his third sentence for the crime describes the occasion preceding his last offense:

> Well, it more or less started out like most of them do: getting high with my buddy there and riding around drinking. Stopped off to get a few Valiums, and we was just riding around here and there. You know, stopped at a buddy's here. It was an all day thing, drinking and driving, driving and drinking. . . . I was in and out [of consciousness]. I would get so drunk he would drive, and then he would get so drunk I would drive while he was sleeping. And just more or less the whole day went on like that.

Offenders encounter many people during their extended parties. As a result, the composition of a group often changes as it proceeds toward crime. Some participants excuse themselves from company suspected to be on a criminal course, whereas others are quick to volunteer. A persistent robber remembers the outcome of his group's plan to rob a gas station: "[t]he other guys backed out, didn't show . . . just me and the guy that worked at the station, we carried out the plan." Continued participation in a scene already construed by others as potentially criminal conveys approval of a criminal course. Restraining influences on a group diminish as those wary of crime and less committed to the party depart. A burglar recalls recognizing the apparent criminal potential in his companions:

> We were at a party and everyone else goes to bed. They go to sleep. We just sittin' around doing nothing. Now, when you have got a bunch of crank heads sitting around at four in the morning with nothing to do, they are scheming. There is nothing to do but scheme.

Experienced offenders are adept at sizing up trustworthiness and criminal willingness in associates (Gould, Walker, Crane, & Lidz, 1974, pp. 45–46; McCarthy et al., 1998, p. 174). Of course, many street offenders are so committed to street life that they can safely assume that those around them are open to criminal proposals. When I asked Greg, a burglar whose most recent conviction contained 32 counts, what happens when his associates refuse to accompany him for a burglary, he answered: "I never had that problem. If they have hit a lick before, they know you can make pretty good money . . . everybody needs more money."

INTERACTIONAL DYNAMICS

Antecedent events and copresent others open group participants' eyes to opportunity, but interaction begins enactment of a criminal course and the more intentional stages of decision making. All interactions are temporally embedded and contextual. Offenders' forward-looking opportunity appraisals are based on the sense they make of situations using contextually relevant precedent and experience (Vaughan, 1998), but actors do not simply apply lessons from experience to static situations. They "continuously engage patterns and repertoires from the past, project hypothetical pathways forward in time and adjust their actions to the exigencies of emerging situations" (Emirbayer & Mische, 1998, p. 1012). How do group offenders interact with each other and their environments to reach a criminal decision?

Subjects described three general styles of interaction that made illicit opportunity apparent and readily accessible. Most crime groups made criminal sense of a scene by referencing group identities, improvisational communicative signals, or conspicuously attractive targets. These styles of decision making are fluid and overlapping; all three considerations play a part in the decisions of many groups. However, qualitative differences in group decisions are apparent. The relative importance of the three recurring considerations in criminal choice is contingent on a group's shared criminal experience and on the experience and motivation of individual participants. Participants in groups with extensive experience frame their situations and opportunities using this experience; groups without shared experience improvise and rely on situational and interactional cues.

INCREMENTAL SIGNALING

In many cases, small decisions and incremental actions made more or less intentionally and by multiple participants alter situations and perceptions until criminal choice is attractive, what I term *incremental signaling*. Offenders without shared experience or on the periphery of street life are especially likely to approach crime gradually using incremental gestural or verbal moves. When offenders are unsure of others' objectives, they use signals to negotiate shared definitions. One offender makes a move toward crime, and then checks others' responses to find out if they see similar potential and are receptive to the directive (Cromwell et al., 1991, p. 67).

Shared contexts and immediate precipitating experiences turn actors' attention to similar reference signals and solutions to mutual problems; signaling articulates these anticipatory courses of action (Hilton & Slugowski, 1998; Wade, 1994). A burglar explains that his partners easily interpreted his otherwise oblique suggestion because their recently incurred obligations made criminal potential apparent:

> I guess I figured they owed me. I mean I wouldn't have cared a bit, the thought would have never crossed my mind if I had went out and bought $100 worth of pot and smoked every bit. I wouldn't have thought [that] they owed me anything. But, I bought $300 worth of rock, and it was gone in like two hours. . . . He shared it [burglary profit] with me because he better have. Bubba was telling Tommy "we have to get some more money." I had spent my whole paycheck on them. So I told them, "Look, I got no more money! All my money was left back in Memphis, it's about time y'all come up with something."

Deliberation begins ambiguously, but escalates quickly. Typically, someone in the group mentions an apparent need for money. The context makes it clear that a suggestion is being made that the group has the potential for acquiring money illegally. Next, a participant mentions a specific type of crime or target. This statement of intent is similar conceptually to a *keynote,* a term familiar to collective behavior scholars. Keynotes are exploratory directives that resonate with those thinking along similar lines, but who are still turning over multiple interpretations of a situation (Turner & Killian, 1987, p. 59). In consequential and urgent situations, keynotes inspire action. Urgent situations are sufficiently ambivalent to encourage actors to turn to others for guidance but convey a finite set of appropriate preferences (Fine, 1979; Kohn & Williams, 1956, p. 173; McPhail, 1991; Turner & Killian, 1987, p. 53). Two robbers recall definitive progressions in verbal deliberation:

> Yeah, it went, "we need some damn money" and then here he sat and told us all. Well, we were all sittin' there, and he was telling us about robberies or whatever, and he told us how to do it.
>
> We was riding around gettin' high, and I was telling them that I needed to make some money for Christmas. They kinda looked at each other and started laughin'. They pretty much said, "you need some easy money, you're with the right people." I said, "that's what I'm talking about." When they said fast and easy, I didn't know they meant armed robbery.

Decisions are based on the style of presentation provided for alternatives as well as on the objective situation (Kuehberger, 1996). Offenders often build confidence using optimistic conversation referred to as "talking it up" or "gassing each other up" (Cromwell et al., 1991, p. 69; Shover, 1996; Tunnell, 1992). Several subjects in this study noted that what is most significant about the optimistic talk preceding crime is what participants do not say. They contend that selective omission of information by some participants reduced fear for others. For example, two burglars reported that the homes they targeted belonged to a co-offender's family members. This information was withheld, however, and the subjects were surprised when their partners were suspected and arrested immediately.

Because conversations are short and criminal consent is often unspoken, many participants are not sure that a crime really will be committed until the last minute (Katz, 1988, p. 225; Matza, 1964, p. 54). A heroin addict engaged in a payroll dispute with his employer approached an older man in his neighborhood with a reputation as a competent thief. He explains how the incremental banter and actions before their robbery allowed the group to work toward a crime and postpone consideration of the risks:

> It is not like you approach him and say "hey, look here, I have this problem." It's more like you are getting high and everything like that. You talkin' about "this son of a bitch who did this to you" and "that son of a bitch that did that to you" and then I said, "I ought to go over there and take my money! Et cetera, et cetera, et cetera." One guy goes, "yeah, yeah, yeah, I ought to!" I ought to do this, and I ought to do that. And one thing leads to another, and basically I find myself in a situation where like I'm laying on the side of a hill saying, "what the hell am I doing this for?"

Criminal proposals are provisional but are often made by those participants who have established a relatively firm definition of a situation. One thief reported that his drug habit did not allow him to be selective about criminal opportunity. When conversations turn to crime, he immediately directs the group toward action with a challenge: "let's go then . . . if they are for real, if they really want to do something, then they will do it right then cuz there ain't no sense talking about it." Because criminal conversations often begin with ambiguous or exploratory statements, the influence of people who speak tersely and forcefully during decision making is substantial, particularly if other participants do not openly oppose their position (DeGrada, Kruglanski, Mannetti, & Pierro, 1999; Turner & Killian, 1987, p. 85). An offender remembers how an outspoken participant influenced his group's decision making:

> He wanted them how he wanted them, and he was the main one who hollered at people to get things done. He said, "let's go do this!" And I tell you, he had a way of talking you into it. He had this way, "oh come on pussy" and this and that and the other. There was one that was real dominant. It was almost like, how do I want to word this? It was almost manipulation as far as getting us to do something that we didn't want to. Like, I'm not saying that any of us didn't want to do what we did; it's like we are skeptical and he would manipulate us into going on into it.

Unchecked assertive directives result in a situation in which "each thinks others are committed" to offending (Matza, 1964, p. 54). Therefore, conversations can rapidly evolve past the point where participants begin to see statements that discourage crime as evidence of cowardice or the speaker's inability to meet the demands of a situation.

TARGET CONVERGENCE

Some groups reach criminal decisions when participants mutually and instantaneously recognize an appealing target, what I term *target convergence*. These groups seemingly converge on a target with only the slightest communication between offenders. The eight subjects whose groups clearly reached their decisions in this manner had participants with extensive criminal experience and exposure to street life. However, none of these groups had committed a robbery or burglary together previously. The groups did not discuss crime because they did not set out to commit one, but when an opportunity appeared, talk was not necessary. Appealing targets trigger a group's partially formed and contingent criminal frame of a situation. Targets stand out against a recently constructed backdrop of illicit potential.

Many spontaneous robbers find conspicuous contrast between their situational understandings and ignorant victims who, without realizing the danger, "flash their money around" or "play [the robbers] for punks" or who simply are "somewhere they don't belong." In these situations, deliberative communication with robbery partners is limited to abrupt gestures, nods, or a few words. A robber recalls that his crime began when an older group of men challenged his friends to a fight. When the younger men did not balk, the groups made a frail peace by mentioning mutual associates and sharing a bottle. The newfound allies, apparently on edge from the averted fight, assaulted a stranger who entered the scene minutes later:

> We were just sitting there chillin', and I asked one of the guys do he got a cigarette. . . . About this time, he says "nah," and he says "but I bet you this dude got one coming down the street." So, I went over there and, you know, asked the dude for a cigarette. One of them dudes comes runnin' across the parking lot and hit him—just Boom! So, when he hit him, [he] hit the ground, and just immediately we started kicking him. While we was beating him, others was going in his pockets gettin' everything he got.

Target convergence typifies mugging and robbery during drug deals, but burglars also can become instantly aware of opportunity. A burglar explains how an encounter with an inviting target during an interstate drug run aligned action in his group:

> I was all high and stuff and seeing tracers and blown away. A big snow come up, and we pulled into this cul-de-sac to stop. There was this hunting lodge or a big house, like an A-frame, and I was sure there was nobody in there. I don't think nothing was even said. I don't know if he said something or I did. We were high and just talking gibberish, like in rhymes. We just ran up there and busted in a window.

ESTABLISHING IDENTITY

Criminality can be a group identity or a mental device shared by participants for organizing events and predicting group action (Cromwell et al., 1991; Short & Strodtbeck, 1965). Participants' knowledge of others in the group, whether gained in firsthand experience or by reputation, frames how a group sees its potential.

The characters inhabiting street scenes often have reputations for criminal capability that precede them. These reputations play a significant part in turning group participants' heads toward illicit opportunity. James, a habitual burglar, reported that a young accomplice probably knew how their group would fund a spontaneous beach vacation: "[t]his is what I do. I am a burglar. He knows that and he knows that if he is with me, we are going to steal." Another experienced burglar reflects on why an accomplice who had never committed a burglary volunteered for their crime: "I am sure he looked at me as someone who could give him an alternative."

Most group offenders have firsthand knowledge of co-offenders' criminal potential. Interaction in these experienced groups retains some of its improvisational character. However, subjects from experienced groups report that their group interaction began and proceeded with the potential for crime in participants' minds. Shared criminal experiences are especially salient in ascribing criminal potential to a group (Wood, Gove, Wilson, & Cochran, 1997; Wright & Decker, 1994, p. 37). Several subjects knew others in their group for years before committing a felony together, but stole every time they were together after the first offense. Although individual criminal careers are usually diverse, crime groups often specialize in method and target selection. This shared specialization suggests that participants associate assembly of the practiced group with particular opportunity (Warr, 1996). An offender with several years' experience installing burglar alarms and with some expertise in burglary reports that after he revealed his skills to younger relatives during a spontaneous theft: "They come to get me to get high about every night. I would have been stealing some, but not near as much."

A modicum of success enthuses some crime groups. A young man remembers the discussion that followed his first burglary: "We sat and joked about it, we was talking about how easy it was . . . hey, we can do this every day."

After many successful crimes, stealing with a group becomes a routine that provides offenders with a sense of security. Confidence in partners and in the group's criminal ability and good fortune reinforces the group's criminal identity. One addict recalls that he regularly met with co-offenders and that theft plans needed no discussion in his group: "we were beginning to use stealing as a job; we got up of a morning; we did us a pill and then we were out and in the process and looking for something to steal."

INFLUENCE AND SCENE SETTING

To this point, I have described how offenders cooperatively negotiate shared recognition of criminal opportunity. Indeed, most subjects took care to assert that crime participants mutually influence each other and that each offender exercises considerable agency in crime choice. Nevertheless, as the preceding discussion of interactional dynamics implies, some participants have more influence on a group's behavior than do others (Warr, 1996). Almost all subjects readily identified the most influential person(s) in their group's decision. Nine interviewees identified themselves as leaders and several more viewed themselves as instigators in their last offense. A self-proclaimed instigator describes a burglary in which he stole a van from a residential garage:

> I don't know him that well. I had the idea of gettin' the van, you know. Whenever I had the idea of getting the van, he went along with it. We were coming from a friend's house. He was just following me. He was ten years younger.

Directives made to a group have the greatest influence when participants attribute relevant expertise or experience to the speaker (Berger, Fisek, Norman, & Zelditch, 1977; Foddy & Smithson, 1996; Levine & Russo, 1987; Maas et al., 1987; Shelley, 1998; Warr, 1996). Offenders sometimes ascribe expertise to partners with a paucity of information, however. Subjects cite co-offenders' age, toughness, confident demeanor, and criminal reputations as sources of influence. Partners' presumed and proven criminal abilities not only lead others to look toward criminal opportunity, but also define power relations in the group. A novice burglar explains that a co-offender's past exploits increased his influence over the group:

> Whether we wanted to do it or not, we would, cuz we figured he was right. I mean, it was like we knew he had been around more than we had. I mean, just getting around into things; like just getting high or stealing or whatever. He wasn't scared of nothin'.

Groups ascribe influence to some participants. In turn, these participants enact their influence. Suspecting that present company and surroundings approximate opportunity, actors adjust the situation to fit their preferred perspective for understanding events (Best, 1982; Goffman, 1969; Heise, 1979).

With motives of helping friends, showing off, and benefitting from task cooperation, some offenders maneuver so that others make criminal sense of a scene. Actors accomplish scene setting by "moving about to confirm that all the parts of a scene are present, . . . or assembling required paraphernalia or mustering human participants, . . . or locomoting to a setting where a required situation exists intact" (Heise, 1979, p. 39).

In some groups, offenders provide drugs and alcohol to reduce fear of criminal participation (Cromwell et al., 1991, p. 64). A severe alcoholic reports that when he refused a criminal proposal, his partner bought more liquor in an attempt to "get me drunk . . . to where I didn't give a damn." Collecting and displaying weapons or other facilitating hardware also elicits criminal ideas and shapes the behavior of others (Carlson, Marcus-Newhall, & Miller, 1990; Lofland, 1969, pp. 69–72). A young man recalls his surprise when his partners suddenly presented tools needed to stage a robbery: "The guns was theirs; they had them and some ski masks already in the car." A habitual burglar explains why it may seem to some offenders that tools suddenly appear in a potentially criminal scene: "Burglary tools, always did have them with me. You never know when you are going to run up on something." A young burglar describes using a set of keys in his effort to recruit accomplices for a burglary:

> Sometimes it just happens to be luck—like one time a store. One day I was in front of the store, it was closed and I walked to the store and tried to open the

doors. It was locked. It was closed, and when I was walking away from the store I happened to look at the ground and seen a set of keys. So . . . I pick up the keys, and I go to the lock and open the door. I lock it back up, go home and tell about two or three friends. We was just livin' across the street from the store. Four of us come back, . . . took all kind of stuff out that store.

Most subjects reported that at least one group participant contemplated or made some preparation for their crime before the group assembled. The consistent finding that many thieves keep a store of potential targets in mind until they need them or an opportune situation arises supports their claim (Maguire, 1982; Wright & Decker, 1994, p. 63, 1997). Six subjects said that before discussing specific criminal plans their group arrived at a target that was preselected by another participant. A home invasion robber contends that until he saw the target, he thought his group's plan was to intimidate a nonpaying drug customer as his partners had implied:

I mean, as soon as we pulled up—and they had gone in and come out to get me— and when I got inside, that's when I first knew. I mean, they didn't tell me outside before I went in; that's the part I couldn't understand about it. All I knew is that the people in there [a wealthy attorney's home] wouldn't mess with these two guys.

Offenders who are the most hesitant or uninformed often become acutely aware of the influence of others on their actions in the instant before they offend. When confronting a target, they realize that their previous decisions and the actions of co-offenders constrain their options. The most motivated offenders in a group often turn from subtle to overt means of influence in an attempt to overcome this late hesitation. When confronting a target, a decisive move finally "brings into relief" criminal definitions and polarizes options (Katz, 1988, p. 305). A burglar reports that his presumed consent placed him in a situation that compelled him to respond:

[By the] time he got the one [partner] and put him through the window, I mean, what am I gonna do, you know? I didn't want to look like a punk and leave. I wouldn't leave them standing there and me a punk. Then, if they got away from it, then I would be a punk for leaving. That's how I was. I mean, I thought I was in a little gang or whatever.

A robber remembers that he was disgusted with his partners' failure to follow through on the group's quickly formulated plan. He explains that frustration led to his decision to take the initiative:

We pulled into a couple of places, and nobody would do it. It was driving me crazy. I can't take that. They were findin' every little thing that could go wrong. I finally said, "all right, by god, pull in the next place you see." I went in and said, "I have a gun" and robbed it.

DISCUSSION

Understanding why people who are not determined to commit a crime one minute become so the next requires attention to the immediate situations that link street life and criminal decisions (Jacobs & Wright, 1999, p. 150; Katz,

1988, p. 3; Short, 1998). This paper shows that interaction with other people in distinctive compositional settings and organizing activities conditions criminal choice. Findings support portrayals of criminal decision making as complex, bounded by the desperate circumstances of offenders' lives, and framed by the pursuit of an escapist party. Moreover, findings suggest that examining offenders' fallible perceptions of costs and benefits or their commitment to conduct norms of street life only begins to capture complexity in criminal decision making.

Inadequate attention to the many sources of extrasituational, situational, and interactional variation in individual offenders' considerations in choosing crime, particularly in studies of target selection, structures research findings and creates an overly rational and simplistic understanding of choice (Bennet & Wright, 1984; Rankin & Wells, 1982; Tunnell, 1992). Burglars obviously scan for signs of occupancy, witnesses, and escape routes in the instant before stealing (Bennet & Wright, 1984). This utilitarian rationality is commensurable with extended, less deliberate, and complex routes to offending. When given freedom to describe events, offenders depict improvisational, contextual, and variable processes leading to their choice. To varying degrees, incremental signaling, target convergence, constraining and enabling actions by others, and the situational dynamics of the criminal setting shape their decisions.

The abstract context of crime is a style of living that creates need for disposable cash and provides few feasible approaches for getting it (Jacobs & Wright, 1999; Wright & Decker, 1994, p. 39). In the immediate context of criminal events, motivation often results from collaboratively constructed perceptions of opportunity. The most insightful and self-reflective thieves refer to both lasting and situational contexts when they report that a learned approach to crime avoidance is "staying out of trouble" or "off the streets." For them, the law-abiding path seems narrow and crime results from inaction and failure to take precautions by avoiding street life, its activities, and potential crime partners.

Many investigators portray criminal motivation either as an enduring predisposition or else as an attraction to offending that remains dormant until an encounter with a target (Jacobs & Wright, 1999, p. 164). Criminological theories suggest models of overdetermined individuals who are driven to crime and waiting for a chance to satisfy their preferences. However, conceptual distinctions between opportunity and motivation blur when ethnographers and situational analysts examine decisions and interaction preceding crime (Athens, 1997; Short & Strodtbeck, 1965; Wolfgang, 1958). Burglars and robbers construct criminal opportunity by comparing recently formulated understandings with developing events and adjusting situations to make events and understanding correspond. Criminal choice "blends indiscriminately into the flow of practical activity" as offenders improvise action and expectations to suit ever-shifting circumstances in informal situations (Emirbayer & Mische, 1998). Some crime groups are more goal directed than are others, but only a few pursue determined and consistent ends known equally to all; more typically, the rational path mutates as options open and close and as participants interact to make sequential choices. Participants in this study contend that the immediate allure of crime is incomprehensible without considering preparation, cajoling, encouragement, and other enabling and constraining action by others.

Findings from investigations of the situational complexities of choice have significant implications for future research. On the one hand, offending results when offenders stumble into developing crime. Therefore, social and geographic proximity to crime groups and situations that precipitate thoughts of crime have causal significance (Fagan, Piper, & Cheng, 1987, p. 588). Those without experience in street life are unlikely to find themselves in the presence of men considering a burglary, but theft groups are difficult for many impoverished young men to avoid. On the other hand, this study reveals that purposive, but contingent, action by some actors often precedes even unplanned crime. Dangerous places, alcohol and drug use, appropriate victims, tools, and supportive co-offenders are correlates of criminal situations, but these elements do not converge in scenes spontaneously (see Sampson & Lauritsen, 1994, p. 39). Actors assemble the elements of criminal situations to direct action, play with danger, and create opportunity.

The complexity of situations and variability in offenders' situational skills and constructions of opportunity receives little empirical attention (Birkbeck & LaFree, 1993). Therefore, the intersections between offenders' lives and the effects of these encounters on variation in their decision making are largely unexplored. For example, many robbers are motivated sufficiently to wait in the car while partners rob a store, but contend that they would never serve as gunmen. Others may never attempt a burglary unless in the presence of people who they assume burglarize routinely. In an event, one offender can be an experienced thief who displays unusual forethought in scouting out a target, whereas his co-offenders are drunken young men who join the decision in its last stages.

Qualitative and interactionist studies of crime have great potential. This paper, however, is not a call for a particular methodology, but for empirical attention to "immediate background and context of offenders' action" (Katz, 1991). Examining event characteristics may support well-worn theories and improve specification of established models. For example, offenders without biographical characteristics correlated with street crime may offend when their lives take a short-term turn for the worse or when they are in the company of those who clearly are at risk of offending. Reducing the accessibility of targets may deter groups without experience. Groups that have committed many crimes may be willing to take on greater risks or only be displaced by a challenging target. In methodologies that examine crime as an outcome of individual offenders' characteristics, potential sources of variation escape notice. Group crimes are an intersection of participants' pathways in which characters and their characteristics meld and interact with environments to shape events.

REFERENCES

Asch, S. E. (1951). Effects of group pressure upon the modification and distortion of judgment. In H. Guetzkow (Ed.), *Groups, leadership and men* (pp. 177–190). Pittsburgh: Carnegie Press.

Athens, L. H. (1997). *Violent criminal acts and actors revisited.* Chicago: University of Chicago Press.

Bennet, T., & Wright, R. T. (1984). *Burglars on burglary: Prevention and the offender.* Aldershot, UK: Bower.

Berger, J., Fisek, M. H., Norman, R. Z., & Zelditch, M. J. (1977). *Status characteristics and social interaction: An expectation-states theory.* New York: Elsevier.

Best, J. (1982). Crime as strategic interaction. *Urban Life, 11,* 107–128.

Birkbeck, C. B., & LaFree, G. (1993). The situational analysis of crime and deviance. *Annual Review of Sociology, 19,* 133–137.

Bureau of Justice Statistics. (1999). *Criminal victimization in the United States.* Washington, DC: Department of Justice.

Carlson, M., Marcus-Newhall, A., & Miller, N. (1990). Effects of situational aggression cues: A quantitative review. *Journal of Personality and Social Psychology, 58,* 622–633.

Carrol, F. M., & Weaver, J. S. (1986). Crime perceptions in a natural setting by expert and novice shoplifters. *Social Psychology Quarterly, 48,* 349–359.

Cloward, R. A., & Ohlin, L. E. (1960). *Delinquency and opportunity.* New York: Free Press.

Cordilia, A. T. (1986). Robbery arising out of a group drinking context. In A. Campbell & J. J. Gibbs (Eds.), *Violent transactions.* New York: Blackwell.

Cornish, D. B., & Clarke, R. V. (1986). *The reasoning criminal: Rational choice perspectives on offending.* New York: Springer-Verlag.

Cromwell, P. F., Olson, J. N., & Avary, D. W. (1991). *Breaking and entering: An ethnographic analysis of burglary.* Newbury Park, CA: Sage.

DeGrada, E., Kruglanski, A. W., Mannetti, L., & Pierro, A. (1999). Motivated cognition and group interaction: Need for closure affects the contents and processes of collective negotiations. *Journal of Experimental Social Psychology, 35,* 346–365.

Deschenes, E. P., Anglin, M. D., & Speckhart, G. (1991). Narcotics addiction: Related criminal careers, social and economic costs. *Journal of Drug Issues, 21,* 405–434.

Eckland-Olson, S., Lieb, J., & Zurcher, L. (1984). The paradoxical impact of criminal sanctions: Some microstructural findings. *Law and Society Review, 18,* 159–178.

Emirbayer, M., & Mische, A. (1998). What is agency? *American Journal of Sociology, 103,* 962–1023.

Erikson, M. L., & Jensen, G. F. (1977). Delinquency is still group behavior: Toward revitalizing the group premise in the sociology of deviance. *Journal of Criminal Law and Criminology, 70,* 102–116.

Fagan, J., Piper, E., & Cheng, Y. (1987). Contribution of victimization to delinquency in inner cities. *Journal of Criminal Law and Criminology, 78,* 586–613.

Faupel, C. E. (1987). Drugs-crime connections: Elaborations from the life of hard-core heroin addicts. *Social Problems, 34,* 54–68.

Feeney, F. (1986). Robbers as decision-makers. In D. B. Cornish & R. V. Clarke (Eds.), *The reasoning criminal: Rational choice perspective on offending.* New York: Springer-Verlag.

Fine, G. (1979). Rethinking subculture: An interactionist analysis. *American Journal of Sociology, 85*, 1–20.

Fleisher, M. S. (1995). *Beggars and thieves: Lives of urban street criminals.* Madison: University of Wisconsin Press.

Foddy, M., & Smithson, M. (1996). Relative ability, paths of relevance, and influence in task oriented groups. *Social Psychology Quarterly, 59*, 40–53.

Gibbs, J. J., & Shelley, P. L. (1982). Life in the fast lane: A retrospective view by commercial thieves. *Journal of Research in Crime and Delinquency, 19*, 299–330.

Giordano, P. C., Cernkovich, S. A., & Pugh, M. D. (1986). Friendship and delinquency. *American Journal of Sociology, 91*, 1170–1202.

Goffman, E. (1969). *Where the action is.* London: Allen Lane.

Gottfredson, M. R., & Hirschi, T. (1990). *A general theory of crime.* Stanford, CA: Stanford University Press.

Gould, L., Walker, A. L., Crane, L. E., & Lidz, C. W. (1974). *Connections: Notes from the heroin world.* New Haven, CT: Yale University Press.

Groves, W. B., & Lynch, M. J. (1990). Reconciling structural and subjective approaches to the study of crime. *Journal of Research in Crime and Delinquency, 27*, 348–375.

Hagan, J., & McCarthy, B. (1992). Street life and delinquency. *British Journal of Sociology, 43*, 533–561.

Heise, D. (1979). *Understanding events: Affect and the construction of social action.* New York: Cambridge University Press.

Hilton, D. J., & Slugowski, B. R. (1998). Judgment and decisionmaking in social context: Discourse processes and rational inference. In T. Connoly & H. R. Arkes (Eds.), *Judgment and decisionmaking: An interdisciplinary reader* (2nd ed.). New York: Cambridge University Press.

Horney, J., Osgood, D. W., & Marshall, I. H. (1995). Criminal careers in the short term: Intra-individual variability in crime and relation to local life circumstances. *American Sociological Review, 60*, 655–673.

Jacobs, B. A., & Wright, R. T. (1999). Stick-up, street culture, and offender motivation. *Criminology, 37*, 149–174.

Kameda, T., & Davis, J. H. (1990). The function of reference point in individual and group risk decision making. *Organizational Behavior and Human Decision Processes, 46*, 55–76.

Katz, J. (1988). *The seductions of crime: Moral and sensual attractions in doing evil.* New York: Basic Books.

Katz, J. (1991). The motivation of persistent robbers. In M. Tonry (Ed.), *Crime and justice: An annual review of research* (Vol. 14, pp. 277–306). Chicago: University of Chicago Press.

Kohn, M. L., & Williams, R. M. (1956). Situational patterning in intergroup relations. *American Sociological Review, 21*, 164–174.

Kuehberger, A. (1996). The influence of framing on risky decisions: A meta-analysis. *Organizational Behavior and Human Decision Processes, 75*, 23–55.

Levine, J. M., & Russo, E. M. (1987). Majority and minority influence. In C. Hendrick (Ed.), *Group processes.* Newbery Park, CA: Sage.

Lofland, J. (1969). *Deviance and identity.* Englewood Cliffs, NJ: Prentice Hall.

Luckenbill, D. F. (1977). Criminal homicide as situated transaction. *Social Problems, 25*, 176–186.

Lyng, S. (1990). Edgework: A social-psychological analysis of voluntary risk-taking. *American Journal of Sociology, 95,* 851–886.

Maas, A., West, S. G., & Cialdini, R. B. (1987). Minority influence and conversion. In C. Hendrick (Ed.), *Group processes.* Newbery Park, CA: Sage.

Maguire, M. (1982). *Burglary in a dwelling.* London: Heinemann.

Matza, D. (1964). *Delinquency and drift.* New York: John Wiley.

McCarthy, B., Hagan, J., & Cohen, L. E. (1998). Uncertainty, cooperation and crime: Understanding the decision to co-offend. *Social Forces, 77,* 155–176.

McPhail, C. (1991). *The myth of the madding crowd.* New York: Aldine de Gruyter.

Miller, J. (1998). Up it up: Gender and accomplishment of street robbery. *Criminology, 36,* 37–66.

Nagin, D., & Paternoster, R. (1993). Enduring individual differences and rational choice theories of crime. *Law and Society Review, 27,* 467–496.

Piliavin, I. M., Gartner, R., Thorton, C., & Matsueda, R. L. (1986). Crime, deterrence and rational choice. *American Sociological Review, 51,* 101–119.

Piquero, A., & Rengert, G. F. (1999). Specifying deterrence with active residential burglars. *Justice Quarterly, 16,* 450–480.

Rankin, J. H., & Wells, L. E. (1982). The social context of deterrence. *Sociology and Social Research, 67,* 18–39.

Reiss, A. J., Jr. (1988). Co-offending and criminal careers. In M. Tonry & N. Morris (Eds.), *Crime and justice: A review of research* (Vol. 10). Chicago: University of Chicago Press.

Reiss, A. J., Jr., & Farrington, D. (1991). Advancing knowledge about co-offending: Results from a prospective longitudinal survey of London males. *Journal of Criminal Law and Criminology, 82,* 360–395.

Sampson, R., & Lauritsen, J. L. (1994). Violent victimization and offending: Individual-, situational-, and community-level risk factors. In A. J. Reiss & J. A. Roth (Eds.), *Understanding and preventing violence* (Vol. 3). Washington, DC: National Academy Press.

Shelley, R. K. (1998). Some developments in expectation states theory: Graduated expectations? In *Advances in Group Processes* (Vol. 15). Stamford, CT: JAI Press.

Sherif, M. (1936). *The psychology of social norms.* New York: Harper & Row.

Short, J. F. (1998). The level of explanation problem revisited. *Criminology, 36,* 1–36.

Short, J. F., & Strodtbeck, F. (1965). *Group process and gang delinquency.* Chicago: University of Chicago Press.

Shover, N. (1996). *Great pretenders: Pursuits and careers of persistent thieves.* Boulder, CO: Westview.

Shover, N., & Henderson, B. (1995). Repressive crime control and male persistent thieves. In H. D. Barlow (Ed.), *Crime and public policy: Putting theory to work.* Boulder, CO: Westview.

Shover, N., & Honaker, D. (1992). The socially bounded decision making of persistent property offenders. *Howard Journal of Criminal Justice, 31,* 276–290.

Taylor, M., & Nee, C. (1988). The role of cues in simulated residential burglary. *British Journal of Criminology, 28,* 396–401.

t'Hart, P. T., Stern, E. K., & Sundelius, B. (1997). *Beyond groupthink: Political group dynamics and policy-making.* Ann Arbor: University of Michigan Press.

Tracy, P. E., Jr. (1987). Race and class differences in self-reported delinquency. In M. E. Wolfgang & T. P. Thornberry (Eds.), *From boy to man, from delinquency to crime.* Chicago: University of Chicago Press.

Tremblay, P. (1993). Searching for suitable co-offenders. In R. V. Clarke & M. Felson (Eds.), *Advances in criminological theory: Routine activity and rational choice* (Vol. 5). New York: Transaction Publishing.

Tunnell, K. D. (1992). *Choosing crime: The criminal calculus of property offenders.* Chicago: Nelson Hall.

Turner, J. C., Wetherall, M. S., & Hogg, M. A. (1989). Referent informational influence and group polarization. *British Journal of Social Psychology, 28,* 135–147.

Turner, R. H., & Killian, L. (1987). *Collective behavior* (3rd ed.). Englewood Cliffs, NJ: Prentice Hall.

Vaughan, D. (1998). Rational choice, situated action, and the social control of organizations. *Law and Society Review, 32,* 501–538.

Wade, A. L. (1994). Social processes in the act of juvenile vandalism. In M. B. Clinard, R. Quinney, & J. Wildeman (Eds.), *Criminal behavior systems: A typology* (3rd ed.). New York: Anderson.

Warr, M. (1996). Organization and instigation in delinquent groups. *Criminology, 34,* 11–37.

Wolfgang, M. E. (1958). *Patterns in criminal homicide.* Philadelphia: University of Pennsylvania Press.

Wood, P. B., Gove, W. R., Wilson, J. A., & Cochran, J. K. (1997). Nonsocial reinforcement and habitual criminal conduct: An extension of learning theory. *Criminology, 35,* 335–366.

Wright, G., & Ayton, P. (1994). *Subjective probability.* Chichester, UK: John Wiley.

Wright, R. T., & Decker, S. (1994). *Burglars on the job: Streetlife and residential break-ins.* Boston: Northeastern University Press.

Wright, R. T., & Decker, S. (1997). *Armed robbers in action.* Boston: Northeastern University Press.

Wright, R. T., Logie, R. H., & Decker, S. (1996). Criminal expertise and offender decision making: An experimental study of the target selection process in residential burglary. *Journal of Research in Crime and Delinquency, 29,* 148–161.

Zimring, F. E. (1981). Kids, groups and crime: Some implications of a well-known secret. *Journal of Criminal Law and Criminology, 72,* 867–885.

CHAPTER 5

Auto Theft and Restrictive Deterrence

Bruce A. Jacobs and Michael C. Cherbonneau

Although researchers have examined the attributes that make offenders more or less responsive to sanction threats, far less attention has centered on the manner in which responsiveness can lead to less detectible crime, or perhaps even more overall crime. Restrictive deterrence is the concept that explains this paradox. We explore it here using qualitative interviews with 35 active auto thieves. Findings suggest that auto thieves' restrictively deterrent decision-making strategies fell into three broad categories: discretionary target selection, normalcy illusions, and defiance. Discussion focuses on the data's conceptual implications for restrictive deterrence and offender decision-making.

INTRODUCTION

Deterrence may be the most-studied theoretical process in all of criminology. The doctrine itself is the wellspring of the discipline, proposed by classical scholars more than 200 years ago (Beccaria, 1963 [1764]; Bentham, 1948 [1789]). The tenets central to the theory, subjective utility, free will, and the hedonic calculus, along with the objective and perceptual properties of sanction threats (i.e., celerity, certainty, and severity) have remained largely unchanged, though not unchallenged, to this day. Although researchers have examined the attributes that make offenders more or less responsive to sanction threats, far less attention has centered on the manner in which responsiveness can lead to less detectible crime, or perhaps even more overall crime. Restrictive deterrence is the concept that explains this paradox. We explore it here using interviews with active auto thieves.

Restrictive Deterrence

Deterrence is at heart a perceptual theory how offenders think about, process, and respond to sanction threats. Restrictive deterrence describes the manner in which offenders manage sanction threats to reduce the risk of detection and

Source: Jacobs, B. A., & Cherbonneau, M. C. (2014). Auto theft and restrictive deterrence. *Justice Quarterly, 31*(2), 344–67.

apprehension. Generally credited with developing the concept, Jack Gibbs (1975, p. 33) explained that restrictive deterrence:

> [I]s the curtailment of a certain type of criminal activity by an individual during some period because in whole or in part the curtailment is perceived by the individual as reducing the risk that someone will be punished as a response to the activity . . .

Although Gibbs (1975, p. 33) argued that the analytic period begins "after the individual's first offense of that type," this is not necessarily correct, as individuals can engage in restrictively deterrent conduct irrespective of prior criminal experience. Certainly, persons with greater experience tend to be more sensitive to the need for restrictive deterrence (because, all else being equal, they are more attuned to the importance of avoiding apprehension), but the ability to engage in restrictively deterrent measures is theoretically a democratic one.

Gibbs implies that restrictive deterrence applies primarily to the frequency of offending: Offenders reduce the number of offenses they commit over a given time period to lower their exposure to sanctions. More recently, Jacobs (2010, p. 433) refined the concept by specifying four distinct dimensions, only the first of which involves offending frequency:

"(1) The offender reduces the number of crimes s/he commits over a particular period of time;

(2) The offender commits crimes of lesser seriousness than the contemplated act, believing that punishment won't be as severe for a 'more minor' infraction . . . ;

(3) The offender engages in situational measures to enhance the probability that the contemplated offense will be undertaken without risk of detection . . . ; [and]

(4) The offender recognizes a risky situational context, which causes him or her to commit the same crime at a different place or time."

METHODS

Data for this study were generated through open-ended qualitative interviews with active auto thieves recruited from the streets of a large midwestern US city. Thirty-five currently active auto thieves were interviewed for the study. The first 30 interviews were conducted during the summer of 2006 and the remaining five one year later. Respondents were located through snowball sampling.

Locating actively involved criminals in this way begins invariably with a gatekeeper, usually one or more key informants with ties to categorically relevant populations (Glassner & Carpenter, 1985). Rather than relying on introductions from criminal justice personnel (i.e., lawyers, police, probation officers, etc.) who have contacts with free-ranging criminal populations (McCall, 1978), we enlisted the help of a street-based fieldworker: an African-American male in his late 20s and a native of the study site. Though in the desistance stage of his criminal career, he was by all accounts a revered member of the criminal order in the area, where he maintained ties to persons involved in street culture and crime. Due to past involvement in similar projects in the area, the recruiter was well practiced in the art of identifying potential respondents, verifying their eligibility, and encouraging their cooperation.

Snowball sampling is a purposive process. Ours was guided by set of inclusion criteria that defined what constitutes an "active" offender as a unit of analysis. It tended toward those with a history of auto theft offending, and above all, those with very recent offending experiences. In order to be eligible for our study, potential interviewees had to: (1) have committed at least one auto theft in the month prior to being interviewed; (2) have committed five or more auto thefts in their lives; and (3) consider themselves to be actively involved in auto theft. Most of the offenders interviewed met all three criteria, but a few did not. They were not excluded, as we did not wish to turn away hard-to-reach respondents with potentially valuable insights. Beyond these criteria, both male and female and adult and juvenile (aged 16 and older) offenders were targeted because perceptions and decision making in auto theft might well be tied to age, gender, and experience (see, e.g., Light et al., 1993; Mullins & Cherbonneau, 2011; O'Connor & Kelly, 2006; Slobodian & Browne, 1997).

The fieldworker initiated the recruitment process by approaching individuals in his immediate network whom he knew to be involved in auto theft. He explained the research objectives and informed prospects in the field that the interview would be confidential, that no legally identifiable information would be sought, and that law enforcement was in no way involved in the research. To expand the sample into new networks (or because eligible participants could no longer be culled from the initial pool of active auto thieves), the recruiter capitalized on referrals provided by initial recruits. In this way, some of the initial recruits served as "sampling seeds" which, in theory, reduces the likelihood of having a sample built entirely from one established network and also guards against having a sample comprised solely of atypical offenders (see Heckathorn, 1997).

The offenders ranged in age from 17 to 49, with a mean age of 27 years. Twenty-seven were male and eight were female. All of the respondents were African-American. The sample, on average, had completed 11 years of education, with two entering the 12th grade at the time of the interview. Though 12 of our subjects were high school dropouts—typically leaving school by the 10th grade, the overwhelming majority (n = 21) had finished high school, a vocational program, or some college. Only eight respondents held a legitimate job at the time of the interview despite the majority having high school or better education. It seemed most were instead committed to an admixture of illegal endeavors for their main source of income, with drug sales and auto theft the most commonly mentioned activities. More than half the sample had one or more dependent children (n = 20), but only two sample members were married.

The average age at which respondents committed their first auto theft was 15, though they were more or less accustomed to stolen cars prior to their first offense—be it from riding in or simply being around cars commandeered by (usually older) family members or peers from their neighborhood. Given the typical early age of onset, it is not surprising that just over half (n = 18) had been arrested for auto theft; some as many as three to six times (n = 5). Of those with criminal justice experience, 11 (61%) were convicted at least once. More often than not, the timing of respondents' first arrest for auto theft came prior to reaching the age of majority, which reportedly landed a handful in juvenile detention. By contrast, probation was a more common punishment than incarceration once offenders had reached the age of majority, which is typically not the case nationwide for felony auto theft convictions (Cherbonneau & Wright, 2009).

Interviews were semi-structured and conducted in a private room. Open-ended questions focused on the circumstances of interviewees' initial involvement in motor vehicle theft and detailed descriptions of their most recent theft(s). Other topics addressed included lifestyle, motivations to commit auto theft, target selection and enactment strategies, methods used to dispose of stolen property, and risk management strategies. The objective in the interview was to create a relaxed and unthreatening atmosphere. This style of interviewing seemed to put respondents at ease, and many were forthright in their conversations, even those who appeared skeptical at first. To provide encouragement for participation, those who consented to the interview were paid $50. The recruiter was paid a higher fee ($75 per interview) for his time and effort, and because he was responsible for transporting respondents to and from the interview.

Interviews varied in length—from 48 to 108 min—but typically lasted an hour and a quarter. They were digitally recorded with the respondent's permission (all granted us permission to record), and three transcriptionists were hired to create a near-verbatim textual account of the interviews. One of the authors proofread each transcript against its audio to limit error from so-called "transcriptionist effects" (see MacLean, Meyer, & Estable, 2004). This ensured accurate and consistent textual documentation of each conversation, especially with regard to auto theft-related terminology, local landmark and ecological descriptions, and street slang. To protect their anonymity and confidentiality, the interviewees were asked to provide us with only an alias—typically a "street" or nickname.

RESTRICTIVE DETERRENCE AMONG AUTO THIEVES

The offenders' restrictively deterrent decision-making strategies fell into three broad categories: discretionary target selection, normalcy illusions, and defiance. Discretionary target selection operated early in the decision-making process and invoked strategies related to the type of vehicles to steal and the venues in which to steal them. Normalcy illusions became relevant once the offenders took possession of the stolen vehicle and pertained to appearance management while in possession of that contraband. Defiance, the third set of tactics, related to flight and became particularly relevant if and/or when the prior two sets of measures failed. Consistent with past research on arrest avoidance, this trilogy of tactics covers restrictively deterrent behavior designed, on the one hand, to "greatly reduce [offenders'] contact with police," and on the other hand, "to decrease their vulnerability to arrest if targeted by police" (Johnson & Natarajan, 1995, p. 50).

DISCRETIONARY TARGET SELECTION

Attention to target selection has long been integral to offender-based research. Prior studies have explored why offenders choose certain targets and/or places and related these choices back to rational processes (Cromwell & Olson, 2004; O'Connor 2006; Rengert & Wasilchick, 1989; Wright & Decker, 1994, 1997). The focus of that research has almost inevitably centered on the perceived benefits of choosing one target, whether it be a person or property, over another. Research seldom has examined target selection in light of the explicit desire to avoid costs. Apprehension risk is a significant cost and oriented the offenders' decision-making strategies with regard to both vehicle type and enactment setting.

The offenders perceived some vehicles to attract more police attention than others. The reasons for the perceived variation related either to the vehicle's type, its overall look, or some combination thereof, and the offenders expressed the need for sensitivity to these factors. Baldy thus liked to steal "something real decent [but] undescriptive. Not something that's gonna be looked at as being stolen but . . . just a plain Jane model . . . [N]othing flashy but nice enough to move." Capone agreed, noting the importance of stealing something that was not too noticeable. "They [the police] ain't gonna trip off this [Chrysler] 300. They up on the Grand Prix, the Bonneville, the Grand Am . . . [T]hey see a little young guy like me riding around they gonna automatically want to flag me." Poo#1 explained that new cars driven by young black males (such as himself) drew unwanted attention. "'We know you ain't got the money for that ['06 Dodge Intrepid, the police say to themselves].' So they gonna pull your ass over." Killa remarked that stealing a car that was too new was unwise because the victim likely had insurance on it and would report it. "[N]ew model cars are always hot . . . Old models are less hot because nobody really cares [to call the police] about a trashy fucked up car." Will similarly selected cars that he perceived would not be called into the police by their owners, although such vehicles were not necessarily mundane:

> I prefer to get a car . . . with custom rims or sounds . . . [T]hem ain't really the cars [of regular 9 to 5 people . . . T]hey don't call them in or where the police don't worry about them type 'cause they ain't just no innocent working 9 to 5 type of people. So you most likely . . . can get away with it quicker than a 9 to 5 person.

Risk sensitivity in target selection was also a matter of the enactment setting. Several offenders underscored the importance of trolling in areas geographically removed from their stomping grounds. "I don't do nothing where I stay," End Dog intoned. "For real . . . I got to lay my head there . . . so I do everything away from there." Capone explained how he would steal cars in "the county" and then take them to "the city" where he lived (the county and city in this research site are geographically and politically separate entities). He claimed that cars stolen in the county would not appear on the city police's "hot sheet" for at least 72 hours, giving him a worry-free experience for at least those three days. He also said that county victims would not go into the city to look for their cars, translating into less risk of informal detection as well:

> [O]nce you steal a car from the county, it takes 3 days for the car to get reported stolen [in the city] . . . So that means we got three free days to ride around in this car. That's 72 hours we got to ride around in this car ain't worrying about the police getting behind us . . . [And] the person in the county ain't gonna ride in the city and look for their car.—Capone

Employing a very similar logic, Juice explained that he stole cars in a town about 30 miles west of where he lived because of the perceived insulation he obtained from that distance:

> [I]f you get a car in [the city] you on pins and needles . . . You don't know when the motherfucker reported it stolen and in the general area is where they [police] are going to look. You go to [the other town] . . . goddamn they ain't looking in [the city] for the car immediately . . . [T]hey'll look around [the distant town instead]. So that's why we had to go down there and get it 'cause we going a distance [and needed to keep the car for a while].—Juice

The offenders not only had to attend to the "what" and "where" of target selection but also to the "when" and "how." Some tactics generated higher risk than others, and the offenders expressed a need for attention to situational factors (see also O'Connor, 2006, pp. 971–972). Red Dog, for example, paid particular heed to police shift work as it related to likely patrol coverage of the areas in which he searched for targets. "There are certain neighborhoods that I won't go through like at certain times," he explained. "Like the police shifts, the shifts of the cops . . . these cops going to be on this shift over here and we know it's hot over there so we stay away from there until they get off . . ." Irrespective of patrol patterns, how offenders operated was potentially as important as when. Juice thus cautioned against "casing" an area before striking. "You don't . . . be like casing the motherfucking joint," he explained, "'cause . . . a motherfucker done checked you out: 'Damn this car hit the corner two or three times . . .' Man that's fucking up your hustle before you even get to it . . ." A number of offenders used lookouts for precisely this reason (see also O'Connor, 2006, p. 973); their utility in spotting potential trouble was undeniable:

> [W]e hit the block a couple of times, weren't no police hide out there, so we go on and went in and I had him looking out for me . . . I got a Nextel, he got a Nextel, and we'll chirp each other. [He'll] look out, sit on the corner . . . where he can see at least two ways and I'll go on and [do the theft] . . . If he hear something he'll chirp, I'll just go on and walk off.—E#2
>
> [My co-offender] will find the car . . . and I'd actually walk and peep the scenery and once I [do] . . . and see that it's good . . . [I] kind of duck back in the bushes and just be watching out. Make sure don't no police come down, you know, ride down on him and stuff . . . —Jasmine King

NORMALCY ILLUSIONS

The second category of restrictively deterrent tactics involved normalcy illusions. Normalcy illusions related to appearance management once the offenders had come into possession of the stolen vehicle. Normalcy illusions invoked a patchwork of tactics designed to prevent authorities from becoming "wise" (Goffman, 1963) to the fact that they were driving a stolen vehicle. The car was an obvious and potent source of discreditation and required careful management.

Arguably the most immediate concern related to the car's license plate coming back "hot" if run by the authorities. Because the "hot sheet" used by police to identify stolen cars reportedly was premised on plate numbers rather than vehicle types, affixing a fresh license plate to the stolen vehicle as quickly as possible after stealing it was desirable. By removing the original plate from the vehicle and replacing it with a different one, the car would not come back "hot." Capone, for example, went to a local junkyard and stole some plates off a car. Then, he found a "crackhead" who was hustling up-to-date (but stolen) registration stickers, which Capone purchased in exchange for a $10 piece of crack. Although Capone did not seem to recognize that the new plate might also come back "hot" (because it too was stolen), he appeared convinced that all that mattered to the "hot sheet" were plates associated with stolen cars: There did not appear to be a "hot sheet" for stolen plates, just for stolen plates linked to stolen cars. That being said, the police could well run the plate through dispatch and discover that it did not belong to that particular car. In the event of detention, poise was key. "You know, [I] got my story together," Jasmine King explained. "[I tell the police]: 'This is my auntie's car . . . she ain't got the money to get her plates.' If you talk to 'em right they'll let you go." Poise certainly was not something to count on, however, and required a degree of aplomb that not all offenders could muster on demand.

For this reason, the offenders focused on how long they retained the vehicle after they stole it. Hot license plate or not, the longer the offenders kept the vehicle, the more exposure they faced. "I had it . . . for a week," Baldy recalled, ". . . and ain't nobody wanted to buy it. Another week passed . . . Now I'm in a position where I don't want to drive it, I'm gonna keep it stashed away . . ." Killa concurred, remarking that, "If you keep them [stolen cars] longer than [a week], you are damn near guaranteed to get caught." But he added that the duration of retention could depend on the nature of the car. "[I]f you got a new[er] model car," he explained, ". . . like if you know it's going to get reported within two days, you might want to only keep it for two or three days." Delivering the stolen vehicle to a drop point rapidly after assuming possession of it was prudent. "[T]hat's why I was trying to go to my place real quick," E#2 explained, "so it ain't no dropped time in between his [victim] waking up, finding his car stolen, calling, call it in stolen." D-Cuz recalled how he had just stolen a car and was in the process of putting it on blocks to strip it when patrolling officers came upon him. "'What y'all doing?" he recalled them asking. "'I had a flat . . . I pulled right here,'" he reportedly responded. "They ran the plates but the plates wasn't . . . com[ing] back stolen. So they went on about they business."

As D-Cuz implies, normalcy illusions were most critical at the point that offenders encountered actual scrutiny from patrolling officers. A stop might be initiated not because of actual knowledge of the offender's guilt, but because the offenders leaked it in their behavior. For the police, contact with offenders was sometimes serendipitous. For offenders, contact might be elicited by attention-grabbing conduct that could be avoided. First and foremost, attention avoidance meant driving sensibly:

> The whole mission is to drive like you got some sense. If you driving like you got some sense, ain't nobody going to trip off you. But when you out here skirting off on lights and running stoplights and running stop signs and shit like that, you looking for trouble ... [If the police get around me,] I just get real nerdy ... The ten and two [on the steering wheel], seatbelt action, and just drive that motherfucker like it's mine ... I'm minding my business ... I'm not gonna be all catted out, you know [gangster-]leaning, music up loud ... —Baldy

Mr. Blackwell similarly discussed the importance of normalcy. "[I]f you don't panic," he professed, "then nothing will happen ... [If you] don't make an obvious move or make a false, you know, mistake about doing something wrong ... then you don't have to worry about none of that there . . .." Indeed, many of the offenders understood the role of dramaturgy in normalcy illusions. Sociologists have long noted the importance of self-presentation in influencing the perceptions of others (Goffman, 1959). Assessments of character and motive are impression-based, so the more normal the offenders could make themselves appear, the less perceived scrutiny they would have to neutralize:

> [I]f I see a police, they get behind me, I'll immediately go down the street and pull over ... Blow the horn, [honk, honk at the adjacent house] and if the police still coming I'll jump out and just knock on anybody's door just like I be looking for somebody. And they be like, "Oh, he going right there, we gonna leave him alone."—Capone

Offenders could influence the opportunity structure of suspicion by choosing their driving routes. They perceived the police to be more active in some areas than others and felt they could decrease the likelihood of being scrutinized by selecting some routes over others. The offenders disagreed, however, as to which type of routes generated more risk. "[O]nce you start going off into these little bitty little side streets where all the houses at," Capone explained, "that's where the police at sitting in the corner because they patrolling the neighborhoods." But Killa and others remarked that back streets were preferable because one was not as noticeable. J also noted that back streets afforded easier escape in the event he had to bail from the car. "[I]f you do hop out and run," he explained, "you know which way to go and what cuts to go through, what fences to jump over ... [O]n the main street, if you hop out and run, you're running in the open. They gonna know where you're at." BB similarly pointed out that:

> On a back street, you can hit 2 or 3 corners and shake 'em and park in the alley and they'll be looking for you, but on a main street ... everybody sees you. I mean they be like, "He went that way" ... —BB

Either way, the importance of manipulating traffic flow to maintain interference between the stolen car and police was essential. E#2 thus explained how he would have a co-offender drive a car directly behind him until he got the stolen car to where it needed to go. "[I]f he [my associate] behind me then they ain't no police behind me," he reasoned. The need for traffic manipulation was less pressing if more "innocent-looking" drivers were enlisted to drive the stolen car in the offenders' stead. A number of male offenders tasked females with this duty. Killa explained how he preferred to have a female drive the vehicle after he stole it because the police did not suspect females of being auto thieves. "The police would mess with a male before they'll mess with a female," he remarked. "[I]f they see a woman, 'Oh, she's just a girl,' you know." J agreed, observing that, "If they see a female driving they'll be like, 'Ah, she ain't steal that car.' . . . So they gonna let her go on about her business." Lil' Bunny, a female respondent, explained that the police "don't ever bother me. They look and smile . . . I look and smile back, maybe flirt . . ." Pulled over in a stolen car once with male associates, Chocolate (another female offender) escaped arrest by playing "it off like I didn't know it was a stolen car . . . as if I didn't know what was going on." As Lavanda concluded that, "We get away with a lot of things 'cause we female." In restrictive deterrence, gender is a resource that female offenders can use to lower the risk of detection and confers a strategic advantage in the effort to thwart law enforcement (Jacobs & Miller, 1998).

As an extension, a number of men (namely those open to working with women) recognized this potential and exploited this gendered advantage through normalcy tactics of their own. T-Raw would often venture out into the county in search of cars to sell to a chop shop located in the city. Concerned that the police in these more affluent communities were wary of vehicles occupied by black males and, unwilling to go at it alone, T-Raw would enlist the company of a female to allay suspicions—which is how he accomplished his most recent theft unscathed:

> On this occasion I went and got one of my little chicks . . . I called her because I was going to the county. Make us at least look like we a couple thang and we out there, we riding or husband and wife handling some business . . . Just throw it off [rather] than two men just riding . . . Now in the city I'll do it . . . with my [male] partner . . . In the city I'm more comfortable. They use to that. That's 24/7—motherfuckers riding four-deep all cats [black males] . . . But, she a better throw off in the county . . . We could be out having errands or something . . . They don't know what the fuck we're doing . . . I can't really have no, loud, obnoxious men in the county. My partners, they loud, they talk, they cuss, they be all "Ooh, ooh Raw, you should do this, [and] Raw, Raw [do that]." I'm like damn, no, you really need to be . . . quiet . . . and that's why I like taking women to [the county].—T-Raw

In the final analysis, men such as Killa, J, and T-Raw were very "forward" in their thinking—they looked beyond the misogyny that is alive and well in the criminal underworld (attitudes that can restrict women's involvement) to anticipate, and capitalize on, a wider range of repertoires to manage sanction threats.

DEFIANCE

Defiance was the last category of restrictively deterrent tactics used by the offenders. Defiance refers to the outright rejection, rather than manipulation, of sanction threats. Typically, it was a tactic of last resort—when the other restrictively deterrent measures failed to achieve detection avoidance. In the context of auto theft, defiance meant flight and focused exclusively on apprehension avoidance.

High-speed chases triggered by refusals to pull over are now common footage across the national airwaves, and the offenders in our sample were no strangers to the phenomenon. Part of the allure of fleeing was flight itself, which permits offenders to showcase driving skills and perceived invincibility (Halsey, 2008). As Capone bragged, "I'm gonna . . . get away 9 times out of 10. I know I'm gonna get away . . . [T]hat's how good I drive." Make no mistake, however. The sensual attractions of fleeing were secondary to the practical mandates of escape itself.

The offenders applied specific tactics during flight—tactics mediated by time, space, and emergent police conduct—to determine when, how, and under what circumstances to flee. Some of the tactics relied on heuristics; others were more spontaneous. All of them, however, shared a fairly developed level of calculation. And that is what sets restrictively deterrent defiance apart from its "traditional" counterpart: In traditional defiance, apprehension avoidance is secondary to the moralistic need to lash out at unfair sanctions or capricious authorities (Sherman, 1993). When defiance is restrictively deterrent, noncompliance with authority is designed to do one thing: avoid arrest. On some level, the offenders seemed to realize that pursuits were not authorized by the police in this jurisdiction, and this provided a measure of comfort in the event the offenders had to take flight:

> [The police] can't do that . . . high-speed chase for real. We know that so . . . we slow up, we speed up, swerve through cars they can't get through, like drive on the shoulder . . . drive on the sidewalk, anything just to get away from 'em.—J

But formal policies are not always adhered to in the real world of policing, and the offenders had to develop contingent strategies accordingly.

A number of these strategies related more to the timing of flight than to flight itself. Like the other restrictively deterrent tactics, the offenders' understanding of what to do and when to do it was sensitive to situational circumstances. Being pulled over need not translate immediately into flight. The decision was more conditional. D-Cuz explained that if pulled over, he would wait to see what the police did before doing anything himself. If the officer immediately exited his vehicle and approached, D-Cuz would wait until the point at which the officer arrived at his (D-Cuz's) door before taking off. But if officers pulled him over and stayed in their vehicle, it meant they were calling for back up and that he should flee immediately. "[T]ake off on their ass . . . cause now they getting the license plate . . . [and] calling for help." Westside, another offender, didn't make as fine a distinction. He simply waited until the officers exited and approached: "Pull over and stop and then wait for them [the police] to get out of the car, come to the car, and then you bake they ass [screech off], you hear me. You bake 'em."

Once a pursuit began, a host of other factors came into play relating to how and where to flee. Criminologists have long recognized the importance of spatial awareness in offending (Brantingham & Brantingham, 1984), and flight from authorities was no exception. Recognizing the potential for a pursuit, Capone claimed that crossing jurisdictional boundaries would effectively bring any chase to a halt:

> [W]e was in the county. We trying to get all the way back to the city . . . Hit the highway get that long stretch on . . . Nine times out of 10 if you get the longer stretch on them you fixing to get away. 'Cause if you get too far from the police . . . and they out their jurisdiction . . . they have to turn their lights off and let us go . . . They do that, they do that. It happened to me a whole bunch of time. I'll stretch on the highway leave they ass goin' about 120 [mph] . . . looking at they asses and laughing . . . They'll just turn their lights off . . .—Capone

But the offenders also had to contemplate what they would do in the event that speed alone did not allow them to escape. E#1 recalled fleeing from the police with co-offenders but not being able to shake them completely. During the chase, E#1 and his associates were able to sneak the vehicle into a stranger's garage right before the police arrived. After pulling the car in and shutting the garage door, they hid for a moment and then walked a few houses down, whereupon the police approached them:

> They chased us down the block and we dipped on their ass, cut up through some lots and pulled up in this garage and let the door down. We heard one [police car] coming down that alley and started looking for us. We sit there in the garage. Then once they went out that alley, we came out . . . and went to . . . my partner's backyard about 2 houses down . . . We sitting there and they come right through the alley . . . "Hey fellas . . . did y'all ever see a car come flying down here?" We be like . . . "Yeah . . . about 15, 20 minutes ago, booting it down here." They be like, "Oh, okay, thanks" [and left].—E#1

For Juice, eluding authorities was similarly focused on the interstice between flight and detention. Fleeing from the police but not able to escape their grasp, he "bailed" from the car before bringing it to a stop. The tactic ensured that the police would pursue the moving car and not him:

> Break it down to 5 [mph], open the door. [The police yell:] "He's gonna bail! He's gonna bail!" You goddamn right I'm fixing to bail, and the car is gonna keep moving. Who you want the worst? Me or the car? . . . I ain't gonna take away the police choice. "Me or the car?" . . . Every time I have done it they went after the car. They didn't have no motherfucking choice . . . You [the police] earning your check with me player . . .—Juice

Other types of misdirection were used. Capone's practice was to secrete cars he had previously stolen in various parts of the city and then use them to permit escape in pursuits. During a pursuit, he would simply drive to one of these vehicles or "stash spots," ditch the vehicle being pursued, and escape in the stashed vehicle:

> That's the main thing when we in a high-speed [chase] is to try to get to where another [stolen] car at. So when we jump out and run we jump in another car and pull off in that car . . . We got cars stashed everywhere . . . Hopefully they

[the police] don't see us get in that car. All they doing is tripping off this car we jumped out of . . .—Capone

Defiance in the form of flight typically was an option of last resort, not first. The offenders would rather prevent situations that required the need for flight. Risk sensitivity in the target selection process, and maintenance of normalcy illusions after coming into possession of the stolen car, were critical to this endeavor. If or when these measures failed, flight became a feasible response. Flight remains, however, the end of the restrictive deterrence process for auto thieves, and when flight fails, so does restrictive deterrence.

DISCUSSION

As noted early in the paper, restrictive deterrence subsumes four dimensions: offense frequency, seriousness, detectability, and displacement. Our research has focused on the latter two dimensions by addressing the extent to which offenders engage in specific tactics to reduce the risk of detection and/or arrest. These tactics fell into three broad categories: discretionary target selection, normalcy illusions, and defiance. Discretionary target selection revolved around prudence in the types of vehicles to steal and the settings in which to steal them. Normalcy illusions related to appearance management once the stolen vehicle was in the offenders' possession. Defiance involved flight—when to flee, how, and under what circumstances.

The picture of risk management painted by the offenders was dynamically contingent. Although the offenders were not necessarily explicit on this issue, the necessity of measures used later in the offending sequence appears to be conditioned by the efficacy of tactics used previously. Thus, when indiscreet targets are selected, normalcy illusions and defiance logically escalate in importance. When normalcy illusions fail, defiance emerges as a seductive fallback strategy. If target choices are beyond perceived suspicion, normalcy illusions become less important, while offenders who believe themselves to be adept in conveying normalcy illusions can conceivably choose riskier vehicles to steal. Although our offenders implied otherwise, restrictive deterrence need not begin with, or travel through, the discretionary selection of targets (if, for example, offenders choose to rely on normalcy illusions or defiance instead). Similarly, although stealing cars in distal areas may make one feel safer, it can increase exposure during the long ride back and elevate the importance of normalcy illusions or defiance. The latter becomes especially relevant if the car's owner sees the offender drive away and alerts the authorities.

Scholars have long known that offender decision making is Bayesian (Pogarsky & Piquero, 2003), prior choices mediate future ones, and the tactics explored here clearly reflect this potential. This is consistent with prior research on threat management in analogous realms, such as drug robbery, where offenders mitigate the risk of retaliation (an informal sanction) by exercising prudence in whom they target and how they carry themselves after they commit the crime (Jacobs, Topalli, & Wright, 2000; see also Topalli & Wright, 2004). Like the offenders in the present study, those offenders betrayed sensitivity to the situated nature of risk and the need to engage in specific measures to attenuate that risk across the offending sequence.

It is important to keep in mind that the measures examined in the present study reflect what the offenders think will thwart the authorities (cf. Cherbonneau & Copes, 2006). Perception may be reality, but perceptions are guided by assumptions. These assumptions reflect a keen sensitivity to codes of conformity, and that is arguably restrictive deterrence's greatest paradox. The more sensitive the offender is to these codes, the better positioned s/he will be to subvert them. In this way, knowledge of the practices of sanctioning agents contributes to, rather than inhibits, crime.

Conspicuously absent from the offenders' accounts was fear. Certainly, offenders can fear sanctions yet remain noncompliant. Noncompliance can flow from a basic lack of respect for sanctions or from situational factors that give rise to resistance (Sherman, 1993). The present data, however, reveal the manner in which noncompliance flows from the tactical neutralization of threat. Although such tactics would not be generated without threat, threat and fear are entirely different. Restrictive deterrence recognizes threat in order to minimize it and take the fear out of it.

In doing so, restrictive deterrence brings the deterrence process itself into relief. This is important because deterrence, as a phenomenon, is otherwise invisible: When crimes do not occur, sanction threats are not necessarily the reason. When crimes do occur, the absence of sanction threats is not necessarily the reason either. This is why Gibbs (1975) argued that deterrence was a theoretical proposition. "Since deterrence is inherently unobservable," he (1975, p. 31) wrote, "rules of inference pertaining to it are unfalsifiable unless stated in the context of a theory." Later, he (1975, p. 32) concluded that, "No definition of deterrence can make it observable nor resolve the evidential problems (i.e., stipulate evidence of deterrence). What is relevant evidence depends entirely on theories about deterrence." The present paper questions these presumptions by highlighting specific tactics offenders use to manipulate the deterrence process. Such tactics exist because of the threat of sanctions. Although their use seemingly indicates deterrence's failure, without sanction threats, these tactics would not develop in the first place. Restrictive deterrence thereby makes deterrence visible in the breach. The data presented here also demonstrate the manner in which restrictive deterrence changes the expression of crime rather than reduces it (cf. Cherbonneau & Copes, 2006). Deterrence is at heart a perceptual process guided by the certainty of detection. The measures explored in this paper address the certainty dimension, but the target of the sanction threat is the one manipulating that dimension, not the sanctioning agent. The past 200 years of deterrence scholarship has assumed that sanction manipulation is unidirectional and comes from the coercers, not the coerced. If deterrence operates through perceptual mechanisms, and if perceived certainty is the most prominent of these mechanisms (Pogarsky, 2002), the manner in which offenders influence these processes should not be underestimated. Ekland-Olson, Lieb, and Zurcher's (1984, p. 177) two-decades-old statement rings as true today as it did then: Deterrence scholarship "must move beyond official indicators of certainty," they wrote. "Further understanding requires data that are sensitive to the dynamic relationship between the organization of the sanctioning process and the adaptive strategies of those who are the target of sanctions."

The auto thieves explored in the present study underscore the situated nature of risk assessment and also the direct link between perception and behavior. Criminologists have long argued that this link exists but rarely provide evidence of it (Pogarsky, Piquero, & Paternoster, 2004). Perceptions relate to how threats influence offenders' thoughts about the risk of apprehension; behavior involves the manner in which these perceptions influence actual conduct. The present paper shows not only how deterrent-relevant behavior flows from perception, but also how perceptions shape that behavior. This dualistic approach explains whether offenders offend and then how they do so. Deterrence scholarship has focused almost exclusively on the "whether" question and largely ignored the manner in which sanction threats shape crime's expression (see also Von Hirsch, Bottoms, Burney, & Wilkström, 1999, pp. 35–37, 46).

The perception–behavior link is particularly relevant in light of the longitudinal nature of auto theft (see Cherbonneau & Wright, 2009). The crime is not limited to the actual stealing of the car but occurs across a much broader temporal and spatial sequence. This is why offenders must embrace both anticipatory (i.e., target selection, appearance management) and reactive (defiance) measures. The present paper supports the contention that sanction risk affects decision making during crime and not just before it. Dynamic risk management is particularly relevant to auto theft because of the manner in which the car, as mobile contraband, permits offenders to elude threats even as it brings other threats right to them. This paradox creates wild potential fluctuations in risk across space and time. Offenders attempt to modulate the amplitude of these risks by taking discrete maneuvers that make a continuous crime manageable in the moment.

REFERENCES

Beccaria, C. (1963 [1764]). *On crimes and punishments* (Henry Paolucci, Trans.). Indianapolis, IN: Bobbs-Merrill.

Bentham, J. (1948 [1789]). *An introduction to the principles of morals and legislation.* New York, NY: Hafner.

Cherbonneau, M., & Wright, R. (2009). Auto theft. In M. Tonry (Ed.), *The Oxford handbook of crime and public policy* (pp. 199–222). New York, NY: Oxford University Press.

Cromwell, P., & Olson, J. (2004). *Breaking and entering: Burglars on burglary.* Belmont, CA: Wadsworth.

Cusson, M., & Pinsonneault, P. (1986). The decision to give up crime. In D. B. Cornish & R.V. Clark (Eds.), *The reasoning criminal: Rational choice perspectives on offending* (pp. 77–82). New York, NY: Springer-Verlag.

Gibbs, J. P. (1975). *Crime, punishment, and deterrence.* New York, NY: Elsevier.

Glassner, B., & Carpenter, C. (1985). *The feasibility of an ethnographic study of property offenders: A report prepared for the National Institute of Justice.* Washington, DC: National Institute of Justice.

Goffman, E. (1963). *Stigma: Notes on the management of spoiled identity.* Englewood Cliffs, NJ: Prentice-Hall.

Halsey, M. (2008). Narrating the chase: Edgework and young peoples' experiences of crime. In T. Anthony & C. Cunneen (Eds.), *The critical criminology companion* (pp. 105–117). Sydney: Hawkins Press.

Heckathorn, D. D. (1997). Respondent-driven sampling: A new approach to the study of hidden populations. *Social Problems, 44,* 174–199.

Jacobs, B. A. (2010). Deterrence and deterrability. *Criminology, 48,* 417–441.

Jacobs, B. A., & Miller, J. (1998). Crack dealing, gender, and arrest avoidance. *Social Problems, 45,* 550–569.

Jacobs, B. A., Topalli, V., & Wright, R. (2000). Managing retaliation: Drug robbery and informal sanction threats. *Criminology, 38,* 171–198.

Johnson, B. D., & Natarajan, M. (1995). Strategies to avoid arrest: Crack sellers' response to intensified policing. *American Journal of Police, 14,* 49–69.

Light, R., Nee, C., & Ingham, H. (1993). *Car theft: The offender's perspective.* Home Office Research Study no. 130. London: Home Office.

MacLean, L. M., Meyer, M., & Estable, A. (2004). Improving accuracy of transcripts in qualitative research. *Qualitative Health Research, 14,* 113–123.

McCall, G. J. (1978). *Observing the law: Applications of field methods to the study of the criminal justice system.* New York, NY: Free Press.

Mullins, C. W., & Cherbonneau, M. (2011). Establishing connections: Gender, motor vehicle theft, and disposal networks. *Justice Quarterly, 28,* 278–302.

O'Connor, C. (2006). Preventing the theft of motor vehicles: The limits of deterrence. *Journal of Passenger Cars: Electronic and Electrical Systems, 115,* 969–978.

O'Connor, C., & Kelly, K. (2006). Auto theft and youth culture: A nexus of masculinities, femininities and car culture. *Journal of Youth Studies, 9,* 247–267.

Pogarsky, G., & Piquero, A. R. (2003). Can punishment encourage offending? Investigating the "resetting" effect. *Journal of Research in Crime and Delinquency, 40,* 95–120.

Rengert, G., & Wasilchick, J. (1989). *Space, time and crime: Ethnographic insights into residential burglary.* Final Report to the National Institute of Justice. Washington, DC: US Department of Justice.

Sherman, L. W. (1993). Defiance, deterrence and irrelevance: A theory of the criminal sanction. *Journal of Research in Crime and Delinquency, 30,* 445–473.

Slobodian, P., & Browne, K. (1997). Car crime as a developmental career: An analysis of young offenders in Coventry. *Psychology, Crime and Law, 3,* 275–286.

Topalli, V., & Wright, R. (2004). Dubs and dees, beats and rims: Carjackers and urban violence. In D. Dabney (Ed.), *Crime types: A text/reader* (pp. 149–169). Belmont, CA: Wadsworth.

Von Hirsch, A., Bottoms, A., Burney, E., & Wilkström, P.-O. (1999). *Criminal deterrence and sentence severity: An analysis of recent research.* Oxford: Hart.

Wright, R. T., & Decker, S. H. (1994). *Burglars on the job: Streetlife and residential break-ins.* Boston, MA: Northeastern University Press.

Wright, R. T., & Decker, S. H. (1997). *Armed robbers in action: Stickups and street culture.* Boston, MA: Northeastern University Press.

Property Crime

If you turn on the television news or open the daily paper, you might conclude that violent crime—muggings, robberies, and assaults—is rampant. It's easy to come to this conclusion: violent crime is what makes news. In reality, property crime and not violent crime makes up the vast majority of crimes reported to the police authorities in the United States. According to the Federal Bureau of Investigation's Uniform Crime Reporting Program (UCR), property crime includes the offenses of burglary, larceny-theft, motor vehicle theft, and arson. Larceny and theft are the most common property offenses reported to police authorities. While the incidence of property crime remains high, it has steadily decreased over the past decade.

The articles featured in this section explore motor vehicle theft, shoplifting, and identity theft. Motor vehicle theft, or auto theft as it sometimes called, is the unlawful taking of a self-propelled road vehicle that is owned by another, with the intent to deprive the owner of it permanently. In 2014, there were an estimated 689,527 motor vehicle thefts reported to the police nationwide (Federal Bureau of Investigation, 2014).

Shoplifting falls under the broad category of larceny-theft. Larceny-theft is simply the unlawful taking of property from another person out of his or her presence. Shoplifting is often considered a "folk crime" because of the high percentage of persons who have committed the offense at least once in their lives. It is perhaps the most widely distributed crime in the United States, with an estimated one in 15 persons having shoplifted in their lifetime.

Burglary is the unlawful or forcible entry or attempted entry of a residence with the intent to commit a crime. It may or may not involve a forcible entry. In 2014, there were an estimated 1,729,806 burglaries—a number down just over 10 percent from the previous year (Federal Bureau of Investigation, 2014).

Identify theft is one of the fastest-growing crimes in the United States. In 2014, over 17 million U.S. residents experienced some form of identity theft (Bureau of Justice Statistics, 2014). Generally, identity theft entails an offender gaining access to the personal information of the victim and then using that information to defraud him or her. Offenders may obtain personal information in a number of ways, including collecting personal information that has been discarded in the trash, intercepting mail, acquiring subscription lists and credit card carbons, using phony telemarketers, and conducting Internet searches (Berghel, 2000). In some cases, the offender acquires a personal item from the victim such as a driver's license number or Social Security card and uses that information to commit a fraud.

In Chapter 6, "Establishing Connections: Gender, Motor Vehicle Theft, and Disposal Networks," Christopher W. Mullins and Michael G. Cherbonneau describe the role that gender plays in motor vehicle theft, and specifically initiation into motor vehicle theft. They argue that while motor vehicle theft is a largely male-dominated offense, women are increasingly participating in this kind of criminal activity. The authors fill an important gap in the literature by examining the gendered nature of motor vehicle theft through direct comparison of qualitative data obtained from 35 juvenile and adult men and women actively involved in auto theft in St. Louis. The authors take an enlightening look at the convergences and divergences of men's and women's experiences in this area of crime.

In Chapter 7, the discussion turns to shoplifters. Paul Cromwell and Quint Thurman ("'The Devil Made Me Do It': Use of Neutralizations by Shoplifters") look at the techniques that shoplifters use to neutralize their crimes. Findings from interviews with 137 apprehended shoplifters reveal a widespread use of techniques of neutralization. The authors identify two new neutralizations, which they term *justification by comparison* and *postponement*. They argue that while earlier formulations of neutralization theory contend that deviants neutralize moral prescriptions prior to committing a crime, research is incapable of determining whether a stated neutralization occurs before or after the fact, and that neutralization more typically follows rather than precedes deviance. This claim parallels Hirschi's (1969) thesis that (1) an after-the-fact rationalization in one instance may be a causal neutralization in another instance, and (2) the assumption that delinquent acts come before justifying beliefs is the more plausible causal ordering.

In Chapter 8 ("Identity Theft: Assessing Offenders' Motivations and Strategies"), Heith Copes and Lynne Vieraitis examine the social, technical, intuitive, and system skills associated with the offense of identity theft. Through interviews with 59 identity thieves incarcerated in the federal prison system, the authors found that identity thieves represent a diverse group and largely come from working-class and middle-class backgrounds. About half of those interviewed had lifestyles similar to those of persistent street offenders, and about half used the proceeds of their crimes to live relatively middle-class lives. Offenders' most frequent way of acquiring information was to buy it from others, steal it from mailboxes or trashcans, or obtain it from persons they knew.

REFERENCES

Baum, K. (2007). *Identity theft, 2005* (NCJ 219411). Washington, DC: Bureau of Justice Statistics, National Crime Victimization Survey, November 2007.

Berghel, H. (2000). Identify theft, social security numbers, and the web. *Communications of the ACM, 43*(2), 17–21.

Bureau of Justice Statistics. (2014). *Victims of identity theft, 2014.* http://www.bjs.gov/

Federal Bureau of Investigation. (2014). *Crime in the United States.* Retrieved October 24, 2015, from: https://www.fbi.gov/about-us/cjis/ucr/crime-in-the-u.s/2014/crime-in-the-u.s.-2014/cius-home

Hirschi, T. (1969). *Causes of delinquency.* Berkeley: University of California Press.

CHAPTER 6

Establishing Connections:
Gender, Motor Vehicle Theft,
and Disposal Networks

Christopher W. Mullins and Michael G. Cherbonneau

As with most other serious street crimes, motor vehicle theft is a male-dominated offense. Nevertheless, women do engage in motor vehicle theft, albeit at a reduced rate of participation. Here we examine the gendered nature of motor vehicle theft through direct comparison of qualitative data obtained from 35 juvenile and adult men and women actively involved in auto theft in St. Louis, Missouri. By tracing similarities and differences between men's and women's pathways of initial involvement, enactment strategies, and post-theft acts, we provide a contextual analysis of offenders' perceptions and behavior. Such an approach allows a more precise discussion of gender's influence (or lack of influence) on motor vehicle theft. Analysis shows that initiation into auto theft and property disposal networks are governed by male gatekeepers, and this leads to some key similarities in techniques between men and women. The ways in which women negotiate male-dominated networks is also discussed, with particular emphasis on the innovative strategies they draw upon to accomplish their crimes within these landscapes and when opportunities are constrained by male gatekeepers.

The past 15 years has witnessed the emergence of a rich body of literature devoted to understanding how gender structures the accomplishment of specific crimes. The preeminent research in this vein uncovers gender similarities and differences through direct comparison of male and female accounts of their participation in street crime (Miller, 2002). The general consensus within comparative work on gender is that while some overlap in men's and women's experiences

Source: Adapted from Mullins, C. W., & Cherbonneau, M. G. (2010). Establishing connections: Gender, motor vehicle theft and disposal networks. *Justice Quarterly, 28*(2), 278–281, 286–302. Used with permission of the publisher.

with street crime exist [sic]—for example, motives and (to a lesser extent) enactment strategies—there is also significant divergence—for example, pathways into
crime, initiation experiences, criminal network ties, and so-called "hypothetical
desistance" (Brookman et al., 2007; Mullins & Wright, 2003; Mullins, Wright, &
Jacobs, 2004; Miller, 1998).

The list of crimes examined to come to these conclusions include male and
female gang members (Campbell, 1993; Miller, 2001), residential burglars (Decker
et al., 1993; Mullins & Wright, 2003), strong-arm and armed robbers (Brookman
et al., 2007; Campbell, 1993; Miller, 1998), and persons involved in retaliatory
and assaultive violence (Mullins, Wright, & Jacobs, 2004). Noticeably absent
from these gendered comparisons of specific crimes is motor vehicle theft. This is
surprising given that "cars have long served as objects for men to position themselves in terms of masculinity, enabling an elaborated performance of the masculine" (Best, 2006, p. 89). In fact, the masculine nature of car culture in general
and car theft in particular is assumed to be masculine in nature. Yet, women *do*
steal cars as well. An understanding of auto theft participation by females can
contribute to existing debates about their role in common street crime and the
ways in which they negotiate the many layers of male-dominated space within
the criminal underworld. It can also shine light on various interactional dynamics that shape motor vehicle theft experiences.

In the pages that follow, we examine the gendered nature of motor vehicle
theft through direct comparison of qualitative data obtained from 35 individuals
actively involved in auto theft in St. Louis, Missouri. By tracing similarities and
differences between men's and women's pathways of initial involvement, enactment procedures, and methods for selling stolen vehicles and vehicle parts,
we provide a contextual analysis of offenders' perceptions and behavior. Such an
approach allows for a more precise discussion of gender's influence (or lack of
influence) on motor vehicle theft.

CONCEPTUAL CONTEXT

Motor vehicle theft is a serious property crime that accounted for 11% of all property offenses reported in 2007, with nearly 1.1 million stolen vehicles—one out
of every 232 registered nationwide—reported stolen in 2007 (Federal Bureau of
Investigation [FBI], 2008; Federal Highway Administration, 2008). Like most
other serious crimes, it is also profoundly gendered in its commission. Among
the 12.6% of auto thefts cleared by arrest in 2007, the ratio of male to female arrestees was 4.6 to 1 (FBI, 2008). While imprecise, the gendered division of motor
vehicle theft in measures of apprehended individuals is corroborated by other
data sources such as "Monitoring the Future" (see *Sourcebook of Criminal Justice
Statistics,* 2003, table 3.44) and also seems to hold in other industrialized nations
(Graham & Bowling, 1995, tables C1, C2; Henderson, 1994; O'Connor & Kelly,
2006; Roe & Ashe, 2008, table 2.1; Walker, Butland, & Connell, 2000; Yates,
2003/4). Despite its commonality, motor vehicle theft is less studied than other

property offenses (Clarke & Harris, 1992). This pattern of neglect has begun to change owing to the score or so of studies published within the past two decades that explore the offense in detail and at varying units of analysis (Cherbonneau & Wright, 2009). Yet, the majority deal directly with offender perceptions, mostly examining offenders from outside the United States (e.g., Australia, Canada, and the United Kingdom). Further, the offender-based literature is dominated by male perspectives (e.g., Copes, 2003).

To date, most work on gender and car theft has focused on the ubiquitous use of stolen cars by young men for so-called "joyriding," attributing these actions to masculinity enactment (Henderson, 1994; Walker, Butland, & Connell, 2000; Williams, 2005). Due to this assumption of masculinity, little prior research has directly compared male and female experiences. To date, only one study situates men and women's experiences in motor vehicle theft within the purview of gender. Drawing from interviews with 17 young people (five women and 12 men) under correctional supervision in Eastern Ontario, O'Connor and Kelly (2006, p. 263) explored the relationship between gender and car stealing, concluding that "the most salient point to understand about young people's participation in auto theft is that it involves an intersection of masculinities, femininities and car culture."

While insightful, O'Connor and Kelly (2006) treated motor vehicle theft as a gendered crime in its own right and framed male and female accounts around the symbolic meanings of car culture and thus did not demonstrate conclusively the impact of gender on auto theft participation. In accordance with a majority of offender-based research on auto theft (Kilpatrick, 1997), the O'Connor and Kelly sample was based on young offenders recruited through criminal justice channels in Canada, and their responses may not be representative of currently active offenders elsewhere. The youthfulness of their sample is also problematic, as perceptions and decision making of auto thieves have been linked to age and experience (Light, Nee, & Ingham, 1993; Slobodian & Browne, 1997; Spencer, 1992; Stephen & Squires, 2003).

Like burglary, auto theft appears to be a "social crime" (see Mullins & Wright, 2003), or at least begins as such; few thieves begin careers stealing cars on their own (Dawes, 2002; Kilpatrick, 1997; Light, Nee, & Ingham, 1993; Spencer, 1992; Stephen & Squires, 2003). Instead, initiation into auto theft is facilitated through interaction with neighborhood peers, usually older and more experienced males. Novices learn from these "technical advisors" (Fleming, Brantingham, & Brantingham, 1994) the skill set needed to steal cars through a role best described as an "apprenticeship" (Light, Nee, & Ingham, 1993; Spencer, 1992). Group status is stratified by skill (but see Stephen & Squires, 2003). Initially, novices typically are relegated to the role of "lookout" and passenger, although in many cases thieves move quickly from apprentices to co-offenders (Fleming, 2003; Light, Nee, & Ingham, 1993). Those who persist may eventually offend independently or form their own crews. Dawes (2002, p. 203) summed it up best stating "the peer group is central in providing the catalyst for [young offenders'] introduction and continuation to car theft and joyriding behavior. . . . [It] provides a structure for the advancement in status for young joyriders to learn the skills of car theft and to graduate to the status of leader of a joyriding crew."

As car theft and disposal are group activities lodged within social networks, the nature and composition of those networks will influence car thieves' lived experiences. The "graduation" Dawes (2002) speaks of will be mediated by the nature of the networks individuals have exposure to and experiences within. Underworld street networks are male dominated, with gatekeepers drawing upon rigid, sexist assumptions about the personalities and abilities of women vis-à-vis criminal action. Thus, women often have difficulty gaining access to street-based criminal networks (Messerschmidt, 1997; Steffensmeier, 1983; Steffensmeier & Terry, 1986). Where women have gained access to these networks, it is often through male relatives or romantic partners who can vouch for their skills and steadfastness (Mullins & Wright, 2003). Thus, these "apprenticeship" experiences should have a situational gendered element to them.

Little is known about tactics and the network experiences of female car thieves, and even less is known about potential interactions of gender with these actions. Recent comparative work has demonstrated that motivation and sometimes enactment strategies can be more similar than different among male and female offenders (Miller, 1998; Mullins & Wright, 2003; Mullins, Wright, & Jacobs, 2004). And while convergence is as important as divergence in establishing the extent that any given behavior is strongly gendered, Miller (2002) cautions about the overapplication of a gendered lens in qualitative analysis as well as reinforcing the need to carefully contextualize social actors' perceptions within both broader and narrower environments. Even though aggregate data suggest that there are clear gender differences in offense participation (which appears to be the case with auto theft), careful exploration of perceptions and experiences of both men and women involved in diverse forms of crime are needed. This idea is the starting point of the analyses presented here. Our goal is to examine female auto thieves' perceptions of their offending in an explicitly comparative fashion by directly comparing women's accounts with those of men involved in motor vehicle theft.

DATA AND METHODS

Data for this study were derived from open-ended qualitative interviews with active auto thieves recruited from the streets of St. Louis, Missouri. The St. Louis Metropolitan Area (which extends into Illinois) has a population of just over 2.8 million, but St. Louis City itself is much smaller, having only about 354,000 residents. St. Louis City is beset by high rates of criminal offending. . . . We recruited and interviewed 35 active auto thieves. Thirty of the interviews were conducted during 2006. The remaining five were done the following year to clarify and amplify empirical issues raised by the earlier interviews. . . .

The auto thieves ranged in age from 17 to 49, with a mean age of 27 years. Twenty-seven were male and eight were female. All of the respondents were

African-American. . . . The sample, on average, had completed 11 years of educa-tion, with two entering the twelfth grade at the time of the interview. Twelve of our subjects were high school dropouts, typically leaving school by the tenth grade, while the majority had at least a high school education, with 15 who com-pleted high school or a GED and another six who completed a vocational pro-gram or some college. Only eight of our subjects held a legitimate job at the time of the interview, despite the high number with high school or higher education. Although some respondents said they were actively looking for work, most were committed to an admixture of illegal endeavors for their main source of income, with drug sales and auto theft being the most common mentioned activities toward this end. The average age at which respondents committed their first auto theft was 15, though many had been in or around stolen cars prior to this. . . .

INITIATION INTO AUTO THEFT

Acquiring the necessary skills to commit a crime begins with the process of being exposed to the crime itself. Almost invariably, the men and women we in-terviewed were initially exposed to auto theft within the context of joyriding. Everyone mentioned riding in stolen cars in their early teens, and doing so with some frequency. Simply, the neighborhoods they grew up in were flush with op-portunities to observe and interact with individuals bearing both the requisite attitudes and knowledge to initiate an individual into motor vehicle theft.

As with other street crime, auto theft requires a basic set of skills. An indi-vidual's introduction to stealing cars coincides with their acquiring this necessary technical expertise. While brute force can be used to gain entry into the vehicle, some dexterity and basic technical skills are required to defeat the vehicle's igni-tion. Complex knowledge is not compulsory, although a familiarity with certain vehicle parts and their operation is essential. As expected, almost everyone in our sample—32 out of 35 respondents—discussed a period of learning how to steal a car; particularly "breaking down" the steering wheel column and/or tampering with ignitions. Thirty-one of the 32 thieves who were coached by others received instruction from neighborhood peers or family members whose source of crimi-nal tutelage was likewise acquired from others in a social context.

Asked how they became involved in auto theft, Goldie's comments were typ-ical, regardless of gender: "Well, hanging out with [a] couple older guys, you know, they showed me the ropes. . . . [W]hat cars to target and what cars you can't steal. . . . That's how I got into it. . . . Just hanging with older guys, they showed me." About half of the sample—both men and women—discussed being taken along on their first theft as a lookout while an older co-offender would physically steal the car. Typically, this role was taken for a few weeks or months before the initiate would be the one responsible for most of the "theft work." Some of the men and women traced a majority of their learning to the time spent riding in cars stolen by peers and observed them start and stop vehicles until they figured out how to replicate the basic procedure. For others, the learning experiences were more structured. Offenders were shown how to effect entry and bypass the ignition, but also informed of the types of cars to target, those that require different techniques, how to check for alarms, and presuppositions about the efforts by police to recover stolen vehicles such as search patterns, "hot sheets," and the length of time in which vehicles can be "safely" displayed in public. Formal learning was common among those who began as lookouts and was especially the case among those affiliated with tight-knit crews. J's initiation into "vehicle-taking" was typical among predominantly male crews:

> When I was doing it my first time it was one person with me. . . . He made sure I did it right and shit. . . . You got to do it real quick so he made sure I get it done and shit. . . . It was sort of like an initiation type of thing . . . once you steal your first car, you know they ain't worried about you stealing your second 'cause . . . you know how to do it and shit. So, I knew they knew I knew how to do it, so that was like my initiation.

Once the basic proficiencies of car stealing were honed, men and women alike tended to pass on this knowledge. One such person was Killa, who, at the time of the interview, was serving as "technical advisor" (Fleming, Brantingham, & Brantingham, 1994) to younger males in his neighborhood:

> KILLA: I'm like switching roles from learning to now teaching.
> INTERVIEWER: Are they the lookout or do they have a more hands-on role during the theft?
> KILLA: Yeah, they'll look out. Some look out, some know how to break it down, some know how to just do it all themselves. It's all in how they learn. . . . You gotta learn from someone, yeah, it's a cycle. . . . It's not that easy. . . . It takes a little finesse.

Comparing experiences reported by the men and women at the time of their first direct participation in taking a vehicle produced some noteworthy themes related to the onset of offending and tutelage. All of the men began offending in sexually homogeneous groups. Overwhelmingly, they were initiated by same-sex peers or same-sex members of their family (again, with one exception). Twenty-six of the 27 males also discussed being taught by other men, either a peer ($n = 22$) or family member ($n = 4$). In all likelihood, this is a reflection of two general social facts. First, criminal networks are largely male in nature. Second, these experiences typically occur in late adolescence—a period where interactional networks display strong gender segregation (especially where illicit activity is a prominent component of the network).

By direct participation, we mean the first time where the interviewee took an active role in the stealing of a car. This includes being a lookout. Due to our interviewees' wide exposure to stolen cars before they began to steal cars themselves, we found it necessary to make this distinction.

In contrast to the men, direct auto theft participation by women occurred in the company of opposite-sex peers. Four of the women first offended within mixed-sex groups (Lavanda, Lil' Bunny, Lil' Bit, and The Beast); Jewells Santana was the only woman in an otherwise all-male group. Two of the women first offended with a single partner, not in a large group; one was with her brother (Tonya James) and one with a romantic partner (Jasmine King). Even Chocolate, the only female to commit her first theft solely in the company of women, admitted, "Someone did teach us how to do it because on another incident a guy was with us and showed us how to do it." The following exchange with Lil' Bit illustrates how, even for a woman who currently worked with a group of women, and was initiated by a mixed-sex group, the technical knowledge necessary to take a car without the proper keys was tied to her interactions with a man.

> INTERVIEWER: These women you got involved with. At first, were you just jumping in cars and driving off in them?
> LIL' BIT: Yeah.
> INTERVIEWER: Is that because you guys [female friends] didn't know how to steal them?
> LIL' BIT: Basically, yeah.
> INTERVIEWER: Did these other girls you were hanging with, did they know how?
> LIL' BIT: No.
> INTERVIEWER: And how did you guys eventually learn how to break down a car?
> LIL' BIT: A boy showed me that used to go steal cars. . . . He was older than me. . . . At first I just used to ride around with them in stolen cars and then I got tired of just riding around [with] boys so I asked him and he told me. Well, he showed me and then he told me.

Thus, even though her current preference was for working with women, Lil' Bit needed to draw on masculine expertise to acquire the needed technical skills to successfully engage in motor vehicle theft.

Early experiences riding in stolen cars were ubiquitous in the interviews for both men and women. Thus, the opportunity to observe an experienced thief at work, as well as have the fundamental techniques explained, was a fairly universal experience. The contextual nature of joyriding and car theft then produced a situation where women did not experience the same sort of gendered barriers to initiation seen with other crimes (i.e., burglary, see Decker et al., 1993; Mullins & Wright, 2003). Some of our female interviewees then circulated these skills and learnt from men within female networks in very much the same way that many men did or were currently doing (such as in the case of Killa, depicted above) among themselves.

ENACTMENT

Unless one purposely targets idling vehicles unattended or otherwise obtains the proper keys, defeating door locks and vehicle ignitions requires a degree of mechanical expertise that surpasses common sense (Copes & Cherbonneau, 2006). The modal enactment method in the sample—discussed equally by men and women—was using a flathead screwdriver to pry off the ignition covering around the keyhole to expose the ignition switch. To start the vehicle, one simply inserts the screwdriver into the exposed ignition and turns clockwise. This constitutes the basics of what men and women learned during their initiation experiences.

While the exact technique varies from one vehicle make to the next, this one reportedly worked well on newer vehicle makes (and models) including, among others, Chrysler–Dodge (Charger, Intrepid, Neon, Stratus), Chrysler–Plymouth (Sebring), General Motors–Buick (LeSabre, Regal), and General Motors–Pontiac (Grand Am, Bonneville, Sunfire). For older vehicles manufactured in the 1980s and early to mid-1990s (General Motors–Chevrolet: Caprice, Blazer/Suburban, Malibu, Monte Carlo; General Motors–Buick: Regal, Riviera; General Motors–Oldsmobile: Cutlass; General Motors–Pontiac: Grand Prix), thieves took advantage of their weak tilt-steering column design, which, when broken, provides access to the ignition switch, which can be easily manipulated by pulling a lever or "horseshoe" and then depressing a coiled spring screw to start up the engine.

Car thieves do engage in a semirational process of target selection. When assessing prospective targets, offenders' primary perceptual filter at work concerns its "stealability" (i.e., one that they can take successfully based on their ability and available on-hand hardware). This filter is grounded in their personal perception of their own skills. As we examine here, those skill sets are gendered, and thus the target selection process drawn upon by our informants is gendered as well.

Although a growing number of newer (and mostly high-end) cars have built-in safeguards to limit ignition tampering, all 27 males and five of the females described using this approach (or a variant of the general script) in a recent theft. However, some of the discourse from these five women suggests that even though they learned how to bypass keyed ignitions from someone else (as discussed previously, typically a male), their knowledge of what was working or why was comparatively limited. For example, Jasmine King recounted her most recent theft of an unlocked Ford Taurus this way:

> I got in there and I had a screwdriver and I took the screwdriver and stuck it in the—you know, where the ignition thing go. . . . Once I stuck it in there . . . some wires fell down, and I just messed with the wire. I never know which wire it is—I guess I just be that nervous. . . . It be about four or five wires—different wires. . . . I cut all of them at the same time, you know, and then after I cut them I just be flicking them together to see which ones work to start it.

Seldom did the men we interview describe this sort of fumbling guesswork in their thefts. Even when asked about general auto theft techniques or prodded about specific enactment strategies, men were able to articulate a more convincing account of their aptitude. Young G's explanation of how to steal a 2000 Dodge Intrepid illustrates this distinction:

> First, you got to get the flathead head in the ignition. Once you get the flathead up in the ignition, you hit it a couple of times before you can get it kind of one-way. . . . It's gonna be loose. . . . You put [the screwdriver] on the other side. Bang it in some more [to] get it loose on that side . . . where you can just stick your

hand in it and pull it [ignition cover] out. Once you do that . . . you stick the flathead up in . . . where the key ignition was . . . and start it up.

While tampering with vehicle ignitions was the modal method discussed for starting a standstill engine, both males and females went after targets that required less effort to obtain. These offenders seized vehicles left idling and unattended by careless owners, thereby eschewing technical effort in favor of patient observation. Jewells Santana, who accomplished her most recent auto theft using this method, explained the general technique:

> I see somebody leave their car running or something with the keys in it . . . I might hop in and just drive off. . . . That's just how easy it is. Just wait until somebody park their car, they'll leave the A/C on or something, run in the store real quick or pay for their gas or something. Just hop in the car and leave.

Taking advantage of momentarily unattended vehicles is an especially common practice when the spontaneity and late-night partying of street-life participation leaves offenders stranded far from home with no means of getting back (Copes, 2003; Copes & Cherbonneau, 2006). In such situations, offenders often lack proper tools to enter vehicles and manipulate ignitions. Poorly equipped for the task at hand, targeting vehicles left running emerges as the "most proximate and performable" (Lofland, 1969, p. 61) way to overcome their current predicaments (c.f., Wright & Decker, 1994, p. 200). Poo#2's description of stealing a Monte Carlo for transportation after he was stranded at a party was exemplary of the circumstances underpinning this style of enactment: "I went there, they all [my ride] got drunk and left, and I got drunk and dozed off. . . . I don't feel much like staying at other people's houses that I ain't comfortable, you know, so I jumped up, got up. It was hopeless and I was looking for anything." Poo#2 proceeded to walk to a nearby familiar gas station where "there's a lot of dudes be going to that filling station, getting out of their cars and going in there to talk" and simply waited until somebody let down their guard. In his words:

> Dude was at the gas station in a Monte Carlo. . . . He's putting gas in there and I just jumped in the shit and drive off. . . . I just needed a ride home. . . . With a young dude in a Monte Carlo, easiest thing in the world. Like taking candy from a baby.

The presentation of "found" opportunities (see Copes & Cherbonneau, 2006) does more than pique the "larceny sense" (Sutherland, 1937) of the casual observer, but, as Poo#2 made clear, these opportunities are tailor-made for would-be thieves seeking to reverse immediate situational misfortunes. The important contrast between men and women who exploited found opportunities is that men were more likely to do so because of some situational (dis)advantage, whereas women were more likely to actively seek them out over more outwardly difficult targets requiring "mechanical" means of enactment.

While pulling away in unattended vehicles is, in some respects, riskier than stealing unoccupied cars (as the owner is almost always assumed to be nearby and to also immediately report the theft to authorities), it nevertheless constitutes a form of theft that requires less technical knowledge. The Beast highlighted how a lack of mechanical finesse could steer one toward different enactment styles. After explaining that she knew how to break down ignitions from working with a male friend, she went on to say that when they were working together she always deferred the task of breaking down targets to him as "he knows more than me," and admitted that doing it on her own took "about 45 minutes to an hour." In a similar vein, Lil' Bit said, "We knew how to break them down but sometimes we don't want to. . . . Breaking it down will take a little longer than just pulling off."

While both men and women either sought out or took advantage of opportunities created by careless car owners, five females (Chocolate, Lavanda, Lil' Bit, Lil' Bunny, The Beast) reported stealing vehicles in ways that men did not. Although the exact techniques varied from one theft to the next, the common thread among enactment procedures described by men was that face-to-face interaction with victims was always avoided, thereby keeping intact the stealth-like quality of the offense (see Donahue, McLaughlin, & Damm, 1994). Women, on the other hand, described thefts in which prior interaction with the victim was an important ruse toward accomplishing the theft. Not surprisingly, men were the targets in all such thefts. Chocolate conned men into leaving their vehicles overnight at a confederate's automotive garage and would return later to steal the vehicle. If confronted by the owner, she claimed ignorance. Chocolate explained the hustle she did "a lot of times" this way:

> You leave the car with me so I can tint it up and dazz[le] it up for you . . . at an auto tint place. . . . I get the word of mouth out. Like a lotta little dudes I know that got nice cars and they're ballin' now. . . . I be bringing by the cars that we had stole [and fixed up at the auto shop] and I let them look at the cars that we got, the spokes, the rims, and the tint all looking good, and they like be like, "Damn whose motherfucking car is that?" I'll be like, "It's mine, I just bought it"; kind of flo-show. "Where'd you get all that shit from?" "[I got it] at such and such place. Come down and leave your car. . . . When you get it back it will look like this." They be like, "They be doing that shit?" I was just like, "Well then leave it," and shit like that. So they leave it and I'd steal their car and shit, and don't fuck with them no more and acting like I don't be knowing what happened.

Chocolate further explained that it is an easy scam for females to pull "versus [males, who] just go out, pick a person, and say 'Yeah you, come over here.' You know a dude gonna talk to a girl long. If she got ass and titties, they gonna talk. There's a lot of males around that want it."

Three females—Lil' Bit, Lil' Bunny, and The Beast—stole vehicles from unknown men who approached them in public settings as they went about their day-to-day activities and solicited their company. Lil' Bunny described one such instance while waiting at a bus stop:

> LIL' BUNNY: Like this one man, wanted to take me for a ride and shit. Wanted to go get some drinks. . . . I just met him waiting on the bus stop. He riding up, "Where you going, little mama?" "Over my friend house." "You wanna go get some drinks?" "Yeah.". . . [I get in his car and he asked]

"What you drinking?" "Absolut and cranberry, you hear me?" He get out the car, leave his keys in the car, I'm gone. I don't want to be with you. You only want one thing: you want to fuck, so I'm gone. . . .

INTERVIEWER: So you kind of set him up?

LIL' BUNNY: He set himself up. Mm-hmm.

INTERVIEWER: Do you usually do it that way?

LIL' BUNNY: Yeah, especially if I ain't stealing them [by breaking down the ignition]. I don't know you. Why am I trying to drink with you? You doing things to me. So I use your ride, I'm gone. . . . I don't know you. You think I'm fixing to drink with you? Hell nah, my pussy ain't free either [laughing].

Chocolate and Lavanda also described situations where they intentionally targeted specific men so that they could create an opportunity to make off with their vehicles. As with Maher's street-level sex workers (1997), the women interviewed here exploited a typical male blind spot—seeing women as little else than sex objects—to accomplish an offense (see also Contreras, 2009; Miller, 1998; Mullins & Wright, 2003).

All in all, most offenders used a narrow range of techniques to steal cars, which they learned from others during their initiation experiences. Of course, a patient thief could steal a car without these skills, though there is a tradeoff in the level of risk incurred while doing so. For example, the women who set up or otherwise took advantage of men entered into more provocative and dangerous situations. While rare, it is telling that the most recent auto thefts described by half of the females we interviewed were accomplished by enactment methods that resulted in obtaining the proper keys. In essence, women's lack of technical expertise led to what appear to be riskier forms of enactment.

DISPOSAL

Nearly all of our interviewees discussed having some relationship or connection to a chop shop of some sort where they would dispose of a stolen car and get paid. Many of these locales were repair garages that did a side business in buying stolen cars to strip down for parts. Interviewees also discussed selling parts to friends, family members, or people on the streets as well. However, in most of these cases, car thieves seemed to take the most valuable portable accessories off the car before taking it to the shop (i.e., radios, speakers, rims).

Three women specifically mentioned that they did not know of a chop shop or garage. Lil' Bunny simply drove the car for recreational use and then abandoned it when she thought it might be on the police "hot sheet" (Topalli & Wright, 2004). Likewise, Lil' Bit drove vehicles for a couple of days but then "after I'm through with the car . . . I sell whatever in the car that could be sold." Asked why she did not sell to chop shops, Lil' Bit replied, "I don't know where no chop shop at. I don't know where no one at. I know they say there's one on the East Side but I never been to it so I don't know where it's at." The third, Tonya James, had a longer history of car theft (compared to Lil' Bunny and Lil' Bit) and used chop shops earlier in her career. When asked about her current use of them, she replied, "I don't know any chop shops. . . . They [the police] caught up with them and they're closed down, that was seven or eight years ago. But man, I don't know none today. . . . I wish I did." With no connections, she stripped valuable accessories off of the cars she stole to sell on the streets (see below). No men specifically mentioned not knowing a chop shop as a personal barrier to disposal; in fact, most discussed how essential it was to have those connections.

Men, however, were likely to dismantle stolen vehicles themselves and sell off specific parts of high value (or those easily sold) on the streets. Only one female mentioned this tactic. In these street disposal approaches, men mentioned specific orders from associates, simply knowing people, or generally trying to sell parts on the streets. JD explained how he sold parts on the street:

> You see a person in a real car you can ask 'em, you know, "I can get you such and such." . . . You gotta ask people. You won't tell him [how] you get it, but you know, [tell them] "I can get it." . . . If I feel like I can't trust you, why ask you? If I feel like it's a problem, I'm not gonna say nothing to you. . . . I approach people I know.

Only one female, Lil' Bit, adopted this disposal technique. Recall, she was one of the females who did not know of any locally run chop shops. Without knowledge of this common outlet, she resorted to selling on the streets, but with a somewhat different approach than JD. Whereas he sought out potential buyers directly, Lil' Bit informed others about the property she had available, who, for the promise of a "finder's fee," helped her locate interested buyers. Asked how she finds people that buy stolen goods, Lil' Bit said:

> I mean, 'cause people tell. Like some of the dudes, that's their white [crack cocaine]. They know that I got some parts and they'll tell who[ever], they'll just go around. If they see somebody they know that like rims and stuff like that then they ask them do they wanna buy a radio, rims, or whatever, and if they do, they'll come and tell me. They'll bring the person who want to buy it to me, and I give them a little money for, you know what I'm saying, bringing them to me. . . . I give them like $30 [on a $100 sale].

It is here that social networks were of upmost importance. In order to be successful, people needed to know where chop shops were and how to approach the operators. They needed to know who would buy stolen auto parts and how best to deal them on their own. This knowledge was typically acquired through other, often more experienced criminal associates. Young G described how he gained entry into these networks:

> I know the owner [through my brother]. . . . My brother was actually the one that . . . will take the car to the shop and I will just come along 'cause he knew the owner well, better than everybody else [in our crew], so that's why he was the ringleader, 'cause all the money, you know what I'm saying, to get the money in the first place it would have to go through him, so that's why he would get paid the most money. 'Cause without him, we wouldn't even be getting paid no

ways.... [The owner] know my brother since birth, so he got a lot of trust in him. That's really what it's all about, trust.

Jasmine King described having to develop this trust over time. "They [the men who ran the chop shop] was cool because they knew who I was. They knew I wasn't no snitch. They knew I wasn't trying to get them in trouble or nothing. They knew I was just wanting some money." She went on to explain that at first she was introduced to the chop shop through her boyfriend at the time, and, once connected, she explained that "I got cool with them and they got to trust you." However, she did reveal that once on her own (having since split up with her boyfriend), the shop owner paid her appreciably less than he did her boyfriend, as illustrated in the following exchange:

INTERVIEWER: How much did the guy [boyfriend] get that you used to work with?

JASMINE KING: He was getting more.

INTERVIEWER: Why is that?

JASMINE KING: I don't know, maybe he was better at it than I was, I don't know. Maybe he didn't have to break 'em down like I did, but I done seen him drive the cars before with a screwdriver in it, you know what I'm saying, so I don't know. I don't know.... I have said something to him [chop shop contact] before like, "Come on now, you know it's worth more than that. You're gonna get more."... [And he says,] "That's the best I can do right now."

INTERVIEWER: Do you have access to any other people like that where you could sell cars?

JASMINE KING: No. He the only person I know.

INTERVIEWER: Do you think he knows that?

JASMINE KING: Yeah.

Without these contacts the ability to profit from auto theft was significantly curtailed. The next profitable source for those who lacked access to these higher outlets was to sell vehicle parts and accessories on the streets. Recall how Tonya James was forced to sell on the streets since she did not know of any chop shops that were currently operating. Yet, even those who sold parts on the street relied upon social networks to either move parts or become aware of customers. The following exchange with Chocolate emphasized the importance of informal network connections:

INTERVIEWER: It seems you got your people setup pretty much—you got your girls . . . and you got people you know you can sell the stuff to.

CHOCOLATE: Yeah. Yeah, exactly.

INTERVIEWER: Do you ever try to look for more connections?

CHOCOLATE: I got more connections now, I just ain't gonna fixing to reveal them. They all good.

INTERVIEWER: But are you always out looking for connections?

CHOCOLATE: Yeah, always looking for something different. If you find something different, you find more money.

We should also note that Chocolate was not dependent on these networks to make car theft profitable; her uncle owned a garage, giving her ready access to a disposal source.

Westside provided a rich description of exactly how these networks can work and how trust is central to their functioning. He described his current involvement in the world of car theft in St. Louis as "an overseer":

> WESTSIDE: Me personally, . . . I oversee it now: "Handle that. Get that. We take this." . . . I mean I got the connect[ion to the chop shop]. [If] the youngsters want to eat how we wanted to eat, they know if they get this certain type of car, they know they can get a certain amount of dollar from it, so they get it, come to me, and I take 'em to where they need to go. . . . I take them to my dude. . . . He sees what he can salvage from them, see if he can strip it down, see what else he . . . can do. Like if this car has rims on it, he'll strip it down and pull all the accessories out, TVs, whatever the case, and just strip it for salvage. . . . Yeah, that's what we do pretty much. . . . We've been working together for damn near seven years, eight years damn near. . . .
>
> INTERVIEWER: I was wondering what's to stop him from . . .
>
> WESTSIDE [INTERRUPTING]: From my little partners going to him? Because nah, we don't do it like that. . . . It's in stone that my guy don't trust nobody but me. For all he know, these little cats could be bringing them folks up in here with them because they get caught up on the jam. . . . You're in a situation where you feel like they probably don't know how to hold they own. You put them in an interrogation room, goddamn they singing and telling every motherfucking thing that need not be told. . . . I remember my dude ain't want to fuck with me back in the day because I was a, you know, he had to just see how I moved. You know what I mean? And you can tell, you can tell who's real and who ain't—pressure bust pipes and bitches too!

Trust is central in establishing connections for criminal disposal of goods, yet these informal social connections in the criminal underworld are often gate-kept by men. This has strong consequences for women's ability to make and maintain these relationships. Steffensmeier (1983) and Steffensmeier and Terry (1986) identified men's negative attitudes toward women as a key barrier to women's inclusion in offending and disposal networks (see also Maher, 1997; Mullins & Wright, 2003). Compared to prior work on the topic, we found much more diversity within men's attitudes toward women in the data.

Over half of the men asked said they did not know any women car thieves, and moreover would not work with them if they did. Typically, they provided a stereotypical explanation that crime in general, and car theft in particular, was a male activity, and that women were "too soft" to be successful criminals. For example, Young G dismissed female offenders by saying that "little chicks just be scared. . . . They just too girly to do something like that. . . . They just don't got what it takes for real." Others suggested that women could not stand up to police questioning and would thus snitch. Killa straightforwardly said, "They [women] can just be broken easily." Thus, if a female associate were caught, she would reveal everything to the police. E#2 agreed, saying that women, "They'll do a switch on you . . . put police in front of them, man, it's over. Yeah, they'll cry."

Others discussed the issue in a more pragmatic fashion. These men did not deny the abilities of women to engage in criminal behavior, but thought that women did not have the exact skill set needed for car theft. J discussed refusing to teach one of his female peers how to steal cars, emphasizing that "I ain't got the time. . . . They [women] don't learn so fast." End Dog made a similar statement, explaining he had worked with a women on a theft once, but "she moved too slow, so no, she was way slow, slower than normal . . . too slow for me. Not going to get caught." Poo#2 combined these themes, saying:

> It's a man thing. . . . It's just not appropriate to take a woman with you to do something like that. . . . It's not safe. . . . It's a dangerous risk. . . . She can't run as fast as you can. If you have to ask her to outrun the police she's gonna get caught, and nine times out of 10, she's gonna tell who you is.

Of those who *knew* female car thieves, all but one said they had no problem working with women. Capone, who had previously worked with Chocolate, insisted that:

> CAPONE: The women I mess with ain't gonna tell—they solid. Just like her [Chocolate],[5] she's solid.
> INTERVIEWER: Do you ever work with her [Chocolate]?
> CAPONE: Couple times. She's cool. She's cool.

Capone was interviewed on the same day and immediately after Chocolate, who at the time of Capone's interview was waiting with the recruiter outside the interview room. Capone also described working with his 19-year-old niece "a couple of times" owing to the fact that she was a competent auto thief. He was also proud to report that much like himself, "she hood. She be high-speeding [eluding police] and everything—she get away."

T-Raw said, "I've worked with some women [who] know more shit than men. A lot of the women stronger than men, you know what I'm saying. . . . A lot of the women they some soldiers, gotta give it to 'em."

This degree of open-mindedness was not just limited to men who had worked with women. Asked if a female could have joined the all-male crew that introduced him to auto theft, Tye said, "Yeah, if she wanted to get down, it was up to her. It's her decision. . . . A female never tried to get with us . . . but I've heard of females that . . . do get down, that's real smooth with it." Thus, there is limited support within criminal networks for working with women, and it is no doubt through these pathways that the women we interviewed gained access to offender and disposal networks.

Taken as a whole, our examination of the data has uncovered several core themes of gender-neutral and gender-specific perspectives and experiences. In general, the motivation and enactment techniques of men and women were very similar. Where women had access to vehicle or parts disposal networks, their experiences tended to be very similar to men's. In the context of the types of groups responsible for offenders' initiation into auto theft and subsequently their access to networks (especially for disposal), strong gender differences emerged.

DISCUSSION

Throughout our analysis we have relied on a tried-and-true method for exploring both the divergences and convergences in the perspectives and experiences of men and women involved in street crime (see Miller & Mullins, 2006). Car theft requires slightly more specialized knowledge to enact than most other street crimes. This information is typically disseminated and acquired in social networks. Car theft also requires knowledge of underground disposal networks to be profitable (though, unlike other forms of theft, there is a utilitarian value to a car in and of itself). Prior work has suggested that women have a social capital disadvantage due to sexist attitudes held by the male gatekeepers of these networks (Messerschmidt, 1997; Mullins & Wright, 2003; Steffensmeier, 1983; Steffensmeier & Terry, 1986). Here we found that this is indeed the case on the streets of St. Louis. Almost universally, individuals learned the basic techniques of car theft and were initiated into social networks that facilitated disposal through male peers or family members. However, unlike prior work, we did find a larger subset of males who were tolerant of women offenders as long as their expertise was similar to males.

Thus, for our male interviewees, their introduction to auto theft occurred within gender-homogenous networks and interaction experiences. The females, however, experienced initiation and socialization into auto theft and disposal networks typically through opposite-sex interactions. While men and women did not describe radical differences in the content of what was learned or how they were treated by others, such initiatory experiences did have gendered ramifications later in the offenders' car theft careers.

As with Mullins and Wright's (2003) work on residential burglary, we found few differences in offense enactment. This is, in all likelihood, a function of the fact that there are only so many ways to take control of a car to steal it. As with most tasks, once an effective technique is found for completion, it is repeated. Auto theft seems to be no different. Men and women alike described the tactic of popping out the ignition and using a screwdriver to start the vehicle. They mentioned learning this technique from others and replicating it due to ease and functionality. As an interesting area of departure, women were the only ones who described specifically seeking out a vehicle left running. Men did rely on these methods, however, both situationally (i.e., they were stranded and/or lacked the necessary tools) and opportunistically (i.e., they chanced upon a vehicle left running and perceived the opportunity too enticing to pass up). It is worth noting that the same females who relied on these techniques most often were also the least integrated into criminal networks. They were the women who mentioned not knowing chop shops and generally not having access to male-dominated networks; thus, their primary use of stolen vehicles was either expressive (i.e., joyriding) or utilitarian (i.e., using them for personal transport)—any profits were serendipitous (i.e., found money or drugs while rummaging a vehicle's interior) or by chance (i.e., a member of their neighborhood network inquired about and offered a small sum for a vehicle stolen for some other purpose). Their lived gendered experiences narrowed the disposal options available and thus constrained opportunities. As we explored previously, this in turn influenced disposal patterns and women's ability to profit from motor vehicle theft, and profit well.

As with many other studies on street life, we also found women taking advantage of men's sexual objectification of them to enact a crime, in this case car theft (see Contreras, 2009; Maher, 1997; Miller, 1998; Mullins & Wright, 2003). This well-confirmed aspect of offender agency highlights how power relationships shape situational interactional contexts, forcing social actors to modify behaviors and adopt innovative interactional strategies for goal accomplishment. Five of our eight female interviewees drew upon this tactic on occasion; it was not resorted to only when the offender lacked other options. As explored previously, those females who had little technical expertise with breaking steering columns down tended to target vehicles left running at convenience stores and gas stations. A general lack of technical expertise lead women to engage in riskier thefts, which also tended to produce less gain.

The issue of similarities and differences are not a zero-sum experience. Women's experiences here were varied. Some were deeply embedded in criminal networks; their interactional experiences provided opportunities to get to be known and trusted by male gatekeepers in the St. Louis underworld. Once established, they were able to engage in and profit from motor vehicle theft; thus, their experiences, techniques, and knowledge overlapped strongly with the men who were interviewed. Two of the women described past exposure to these networks. While some avenues of profitability were no longer open to them, as these earlier connections had since dried up, they still drew upon the skills acquired while attached to active criminal networks. Two of the females interviewed here had no real access to active crime groups; their techniques of commission and disposal reflected this dual lack of technical and social capital, as did their use of the vehicle once stolen (i.e., utilitarian usage versus selling for profit). Further, two others only had access to disposal networks through males. As a group, women's experiences were far more diverse in nature than men's experiences. We conclude that this is a product, in part, of what social ties and connections they were able to establish and maintain throughout their criminal careers.

CONCLUSION

This paper has examined the convergences and divergences of men's and women's experiences in motor vehicle theft, adding to the qualitative literature on street-life subculture, street crime, and the experiences of gender within each and at the intersection of both domains. As other recent work has shown (Brookman et al., 2007; Miller, 1998; Miller, 2002; Mullins & Wright, 2003; Mullins, Wright, & Jacobs, 2004), men and women share many motivational drives and enactment techniques for committing crime. Such findings speak directly to broader theorizations of crime that either postulate gender-specific motivations for criminal involvement or suggest that there is a more universal criminal experience. In terms of initiation into car crimes, our data here highlight the generally criminogenic nature of certain neighborhood situations and experiences and show them influencing both women and men in similar fashion (at least the women interviewed in this project).

Yet, despite similarities of early crime experiences, our findings support prior work that establishes a strong set of misogynistic attitudes toward women that shapes female experiences with offending and within offender networks (and more generally of life lived within neighborhoods inhabited by offenders— see Miller, 2008). We do not doubt these attitudes preclude some women from getting involved at all in criminal activities (thus contributing to the wide gender gap in motor vehicle theft) and that those women who do become involved are frequently presented with negative social stimuli that push some toward (if not outright into) criminal desistence. Yet, unlike other work, our findings highlight some diversity of men's opinions of female peers, with a minority judging potential women co-offenders by skill set and not by sex category. This is an area which requires more investigation. Much of the early (and even recent) work establishing pervasive misogyny on the streets is grounded in data which are older (i.e., Mullins & Wright's 2003 data were collected in 1989 and 1990). There is no reason to believe that attitudes in street-life social networks remain static over time. They should exhibit the same dynamic characteristics that mainstream norms do. Thus, to a small degree, attitudes toward female offenders may be changing. More work is needed to explore how individuals respond to initially negative experiences with these gendered barriers then decide to either seek entry into networks anyway or who decide to either forgo crime in general or crimes with gatekeepers (i.e., burglary, drug selling, and auto theft).

An immutable limitation of the data presented here is undoubtedly sample size, particularly in the number of female participants. Moreover, due to the nature of nonprobabilistic sampling using "snowball" and chain-referral methods, we gained the views of a number of women within one established street-life network. We cannot make broad generalizations of our findings here beyond the data themselves. Be that as it may, the current findings confirm themes and experiences reported in other criminological research using qualitative methods—be they gender-specific or mixed-gender offender-based examinations of street crime in general. Further, Guest, Bunce, and Johnson (2006) establishes experimentally that most major themes in qualitative interviewing tend to be uncovered and saturated early during data collection—especially with regard to the types of meta-themes dealt with here. With the experimental work of Guest and co-authors (2006) in mind, we are confident in the validity of the information we uncovered in the female narratives. Hopefully more work on female experiences in crime in general and car crime specifically will provide further insight into our findings.

Our uncovering of a high diversity of female experiences within criminal social networks contributes to the current debates within feminist criminology concerning the divergence and convergence of male and female experiences of street life. As described by both male and female interviewees, in some social groups femininity is not necessarily the barrier to entry and cooperation that some work has suggested. However, women are still not universally respected on the streets and there is still a strong culture of misogyny held and perpetuated by criminally involved men of all ages (Miller, 1998; Miller & Mullins, 2006; Mullins, 2006). As discussed, such negative perceptions and experiences were prominent in the data explored here. Our understanding of the conditional nature of these attitudes and what factors shape men's attitudes toward women in criminal social networks would benefit from a closer look at these variant contexts and experiences.

Such contexts and experiences are of the utmost importance to understand as criminology continues to explore both the prominent gender gap in offending and the manner in which experiences within criminal networks influence criminal career trajectory. Opportunity structures on the streets clearly frame both of these issues. Offender decision making is situated within the context of street-life social networks. If and how gender shapes such networks will feed back into decision-making events. Gendered perceptions, knowledge, and opportunities will shape if, and if so how, individuals offend. Such forces will also affect how offenders negotiate post-offense actions, especially transforming ill-gotten goods into money or other desired goods. Hopefully future research will continue to explore how gender at the macro and meso levels intersects with micro-level offending decisions and actions.

REFERENCES

Best, A. L. (2006). *Fast cars, cool rides: The accelerating world of youth and their cars.* New York: New York University Press.

Brookman, F., Mullins, C. W., Bennett, T., & Wright, R. (2007). Gender, motivation and the accomplishment of street robbery. *British Journal of Criminology, 47,* 861–884.

Campbell, A. (1993). *Men, women, and aggression.* New York: Basic.

Cherbonneau, M., & Wright, R. (2009). Auto theft. In M. Tonry (Ed.), *The Oxford handbook of crime and public policy* (pp. 191–222). New York: Oxford University Press.

Clarke, R. V., & Harris, P. (1992). Auto theft and its prevention. In M. Tonry (Ed.), *Crime and justice: A review of research* (vol. 16, pp. 1–54). Chicago: University of Chicago Press.

Contreras, R. (2009). "Damn, yo—who's that girl?": An ethnographic analysis of masculinity in drug robberies. *Journal of Contemporary Ethnography, 38,* 465–492.

Copes, H. (2003). Streetlife and the rewards of auto theft. *Deviant Behavior, 24,* 309–332.

Copes, H., & Cherbonneau, M. (2006). The key to auto theft: Emerging methods of auto theft from the offenders' perspective. *British Journal of Criminology, 46,* 917–934.

Dawes, G. (2002). Figure eights, spin outs and power slides: Aboriginal and Torres Strait Islander youth and the culture of joyriding. *Journal of Youth Studies, 5,* 195–208.

Decker, S., Wright, R., Redfern, A., & Smith, D. (1993). A woman's place is in the home: Females and residential burglary. *Justice Quarterly, 10,* 143–162.

Donahue, M., McLaughlin, V., & Damm, L. 1994. Accounting for carjacking: An analysis of police records in a southeastern city. *American Journal of Police, 13*(4), 91–111.

Federal Bureau of Investigation (FBI). (2008). *Uniform crime report: Crime in the United States, 2007.* Washington, DC: U.S. Department of Justice.

Federal Highway Administration. (2008). *Highway statistics, 2007.* Washington, DC: U.S. Department of Transportation.

Fleming, Z. (2003). "The thrill of it all": Youthful offenders and auto theft. In P. Cromwell (Ed.), *In their own words: Criminals on crime* (3rd ed., pp. 99–107). Los Angeles: Roxbury.

Fleming, Z., Brantingham, P., & Brantingham, P. (1994). Exploring auto theft in British Columbia. In R. V. Clarke (Ed.), *Crime prevention studies* (Vol. 3, pp. 47–90). Monsey, NY: Criminal Justice Press.

Graham, J., & Bowling, B. (1995). *Young people and crime.* Home Office Research Study, 145. London: Home Office.

Guest, G., Bunce, A., & Johnson, L. (2006). How many interviews are enough? An experiment with data saturation and variability. *Field Methods, 18*(1), 59–82.

Henderson, J. (1994). Masculinity and crime: The implications of a gender-conscious approach to working with young men involved in "joyriding." *Social Action, 2*(2),19–26.

Kilpatrick, R. (1997). Joy-riding: An addictive behaviour. In J. E. Hodge, M. McMurran, & C. Hollin (Eds.), *Addicted to crime?* (pp. 165–190). New York: John Wiley & Sons.

Light, R., Nee, C., & Ingham, H. (1993). *Car theft: The offender's perspective.* Home Office Research Study 130. London: Home Office.

Lofland, J. (1969). *Deviance and identity.* Englewood Cliffs, NJ: Prentice-Hall.

Maher, L. (1997). *Sexed work: Gender, race and resistance in a Brooklyn drug market.* Oxford: Oxford University Press.

Messerschmidt, J. W. (1997). *Crime as structured action: Gender, race, class, and crime in the making.* Thousand Oaks, CA: Sage.

Miller, J. (1998). Up it up: Gender and the accomplishment of street robbery. *Criminology, 36*(1), 37–66.

———. (2001). *One of the guys: Girls, gangs and gender.* New York: Oxford University Press.

———. (2002). The strengths and limits of "doing gender" for understanding street crime. *Theoretical Criminology, 6,* 433–60.

———. (2008). *Getting played: African American girls, urban inequality and gendered violence.* New York: New York University Press.

Miller, J., & Mullins, C. W. (2006). The status of feminist theories in criminology. In F. T. Cullen, J. P. Wright, & K. R. Blevins (Eds.), *Taking stock: The status of criminological theory, advances in criminological theory* (vol. 15, pp. 217–249). New Brunswick, NJ: Transaction Publishers.

Mullins, C. W. (2006). *Holding your square: Masculinities, streetlife and violence.* Cullompton, Devon, UK: Willan.

Mullins, C. W., & Wright, R. T. (2003). Gender, social networks, and residential burglary. *Criminology, 41*(3), 813–840.

Mullins, C. W., Wright, R. T., & Jacobs, B. A. (2004). Gender, streetlife, and criminal retaliation. *Criminology, 42*(4), 911–940.

O'Connor, C., & Kelly, K. (2006). Auto theft and youth culture: A nexus of masculinities, femininities and car culture. *Journal of Youth Studies, 9,* 247–267.

Roe, S., & Ashe, J. (2008). *Young people and crime: Findings from the 2006 Offending, Crime and Justice Survey.* London: Home Office.

Slobodian, P., & Browne, K. (1997). Car crime as a developmental career: An analysis of young offenders in Coventry. *Psychology, Crime and Law, 3,* 275–286.

Sourcebook of Criminal Justice Statistics. 2003. High school seniors reporting involvement in selected delinquent activities in last 12 months. Retrieved June 4, 2012, from http://www.albany.edu/sourcebook/pdf/t344.pdf.

Spencer, E. (1992). *Car crime and young people on a Sunderland housing estate.* Crime Prevention Unit Series paper no. 40. London: Home Office.

Steffensmeier, D. (1983). Organization properties and sex-segregation in the underworld: Building a sociological theory of sex differences in crime. *Social Forces, 61,* 1010–1032.

Steffensmeier, D., & Terry, R. (1986). Institutional sexism in the underworld: A view from the inside. *Sociological Inquiry, 56,* 304–323.

Stephen, D., & Squires, P. (2003). "Adults don't realize how sheltered they are." A contribution to the debate on youth transitions from some voices on the margins. *Journal of Youth Studies, 6,* 145–164.

Topalli, V., & Wright, R. (2004). Dubs and dees, beats and rims: Carjackers and urban violence. In D. Dabney (Ed.), *Crime types: A text reader* (pp. 149–169). Belmont, CA: Wadsworth.

Walker, L., Butland, D., & Connell, R. W. (2000). Boys on the road: Masculinity, car culture and road safety education. *Journal of Men's Studies, 8*(2), 153–169.

Williams, C. (2005). *Stealing a car to be a man: The importance of cars and driving in the gender identity of adolescent males.* Unpublished Ph.D. diss., Queensland University of Technology, School of Psychology and Centre for Counseling.

Wright, R. T., & Decker, S. H. (1994). *Burglars on the job: Streetlife and residential break-ins.* Boston: Northeastern University Press.

Yates, J. (2003/4). Adolescent males: Masculinity and offending. *IUC Journal of Social Work Theory and Practice, 8,* 13 pages.

CHAPTER 7

"The Devil Made Me Do It": Use of Neutralizations by Shoplifters

Paul Cromwell and Quint Thurman

This study is based on 137 interviews with shoplifters obtained over a period of 12 months in 1997–1998 in a Midwestern city of approximately 360,000. The authors obtained access to a court-ordered diversion program ostensibly for adult "first offenders" (although few were actually first offenders) charged with theft. Of these, most were charged with misdemeanor shoplifting and required to attend an eight-hour therapeutic/education program as a condition of having their record expunged. The average group size was 18 to 20 participants. The participants were encouraged to discuss with the group the offense that brought them to the diversion program, why they did what they did, and how they felt about it. A series of educational exercises and role-playing activities completed each session's activities. The authors participated in the sessions as observers, recording their stories and experiences and occasionally asking questions. The participants were told that we were researchers studying shoplifting. At the conclusion of each daily session, participants were approached and asked if they would agree to a one-on-one interview. Interviews were obtained with 137 subjects. The mean age of the sample was 26. The age range was 18 to 66 years of age. Forty-eight were male and 49 were female. Seventy-eight were non-Hispanic white, 17 were Hispanic, and 42 were African-American.

> You know that cartoon where the guy has a little devil sitting on one shoulder and a little angel on the other? And one is telling him "Go ahead on, do it," and the angel is saying, "No, don't do it." You know? . . . Sometimes when I'm thinking about boosting something, my angel don't show up.
>
> —30-YEAR-OLD MALE SHOPLIFTER

Source: Cromwell, P., & Thurman, Q. (2003). "The devil made me do it": Use of neutralizations by shoplifters. *Deviant Behavior, 24*, 535–550. Used with permission of the publisher.

Nearly five decades ago Gresham Sykes and David Matza (1957) introduced neutralization theory as an explanation for juvenile delinquency. At that time, delinquency theory was the central attraction of criminology, with theorists such as Albert Cohen, Walter Miller, Edwin Sutherland, Richard Cloward and Lloyd Ohlin, and Sheldon and Eleanor Glueck establishing a foundation upon which subsequent theorists would build. The challenge then, as it still exists today, was to explain the unconventional behavior of juveniles. This paper examines Sykes and Matza's theory as it might apply to a specific form of criminal activity that is highly popular among juveniles and young adults. Here we look at offenders who shoplift and explore the justifications that they say they rely upon to excuse behavior they also acknowledge as morally wrong.

THE PROBLEM

Shoplifting may be the most serious crime with which the most people have some personal familiarity. Research has shown that one in every 10 to 15 persons who shops has shoplifted at one time or another (Lo, 1994; Russell, 1973; Turner & Cashdan, 1988). Further, losses attributable to shoplifting are considerable, with estimates ranging from 12 to 30 billion dollars lost annually (Klemke, 1982; Nimick, 1990; Griffin, 1988). Shoplifting also represents one of the most prevalent forms of larceny, accounting for approximately 15% of all larcenies according to data maintained by the Federal Bureau of Investigation (Freeh, 1996).

Unlike many other forms of crime, people who shoplift do not ordinarily require any special expertise or tools to engage in this crime. Consequently, those persons who shoplift do not necessarily conform to most people's perception of what a criminal offender is like. Instead, shoplifters tend to be demographically similar to the "average person." In a large study of nondelinquents, Klemke (1982) reported that as many as 63% of those persons he interviewed had shoplifted at some point in their lives. Students, housewives, business and professional persons, as well as professional thieves constitute the population of shoplifters. Loss prevention experts routinely counsel retail merchants that there is no particular profile of a potential shoplifter. Turner and Cashdan (1988) conclude, "While clearly a criminal activity, shoplifting borders on what might be considered a 'folk crime.'" In her classic study, Mary Cameron (1964) wrote:

> Most people have been tempted to steal from stores, and many have been guilty (at least as children) of "snitching" an item or two from counter tops. With merchandise so attractively displayed in department stores and supermarkets, and much of it apparently there for the taking, one may ask why everyone isn't a thief. (p. xi)

Because of its somewhat normative nature, shoplifting provides an excellent forum for criminologists to study various theories for explaining why some people commit crime and others do not since it appears to cross racial, ethnic, gender, and class lines and is frequently committed by "otherwise noncriminal" persons.

Furthermore, since shoplifting is a crime that is widely distributed across the general population by people whose values are thought to be generally consistent with the conventional moral code, it also represents an excellent choice for testing the merits of one theory in particular, that is, the theory of neutralization.

Neutralization theory argues that "ordinary" individuals who engage in deviant or criminal behavior may use techniques that permit them to recognize extenuating circumstances that enable them to explain away delinquent behavior. Without worrying about guilty feelings that would stand in their way of committing a criminal act, the theory asserts that those persons are free to participate in delinquent acts that they would otherwise believe to be wrong.

THEORETICAL CONSIDERATIONS

American criminology in the 1950s focused on whether or not juvenile delinquents in particular shared a common American culture or somehow belonged to another culture or had in fact formed their own subculture. Did they belong to the underclass culture that William Julius Wilson (1987) would identify some years later in *The Truly Disadvantaged* or had they somehow made a poor adaptation to a conventional culture that they did not fit, and thus, become their own youth subculture or counterculture as Howard Becker (1963) suggested in *Outsiders*?

Sykes and Matza's theory is an elaboration of Edwin Sutherland's proposition that individuals can learn criminal techniques, and the "motives, drives, rationalizations and attitudes favorable to violations of the law." Sykes and Matza argued that these justifications or rationalizations protect the individual from self-blame and the blame of others. Thus, the individual may remain committed to the value system of the dominant culture while committing criminal acts without experiencing the cognitive dissonance that might be otherwise expected. He or she deflects or "neutralizes" guilt in advance, clearing the way to blame-free crime. These neutralizations also protect the individual from any residual guilt following the crime. It is this ability to use neutralizations that differentiates delinquents from nondelinquents (Thurman, 1984).

While Sykes and Matza do not specifically maintain that only offenders who are committed to the dominant value system make use of these techniques of neutralizations, they appear to contend that delinquents maintain a commitment to the moral order and are able to drift into delinquency through the use of "techniques of neutralization." This approach assumes that should delinquents fail to internalize conventional morality, neutralization would be unnecessary, since there would be no guilt to neutralize. However, Hirschi (1969) argued that there is wide variation in the commitment to the conventional moral order. Furthermore, subsequent research implies that both delinquents and nondelinquents make use of neutralization strategies (Austin, 1977; Mannle & Lewis, 1979).

Thurman (1984) contends that commitment to conventional values and neutralization is empirically and conceptually distinct. Using this line of reasoning, individuals at any point on the committed/noncommitted continuum might utilize neutralization strategies. The specific purpose of the neutralization could be to reduce cognitive dissonance arising from guilt, to maintain self-image in the face of condemnation by others, to establish a defense against possible prosecution, or to facilitate subsequent offenses. Mannle and Lewis (1979) and Austin (1977) found that unconventional boys are most likely to neutralize, suggesting that neutralization is inversely related to moral commitment. Thurman (1984) supplies a logical rationale to this contradictory finding. He suggests that when "moral commitment is high, the level of guilt operates as a formidable obstacle to deviance which neutralizations cannot effectively reduce. Conversely, when commitment is low, guilt exists at levels susceptible to neutralization strategies" (p. 295).

One issue that has not been satisfactorily settled is when neutralization occurs. Sykes and Matza (1957) and social learning theory (Akers, 1985) contend that deviants must neutralize moral prescriptions prior to committing a crime. However, most research is incapable of determining whether the stated neutralization is a before-the-fact neutralization or an after-the-fact rationalization. As Hirschi (1969) surmises, an after-the-fact rationalization in one instance may be a causal neutralization in another instance. He states, "The assumption that delinquent acts come before justifying beliefs is the more plausible causal ordering" (p. 208).

While Sykes and Matza's work referred to juvenile offenders, subsequent research has found that adult offenders also make use of neutralization techniques (Nettler, 1974; Geis & Meier, 1977; Zeitz, 1981; Thurman, 1984; Coleman, 1985; Benson, 1985; Jesilow, Pontell, & Geis, 1993; Dabney, 1995; Gauthier, 2001). This appears to be particularly true for white-collar offenders whose otherwise conventional lifestyles and value systems would not countenance criminal involvement.

TECHNIQUES OF NEUTRALIZATION

Sykes and Matza (1957) identified five techniques of neutralization commonly offered to justify deviant behavior: *denial of responsibility, denial of the victim, denial of injury, condemning the condemners,* and *appeal to higher loyalties.*

Five additional neutralization techniques have since been identified. These include *defense of necessity* (Klockars, 1974), *metaphor of the ledger* (Minor, 1981), *denial of the necessity of the law, the claim that everybody else is doing it,* and *the claim of entitlement* (Coleman, 1994).

The purpose of this study is to determine the extent to which adult shoplifters use techniques of neutralizations and to analyze the various neutralizations available to them.

FINDINGS

The informants appeared to readily use neutralization techniques. We identified nine categories of neutralizations; the five Sykes and Matza categories, the *defense of necessity* and *everybody does it* neutralizations identified by Coleman (1994) and two additional neutralizations that we labeled *justification by comparison* and *postponement*. Only five of the 137 informants failed to express a rationalization or neutralization when asked how they felt about their illegal behavior. All but one stated that they felt that stealing was morally wrong. In many cases, the respondent offered more than one neutralization for the same offense. For example, one female respondent stated, "I don't know what comes over me. It's like, you know, it's somebody else doing it, not me" (denial of responsibility). "I'm really a good person. I wouldn't ever do something like that, stealing, you know, but I have to take things sometimes for my kids. They need stuff and I don't have any money to get it" (defense of necessity). They frequently responded with a motivation ("I wanted the item and could not afford it") followed by a neutralization ("Stores charge too much for stuff. They could sell things for half what they do and still make a profit. They're just too greedy"). Thus, in many cases, the motivation was linked to the excuse in such a way as to make the excuse a part of the motivation. The subjects were in effect explaining the reason the deviant act occurred and justifying it at the same time. The following section illustrates the neutralizations we discovered in use by the informants.

Denial of Responsibility (I Didn't Mean It)

Denial of responsibility frees the subject from experiencing culpability for deviance by allowing him or her to perceive themselves as victims of their environment. The offender views him- or herself as being acted upon rather than acting. Thus, attributing behavior to poor parenting, bad companions, or internal forces ("the devil made me do it") allows the offender to avoid disapproval of self or others, which in turn diminishes those influences as mechanisms of social control. Sykes and Matza (1957) describe the individual resorting to this neutralization as having a "billiard ball conception of himself in which he see himself as helplessly propelled into new situations" (p. 666).

> I admit that I lift. I do. But, you know, it's not really me—I mean, I don't believe in stealing. I'm a churchgoing person. It's just that sometimes something takes over me and I can't seem to not do it. It's like those TV shows where the person is dying and he goes out of his body and watches them trying to save him. That's sorta how I feel sometimes when I'm lifting. (26-year-old female)
>
> I wasn't raised right. You know what I mean? Wasn't nobody to teach me right from wrong. I just ran with a bad group and my mamma didn't ever say nothin' about it. That's how I turned out this way—stealin' and stuff. (22-year-old female)
>
> If I wasn't for the bunch I ran with at school, I never would have started taking things. We used to go the mall after school and everybody would have to steal something. If you didn't get anything, everybody called you names—chicken-shit and stuff like that. (20-year-old male)

Many of the shoplifter informants neutralized their activities citing loss of self-control due to alcohol or drug use. This is a common form of denial of responsibility. If not for the loss of inhibition due to drug or alcohol use, they argue, they would not commit criminal acts.

I was drinking with my buddies and we decided to go across the street to the [convenience store] and steal some beer. I was pretty wasted or I wouldn't done it. (19-year-old white male)

I never boost when I'm straight. It's the pills, you know? (30-year-old white female)

Denial of Injury (I Didn't Really Hurt Anybody)

Denial of injury allows the offender to perceive his or her behavior as having no direct harmful consequences to the victim. The victim may be seen as easily able to afford the loss (big store, insurance company, and wealthy person), or the crime may be semantically recast, as when auto theft is referred to as joyriding, or vandalism as a prank.

They [stores] big. Make lotsa money. They don't even miss the little bit I get. (19-year-old male)

They write it off their taxes. Probably make a profit off it. So, nobody gets hurt. I get what I need and they come out O.K. too. (28-year-old male)

Them stores make billions. Did you ever hear of Sears going out of business from boosters? (34-year-old female)

Denial of the Victim (They Had It Coming)

Denial of the victim facilitates deviance when it can be justified as retaliation upon a deserving victim. In the present study, informants frequently reported that the large stores from which they stole were deserving victims because of high prices and the perception that they made excessive profits at the expense of ordinary people. The shoplifters frequently asserted that the business establishments from which they stole overcharged consumers and thus deserved the payback from shoplifting losses.

Stores deserve it. It don't matter if I boost $10,000 from one, they've made ten thousand times that much ripping off people. You could never steal enough to get even. . . . I don't really think I'm doing anything wrong. Just getting my share. (48-year-old female)

Dillons [food store chain] are totally bogus. A little plastic bag of groceries is $30, $25. Probably cost them $5. . . . Whatta they care about me? Why should I care about them? I take what I want. Don't feel guilty a bit. No, sir. Not a bit. (29-year-old female)

I have a lot of anger about stores and the way they rip people off. Sometimes I think the consumer has to take things into their own hands. (49-year-old female)

Condemning the Condemners (The System Is Corrupt)

Condemning the condemners projects blame on lawmakers and law-enforcers. It shifts the focus from the offender to those who disapprove of his or her acts. This neutralization views the "system" as crooked and thus unable to justify making and enforcing rules it does not itself live by. Those who condemn their behavior are viewed as hypocritical since many of them engage in deviant behavior themselves.

> I've heard of cops and lawyers and judges and all kind of rich dudes boosting. They no better than me. You know what I'm saying. (18-year-old male)
>
> Big stores like J.C. Penney—when they catch me with something—like two pairs of pants, they tell the police you had like five pairs of pants and two shirts or something like that. You know what I'm saying? What they do with the other three pairs of pants and shirts? Insurance company pays them off and they get richer—they's bigger crooks than me. (35-year-old female)
>
> They thieves too. Just take it a different way. They may be smarter than me—use a computer or something like that—but they just as much a thief as me. Fuck 'em. Cops too. They all thieves. Least I'm honest about it. (22-year-old male)

Appeal to Higher Loyalties (I Didn't Do It for Myself)

Appeal to higher loyalties functions to legitimize deviant behavior when a nonconventional social bond creates more immediate and pressing demands than one consistent with conventional society. The most common use of this technique among the shoplifters was pressure from delinquent peers to shoplift and the perceived needs of one's family for items that the informant could not afford to buy. This was especially common with mothers shoplifting for items for their children.

> I never do it 'cept when I'm with my friends. Everybody be taking stuff and so I do too. You know—to be part of the group. Not to seem like I'm too good for 'em. (17-year-old female)
>
> I like to get nice stuff for my kids, you know. I know it's not O.K., you know what I mean? But, I want my kids to dress nice and stuff. (28-year-old female)

The Defense of Necessity

The defense of necessity (Coleman, 1998) serves to reduce guilt through the argument that the offender had no choice under the circumstances but to engage in a criminal act. In the case of shoplifting, the defense of necessity is most often used when the offender states that the crime was necessary to help one's family.

> I had to take care of three children without help. I'd be willing to steal it to give them what they wanted. (32-year-old female)
>
> I got laid off at Boeing last year and got behind on all my bills and couldn't get credit anywhere. My kids needed school clothes and money for supplies and stuff. We didn't have anything and I don't believe in going on welfare, you know. The first time I took some lunch meat at Dillons [grocery chain] so we'd have supper one night. After that I just started to take whatever we needed that day. I knew it was wrong, but I just didn't have any other choice. My family comes first. (42-year-old male)

Everybody Does It

Here the individual attempts to reduce his or her guilt feelings by arguing that the behavior in question is common (Coleman, 1998). A better label for this neutralization might be "diffusion of guilt." The behavior is justified or the guilt is diffused because of widespread similar acts.

Everybody I know do it. All my friends. My mother and her boyfriend are boosters and my sister is a big-time booster. (19-year-old female)

All my friends do it. When I'm with them it seems crazy not to take something too. (17-year-old male)

I bet you done did it too . . . when you was coming up. Like 12, 13 years old. Everybody boosts. (35-year-old female)

Justification by Comparison (If I Wasn't Shoplifting, I Would Be Doing Something More Serious)

This newly identified neutralization involves the offender justifying his/her actions by comparing his/her crimes to more serious offenses. While it might be argued that justification by comparison is not a neutralization in the strict Sykes and Matza sense, in that these offenders are not committed to conventional norms, they are nonetheless attempting to maintain their sense of self-worth by arguing that they could be worse or are not as bad as some others. Even persons with deviant lifestyles may experience guilt over their behavior and/or feel the necessity to justify their actions to others. The gist of the argument is that "I may be bad, but I could be worse."

I gotta have $200 every day—day in and day out. I gotta boost $1000, $1500 worth to get it. I just do what I gotta do. . . . Do I feel bad about what I do? Not really. If I wasn't boosting, I'd be robbing people and maybe somebody would get hurt or killed. (40-year-old male)

Looka here. Shoplifting be a little thing. Not a crime really. I do it 'stead of robbing folks or breaking in they house. [Society] oughta be glad I boost, stead of them other things. (37-year-old male)

It's nothing. Not like it's "jacking" people or something. It's just a little lifting. (19-year-old male)

Postponement

In a previous study, one of the present authors (Thurman, 1984) suggested that further research should consider the excuse strategy of postponement, by which the offender suppresses his or her guilt feelings—momentarily putting them out of mind to be dealt with at a later time. We found this strategy to be a common occurrence among our informants. They made frequent statements that indicated that they simply put the incident out of their mind. Some stated that they would deal with it later when they were not under so much stress.

I just don't think about it. I mean, if you think about it, it seems wrong, but you can ignore that feeling sometimes. Put it aside and go on about what you gotta do. (18-year-old male)

Dude, I just don't deal with those kinda things when I'm boosting. I might feel bad about it later, you know, but by then it's already over and I can't do anything about it then, you know? (18-year-old male)

I worry about things like that later. (30-year-old female)

DISCUSSION AND CONCLUSION

We found widespread use of neutralizations among the shoplifters in our study. Even those who did not appear to be committed to the conventional moral order used neutralizations to justify or excuse their behavior. Their use of neutralizations was not so much to assuage guilt but to provide them with the necessary justifications for their acts to others. Simply because one is not committed to conventional norms does not preclude their understanding that most members of society do accept those values and expect others to do so as well. They may also use neutralizations and rationalizations to provide them with a convincing defense for their crimes that they can tell to more conventionally oriented others if the need arises.

As stated earlier, our research approach could not determine whether the informants neutralized before committing the crime or rationalized afterwards. We suggest, however, that Hirschi (1969) was correct in stating that a postcrime rationalization may serve as a precrime neutralization the next time a crime is contemplated. Whether neutralization allows the offender to mitigate guilt feelings before the crime is committed or afterwards, the process still occurs. Once an actor has reduced his or her guilt feelings through the use of techniques of neutralization, he or she can continue to offend, assuaging guilt feelings and cognitive dissonance both before and after each offense. It would follow that continued utilization of neutralization and rationalization habitually over time might serve to weaken the social bond, reducing the need to neutralize at all.

Our exploratory study of shoplifters' use of neutralization techniques also suggests that neutralization (theory) may not be so much a theory of crime but rather a description of a process that represents an adaptation to morality that leads to criminal persistence. Neutralization focuses on how crime is possible, rather than why people might choose to engage in it in the first place. In a sense, neutralization serves as a form of situational morality. While the offender knows an act is morally wrong (either in his or her eyes or in the eyes of society), he or she makes an adaptation to convention that permits deviation under certain circumstances (the various neutralizations discussed). Whether the adaptation is truly neutralizing (before the act) or rationalizing (after the act) the result is the same—crime without guilt.

REFERENCES

Akers, R. (1985). *Deviant behavior: A social learning approach.* Belmont, CA: Wadsworth.

Austin, R. L. (1977). Commitment, neutralization and delinquency. In T. N. Ferdinand (Ed.), *Juvenile delinquency: Little brother grows up* (pp. 121–137). Newbury Park, CA: Sage.

Becker, H. S. (1963). *Outsiders: Studies in the sociology of deviance.* New York: Free Press.

Benson, M. (1985). Denying the guilty mind: Accounting for involvement in white-collar crime. *Criminology, 23*(4), 589–599.

Cameron, M. (1964). *The booster and the snitch.* New York: Free Press.

Coleman, J. W. (1985). *The criminal elite: The sociology of white collar crime*. New York: St. Martin's.

———. (1994). Neutralization theory: An empirical application and assessment. Ph.D. diss., Oklahoma State University.

———. (1998). *Criminal elite: Understanding white collar crime*. New York: St. Martin's.

Dabney, D. (1995). Neutralization and deviance in the workplace: Theft of supplies and medicines by hospital nurses. *Deviant Behavior, 116*, 312–321.

Freeh, L. (1996). *Crime in the United States—1995*. Washington, DC: U.S. Department of Justice.

Gauthier, D. K. (2001). Professional lapses: Occupational deviance and neutralization techniques in veterinary medical practice. *Deviant Behavior, 21*, 467–490.

Geis, G., & Meier, R. (1977). *White collar crime*. New York: Free Press.

Griffin, R. (1988). *Annual report: Shoplifting in supermarkets*. Van Nuys, CA: Commercial Service Systems.

Hirschi, T. (1969). *Causes of delinquency*. Berkeley: University of California Press.

Jesilow, P., Pontell, H. M., & Geis, G. (1993). *Prescriptions for profit: How doctors defraud Medicaid*. Berkeley, CA: University of California Press.

Klemke, L. W. (1992). *The sociology of shoplifting: Boosters and snitches today*. Westport, CT: Praeger.

Klockars, C. B. (1974). *The professional fence*. New York: Free Press.

Lo, L. (1994). Exploring teenage shoplifting behavior. *Environment and Behavior, 26*(5), 613–639.

Mannle, H. W., & Lewis, P. W. (1979). Control theory reexamined: Race and the use of neutralizations among institutionalized delinquents. *Criminology, 17*(1), 58–74.

Minor, W. W. (1981). Techniques of neutralization: A reconceptualization and empirical examination. *Journal of Research in Crime and Delinquency, 18*, 295–318.

Nettler, G. (1974). Embezzlement without problems. *British Journal of Criminology, 14*, 70–77.

Nimick, E. (1990). Juvenile court property cases. In U.S. Department of Justice (Ed.), *OJJDP Update on Statistics* (pp. 1–5). Washington, DC: U.S. Department of Justice.

Russell, D. H. (1973). Emotional aspects of shoplifting. *Psychiatric Annals, 3*, 77–79.

Sykes, G. M., & Matza, D. (1957). Techniques of neutralization: A theory of delinquency. *American Sociological Review, 22*(6), 664–670.

Thurman, Q. C. (1984). Deviance and neutralization of moral commitment: An empirical analysis. *Deviant Behavior, 5*, 291–304.

Turner, C. T., & Cashdan, S. (1988). Perceptions of college students' motivations for shoplifting. *Psychological Reports, 62*, 855–862.

Wilson, W. J. (1987). *The truly disadvantaged*. Chicago: University of Chicago Press.

Zeitz, D. (1981). *Women who embezzle or defraud: A study of convicted felons*. New York: Praeger.

CHAPTER 8

Identity Theft: Assessing Offenders' Motivations and Strategies

Heith Copes and Lynne Vieraitis

Despite rates of identity theft, little is known about those who engage in this crime. The current study is exploratory in nature and is designed to shed light on the offenders' perspectives. To do this, we interviewed 59 identity thieves incarcerated in federal prisons. Results show that identity thieves are a diverse group, hailing from both working-class and middle-class backgrounds. Nearly half of those we interviewed led lifestyles similar to those of persistent street offenders. The rest used the proceeds of their crimes to live "respectable" middle-class lives. Regardless of their chosen lifestyle, offenders were primarily motivated by the quick need for cash and saw identity theft as an easy, relatively risk-free way to get it. They employed a variety of methods to both acquire information and convert it to cash. The most common methods of acquiring information were to buy it from others, steal it from mailboxes or trashcans, or obtain it from people they knew. Identity thieves developed a set of skills to enable them to be successful at their crimes. These skills included social skills, technical skills, intuitive skills, and system knowledge. By developing these skills they thought they could commit identity theft with impunity.

Over the past several years, the United States has enjoyed a significant decline in rates of serious street crime. However, crimes of fraud continue to increase and with emerging opportunities for economic crime this trend is expected to continue (Shover & Hochstetler, 2006). In the last 10 years, one form of

Source: Excerpted and adapted from Copes, H., & Vieraitis, L. (2007). *Identity theft: Assessing offenders' strategies and perceptions of risk.* Project funded by the National Institute of Justice, Grant # 2005-IJ-CX-0012. For a complete version of the study, go to http://www.ncjrs.gov/App/Publications/Abstract.aspx?ID=240910. Used with permission of the authors.

fraud, identity theft, has garnered America's attention as it became one of the most common economic crimes in the nation (Bernstein, 2004; Perl, 2003). According to recent data from the Federal Trade Commission, 685,000 complaints of fraud were reported in 2005. Thirty-seven percent of these complaints (255,565) were for identity theft, making it the most prevalent form of fraud in the United States (Federal Trade Commission [FTC], 2006).

To combat these rising rates, Congress passed the Identity Theft and Assumption Deterrence Act (ITADA) in 1998. According to ITADA, it is unlawful if a person:

> knowingly transfers or uses, without lawful authority, a means of identification of another person with the intent to commit, or to aid or abet, any unlawful activity that constitutes a violation of Federal law, or that constitutes a felony under any applicable State or local law.

This law made identity theft a separate crime against the person whose identity was stolen, broadened the scope of the offense to include the misuse of information and documents, and provided punishment of up to 15 years of imprisonment and a maximum fine of $250,000. Under U.S. Sentencing Commission guidelines a sentence of 10 to 16 months incarceration can be imposed even if there is no monetary loss and the perpetrator has no prior criminal convictions (U.S. General Accounting Office, 2002).

In 2004, the Identity Theft Penalty Enhancement Act established a new federal crime, aggravated identity theft. Aggravated identity theft prohibits the knowing and unlawful transfer, possession, or use of a means of identification of another person during and in relation to any of more than 100 felony offenses, including mail, bank, and wire fraud; immigration and passport fraud; and any unlawful use of a Social Security number. The law mandates a minimum two years in prison consecutive to the sentence for the underlying felony. In addition, if the offense is committed during and in relation to one of the more than 40 federal terrorism-related felonies, the penalty is a minimum mandatory five years in prison consecutive to the sentence for the underlying felony.

Identity theft occurs when a criminal appropriates an individual's personal information such as name, address, date of birth, or Social Security number to assume that person's identity to commit theft or multiple types of fraud. Identity thieves utilize a variety of methods to acquire victims' identities, most of which are "low-tech" (Newman & McNally, 2005). These methods include stealing wallets or purses, dumpster diving, stealing mail from residential and business mailboxes, and buying information on the street or from employees with access to personal information. More sophisticated methods or "high-tech" methods include hacking into corporate computers and stealing customer and/or employee databases, skimming, and using the Internet to purchase information from websites or trick consumers into divulging account information (Newman & McNally, 2005).

By exploiting personal and financial information, an identity thief can obtain a person's credit history; access existing financial accounts; file false tax returns; open new credit accounts, bank accounts, charge accounts, and utility accounts; enter into a residential lease; and even obtain additional false identification documents such as a duplicate driver's license, birth certificate, or passport. Identity theft also occurs when an offender commits crimes in the victim's name and gives that person a criminal record. Identity thieves may use the victim's personal information "to evade legal sanctions and criminal records (thus leaving the victim with a wrongful criminal or other legal record)" (Perl, 2003).

Although estimates of the costs vary, identity theft is one of the most expensive financial crimes in America, costing consumers an estimated $5 billion and businesses $48 billion each year. The FTC Identity Theft Clearinghouse estimates the total financial cost of identity theft to be over $50 billion a year, with the average loss to businesses being $4,800 per incident and an average of $500 to the victim whose identity is misused (FTC, 2006).

Despite the fact that identity theft is one of the fastest-growing economic crimes in the United States, researchers have devoted little attention to understanding those who engage in this offense. To date, no one has conducted a systematic examination of a sample of offenders to ascertain a reliable or comprehensive picture of identity theft and how it can be controlled more effectively (for an exception, see Allison, Schuck, & Lersch, 2005). The goal of the current research is to explore the offenders' perspectives. Through semi-structured interviews with 59 identity thieves incarcerated in federal prisons, we examine their life experiences and criminal careers, the apparent rewards and risks of identity theft, and measures employed to carry out their crime. Because so little is known about those who commit identity theft, the current study is exploratory and is designed to act as a springboard for future research on identity theft.

DESCRIPTIVE STATISTICS

The common perception of identity thieves is that they are more akin to white-collar fraudsters than they are to street-level property offenders. That is, they hail disproportionately from the middle classes, they are college educated, and they have stable family lives. To determine if identity thieves, at least the ones we interviewed, resemble other fraudsters, we collected various demographic characteristics, including age, race, gender, employment status, and educational achievement. We also asked offenders about their socioeconomic status, family status, and criminal history, including prior arrests, convictions, and drug use. Overall, we found identity theft to be quite democratic, with participants from all walks of life. In fact, they were just as likely to resemble persistent street offenders as they were middle-class fraudsters.

Gender, Race/Ethnicity, and Age

Our final sample of 59 inmates included 23 men and 36 women. This discrepancy in gender is likely a result of our sampling strategy and the higher response rate from female inmates rather than the actual proportion of identity theft offenders.

In addition, more males were unavailable for interviews because of disciplinary problems and/or prison lockdowns. Offenders in our sample ranged in age from 23 to 60 years, with a mean age of 38 years. They included 18 white females, 16 black females, two Asian females, eight white males, and 15 black males.

MOTIVATIONS FOR IDENTITY THEFT

Numerous studies of street-level property offenders and fraudsters find that the primary motivation for instigating these events is the need for money (Shover, 1996; Shover, Coffey, & Sanders, 2004; Wright & Decker, 1994). When asked what prompted their criminal involvement, the overwhelming response was money. Lawrence probably best reflects this belief: "It's all about the money. That's all it's about. It's all about the money. If there ain't no money, it don't make sense." Indeed, identity theft is financially rewarding. Gladys estimated that she could make "$2000 in three days." Lawrence made even larger claims: "I'll put it to you like this, forging checks, counterfeiting checks . . . in an hour, depending on the proximity of the banks—the banks that you're working—I have made $7000 in one hour." These estimates were consistent with those given by other offenders in the sample and with previous estimates (Bureau of Justice Statistics, 2006).

Although estimates on how much they made from their crimes varied widely among respondents, most brought in incomes greater than they could have earned with the types of legitimate work they were qualified for or from other illegal enterprises. In fact, several of them described how they gave up other criminal endeavors for identity theft because they could make more money. When asked why she stopped selling drugs, Bridgette answered, "[Selling drugs is] not the answer. That's not where the money is." Dale switched from burglaries to identity theft arguing, "[Identity theft] is easier and you keep the money, you know. You keep a lot of money."

But how did they spend the money gained through their illegal enterprises? Ethnographic studies of street offenders indicate that few "mentioned needing money for subsistence" (Wright, Brookman, & Bennett, 2006, p. 6). This was also true for the majority of those with whom we spoke. Jacob said that he spent most of his money on "a lot of nice clothes." When asked what he did with the money, Lawrence replied, "Partying. Females. I gave a lot of money away. I bought a lot of things." Finally Carlos said, "We're spending it pretty much as fast as we can get it, you know?" The majority of them spent the money on luxury items, drugs, and partying.

But not all identity thieves were so frivolous with their proceeds. In fact, many of them claimed that they spent money on everyday items. When asked what he did with the money, Jake answered, "Nothing more than living off it, putting it away, saving it. . . . Nothing flashy. Just living off it." Similarly, Bonnie responded, "Just having extra money to do things with . . . but nothing extravagant or anything like that." Oscar simply stated, "Just pay bills, you know."

Identity thieves used the proceeds of their crimes to fund their chosen life-styles. Much has been written describing the self-indulgent lifestyles of persistent street offenders. Of the 54 for which we had information about their lifestyle, 23 led lifestyles similar to persistent street offenders. Like their street offender counterparts, these individuals led a "life of party." Proceeds were more likely to be spent maintaining partying lifestyles filled with drug use and fast living than putting money aside for long-term plans. Bridgette explained succinctly why she committed identity theft: "Getting money and getting high." This lifestyle was described by Lawrence:

> I made a lot of money and lost a lot of money. It comes in and you throw it out.
> . . . A lot of people put things in their names. . . . Back and forth to Miami, to Atlanta. I mean it's a party. . . . Just to party, go to clubs, strip clubs and stuff. Just to party.

The ease with which money was made and spent is reflected in the words of Sheila:

> I was eating great food, buying clothes, going shopping, getting my hair done, you know, wasting it. I wish I would have bought a house or something like that, but it probably would have got taken away anyways.

However, not all indulged in such a lifestyle. In fact, some showed restraint in their spending. Nearly half of those we had lifestyle information on used the money they gained from identity theft to support what could be considered conventional lives ($n = 24$). In addition, seven others could be classified as drifting between a party lifestyle and a more conventional one. These offenders made efforts to conceal their misdeeds from their friends and family and to present a law-abiding front to outsiders. They used the proceeds of identity theft to finance comfortable middle-class lives, including paying rent or mortgages, buying expensive vehicles, and splurging on the latest technological gadgets. Bruce engaged in identity theft "to maintain an upper-class lifestyle. To be able to ride in first class, the best hotels, the best everything." Their lifestyles were in line with the telemarketers interviewed by Shover, Coffey, and Sanders (2004). This is not to say that they did not indulge in the trappings of drugs and partying. Many did. As Denise explains, "I didn't do a lot of partying. I bought a lot of weed, paid out a lot, kept insurance going and the car note, put stereos in my car." Nevertheless, they put forth an image of middle-class respectability.

Offenders have a variety of options when seeking means to fund their chosen lifestyles. Regardless of their lifestyle, offenders are often confronted with a perceived need for quick cash. This was certainly true for the identity thieves we spoke with, regardless of their lifestyle. These self-defined desperate situations included drug habits, gambling debts, family crises, and loss of jobs. Shover's (1996, p. 100) description is applicable here: "Confronted by crisis and preoccupied increasingly with relieving immediate distress, the offender may experience and define himself as propelled by forces beyond his control." Edgar succinctly described why he engaged in identity theft: "Poverty. Poverty makes you do things." When asked how she got involved in identity theft, Sherry explained, "Well, let's see. I had been laid off at work, my son was in trouble, about to go to jail. I needed money for a lawyer." Sylvia described the situations that led her to start her crimes:

> I had a mortgage company that went under. My partner embezzled a bunch of money. Certain events happened and you find yourself out there almost to be homeless, and I knew people that did this, but they never went to jail. And back then they didn't go to jail, so it was a calculated risk I took.

In the face of mounting financial problems, she, like other identity thieves, thought identity theft could offer hope of relief, even if only temporarily.

For those who were addicted to alcohol or other drugs ($n = 22$), their addictions led them to devote increasing time and energy to the quest for monies to fund their habits. For identity thieves, as for other offenders, the inability to draw on legitimate or low-risk resources eventually may precipitate a crisis that they believe can only be relieved through crime. Penni explained, "I started smoking meth and then when I started smoking meth, I stopped working, and then I started doing this for money." In explaining how she and her husband relapsed into drug use, Sherry said, "My husband had lost his job at [an airline] and I was working at a doctor's office, and then I lost my job. So we were both on unemployment." The loss of both sources of income set them onto a path of drug use and identity theft. Finally, Heidi claimed that her relapse precipitated her crimes. In her words, "I was clean for three and a half years before I relapsed on methamphetamines, and that's what brought me back into this."

In addition to the financial rewards of identity theft, there are also intrinsic ones. Criminologists should not forget that crime can be fun and exciting (Katz, 1988). Eleven interviewees mentioned that they found identity theft "fun" or "exciting." These offenders said that they enjoyed the "adrenaline rush" provided by entering banks and stores and by "getting over" on people. Bruce describes what it was like going into banks, "It was fairly exciting to ... I mean, every time you went to a retail establishment and you gave them the credit card, you don't know what's going to happen." Similarly, Cori described, "It's just, it was, it was like a rush. ... At first it was kind of fun. The lifestyle is addicting, you know." Bridgette described what it was like: "It was like a high. ... It's all about getting over." When asked to describe the rush he felt from engaging in identity theft, Lawrence replied:

> It's money. It's knowing I'm getting over on them. Knowing I can manipulate the things and the person I got going in there. It's everything. It wasn't just ... I guess you can say it is a little fear, but it's not fear for me, though. It's fear for the person I got going in there. I don't know. It's kind of weird. I don't know how to explain it. ... But it's the rush. Knowing that I created this thing to manipulate these banks, you know what I'm saying? They're going to pay me for it and I'm going to manipulate this dude out of the money when they cashing those checks.

Dustin attributed his continuance with identity theft to the thrill:

> I like to go out with money. But eventually it got to the point where I didn't need money. I was just doing it for the high. But that is basically what it was. The rush of standing there in her face and lying. [Laughter.] That's what it was. I'm being honest. I didn't need the money. I had plenty.

But even for these individuals, except Dustin, the thrill factor of identity theft was a secondary motivation to the money. Thrills alone did not instigate or propel identity theft. It is possible, however, that offenders persisted with identity theft because of the excitement of these crimes.

Previous reports on identity theft have pointed out that some of these crimes are precipitated by the desire to hide from the law or to get utilities or phone service activated (Newman, 2004). Only three people with whom we spoke mentioned such reasons. Jolyn told us that she had a warrant out so she used another's identity to get a telephone. Although her crimes started as a means to get telephone services, she eventually used this information to garner Social Security benefits. Additionally, Jamie said, "I needed my utilities on. [I did it] for that reason. I've never used it as far as applying for a credit card, though, because I knew that was a no."

METHODS AND TECHNIQUES OF IDENTITY THEFT

Acquiring Information

Offenders in our sample utilized a variety of methods to procure information and then convert this information into cash and/or goods. In fact, most did not specialize in a single method; instead, they preferred to use a variety of strategies. Although some offenders in our sample acquired identities from their place of employment (35%), mainly mortgage companies, the most common method of obtaining a victim's information was to buy it ($n = 13$). Offenders in our sample bought identities from employees of various businesses and state agencies who had access to personal information such as name, address, date of birth, and Social Security number ($n = 5$). Information was purchased from employees of banks, credit agencies, a state law enforcement agency, mortgage companies, state departments of motor vehicles, hospitals, doctor's offices, a university, car dealerships, and furniture stores. Those buying information said that it was easy to find someone willing to sell them what they wanted. According to Gladys, "It's so easy to get information, and everybody has a price." Penni said:

> People that work at a lot of places, they give you a lot of stuff . . . hospitals, DMV, like Wal-Mart, a lot of places, like [local phone company]. People fill out applications. A lot of stuff like that, and you get it from a lot of people. There's a lot of tweekers [drug addicts] out there, and everybody's trying to make a dollar and always trading something for something.

When describing how she obtained information from a bank employee, Kristin said:

> She was willing to make some money too, so she had the good information. She would have the information that would allow me to have a copy of the signature card, passwords, work address, everything, everything that's legit.

Eight offenders who purchased information did so from persons they knew or who they were acquainted with "on the streets." Lawrence explained, "[People on the streets] knew what I was buying. I mean any city, there's always somebody buying some information." The identity thieves bought information from other offenders who obtained it from burglaries, thefts from motor vehicles, prostitution, and pickpocketing. One offender purchased information from boyfriends or girlfriends of the victims. For the most part, those with whom we spoke did not know nor care where their sellers obtained their information. As long as the information was good they asked no questions.

Five individuals obtained information by using the mailbox method, and another two got information by searching trashcans. Those offenders typically stole mail from small businesses such as insurance companies or from residential mailboxes in front of homes or apartments. Some offenders simply drove through residential areas and pulled mail out, often taking steps to appear to be legitimate, that is, they placed flyers advertising a business in mailboxes. Mailboxes and trashcans for businesses that send out mail with personal information (account numbers, Social Security numbers, and date of birth) such as insurance companies were also popular targets.

Although most of the offenders we interviewed did not know their victims, of those who did six said that the victim willingly gave them the information in exchange for a cut of the profits. In these cases, the "victim" gave the offender information to commit the identity theft and then reported that their identity had been stolen. According to Lawrence, "What I did was I had got this guy's personal information, he actually willingly gave it to me." Five offenders used family members' information without their knowledge, and in one case the information was on family members who were deceased. Another five stole from friends or acquaintances without their knowledge.

Other methods of acquiring victims' information included various thefts (house and car burglary, purse-snatching) ($n = 3$) and socially engineering people to get their information ($n = 2$). One individual set up a fake employment site to get information from job applicants. Another used the birth announcements in newspapers to get the names of new parents and, posing as an insurance representative, called the parents to get information for "billing purposes." Interestingly, the offender made the phone calls from the waiting room of the hospitals where the infants were born so that the name of the hospital would appear on the victims' caller ID if they had it. Another offender used rogue Internet sites to run background checks and order credit reports on potential victims.

In addition, nine individuals claimed to work in a group where others obtained information. These thieves chose not to ask where the information came from.

Converting Information

After they obtain a victim's information the offender must convert that information to cash or goods. Most commonly, offenders used the information to acquire or produce additional identity-related documents such as driver's licenses or state identification cards. Some offenders created the cards themselves with software and materials, for example, paper and ink, purchased at office supply stores or given to them by an employee of a state department of motor vehicles. Other offenders knew someone or had someone working for them who produced IDs. Identification cards were needed to withdraw cash from the victim's existing bank account or to open a new account.

Offenders used a variety of methods to profit from the stolen identities. The most common strategies were applying for credit cards in the victims' names (including major credit cards and department store credit cards), opening new bank accounts and depositing counterfeit checks, withdrawing money from existing bank accounts, applying for loans, and applying for public assistance programs. Identity thieves often used more than one technique when cashing in on their crimes.

The most common strategy for converting stolen identities into cash was by applying for credit cards. Twenty-three offenders used the information to order new credit cards. In a few cases, the information was used to get the credit card agency to issue a duplicate card on an existing account. They used credit cards to buy merchandise for their own personal use, to resell the merchandise to friends and/or acquaintances, or to return the merchandise for cash. Offenders also used the checks that are routinely sent to credit card holders to deposit in the victim's account and then withdraw cash or to open new accounts. Offenders also applied for store credit cards at places such as department stores and home improvement stores. According to Emma:

> [I would] go to different department stores, or most often it was Lowes or Home Depot, go in, fill out an application with all the information, and then receive instant credit in the amount from say $1,500 to $7,500. Every store is different. Every individual is different. And then at that time, I would purchase as much as that balance that I could at one time. So if it was $2,500, I would buy $2,500 worth of merchandise.

Another common strategy is to produce counterfeit checks. Sixteen offenders either made fraudulent checks on their own or knew someone who would produce these checks for them. Although most offenders who counterfeited checks made personal checks, others made insurance checks or payroll checks. They cashed these checks at grocery stores, purchased merchandise, and paid bills such as utilities or cell phones.

Sometimes identity thieves would use the stolen identities to either open new bank accounts as a way to deposit fraudulent checks or to withdraw money from an existing account. Sixteen of the people we interviewed used this approach.

Using this strategy required the offender to have information about the victims' bank account.

Another method of conversion included applying for and receiving loans. Fourteen individuals used this strategy. The majority of those who applied for loans engaged in some type of mortgage fraud. These types of scams often involved using victims' information to purchase homes for themselves. In one case, the offenders were buying houses and then renting them for a profit. Others applied for various auto loans, home equity loans, or personal loans.

SKILL SETS

As with any behavior, skills improve with experience. With practice, persistent burglars learn to assess the risks and value of homes almost instantaneously, crack dealers and prostitutes learn to discern undercover officers, and hustlers learn to recognize potential marks. Identity thieves have also developed a skill set to successfully accomplish their crimes. Four broad categories of skills emerged in our analysis of the interviews: (1) social skills, (2) intuitive skills, (3) technical skills, and (4) system knowledge.

Good social skills are perhaps the most important skills that identity thieves claim to possess. Social skills are the ability to manipulate the social situation through verbal and nonverbal communication. To be successful, an identity thief must possess the ability to "pass" as a regular customer in stores and banks and "be" the person they claim to be. This ability allows identity thieves to construct a larcenous situation as real and remove any doubts about the legitimacy of the situation. Identity thieves accomplish this through dress, mannerisms, and speech. When questioned as to what skills make a "good" identity thief, Gladys responded:

> I mean I can go into a place. . . . Knowing how to look the part in certain situations . . . you go up to a place and you look in there and get the feeling about how a person would look, and I'd take off a ring or something, put on a ring, take off some of your make-up, or go put on a hat or a scarf, put some glasses on.

Bridgette also made sure that whomever she sent into the bank was dressed to appear to be the person he/she claimed to be.

> I always made them dress accordingly, if you're going in to cash an insurance check, I want to dress nice and casual. If you were cashing a payroll check, you got to wear a uniform. I always try to find a uniform that match whatever company we were using. With the lab tech, we went right to the uniform shop and got it, the little nurse scrub sets and everything.

Tameka also "dressed" the part, "I might have on a nurse uniform, a lot of these they had me on I had on a nurse uniform." In describing what it was like interacting with bank and store employees, Bruce, an experienced thief, said:

> You definitely have to be adaptable. It's not even being pleasant with people. It's just having authority. You have to have authority of whatever situation you are

in. And if you have that authority, people will not go any further than to peripherally question you. That's about it.

Emma explained:

> I would just act as if I were that person and I would go in and I'd be talking to
> the person processing the application and, say if it were at Home Depot, I would
> be saying, "Oh, we're doing some remodeling of our home" or something like
> that, and I'd engage the people.

The ability to socially engineer people and situations is especially important
when things go wrong. When describing how she would conduct herself in a
bank when questioned by employees, Tameka said:

> If it was a tricky question, you should be able to talk to the bank manager, cause
> there were times when I asked to speak to the manager if I was withdrawing a
> large sum of money. In essence, you had to become these people.

A second skill that identity thieves develop is intuitive skills, which can be
defined as "an acute sensitization to and awareness of one's external surrounding"
(Faupel, 1986). Some offenders superstitiously believed they have developed the
ability to sense trouble, believing that if they do not "feel bad" about a crime, then
they are safe. April replied, "You kind of get, I don't know, almost like you dreaded
walking into it." The ability to recognize criminal opportunity, sense danger, and
know when to call off a criminal plan has been referred to as "larceny sense," "grift
sense," and "intuitive sense" (Faupel, 1986; Maurer, 1951; Sutherland, 1937). When
asked how he got better at identity theft, Bruce responded:

> Sensing . . . sensing what was going on within a situation, like at a bank, like I
> could sense what was going on with tellers. I could tell how they were looking at
> the screen, how long they were looking at it, and I could sense whether some-
> thing had been written or if I was cashing too many checks. Just a sense of how
> people react in situations and then also just the situations themselves. As many
> as they presented themselves, I would find a way around them. So I guess just
> honing the thinking on your feet . . . in the situations that came up.

Several offenders in this study believed they would not have been caught if
they had paid attention to their premonitions. For instance, Kimi described the
moments before she was arrested:

> I knew the detectives were watching. I knew that and I had the feeling and I told
> [my co-defendant], but he was trying to kick heroin that day. And this stupid
> fool was shooting, and I'm all surrounded by heroin addicts. So one person, up
> all night, she was smoking meth and smoking weed, but everyone else was
> shooting heroin, and I'm surrounded by them. And I told him, I said, we got to
> leave. I have this freaking feeling something's going to go wrong.

Whether or not repeat offenders have a heightened ability to sense danger is
less important than the fact that many believe they do.

A third type of skill identity thieves develop are technical skills. This refers to the technical knowledge needed to produce fraudulent documents such as identification, checks, and credit applications. Making these documents look real is an increasingly difficult task. For example, determining the right types of paper to print checks on, how to replicate watermarks, and matching the colors on driver's licenses are necessary skills that must be learned. Lawrence described:

> I use a different type of paper. I use a regular document. The paper always came straight from the bank. A lot of people, they would get paper out of like Target or Office Max or places like that. That kind of paper right there, it's not always efficient. Nine times out of 10, the bank may stop it. They want to check the company payroll.

Although many identity thieves contract out for their documents, a sizable number learn these tricks through experimentation and practice. Kimi described her process:

> We studied IDs, then I went to the stamp shop, the paint shop, got the logos right, and I know the [bank] was one of the hardest banks for us to get money out, but when I found out about the logos, when I passed it through the black light, it became real easy. . . . I went to the stamp shop and bought a stamp and sat there for hours and hours with the colors, and I made like seven different IDs before it come through under the black light.

The final skill discussed by identity thieves is system knowledge. This includes knowing how banks and credit agencies operate and knowing which stores require identification when cashing checks. Sherry said:

> You have to have an idea of how banks work. At some point in your life, live a normal life and understand how credit is extended and things like that.
>   I was a bank teller. I knew how to approach a person. I knew the insights, you know, what they would look for, how much I could get, when to go out. (Sheila)

The development of these various skills plays an important role in crime persistence. By developing these skills, identity thieves increase their chances of being successful at crime; that is, these skills allow them to avoid the formal sanctions associated with identity theft. Those who commit crime with impunity have overly optimistic views of their crimes (Cusson, 1993; Paternoster et al., 1982), which was the case for many of those we interviewed. Offenders came to believe that they could continue offending because they could rely on their skills to evade sanctions, thereby nullifying the deterrent effects of criminal sanctions.

CONCLUSION

Our interviews with 59 offenders incarcerated in federal prisons revealed information about their motivations for identity theft and the methods they employ to acquire information and convert it into cash and/or goods. Results show that identity thieves are a diverse group. Offenders are primarily motivated by the quick need for cash and see identity theft as an easy, relatively risk-free way to get it. They employ a variety of methods to both acquire information and convert it to cash and have developed a set of skills to enable them to do so successfully.

REFERENCES

Allison, S. F. H., Schuck, A. M., & Lersch, K. M. (2005). Exploring the crime of identity theft: Prevalence, clearance rates, and victim/offender characteristics. *Journal of Criminal Justice, 33,* 19–29.

Bernstein, S, E. (2004). New privacy concern for employee benefit plans: Combating identity theft. *Compensation and Benefits Review, 36,* 65–68.

Bureau of Justice Statistics. (2006). *Identity theft, 2004* (NCJ 212213). Washington, DC: U.S. Department of Justice.

Cusson, M. (1993). Situational deterrence: Fear during the criminal event. In R. Clarke (Ed.), *Crime prevention studies* (Vol. 1, pp. 55–68). Monsey, NY: Willow Tree.

Faupel, C. E. (1986). Heroin use, street crime, and the "main hustle": Implications for the validity of official crime data. *Deviant Behavior, 7,* 31–45.

Federal Trade Commission (FTC). (2006). *Consumer fraud and identity theft complaint data: January–December 2005.* Retrieved December 9, 2008, from http://www.consumer .gov/sentinel/pubs/Top10Fraud2005.pdf.

Katz, J. (1988). *Seductions of crime.* New York: Basic.

Maurer, D. W. (1951). *Whiz mob: A correlation of the technical argot of pickpockets with their behavior patterns.* Gainesville, FL: American Dialect Society.

Newman, G. R. (2004). *Identity theft.* Washington, DC: U.S. Department of Justice.

Newman, G. R., & McNally, M. M. (2005). *Identity theft literature review.* Presented at the National Institute of Justice Focus Group Meeting. Retrieved December 9, 2008, from http://www.ncjrs.gov/pdffiles1/nij/grants/210459.pdf.

Paternoster, R., Saltzman, L., Chiricos, T., & Waldo, G. (1982). Perceived risk and deterrence: Methodological artifacts in perceptual deterrence research. *Journal of Criminal Law and Criminology, 73,* 1238–1258.

Perl, M. W. (2003). It's not always about the money: Why the state identity theft laws fail to address criminal record identity theft. *Journal of Criminal Law and Criminology, 94,* 169–208.

Shover, N. (1996). *Great pretenders: Pursuits and careers of persistent thieves.* Boulder, CO: Westview.

Shover, N., Coffey, G., & Sanders, C. (2004). Dialing for dollars: Opportunities, justifications and telemarketing fraud. *Qualitative Sociology, 27,* 59–75.

Shover, N., & Hochstetler, A. (2006). *Choosing white-collar crime.* Cambridge, UK: Cambridge University Press.

Sutherland, E. (1937). *The professional thief.* Chicago: University of Chicago Press.

U.S. General Accounting Office. (2002). *Identity theft: Prevalence and cost appear to be growing.* GAO 02–363. Washington, DC: Author.

Wright, R. T., Brookman, F., & Bennett, T. (2006). The foreground dynamics of street robbery in Britain. *British Journal of Criminology, 46,* 1–15.

Wright, R., & Decker, S. (1994). *Burglars on the job.* Boston: Northeastern University Press.

Violent Crime

While the last section examined property crimes, Section IV takes a look at violent crime. According to the FBI's Uniform Crime Reporting Program, violent crime is composed of four offenses: murder and nonnegligent manslaughter, forcible rape, robbery, and aggravated assault. Violent crimes such as robbery, assault, and murder have profoundly affected the way we live and have clearly altered our lifestyles. In 2014, over 1.1 million violent crimes were reported to police nationwide. This represents a slight decrease compared with 2013 numbers (Federal Bureau of Investigation, 2014).

Violent crime is often considered less rationally conceived than property crime. Violent behavior is often expressed in the "heat of passion," during periods of great emotional turmoil. The violent act is thought to be more expressive than instrumental, having no real functional purpose or acceptable rationale. However, as the three studies featured in this section demonstrate, violent crime has both expressive and instrumental roots. These chapters discuss the motives for offenders' behavior, strategies they use to accomplish their crimes, and rationalizations used to avoid responsibility for their acts.

The first article in this section, Kristin L. Anderson and Debra Umberson's "Gendering Violence: Masculinity and Power in Men's Accounts of Domestic Violence," looks at domestic violence. Domestic violence has long been problematic. Prior to the passage of legislation mandating that police authorities follow certain protocols in the investigation of domestic violence, including mandatory arrests, domestic violence received a less-than-effective response from the criminal justice system. In many cases, the police deemed domestic violence an issue that should be handled within the family. Consequently, these cases were "resolved" by having one of the parties leave for the evening until "things cooled down." Approaches such as these were ineffective and provided only short-term resolutions. In essence, the manner in which the criminal justice system handled domestic violence was at times devastating and occasionally fatal for victims.

Academic treatments of domestic violence have devoted a great deal of attention to its victims. While this is an important step in developing an understanding of the crime from the victim's perspective, it is also critical that researchers construct an understanding of the offender's perspective. Anderson and Umberson's article does just that, examining the construction of gender in men's accounts of domestic violence. This postmodern treatment of domestic violence discusses both masculinity and power in men's accounts of domestic violence. The authors interviewed 33 heterosexual male domestic violence offenders and found that these batterers blamed their female partners for the violence in their relationship. These men identified themselves as victims of a biased criminal justice system. According to the study, "the men excused, justified, rationalized, and minimized their violence against their female partners." These offenders constructed their battering as an appropriate response to "extreme provocation, loss of control, or an incident blown out of proportion." This is similar to one other study that examined court files from 1,873 protection-from-abuse orders in domestic violence cases and found that abusers overwhelmingly used neutralizations to justify their actions (Etter & Birzer, 2007). Anderson and Umberson have made a substantial contribution to the domestic violence literature. Moreover, their research provides an alarming glimpse into male batterers' constructions of their own offending.

In Chapter 10 ("Serendipity in Robbery Target Selection"), Bruce A. Jacobs argues that rational-choice theory downplays the phenomenological forces that undermine reasoned calculation. Rational-choice theory proposes that offenders make conscious decisions to commit crimes based on a calculated weighing of risks and benefits. According to this theory, if the benefits outweigh the risks involved in committing the crime, the offender will carry out the crime. Jacobs argues that this is a "sterile view" of criminal offending. Using data collected from interviews of unincarcerated robbery offenders who specialize in carjacking and drug robbery, he finds that in many cases, victims became victims after crossing paths with offenders at the right or wrong time, or converging along "an axis of serendipity." Thus, serendipity speaks to the nondeterministic nature of the offender's decision making, and that opportunity is often unpredictable and must be appraised. Jacobs is onto something salient here. If we were to ask those who regularly interact with offenders (i.e., police and probation or parole authorities), those who see firsthand what Katz (1988) refers to as "the seductions of crime," it's possible that they would inform us that offenders' calculations to commit a crime would involve more than a simple weighing of risks and benefits. It would seem that there are indeed many phenomenological factors that may confound the risk and benefit calculation.

In Chapter 11, Heith Copes, Andy Hochstetler, and Craig J. Forsyth advance the literature giving attention to the role that codes for violence play in generating crime. The authors illuminate codes of violence as part of a system of order and honor as articulated by a group of white, working-class males. As generally stated by the authors, their findings suggest that the code these men use actually prohibits predatory violence, and constrains the level of violence in a fight.

REFERENCES

Etter, G. W., & Birzer, M. L. (2007). Domestic violence abusers: A descriptive study of the characteristics of defenders in protection from abuse orders in Sedgwick County, Kansas. *Journal of Family Violence, 22,* 113–9.

Federal Bureau of Investigation. (2014). *Crime in the United States.* Retrieved October 24, 2015, from https://www.fbi.gov/about-us/cjis/ucr/crime-in-the-u.s/2014

Katz, J. (1988). *Seductions of crime: Moral and sensual attractions in doing evil.* New York: Basic.

CHAPTER 9

Gendering Violence: Masculinity and Power in Men's Accounts of Domestic Violence

Kristin L. Anderson and Debra Umberson

This chapter examines the construction of gender within men's accounts of domestic violence. The analyzed data was gathered through in-depth interviews conducted with 33 domestically violent heterosexual men recruited through the Family Violence Diversion Network, a nonprofit organization located in a mid-sized Southwestern city. The analysis indicated that these batterers used diverse strategies to present themselves as nonviolent, capable, and rational men. They claimed that female partners were responsible for the violence in their relationships and constructed men as victims of a biased criminal justice system. The men excused, justified, rationalized, and minimized their violence against their female partners, constructing their violence as a rational response to extreme provocation, loss of control, or an incident blown out of proportion. This study suggests that violence against female partners is a means by which batterers reproduce a binary framework of gender.

INTRODUCTION

In the 1970s, feminist activists and scholars brought wife abuse to the forefront of public consciousness. Published in the academic and popular press, the words and images of survivors made one aspect of patriarchy visible: male dominance was displayed on women's bruised and battered bodies (Dobash & Dobash, 1979; Martin, 1976). Early research contributed to feminist analyses of battery as part

Source: Anderson, K. L., & Umberson, D. (2001). Gendering violence: Masculinity and power in men's accounts of domestic violence. *Gender & Society, 15,* 358–380. © 2001 Sociologists for Women in Society. Used with permission of the publisher.

of a larger pattern of male domination and control of women (Pence & Paymar, 1993; Yllo, 1993). Research in the 1980s and 1990s has expanded theoretical understandings of men's violence against women through emphases on women's agency and resistance to male control (Bowker, 1983; Kirkwood, 1993); the intersection of physical, structural, and emotional forces that sustain men's control over female partners (Kirkwood, 1993; Pence & Paymar, 1993); and the different constraints faced by women and men of diverse nations, racial ethnic identities, and sexualities who experience violence at the hands of intimate partners (Eaton, 1994; Island & Letellier, 1991; Jang, Lee, & Morello-Frosch, 1998; Renzetti, 1992). This work demonstrates ways in which the gender order facilitates victimization of disenfranchised groups.

Comparatively less work has examined the ways in which gender influences male perpetrators' experiences of domestic violence (Yllo, 1993). However, a growing body of qualitative research critically examines batterers' descriptions of violence within their relationships. Dobash and Dobash (1998), Hearn (1998), and Ptacek (1990) focus on the excuses, justifications, and rationalizations that batterers use to account for their violence. These authors suggest that batterers' accounts of violence are texts through which they attempt to deny responsibility for violence and to present nonviolent self-identities.

Dobash and Dobash (1998) identify ways in which gender, as a system that structures the authority and responsibilities assigned to women and men within intimate relationships, supports battery. They find that men use violence to punish female partners who fail to meet their unspoken physical, sexual, or emotional needs. Lundgren (1998) examines batterers' use of gendered religious ideologies to justify their violence against female partners. Hearn (1998, p. 37) proposes that violence is a "resource for demonstrating and showing a person is a man." These studies find that masculine identities are constructed through acts of violence and through batterers' ability to control partners as a result of their violence.

This article examines the construction of gender within men's accounts of domestic violence. Guided by theoretical work that characterizes gender as performance (Butler, 1990; Butler, 1993; West & Fenstermaker, 1995), we contend that batterers attempt to construct masculine identities through the practice of violence and the discourse about violence that they provide. We examine these performances of gender as "routine, methodical, and ongoing accomplishment[s]" that create and sustain notions of natural differences between women and men (West & Fenstermaker, 1995, p. 9). Butler's concept of performativity extends this idea by suggesting that it is through performance that gendered subjectivities are constructed: "Gender proves to be performative—that is, constituting the identity it is purported to be. In this sense, gender is always a doing, though not a doing by a subject who may be said to preexist the deed" (1990, p. 25). For Butler, gender performances demonstrate the instability of masculine subjectivity; a "masculine identity" exists only as the actions of individuals who stylize their bodies and their actions in accordance with a normative binary framework of gender.

In addition, the performance of gender makes male power and privilege appear natural and normal rather than socially produced and structured. Butler (1990) argues that gender is part of a system of relations that sustains heterosexual male privilege through the denigration or erasure of alternative (feminine/gay/lesbian/bisexual) identities. West and Fenstermaker (1995) contend that cultural beliefs about underlying and essential differences between women and men, and social structures that constitute and are constituted by these beliefs are reproduced by the accomplishment of gender. In examining the accounts offered by domestically violent men, we focus on identifying ways in which the practice of domestic violence helps men to accomplish gender. We also focus on the contradictions within these accounts to explore the instability of masculine subjectivities and challenges to the performance of gender.

FINDINGS

How do batterers talk about the violence in their relationships? They excuse, rationalize, justify, and minimize their violence against female partners. Like the batterers studied by previous researchers, the men in this study constructed their violence as a rational response to extreme provocation, a loss of control, or a minor incident that was blown out of proportion. Through such accounts, batterers deny responsibility for their violence and save face when recounting behavior that has elicited social sanctions (Dobash & Dobash, 1998; Ptacek, 1990).

However, these accounts are also about the performance of gender. That is, through their speech acts, respondents presented themselves as rational, competent, masculine actors. We examine several ways in which domestic violence is gendered in these accounts. First, according to respondents' reports, violence is gendered in its practice. Although it was in their interests to minimize and deny their violence, participants reported engaging in more serious, frequent, and injurious violence than that committed by their female partners. Second, respondents gendered violence through their depictions and interpretations of violence. They talked about women's violence in a qualitatively different fashion than they talked about their own violence, and their language reflected hegemonic notions of femininity and masculinity. Third, the research participants constructed gender by interpreting the violent conflicts in ways that suggested that their female partners were responsible for the participants' behavior. Finally, respondents gendered violence by claiming that they are victimized by a criminal justice system that constructs all men as villains and all women as victims.

Gendered Practice

Men perpetrate the majority of violence against women and against other men in the United States (Bachman & Saltzman, 1995). Although some scholars argue that women perpetrate domestic violence at rates similar to men (Straus, 1993), feminist scholars have pointed out that research findings of "sexual symmetry" in domestic violence are based on survey questions that fail to account for sex differences in physical strength and size and in motivations for violence (Dobash et al., 1992; Straton, 1994). Moreover, recent evidence from a large national survey suggests that women experience higher rates of victimization at the hands of partners than men, and that African American and Latina women experience higher rates of victimization than European American women (Bachman & Saltzman, 1995).

Although the majority of respondents described scenarios in which both they and their partners perpetrated violent acts, they reported that their violence was more frequent and severe than the violence perpetrated by their female partners. Eleven respondents (33%) described attacking a partner who did not physically resist, and only two respondents (6%) reported that they were victimized by their partners but did not themselves perpetrate violence. The 20 cases (61%) in which the participants reported "mutual" violence support feminist critiques of "sexual symmetry":

> We started pushing each other. And the thing is that I threw her on the floor. I told her that I'm going to leave. She took my car keys, and I wanted my car keys, so I went and grabbed her arm, pulled it, and took the car keys away from her. She—she comes back and tries to kick me in the back. So I just pushed her back and threw her on the floor again. (Juan)

Moreover, the respondents did not describe scenarios in which they perceived themselves to be at risk from their partners' violence. The worst injury reportedly sustained was a split lip, and only five men (15%) reported sustaining any injury. Female partners reportedly sustained injuries in 14 cases (42%). Although the majority of the injuries reportedly inflicted on female partners consisted of bruises and scratches, a few women were hospitalized, and two women sustained broken ribs. These findings corroborate previous studies showing that women suffer more injuries from domestic violence than men (Langhinrichsen-Rohling, Neidig, & Thorn, 1995). Moreover, because past studies suggest that male batterers underreport their perpetration of violence (Dobash & Dobash, 1998), it is likely that respondents engaged in more violence than they described in these in-depth interviews.

Domestic violence is gendered through social and cultural practices that advantage men in violent conflicts with women. Young men often learn to view themselves as capable perpetrators of violence through rough play and contact sports, to exhibit fearlessness in the face of physical confrontations, and to accept the harm and injury associated with violence as "natural" (Dobash & Dobash, 1998; Messner, 1992). Men are further advantaged by cultural norms suggesting that women should pair with men who are larger and stronger than themselves (Goffman, 1977). Women's less pervasive and less effective use of violence reflects fewer social opportunities to learn violent techniques, a lack of encouragement for female violence within society, and women's size disadvantage in relation to male partners (Fagot et al., 1985; McCaughey, 1998). In a culture that defines aggression as unfeminine, few women learn to use violence effectively.

Gendered Depictions and Interpretations

Participants reported that they engaged in more frequent and serious violence than their partners, but they also reported that their violence was different from that of their partners. They depicted their violence as rational, effective, and explosive, whereas women's violence was represented as hysterical, trivial, and ineffectual. Of the 22 participants who described violence perpetrated by their partners, 12 (55%) suggested that their partner's violence was ridiculous or ineffectual. These respondents minimized their partners' violence by explaining that it was of little concern to them:

> I came out of the kitchen, and then I got in her face, and I shoved her. She shoved, she tried to push me a little bit, but it didn't matter much. (Adam)
>
> I was seeing this girl, and then a friend of mine saw me with this girl and he went back and told my wife, and when I got home that night, that's when she tried to hit me, to fight me. I just pushed her out of the way and left. (Shad)

This minimizing discourse also characterizes descriptions of cases in which female partners successfully made contact and injured the respondent, as in the following account:

> I was on my way to go to the restroom. And she was just cussing and swearing, and she wouldn't let me pass. So, I nudged her. I didn't push her or shove her, I just kind of, you know, just made my way to the restroom. And, when I done that she hit me, and she drew blood. She hit me in the lip, and she drew blood. . . . I go in the bathroom and I started laughing, you know. And I was still half lit that morning, you know. And I was laughing because I think it maybe shocked me more than anything that she had done this, you know. (Ed)

Although his partner "drew blood," Ed minimized her violence by describing it as amusing, uncharacteristic, and shocking.

Even in the case of extreme danger, such as when threatened with a weapon, respondents denied the possibility that their partners' violence was a threat. During a fight described by Steve, his partner locked herself in the bathroom with his gun:

> We were battering each other at that point, and that's when she was in the bathroom. This is—it's like 45 minutes into this whole argument now. She's in the bathroom, messing with my [gun]. And I had no idea. So I kicked the door in—in the bathroom, and she's sitting there trying to load this thing, trying to get this clip in, and luckily she couldn't figure it out. Why, I don't—you know, well, because she was drunk. So, luckily she didn't. The situation could have been a whole lot worse, you know, it could have been a whole lot worse than it was. I thank God that she didn't figure it out. When I think about it, you know, she was lucky to come out of it with just a cut in her head. You know, she could have blown her brains out or done something really stupid.

This account contains interesting contradictions. Steve stated that he had "no idea" that his partner had a gun, but he responded by kicking down the door to reach her. He then suggested that he was concerned about his partner's safety and that he kicked in the door to save her from doing "something really stupid" to herself. Similarly, Alejandro minimized the threat in his account of an incident in which his partner picked up a weapon:

> So, she got angry and got a knife, came up at me, and I kick her. [*And then what happened?*] Well, I kick her about four times because she—I kick her, and I say "Just stop, stay there!" and she stand up and come again and I had to kick her again. Somebody called the police, somebody called the police. I guess we were making a lot of noise. And I couldn't go out, I couldn't leave home, because I was not dressed properly to go out. And so I couldn't go, so the only alternative I had at this moment was to defend myself from the knife. So I had to kick her.

Alejandro suggested that his partner's attack with a knife was not enough of a threat to warrant his leaving the house when he was "not dressed properly to go out."

In addition to emphasizing their partners' incompetence in the practice of violence, some respondents depicted the violence perpetrated by their partners as irrational:

> She has got no control. She sees something and she don't like it, she'll go and pull my hair, scratch me, and [act] paranoid, crazy, screaming loud, make everybody look at her, and call the police, you know. Just nuts. (Andrew)
>
> She came back and started hitting me with her purse again so I knocked the purse out of her hand, and then she started screaming at me to get out. I went back to the room, and she came running down the hall saying she was going to throw all my stuff out and I'd just had enough, so I went and grabbed her, pulled her back. And grabbed her back to the bed and threw her on the bed and sat on her—told her I wasn't going to let her up until she came to her senses. . . . She came back up again, and I just grabbed her and threw her down. After that, she promised—she finally said that she had come to her senses and everything. I went into the other room, and she went out to clean up the mess she had made in the living room, and then she just started just crying all night long, or for a while. (Phil)

Phil and Andrew described their partners' acts as irrational and hysterical. Such depictions helped respondents to justify their own violence and to present themselves as calm, cool, rational men. Phil described his own behavior of throwing his partner down as a nonviolent, controlled response to his partner's outrageous behavior. Moreover, he suggests that he used this incident to demonstrate his sense of superior rationality to his partner. Phil later reported that a doctor became "very upset" about the marks on his wife's neck two days after this incident, suggesting that he was not the rational actor represented in his account.

In eight other cases (36%), respondents did not depict their partner's violence as trivial or ineffectual. Rather, they described their partner's behavior in matter-of-fact terms:

> Then she starts jumping at me or hitting me, or tell[ing] me "Leave the house, I don't want you, I don't love you" and stuff like that. And I say, "Don't touch me,

don't touch me." And I just push her back. She keeps coming and hit me, hit me. I keep pushing back, she starts scratch me, so I push hard to stop her from hurting me. (Mario)

Other respondents depicted their partner's violence in factual terms but emphasized that they perceived their own violence as the greater danger. Ray took his partner seriously when he stated that "she was willing to fight, to defend herself," yet he also mentioned his fears that his own violence would be lethal: "The worst time is when she threw an iron at me. And I'm gonna tell you, I think that was the worst time, because, in defense, in retaliation, I pulled her hair, and I thought maybe I broke her neck." Only two respondents—Alan and Jim—consistently identified as victims:

> One of the worst times was realizing that she was drunk and belligerent. I realized that I needed to take her home in her car and she was not capable of driving. And she was physically abusive the whole way home. And before I could get out of the door or get out of the way, she came at me with a knife. And stupidly, I defended myself—kicked her hand to get the knife out. And I bruised her hand enough to where she felt justified enough to call the police with stories that I was horribly abusing. (Jim)

Jim reported that his partner has hit him, stabbed him, and thrown things at him. However, he also noted that he was arrested following several of these incidents, suggesting that his accounts tell us only part of the story. Moreover, like Steve and Alejandro, he did not describe feelings of fear or apprehension about his partner's use of a knife.

Although female partners were represented as dangerous only to themselves, the participants depicted their own violence as primal, explosive, and damaging to others:

> I explode for everything. This time it was trying to help my daughter with her homework; it was a Sunday, and she was not paying any attention, and I get angry with my daughter, and so I kick the TV. . . . I guess I broke the TV, and then I kick a bookshelf. My daughter tried to get into the middle, so I pushed her away from me and I kicked another thing. So, she [his partner] called the police. I am glad she called the police because something really awful could have happened. (Alejandro)
>
> She said something, and then I just lost control. I choked her, picked her up off her feet, and lifted her up like this, and she was kind of kicking back and forth, and I really felt like I really wanted to kill her this time. (Adam)
>
> I feel that if there had been a gun in the house, I would have used it. That's one reason also why I refuse to have a gun. Because I know I have a terrible temper and I'm afraid that I will do something stupid like that. (Fred)

In contrast to their reported fearlessness when confronted by women wielding weapons, respondents constructed their own capacity for violence as something that should engender fear. These interpretations are consistent with cultural constructions of male violence as volcanic—natural, lethal, and impossible to stop until it has run its course.

Respondents' interpretations of ineffectual female violence and lethal male violence reflect actual violent practices in a culture that grants men more access to violence, but they also gender violence. By denying a threat from women's violence, participants performed masculinity and reinforced notions of gender difference. Women were constructed as incompetent in the practice of violence, and their successes were trivialized. For example, it is unlikely that Ed would have responded with laughter had his lip been split by the punch of another man (Dobash & Dobash, 1998). Moreover, respondents ignored their partners' motivations for violence and their active efforts to exert change within their relationships.

In her examination of Irigaray's writings on the representation of women within the masculine economy, Butler (1993, p. 36) writes that "the economy that claims to include the feminine as the subordinate term in a binary opposition of masculine/feminine excludes the feminine—produces the feminine as that which must be excluded for that economy to operate." The binary representation of ineffectual, hysterical female behavior and rational, lethal male violence within these accounts erases the feminine; violence perpetrated by women and female subjectivity are effaced in order that the respondents can construct masculinities. These representations mask the power relations that determine what acts will qualify as "violence" and thus naturalize the notion that violence is the exclusive province of men.

Gendering Blame

The research participants also gendered violence by suggesting that their female partners were responsible for the violence within their relationships. Some respondents did this by claiming that they did not hit women with whom they were involved in the past:

> I've never hit another woman in my life besides the one that I'm with. She just has a knack for bringing out the worst in me. (Tom)
>   You know, I never hit my first wife. I'm married for five years—I never hit her. I never struck her, not once. (Mitchell)

Respondents also shifted blame onto female partners by detailing faults in their partners' behaviors and personalities. They criticized their partners' parenting styles, interaction styles, and choices. However, the most typically reported criticism was that female partners were controlling. Ten of the 33 respondents (30%) characterized their partners as controlling, demanding, or dominating:

> She's real organized and critiquing about things. She wanna—she has to get it like—she like to have her way all the time, you know. In control of things, even when she's at work in the evenings, she has to have control of everything that's going on in the house. And—but—you know, try to get, to control everything there. You know, what's going on, and me and myself. (Adam)
>   You know, you're here with this person, you're here for five years, and yet they turn out to be aggressive, what is aggressive, too educated, you know. It's the reason they feel like they want to control you. (Mitchell)

In a few cases, respondents claimed that they felt emasculated by what they interpreted as their partners' efforts to control them:

> She's kind of—I don't want to say dominating. She's a good mother, she's a great housekeeper, she's an excellent cook. But as far as our relationship goes, the old traditional "man wears the pants in the family," it's a shared responsibility. There's no way that you could say that I wear the pants in the family. She's dominating in that sense. (Ted)
>
> You ask the guy sitting next door to me, the guy that's down the hall. For years they all say, "Bill, man, reach down and grab your eggs. She wears the pants." Or maybe like, "Hey man, we're going to go—Oh, Bill can't go. He's got to ask his boss first." And they were right. (Bill)

These representations of female partners as dominating enabled men to position themselves as victims of masculinized female partners. The relational construction of masculinity is visible in these accounts; women who "wear the pants" disrupt the binary opposition of masculinity/femininity. Bill's account reveals that "one is one's gender to the extent that one is not the other gender" (Butler 1990, p. 22); he is unable to perform masculinity to the satisfaction of his friends when mirrored by a partner who is perceived as dominating.

Moreover, respondents appeared to feel emasculated by unspecified forces. Unlike female survivors who describe concrete practices that male partners utilize to exert control (Kirkwood, 1993; Walker, 1984), participants were vague about what they meant by control and the ways in which their partners exerted control:

> I don't think she's satisfied unless she has absolute control, and she's not in a position to control anyway, um, mentally.... [*When you said that, um, that she wasn't really in a position to control, what did you mean by that?*] Well, she's not in a position to control, in the fact that she's not, the control that she wants, is pretty much control over me. I'm pretty much the only person that she sees every day. She wants to control every aspect of what I do, and while in the same turn, she really can't. (George)

Respondents who claimed that their partners are controlling offered nebulous explanations for these feelings, suggesting that these claims may be indicative of these men's fears about being controlled by a woman rather than the actual practices of their partners.

Finally, respondents gendered violence through their efforts to convince female partners to shoulder at least part of the blame for their violence. The following comments reflect respondents' interpretations of their partners' feelings after the argument was over:

> Finally, for once in her life, I got her to accept 50/50 blame for the reason why she actually got hit. You know, used to be a time where she could say there was never a time. But, she accepts 50/50 blame for this. (Tom)
>
> She has a sense that she is probably 80 to 90% guilty of my anger. (Alejandro)

Contemporary constructions of gender hold women responsible for men's aggression (Gray, Palileo, & Johnson, 1993). Sexual violence is often blamed on women, who are perceived as tempting men who are powerless in the face of their primal sexual desires (Scully, 1990). Although interviewees expressed remorse for their violent behavior, they also implied that it was justified in light of their partners' controlling behavior. Moreover, their violence was rewarded by their partners' feelings of guilt, suggesting that violence is simultaneously a performance of masculinity and a means by which respondents encouraged the performance of femininity by female partners.

THE LAW IS FOR WOMEN: CLAIMING GENDER BIAS

Participants sometimes rationalized their violence by claiming that the legal system overreacted to a minor incident. Eight of the 33 interviewees (24%) depicted themselves as victims of gender politics or the media attention surrounding the trial of O. J. Simpson:

> I think my punishment was wrong. And it was like my attorney told me—I'm suffering because of O. J. Simpson. Mine was the crime of the year. That is, you know, it's the hot issue of the year because of O. J. Two years ago they would have gone "Don't do that again." (Bill)
>
> I'm going to jail for something I haven't even done because the woman is always the victim and the guy is always the bad guy. And O. J., I think, has made it even worse—that mentality. I know that there's a lot of bad, ignorant, violent guys out there that probably think that it's wonderful to batter their wife on a regular basis, but I think there's a lot of reverse mentality going on right now. (Jim)
>
> I don't necessarily agree with the jail system, which I know has nothing to do with you guys, but you have to sign a form saying that you'll come to counseling before you've ever been convicted of a crime. And, like I said, here I am now with this [inaudible] that I have to come to for 21 weeks in a row—for what could amount to some girl calling—hurting herself and saying her boyfriend or husband did it. (Tom)

These claims of gender bias were sometimes directly contradicted by respondents' descriptions of events following the arrival of the police. Four participants (12%) reported that the police wanted to arrest their female partner along with or instead of themselves—stories that challenged their claims of bias in the system. A few of these respondents reported that they lied to the police about the source of their injuries to prevent the arrest of their partners. Ed, the respondent who sustained a split lip from his partner's punch, claimed that he "took the fall" for his partner:

> They wanted to arrest her, because I was the one who had the little split lip. And I told them that—I said, "No, man, she's seven months pregnant." I told the officer, you know, "How can you take her to jail? She's seven months pregnant!" And I said, "Look, I came in here—I started it, I pushed her. And she hit me." You know, I told them that I had shoved her. And after that they said, "Okay, well, we have to remove, move you out of this—out of this situation here."

Something about the law. So, I said, "Well, you know. I started it." I told them I had started it, you know. And, they said, "Okay, well, we'll take you then." So I went to jail. (Ed)

When the police arrived, these respondents were in a double bind. They wanted to deny their own violence to avoid arrest, but they also wanted to deny victimization at the hands of a woman. "Protecting" their female partners from arrest allowed them a way out of this bind. By volunteering to be arrested despite their alleged innocence, they became chivalrous defenders of their partners. They were also, paradoxically, able to claim that "gender bias" led to their arrest and participation in the Family Violence Diversion Network (FVDN) program. When Ed argued that the criminal justice system is biased toward women, we confronted him about this contradiction:

ED: I am totally against, you know,—ever since I stepped foot in this program and I've only been to the orientation—[that] it speaks of gender, okay, and everything that—it seems like every statement that is made is directed toward men, toward the male party. . . . As I stated earlier, the law is for women. In my opinion, it—

INTERVIEWER: Although, they would have arrested her if you hadn't intervened.

ED: They would, that's right. That's another thing. That's right, that's right. They would have arrested her. But, you know even, even with her statement saying, look this is what, this is what happened, I'm not pressing charges. The state picked up those charges, and, they just took it upon themselves, you know, to inconvenience my life, is what they did.

INTERVIEWER: Okay. And the other alternative would have been that she would have been going through this process instead of you.

ED: Well, no, the other alternative, that was, that was, that would come out of this, is [that] I would have spent 30 days in jail.

Ed repeatedly dismissed the notion that the legal system would hold his partner accountable for her actions, despite his own words to the contrary. His construction of men as victimized by an interfering justice system allowed him to avoid the seemingly unacceptable conclusion that either he or his partner was a victim of violence.

Another respondent, Jim, reportedly prevented his partner's arrest because he felt it to be in his best interests:

She was drunk and behind the wheel and driving erratically while backhanding me. And a cop pulled us over because he saw her hit me. And I realized that she was gonna get a DWI [driving while intoxicated], which would have been her second and a major expense to me, besides, you know, I think that there's a thin line between protecting somebody and possessing somebody. But I protect her, I do. I find myself sacrificing myself for her and lying for her constantly. And I told the cops that I hit her just because they saw her hit me and I figured that if

> I told them that I hit her, rather than her get a DWI, that we would both go to jail over an assault thing. Which is what happened. (Jim)

When batterers "protect" their partners from arrest, their oppressor becomes a powerful criminal justice system rather than a woman. Although even the loser gains status through participation in a fight with another man, a man does not gain prestige from being beaten by a woman (Dobash & Dobash, 1998). In addition, respondents who stepped in to prevent their partners from being arrested ensured that their partners remained under their control, as Jim suggested when he described "the thin line between being protected by somebody and possessing somebody." By volunteering to be arrested along with his partner, Jim ensured that she was not "taken into possession" (e.g., taken into custody) by the police.

By focusing the interviews on "gender bias" in the system, respondents deflected attention from their own perpetration and victimization. Constructions of a bias gave them an explanation for their arrest that was consistent with their self-presentation as rational, strong, and nonviolent actors. Claims of "reverse mentality" also enabled participants to position themselves as victims of gender politics. Several interviewees made use of men's rights rhetoric or alluded to changes wrought by feminism to suggest that they are increasingly oppressed by a society in which women have achieved greater rights:

> I really get upset when I watch TV shows as far as, like, they got shows or a TV station called Lifetime and there are many phrases "TV for women." And that kind of made me upset. Why is it TV for women? You know, it should be TV for everyone, not just women. You don't hear someone else at a different TV station saying, "TV for men." . . . As far as the law goes, changing some of the laws goes too, some of the laws that guys are pulled away from their children. I kind of felt sorry for the guys. (Kenny)

A number of recent studies have examined the increasingly angry and antifeminist discourse offered by some men who are struggling to construct masculine identities within patriarchies disrupted by feminism and movements for gay/lesbian and civil rights (Fine et al., 1997; Messner, 1998; Savran, 1998). Some branches of the contemporary "men's movement" have articulated a defensive and antifeminist rhetoric of "men's rights" that suggests that men have become the victims of feminism (Messner, 1998; Savran, 1998). Although none of our interviewees reported participation in any of the organized men's movements, their allusions to the discourse of victimized manhood suggest that the rhetoric of these movements has become an influential resource for the performance of gender among some men. Like the angry men's rights activists studied by Messner, some respondents positioned themselves as the victims of feminism, which they believe has co-opted the criminal justice system and the media by creating "myths" of male domination. The interviews suggest that respondents feel disempowered and that they identify women—both the women whom they batter and women who lead movements to criminalize domestic violence—as the "Other" who has "stolen their presumed privilege" (Fine et al., 1997, p. 54): "Now girls are starting to act like men, or try and be like men. Like if you hit me, I'll call the cops, or if you don't do it, I'll do this, or stuff like that" (Juan). Juan contends that by challenging men's "privilege" to hit their female partners without fear of repercussions, women have become "like men." This suggests that the construction of masculine subjectivities is tied to a position of dominance, and that women have threatened the binary and hierarchical gender framework through their resistance to male violence.

DISCUSSION: SOCIAL LOCATIONS AND DISCOURSES OF VIOLENCE

Respondents' descriptions of conflicts with female partners were similar across racial, ethnic, and class locations. Participants of diverse socioeconomic standings and racial ethnic backgrounds minimized the violence perpetrated by their partners, claimed that the criminal justice system is biased against men, and attempted to place responsibility for their violence on female partners. However, we identified some ways in which social class influenced respondents' self-presentations.

Respondents of higher socioeconomic status emphasized their careers and the material items that they provided for their families throughout the interviews:

> We built two houses together and they are nice. You know, we like to see a nice environment for our family to live in. We want to see our children receive a good education. (Ted)
>
> That woman now sits in a 2,700-square-foot house: She drives a Volvo. She has everything. A brand-new refrigerator, a brand-new washer and dryer. (Bill)

Seven respondents fit these criteria. We define disenfranchised respondents as those who report personal earnings of less than $15,000 per year and who have not completed a two-year college program. Nine respondents fit these criteria. Conversely, economically disenfranchised men volunteered stories about their prowess in fights with other men. These interviewees reported that they engaged in violent conflicts with other men as a means of gaining respect:

> Everybody in my neighborhood respected me a lot, you know. I used to be kind of violent. I used to like to fight and stuff like that, but I'm not like that anymore. She—I don't think she liked me because I liked to fight a lot, but she liked me because people respected me, because they knew that they would have to fight if they disrespected me. You know, I think that's one thing that turned her on about me; I don't let people mess around. (Tony)
>
> My stepson's friend was there, and he start to push me too. So I started to say, "Hey, you know, this is my house, and you don't tell me nothing in my house." So I start fighting, you know, I was gonna fight him. (Mario)

The use of violence to achieve respect is a central theme in research on the construction of masculinities among disenfranchised men (Messerschmidt, 1993; Messner, 1992). Although men of diverse socioeconomic standings valorize fistfights between men (Campbell, 1993; Dobash & Dobash, 1998), the extent to which they participate in these confrontations varies by social context. Privileged young men are more often able to avoid participation in social situations that require physical violence against other men than are men who reside in poor neighborhoods (Messner, 1992).

We find some evidence that cultural differences influence accounts of domestic violence. Two respondents who identified themselves as immigrants from Latin America (Alejandro and Juan) reported that they experienced conflicts with female partners about the shifting meanings of gender in the United States:

> She has a different attitude than mine. She has an attitude that comes from Mexico—be a man, like, you have to do it. And it's like me here, it's 50/50, it's another thing, you know, it's like "I don't have to do it." . . . I told her the wrong things she was doing, and I told her, "It's not going to be that way because we're not in Mexico, we're in the United States." (Juan)

Juan's story suggests that unstable meanings about what it means to be a woman or a man are a source of conflict within his relationship, and that he and his partner draw on divergent gender ideologies to buttress their positions. Although many of the respondents expressed uncertainty about appropriate gender performances in the 1990s, those who migrated to the United States may find these "crisis tendencies of the gender order" (Connell, 1992, p. 736) to be particularly unsettling. Interestingly, Juan depicts his partner as clinging to traditional gender norms, while he embraces the notion of gender egalitarianism. However, we are hesitant to draw conclusions about this finding due to the small number of interviews that we conducted with immigrants.

Race or ethnicity, class, and gender matter in the context of the interview setting. As white, middle-class, female researchers, we were often questioning men who resided in different social worlds. Like other female researchers who have interviewed men with histories of sexual violence, we found that the interviewees were usually friendly, polite, and appeared relatively comfortable in the interview setting (Scully, 1990). Unlike Ptacek, a male researcher who interviewed batterers, we did not experience a "subtext of resistance and jockeying for power beneath the otherwise friendly manner these individuals displayed in our initial phone conversations" (1990, p. 140). However, respondents may have offered more deterministic accounts of gender and assumed more shared experiences with the interviewer had they been interviewed by men rather than women (Williams & Heikes, 1993). For example, whereas Ptacek (1990) found that 78% of the batterers that he interviewed justified their violence by complaining that their wives did not fulfill the obligations of a good wife, participants in this study rarely used language that explicitly emphasized "wifely duties."

Previous studies also suggest that when white, middle-class researchers interview working-class people or people of color, they may encounter problems with establishing rapport and interpreting the accounts of respondents (Edwards, 1990). Riessman (1987) found that white researchers feel more comfortable with the narrative styles of white and middle-class respondents and may misinterpret the central themes raised by respondents of color. These findings suggest that shared meanings may have been less easily achieved in our interviews conducted with Latino, Native American, and African American men. For example, there is some evidence that we attempted to impose a linear narrative structure on our interviews with some respondents who may have preferred an episodic style (see Riessman, 1987):

> We just started arguing more in the house. And she scratched me, and I push her away. Because I got bleeding on my neck and everything, and I push her away. And she called the police and I run away so they don't catch me there. There's a lot of worse times we argued. She tried to get me with the knife one time, trying to blame me that I did it. And the next time I told her I was going to leave her, and she tried to commit suicide by drinking like a whole bunch of bottles of Tylenol pill. And I had to rush her to the hospital, you know. That's about it. [*So, in this worst fight, she scratched you and you pushed her. She called the police?*] A few times she kicked me and scratched me on my neck and everything, and my arms. (Andrew)

Andrew, who identifies as Latino, recounts several episodes that are salient to his understanding of the problems within his relationship. The interviewer, however, steers him toward a sequential recounting of one particular incident rather than probing for elaboration of Andrew's perceptions of these multiple events.

In contrast, racial ethnic locations can shape what interviewers and interviewees reveal. One way in which this dynamic may have influenced the interviews was suggested by Tom, who identified as African American:

> I've never dated a black woman before. Not me. That was my choice—that's a choice I made a long time ago. . . . I tend to find that black women, in general, don't have any get-up-and-go, don't work. I can't say—it's just down players. But I just don't see the desire to succeed in life.

Tom introduced the issue of interracial dating without prompting and went on to invoke a variety of controlling images to represent black women (Collins, 1991). It is difficult to imagine that Tom would have shared these details if he had been interviewed by an African American woman or perhaps even a white man. Given the middle-class bias of our sample and our own social locations, future research ought to compare accounts received by differently located interviewers and a wider class and racial ethnic range of respondents.

CONCLUSIONS

Many scholars have suggested that domestic violence is a means by which men construct masculinities (Dobash & Dobash, 1998; Gondolf & Hannekin, 1987; Hearn, 1998). However, few studies have explored the specific practices that domestically violent men use to present themselves as masculine actors. The respondents in this study used diverse and contradictory strategies to gender violence, and they shifted their positions as they talked about violence. Respondents sometimes positioned themselves as masculine actors by highlighting their strength, power, and rationality compared with the "irrationality" and vulnerability of female partners. At other times, when describing the criminal justice system or "controlling" female partners, they positioned themselves as vulnerable and powerless. These shifting representations evidence the relational construction of gender and the instability of masculine subjectivities (Butler, 1990).

Recently, performativity theories have been criticized for privileging agency, undertheorizing structural and cultural constraints, and facilitating essentialist readings of gender behavior: "Lacking an analysis of structural and cultural context, performances of gender can all too easily be interpreted as free agents acting out the inevitable surface manifestations of a natural inner sex difference" (Messner, 2000, p. 770). Findings from our study show that each of these criticisms is not necessarily valid.

First, although the batterers described here demonstrate agency by shifting positions, they do so by calling on cultural discourses (of unstoppable masculine aggression, of feminine weakness, and of men's rights). Their performance is shaped by cultural options.

Second, batterers' performances are also shaped by structural changes in the gender order. Some of the batterers interviewed for this study expressed anger and confusion about a world with "TV for women" and female partners who are "too educated." Their arrest signaled a world askew—a place where "the law is for women" and where men have become the victims of discrimination. Although these accounts are ironic in light of the research documenting the continuing reluctance of the legal system to treat domestic violence as a criminal act (Dobash & Dobash, 1979), they demonstrate the ways in which legal and structural reforms in the area of domestic violence influence gender performances. By focusing attention on the "bias" in the system, respondents deflected attention from their own perpetration and victimization and sustained their constructions of rational masculinity. Therefore, theories of gender performativity push us toward analyses of the cultural and structural contexts that form the settings for the acts.

Finally, when viewed through the lens of performativity, our findings challenge the notion that violence is an essential or natural expression of masculinity. Rather, they suggest that violence represents an effort to reconstruct a contested and unstable masculinity. Respondents' references to men's rights movement discourse, their claims of "reverse discrimination," and their complaints that female partners are controlling indicate a disruption in masculine subjectivities. Viewing domestic violence as a gender performance counters the essentialist readings of men's violence against women that dominate U.S. popular culture. What one performs is not necessarily what one "is."

Disturbingly, however, this study suggests that violence is (at least temporarily) an effective means by which batterers reconstruct men as masculine and women as feminine. Participants reported that they were able to control their partners through exertions of physical dominance and through their interpretive efforts to hold partners responsible for the violence in their relationships. By gendering violence, these batterers not only performed masculinity but reproduced gender as dominance. Thus, they naturalized a binary and hierarchical gender system.

REFERENCES

Bachman, R., & Saltzman, L. E. (1995). *Violence against women: Estimates from the redesigned survey, August 1995* (NCJ-154348 Special Report). Washington, DC: Bureau of Justice Statistics.

Bowker, L. H. (1983). *Beating wife-beating.* Lexington, MA: Lexington Books.

Butler, J. (1990). *Gender trouble: Feminism and the subversion of identity.* New York: Routledge.

———. (1993). *Bodies that matter: On the discursive limits of sex.* New York: Routledge.

Campbell, A. (1993). *Men, women, and aggression.* New York: Basic.

Collins, P. H. (1991). *Black feminist thought: Knowledge, consciousness, and the politics of empowerment.* New York: Routledge.

Connell, R. W. (1992). A very straight gay: Masculinity, homosexual experience, and the dynamics of gender. *American Sociological Review, 57,* 735–751.

Dobash, R. E., & Dobash, R. P. (1979). *Violence against wives: A case against the patriarchy.* New York: Free Press.

Dobash, R. E., & Dobash, R. P. (1998). Violent men and violent contexts. In R. E. Dobash & R. P. Dobash (Eds.), *Rethinking violence against women.* Thousand Oaks, CA: Sage, 358–380.

Dobash, R. P., Dobash, R. E., Wilson, M., & Daly, M. (1992). The myth of sexual symmetry in marital violence. *Social Problems, 39,* 71–91.

Eaton, M. (1994). Abuse by any other name: Feminism, difference, and intralesbian violence. In M. A. Fineman & R. Mykitiuk (Eds.), *The public nature of private violence: The discovery of domestic abuse.* New York: Routledge, 199–215.

Edwards, R. (1990). Connecting method and epistemology: A white woman interviewing black women. *Women's Studies International Forum, 13*(5), 477–490.

Fagot, B., Hagan, R., Leinbach, M. B., & Kronsberg, S. (1985). Differential reactions to assertive and communicative acts of toddler boys and girls. *Child Development, 56,* 1499–1505.

Fine, M., Weis, L., Addelston, J., & Marusza, J. (1997). (In)secure times: Constructing white working-class masculinities in the late 20th century. *Gender & Society, 11,* 52–68.

Goffman, E. (1977). The arrangement between the sexes. *Theory & Society, 4*(3), 301–331.

Gondolf, E. W., & Hannekin, J. (1987). The gender warrior: Reformed batterers on abuse, treatment, and change. *Journal of Family Violence, 2,* 177–191.

Gray, N. B., Palileo, G. J., & Johnson, G. D. (1993). Explaining rape victim blame: A test of attribution theory. *Sociological Spectrum, 13,* 377–392.

Hearn, J. (1998). *The violences of men: How men talk about and how agencies respond to men's violence against women.* Thousand Oaks, CA: Sage.

Island, D., & Letellier, P. (1991). *Men who beat the men who love them: Battered gay men and domestic violence.* New York: Harrington Park.

Jang, D., Lee, D., & Morello-Frosch, R. (1998). Domestic violence in the immigrant and refugee community: Responding to the needs of immigrant women. In S. J. Ferguson (Ed.), *Shifting the center: Understanding contemporary families.* Mountain View, CA: Mayfield, 481–491.

Kirkwood, C. (1993). *Leaving abusive partners: From the scars of survival to the wisdom for change.* Newbury Park, CA: Sage.

Langhinrichsen-Rohling, J., Neidig, P., & Thorn, G. (1995). Violent marriages: Gender differences in levels of current violence and past abuse. *Journal of Family Violence, 10,* 159–176.

Lundgren, E. (1998). The hand that strikes and comforts: Gender construction and the tension between body and symbol. In R. E. Dobash & R. P. Dobash (Eds.), *Rethinking violence against women.* Thousand Oaks, CA: Sage, 141–168.

Martin, D. (1976). *Battered wives.* New York: Pocket Books.

McCaughey, M. (1998). The fighting spirit: Women's self-defense training and the discourse of sexed embodiment. *Gender & Society, 12,* 277–300.

Messerschmidt, J. (1993). *Masculinities and crime: A critique and reconceptualization of theory.* Lanham, MD: Rowman & Littlefield.

Messner, M. A. (1992). *Power at play: Sports and the problem of masculinity.* Boston, MA: Beacon.

———. (1998). The limits of the "male sex role": An analysis of the men's liberation and men's rights movements' discourse. *Gender & Society, 12,* 255–276.

———. (2000). Barbie girls versus sea monsters: Children constructing gender. *Gender & Society, 14,* 765–784.

Pence, E., & Paymar, M. (1993). *Education groups for men who batter: The Duluth model.* New York: Springer.

Ptacek, J. (1990). Why do men batter their wives? In K. Yllo & M. Bograd (Eds.), *Feminist perspectives on wife abuse.* Newbury Park, CA: Sage, 133–157.

Renzetti, C. M. (1992). *Violent betrayal: Partner abuse in lesbian relationships.* Newbury Park, CA: Sage.

Riessman, C. K. (1987). When gender is not enough: Women interviewing women. *Gender & Society, 1,* 172–207.

Savran, D. (1998). *Taking it like a man: White masculinity, masochism, and contemporary American culture.* Princeton, NJ: Princeton University Press.

Scully, D. (1990). *Understanding sexual violence: A study of convicted rapists.* Boston, MA: Unwin Hyman.

Straton, J. C. (1994). The myth of the "battered husband syndrome." *Masculinities, 2,* 79–82.

Straus, M. A. (1993). Physical assaults by wives: A major social problem. In R. J. Gelles & D. R. Loseke (Eds.), *Current controversies on family violence.* Newbury Park, CA: Sage, 55–77.

Walker, L. (1984). *The battered woman syndrome.* New York: Springer.

West, C., & Fenstermaker, S. (1995). Doing difference. *Gender & Society, 9,* 8–37.

Williams, C. L., & Heikes, E. J. (1993). The importance of researcher's gender in the in-depth interview: Evidence from two case studies of male nurses. *Gender & Society, 7,* 280–291.

Yllo, K. (1993). Through a feminist lens: Gender, power, and violence. In R. J. Gelles & D. R. Loseke (Eds.), *Current controversies on family violence.* Newbury Park, CA: Sage, 35–54.

CHAPTER 10

Serendipity in Robbery Target Selection

Bruce A. Jacobs

Drawing from interviews with 57 unincarcerated robbers, most of whom special-
ized in either carjacking or drug robbery, this chapter explores the role of seren-
dipity in the process of selecting a robbery target. Serendipity is defined as the art
of finding something valuable while engrossed in something different (Roberts,
1989). On average, the robbers were in their 20s. The majority had no high school
degree. Most were unmarried. Although respondents typically were involved with
drugs and committed a wide variety of offenses, they were recruited specifically
because of their prior experience with drug robbery and carjacking.

Criminologists long have argued that the selection of predatory robbery tar-gets is guided by rational choice. Offenders weigh the costs and benefits of contemplated conduct and proceed when the latter exceed the former (see, e.g., Carroll & Weaver, 1986; Cornish & Clarke, 1986). This relatively sterile view of offender decision making downplays the phenomenological forces that under-mine reasoned calculation. Time pressure, uncertainty, emotion, and needs of various kinds can "bound" rationality and give rise to choices that are more or less spontaneous (Bennett & Wright, 1984). The dynamic tension between reflex-ive action and reasoned calculation comes into particular relief when opportu-nity and motivation converge along an axis of serendipity—chance circumstances that align to energize predatory conduct. It is this convergence and its implica-tions for offender decision making that concern the present paper.

TARGET SELECTION

Any crime requires the intersection of suitable targets and motivated offenders (Felson, 1998), and robbery is no exception. Which targets are perceived to be

Source: Adapted from Jacobs, B. A. (2010). Serendipity of robbery target selection. *British Journal of Criminology, 50*(3), 514–529. Used with permission of the publisher.

suitable, when, and under what circumstances varies across situations and even within them. Contextual factors are labile and subjectively perceived.

As a criminological construct, target selection implies that something is being selected and someone is doing the selecting. Both presume agency. Understandably, the offender is the locus of much of this inquiry (see, e.g., Cornish & Clarke, 1986). Offenders' target selection strategies vary in their sophistication, calculation, focus, and degree of planning. Planning is of particular concern to criminologists because of assumptions of offender rationality and, more specifically, the belief that target selection hinges on offenders' objective information-processing capabilities. As Hochstetler (2002, p. 46) observes, "Decision-making investigators focus on offenders' agency and perceptual construction of situations as illicit opportunity. These investigators view crime as the outcome of purposeful action resulting from assessments of risk and reward."

That being said, a growing body of research in the offender decision-making tradition shows how the selection of predatory robbery targets is awash in ambiguity (Wright & Decker, 1997). Phenomenological forces like emotion and impulsivity destabilize choice and give rise to miscalculations of risk and reward. Offenders may not think about the prospects of sanctions, may think about the prospects but dismiss them, may inflate anticipated rewards, or may focus on anticipated rewards to the exclusion of risks (Bennett & Wright, 1984). All of these possibilities are consistent with a general lack of planning. Indeed, "street robbery is characterized as a spontaneous, impulsive [affair] more often than it involves real [preparation]" (Alarid, Burton, & Hochstetler, 2009, p. 7). Offenders typically "do not plan their crimes or spend only a few minutes planning" (Hochstetler 2001, p. 744; see also Feeney, 1986; Wright, Brookman, & Bennett, 2006).

Target selection can be an artifact of opportunity, but the lens through which opportunities are perceived is no doubt influenced by need. Prior researchers (Bennett & Wright, 1984; Topalli & Wright, 2004) have offered the terms "alert" and "motivated" opportunism to encapsulate the dynamic interplay between need and opportunity. Alert opportunism describes offenders who face needs that are present but not necessarily pressing. Offenders are not desperate, "but they anticipate need in the near term and become increasingly open to opportunities that may present themselves during the course of their day-to-day activities" (Topalli & Wright, 2004, pp. 156–157). By contrast, motivated opportunism is characterized by needs that are, or soon will be, acute. "Attention and openness to possibilities expands [sic] to allow offenders to tolerate more risk. Situations that previously seemed unsuitable start to look better" (Topalli & Wright, 2004, p. 157).

The distinction between alert and motivated opportunism is murky in street culture. Street culture promotes anomic, cash-intensive living that creates an endless supply of deficits and an equally endless need to extend surpluses so that they don't become deficits (Jacobs & Wright, 1999). The confluence of need and inducement gives rise to perpetual searches for scores big and small. Thus, alert and motivated opportunism presuppose a conceptual distinction between offenders who have to make something happen and offenders who face situations that simply "happen." In so doing, the two constructs fail to specify the role of serendipity in alert opportunism and downplay its potential relevance to motivated opportunism. Serendipity, for example, can be manufactured in probabilistic ways, and this manufacturing process need not flow from desperation or truncated rationality (as motivated opportunism implies). By the same token, alert opportunism can involve considerable time pressure if prevailing circumstances are "right" but fleeting. The role of serendipity in mediating these processes is of considerable interest.

Serendipity

Traditionally, serendipity has been interpreted as the art of finding something valuable while engrossed in something different (Roberts, 1989). The discovery is unanticipated, unexpected, and anomalous (Merton & Barber, 2006). The challenge of serendipity is to recognize the inherent value of the unexpected discovery lest it be perceived as just another failed experiment or finding of residual but apparent insignificance. Horace Walpole, credited for coining the word serendipity, refers to this ability as "sagacity" (Roberts, 1989, p. 244). Serendipity promises success from setbacks but only for those wise enough to recognize that in setbacks there are opportunities.

Many of science and industry's most important discoveries have been products of serendipity. These include penicillin, X-rays, vulcanized rubber, and infrared radiation (Roberts, 1989). Serendipity also has been implicated in numerous product developments that arguably have become indispensable to Western popular culture—everything from Post-it Notes and NutraSweet to Ivory Soap and Velcro. Chance is implicated in these discoveries, but chance lies at the confluence of effort and preparation. As Louis Pasteur was once quoted as saying, "Chance favors only the prepared mind" (in Van Andel, 1994, p. 635). The fact that serendipity is deemed a faculty suggests that it is a skill that can be cultivated, exercised, and harnessed for positive ends. Serendipity and luck are not necessarily the same thing, though they are related. Luck is perceptual and "constructed" in the sense that emergent outcomes, be they positive or negative, are ascribed to good or bad luck. Luck implies fatalism—the belief that one's destiny is beyond his or her control (Miller, 1958). Yet some people are more lucky than others, and these people may be doing things that enhance their opportunity structure for luck. They may have a unique ability to recognize chance opportunities when they arise. Or, they have access to networks that convey relevant information, are more open to new experiences than others, and have a better-developed intuitive capacity. Lucky people also tend to be optimistic in the sense that expectations of good fortune often produce good fortune. When bad fortune comes instead of good fortune, optimists reframe the experience in positive ways (Wiseman, 2003).

In street culture, serendipity's meaning is more nuanced. Certainly, serendipity is an artifact of finding something valuable when looking for something unrelated. But serendipity also is about how offenders transform unfavorable developments into valued outcomes. Analysts may call this luck, but some settings are "more lucky" than others, and, not infrequently, this will be determined by the position in which offenders place themselves and how they react once they are there. In other social settings, serendipity affords a built-in temporal cushion between discovery, recognition, and action. In street culture, such phases are more or less coterminous. Targets of predatory robbery are there one moment and gone the next, requiring decisive action. The alternative is to "manufacture" serendipity, adopting targeting strategies that are sensitive to time and space in order to *make* things happen. Not infrequently, the decision to do this will be energized by negative situations that offenders realize they can transform into positive ones. The extent to which robbery targets emerge spontaneously (pure serendipity) or through some degree of manipulation (manufactured serendipity) offers a window into the offender decision-making process that in turn sheds light on the conceptual interface between perception, need, opportunity, and rational choice. Two forms of robbery—carjacking and drug robbery—provide a medium to explore this interface.

Pure Serendipity

One of the most striking findings to emerge from the interviews is the extent to which targets of predatory robbery materialized almost magically in time and space. Victims "became" victims after crossing paths with offenders at the right— or wrong (depending on one's perspective)—time. In a number of cases, serendipity made the target selection process appear to be almost effortless.

Driving around one afternoon, one respondent was approached by a young man who broached the idea of a drug sale. Although the respondent did need drugs and also had a firearm on his person, his explicit intention was not to commit a robbery (at the time, he was driving to his girlfriend's house and attempting to meet a friend there). When the would-be victim introduced the idea of a drug transaction, the respondent realized that he could simply take what he would otherwise have had to buy and secure more than he could have purchased in the process. Robbery was the inevitable result:

> Well one of these young guys come up to my car asking me if I wanted to buy some drugs. . . . I had wanted me some drugs that day and I didn't have enough money and I happened to see the little guy on the street, so he had me just pull over. I was going to see a friend of mine. . . . I needed to go to a friend of mine and get something. . . . So he [the friend] wasn't at home, so I saw him [the victim] and he happened to run up to my car. So I said yes, I would like to buy some. So he got in the car with me, he wasn't aware that I had a gun in the car. So I told him, "You know what time it is, this is a robbery." So I stuck my gun up in his face to let him know that I wasn't playing. So he gave me $450 cash, he gave me five grams of Boy [heroin] . . . and four tenths and about 20 pills. (Blackwell)

Another respondent described a strikingly similar encounter, also unfolding as the respondent roamed the streets in unrelated pursuits. The eventual victim approached the respondent and his brother's vehicle at a red light, soliciting a drug sale. This simple interrogatory transformed the offenders' decision-making calculus, implanted the robbery idea, and unleashed the offense:

> No, we [were not looking to rob anybody]. We just out riding and then we stopped at a red light and he [the eventual victim] walked up on us talking about did you want to buy something, so he [my brother] pulled out a gun. . . . He didn't say nothing, he just pulled it [the gun] out. . . . And then when he pulled the gun on him, then he told me to get out of the car and take his little stuff. . . . I think he [my brother] really thought he had rocks or something, but he only had like six packs of weed . . . [and] like $600 something. . . . Just took his stuff and we just pulled off. (V-O)

As Roberts (1989, p. 244) points out, persons attuned to the prospects of serendipity will observe a phenomenon that is unexpected and take note of it "rather than dismiss it as trivial or annoying." This faculty is particularly valuable in carjacking, the other modality of robbery explored in this paper. By its nature, carjacking is less dependent on the mobility of the offender than of the victim (Jacobs, Topalli, & Wright, 2003). For perpetrators, the trick is to have the "sagacity" (Roberts, 1989) to recognize opportunities when they appear. As Joseph Henry once remarked, "The seeds of great discovery are constantly floating around us, but they only take root in minds well prepared to receive them" (in Roberts, 1989, p. 65). Edwin Sutherland (1937) famously called this the "larceny sense" (see also Copes & Cherbonneau, 2006). Little Tye illustrates it emphatically below:

> My partner, he wanted him some rims. He had just bought this little Malibu and he just wanted rims. I needed a radio and some speakers, so it all came down like, they were goin' over there. We saw this little cat over there by a little liquor store . . . with his gal over there, pumping his beats, riding his rims, goddamn, me and my partner got on [it]. . . . It's just something we wanted to do. [We had money but] we'd rather go take it than spend the money in our pockets. . . . That's what I'm saying, we don't need no money. We have money. We're selling dope, we got money. We stay in the projects, we got money. It's just something, we steal cars, I mean that's what we want. We don't want it, we go sell it. I mean we don't give it away, we go sell it to get more money. . . . You know what happens, when you see, like, a baby when they see someone, they get surprised and so happy. When they see something they want, they're gonna cry for it, they want it. [That's like us.] That's how we live, I mean. . . . You can never have enough of money.

Unlike other forms of street robbery that emerge by chance, carjacking puts a particular premium on spontaneity. A "regular" robbery victim might be banked in a perceptual reservoir for future consideration (see, e.g., Hochstetler 2001; Wright & Decker, 1994; Wright & Decker, 1997), but a desirable car is there one minute and gone the next. Acting decisively can mean the difference between hitting a "lick," as offenders refer to it, or going home empty-handed. Carjacking is rapid and simple, and the reward doubles as an escape mechanism:

> I was coming from the club and I was drunk and high . . . you know, everybody go to the East Side to go see girls and stuff, you know, meet girls. . . . We was coming back to [town]. We was leaving [one place and] coming back in to [town]. We seen him [the eventual victim] on our way to [town]. We had seen him at a stoplight. . . . It was like at night, real late at night, about 2:00 in the morning. . . . He was just riding through and he stopped at a stoplight. . . . I was like, man, I like that car, man, and I love [the color] red. . . . It [the idea to car-jack] . . . come in my head once I see the car. I say I want that and I'm gonna go get that. . . . He [the victim] looked like a punk. I wanted to take the car from him, you know, so we went over there and took it. . . . I already got what I need, a gun . . . ran up to him and put the gun to his head, "Get out of the car." He got out of the car and we was up on him, we skirted off. (C-Ball)

MANUFACTURING SERENDIPITY

The foregoing accounts reveal the fluidity and open-endedness of target selection when serendipity is more or less "pure." While it is an overstatement to suggest that targets select themselves in such cases, their situated vulnerability moves offenders from an indifferent state to one in which they are determined to act (c.f. Topalli & Wright, 2004). Although happenstance certainly produces moments of pure serendipity, more typically, effort is required to convert opportunities into scores. Effort requires knowledge of when, where, and under what circumstances strategies for manipulating time and space will produce favorable outcomes. To outsiders uninitiated in the ways of the street, the process can be difficult to master. To offenders accustomed to street-level dynamics, it can become almost second nature.

At the most basic level, manufacturing serendipity requires that offenders have a reasonably well-developed "perceptual shorthand" (Skolnick, 1966) to identify the likely emergence of predatory targets based on time, place, and circumstance. Palpable to the offenders who exercise it but difficult for many to articulate, it is a shorthand that maximizes the efficiency of effort relative to expected rewards.

By manufacturing serendipity, I mean fashioning circumstances that create fortuitous accidents. Manufacturing serendipity requires that offenders manipulate activity patterns in ways that produce temporal and spatial convergence with would-be crime targets. The convergence is anticipatory because it is based on probabilistic assessments of likely target-rich times and places (see also Branting-ham & Brantingham, 1978; Copes & Cherbonneau, 2006; Topalli, 2005). The convergence is historical in the sense that it draws from experiential knowledge of the perceived suitability of such venues. Offenders are passive-aggressive "foragers" who move with purpose and logic (Bernasco & Block, 2009, p. 95) even as their activity appears random. Offenders rely on emergent and difficult-to-predict circumstances while manipulating activity patterns in ways that permit exploitation of the targets that do emerge. This curious mix of agency and constraint can result in substantial bounties:

> I cruise around neighborhoods mostly every day like that to find out where the dope dealers are you know. . . . When I left out of [one area], I'm coming up from [street] going towards [street]. I make a left on [street]. See, first I started in [one area] looking. Couldn't find nobody in [that area], so I go over on [street]. See I know these little cats on [street], they usually be out. I didn't see them. So I say, ok, it was about 12:00. I'm gonna find somebody, you know. I go up on [street] and [street], that dude standing out flagging you know. . . . So he flagged me down. He said, "Hey brother, what's up, you looking?" I told him, "Yeah, I'm looking." He said, "What you looking for?" Told him, "I'm looking for some Boy [heroin] and some rock." He said, "All right, look, check this here out. You don't mind if I get in your car?" I told him, "No, come on, get on in there." He said, "Drive around the corner." I take him around the corner, instead of going right around the corner, go right around the corner, jump right on [street], jump on [the Interstate. . . . He said], "Hey, brother, what's up, what's up?" "You know what's up, you know what's up now. You can't get out of the car. Say, what's up. You gonna get out of the car when we doing 65 miles an hour on the highway, can't get out of the car, you know what's up, you know." So he say, "Don't kill me, man, don't kill me." "I'm not gonna kill you, I just want your dope and your money, man, that's all I want and be kind enough to take you back down on [street] and drop you off by the highway." That's how I got him. (Do-dirty)[1]

Bennett and Wright's (1984) "searchers" acted in a reasonably similar manner, but unlike the offenders explored here, their offenders waited before exploiting targets. Offenders who manufacture serendipity act more or less contemporaneously after spotting the target.

Whereas the above respondent discusses the importance of circulating generally within a target-rich environment, other offenders applied a more direct approach. Manufacturing serendipity could be quite purposive in this regard. The logic that drives the selection process is the same—putting oneself in a position to capitalize on emergent opportunities that are uncertain but possible and drawing from experiential knowledge to do so—but the selection process itself is less random. Thus, one respondent, Goldie, received information about the possible emergence of a carjacking target. Although the information was not precise, it was sufficiently specific to get him to lurk. Pure serendipity may be about finding something fortuitous while looking for something different, but manufactured serendipity creates an opportunity structure for fortuity by merging luck with preparation. As Roberts (1989, p. 119) notes, "Discoveries have been made, not only 'by really trying,' but also by clever design or *conception*."[2] Goldie illustrates this logic as it relates to his hunch about a carjacking target:

> I'm standing across the street like I'm waiting on a bus or something sitting at this stoplight. . . . I got the drop that he [a car] usually come through this certain place, [street] and [street] around this time. I was standing at the bus stop

waiting on him, you know. . . . I'm standing there hoping, and if he don't come, you know, but he did. . . . Just chilling and he pulled up, you know, and the [stop] light changed just in time. I ran up over there, put the gun to his head, asked him if he was going to get out or die, you know what I'm saying, either one, you going to get out this motherfucker or die? . . . First night [waiting for him]. First night got his ass. . . . [Lucky.] Yeah.

Manufacturing serendipity can be particularly important when predatory robberies flow from moralistic concerns. Criminologists have long recognized that robbery and assault serve as social control devices for offenders who are wronged by others (Black, 1983). The need to manufacture serendipity for moralistic reasons can on occasion be quite reflexive—a product of provocative target behavior at a discrete moment in time. Although in purely serendipitous incidents, would-be victims also play a role in their own selection, in those incidents, being at the right place results less from victim precipitation than bad timing. In a moralistically energized incident, the target behaves in a way that creates a specific imbalance in need of rectification. The offender transforms the imbalance into an opportunity for gain. Being aggrieved certainly is not invited or appreciated by respondents (which the notion of serendipity can, at times, imply), but the affront does permit offenders to turn something unwelcome into something propitious, and that lies at the core of serendipity as a situational process. J Rock thus explains what he did to a drug dealer who "disrespected" him:

Like I ask them [for drugs] for something and they don't give it to me, I'll tell 'em, "I'm coming back for your ass," and I come back. You think I'm bullshitting, I'll rob his ass. Come right back. . . . [Put the gun in their face] "Give me all your dope and all your money now. I asked for something and you wouldn't give me nothing, so now I want it all." . . . . Don't fuck with me, nobody, nobody, nobody.

Although objective financial need certainly primes the selection process (as the above respondent implies), manufacturing serendipity requires a perceptual trigger to generate awareness of debasement (Tittle, 1995). In street culture, sensitivity is high, so such triggers are in ample supply. This is especially true of carjacking because imbalances are frequently created by mobile displays of wealth perceived by would-be offenders to be insulting. Flossing, as it is sometimes called, constitutes both a putdown and a provocation (Jacobs, Topalli, & Wright, 2003) and creates an imbalance that cries out for rectification. The provocation may not be welcome, but the opportunity to make something fortuitous come out of it is:

We were tired of seeing them just coming through, always trying to floss as they went past . . . always wanting to go somewhere and stare, or always showing off, talking a lot. . . . Me and my partner, we saw him pull up to the lot [while we were sitting in a park next door]. . . . He [the victim] went into the [gas station], and he was pumping the gas. His partner was listening to the news. . . . It was late, round about 2, 2:30. . . . Boy I knew he had some money. . . . People drive around like that. . . . From his pockets, we took about five Gs. . . . You floss it too much, you get robbed. . . . He tried to floss, man. (Snake)

DISCUSSION

The methods and motives of robbery are well understood. Less clear are the situational factors that give rise to perceptions of opportunity irrespective of method or motive. The objective of this paper has been to refocus attention on this situated convergence through the concept of serendipity.

Robberies have long been described as "low-level, desperate, and impulsive exploits" that rarely involve advance planning (Alarid, Burton, & Hochstetler, 2009, p. 2; see also Feeney, 1986). Although prior research emphasizes the role of opportunity in triggering such events, only recently have studies begun in earnest to identify the situated manner in which opportunity is constructed (see, e.g., Hochstetler, 2001). The present paper has sought to expand this line of inquiry by sensitizing readers to the notion of serendipity.

Serendipity requires that offenders both make, and let, things happen. The latter is especially consequential given the frequency with which moments of pure serendipity arise. The transition from relative indifference to committed action is rapid, and the capacity for motivation to "flex" in this way has not been examined in any great detail by prior etiological studies of crime. Likely, this is because criminologists view offender motivation through static risk factors. Risk factors create predispositions to crime, but they neither cause nor shape crime in the offending moment. The offending moment is the magical instant by which indifference transforms into committed action. The speed of this transformation can be torrid, as this paper has demonstrated.

Spontaneity may imply irrationality, but the spontaneity that drives serendipity is firmly rooted in reasoned calculation, a process long associated with rational choice. Over two centuries ago, this tradition embarked with two seminal treatises in utilitarian theory—Beccaria's 240-year-old *An Essay on Crimes and Punishment* and Bentham's comparably historic *An Introduction to the Principles of Morals and Legislation*. By focusing on sanction threats and how would-be offenders react to them, Beccaria (1764/1963) presumed that offenders ponder what they are going to do and how they are going to do it before they do it. Bentham (1789) similarly opined that would-be offenders exercise a "quantum of sensibility" in how they construct, define, and respond to criminogenic circumstances.

Over the years, rational-choice theorists have refined the focus by adding concepts like decision frames (Tversky & Kahneman, 1981), editing/evaluation (Kahneman & Tversky, 1979) and noncompensatory strategizing (Johnson & Payne, 1986). Decision frames come from "prospect theory" (Lattimore & Witte, 1986), an approach that explores how offenders discern among various conduct options based on the discrete outcome probabilities of each. Editing/evaluation is a more complicated process in which offenders code, combine, segregate, cancel, simplify, and detect dominance in relation to some anticipated action. This analytic process requires that offenders be sensitive to things such as decision weights, value functions, and risk perceptions as each relates to outcome probabilities (Lattimore & Witte, 1986).

Noncompensatory strategizing, the third approach, is simpler and more relevant to serendipity. It holds that offender rationality is limited, and that offenders weigh but a few aspects of a few alternatives and ignore the rest (Johnson & Payne, 1986, p. 173). Noncompensatory strategizing promotes "standing decisions" (Cook, 1980) that offenders cultivate over time and which they invoke on command. Steeped in "iterative agency" (Emirbayer & Mische, 1998), standing decisions sensitize offenders to patterns and practices and permit efficient reaction to emergent cues (Emirbayer & Mische, 1998). Offenders learn "which discriminative cues are associated with 'good' targets," and these cues "then serve as a 'template'" applied in subsequent actions (Cromwell & Olsen, 2004, p. 19). Expertise may play a role in this process (Topalli, 2005), although the nature of expertise's role is unclear. Novice offenders, for example, may be less constrained by biases and more apt to "go with the flow," which can expand choice and the universe of would-be crime opportunities to recognize.

Despite its centrality to offender decision making, theorists have largely ignored serendipity's function in the noncompensatory strategic toolkit. Certainly, opportunities arise, but opportunities mean nothing unless or until they are perceived, recognized, and acted upon by offenders. Serendipity bridges the gap between the emergence of opportunity and opportunity's exploitation because it is a faculty that offenders exercise.

Prior research mistakes serendipity for opportunity and fails to grasp the distinction between the two. Opportunity is inherent; serendipity is referential. Opportunity is situation-focused; serendipity nests offenders in those situations. Opportunity is fixed; serendipity is adaptable. Opportunity is an event; serendipity is a capacity. Even when prior research explores opportunity, it does so almost exclusively through the lens of need (see, e.g., Hochstetler 2001; Topalli & Wright, 2004). Thus, studies repeatedly emphasize how intense pressures energize offending decisions and distort the manner in which offenders reach these decisions. Wright and Decker (1994, pp. 200–201) found that all but a few of their offenders typically "began to contemplate the commission of their [offenses] while under intense emotional pressure to obtain money as quickly as possible." This required them to develop a repository of crime targets they could tap when desperation inevitably set in. Only one person in Wright and Decker's sample of over 100 offenders qualified as purely opportunistic (i.e., serendipitously minded)—someone who "'just happen[ed] upon' a vulnerable target and, as a result, commit[ted] an offense on the spur of the moment" (1994, p. 99). Moreover, nearly 90% of their sample had a *specific target* in mind before setting out to offend (Wright & Decker, 1994, p. 63). In an earlier study of British offenders, Bennett and Wright (1984) found similarly that only 7% of their sample fit the "opportunist" category—equivalent to someone who responded reflexively to unexpected but favorable situational cues, that is, someone who responded seren-dipitously. It is precisely because desperate offenders cannot predict when and under what circumstances opportunities will arise that serendipity was a residual category in these studies.

The robbery literature is afflicted similarly by its disproportionate focus on need and how opportunity passively works through it (see Wright & Decker, 1997). The robbery literature is peppered with descriptions of desperate offenders trolling the streets seeking to attack the first suitable target into which they run. Thus, Jacobs' robbers were "very much spinning out of control" (2000, pp. 42–43). Wright and Decker's (1997) robbers lurched from one crisis to the next. Topalli and Wright's (2004) carjackers sacrificed prudence for immediacy. Feeney's (1986) robbers, at times, careened into crimes.

None of these studies explore serendipity as an empirical process or mean-ingfully link it to the construction of criminal opportunity *in situ*. Part of the problem is that studies on criminality in general, and on offender decision making in particular, conflate desperation with impulsivity and imply that the latter and former are one and the same. Concomitantly, these studies presume that desperation so limits rationality that serendipity, as a faculty, cannot mean-ingfully be exercised. The renowned lack of planning on the part of many rob-bery offenders is thought to be *prima facie* evidence of their recklessness. Certainly, the present study does not wish to disabuse readers of the urgency that frequently imbues robbery offenders' actions. It does, however, wish to sensitize readers to the distinction between impulsivity and recklessness so that serendip-ity's conceptual import can better be grasped.

Impulsivity lies at the heart of street crime, and robbery tends to be no ex-ception. Impulsive people want things the easy way; they are risk seeking, at-tracted to thrills, and unable to defer gratification (Gottfredson & Hirschi, 1990). Numerous scholars (see, e.g., Nagin & Pogarsky, 2003) have noted how present orientation interferes with the ability to process potential setbacks, setbacks being critical to understanding how serendipity operates as a faculty. In particu-lar, impulsivity subsumes a "here and now" worldview and the "commensurate tendency to devalue or discount delayed consequences" (Pogarsky & Piquero, 2004, p. 374).

> By seeking immediate gratification, those [with high levels of impulsivity] are relatively unmoved by the potential pains of punishment that are both uncer-tain and removed in the future. As such, the "emotional force" of present desires overwhelms the apprehension of pain in the future. (Wright et al., 2004, p. 182)

But the present orientation that guides the serendipitous exploitation of crime targets underscores a sensitivity to future consequences, not an ignorance of them. Indeed, the longer-term outlook that mediates serendipitous conduct arguably is risk averse, not risk seeking. Not only have choice theorists failed to appreciate this wrinkle in offender decision making, they have emphasized just the opposite:

> In decision making parlance, the criminal opportunity presents a choice between a sure thing (restraint from the criminal act), and a gamble that arises because the contemplated conduct can produce a gain with some probability and a loss with complementary probability. Individuals who tend more toward the safety of a sure thing rather than risk a loss are considered risk-averse. In contrast, individuals with the opposite propensity, namely, to risk a loss for even the slightest chance of reward, are considered risk-seeking. (Nagin & Pogarsky, 2001, p. 885)

Offenders who act serendipitously, and particularly those who do not face pressing needs at the time, capitalize on a "sure thing" *and* make moot the uncertainty of the crime target's reemergence. By forestalling the emergence of desperation that ultimately will *require* them to act, offenders reveal the forward-thinking potential of impulsive action.

Impulsivity can also affect the manner in which serendipity is enacted. Conventional criminological wisdom holds that offenders living in and for the moment will be hard pressed to focus on anything but that moment (Gottfredson & Hirschi, 1990). Conventional wisdom also holds that "bounded rationality" is especially problematic in high-velocity, uncertain environments imbued with desperation (such as street culture). On their face, such conditions would seem to restrict the functional expression of serendipity because they compromise choice. The present study brings this into question and is supported by research in cognitive psychology, which suggests that bounded rationality may improve rather than undermine the perceptual clarity upon which serendipity relies to operate. Actors who face strict limits on the factors they can realistically attend to can discern emergent cues more efficiently. When information loads lighten, decision-makers are better able to ignore irrelevant data and focus on cues of real substance (see, e.g., Khatri & Ng, 2000). Bounds on rationality may thereby encourage offenders to lock into discrete moments and discern them resourcefully and creatively, sharpening serendipity's edge and the strategic vision necessary to invoke it.

That being said, two essential links in offender decision making must be addressed if analysts ever are to understand why offenders perceive things the way they do and how they act once the perception is made (Piquero & Pogarsky, 2002). The first is the manner by which information known to an actor becomes a judgment. The second is the manner by which such judgments influence actual behavior (Piquero & Pogarsky, 2002, p. 154). Research on offender decision making has left these processes largely untapped. When it does explore them, the bulk of the focus is on person-based traits as opposed to situations (see, e.g., Nagin & Pogarsky, 2003). Because serendipity explores persons nested in situations, the oversight is problematic.

A cursory review of the data presented in the current paper reveals the prominence of situational factors. A number of factors were relevant, but the role of weapon availability and co-offenders was especially germane. Firearms routinely transformed indifference into committed action, irrespective of objective needs. Firearms obviously inflict serious injury, they can do it from a distance, and everyone knows that firearms have these attributes, which makes for a highly effective contingent threat (Cook, 1982) and a rapid way to convert nascent motives into action. Co-offenders were equally powerful in catalyzing the process, which is understandable given that decision-makers in group settings "do not respond passively to situational opportunity; they create it by selecting and transforming the situations they confront" (Hochstetler, 2001, p. 740). In particular, co-offenders encourage accomplices to take risks. They embolden behavior, diffuse responsibility, and enhance perceptions of dominance—all of which entice decision-makers to seek out opportunity with greater vigor and manufacture it with more intense resolve. Co-offenders, finally, quicken the pace by which actual decisions are made, which can reveal serendipitous circumstances more readily or encourage offenders to act on them with less regret. Certainly, the cases of V-O, Little Tye, and C-Ball highlight this powerful process of "social exchange" (McCluskey & Wardle, 1999; see also Alarid, Burton, & Hochstetler, 2009).

Because serendipity is a faculty that involves the situated capacity to turn setbacks into opportunities, the manner in which "setback experiences" influence serendipity's structure and process warrants empirical attention. Deterrence theorists have made analogous arguments regarding the relationship between prior punishment experiences and future criminality (see, e.g., Paternoster & Piquero, 1995): punishment experiences can influence the manner in which offenders contemplate additional crime (see Minor & Harry, 1982, on the "experiential effect") by promoting more nuanced decisions that carry a lower risk of detection. Setback experiences may similarly sensitize offenders in the realm of opportunity perception and perhaps promote greater efficacy in serendipity's exercise. We know this happens in the "real world." Research on entrepreneurship, for example, shows a direct correlation between prior failures and innovation potential (Minniti & Bygrave, 2001). The most prolific entrepreneurs the world over typically experience setback after setback before tasting success, and only taste success because failure is pedagogical (Roberts, 1989). Street offenders are widely perceived to be failures in almost every sense of the word. Maybe it is failure that makes serendipity possible and real.

Experiential effects highlight this "accretive" potential (Zimring & Hawkins, 1973) of serendipity. Accretion is important because it implies dynamic interplay and/or conditional interaction between different forms of serendipity, both of which ultimately influence how or when serendipity is expressed. For example, having a crime target fall onto one's lap doesn't mean that serendipity won't be manufactured a moment later if a previously established target emerges or if some affront moves offenders from a neutral state to one in which they are determined to act. Crime targets may also emerge one after another in a purely serendipitous manner, which can alter the trajectory of serendipity-based decision making: a series of purely serendipitous encounters can make offenders "resistant" to incidents that might otherwise require serendipity to be manufactured (e.g., in response to an affront). Conversely, frustration tolerances may rise after a spate of good but unexpected fortune, permitting offenders to develop greater cognitive clarity in how they exercise serendipity: a series of positive outcomes can liberate the psyche from worry and allow offenders to devote energy to cultivating chance encounters that bear yet more fruit. At the same time, bad fortune can also make offenders more attuned to their environment, more sensitive to affronts, and more apt to manufacture serendipity from negative events. Whether hypersensitivity "primes" reactions in general, or makes offenders more discerning of crime targets in particular, is unclear and merits additional research attention.

In the final analysis, serendipity speaks to the nondeterministic nature of offender decision making. Although opportunity may, in some cases, "make the thief" (as the nineteenth-century French saying holds; see Fattah, 1993, p. 246), opportunity is unpredictable and must be appraised. Appraisals are based on the sense that offenders "make of situations using contextually relevant precedent and experience." Indeed, offenders "construct criminal opportunity by comparing recently formulated understandings [against] developing events and adjusting situations to make events and understanding correspond" (Hochstetler, 2001, pp. 747, 756). By definition, uncertain events rarely occur in predictable frequencies, but emergent cues can be recognized, processed, and manipulated for productive ends. Serendipity hinges on this curious combination of agency and constraint. When action and receptivity interact in such a way, favorable outcomes result from unexpected and even negative events.

NOTES

1. Bennnett and Wright's (1984) "searchers" acted in a reasonable similar manner, but unlike the offenders explored here, their offenders waited before exploiting targets. Offenders who manufacture serendipity act more or less contemporaneously after spotting the target.

2. This is why building contractors occasionally hire archaeologists to be on site during certain excavations. The frequency with which artifacts of one sort or another are unearthed while digging makes the occurrence predictable. Such a practice betrays the inherent recognition of a likely serendipitous find simply by preparing for it (Roberts, 1989, p. 106).

REFERENCES

Alarid, L. F., Burton, V. S., & Hochstetler, A. L. (2009). Group and solo robberies: Do accomplices shape criminal form? *Journal of Criminal Justice, 37,* 1–9.

Beccaria, C. (1764/1963). *On crimes and punishments.* Trans. H. Paolucci. Indianapolis: Bobbs-Merrill.

Bennett, T., & Wright, R. (1984). *Burglars on burglary: Prevention and the offender.* Aldershot: Gower.

Bentham, J. (1789). *An introduction to the principles of morals and legislation.* London: Hafner.

Bernasco, W., & Block, R. (2009). Where offenders choose to attack: A discrete choice model of robberies in Chicago. *Criminology, 47,* 93–130.

Black, D. (1983). Crime as social control. *American Sociological Review, 48,* 34–45.

Brantingham, P. J., & Brantingham, P. L. (1978). A theoretical model of crime site selection. In M. D. Krohn & R. X. Akers (Eds.), *Crime, law and sanctions* (pp. 105–118). Beverly Hills, CA: Sage.

Carroll, J., & Weaver, F. (1986). Shoplifters' perceptions of crime opportunities: A process-tracing study. In D. B. Cornish & R. V. G. Clarke (Eds.), *The reasoning criminal: Rational choice perspectives on offending.* New York: Springer-Verlag, 19–37.

Cook, P. J. (1980). Research in criminal deterrence: Laying the groundwork for the second decade. In M. Tonry and N. Morris (Eds.), *Crime and justice: An annual review of research* (Vol. 2). Chicago: University of Chicago Press, 211–268.

———. (1982). The role of firearms in violent crimes: An interpretative review of the literature, with some new findings and suggestions for further research. In M. E. Wolfgang & N. A. Weiner, *Criminal violence* (pp. 236–291). Beverly Hills, CA: Sage.

Copes, H., & Cherbonneau, M. (2006). The key to auto theft: Emerging methods of auto theft from the offenders' perspective. *British Journal of Criminology, 46,* 917–934.

Cornish, D. B, & Clarke, R. V. (1986). *The reasoning criminal: Rational choice perspectives on offending.* New York: Springer-Verlag.

Cromwell, P., & Olson, J. N. (2004). *Breaking and entering: Burglars on burglary.* Belmont, CA: Wadsworth.

Emirbayer, M., & Mische, A. (1998). What is agency? *American Journal of Sociology, 103,* 962–1023.

Fattah, E. A. (1993). The rational choice/opportunity perspectives as a vehicle for integrating criminological and victimological theories. In R. V. Clarke & M. Felson (Eds.), *Routine activity and rational choice: Advances in criminological theory* (pp. 225–258). New Brunswick, NJ: Transaction.

Feeney, F. (1986). Robbers as decision-makers. In D. Cornish & R. Clarke (Eds.), *The reasoning criminal: Rational choice perspectives on offending* (pp. 53–71). New York: Springer-Verlag.

Felson, M. (1998). *Crime and everyday life* (2nd ed.). Thousand Oaks, CA: Pine Forge.

Gottfredson, M., & Hirschi, T. (1990). *A general theory of crime.* Palo Alto, CA: Stanford University Press.

Hochstetler, A. (2001). Opportunities and decisions: Interactional dynamics in robbery and burglary groups. *Criminology, 39,* 737–764.

———. (2002). Sprees and runs: The construction of opportunity in criminal episodes. *Deviant Behavior, 23,* 45–74.

Jacobs, B. A. (2000). *Robbing drug dealers: Violence beyond the law.* New York: Aldine de Gruyter.

Jacobs, B. A., Topalli, V., & Wright, R. (2003). Carjacking, street life, and offender motivation. *British Journal of Criminology, 43,* 673–688.

Jacobs, B. A., & Wright, R. (1999). Stick-up, street culture, and offender motivation. *Criminology, 37,* 149–173.

Johnson, E., & Payne, J. (1986). The decision to commit a crime: An information-processing analysis. In D. B. Cornish & R. V. Clarke (Eds.), *The reasoning criminal* (pp. 170–185). New York: Springer-Verlag.

Kahneman, D., & Tversky, A. (1979). Prospect theory: An analysis of decisions under risk. *Econometrica, 47,* 313–327.

Khatri, N., & Ng, H. A. (2000). The role of intuition in strategic decision making. *Human Relations, 53,* 57–86.

Lattimore, P., & Witte, A. (1986). Models of decision making under uncertainty: The criminal choice. In D. B. Cornish & R. V. Clarke (Eds.), *The reasoning* (pp. 130–155). New York: Springer-Verlag.

McCluskey, K., & Wardle, S. (1999). The social structure of robbery. In D. Canter & L. Alison (Eds.), *The social psychology of crime: Groups, teams, and networks* (pp. 247–285). Aldershot, UK: Ashgate/Dartmouth.

Merton, R. K., & Barber, E. (2006). *The travels and adventures of serendipity: A study in sociological semantics and the sociology of science.* Princeton, NJ: Princeton University Press.

Miller, W. (1958). Lower-class culture as a generating milieu of gang delinquency. *Journal of Social Issues, 14,* 5–19.

Minniti, M., & Bygrave, W. (2001). A dynamic model of entrepreneurial learning. *Entrepreneurship Theory and Practice, 25,* 5–16.

Minor, W. W., & Harry, J. (1982). Deterrent and experiential effects in perceptual deterrence research: A replication and extension. *Journal of Research in Crime and Delinquency, 19,* 190–203.

Nagin, D. S., & Pogarsky, G. (2001). Integrating celerity, impulsivity, and extralegal sanction threats into a model of general deterrence: Theory and evidence. *Criminology, 39,* 865–889.

———. (2003). An experimental investigation of deterrence: Cheating, self-serving bias, and impulsivity. *Criminology, 41,* 167–191.

Paternoster, R., & Piquero, A. R. (1995). Reconceptualizing deterrence: An empirical test of personal and vicarious experiences. *Journal of Research in Crime and Delinquency, 32,* 251–286.

Pogarsky, G., & Piquero, A. R. (2004). Studying the reach of deterrence: Can deterrence theory help explain police misconduct? *Journal of Criminal Justice, 32,* 371–386.

Roberts, R. M. (1989). *Serendipity: accidental discoveries in science.* New York: John Wiley & Sons.

Skolnick, J. H. (1966). *Justice without trial: Law enforcement in democratic society.* New York: Wiley.

Sutherland, E. H. (1937). *The professional thief.* Chicago: University of Chicago Press.

Tittle, C. R. (1995). *Control balance.* Boulder, CO: Westview.

Topalli, V. (2005). Criminal expertise and offender decision-making: An experimental analysis of how offenders and non-offenders differentially perceive social stimuli. *British Journal of Criminology, 45,* 269–295.

Topalli, V., & Wright, R. (2004). Dubs, dees, beats, and rims: Carjacking and urban violence. In D. Dabney (Ed.), *Crime types: A text reader.* Belmont CA: Wadsworth, 149–169.

Tversky, A., & Kahneman, D. (1981). The framing of decisions and the psychology of choice. *Science, 211,* 453–458.

Van Andel, P. (1994). Anatomy of the unsought finding: Serendipity: Origin, history, domains, traditions, appearances, patterns and programmability. *British Journal for the Philosophy of Science, 45,* 631–648.

Wiseman, R. (2003). *The luck factor.* London, UK: Random House.

Wright, B. R. E., Caspi, A., Moffitt, T. E., & Paternoster, R. (2004). Does the perceived risk of punishment deter criminally prone individuals? Rational choice, self-control, and crime. *Journal of Research in Crime and Delinquency, 41,* 180–213.

Wright, R., Brookman, F., & Bennett, T. (2006). The foreground dynamics of street robbery in Britain. *British Journal of Criminology, 46,* 1–15.

Wright, R., & Decker, S. H. (1994). *Burglars on the job.* Boston: Northeastern University Press.

———. (1997). *Armed robbers in action: Stickups and street culture.* Boston: Northeastern University Press.

Zimring, F. E., & Hawkins, G. J. (1973). *Deterrence: The legal threats in crime control.* Chicago: University of Chicago Press.

CHAPTER 11

Peaceful Warriors: Codes for Violence Among Adult Male Bar Fighters

Heith Copes, Andy Hochstetler, and Craig J. Forsyth

Considerable theoretical and empirical inquiry has focused on the role codes for violence play in generating crime. A large part of this work has examined the attitudes and codes condoning retaliation and violence as well as the prevalence of these among minorities residing in impoverished neighborhoods. Much about the nature of codes remains unknown, however, and this may in part reflect a narrow interest in beliefs about provocation and uses of violence among the inner-city poor. In this study, we elaborate on a code of violence as part of a system of order and honor as articulated by a network of white, working-class males in a southern U.S. city who participate in bar fights. The findings suggest that the code these men use prohibits predatory violence, puts exclusive limitations on situations that warrant violence, and constrains the level of violence in a fight. We detail the contours of this code (e.g., purpose of fighting, the rules of honorable fighting, and justifications for violating these rules) and discuss the code as both a cause and a consequence of behavior.

INTRODUCTION

The maturing "cultural turn" in the social sciences has reinvigorated interest among criminologists in the narratives and lives of offenders (Agnew, 2006; Presser, 2010; Sandberg, 2009a, 2010). This interest has been occurring alongside renewed attention to classic works on subculture and contemporary efforts to sketch beliefs and codes that encourage violence among certain groups. Reinvigoration of attention to culture and subculture has included recognition of

Source: Copes, H., Hochstetler, A., & Forsyth, C. (2013). Peaceful warriors: Codes for violence among adult male bar fighters. *Criminology, 51*(3), 761–794. Used with permission of publisher.

variation in adherence to behavioral codes that endorse the application of violence and differing views on the genesis and purpose of these codes. Whether investigators have conceptualized such codes for violence as understandings of the self, situational scripts for action, or culturally available toolkits, they have concurred that actors' thoughts on how to behave appropriately *in situ* intervene between cultural forms and action to determine when, where, and how actors behave. Most have agreed that subcultural codes contain general understandings of how to live and provide situational guidelines for action (Anderson, 1999; Stewart, Simmons, and Conger, 2002; Swidler, 1986).

Although it is apparent that subjective interpretations and meanings play a prominent part in violent crime commission, and this is clearly so for assaults (Athens, 1997), codes for violence are not as well understood as one might assume. There are exceptions that give thorough theoretical attention to offenders' views on the use of violence and what they are trying to accomplish by it (e.g., Athens, 1997; Katz, 1988). However, most analyses of codes for violence have focused on those found among minorities living in large metropolitan areas and typically have contained imprecise connections between codes and high rates of violent crimes in these locations (e.g., Anderson, 1999; Garot, 2010; Horowitz, 1983; Jacobs and Wright, 2006). Emphasis on the urban underclass belies the importance of codes for all people, including those living in areas outside the inner city (Jackson-Jacobs, 2013).

Additionally, despite considerable evidence for the predictive importance of adherence to a code for violence on subsequent behavior, investigators have not been in agreement about just what the codes are or how they constrain behavior. Even within a single work, it often is not clear. In a critique of Anderson's work on the code of the street, Wacquant (2002: 1491) wrote that, "The code is variously described as a set of 'informal rules,' an 'etiquette,' a 'value orientation,' an 'oppositional culture' and the objective regularities of conduct they prescribe, but also as a 'script,' a set of roles and their patterned expectations, a personal identity, a 'milieu,' and even as the 'fabric of everyday life.'" Questions about whether the code is a way that inhabitants navigate local cultural context strategically, an acculturated presentation of self, a set of attitudes about acceptability of violence, or a resource to aid rationalization after the fact reflect this ambiguity.

In this study, we contribute to the growing literature on codes for violence by examining how one network of adult, White males in a midsized southern U.S. city make sense of their participation in bar fights. We argue that examining common narratives in a purposively selected group provides insight into the structure and content of codes for violence, and into how actors connect personal identity with subcultural identities. Specifically, we focus on themes that actors use when discussing their reasons for fighting, rules that determine whether they cast violence as a respectable and necessary activity, and how understandings that endorse restrictive uses of violence lead to combat that may or may not fit the ideal form. We reveal an idealized code of acceptable violence in this group as well as a capacity to support and endorse the code despite inherent difficulties and evident contradictions when explaining fights.

Our findings speak not only to a particular code for violence but also to how codes guide individuals more generally. Our participants are conventional in most aspects and strive to use force in a way that they and their audiences deem reasonable. We conclude with a discussion of how codes affect these actors and how they use their code as a resource to construct meaningful identities. Participants do not consider their code a strict determinant of behavior, a purely practical response to their environment, or a simple set of attitudes about when to use violence. Rather, they imbue it with significant meaning as a reflection of inner integrity and honor, and they cast their fights as more or less successful attempts to follow it.

An investigator can observe the form of a code or cultural belief when individuals relay thematically similar stories or refer to patterned behavior and thinking among groups with whom they identify. One reason for interviewing offenders is that they use recurring storylines to explain who they are and what they do. That is, actors rely on shared narratives or storylines to situate their actions and selves within larger structures. Loseke (2007) described how formula stories (which exist at a cultural level) are essential for the construction and representation of identities.

FORMULA STORIES AND BEHAVIORAL CODES

Formula stories refer to "narratives of typical actors engaging in typical behaviors within typical plots leading to expectable moral evaluations" (Loseke, 2007: 664). They help people perpetuate symbolic codes and reveal what people value, what they know, and how they should behave. By relying on formula stories, actors link personal experiences and behaviors with a culturally meaningful group (one that listeners understand) for effective communication.

For offenders, formula stories can be convenient devices to show that their behaviors are not unusual or are easily understandable, if not benign and honorable, if considered in the proper cultural context. Such stories reflect larger cultural goals and values, and they situate individuals in specific cultures. Thus, street offenders articulate the code of the street to justify violence, real hustling dope fiends separate themselves from incapable sick addicts (Faupel, 1991), and white-collar offenders tell stories of providing middle-class lifestyles for their families when accounting for crimes (Klenowski, Copes, and Mullins, 2011). Brookman, Copes, and Hochstetler (2011) discussed how robbers use the code of the street to plot stories of instrumental violence. They argued that the conversational use of this code allows violent offenders to present themselves in the best possible light and aids in contextualizing acts. By demonstrating that their violence emerged from the disrespect or gullibility of victims, offenders save face, construct identity, and impart a great deal about the contexts and environments where they operate.

As formula stories are general forms, the fit of an individual narrative to a formula story often is something that speakers negotiate and work out as the story unfolds. Whether fitting a narrative to such a story or playing it against the story by explaining and rationalizing unexpected departures, narrators affirm codes relevant to themselves and the audience. Thereby, they depict experiences generally and simultaneously portray themselves as upholders of a pattern of beliefs and related lines of action.

In this study, we use explanations of fights by a small network of working class, White males residing in the American South to add to our understanding of codes for violence. By focusing on a group seldom studied when examining violence, we show that such codes are not restricted to the urban underclass and minorities. In addition to detailing the content of a code, we seek to contribute to understandings of how acceptance of codes contributes to discrete violent acts and how individuals use codes to make sense of actions retrospectively.

METHODS

We base our findings on the narratives of 23 men who had been in multiple fights with nonfamily members as adults. These individuals lived in or near the city Lafayette, Louisiana (population 120,623 as of 2010). Like most midsized cities in the southern United States, Lafayette has above-average crime rates, especially violent crime. The number of assaults per 100,000 people in Lafayette was 579, whereas across the United States it was 254. The city's population is primarily White (63.5%) and Black (30.9%). The poverty rate is high (19.8% in 2010). The most central industry in the town is oil and gas extraction. We located interviewees with the help of a lifelong resident who has a history of offenses related to drinking and fighting, and who is known for being a street fighter. He reported being in numerous bar fights (too many to list precisely), and several tavern owners have banned him entry for fighting. Although he has been arrested for disorderly conduct (including fighting), he denied taking part in other illegal activities and had no felony record. The recruiter relied on personal contacts and snowball sampling to locate the sample.

PURPOSES OF FIGHTING

The participants portrayed themselves as "peaceful warriors" who neither sought out violent confrontations nor ran from them. They described acceptable purposes for violence that went beyond the obvious notion of protection, although this was an important reason. Even when they provided protection as justification, the narrator imbued the moral of the account with broader notions of respect and the necessity of standing up against aggressors as a matter of principle. Often, they wove motives for violence together with judgments of honorable behavior and the ability to back up claims, and they presented much of this by referring to appropriate manly behavior. Fighting also meant solving problems immediately, without lingering discussions, and it avoided uncomfortable or emotional negotiations. Participants depicted it as a pragmatic deterrent of future insults and altercations: Violence taught lessons to those who insulted and those who might consider insulting in the future.

VERIFYING MASCULINE CHARACTER

Defending and verifying character is a major motivator for violence among urban and rural residents in the United States and abroad (Anderson, 1999; Brookman et al., 2011; Nisbett and Cohen, 1996). Our participants were not exceptions, and many tied this belief directly to masculinity. When asked why it was important to fight when confronted, Kevin said:

> I think it's important to show who you are as a man, how you feel about yourself, and how you feel about your friends and loved ones. [To show] that you're there to protect them. People, even your friends, need to know that you're there for them, that you're there for yourself, that you have the strength to stand up for yourself and kinda prove you're a man.

David said the willingness to fight allows people to "keep their pride intact. Just sayin' that they're not chumps." Participants asserted that principled individuals know that their character is worth defending physically (Jackson-Jacobs, 2013). They believed that fights were an important part of maintaining self-image. This belief was evident when we asked what they would think of themselves if they did not fight when insulted. In response to this question, David said, "I hate to use the word, but the word pussy comes to mind. . . . That you punked out and you couldn't handle your own business." Similarly, Kevin answered:

> I'd feel guilty. I'd feel weak. I'd feel like I let myself down. I'd feel like I let anybody else that was involved down. I'd feel like the other person involved got the upper hand. I'd feel like I lost something. And most of all I wouldn't feel like a man.

Eric said that if he did not fight he would think:

> That I just wasn't a man, straight and simple. I feel like if I'm tested and I walk away, if I didn't fight that person or prove myself, you know, I'd just feel real down on myself and feel like I'm kind of a coward. They ain't nothin' more that I hate than feelin' like a coward. So, if I'm tested, I'm gonna do what I gotta do to not feel like a coward.

Fighting affirmed a sense of self as a capable and dependable man, but also it fended off powerful negative emotions and shame from refusal to meet the call when provoked.

Being perceived as men who are willing to defend principles was important for participants' sense of self. Using violence was more than saving face; it served internalized and private purposes. A desire to uphold their character led several participants to say that at times they were disappointed deeply in themselves for not fighting. Kevin explained:

> There's times when I kicked myself for days for not hurtin' somebody because I felt they disrespected me in front of people. And just to myself, I felt less of a man. I felt guilty for not doing anything. I felt like a chump. All around it affected me for a while.

Such statements reflect the idea that regret and damage to self-concept and masculinity may linger longer than the pain caused by being struck or worries about legal consequences of a public fight. The imperative to fight in some situations buttressed notions of courage and the value of principled stances. As Dana put it, "You have to stand up for your principles. You have to stand up. That's it." Participants used fighting to reinforce valued identities and considered it part of what it meant to be a man of conviction.

Willingness to fight reportedly is not the same as eagerness to use aggression unprovoked or for felonious purposes (Jackson-Jacobs, 2013). These men condemned those who were set on fighting before they encountered a legitimate conflict. They believed that men should not contrive arguments only to demonstrate fighting prowess, and assault for robbery was inexcusable. Participants often expressed these sentiments using stereotypes of criminals and brutes for contrast and by emphasizing a generally peaceful demeanor (Hochstetler, Copes, and Williams, 2010). Dennis cast himself as a "peaceful warrior" in contrast to "agro dudes that have something to prove and are just looking for trouble." Similarly explaining the distinction between the violent and the peaceful, Renee said:

> Guys that work out and they just go out to the bars with their tight shirts that show their muscles, and they get drunk, and they go out, they lookin' for a fight. That's why they go out that night. You can tell when you see 'em. You know they lookin' for something. That's the type of people that I think are like street people, thugs, you know. I consider them violent people.

DETERRENCE

There was a pragmatic reason for a firm and unyielding stance in the face of challenge or insult. Fighters believed that by violently responding to affronts they could prevent future insults and deter potential victimizers (Topalli, Wright, and Fornango, 2002). Kelly said that, "Without doing it [fighting], you'd just be a sitting duck. You'd be the one getting beaten up. Incidentally, laying the foundation to get beat up again, picked on, taken advantage of, or exploited later." Fred indicated that his latest fight was because, "I didn't want them to think that I was just some pussy. I wanted to show that I could take care of my business." In short, some violence was motivated by the desire to communicate that aggressors had selected the wrong person to confront.

Beaten rivals from the past also show that violence can be an effective specific deterrent. As Dana said:

> [If] you tell somebody not to keep hittin' on your wife, and they're not listenin' there's gotta be consequences. . . . I told him to back off, and he didn't so I knocked him out. After that he never fucked with her again. . . . [The police] wouldn't have solved anything. Really, I solved it. Maybe it wasn't the way everybody wants it to be handled, but it was handled. I got my point across and it never happened again.

Renee emphasized that his violence was a response to an insult, and for him the important thing was to show aggressors that they cannot insult with impunity:

> You give a man a warning, you ask him to respect it, and he doesn't want to listen to you, that's almost a sign of disrespect again. And if he already disrespected you once, he's gonna disrespect you again, and he's gonna always disrespect you. So you almost have to use physical violence, not to say teach him a lesson, but show him that you're not playin' around, and that you are willing to stand your ground and do it every time you see him.

Participants believed that willingness to fight and decisiveness when threatened deterred a great deal of trouble, but winning drove home the message that they could meet infractions with painful consequences. Therefore, it was sometimes important to demonstrate dominance, and not only willingness to engage. Al said, "If you half-ass kick somebody's ass, they gonna snap and come back and beat the shit out of you or kill you or what-not. There's no halfway ass kickin'." In response to a theft, Renee said that he had to teach the culprit a lesson by force and afterward added a verbal reprimand:

> He tried talkin' his way out of it, but I didn't want to hear his talkin'. So, as soon as he was done talkin', I just hit him, and I hit him 'til I cut his eye, and I stopped. I told him, "Take your ass-beatin' like a man," and I walked back to the bar and he left.

By telling his opponent to follow the rule against retaliation for an honorable fight, he affirmed that the contest had ended, that the conflict was settled, and that no future violence should follow.

For those who believe in the deterrent value of fighting, the fear of combat can be far less worrisome than the lasting effects of failure to respond violently. Participants considered failure to fight when provoked as shameful and believed that when a persistent adversary who might respond to perceived weakness with increased aggression is not bested or at least fought to conclusion, it could lead to further trouble.

Hierarchies and Natural Order

Those interviewed portrayed fighting as a natural occurrence and as a means to establish hierarchies of physical dominance. Multiple respondents made reference to primitive man or the animal kingdom to show that physical confrontation and dominance contests are natural. The point was that fighting is what humans do to establish rank. Kelly said:

> Defending yourself will expand and trickle through all aspects of your life. It can start with physical defense. To not defend yourself is equal to being defenseless. You would be equal to a sitting duck. The same way sharks smell blood and animals smell fear. People see fear and capitalize on it. You know big fish, little fish kind of thing.

His statement reflects a belief that the assertiveness reflected in a willingness to fight leads to other successes in a competitive world. Participants seemed comfortable with the idea that physical dominance is part of the human condition and particularly significant in their social surroundings. According to Fred, "I think it's part of human nature. Part of people are animals just like any other animal. That's how you figure out dominance and who's right and who's wrong." Thus, they considered fighting an important part of establishing and challenging a pecking order and of building a social environment where the order of respect is known. Curiously, most participants placed themselves in the middle range of fighting ability and said that they were not particularly tough guys. Their willingness to stand up and fight was sufficient to place them in a relatively respectable position in this order.

Although most of the men said that flaunting the ability and willingness to fight was a mark of immaturity, it was good to make a habit of being strong and at the ready for violence. This demeanor improves one's social position, reinforces a manly image, increases confidence in diverse settings, and wards off trouble by garnering respect. This is important to those who perceive their neighborhood barroom as a setting where aggressors inevitably will try to demonstrate mettle and intimidate if they think they can.

Letting Bad Blood

Most of the men we interviewed considered fighting a likely and reasonable outcome of many exchanges of insults or disputes. They believed that lingering animosities, yelling, shoving matches, and verbal battles served no purpose. Arguing is unproductive, but fighting can bring conflicts to resolution and reduce the likelihood of an uncomfortable series of interactions (see Ferguson, 2001). Jason perceived little value in debating foes and assumed that most arguments of any duration in public will lead to fist fights. In his words, "What's the point of arguing back and forth for thirty minutes or an hour? Just fight and it's over in a few minutes." Once disputants established dominance and demonstrated courage, they could consider the matter settled. Fights also prevented prolonged conflict and animosity, and they avoided expression of emotion that audiences will not receive well. Of his decision to fight, Renee said, "A friend just told me, 'If you feel that you need to do it, just go ahead and do it. Stop stressing out about it. You're gonna see this person, so you might as well just do it and get it over with.'"

Fighting also was perceived as cathartic. Adversaries can release the stress of tense situations with a flurry of punches. After the violence, emotions settle. Even on the losing side of the fight, these men accepted that they could resolve conflicts with violence and that it could prevent lasting conflict. Indeed, most believed that dangerous animosity was unlikely to last beyond the incident. In their circles, fights happen, and in most cases, people get over them. In describing a particular fight, Fred said:

> Nobody got seriously hurt. It was just kinda one of those things where we took care of what had to be taken care of. It's kinda funny 'cause I did end up runnin' into the guy two days later, and he bought me some drinks, and we kinda just talked for a minute. It's not like we sat there and made up, but at the same time he was like, "Man, that was stupid," and I was like, "Yeah, that was stupid." But at that point in time we did what had to be done, I guess.

To these men, fights were useful voluntary contests for settling disputes and were more likely to resolve conflicts than prolong them. Charlie expressed the idea that fights should not lead to cycles of retaliation or lasting animosity. He said, "I guess after the fight, it's over. Just the way I grew up, if you got beat up and it's pretty bad, there's no reason to press charges." Such resolutions extended even to situations when the speaker provoked a fight. As Cain said, "If you're the person who starts it and you end up getting your ass handed to you, you get what you deserve. You feel stupid you know, but you know you had it comin'."

They believed that fighting could settle some problems and onlookers should allow them to conduct their contests without interference, especially from police. Dennis elaborated on his belief that fights allow resolution of conflict by "working out" problems through competition:

> It's a timeless tradition. Two people duking it out goes back to dudes slappin' people with gloves and challenging them to a duel and probably way before that, cavemen and stuff. That's what men do. Some things can just be worked out like that.

Many participants thought that police involvement would undermine the purpose of fighting and that witnesses should only call police under strict conditions where fights were not for settling disputes (e.g., robberies or unfair and merciless attacks).

CONDUCT IN COMBAT

Participants claimed that honorable fighters should follow rules. Almost all said that the point of fighting was not to hurt the other person as severely as possible. Clearly, their intent was to win and cause pain to opponents, but it was not to cause lasting injury or death. For this reason, they attempted to follow specific rules of combat and expected others to do so. They claimed that those who fight honorably stop when their opponent is bested, only fight equally matched opponents, and fight with equal numbers of combatants. They believed that failing to do so impugned claims of being peaceful warriors and cast them as violent, a label they avoided.

Give Quarter

Several interviewees said that they took the threat of causing severe and permanent injury seriously and believed that it was the worst possible outcome of a fight. Avoiding tragedy was part of the reason they tried to conduct fights fairly, put limitations on violence, and stopped once they earned a victory (Jackson-Jacobs, 2013). These offenders said that the level of accepted aggression was high and that fighting aggressively was fine, but they still emphasized the importance of restraint when fighting. As Chris said, "I'm not tryin' to kill nobody." Renee said, "I mean, I wouldn't want to seriously kill somebody, but bones heal. You can get teeth fixed. Bloody nose ain't gonna kill anybody." They believed it important to stop when one fighter clearly has bested their opponent, so that combatants land no potentially deadly blow against the defenseless. As Charlie said, "I never felt like I inflicted more pain than needed to be inflicted on somebody. I felt like once I did enough damage to 'em, you know, I didn't do any more."

Most respondents said that once the winner of a fight was established, the honorable thing to do was desist. The signs that they should cease were when their adversary yielded, went to ground, became too tired to compete, or could no longer defend himself (Jackson-Jacobs, 2013). Charlie elaborated:

> I think a fist fight in the street or in a bar . . . should be done with when somebody can't get up, when they can't defend themselves anymore. If you take it beyond that, where somebody needs to go to the hospital for head injuries or bleedin' to death, that's takin' it way too far.

When asked when fighting should stop, Cain said:

> One person just giving up; throwing their hands up saying they've had enough. When a person just can't defend themselves, that's a sign that they're done. What constitutes it for me, I guess, is just knowing that if I've gotten into it with someone, and they stop throwing back, and they start talking like in between, it's kinda like they saying I quit.

Jason relayed two stories that supported this claim: one where he showed mercy and the other where he benefited from mercy. In the first, he discussed landing the first blow that "dropped" his opponent, and then instead of further attacks, he verbally reinforced the demand to yield and not come back. In the second, he said he was tackled and suffered a broken shoulder. Afterward, he threw a punch but the pain from the break brought him to his knees. He said that he was defenseless and grateful that his opponent recognized the proper moment to stop.

Equal Combatants

One way to determine a "fair" fight was whether the combatants were matched equally, at least by appearances (see Garot, 2010). As Kelly said, "A fair fight is when [they're] equally matched in physical stature, strength, age. Unfair would be age, physical stature, intoxication, outnumbered." Although any touching or attempt to intimidate by invading space during confrontation might set off a fight, participants claimed that they avoided throwing a first blow and would attempt to deescalate conflict when their opponent had lost the chance to win. Exceptions to the dictate to avoid the first blow were when they believed they were far outmatched and the fight was inevitable. They claimed that throwing the first blow in these situations might give a "puncher's chance" to escape unharmed. Still, several participants said that there is little purpose in fighting when there is no chance of winning, such as when a far superior fighter insults you. It is very bad form to bully far outside one's size and fighting ability; if personal pride allows, then there is little shame in letting it go when it happens. As Chris said, "If you're definitely gonna get your ass whipped, there's no point in fightin'. You might as well just walk away." It is possible to walk away from a fight and avoid humiliation when unquestionably outmatched (Garot, 2010).

We asked participants when they thought it was wrong to fight. Their answers supported the claim that fighting easily outmatched opponents was wrong and did not convey their ideals of honor. David said you should not fight:

> Somebody that's a whole lot smaller than you, that you could easily kick their ass for no reason, you know just to make them look dumb. I guess you would kinda feel a little guilty after that, just to fight, just for that. So I guess I would consider that kinda wrong, an unfair match.

Eric said, "If you can already beat somebody up, it's not necessary for you to follow through with it." He explained that it would be acceptable to walk away when provoked by those who clearly were not contenders for victory because they could not have intended insult with a clear head. If insulted parties believe that the aggressor does not comprehend the consequences of an affront or is insincere, then they can forgive slights:

> If somebody's eggin' you on to fight but you really know they don't want to fight, then you feel like you could just give 'em exactly what they're askin' for. Maybe they want to fight knowing they're gonna get beat up, and they just want to get beat up. I'm not gonna do that to somebody, I'll walk away from a fight when I know it's not worth it. Some people just aren't worth beatin' up or fightin' with because I don't want to hurt 'em and I know they really don't want to fight in the first place. They're just drunk.

Several mentioned that they can detect reluctance from the fearful, outmatched, or unintentional insulter, and in these situations, the right thing to do is to deescalate conflict. Dana indicated that adversaries attempting to deescalate or who have done no significant wrong are among the reasons for deciding not to fight as a conflict begins: "[I]t's okay to walk away from a fight. Number one, if you know you can't win. Number two, if the principle isn't there." When asked if he thought there are times when it is acceptable to walk away, Charlie responded:

Definitely. A lot of times you walk away when you know you could beat someone up or they're drunk—too drunk. Or you just feel like they really don't—you can see sometimes in people's eyes—they really don't want to get in a fight with you, but they just feel like they have to.

Equal Numbers

To establish reputations and reinforce the idea that they uphold rules of accepted behaviors, fighters argued that you should go it alone. They framed having friends join the fight as an ineffective way to convey reputations worthy of respect. In fact, having friends join an otherwise fair fight reportedly diminished your reputation. Kevin claimed that he did not approve when a friend came to his aid. As he explained, "[Being] jumped by multiple people is not very fair. And sometimes it's hard to stay away from that 'cause if you're with a group of people, friends usually jump in, and it may turn out to be unfair when multiple people are jumpin' on one guy." According to Charlie, "I think a fair fight is if it's one-on-one. Just fists, you know, fighting straight up. If someone has a weapon or if someone has more friends, like if another friend jumps in, I think that's unfair." When asked if he would jump in a fight to help a friend, Kevin replied:

> I usually see what is happening, try and watch the situation, and if my friend's handlin' it's okay and if nobody else on the other guy's side is jumpin' in, I usually watch and make sure nobody else jumps in. If he's getting hurt bad enough, I'll jump in to try and help him or stop him.

EXCEPTIONS TO RULES

Although participants articulated rules of combat, they also said that they sometimes abandoned these rules. Several indicated that for some transgressions—a sexual crime or other serious offense against those held close—the injured can cast rules aside. It may be acceptable to approach with stealth, gang up on, blindside, or pull a weapon first when the sole objective is vengeance and inflicting pain on dishonorable and egregious offenders who deserve it, but such events were rare among this group. Departures from the code also occurred for less intentional reasons; these events are much more common and received considerably more attention from participants. Here, we elaborate on the situations and circumstances where the participants did not follow the accepted rules of fighting.

Loyalty

Loyalty to friends or the unprotected can conflict with the imperative that fights be fair. Fighters often recognize that despite the need to let a fight proceed to culmination without interference, they should not let friends be injured severely or humiliated. Louis said that one must assist a friend in the fray "if they need it—if they're getting hurt or losing." David explained that he is sure to intervene in fights if a friend is outnumbered, but he said also that he would aid as a gesture of friendship and unwillingness to watch a compatriot suffer:

> Oh yeah, you jump in to help. Why? Because I guess it's your friend and it all depends, you know, how many friends they got with 'em. But yeah, I'd jump in for a friend of mine just 'cause it's your friend. You don't want to see them get hurt, get beat up.

Onlookers are attentive to how a battle unfolds and whether those with whom they side have the upper hand. If they judge that significant injury to their side is occurring or impending, or that the situation requires a demonstration of loyalty, then they may violate the abstract belief that people should fight their own battles. They cast such violations as reluctant, however. The following dialogue with Sal reflected his decision-making process for determining when to violate the ethic of fighting fair:

> INTERVIEWER: Would you jump in even if it was a fair fight?
> SAL: Well, I guess it depends. I guess you'd have to be in the situation, see what it calls for.
> INTERVIEWER: Let's say it's a fair fight and your friend's winning, would you jump in?
> SAL: No, I wouldn't jump in. I'd let him handle his business.
> INTERVIEWER: But if he was getting beat up?
> SAL: I'd probably jump in, yeah.

Jason relied on loyalty to explain the use of a weapon in a fight where he normally would avoid it. He relayed a story of smashing a glass on an antagonist's head:

> This big dude was harassing a guy I knew, who was pretty small. I told him, "Don't worry, that dude won't do nothing." Right after I said that, the big dude pushed my friend hard against the wall. I was like, "Fuck man, I just told him nothin' was going to happen to him." I had to do something. So I smashed my drink over the dude's head.

The participants were not blind to conflicting imperatives that shape how they should respond to a fight. Reportedly, it is a complicated decision determining when to intervene in an ongoing fight. The decision requires speedily considering the entirety of the situation; a significant part of the calculation is how much punishment one allows a friend who has lost momentum in a fight to take before intervening to assist. Onlookers should allow fights to proceed in most cases, but at some point, the beating of a friend must stop.

Alcohol and Drugs

Many fighters said that they were ashamed of the times they had provoked another person because of their own intoxication. When they portrayed their fights as shameful or immature events, it was typically because they had provoked another needlessly and being drunk was usually the reason for it. Eric recalled:

I beat up some guy one night just because I was intoxicated. It had nothing to do with him. It had somethin' to do with his family member. It had to do with a girl, and if I wouldn't have been in the state of mind I was in, I would've never done that to that person. He didn't deserve that.

As Kevin noted, when fights occur because of drunkenness, the fighter may experience guilt. It is not the fight that inspires regret, but the realization that it occurred for "irrational" reasons:

There's times when I definitely didn't think it was the right thing to do, and maybe too much alcohol was involved and I had a hot head, and if I was sober that probably wouldn't have happened. So there's times I feel guilty for doin' it when I'm drunk or something.

The fighters noted that drugs and alcohol interfere with decision making and have a great deal to do with why some of their fights occur. However, in several cases, they reconciled this with the belief that they fight in response to insults. Alcohol-induced sensitivity and intolerance to insults probably means only that they might have chosen to ignore real infractions if sober. When asked what instigated his most recent fight, Rob said:

I think it [alcohol] influenced me to the point where I thought I reacted really fast. I mean I got mad quick. It just all happened, and I just did whatever felt like I had to do right away. My adrenaline started pumping faster because I was drunk. Had I been calm and had some food in me and somewhat normal I might have tried the situation slightly different. I don't know how that would've ended up. I think overall because I had been drinkin' so much, it was just a quick reaction and the only way I saw fit to handle it.

Quick Judgements and Overwhelming Emotions

Many fights occurred quickly. Therefore, the fighters often cast the decision to fight as a spur-of-the-moment, physiological reaction rather than the result of deliberation. They weighed their decision to fight against a cultural backdrop of right and wrong behavior, but also they knew that there was little time to measure guidance for using violence against developing conflicts. They were aware that outcomes often do not fit cultural imperatives neatly and that sometimes they made mistakes. It usually was after the fight that these fighters measured their actions against the standards of whether it should have occurred and how it should have proceeded. After such careful examination, many experience regret. Dennis regretted the level of violence he used in a fight that his friend provoked:

So my friend's all drunk at the bar, bouncin' around screamin', and these dudes walk up behind him and start shit with him. He starts fightin' one of the dudes, and then two of that guy's friends jumped in. I mean, like I said, my friend was in the wrong, but we all jumped in anyway. It was a couple of us, and that's when I made the dude's ear bleed.

Kevin reconciled his beliefs that fights should not include weapons and should end before serious injury with contradictory behavior by referring to fights as charged situations where a person can lose control:

> You kinda lose yourself in the moment and codes go out the window. There's been times when I probably should've stopped before I did, or somebody should've stopped something, but you kinda lose yourself. You don't really realize what you're doing sometimes, and it's not really about a code at that point.

Emotions often cause bystanders to jump into what were fair fights initially or to escalate more than the situation demands. Jerry explained that he regretted injuring his opponent but that this experience had taught him that fights sometimes progress in this manner. The natural flash of anger that is an emotional response to pain and fear when under attack means that he need not deeply regret exceeding his limitations for violence:

> Sometimes, everybody gets their adrenaline pumpin' and you don't think too rationally. So, you know, it didn't bother me afterward. Usually that's the way things happen. . . . I wasn't tryin' to hurt him at all. At first I just felt like I was tryin' to defend myself. But once I got him on the ground, I hit him four more times with the intent to hurt him, but also with the intent just to keep him from comin' back at me, and when he came back at me, I meant to hurt him that last time and I did hurt him.

Rob said that limits on the injuries one tends to inflict and the level of escalation allowed may be set aside instantaneously when things do not progress as expected:

> I don't want to get in a situation where I put some dude in a coma and spend my days in jail and go through all of that. That's definitely not the goal. But sometimes it's hard to go with that idea even if that's how you feel about it normally. You get in that situation, and somebody takes a swing at you with a baseball bat, and all of a sudden things change. I don't know that there's clear-cut limits in my head. I hope to have a limit and never do anything too permanent.

In fact, several offenders noted that their personal response to the anger, fear, and associated biochemical arousal that occurs in a fight makes them lose touch completely with personal restrictions and ostensive rules of combat. Experience had taught these men that there was a risk that they would lose control when fighting and that the limitations on conduct when fighting were uncertainties even for themselves. Fred said:

> I kinda lose touch with myself as a human being when I fight and I just kinda lose my mind for a minute and whatever happens, happens. I don't even know what happened sometimes. It's kinda like you just turn into an animal.

Combatants said that they (and others) may lose sight of the rules of combat they try to follow but that they still must trust their instinct to fight when provoked. Participants easily cast many fights that do not follow the form of fair contests, as situations that result either from purposive violations, usually by the other side, or from accidental failure to follow the rules. Failure to adhere to rules, although occurring frequently, does not undermine the belief that opponents can, should, and often do perform fights as honorable contests.

DISCUSSION

Ethnographies that focus on singular aspects of a group's life tend to portray the participants as one-dimensional. For instance, Sandberg (2009b) argued that much ethnographic work on violent street offenders highlights their gangster or violent sides and ignores other dimensions of their lives. Because our interviews focused on violence, our findings may lead the reader to overestimate the degree to which fighting was a part of their lives. Readers can garner the complexity of participants at times from the quotes we present, but many participants made efforts to construct themselves as not being truly violent in other parts of the interviews that are not included in this article. They engage in violence, endorse some forms of violence, and articulate a code governing such behavior, but other dimensions of their lives having little to do with crime take precedence in defining how they perceive themselves. Fighting is but one aspect of their complicated lives and identities.

Our aims with this research were to explore the content and implementation of codes for fighting among a group of adult, working-class, White males and to determine how they talk about such codes in relation to constructing identities. In describing the content of their code for violence, participants said fighting was a means of constructing an identity as someone deserving respect, but only when conducted acceptably. They emphasized how defending honor, seeking quick conflict resolution, and establishing admirable qualities motivated them to fight. They were proud of their willingness and ability to oppose adversaries with violence when protecting honorable positions or defending character. They thought people should not seek out violence, but they should not back down from it either. They saw value in fighting to defend honor and to establish order. Defending themselves under the right circumstances enhanced self-respect and confidence that they were men of character and good repute. Failure to fight in appropriate circumstances led to self-doubt and regret.

They believed that fighting served functions beyond building a reputation, however. To them, fighting bolstered a confident demeanor, gave advantage in daily nonviolent interactions, and warded off future disrespectful interactions. They portrayed fighting as a reasonable means for dispute resolution because it ended verbal confrontation, brought conflicts to conclusion, and brought grudges out in the open. Completed fights settled disputes that if left untendered could fester and lead to nastier consequences, including shame associated with feeling cowed, gossip and other harmful talk, or sneaky vengeance. For these reasons and because fighting was an intimidating event, many believed it was the better strategy and found it psychologically easier to charge ahead and be done than to wait or act in hesitation.

They perceived fighting as an indicator of their character, but it was most effective for building a desired reputation when conducted following rules. They frowned on unfair contests, believing that fights should not result from inadvertent insults or when one's opponent is attempting to deescalate, apologize, or back down. Combatants should grant quarter and avoid permanent damage to opponents. Participants considered ruthless or extreme escalation of violence in what should be an ordinary fight as unacceptable (Jackson-Jacobs, 2013). Their fights were intended to inflict punishment but not to cause long-term damage. In short, they articulated and sought to adhere to a code that was restrictive in allowances of when to fight and for the acceptable amount of force. None portrayed themselves as innately violent or as generally criminal.

In describing this code for violence, participants referred to the necessity of general and specific deterrence of aggressors and to fighting as a form of self-protection. However, their explanations of it had much more to do with conducting oneself honorably and with maintaining respectable status, reputation, and character than it did with preventing impending physical injury or the desire to keep order. They did not portray their fights as being necessary for survival in their environments. In most instances, they were seeking to defend status and pride more than their bodies. They were proud of fighting for reputation and imbued willingness to defend their character in a physical way with great meaning. Although they described serious reputational stakes for responding properly when insult to honor was clear, they also believed that escalating petty disagreements and maintaining grudges call honor into question.

They believed that some confrontational situations require violence but not all. There were allowances in the code for tolerating insults (Garot, 2010). For instance, violence was not necessary when the opponent is weak physically or the insult slight, and participants said people understood if one tolerates insult from a clearly superior fighter. Conversely, an adept fighter who decided to let an affront pass from a foolish or drunken challenger likely gained respect for mercy. Scrutinizers will not always deem walking away from provocations or intimidating encounters as an exhibition of weakness and, therefore, doing so brings neither increased threat nor future challenges. Perhaps calls for violence in response to threats and insults acquired significance in part because these men believed that insults that demand a fight fall within a narrow range.

Despite the vagaries of when and how they draw on the code, willingness to fight is a foundation on which participants construct both accounts of abidance and departures from their code for settling disputes violently but with honor. A general willingness to fight is a primary component of judging action and is foundational for claiming the code and the image these men want to convey. They often try to establish that they generally are willing to fight when describing both conflicts they avoided and those that eventuated in fights. Although seeking fights regularly and proactively is a mark against character, clear demonstrations of cowardice in a confrontation where observers would judge violence justifiable is difficult to excuse.

These men articulated a clear code for violence, but our results also suggest that their application of it is improvisational and spontaneous. A code may fit situations imperfectly, and because it contains few immutable rules, actors may take liberties in application. Often, codes provide only the loosest guidance for navigating a series of provisional interactions. One can fight when insulted, but actors have a great deal of freedom in deciding precisely when an insult rises to the level that demands escalation. Once a conflict is underway, violence heightens emotions, and fighters can lose track of acceptable motives and rules. Fights are precarious, uncertain, and emotional interactions that "get out of control," escalate beyond what was intended, and sometimes elicit unplanned action. An imperfect fit between ideals for applying the code, and their own experiences with errant application to situations, does not disrupt claims to adhere to the code. The code of honorable fighting is important and valued, but they know that given the complexities of conflicts, they are likely to apply it imperfectly.

Many who have examined subcultural codes recognize that they are not followed precisely or certainly (Garot, 2010; Topalli, 2005), and our participants knew this as well. Nevertheless, the guilt expressed by participants when acting in discord with the code and the effort they put into making sense of action according to codes evidences its importance. They discussed fights that occurred for the right reasons and that followed the acceptable rules with pride. They expressed guilt and regret when they provoked fights or when they used violence beyond what was seen as honorable. When they engaged in unfair fighting methods, they offered excuses and justifications for why their actions were not acceptable in general but were in this situation. The participants' need to excuse inconsistent behavior suggests commitment to a code in the same way that those committed to conventional values excuse and justify their norm-violating behavior or that persistent street offenders excuse behaviors such as snitching (Rosenfeld, Jacobs, and Wright, 2003; Topalli, 2005).

In addition to detailing the contours of this code for violence, we also believe that our findings speak to larger issues pertaining to why it departs from those codes discussed elsewhere. Previous discussions of codes for violence have located their origins in the historical inaccessibility or unresponsiveness of agents of the law (Anderson, 1999; Nisbett and Cohen, 1996). If the genesis of participants' belief in pragmatic violence was in these conditions, then they recognized that today legal protection is available to members of their class. In fact, they condoned the use of the formal law for infractions deemed more criminal than their own, such as burglary or robbery.

These men do not need to be on a constant campaign for respect or to establish reputations as extremely dangerous persons to protect themselves from victimization. In fact, they hold little regard or respect for those who portray themselves as violent or potentially homicidal. They consider persons who flaunt violent potential as immature or as criminals. Participants here had some access to conventional, formal dispute resolutions and perceived themselves as conventional citizens and as average working men. Excessive violence or fighting in ways that fundamentally violate their restrictive code for violence threatened this conventional, nonviolent identity. An identity or reputation that is overly aggressive, quick to fight, and brutal may ward off future insults, but also it may damage social relations. Such reputations, especially if they come with arrests and incarceration, threaten the conventional lives, identities, and outcomes they seek. Broken jaws and teeth may lead to local acclaim for these offenders, and even victims may not consider them significantly consequential, but stabbing, shooting, or severely injuring victims could destroy what these men have. If codes lie on a continuum, then we would expect those with more to lose to perceive violence as acceptable in fewer situations and to exhibit greater restraint, and more marginalized persons with fewer prospects to be quicker to violence and relatively comfortable with dangerous reputations.

The participants in this study presented a code for violence tempered by restraints on acceptable motives and methods. Undoubtedly, the code of violence held by these men shaped how they perceived themselves and how they handled interpersonal conflict. Notions of strength, capability, tradition, and honor, which are one aspect of a broader shared identity for these working men, undergird this code. Their identity rests on an ethic of being generally law abiding but rugged and, within bounds, dangerous in some circumstances. Their form of a code for violence might be linked to their region historically, and their views probably are grounded in structural positions tied directly to the blue-collar labor market rather than to the streets, but shared beliefs and ways of understanding violence reinforce and define how they want to be perceived in daily contexts and social life. Their conduct in leisurely settings and enactment of these beliefs reinforced their identity and securely positioned their place locally and among friends. Their code compelled them to action, had a strong influence on how they interpreted situations, and shaped how they made decisions to engage in violence.

Our findings also suggest that codes are accounts or vocabularies of motive fighters used to explain, rationalize, or make sense of their behaviors (Jimerson and Oware, 2006). When their behaviors were inconsistent with their code, the fighters reframed their actions as exceptions or mistakes. By verbally aligning their behavior with behavioral expectations by explanations, they show that they remain worthy of respect (Stokes and Hewitt, 1976). In conversation and action, they used codes directly and as a sensitizing device to grasp or explain situations. In deeds and words, they loosely improvised and played on codes as they decided either what to do in conflicts or how to explain their choices.

Codes are not only attitudes that predict action, but also they act as sense-making devices. They affect the way people interpret and respond to situations and are "acculturated linguistic devices that . . . actors use to present a consistent image of self when asked to explain behavior" (Brookman, Copes, and Hochstetler, 2011: 403). Considering codes this way highlights that people *use* codes to evaluate actions prospectively and retrospectively. Whether done prospectively or retrospectively, this takes interpretive or creative effort on the part of the implementer. In short, when actors are "telling the code," they draw on culturally relevant normative expectations, attitudes, and conceptions (i.e., formula stories) to justify their behavior and to construct meaningful identities (Wieder, 1974). Therefore, we do not perceive codes simply as unidirectional determinants of action. Rather, culturally prevalent codes of behavior shape thoughts, decisions, and actions.

Analyses of the codes that pertain to violence often contrast subcultural codes, which analysts cast as those that condone or allow violence, with those of the dominant culture, which they presume to proscribe violence. Our interviews imply that codes that are conducive to crime in some ways can be prohibitive in others. In some circumstances, a code for violence dissuades violent responses and limits the insults that lead to them. Therefore, a code may be useful to people who live within the law in general and think about the future; our participants defend it thus. Undoubtedly, few persons endorse codes for violence that condone ruthlessness, brutality, killing, and long-running cycles of escalating retaliation. Certainly, more individuals, like our participants, believe measured violence is appropriate when faced with certain insults and in a narrowly defined range of contexts. Restrictive codes for the use of violence may be enthusiastically perpetuated not only by the down-and-out but also by those rungs above on the class structure—say men who are solidly working class or pursuing college educations. Allowances for violence contained in these codes can contribute to violence, or help rationalize it, in situations clearly defined as appropriate and even in situations where misapplication occurs. Fighters often feel no regret when the former applies, as a code provides neat rationale, but in other cases, they may rest on good intentions, understandable mistakes, and circumstantial complexities. Flexibility in the implementation of codes and as a device for framing diverse violent events surely is one reason that codes for violence endure in so many contexts. For those avoiding callous or criminal reputations, the code may be durable and defensible not for its allowance but because of the restrictions it contains.

REFERENCES

Agnew, Robert. 2006. Storylines as a neglected cause of crime. *Journal of Research in Crime and Delinquency*, 43:119–47.

Anderson, Elijah. 1999. *Code of the Street: Decency, Violence, and the Moral Life of the Inner City*. New York: Norton.

Athens, Lonnie. 1997. *Violent Criminal Acts and Actors Revisited*. Champaign: University of Illinois Press.

Brookman, Fiona, Heith Copes, and Andy Hochstetler. 2011. Street codes, accounts, and rationales for violent crime. *Journal of Contemporary Ethnography*, 40:397–424.

Faupel, Charles E. 1991. *Shooting Dope: Career Patterns of Hardcore Heroin Users*.

Garot, Robert. 2010. *Who You Claim? Performing Gang Identity in School and on the Streets*. New York: New York University Press.

Hochstetler, Andy, Heith Copes, and Patrick Williams. 2010. That's not who I am: How offenders commit violent acts and reject authentically violent selves. *Justice Quarterly*, 27:492–516.

Horowitz, Ruth. 1983. *Honor and the American Dream: Culture and Identity in a Chicano Community*. Newark, NJ: Rutgers University Press.

Jackson-Jacobs, Curtis. 2013. Constructing physical fights: An interactionist analysis of violence among affluent, suburban youth. *Qualitative Sociology*, 36:23–52.

Jacobs, Bruce A., and Richard Wright. 2006. *Street Justice: Retaliation in the Criminal Underworld*. New York: Cambridge University Press.

Katz, Jack. 1988. *Seductions of Crime*. New York: Basic Books.

Klenowski, Paul, Heith Copes, and Christopher Mullins. 2011. Gender, identity and accounts: How white collar offenders do gender when they make sense of their crimes. *Justice Quarterly*, 28:46–69.

Nisbett, Richard, and Dov Cohen. 1996. *Culture of Honor: The Psychology of Violence in the South*. Boulder, CO: Westview Press.

Presser, Lois. 2010. Collecting and analyzing the stories of offenders. *Journal of Criminal Justice Education*, 21:431–46.

Rosenfeld, Richard, Bruce Jacobs, and Richard Wright. 2003. Snitching and the code of the street. *British Journal of Criminology*, 43:291–309.

Sandberg, Sveinung. 2009a. A narrative search for respect. *Deviant Behavior*, 30:487–510.

Sandberg, Sveinung. 2009b. Gangster, victim or both? The interdiscursive construction of sameness and difference in self-presentations. *British Journal of Sociology*, 60:523–42.

Sandberg, Sveinung. 2010. What can "lies" tell us about life? Notes towards a framework of narrative criminology. *Journal of Criminal Justice Education*, 21:447–65.

Stewart, Eric A., Ronald L. Simons, and Rand Conger. 2002. Assessing neighborhood and social psychological influences on childhood violence in an African-American sample. *Criminology*, 40:801–30.

Stokes, Randall, and John Hewitt. 1976. Aligning action. *American Sociological Review*, 41:838–49.

Swidler, Ann. 1986. Culture in action: Symbols and strategies. *American Sociological, Review*, 51:273–86.

Topalli, Volkan. 2005. When being good is bad: An expansion of neutralization theory. *Criminology*, 43:797–836.

Topalli, Volkan, Richard Wright, and Robert Fornango. 2002. Drug dealers, robbery, and retaliation: Vulnerability, deterrence and the contagion of violence. *British Journal of Criminology*, 42:337–351.

Wacquant, Loic. 2002. Scrutinizing the street: Poverty, morality, and the pitfalls of urban ethnography. *American Journal of Sociology*, 107:1468–532.

Wieder, D. Lawrence. 1974. *Language and Social Reality: The Case of Telling the Convict Code*. The Hague, the Netherlands: Mouton.

Occupational and White-Collar Crime

Section V examines occupational and white-collar crime. The term *occupational crime* refers to crimes committed through opportunities created in the course of a legal occupation. In the past, the label *white-collar crime* almost always connoted crimes committed by the rich and powerful. Today, most criminologists have broadened the term to refer to crimes committed by persons in a wide range of situations. The focus today is on the nature of the crime and not the person committing it, thus the term *occupational crime*.

On June 29, 2009, Bernard Madoff was sentenced by a federal judge to 150 years in prison for the largest Ponzi scheme in recent history. His sentence represents the maximum allowed under federal sentencing law. Madoff, founder of the Bernard L. Madoff Investment Securities, Inc., a Wall Street–affiliated investment firm, had previously pled guilty to numerous charges that stemmed from an investment fraud that prosecutors estimated to be over $50 billion. Federal authorities identified over 1,300 investors who had losses exceeding $13 billion.

Occupational and white-collar crimes are not victimless crimes. Not every white-collar crime results in the incredible dollar loss of the Madoff scandal, but nevertheless, victims suffer both financially and emotionally. These crimes arguably result in more harm in terms of dollar loss and emotional turmoil than street crime, which almost always receives the bulk of media attention. White-collar offenders can skillfully carry out crimes with the potential to destroy companies and devastate families. A single white-collar criminal can wipe out a victim's life savings or cost investors billions of dollars. Fraud schemes represent some of the most sophisticated of these crimes. While white-collar crime is nonviolent, the effects of these financially motivated crimes can be just as devastating.

Much of the research reported in this book tends to support the idea that many offenders accept responsibility for their crimes. However, the most consistent theme in the following articles on occupational crime is that these offenders concoct elaborate justifications, excuses, and rationalizations to avoid accepting responsibility for their criminal behavior. Perhaps that is because the primary identity of most of these offenders is noncriminal. They are health care workers, lawyers, bankers, stockbrokers, and so on. For these people to conceive of themselves as criminals is difficult, if not impossible.

In Chapter 12, "Crime on the Line: Telemarketing and the Changing Nature of Professional Crime," Neal Shover, Glenn S. Coffey, and Dick Hobbs examine the world of telemarketing fraud. In perhaps one of the most insightful studies of telemarketing offenders to date, Shover and his associates interviewed 47 criminal telemarketers. The authors found that unlike their fellow thieves, telemarketing criminals are disproportionately drawn from the middle class. They are drawn to the business of telemarketing crime because they find the work attractive and rewarding. They are also drawn to the lifestyle and the income it provides. The authors note that their subjects, like those who engage in "street crimes," pursue a hedonistic lifestyle featuring alcohol, drugs, and conspicuous consumption.

In Chapter 13, "Drugged Druggists: The Convergence of Two Criminal Career Trajectories," Dean A. Dabney and Richard C. Hollinger take a fascinating look at the paths of entry into prescription drug abuse by pharmacists. They conducted interviews with 50 recovering drug-addicted pharmacists in order to describe and construct meaning for their onset of and progression into illicit pharmaceutical drug abuse. The authors discovered that pharmacists had two distinct paths of entry into drug use. One group, which they named "recreational abusers," began using prescription drugs for their euphoric effects. The other group, identified as "therapeutic self-medicators," began using prescription drugs much later in their careers for primarily medicinal reasons. What is especially salient in Dabney and Hollinger's study is that once both groups became addicted, the distinguishing characteristics between the two groups disappeared. This, according to the authors, reveals a "dynamic convergence into a single pattern for the mature deviant." Thus, the authors argue that their findings suggest that previous scholarship in this area may have falsely assumed the discovery of multiple static types of offenders, when it may have been that they were really observing a single criminal career at different points along its dynamic trajectory.

The two studies presented in this section are somewhat unusual in that ethnographic research of crime "in the suites" is much more difficult to accomplish than studies of crime "in the streets." Potential subjects are less likely to talk with researchers and are not as easily approached. Thus, the pool of field studies of so-called white-collar crime is small; however, the papers included here are excellent examples of what can be accomplished with a difficult population.

CHAPTER 12

Crime on the Line: Telemarketing and the Changing Nature of Professional Crime

Neal Shover, Glenn S. Coffey, and Dick Hobbs

Although it has become an important part of the legitimate economy, criminals also have been quick to exploit the opportunities presented by telemarketing. Although it was nearly unheard of until recent decades, few adults today are unfamiliar with telemarketing fraud. There are countless variations on the basic scheme, but typically a consumer receives a phone call from a high-pressure salesperson who solicits funds or sells products based on untrue assertions or enticing claims. Callers offer an enormous variety of products and services and often use names that sound similar to those of bona fide charities or reputable organizations. Goods or services either are not delivered at all or are substantially inferior to what was promised. Telemarketing fraud touches the lives of many citizens, but the criminological consequences of this development are poorly charted. In this chapter, the authors examine offenders who have stepped forward to exploit these new opportunities. Drawing from interviews with 47 criminal telemarketers, the authors present a picture and interpretation of them, their pursuits, and their lifestyles. As vocational predators, they share several important characteristics with the professional thieves sketched by earlier generations of investigators. Like the latter, they pursue a hedonistic lifestyle featuring illicit drugs and conspicuous consumption and acquire and employ an ideology of legitimation and defense that insulates them from moral rejection. Unlike professional thieves, however, telemarketing criminals disproportionately are drawn from middle-class, entrepreneurial backgrounds. They are markedly individualistic in their dealings with one another and with law enforcement. Finally, their work organizations are more permanent and conventional in outward appearance than the

Source: Shover, N., Coffey, G. S., & Hobbs, D. (2003). Crime on the line: Telemarketing and the changing nature of professional crime. *British Journal of Criminology*, 43(3), 489–505.

criminal organizations created by blue-collar offenders, which were grounded in the culture of the industrial proletariat. The findings show how the backgrounds and pursuits of vocational predators reflect the qualities and challenges of contemporary lucrative criminal opportunities. Like the markets they seek to manipulate and plunder, the enacted environments of professional criminals embrace infinite variations and are largely indistinguishable from the arenas that capacitate legitimate entrepreneurial pursuits.

Writing at the dawn of the twentieth century, E. A. Ross (1907, p. 3) was one of the first sociologists to call attention to the fact that crime "changes its quality as society develops." Ross focused specifically on growing social and economic interdependence and the variety of ways this permits both exploitation of trust and the commission of crime at a distance from victims. The transformative social and economic changes he noted only gained speed as the century progressed. In the United States and other Western nations, the middle decades of the century saw the emergence or the expansion of state policies and corporate practices with enormous criminological significance. These included a fundamental shift in the state's public welfare functions, which had the effect of expanding programs and subsidies for citizens across the income spectrum. One measure of this is the fact that by 1992, 51.7% of American families received some form of federal payments, ranging from Social Security, Medicare, and military retirement benefits to agricultural subsidies (Samuelson, 1995, p. 158).

In addition, the years following World War II witnessed a rapid growth of the domestic economy, which made available goods that either were unknown or were unattainable by most citizens just a decade earlier. Houses, automobiles, refrigerators, television sets, and a host of other commodities now were within the reach of a growing segment of the population. The disposable income available to the new owners of these commodities allowed them also to purchase the new comprehensive insurance policies offered by insurance underwriters. Increasingly, the middle-class family now was insured against not only major hazards to life, home, and business, but also loss of or damage to household items (Clarke, 1990).

As the century drew to a close, there were fundamental changes also in the structure and dynamics of economic relationships and in communications technology (Adler, 1992; Lash & Urry, 1994). Most important, widespread use of telecommunications (Batty & Barr, 1994; Turkle, 1995), electronic financial transactions, and consumer credit (Tickell, 1996) presaged a depersonalized, cashless economy. Electronic financial transfers among banks and businesses, automatic teller machines (Hirschhorn, 1985), and home banking increasingly are used across the globe (Silverstone, 1991). In the new world of personal computers and virtual identities, individuals and organizations conduct business with remote others whose credentials and intentions cannot be easily determined.

The net result of these political and economic developments is a cornucopia of new criminal opportunities (Grabosky, Smith, & Dempsey, 2001; Taylor, 1999).

Federally funded health care programs, for example, have given physicians and hospitals access to new pools of tax revenue for which oversight is so weak that it has been called a "license to steal" (Sparrow, 1996). The growth of health insurance fraud, therefore, can be seen as "emblematic of the emerging forms of . . . crime that reflect the changing economy of the late twentieth century" (Tillman, 1998, p. 197). The new criminal opportunities extend far beyond health care, however.

The changing landscape of criminal opportunities is strikingly apparent in crimes of fraud. Fraud is committed when misrepresentation or deception is used to secure unfair or unlawful gain, typically by perpetrators who create and exploit the appearance of a routine transaction. Fraud violates trust, it is nonconfrontational, and it can be carried out over long distances. In organizational complexity and reach, it ranges from itinerant vinyl siding scamsters to international banking crimes that can destabilize national economies. The number of Americans victimized by it is large and substantially exceeds the number victimized by serious street crime (Rebovich et al., 2000; Titus, 2001). A 1991 survey of U.S. households found that compared to crimes of burglary, robbery, assault, and theft, fraud "appears to be very common" (Titus, Heinzelmann, & Boyle, 1995, p. 65). Although a number of methodological shortcomings limit confidence in the findings of previous studies of fraud victimization, there seems little doubt that it is an increasingly commonplace crime.

TELEMARKETING AND FRAUD

The rapid growth of telemarketing is one of several consequential changes in the nature of economic relationships in recent decades. In 2000, telemarketing sales accounted for $611.7 billion in revenue in the United States, an increase of 167% over comparable sales for 1995. Total annual sales from telephone marketing are expected to reach $939.5 billion by the year 2005 (Direct Marketing Association, 2001). The reasons for the growth of telemarketing are understood easily in context of the "general acceleration of everyday life, characterized by increasingly complicated personal and domestic timetables" (Taylor, 1999, p. 45). The daily schedule no longer permits either the pace or the style of shopping that were commonplace a few decades ago, and the need to coordinate personal schedules and to economize on time now drives many household activities. In the search for convenience, telemarketing sales have gained in popularity.

But although it has become an important part of the legitimate economy, criminals also have been quick to exploit the opportunities presented by telemarketing. Although it was nearly unheard of until recent decades, few adults today are unfamiliar with telemarketing fraud. There are countless variations on the basic scheme, but typically a consumer receives a phone call from a high-pressure salesperson who solicits funds or sells products based on untrue assertions or enticing claims. Callers offer an enormous variety of products and services, and often they use names that sound similar to bona fide charities or reputable organizations (U.S. Senate, 1993). Goods or services either are not delivered at all, or they are substantially inferior to what was promised. Telemarketing fraud touches the lives of many citizens. A 1992 poll of a national sample of Americans showed that 2% of respondents had been victimized in the preceding six months (Harris, 1992).

FINDINGS

Of all who begin employment in criminal telemarketing, some quickly discover it is not their cup of tea; they dislike it or they do not perform well. Others find the work attractive and rewarding but see it only as a means to other life and career goals. Most, therefore, pursue it only temporarily. Others, however, discover they are good at fraudulent telephone sales, and they are drawn to the income and the lifestyle it can provide. On average, the members of our interview sample were employed in these endeavors for 8.25 years. Their ages when interviewed range from 26 to 69, with a mean of 42.4 years. Their ranks include 38 white males, 3 African American males, and 6 white females. Nearly all have been married at least once, and most have children.

Organization and Routine

Like its legitimate forms, criminal telemarketing is a productive enterprise that requires the coordinated efforts of two or more individuals. To work in it, therefore, is to work in an organizational setting (Francis, 1988; Schulte, 1995; Stevenson, 2000). The size of criminal telemarketing organizations can vary substantially. Some are very small, consisting of only two or three persons, but others are considerably larger (see, e.g., *Atlanta Journal-Constitution,* 2000). Their permanence and mobility vary also, ranging from those that operate and remain in one locale for a year or more to others that may set up and operate for only a few weeks before moving on. These "rip and tear" operators count on the fact that up to six months' time may pass before law enforcement agencies become aware of and target them. "Boiler rooms," operations featuring extensive telephone banks and large numbers of sales agents, have become less common in the United States in recent years, largely because of the law-enforcement interest they attract. There is reason to believe, however, that criminal telemarketers increasingly are locating them in countries with weak laws and oversight and operating across international borders (see, e.g., Australian Broadcasting Corporation, 2001).

Larger telemarketing operations commonly take on the characteristics and dynamics of formal organizations; they are hierarchical, with a division of labor, graduated pay, and advancement opportunities. Established by individuals with previous experience in fraudulent sales, they generally employ commissioned sales agents to call potential customers, to make the initial pitch, and to weed out the cautious and the steadfastly disinterested. We took steps to ensure that our offender interview sample included persons who formerly held a variety of positions in criminal telemarketing firms. It includes 22 owners, eight managers, and 17 sales agents.

Experienced telemarketers generally do not call individuals randomly but work instead from "lead lists" (also known as "mooch lists"). These are purchased from any of dozens of businesses that compile and sell information on consumer behavior and expressed preferences. Individuals whose names appear on lead lists typically are distinguished by past demonstrated interest or participation in promotions of one kind or another. When a person is contacted by telephone, the sales agent generally works from a script. Scripts are written materials that lay out both successful sales approaches and responses to whatever reception sales agents meet with from those they reach by phone. Promising contacts are turned over to a "closer," a more experienced and better-paid sales agent. "Reloaders" are the most effective closers; much like account executives in legitimate businesses, they maintain contacts with individuals who previously sent money to the company (i.e., "purchased" from it) in hopes of persuading them to send more. As one subject told us:

> I had it so perfected that I could get these customers to buy again. . . . I made sure they were happy so I could sell them again. It didn't do me—I didn't want the one time, I didn't want the two-timer. I wanted to sell these people 10 times.

The organization of larger telemarketing firms and the routine employees follow when handling promising calls explains why those who "buy" from them typically report contact with multiple "salespersons" (American Association of Retired Persons, 1996).

The products and services offered by criminal telemarketers span a wide gamut. In one scam, subjects identified and located unaware owners of vacant property, led them to believe that buyers for the property could be found easily, and then charged high fees to advertise it. Other schemes we encountered included collection for charities, drug education programs, and sale of "private" stocks. One subject sold inexpensive gemstones with fraudulent certificates of grossly inflated value and authenticity. The stones were sealed in display cases such that purchasers would have difficulty getting them appraised, particularly since they were told that if they broke the seal, the value of the stones would decrease and the certificate of authenticity would become invalid. "Private stocks" by definition are not listed or traded on a stock exchange, but telemarketers are able to entice investors with smooth talk and promising prospectives. Dependent on their salesmen for market reports, those who purchase soon discover that the nonexistent stocks take a nosedive, and they lose their investments. A high proportion of the companies represented by our interview subjects promised that those who purchased products from them were odds-on winners of a prize soon to be awarded once other matters were settled. Typically, this required the customers to pay fees of one kind or another. Some of our subjects solicited money for nonexistent charities or legitimate organizations they did not represent. In the products they sell, criminal telemarketers clearly are limited only by the human imagination.

BACKGROUNDS AND CAREERS

A substantial body of research into the lives and careers of street criminals has shown that many are products of disadvantaged and disorderly parental homes. We were interested in determining if the homes in which our subjects were reared reveal similar or functionally equivalent criminogenic characteristics. They do not. Overwhelmingly, the members of our sample describe their parents as conventional and hardworking and family financial circumstances as secure, if not comfortable. Their parental families were traditional in nature, with the father providing the main source of income. Nevertheless, one-half of the mothers also were employed outside the home. Although the fathers' reported occupations ranged from machinist to owner of a chain of retail stores, 32 were business owners or held managerial positions. A substantial proportion of our subjects was exposed to and acquired entrepreneurial perspectives and skills while young. Business ownership appealed to many of them:

> You're always pursuing more money, most of us are. We're raised that way, we are in this country. And that's the way I was raised. But I also wanted to do my own thing. I wanted to be in business for myself, I wanted the freedom that came with that.

Clearly, telemarketing criminals are not drawn from the demographic pools or locales that stock and replenish the ranks of street criminals. Although we questioned them at length about their early and adolescent years, their responses reveal little that distinguishes them from others of similar age and class background. Certainly, the disadvantages and pathologies commonplace in the early lives of most street criminals are in scant evidence here.

If our subjects' early years reveal few clues to their later criminality, there also are few signs that they distinguished themselves in conventional ways. Their educational careers, for example, are unremarkable; eight dropped out of high school, although most graduated. Twenty-one attended college, but on average they invested only two years in the quest for a degree. Five claimed a baccalaureate degree. When invited to reflect on how they differ from their siblings or peers, many reported they were aware of an interest in money from an early age. One subject told us:

> I had certain goals when I was a teenager, you know. And I had a picture of a Mercedes convertible on my bedroom mirror for years. You know, I do have a major addiction, and I don't think I'll ever lose it. And I don't think there's any classes [treatment] for it. And it's money, it's Ben Franklin.

He and others like him were aware also that there are ways of earning a good income that do not require hard work and subordination to others.

Another subject said:

> You know, I was, I've never been a firm believer [that] you got to work for a company for 30 years and get a retirement. Like my dad thinks. I'm all about

going out [and] making that million and doing it, doing it very easily. And there's a lot of ways to do it.

Typically, they began working for pay while young and maintained employment throughout their adolescent years.

None of our subjects said that as children they aspired to a career in telemarketing, either legitimate or criminal. Some had previous sales experience before beginning the work, but most did not. Their introduction to it was both fortuitous and fateful; while still in high school or, more commonly, while in college, they either responded to attractive ads in the newspaper or were recruited by friends or acquaintances who boasted about the amount of money they were making.

> [A former acquaintance] . . . looked me up, found me and said, "You gotta come out here. . . . We're gonna make a ton of money." I went out for three weeks—left my wife back home. And I got on the phones, and I was making a thousand dollars a week. I'm like, "Oh, my God, Jenni, pack the stuff, we're going to Arizona." . . . He was like, "Man, you're, you're a pro at this shit." And I just, I don't know what it was. I was number one. . . . I don't know, I loved it.

The influence of others is remarkably similar to what is known about the criminal careers of street criminals, particularly those who go on to pursue crime with a high degree of skill and success (Hobbs, 1995, ch. 2; Winlow, 2001, pp. 66–86).

For our subjects, many of whom were foundering on conventional paths, criminal telemarketing was a godsend; it came along at a time when they needed to show that they could make something of themselves. In the words of one of them, it was "a salvation to me as a means of income. And being able to actually accomplish something without an education." Criminal telemarketing was the reason some reported for dropping out of college:

> [It] was just something I picked up as a part-time job, when I was 16. . . . When I was in college, my second year in college, [fellow students] were talking about finishing their four years of college and making $28,000 or $30,000 a year. And I was making $1,000 a week part time, you know. . . . And I just couldn't see doing it. I mean, I wound up, after the end of my second year of college, I never went back. I was making too much money. It just seemed so easy.

New recruits generally start as sales agents, although most of our subjects later worked also as closers and reloaders. Employment mobility is common; individuals move from one firm to another, with some eventually taking managerial positions (Doocy et al., 2001).

After gaining experience, former managers told us, they were confident they knew enough about the business to strike out on their own. They did so expecting to increase their income substantially. As one put it:

> In my mind I believed I was smarter than the owners of these other companies that were making millions of dollars. And I just said, "I can do this on my own."

Typically, defectors lure productive personnel from their current employer with promises of more money, and on the way out, they are not above plundering the business's files and lead lists:

> I downloaded every lead in his file. I took it all. I opened up . . . my own office, took all those people, and said, "Now, watch me."

Based in part on the widely shared assumption that the market is never saturated, they generally open a company based on similar products and sales approaches.

What about the criminal histories of fraudulent telemarketers? Information elicited in the interviews and a review of information contained in presentence investigation reports shows that 13 of our subjects had previous criminal records, seven for minor offenses (e.g., petty theft and possession of marijuana) and six for felonies. Of the latter, three were convicted previously of telemarketing offenses. Clearly, many of our subjects are not one-time or accidental violators; they have histories of multiple arrests and convictions. Others have reported similar findings. Thirty percent of 162 sales agents employed by a California-based fraudulent telemarketing firm, for example, had records of at least one criminal offense, and another 16.4% had records of alcohol or drug offenses (Doocy et al., 2001). For members of our sample who have previous arrests, the age of onset for criminal activity is considerably higher than for street criminals. Our data do show persuasively, however, that many appear to have recurrent trouble with the law, and, like street criminals, they are persistent users of alcohol and other drugs. This picture is confirmed also by information contained in their presentence reports.

Attractions and Lifestyles

Overwhelmingly, our subjects told us they got into and persisted at telemarketing for "the money." How well does it pay? Only one subject reported earning less than $1,000 weekly, and most said their annual earnings were in the range of $100,000 to $250,000. Five told us their annual earnings exceeded $1 million. The fact that they can make money quickly and do so without incurring restrictive responsibilities adds to the attractiveness of the work. They find appealing both the flexible hours and the fact that it requires neither extensive training nor advanced education. Few employers impose rigid rules or strictures; generally, there are neither dress codes nor uniforms. The work can be done in shorts and a tee shirt (Doocy et al., 2001).

As important as the income it yields and the casual approach to employment it permits, criminal telemarketing appeals to many who persist at it for reasons of career and identity. Despite class and parental expectations, most of our subjects had not previously settled upon promising or rewarding occupations. Asked what he "liked about telemarketing," one subject's reply was typical: "Well, obviously, it was the money." Immediately, however, he added, "It gave me a career, [and] to me it was my salvation." As with him, criminal telemarketing enables others to own their own business despite their unimpressive educational background, their limited credentials, and the absence of venture capital. As president of their own corporation, telemarketing provides both outward respectability and an income sufficient to maintain the good life.

Other aspects of the work are attractive as well. Its interpersonal and psychological challenge, for example,

> [It] has strong appeal to many salespersons. The ability to impose one's will upon another person—and to achieve a measurable financial reward for doing so—is highlighted in many of the reports of illegal telemarketing practices. . . . Enforcement officials told us that sellers often have mirrors in the cubicles in which they work. They are told to look into the mirror and see the face of a hot shot salesperson. Sometimes there will be a motto on the wall, such as: "Each No gets me closer to the Yes I want." Boiler room owners and managers . . . may put large bills on a bulletin board and say that the next sale or the highest total for the day will qualify for this extra reward. Often the sales people have to stand up when they consummate a transaction, so that the boss can note them and they can take pleasure in the achievement. (Doocy et al., 2001, p. 17)

Characteristically, our subjects believe they are outstanding salespersons; they are supremely confident of their ability to sell over the telephone despite resistance from those they contact. Doing so successfully is a high. One subject told us:

> You could be selling a $10,000 ticket, you could be selling a $49.95 ticket. And it's the same principle, it's the same rules. It's the same game. I like to win. I like to win in all the games I play, you know. And the money is a reason to be there, and a reason to have that job. But winning is what I want to do. I want to beat everybody else in the office. I want to beat that person I am talking to on the phone.

His remarks were echoed by others:

> [I] sold the first person I ever talked to on the phone. And it was just like that first shot of heroin, you know. I'm not a heroin addict. . . . I've only done heroin a couple of times. But it was amazing. It was like, "I can't believe I just did this!" It was incredible. It was never about the money after that. . . . Yeah, it was about the money initially, but when I realized that I could do this every day, it was no longer about the money. It was about the competition, you know. I wanted to be the best salesman, and I want to make the most money that day. And then it became just the sale. It wasn't the money. I didn't even add the figures in my head anymore. It was just whether or not I can turn this person around, you know, walk him down that mutual path of agreement, you know. That was exciting to me. It was power, you know; I can make people do what I wanted them to do. And they would do it.

> It was the money, but it was [also] the ability to control people, to be able to say over the phone, "John, go pick up your pen and write this down." And you write it down! You do exactly like a robot—they would do exactly what they were told to do. And they would do it pleasingly, they would do it without hesitation, because, again, they had enough confidence and faith in you to believe that you were gonna do the right thing about it.

Another subject said simply that the work "gives you power. It gives you power." The importance of this dimension of the payoff from fraud has been commented on by others as well (e.g., Duffield & Grabosky, 2001).

Criminal telemarketers generally distinguish between working hard and "working smart." When asked, therefore, how he viewed those who work hard for modest wages, one replied, "I guess somebody's gotta do it." By contrast, work weeks of 20 to 30 hours are common for them, and even for owners and managers, the need for close oversight of operations decreases substantially once things are up and running. The short work week and their ample income provide considerable latitude in the use of leisure time and in consumption patterns.

The lifestyles of telemarketing participants vary by age and the aspects of the work that employees find most appealing, but ostentatious consumption is common to all. The young, and those attracted to the work and leisure it permits, live life as party (Shover, 1996). Use of cocaine and other illicit drugs is common among this segment of the criminal telemarketing workforce.

> The hours were good. You'd work, sometimes, from about 9:00 to 2:00, 9:00 to 3:00, sometimes from 12:00 to 4:00. Basically, we set our own hours. It was freedom. The money was fantastic. . . . You got the best of the girls. For me, it wasn't really about the job, it was a way of life. . . . I had an alcohol problem at a young age, and to be able to support the alcohol and drug habit with the kind of money that we were making seems to go hand in hand. And then you've got the fast lifestyle . . . up all night, sleep all day, you know. So, everything kinda coincided with that fast lifestyle, that addictive lifestyle.

Asked how he spent the money he made, another subject responded saying:

> Houses, girls, just going out to nightclubs. And a lot of blow [cocaine]. . . . Lots and lots of blow, enormous amounts. And other than that, you know, I look back, I get sick when I think about how much we spent, where the hell I put it all. I'm making all this money [but] I don't have a whole hell of a lot to show for it, you know. That lifestyle didn't allow you to save.

Heavy gambling is commonplace. One subject said that they "would go out to the casinos and blow two, three, four, five thousand dollars a night. That was nothing—to go spend five grand, you know, every weekend. And wake up broke!" Commenting on one of his employees, a subject who owned a telemarketing firm when he was arrested said that the man

> had a Porsche Speedster after he sold his Porsche 911. He had a Dodge Viper, he had a Ferrari 348, he had a Lexus LS400, he had a BMW 850i, he had a Jeep Grand Cherokee. He liked his cars. Now, he didn't have all these at one time, but he ran through them, you know. He traded the Dodge Viper . . . in for the Ferrari. He always had a Porsche.

What we learned about the lifestyles and spending habits of criminal telemarketers differs little from what is known about street criminals and other vocational predators. It also confirms what has been learned about the relationship between easy, unearned income and profligacy: "The way money is acquired is a powerful determinant of how it is defined, husbanded, and spent" (Shover, 1996, p. 104).

The lifestyles of telemarketers change somewhat as they get older and take on more conventional responsibilities:

> I started to realize that, as I was getting older in the industry, it was affecting my children and my relationship with my wife. To the point that it wasn't what I wanted. I wanted more of a home-type of family, where I got home at 6:00 and have dinner and spend time with my wife and children. And with that industry, it doesn't really do that. My lifestyle? Play golf, go to the lake, you know. I had a family, but . . . I was also, you know, making good money. And I wanted to party and that kind of thing. So, I did that a lot. We got together and partied a lot and went here and there and went to, you know—nightlife, go out to clubs occasionally, But, when you're married and have kids, it's limited. It changes. It changed a lot over those years.

For older and more experienced telemarketers, the lifestyle centers around home and family and impressing others with signs of their apparent success:

> I played some golf. [In the summer] water skiing, fishing. I'm real heavy into bass fishing, me and my dad and my brothers. Hunting. Doing things with my wife and kids. I spent a lot of time with them. Evenings, maybe just walking the golf course, or whatever. Watching the sunset.

Another subject told us that after he moved up in the telemarketing ranks, "My partner and I played, we played a lot of golf. The office was right down from the golf course. We'd go to the golf course and play two or three times a week." Save for the unrestrained hedonism of their lives when young and neophytes at criminal telemarketing, the broad outlines of their occupational careers, particularly for those who went on to form their own businesses, resemble the work careers of more conventional citizens.

Legitimation and Defense

Doocy et al. (2001, p. 18) remark that the telemarketing offender they interviewed "conveyed the assured appearance of a most respectable entrepreneur" and "conveyed no hint that what he was doing might not be altogether legitimate." Our subjects are no different. Notwithstanding the fact that all were convicted felons, most reject the labels *criminal* and *crime* as fitting descriptions of them and their activities. They instead employ a range of mitigating explanations and excuses for their offenses, although claims of ignorance figure in most (Scott & Lyman, 1968; Sykes & Matza, 1957). Some former business owners told us, for example, that they set out to maintain a legitimate operation, emulated the operations of their previous employers, and assumed, therefore, that their activities violated no laws. Others said they are guilty only of expanding their business so rapidly that they could not properly oversee day-to-day operations. Some said that indulgence in alcohol and illicit drugs caused them to become neglectful of or indifferent toward their businesses. Most claimed that the allure of money caused them to "look the other way." Those who owned or managed firms are prone also to blame rogue sales agents for any fraudulent or deceptive activities. As one put it: "The owners are trying to do the right thing. They're just attracting the wrong people. It's the salesmen." Another subject likewise suggested: "I guess I let the business get too big and couldn't watch over all of the agents to prevent what they were doing." For their part, sales agents charge that their owners and managers kept them in the dark about the business and its criminal nature.

Fraud offenders typically derive moral justification for their activities from the fact that their crimes cannot succeed without acquiescence or cooperation from their victims; unlike victims of burglary and robbery, those who fall prey to fraud usually are willing, if halting or confused, participants in their own victim- ization (Goffman, 1952). Chief among the legitimating and defensive tenets of telemarketing criminals is the belief that "the mooch is going to send his money to someone, so it might as well be me" (Sanger, 1999, p. 9). In other words, "cus- tomers" are thought to be so greedy, ignorant, or incapable that it is only a matter of time before they throw away their money on something impossible. The ten- dency of fraud offenders to see their victims as deserving of what befalls them was noted by Maurer (1940) more than six decades ago, and it remains true of contemporary telemarketing criminals. One of our subjects told us, "They know what they're doing. They're bargaining for something, and when they lose, they realize that they were at fault." There is neither concern nor sympathy for them. Another subject said:

> If these people can't read, so be it. Screw them, you know. It [doesn't say] every- body's gonna get the diamond and sapphire tennis bracelet. They're dumb enough not to read, dumb enough to send me the money, I really don't care, you know. I'm doing what I have to do to stay out of jail. They're doing what they have to do to fix their fix. They're promo junkies, and we're gonna find them and get them, and we're gonna keep getting them. And they're gonna keep buying. And, you know what I used to say, "They're gonna blow their money in Vegas, they're gonna spend it somewhere. I want to be the one to get it."

Telemarketing criminals selectively seize on aspects of their victims' behav- ior and point to these as a justification or excuse for their crimes. They maintain that they were not victimizing their customers but engaging in a routine sales transaction, no different than a retail establishment selling a shirt that is marked up 1,000%. Telemarketing fraud is therefore construed by its practitioners as per- fectly in tune with mainstream commercial interactions: a "subculture of busi- ness" (Ditton, 1977, p. 173).

Ensconced in their outwardly respectable and self-indulgent lifestyles, our subjects professed belief that, so far as the law was concerned, they were risking nothing more severe than a fine, an adverse civil judgment, or a requirement they make restitution. They claim the entire problem more appropriately was a "civil matter" and "should not be in criminal court." As one put it: "If you have people that are not satisfied, we would be happy to give their money back."

INTERPRETATION

Our description of telemarketing crime and criminals is noteworthy for several reasons, but principally for what it reveals about the relationship between social change and the changing character of lucrative professional theft (Taylor, 1999). Defined by cultural criteria rather than legal yardsticks (see Sykes, 1978, p. 109), the concept of professional crime has become infused with contradiction and ambiguity by the evolution of this new kind of "respectable" predator.

Sociological debate over the descriptive validity of professional theft has been carried out largely as a dialogue with the tradition of Sutherland (1937), who located a behavior system of criminal specialists featuring technical skill, consensus via a shared ideology, differential association, status and, most important, informal organization grounded in a shared cultural identity. Subsequently, scholars presented alternative perspectives regarding crimes other than theft (Einstadter, 1969; Lemert, 1958). However, Shover (1973) perhaps came closest to Sutherland's original conception by locating the social organization of burglary based on highly instrumental and constantly evolving networks of dependency as the key variable. In his view, these networks continue to evolve due to innovative strategies in policing, security, and technology, and telemarketing fraudsters resemble Shover's professional burglar in their adaptive pragmatic organization.

Telemarketers also share many core characteristics with "hustlers" (President's Commission on Law Enforcement and Administration of Justice, 1966; Shover, 1996), or "rounders" (Letkemann, 1973), offenders whose lack of commonality or consensus contradicts the notion of a cohesive, tightly knit behavior system (see also Holzman, 1983; Polsky, 1964; Roebuck & Johnson, 1962). Yet Letkemann (1973) suggests that explicit commitment to criminal activity as a means of making a living is the best criterion for differentiating between professional and nonprofessional criminals, which also echoes Sutherland's classic work, and offers some support for the notion of an occupational group defined by members' commitment to illegal economic activities (Becker, 1960).

Although the investigation of professional thieves and their pursuits has a long history in criminology, the canon is replete with portraits of offenders who have passed from the scene. However, for contemporary observers, "fraud masters" (Jackson, 1994) deservedly command more attention than "cut purses" (Tobias, 1967), "cannons" (Maurer, 1964), and "good burglars" (Shover, 1973). Economic and social change inevitably transform the worlds in which offenders entertain options and organize for pursuit of criminal income (Hobbs, 1997; McIntosh, 1975; Shover, 1983). The classic criminal subcultures of shared practices and beliefs as the basis of criminal community have met the same fate as blue-collar communities based on traditional industries (Soja, 1989). The new entrepreneurial milieu is an enabling environment for a great range and variety of money-making schemes (Ruggiero & South, 1997), and the perceptual templates of contemporary professional criminals feature cues that are geared to success in a sphere emptied out of anachronistic practice (Wright & Decker, 1994).

Automobile theft and "chop shops" were not found in nineteenth-century society, for the obvious reason that there were no automobiles to steal or sell. The shift to a postindustrial order inevitably changed selectively the human qualities and social capital requisite for successful exploitation of criminal opportunities. Traditional professional thieves hailed from locations in the class and social structure where the young generally do not acquire the human capital requisite to success in the world of well-paid and respectable work. The blue-collar skills of an industrial society, however, are not equal to the challenge of exploiting contemporary, increasingly white-collar criminal opportunities. The postindustrial service-oriented economy instead places a premium on entrepreneurial, interpersonal, communicative and organizational skills, and it is the children of the middle class who are most likely to be exposed to and acquire these.

The knowledge and skills needed to exploit criminal opportunities vocationally and successfully do not differ greatly from those required for success in the legitimate world. Like the professional thief, the new and increasingly white-collar vocational predators commit planned violations of the law for profit (Van Duyne, 1996), but they do so in the style of the middle class. They take on and publicly espouse a belief system that defends against moral condemnation from outsiders, and they are dismissive of both the world of hourly employment and the lives of those confined to it. But although the professional thieves of an earlier era publicly endorsed and were expected to adhere to norms of loyalty and integrity in dealings with one another (Cohen & Taylor, 1972; Irwin, 1970; Irwin & Cressey, 1962; Mason, 1994; Maurer, 1964; McVicar, 1982; Shover, 1973; Taylor, 1984), criminal telemarketers by contrast are extremely individualistic and self-centered in their contacts with criminal justice officials and agencies. Whether this is because of their privileged backgrounds or because the nature of criminal relationships has been "transformed by the advent of a market culture," their illicit pursuits manifest qualities not only of entrepreneurial creativity but also independence and "possessive individualism" (Taylor, 1999).

Professional thieves of earlier eras found a measure of success in crime despite their humble beginnings, and much about what they made of themselves is understandable in the light of their blue-collar roots. The lives they constructed emphasized freedom to live "life as party" (Shover & Honaker, 1991) by "earning and burning money" (Katz, 1988, p. 215), to roam without restraint, and to celebrate these achievements with others of similar perspective. The class origins of contemporary garden-variety white-collar criminals are more advantaged, but they live their lives in substantially similar fashion. Unlike the "foot pads" of Elizabethan England, they generally do not gravitate to a criminal netherworld or a self-contained criminal fraternity. Nor do they confine their leisure pursuits to others of similar work. The proletarian underworld was an essential network for exchanging, controlling, and disseminating information (Hobbs, 1995, pp. 21–23; McIntosh, 1971), but the telemarketing fraudster depends on networks of information that are largely indistinguishable from those that underpin the noncriminal sector.

What Benney (1981, p. 263) called "the fabulous underworld of bourgeois invention" ironically has been decimated by the embourgeoisement of crime. Criminals now emerge from the economic mainstream and engage both socially and pragmatically with derivations of normative economic activity. The acquisitive entrepreneurial ethic that underpins both legal and illegal performances within the postindustrial marketplace thrives upon "new technical, social, psychological and existential skills" (Bauman, 1992, p. 98), which in turn are bordered by new configurations of cultural and technological capital.

Although the old underworld was safely ensconced in the locales, occupational practices, leisure cultures, and oppositional strategies of the industrial proletariat (Hobbs, 1997; Samuel, 1981), it is the bourgeois who have emerged with the education and ideological flexibility to engage with lucrative contemporary professional crime, which is located not within a proletarian outpost of traditional transgression, but within rhetorics that legitimate and enable the entire "spectrum of legitimacy" (Albanese, 1989, p. 101).

Telemarketing fraudsters should be seen as "fluid sets of mobile marauders in the urban landscape, alert to institutional weakness in both legitimate and illegitimate spheres" (Block, 1983, p. 245). These spheres are pliant and not territorially embedded (Chaney, 1994, p. 149). Detached from an "underworld" (Haller, 1990, pp. 228–29), contemporary professional crime has mutated from an overworld in which the bourgeoisie rather than blue-collar culture is sovereign. This helps explain why telemarketing fraudsters, unlike the professional thieves of previous generations, are likely to spend their weekends on the lake, playing golf, or having friends over for a barbeque. Still, they blow their earnings on drugs, gambling, fast living, and conspicuous consumption. They earn a reasonably good return from crime, but like "box men" of yore, few spend appreciable time in jails and prisons.

REFERENCES

Adler, P. S. (1992). *Technology and the future of work*. New York: Oxford University Press.

Albanese, J. (1989). *Organized crime in America*. Cincinnati, OH: Anderson.

American Association of Retired Persons. (1996). *Telemarketing fraud and older Americans: An AARP survey*. New York: Author.

Atlanta Journal-Constitution. (2000). Alleged scam on elderly by telemarketers is revealed. September 6, B3.

Australian Broadcasting Corporation. (2001). *Beyond the boiler room*. Retrieved September 24, 2003, from www.abc.net.au/4corners/.

Batty, M., & Barr, B. (1994). The electronic frontier: Exploring and mapping cyberspace. *Futures, 26*(7), 699–712.

Bauman, Z. (1992). *Intimidations of modernity*. London: Routledge.

Becker, H. (1960). Notes on the concept of commitment. *American Journal of Sociology, 66*, 32–40.

Benney, M. (1981). *Low company*. Sussex, UK: Caliban.

Block, A. (1983). *East Side–West Side: Organizing crime in New York, 1930–1950*. Newark, NJ: Transaction.

Chaney, D. (1994). *The cultural turn*. London: Routledge.

Clarke, M. (1990). Control of insurance fraud: A comparative view. *British Journal of Criminology, 30,* 1–3.

Cohen, S., & Taylor, L. (1972). *Psychological survival*. Harmondsworth: Penguin.

Direct Marketing Association. (2001). Retrieved June 5, 2012, from http://www.thedma.org.

Ditton, J. (1977). *Part time crime*. London: Macmillan.

Doocy, J., Schichor, D., Sechrest, D., & Geis, G. (2001). Telemarketing fraud: Who are the tricksters and what makes them trick? *Securities Journal, 14,* 7–26.

Duffield, G., & Grabosky, P. (2001). *The psychology of fraud*. Paper 199. Griffith, Canberra: Australian Institute of Criminology.

Einstadter, W. J. (1969). The social organization of armed robbery. *Social Problems, 17,* 54–83.

Francis, D. (1988). *Contrepreneurs*. Toronto: Macmillan.

Goffman, E. (1952) On cooling the mark out: Some aspects of adaptation to failure. *Psychiatry, 15,* 451–463.

Grabosky, P. N., Smith, R. G., & Dempsey, G. (2001). *Electronic theft: Unlawful acquisition in cyberspace*. New York: Cambridge University Press.

Haller, M. (1990). Illegal enterprise: A theoretical and historical interpretation. *Criminology, 28*(2), 207–235.

Harris and Associates, Inc. (1992). *Telemarketing fraud*. Charlotte: University of North Carolina, Institute for Research in Social Science.

Hirschhorn, L. (1985). Information technology and the new services game. In M. Castells (Ed.), *High technology, space, and society* (pp. 172–190). Beverly Hills, CA: Sage.

Hobbs, R. (1995). *Bad business: Professional crime in contemporary Britain*. Oxford: Oxford University Press.

———. (1997). Professional crime: Change, continuity, and the enduring myth of the underworld. *Sociology, 31,* 57–72.

Holzman, H. (1983). The serious habitual property offender as moonlighter: An empirical study of labor force participation among robbers and burglars. *Journal of Criminal Justice Law and Criminology, 73,* 1774–1792.

Irwin, J. (1970). *The felon*. Upper Saddle River, NJ: Prentice Hall.

Irwin, J., & Cressey, D. (1962). Thieves, convicts and the inmate culture. *Social Problems, 10,* 142–55.

Jackson, J. (1994). Fraud masters: Professional credit card offenders and crime. *Criminal Justice Review, 19,* 24–55.

Katz, J. (1988). *Seductions of crime*. New York: Basic.

Lash, S., & Urry, J. (1994). *Economies of signs and space*. London: Sage.

Lemert, E. (1958). The behavior of the systematic check forger. *Social Problems, 6,* 141–149.

Letkemann, P. (1973). *Crime as work*. Upper Saddle River, NJ: Prentice Hall.

Mason, E. (1994). *Inside story*. London: Pan.

Maurer, D. W. (1940). *The big con*. Indianapolis, IN: Bobbs-Merrill.

———. (1964). *Whiz mob*. New Haven, CT: College and University Press.

McIntosh, M. (1971). Changes in the organization of thieving. In S. Cohen (Ed.), *Images of deviance*. Harmondsworth: Penguin.

———. (1975). *The organization of crime*. New York: Macmillan.

McVicar, J. (1982). Violence in prisons. In P. Marsh & A. Campbell (Eds.), *Aggression and violence*. Oxford: Blackwell.

Polsky, N. (1964). The hustler. *Social Problems, 12*, 3–15.

President's Commission on Law Enforcement and Administration of Justice. (1966). Professional crime. In *Task force report* (ch. 7). Washington, DC: US Government Printing Office.

Rebovich, D., Layne, J., Jiandani, J., & Hage, S. (2000). *The national public survey on white collar crime*. Glen Allen, VA: National White Collar Crime Center.

Roebuck, J., & Johnson, R. (1962). The jack of all trades offender. *Crime & Delinquency, 8*, 172–181.

Ross, E. A. (1907). *Sin and society: An analysis of latter-day iniquity*. Boston: Houghton Mifflin.

Ruggiero, V., & South, N. (1997). The late modern city as a bazaar. *British Journal of Sociology, 48*, 54–70.

Samuel, R. (1981). *East End underworld: The life and times of Arthur Harding*. London: Routledge and Kegan Paul.

Samuelson, R. J. (1995). *The good life and its discontents*. New York: Random House.

Sanger, D. (1999). Confessions of a phone-scam artist. *Saturday Night, 114*, 86–98.

Schulte, F. (1995). *Fleeced! Telemarketing rip-offs and how to avoid them*. Essex, UK: Prometheus.

Scott, M. B., & Lyman, M. L. (1968). Accounts. *American Sociological Review, 33*, 46–62.

Shover, N. (1973). The social organization of burglary. *Social Problems, 20*, 499–514.

———. (1983). Professional crime: Major offender. In S. H. Kadish (Ed.), *Encyclopedia of crime and justice* (pp. 1263–1271). New York: Macmillan.

———. (1996). *Great pretenders: Pursuits and careers of persistent thieves*. Boulder, CO: Westview.

Shover, N., & Honaker, D. (1991). The socially bounded decision making of persistent property offenders. *Howard Journal, 31*, 276–293.

Silverstone, R. (1991). *Beneath the bottom line: Households and information and communication technologies in the age of the consumer*. London: Brunel University Centre for Research on Innovation, Culture, and Technology.

Soja, E. (1989). *Postmodern geographies*. London: Verso.

Sparrow, M. K. (1996). *License to steal: Why fraud plagues America's health care system*. Boulder, CO: Westview.

Stevenson, R. J. (2000). *The boiler room and other telephone sales scams*. Urbana: University of Illinois Press.

Sutherland, E. H. (1937). *The professional thief*. Chicago, IL: University of Chicago Press.

Sykes, G. (1978). *Criminology*. New York: Harcourt Brace Jovanovitch.

Sykes, G., & Matza, D. (1957). Techniques of neutralization: A theory of delinquency. *American Sociological Review, 22*, 667–670.

Taylor, I. (1999). *Crime in context: A critical criminology of market societies*. Boulder, CO: Westview.

Taylor, L. (1984). *In the underworld*. Oxford: Blackwell.

Tickell, A. (1996). Taking the initiative: Leeds' Financial Centre. In G. Haughton & C. Williams (Eds.), *Corporate city? Partnerships, participation in urban development in Leeds*. Aldershot, UK: Avebury.

Tillman, R. (1998). *Broken promises: Fraud by small business health insurers*. Boston: Northeastern University Press.

Titus, R. (2001). Personal fraud and its victims. In N. Shover & J. P. Wright (Eds.), *Crimes of privilege: Readings in white collar crime* (pp. 57–67). New York: Oxford University Press.

Titus, R. M., Heinzelmann, F., & Boyle, J. M. (1995). Victimization of persons by fraud. *Crime & Delinquency, 41*, 54–72.

Tobias, J. J. (1967). *Crime and industrial society in the 19th century*. London: Batsford.

Turkle, S. (1995). *Life on the screen: Identity in the age of the Internet*. New York: Simon and Schuster.

U.S. Senate. (1993). *Telemarketing fraud and section 568, The Telemarketing and Consumer Fraud and Abuse Protection Act*. Hearing before the Subcommittee on Consumer of the Committee on Commerce, Science, and Transportation. 103d Cong.

Van Duyne, P. (1996). The phantom and threat of organized crime. *Crime, Law, and Social Change, 21*, 241–277.

Winlow, S. (2001). *Badfellas*. Oxford, UK: Berg.

Wright, R., & Decker, S. (1994). *Burglars on the job: Streetlife and residential break-ins*. Boston: Northeastern University Press.

CHAPTER 13

Drugged Druggists: The Convergence of Two Criminal Career Trajectories

Dean A. Dabney and Richard C. Hollinger

The authors interviewed 50 recovering drug-addicted pharmacists to help under-stand the onset of and progression into illicit prescription pharmaceutical drug abuse. Two distinct paths of entry into drug use were found. Nearly half (n = 23) of the pharmacists first used street and/or prescription drugs before entering their professional careers. This first group ("recreational abusers") began using pre-scription drugs principally for their euphoric effects, exploiting their newly discovered access to and knowledge about pharmaceuticals. The remaining 27 pharmacists ("therapeutic self-medicators") began using prescription drugs much later in their careers and primarily for medicinal reasons. These two dis-tinct modes of entry eventually converged into a single, common criminal career trajectory. Once addicted, the distinguishing characteristics between the two groups begin to disappear and common themes emerged, indicating dynamic convergence into a single pattern for the mature deviant. The authors conclude that early differentiation followed by subsequent convergence of behaviors and motivations suggests that some theorists and practitioners alike have erroneously concluded that they have discovered multiple static types of crime and criminals when in some cases they are examining a single criminal/deviant career at differ-ent points along its dynamic trajectory.

INTRODUCTION

Self-report studies reveal that between 40% and 65% of all practicing pharma-cists engage in some form of illicit drug use at least once during their profes-sional careers. Approximately 20% of pharmacists in earlier studies report using

Source: Dabney, D. A., & Hollinger, R. C. (2002). Drugged druggists: The convergence of two criminal career trajectories. *Justice Quarterly, 19*, 182–213.

217

drugs regularly enough that they experienced negative life consequences, such as missing work, blackouts, health problems, or difficulties with interpersonal relationships. Interestingly, only 5% to 10% of these "regular" users consider themselves to be "drug abusers" (Dabney, 1997; Dabney, 2001; McAuliffe et al., 1987; Normack et al., 1985).

Although scholars generally agree about the high incidence and prevalence, substantial knowledge gaps prevent us from fully understanding the complex causal etiology of criminal drug use among this particular category of health care professionals. Most vexing is the limited understanding of how these individuals come to initially use and then abuse the prescription substances that they are entrusted to dispense. The present study is an attempt to fill this current knowledge void by identifying the underlying causes of illicit prescription drug use among practicing pharmacists.

This is the first empirical inquiry designed to systematically identify the reasons why pharmacists begin, and subsequently continue to use unauthorized prescription medicines. Our substantive objectives are two-fold. We begin by exploring the ways in which criminal/deviant roles and associations develop and evolve within the personal and professional worlds of these addicts. Specifically, we draw upon the personal experiences of 50 recovering drug-impaired pharmacists using lengthy, face-to-face interviews in order to map out the criminal career trajectory of pharmacists who become addicted to prescription medicines. The lessons learned from these data will then be applied to contemporary theory on criminal careers in an effort to expand conceptual understanding of this phenomenon.

Drug-Addicted Pharmacist Literature

Various explanations have been offered to explain illicit drug use among pharmacists. For example, existing drug abuse hypotheses include inadequate professional socialization, occupational role conflicts, low risk of detection, minimal negative consequences, and a profession-wide atmosphere of denial (Bissell, Haberman, & Williams, 1989; Dabney & Hollinger, 1999; Gallegos et al., 1988; Hankes & Bissell, 1992; McAuliffe, 1984; Penna & Williams, 1985; Quinney, 1963; Sheffield, 1988). Still, uncertainty exists regarding (1) what factors are most influential in explaining pharmacists' initial entry into theft and addiction and (2) what stimuli facilitate an ongoing pattern of drug theft and abuse that eventually results in addiction.

The explanations most commonly found in the scholarly literature regarding medical professionals' drug abuse can be divided into two generic conceptual categories, "recreational abuse" and "therapeutic self-medication." Some of the first studies of the phenomenon of illicit prescription drug abuse suggested that health care professionals engage in prescription drug theft and use primarily for recreational reasons, exacerbated by nearly unlimited access to prescription medications and combined with a perceived invincibility to drug addiction (McAuliffe, 1984; McAuliffe et al., 1987). However, the momentum has turned away from "recreational abuser" explanations, and instead, a less judgmental model has come to flourish. Today, most scholars and practitioners alike assume that the vast majority of health care professionals steal and use prescription drugs principally for therapeutic reasons (Bissell, Haberman, & Williams, 1989; Chi, 1983; Gallegos et al., 1988; Normack et al., 1985; Sheffield, O'Neill, & Fisher, 1992; Winick, 1961). In the case of the pharmacist, factors such as work-related stress, heightened access to drugs, and the physical and emotional demands of pharmacy practice are thought to be the impetus for early forays into illegal drug use. Driven by pitfalls of drug tolerance, levels of use escalate and the pharmacist draws upon his/her vast clinical knowledge as a means of regulating his/her use and convincing him/herself that he/she is in control of an ever-growing drug habit (Dabney & Hollinger, 1999; Hankes & Bissell, 1992).

The principal objective of this research was to ascertain which of these two competing models, recreational or therapeutic, is the most accurate in explaining the illicit prescription drug use careers of practicing pharmacists. Despite the pervasiveness of both explanations in the literature, we quickly recognized that perhaps neither was entirely correct. In fact, we ultimately realized that both models were partially accurate. As we shall see, one can readily identify two very different paths of entry among drug using pharmacists. However, as drug theft and use gives way to drug abuse and eventually uncontrollable addiction, these two deviant career trajectories converge and we see that the motivational and behavioral patterns of mature deviants appear very much the same.

Criminal Career Literature

We turn to the broader criminological literature for conceptual clarification. Analogous to an occupational career, it has become increasingly popular to use the term "career" in speaking about various forms of criminal or deviant behavior that occur over a period of time (Becker, 1963; Nettler, 1982). Our current understanding of this concept can be traced to scores of scholarly efforts wherein academics have repeatedly shown patterned aspects to how offenders enter into and then proceed through their deviant or criminal routines (see Greenberg, 1996, for a sampling). We note that these career-based inquiries have often targeted samples of drug offenders (Adler, 1993; Becker, 1953; Blackwell, 1983; Coombs, 1981; Faupel, 1987; Faupel, 1991; Rubington, 1967; Smith & Smith, 1984; Waldorf, 1983). For example, Adler (1993) and others (Hafley & Tewksbury, 1996) have written at length about the various "career" stages (i.e., entry, escalation, and exit) that go along with using and dealing marijuana. Similarly, Faupel and Klockars (1987) identified a four-step career progression that was observed in a sample of hard-core heroin users. We have learned a lot from these offender-based studies. Namely, we have learned that not all heroin or marijuana users think or act the same. At the same time, we have come to identify shared ideals, motivations, and behaviors that serve to reinforce our stereotypical images of a given type of criminal subculture.

These latter realizations have given way to several more generic efforts at theorizing. Scholars such as Best and Luckenbill (1994) and, more recently, Tittle and Paternoster (2000) provide us with conceptual models of "criminal/deviant careers." These works seek to summarize the lessons that we have learned from past research efforts and thus crystallize our understanding of this important dimension of the criminological enterprise. In the tradition of deductive reasoning, these scholars begin by identifying and defining a set of core components (i.e., fundamental motivational and behavioral dimensions) that they see as being common to all crimes. This underlying framework is then used to funnel seemingly different criminal acts and actors into a series of abstract conceptual categories. As an abbreviated example, Tittle and Paternoster (2000) argue that there are nine underlying dimensions to criminal behavior: sociality, pervasiveness, communication, differentiation, culture, self-identity, philosophical integration, self-control from within group, and recruitment. While they recognize that each criminal and crime type possesses its own unique combination of these nine factors, they contend that all criminal behavior can be organized along a three-point continuum. This continuum places "individualized deviance" is at one end, "subcultural deviance" in the center, and "fully organized deviance" at the other end. The authors list suicide and serial murder as examples of individualized deviance, the deviant behaviors of recreational drug users and street gang members as examples of subcultural deviance, and racketeering and collective terrorism as examples of fully organized forms of deviance.

Several years earlier, Best and Luckenbill (1994) also introduced a conceptual framework that seeks to organize both deviant individuals and their deviant behaviors within a career-based context. Deviant acts, or what they term "transactions," are said to manifest themselves in one of three forms: individualized deviance, deviant exchanges, or deviant exploitation. Secrecy and solitude are the hallmarks of individualized deviance. Collectivity and cooperation are central to deviant exchanges. And deviant exploitation takes on a coercive quality, as when an unsuspecting victim is surreptitiously targeted by a stealthy offender.

Best and Luckenbill (1994) also outline a series of generic motivational categories that go along with their behavioral scheme. The authors theorize that different types of generic motives (defensive, adventurous, and mental calculations) should be present in different types of deviant transactions and thus coin the term "sociology of deviance" to describe the patterned forms of behavior and motivation that are indigenous to a given type of crime or deviance.

Once they have finished describing the behavioral and motivational elements of deviant acts, Best and Luckenbill (1994) shift the unit of analysis to the individual. The authors' discussion of deviant actors, or what they term the "sociology of deviants," applies the abovementioned framework and thus seeks to demonstrate the way that an individual's behaviors are patterned and interconnected within "a network of social relations" (Best & Luckenbill, 1994, p. 5). The term "social organization" speaks to the way that one's motives, associations, and transactions dictate the types of dynamic roles that are experienced while engaging in both deviant and non-deviant activities. This line of reasoning leads Best and Luckenbill to conclude that different types of deviant activities will produce different roles and associations for those who choose to engage in them. They go so far as to categorize deviant actors and relationships within a five-category typology. These categories are placed on a continuum delineated by differing levels of sophistication in social organization. Moving from the least sophisticated level of social organization to the most, this list includes (1) loners, (2) colleagues, (3) peers, (4) teams, and (5) formal organizations. Best and Luckenbill (1994) see the deviant or criminal career as the synthesized reality in which actors and their actions come to be patterned and regimented over time. In short, the nature of the behavior interacts with the social organization of the perpetrators (i.e., their deviant roles and associations) to produce somewhat predictable career paths.

The conceptual models provided to us by Best and Luckenbill (1994) and Tittle and Paternoster (2000) occupy an important place in our understanding of criminal careers, especially those involving drug users. First and foremost, these discussions elevate the empirical lessons that we have learned from street ethnographies of drug users to a higher level of abstraction. In doing so, they allow us to group similar offenders and offenses into categories. In turn, these categories provide direction about the types of behaviors and motivations that one might encounter when seeking to enforce or prevent specific or general categories of acts or actors. One must be careful, however, not to lose sight of the fact that these categories are theoretical abstractions that will not always fare so well when superimposed onto complex social realities. Best and Luckenbill (1994) emphasize this point when they speak of the fluid nature of deviant careers and how circumstances might lead to an individual or individuals experiencing noticeable vertical or lateral shifts across their criminal career trajectory. Tittle and Paternoster (2000) make scant mention of career fluidity and relativity.

The existing literature provides little hard evidence on if and how the notions of career fluidity and relativity might manifest themselves in real-life situations. Given that our inquiry uncovered a clear instance of career fluidity and relativity in action, we were left with the task of filling in the conceptual space on our own. What follows is an effort to clarify and extend the implied conceptual flexibility of the criminal career hypothesis. Namely, we use the details of criminal career trajectories observed in 50 drug-recovering pharmacists to elucidate the strengths and weaknesses of the career-based notion of drug abuse and thus provide valuable evidence of the types of shifts and fluidity that exist therein.

STUDY GROUP DEMOGRAPHICS

The pharmacists that were interviewed represented a variety of social and demographic backgrounds. For example, 78% were men and 22% were women. The vast majority (48) of interviewees were white, with the exception of one Hispanic and one African American individual. A broad age range was present, with 8% being under the age of 30, 38% in their 30s, 36% in their 40s, 12% in their 50s, and 6% over the age of 60.

Table 13.1 Defining Characteristics of Pharmacists' Illicit Prescription Drug Use Motivation and Behaviors

SIGNIFICANT CHARACTERISTICS	TYPE I (N = 23) RECREATIONAL ABUSERS	TYPE II (N = 27) THERAPEUTIC SELF-MEDICATORS
(1) Nature of drug use	Recreational	Therapeutic/medicinal
(2) Onset of drug use	Prior to or during Rx school—early in pharmacy careers	Post Rx school—well into pharmacy careers
(3) General trajectory of drug use	Rapid, steep trajectory	Slow, progressive trajectory
(4) Principal mode of rationalization	"Better living through chemistry—live your work"	"I know enough to monitor and control my self-medication"
(5) Scope of the drug use	Indiscriminate experimentation	Selective drug types/schedules
(6) Social organization of deviant transactions	Deviant exchanges turning into individual deviance	Individual deviance
(7) Underlying motive for drug use	Adventurous motives based in permissive drug use ideals followed by defensive motives aimed at survival	Defensive motives aimed first at job-related pain or stress relief, then survival
(8) Social organization of deviants	Peers → colleagues → loners	Loners

Turning to issues of professional status, we note that 86% held bachelor's degrees in pharmacy, while 16% held some advanced pharmacy degree. While many of the pharmacists moved from job to job and crossed over different practice settings, they categorized their "primary practice setting" as follows: 36% hospital pharmacy, 28% independent retail pharmacy, 26% chain retail pharmacy, 4% home infusion pharmacy, 4% nursing homes, and 2% employed as temporary contract pharmacists. These demographic characteristics closely resemble the descriptive elements that were revealed in a 1992 nationwide study of 179,445 of the 194,570 pharmacists who were licensed to practice at the time (Martin, 1993).

TWO PATHS OF ENTRY INTO A DEVIANT CAREER

Given our specific interest in the various career aspects of deviant behavior, a significant portion of each interview was focused on the pharmacist's entry into illicit drug use. After examining the transcripts of the interviews, it quickly became apparent that their initial deviant drug use took on two distinct forms. Nearly one half of the pharmacists began using prescription drugs recreationally to "get high." These individuals usually had a history of "street" drug use prior to their even beginning the formal pharmacy education process. Alternatively, the other half of the pharmacists interviewed described how they began using prescription drugs much later for therapeutic purposes when confronted with some physical malady while on the job.

Recreational Abusers

Of the 50 pharmacists interviewed, nearly half (23, or 46%) could be classified as "recreational abusers." One of the defining characteristics of these individuals is that they all began experimenting with street drugs during their teenage years. They each described their early drug use experiences as being "recreational" in nature. These respondents commonly experimented with "street" drugs such as marijuana, cocaine, alcohol, and various psychedelics while in high school and during their early college years. The motivation behind this use was quite simple; they were adventurous and wanted to experience the euphoric, mind-altering effects that the drugs offered. Due to procurement problems, these individuals reported that they engaged in little, if any, prescription drug use before entering pharmacy school.

Initial Prescription Drug Use

For the recreational abuser, the onset of the illicit prescription drug use career usually began shortly after entering pharmacy training. These respondents were quick to point to the recreational motivations behind their early prescription drug use. As one 42-year-old male pharmacist stated, "I just wanted the effect, I really just wanted the effect. I know what alcohol is. But what if you take a Quaalude and drink with it? What happens then?" Similarly, a 36-year-old male pharmacist said:

> It was very recreational at first, yeah. It was more curiosity . . . experimental. I had read about all these drugs. Then I discovered I had a lot of things going on with me at that time and that these [drugs] solved the problem for me instantly. I had a lot of self-exploration issues going on at that time.

Trends in the data indicate that pharmacy school provided these individuals with the requisite access to prescription drugs. They recalled how they exploited their newly found access to prescription drugs in an effort to expand or surpass the euphoric effects that they received from weaker street drugs. For example, a 27-year-old male pharmacist said:

> It was a blast. It was fun. . . . It was experimentation. We smoked a little pot. And then in the "model pharmacy" [a training facility in college], there was stuff [prescription drugs] all over the place. "Hey this is nice . . . that is pretty nice." If it was a controlled substance, then I tried it. I had my favorites, but when that supply was exhausted, I'd move on to something else. I was a "garbage head"! It was the euphoria. . . . I used to watch Cheech and Chong [movies]. That's what it was like. I wasn't enslaved by them [or so I thought]. They made the world go round.

Pharmacy as a Drug Access Career Choice

It is important to note that the majority of the recreational abusers claimed that they specifically chose a career in pharmacy because it would offer them an opportunity to expand their drug use behaviors. For example, a 37-year-old male pharmacist said: "That's one of main reasons I went to pharmacy school, because I'd have access to medications if I needed them." Further evidence of this reasoning can be seen in the comments of a 41-year-old male pharmacist:

> A lot of my friends after high school said, "Oh great, you're going into pharmacy school. You can wake up on uppers and go to bed on downers," all that stuff. At first, [I said] no. The first time I ever [used prescription drugs], I thought, "No, that's not why I'm doing it [enrolling in pharmacy school]. No, I'm doing it for the noble reasons." But then after a while I thought, well, maybe they had a point there after all. I [had to] change my major. So I [based my choice] on nothing more than: "Well, it looks like fun and gee, all the pharmacy majors had drugs." The [pharmacy students] that I knew . . . every weekend when they came back from home, they would unpack their bags, and bags of pills would roll out. I thought, "Whoa, I got to figure out how to do this." [I would ask:] "How much did you pay for this?" [They would respond:] "I haven't paid a thing, I just stole them. Stealing is okay. I get shit wages so I got to make it up somehow. So we just steal the shit." Well, I thought, "This is it; I want to be a pharmacist." So I went into pharmacy school.

This trend was observed over and over again among recreational abusers. Namely, access to prescription drugs was a critical factor in their career choice.

Learning by Experimentation

Once in pharmacy school, the recreational abusers consistently described how they adopted an applied approach to their studies. For example, if they read about a particularly interesting type of drug in pharmacy school, they often would indicate that they wanted to try it. Or, if they were clerking or interning in a pharmacy, which offered access to prescription medicines, they would describe how they stole drugs just to try them. If a teacher or employer told them about the unusual effects of a new drug, interviewees would state that this piqued their interest. This pattern of application-oriented learning is exemplified in the comments of a 49-year-old male pharmacist:

> I began using [prescription drugs] to give myself the whole realm of healing experience . . . to control my body, to control the ups and the downs. . . . I thought I could chemically feel, do, and think whatever I wanted to if I learned enough about these drugs and used them. Actually, I sat in classes with a couple of classmates where they would be going through a group of drugs, like, say, a certain class of muscle relaxants, skeletal muscle relaxants, and they would talk about the mechanism of pharmacology and then they would start mentioning different side effects, like drowsiness, sedation, and some patients report euphoria, and at a high enough dose, hallucinations and everything. Well, hell, that got highlighted in yellow. And then that night, one of us would take some [from the pharmacy], and then we would meet in a bar at 10:00 or in somebody's house and we would do it together.

The above quote stands as an example of how recreational abusers often superimposed an educational motive onto their progressive experimentation with prescription drugs in pharmacy school. They explained that they wanted to experience the drug effects that they read about in their pharmacy textbooks. These individuals adeptly incorporated their scientific training and professional socialization in such a way that allowed them to excuse and redefine their recreational drug use. Many went as far as to convince themselves that their experimental drug use was actually beneficial to their future patients. This adaptation strategy is illustrated in the comments of a 59-year-old male recreational abuser:

> In a lot of ways, [college drug use] was pretty scientific. [I was] seeing how these things affected me in certain situations . . . [just] testing the waters. I thought that I'll be able to counsel my patients better the more I know about the side effects of these drugs. I'll be my own rat. I'll be my own lab rat. I can tell [patients] about the shakes and chills and the scratchy groin and your skin sloughing off. I can tell you all about that stuff.

SOCIALLY ACCEPTABLE RECREATIONAL DRUG USE IN PHARMACY SCHOOL

The recreational abusers unanimously agreed that there was no shortage of socially acceptable experimental drug use while in pharmacy school. They recalled liberal use of alcohol and street drugs among many of their fellow pharmacy students. Moreover, all 23 claimed that it was not uncommon for students to use amphetamines to get through all-night study sessions once or twice each semester. Many of the recreational abusers recalled that they were not satisfied with this type of controlled drug use. They were more interested in expanding their usage. One 48-year-old male pharmacist described the make-up of his pharmacy school cohort as follows:

> There were a third of the pharmacy students in school because Mom and Dad or Grandfather or Uncle Bill were pharmacists. They looked up to them and wanted to be one [too]. A [second] third had been in the [Vietnam] war. They were a pharmacy tech in the war or had worked in a pharmacy. They had the experiential effect of what pharmacy is and found a love for it or a desire to want it. Then you had the other third . . . and we were just drug addicts. We didn't know what the practice was all about, but we did know that we got letters after our names, guaranteed income if we didn't lose our letters. And we had access to anything [prescription drugs] we needed.

Many of the recreational abusers claimed that they specifically sought out fellow pharmacy students who were willing to use prescription drugs. The most common locus of these peer associations was in pharmacy-specific fraternities. The interviewees said that there was usually ample drug use going on in these organizations, allowing them the opportunity to cautiously search out and identify other drug users. Once they were connected with other drug users, the prescription drug use of all involved parties increased. This type of small group drug use allowed for access to an expanded variety of drugs, a broader pharmacological knowledge base, and even larger quantities of drugs. However, numerous respondents were quite clear about the fact that these drug-based associations were tenuous and temporary in nature. Over time, as the intensity of their drug use increased, the recreational abusers described how they became more reclusive. They became more guarded and selective with their relationships, fearing that their heightened prescription drug use would come to be defined as problematic by fellow pharmacy students. One 43-year-old male pharmacist said:

> You get the sense pretty quickly that you are operating [using] on a different level. Those of us that were busily stealing [prescription drugs] from our internship sites began to tighten our social circle. We might party a little bit with the others, but when it came to heavy use, we kept it hush, hush.

Unlike other pharmacy students who were genuinely experimenting with drugs on a short-term basis, these recreational abusers observed that there was an added intensity associated with their own prescription drug use. While most of these recreational abusers entered pharmacy school with some prior experiences in recreational street drug use, their precollege prescription drug use was usually not extensive. As such, it was not until they got into pharmacy school that they began to develop more pronounced street and prescription drug use habits. A 38-year-old female pharmacist discusses this transition into increased usage in the following interview excerpt:

> I went off to pharmacy school. That was a three-year program. I had tried a few things [before that], but I would back off because it was shaming for me not to get straight As. The descent to hell started when I got to pharmacy school. There were just so many things [prescription drugs] available and so many things that I thought I just had to try. It might be a different high; it might be a different feeling, anything to alter the way that I just felt. I was pretty much using on a daily basis by the time I got to my last year.

Pharmacy Practice Yields Even More Drug Access and Use

Pharmacy school was just the beginning of the steep career trajectory for the recreational abusers. School was followed by pharmacy practice that offered even greater access to prescription medicines. Daily work experiences meant exposure to more new drugs. Introduction to a newly developed compound was followed by some quick research on the effects of the drug and then almost immediate experimentation. This is well illustrated by a 37-year-old male pharmacist describing his early work experience:

> In '82, I remember I came down here and applied for a job . . . in May of '82. I remember even then, I went out to the satellite [pharmacy facility] and I heard about this one drug, Placidyl. As soon as I got to the interview, they were showing me around. A friend took me around . . . and I saw a Placidyl on the shelf there. . . . I took a chance, kind of wandering around, and I went back and took

some off the shelf. So even then, I was [stealing and misusing]. You know, why would you do that in the middle of interviewing for a job? I took it even then. I just jumped at the chance.

Once recreational abusers got into a permanent practice setting, most described how they quickly realized that they had free rein over the pharmacy stock. At first, these individuals relied upon other more experienced pharmacists for guidance in gaining access to (or in using) newly available prescription drugs. Later, their nearly unrestricted access meant that they could now try any drugs that they pleased. And most did. More importantly, increased access allowed the pharmacists-in-training to secretly use the drugs that they most liked. No longer did they have to worry about others looking over their shoulders. Not surprisingly, the level of their drug use usually skyrocketed shortly after entering pharmacy practice. This trend is demonstrated in the comments of a 41-year-old male pharmacist:

> By the time I got to pharmacy school in 1971, I was smoking dope [marijuana] probably every day or every other day, and drinking with the same frequency, but not to the point of passing out kind of stuff. Then, in 1971, that was also the year that I discovered barbs [barbiturates]. I had never had barbs up until I got to pharmacy school. So it was like '75 or '76 [when I got out of pharmacy school], I was using heavy Seconals and Quaaludes and Ambutols [all barbiturates]. I withdrew and it [the heavy abuse] just took off.

At the start, the recreational abusers' drug use was openly displayed and took on an air of excitement, much like others' experimentation with street or prescription drugs. However, as it intensified over time, the majority described how they slowly shielded their use from others. They thought it important to appear as though they still had the situation under control. As physical tolerance and psychological dependence increasingly progressed, these individuals began to lose control. Virtually all of the recreational abusers eventually developed serious prescription drug use habits. Using large quantities and sometimes even multiple drug types, their prescription drug use careers were usually marked by a steep downward spiral. This trend was clearly evidenced in the hand-sketched timeline that was drawn by each respondent. What started out as manageable social drug experimentation persistently progressed to increasingly more secretive drug abuse. In almost all of the cases, it took several years for the drug use to reach its peak addictive state. The intense physical and psychological effects of the drug use meant that the recreational abuser's criminal/deviant career was punctuated by a very "low bottom." Commonly identified signs of "bottoming out" included life-threatening health problems, repeated dismissal from work, having action taken against their pharmacy license, habitual lying, extensive cover-ups, divorce, and suicide attempts. By all accounts, the personal and professional lives of these recreational abusers suffered heavily from their drug abuse. In the end, most were reclusive and paranoid—what started out as collective experimentation ended in a painful existence of solitary addiction.

Therapeutic Self-Medicators

The criminal/deviant career paths of the remaining 27 (54%) interviewees fit a different substantive theme. To differentiate these individuals from the recreational abusers, we call this latter group of pharmacists "therapeutic self-medicators." One of the defining characteristics of this group was that they had little or no experience with street or prescription drug use prior to entering pharmacy school. In fact, many of these individuals did not even use alcohol. What little drug involvement they did report was usually occasional experimentation with marijuana. If they had ever used prescription drugs, it was done legitimately under the supervision of a physician. Members of this group did not begin their illicit prescription drug use until they were well into their formal pharmacy careers.

The onset of the therapeutic self-medicators' drug use was invariably attributed to a problematic life situation, accident, medical condition, or occupationally related pain. When faced with such problems, these pharmacists turned to familiar prescription medicines for immediate relief. Rather than reporting a recreational, hedonistic, or pleasure motivation, these pharmacists had simply decided to use readily available prescription drugs to treat their own medical maladies.

Therapeutic Motives for Prescription Drug Use

The therapeutic self-medicators unanimously insisted that their drug use was never recreational. They never used drugs just for the euphoric effects. Instead, their drug use was focused on specific therapeutic goals. This is illustrated in the comments of a 33-year-old male pharmacist:

> There was no recreation involved. I just wanted to press a button and be able to sleep during the day. I was really having a tough time with this sleeping during the day. I would say by the end of that week I was already on the road [to dependency]. The race had started.

Other pharmacists described how their drug use began as a way of treating insomnia, physical trauma (e.g., a car accident, sports injury, or a broken bone), or some chronic occupationally induced health problem (e.g., arthritis, migraine headaches, leg cramps, or back pain).

It is important to point out that during the earliest stages of their drug use, these individuals appeared to be "model pharmacists." Most claimed to have excelled in pharmacy school. Moreover, occupational and career success usually continued after they entered full-time pharmacy practice. Personal appraisals, as well as annual supervisory evaluations, routinely described these individuals as hardworking and knowledgeable professionals.

Since they were usually treating the physical pain that resulted from the rigors of pharmacy work, all of the therapeutic self-medicators described how their early prescription drug use began under seemingly innocent, even honorable, circumstances. Instead of taking time off from work to see a physician, they chose to simply self-medicate their own ailments. Many felt that they could not afford to take the time off to get a prescription from a doctor who often knew less about the medications than they did. A 50-year-old male pharmacist described this situation as follows:

> When I got to [a job at a major pharmacy chain], the pace there was stressful. We were filling 300 to 400 scripts a day with minimal support staff and working 12- to 13-hour days. The physical part bothered me a lot. My feet and my back hurt. So, I just kept medicating myself until it got to the point where I was up to six to eight capsules of Fiorinol-3 [narcotic analgesic] a day.

Peer Introductions

Without exception, the therapeutic self-medicator pharmacists described how there was always a solitary, secretive dimension to their drug use. While they usually kept their drug use to themselves, it was not at all uncommon for the pharmacists to claim that their initial drug use was shaped by their interactions with co-workers. Many interviewees described how they got the idea to begin self-medicating from watching a co-worker do so. Others claimed that they merely followed the suggestion of a concerned senior pharmacist who was helping them remedy a physical malady, such as a hangover, anxiety, or physical pain. For example, a 38-year-old male pharmacist described an incident that occurred soon after being introduced to his hospital pharmacy supervisor:

> I remember saying one time that I had a headache. [He said,] "Go take some Tylenol with codeine elixir [narcotic analgesic]." I would never have done that on my own. He was my supervisor at the time, and I said to myself, "If you think I should?" He said, "That's what I would do." I guess that started the ball rolling a little bit mentally.

Members of the therapeutic self-medicator group took notice of the drug-related behaviors and suggestions of their peers but never acted upon them in the company of others. Instead, they maintained a public front condemning illicit prescription drug use but quietly followed through on the suggestive behaviors when in private.

Perceived Benefits of Self-Medication

The recreational abusers used drugs to get high. Conversely, the therapeutic self-medicators saw the drug use as a means to a different end. Even as their drug use intensified, they were able to convince themselves that the drugs were actually having a positive, rather than negative, effect on their work performance. This belief was not altogether inaccurate, since they began using the drugs to remedy a health problem that was detracting from their work efficiency.

Some therapeutic self-medicators looked to their notion of professional obligation to justify their illegal drug use. For example, in describing his daily use of Talwin, a Schedule II narcotic analgesic, a 43-year-old male pharmacist maintained: "I thought I could work better. I thought I could talk better with the nurses and patients. I thought I could socialize better with it."

A Slippery Slope

At first, these pharmacists reported that their secretive and occasional therapeutic self-medication seemed to work well. The drugs remedied the problematic situation (i.e., pain, insomnia, etc.) and thus allowed them to return to normal functioning. However, over time, they invariably began to develop a drug tolerance. This meant that they had to take larger quantities to achieve the same level of relief. In the end, each had to face the fact that the regular use of a seemingly harmless therapeutic medicine had resulted in a serious and addictive drug abuse habit. The following interview excerpt from a 50-year-old male pharmacist offers a good overview of the life history of a therapeutic self-medicator:

> Well, I didn't have a big problem with that [early occasional self-medication behavior]. I wasn't taking that much. It was very much medicinal use. It was not an everyday thing. It really was used at that point for physical pain. But that's when I started tampering with other things and started trying other things. I would have trouble sleeping, so I would think, "You know, let's see what the Dalmane [benzodiazepine] is like?" When I was having weight problems . . . "Let's give this Tenuate [amphetamine] a try." And I just started going down the line treating the things that I wanted to treat. And none of it got out of hand. It wasn't until I came down here [to Texas] . . . that things really started to go wild.

It generally took between five and 10 years for these pharmacists to progress into the later stages of drug abuse. Such a timeframe suggests that the therapeutic self-medicators were able to prevent their drug abuse from interfering with their personal or professional lives for a considerable time. For example, consider the exchange that occurred between the interviewer (I) and a 42-year-old male pharmacist (P):

> P: Every time I drink even two martinis, I throw up. I get diarrhea and I puke and I'm sick. So I took some Zantac [antacid]. I tried to cure my hangovers a little bit.
>
> I: These were just for medicinal purposes?
>
> P: Yeah, medicinal. Zantac [antacid], I mean, how can that hurt? And I go to work, but I'm sick and I don't want to go smelling like alcohol. Now I am deeply trying to just make it by. So now I begin to take pills to cure being sick so I can go to work. First I'm taking things strictly to cure hangovers, which began happening with practically drinking nothing and it's scaring me to death. . . . So I start working and I start to take a few pills. I feel a little better. Now the [mood-altering] meds start to happen. I take a couple V's [Valium, a benzodiazepine] now and then. I'm taking a few Xanax [benzodiazepine]. Next, I'm taking some Vicodin [narcotic analgesic]. It took years [for the usage pattern] to go anywhere. Then somebody comes in with drugs and says, "These are my mother-in-law's prescriptions, she passed away, she had cancer." I look at it, and it's all morphine. She says, "I don't know what to do. Will you please take it for me?" [The respondent replies, laughing], "We'll destroy the drugs, don't worry."

With the exception of their unauthorized self-medication, most individuals continued to serve the role of the "model pharmacist." Despite their progressive drug use, they usually continued to garner the respect and admiration of their peers and employers alike. It was not uncommon for them to be promoted into senior management positions, even after their prescription drug use became a daily occurrence. The bulk of the self-medicator group experienced a slow, progressive transition from occasional therapeutic drug use to a schedule of repeated daily dosage intake. In retrospect, they attributed their increased usage to the body's tendency to develop a chemical tolerance to the medications. This situation necessitated larger and more frequent dosage units to achieve the desired therapeutic effects.

A handful of therapeutic self-medicators were not so lucky. For them, there was less time between the onset of their use and manifestation of drug addiction. Their abuse progression was much faster. This is illustrated by the comments of a 49-year-old male pharmacist:

> About two or three years after I had my store, I was working long, long hours. Like 8:00 to 8:00 Monday through Saturday and some hours on Sunday. And my back hurt one day. It was really killing me. . . . I started out with two Empirin-3 [narcotic analgesic]. Just for the back pain. I mean, I hurt, my back hurt, my head hurt. I don't know why, but I just reached for that bottle, and I knew it was against the law to do that, but I did it anyway. Man, I felt good. I was off and running. This was eureka. This was it. It progressed. I started taking more and more.

The key to a self-medicator's fast-paced progressive drug use seemed to lie in the given individual's perceived need to treat a wider and growing array of physical ailments. In fact, it got to the point that many "drug-thirsty" pharmacists now recognized that they were actively inventing ailments to treat. As a 40-year-old female pharmacist put it, "I had a symptom for everything I took."

There were 27 pharmacists who could be classified as therapeutic self-medicators. These pharmacists entered their pharmacy careers admittedly as extremely naive about drug abuse. They were either counseled or had convinced themselves that there was no harm in the occasional therapeutic use of prescription medicines. In short, the normative and behavioral advances in their criminal and deviant behavior were largely the result of a well-intentioned exploitation of their professional position and knowledge. The justifications for their drug use were firmly entrenched in a desire to excel in their jobs while always efficiently caring for their patients. The therapeutic self-medicators always used their drugs in private, carefully disguising their addiction from others around them. Over time, their false confidence and self-denial allowed their drug use to progress significantly into addiction. Once their façade was broken, these pharmacists awoke to the stark reality that they were now chemically dependent on one or more of the drugs that they so confidently had been "prescribing" for themselves.

COMMON COGNITIVE AND BEHAVIORAL THEMES

We found clear evidence of two very different modes of entry among the respondents, namely recreational abusers and therapeutic self-medicators. However, it is important to note that these were *not* mutually exclusive categories of offenders. In other words, these two categories were not completely dichotomous. As is usually the case, real life seldom fits cleanly into nice, neat categories. In fact, we were able to identify a number of cognitive and behavioral themes that were common to almost all of the drug-using pharmacists interviewed. These themes were expressed by nearly all of the drug-abusing pharmacists that we interviewed, regardless of how the individual initially began their illicit drug abuse career. The existence of these common themes suggests that pharmacy-specific occupational contingencies play a central role in the onset and progression of illicit use of prescription medicines. Let us examine the three most common of these cognitive and behavioral themes in more detail.

I'm a Pharmacist, So I Know What I Am Doing

Intuitively, it should not be surprising that pharmacists would steal prescription medicines as a way of treating their own physical ailments. After all, they have been exposed to years of pharmacy training that emphasized the beneficial, therapeutic potential of prescription medicines. Each pharmacist has dispensed medicines to hundreds of patients and then watched the drugs usually produce the predicted beneficial results. They all have read the literature detailing the drug's chemical composition and studied the often times dramatic beneficial, curative effects of these chemical substances. Pharmacists, more so than any other member of society, are keenly aware of how and why drugs work. There was strong evidence to suggest that both the therapeutic self-medicators and the recreational abusers actively utilize the years of pharmacological knowledge that they had acquired. So, when health or emotional problems occurred, it makes perfect sense that they should put their knowledge to work on themselves. This personal application of pharmaceutical information can be seen clearly in the comments of a 40-year-old female self-medicator:

> So, in 1986, I was sent to the psychologist. That was when I was forced to recognize that I had an alcohol problem. And I recognized that I had to do something. And in my brilliant analysis, I made a decision that since alcohol was a central nervous system depressant, the solution for me was to use a central nervous system stimulant. That would solve my alcohol problem. So I chose the best stimulant that I had access to, and that was [pharmaceutical-grade] cocaine. I started using cocaine in 1986. I never thought that it would progress. I never thought it was going to get worse. I thought, "I'm just going to use it occasionally."

Similar trends were observed among the recreational abuser group, only here, the applied use of drugs was based upon more recreational motives.

Virtually all of the therapeutic self-medicators and the recreational abusers described how they became masters at quickly diagnosing their own ailments or emotional needs, then identifying the appropriate pharmacological agent that would remedy the problem. Moreover, as professionals, they were quite confident that they would be able to limit or self-regulate their drug intake as to never become addicted. All of the respondents drew upon their social status as pharmacists to convince themselves that their drug use would not progress into dependency. As a 40-year-old female self-medicator put it, "I'm a pharmacist, I know what I am doing." To a person, the interviewees agreed that a well-trained, professional pharmacist could not possibly fall prey to drug addiction. They recall being even more adamant in their view that personally they were immune from such problems, believing that only stupid, naive people became addicted to drugs. This distinct form of denial is illustrated in the remarks of a 35-year-old male recreational abuser:

> Yeah, I thought, "It [addiction] can't happen to me because I know too much." We somehow think that knowledge is going to prevent it from happening to us when [we know that] knowledge has nothing to do with it. It's like heart disease or anything else. It's like, "Well, I know about this so it can't happen to me." [In fact,] . . . now I teach pharmacy. I developed a chemical dependency curriculum at our pharmacy school. I do a clerkship in it and I don't think there is one in the country, except for mine, that deals with some of that. Maybe they [the students] can personalize [pharmacists' drug abuse] a little bit.

One 39-year-old male self-medicator went so far as to say: "I mean, we know more [about the effect of drugs] than doctors. We have all the package inserts. We have the knowledge. We know a lot about the drugs, so what's the big deal?" Interviewees did not understand why they should use personal sick leave to go to a doctor and pay money to acquire a written prescription to dispense a drug that was on the shelves right behind them. This just did not make any sense, since they firmly believed that pharmacists knew more about dispensing medicines than most doctors. Elsewhere (Dabney & Hollinger, 1999), we refer to this denial mechanism as a "paradox of familiarity," arguing that familiarity can breed consent, not contempt toward prescription drug use.

No Cautionary Tales or Warnings

Remarkably, the vast majority of both the recreational abusers and therapeutic self-medicators claimed that they never had been warned about the dangers of drug addiction. Rather, they insisted that their formal training had only stressed the beneficial side of prescription medicines. For example, a 48-year-old male recreational abuser stated:

> I never had anybody come right out and tell me that [prescription drug abuse] was probably unethical and illegal, because they assumed that we knew that. But nobody ever said this is something that is not done.

Left without precise ethical guidance on the issue, some pharmacists assumed that their drug use was acceptable behavior. In explaining this point of view, a 39-year-old female self-medicator stated:

> It's [self-medication] . . . just part of it [the pharmacy job]. It's just accepted because we know so much. I'm sure it's the same way when the doctors do it. It wasn't a big stretch to start [thinking,] "You know, I got a headache here, maybe I should try one of these Percocets [narcotic analgesic]?"

In fact, many pharmacists spoke about their theft of prescription drugs as if they were a "fringe benefit" that went along with the job. Much like a butcher always eats the best cuts of meat or a car dealer drives a brand-new automobile, pharmacists always will have access to free prescription drugs. This theme is illustrated in the comments of a 45-year-old male pharmacist:

> Why take plain aspirin or plain Tylenol when you've got this [Percocet—narcotic analgesic]? It works better . . . [so] you don't even have to struggle with it. I really believed that I had license to do that . . . as a pharmacist. I mean with all that stuff sitting there, you know. Oh, my back was just killing me during that period of time, and this narcotic pain reliever is sitting right there. I thought, "Why should [I] suffer through back pain when I have this bottle of narcotics sitting here?"

Out-of-Control Addiction

The abovementioned themes involve cognitive dimensions of the pharmacists' drug abuse in that they speak to common motivational and justification themes that were present in all of the interviews. Perhaps more important is the fact that there was a common behavioral characteristic shared by all 50 pharmacists. In every case, occasional prescription drug abuse eventually gave way to an advanced addictive state that was marked by an enormous intake of drugs, unmistakable habituation, and the constant threat of physical withdrawal. Members of the recreational abuser and therapeutic self-medicator groups alike routinely reported daily use levels exceeding 50 to 100 times the recommended daily dosage. One pharmacist reported that his drug use regimen progressed to 150 Percocets (a strong narcotic analgesic) per day. Another individual reported injecting up to 200 mg of morphine each day. Still another respondent described a daily use pattern that, among other things, included five grams of cocaine.

Invariably, these advanced levels of drug use led to clear signs of habituation and the constant threat of physical withdrawal. At this point, the individuals recall growing increasingly desperate. Consider the following quote from a 44-year-old male pharmacist who was in charge of ordering the narcotics at the independent retail pharmacy where he worked:

> I was ordering excessive quantities and chasing down drug trucks. That's what I used to do. I was really reaching my bottom. I would chase these delivery trucks down in the morning, because I didn't come to my store until midafternoon. I was in withdrawal in the morning, and I was without drugs, so

I had to have it. I was just going nuts. Many mornings I had gone to work sweating. It would be 30 degrees, it would be January, and the clerk would say, "You look sick," and I would say, "It's the flu." So I would pay the delivery guys extra money to deliver my drugs first, or I would chase the delivery trucks down in the morning. I knew the trucks delivered at six in the morning, they came by my area, and I would get up early and chase the trucks down the highway. I would go in excess of 100 miles an hour trying to catch up with this truck and flag it down.

The advanced stages of addiction almost always produced traumatic physical and psychological events. Take, for example, the following comments that were made by a 39-year-old male pharmacist:

I was out of control for four years. I was just lucky that I never got caught. I don't know how I didn't get caught. I fell asleep twice coming home on Interstate 95. I fell asleep at the wheel doing 70 once and then I scraped up the side of the car and blew out the tires. I also tried to kill myself with a shotgun. She [my wife] was going to leave me. My world was falling apart, but I couldn't do anything about it. I didn't know what to do.

These "out of control" drug use patterns along with the realization of chemical dependency left the pharmacists in a problematic mental state. It was at this point that all of the pharmacists recalled coming to grips with their addiction. This personal realization was accompanied by a shift in the way that they thought about their drug use. They no longer denied the situation by drawing upon recreational or therapeutic explanations. Instead, they finally admitted the dire nature of their situation and became more and more reclusive. In short, all of the respondents grew to realize that they had a drug problem, turning then to fear and ignorance to foster the final weeks or months of their drug addiction.

THEORETICAL IMPLICATIONS—A CONTEXTUALIZED UNDERSTANDING OF DEVIANT CAREERS

Let us now consider how the present research serves to inform the existing literature on deviant and/or criminal careers. We believe that this is best achieved by applying the Best and Luckenbill (1994) conceptual framework to the realities of the 50 drug-using pharmacists that we studied. We chose the Best and Luckenbill (1994) model because (1) it is particularly apropos to the issue of drug use careers, (2) it is positioned at the forefront of the broader literature on criminal careers, and (3) it helps make sense of multiple dimensions and types of social organization. In short, these authors provide a series of valuable conceptual tools that can be used to organize and understand the nature and dynamics of a criminal career, especially one involving drug use. Notwithstanding these merits, there is a paucity of research that attempts to systematically validate these conceptual claims that are inherent in their five-part typology. The present analysis is an attempt to fill this void.

In general, we find strong support for Best and Luckenbill's conceptual claim that there exists patterned organization to both deviants and deviance. Nevertheless, the data expand upon the existing understanding of drug use careers in three very important ways. First, by looking at prescription drug use among pharmacists, we blur the lines between the concepts of crime and deviance, as the individuals are routinely violating both norms and laws. Second, we discovered that a single category of criminal/deviant action (i.e., illicit prescription drug use) within a single category of criminal/deviant actors (practicing pharmacists) could begin and progress under different behavioral and motivational pretenses. Thus, even under the most constrained substantive focus, there can exist variation in the social organization of deviance and deviants.

At the same time, our data suggest that divergent criminal/deviant career trajectories eventually converge to produce very similar behavioral and motivational manifestations in mature offenders. This third observation suggests that there can be a two-way fluidity to the social organization of deviance and deviants, even within the most narrowly defined criminal/deviant phenomena (i.e., illicit prescription drug use among pharmacists). We provide the following discussion to illustrate these assertions.

Therapeutic Self-Medicators—Loners to the End

Best and Luckenbill (1994) identify physician drug addicts as examples of the "loner" category. They contend that the physician's repeated drug thefts and drug usage lead him/her to refine his/her techniques while at the same time solidifying their denial or justifications for on-the-job offending. Given the secretive nature of the loner's crime and deviance, the authors suggest that he/she will become more and more efficient at manipulating and distorting norms and routines within their conventional lifestyles in order to reinforce their unconventional needs. They submit that the techniques and justifications for continued and progressive drug use can be largely traced to the individual's ability to manipulate or exploit their professional standing. These characteristics produce long, drawn-out criminal careers whereby the individual slowly plods along with their wrongdoing.

Drawing also upon earlier work by Winick (1961) to articulate the systematic loner category of deviants, the present analysis offers valuable empirical evidence substantiating the authors' theoretical proposition. Namely, the analysis reveals how some drug-using pharmacists always use prescription drugs in private. They manipulate their access, knowledge, and the messages from other pharmacists to sustain these deviant ways. Moreover, they develop and impose various denial and/or rationalization frameworks to protect them from the shame and hazards of their considerable drug habits. Thus, the effectiveness of these cognitive denial structures is conveniently reinforced by the efficient and secretive nature of their habitual offending.

In summary, we submit that the drug use careers of the 27 therapeutic self-medicators are clearly representative of Best and Luckenbill's (1994) loner category.

Specifically, they are secretive deviants with defensive motives who adeptly manipulate and distort aspects of their conformist lives to facilitate their deviance. More importantly, there is a consistency to the social organization of their criminal and deviant acts and interactions throughout the course of their criminal/deviant careers. These individuals never displayed characteristics that would warrant their classification within any of the other four categories of deviant careers, motivations, or transactions.

Recreational Abusers—Peers to Colleagues to Loners

Our discussion of therapeutic self-medicators clearly surpasses what is found in the existing literature. However, we argue that it is our documentation of the recreational abuser category that provides the more exciting findings. Unlike the therapeutic self-medicators, we encountered difficulty when attempting to classify the 23 recreational abusers within Best and Luckenbill's (1994) five-point continuum. We observe that these pharmacists do not neatly fit within any single category. Instead, the members of the recreational abuser group followed a more dynamic and evolving career path. Over time, this group seemed to move across at least three of Best and Luckenbill's five categories—from peers, to colleagues, and then finally to loners. Corresponding changes are also seen in the nature of their deviant motivations and transactions.

Best and Luckenbill assert that "peers" differ from loners in that there is a collective interaction dimension to their deviance. They use the term "deviant exchanges" to describe the cooperative deviant roles that exist in these relationships. The authors reference recreational drug users as examples of peer-based deviants. Not only are recreational drug users afforded the normative subculture that accompanies a collegial relationship, but also the collective nature of their deviant activities provides them direct and continued social support for their actions and justifications. In other words, shared participation in deviance results in a more stable, closer-knit subculture. This yields a more complete socialization process and an even more rapid career trajectory than loners or colleagues.

In the initial days of their illicit prescription drug use, most all of the recreational abusers actively sought out collective opportunities to engage in crime and deviance. Limited access to medications forced drug users to become more reliant on friends or fellow pharmacy students to supply them with prescription drugs. In these earlier stages of the recreational abusers' career, drug-using pharmacists were able to structure deviant acts in the form of "deviant exchanges." That is, while their usage levels were within socially acceptable limits, they knew that they could turn to fellow drug-using peers or colleagues to supply them with drugs and/or the necessary deviant justifications.

The progressive nature of their prescription drug use meant that they came to rely on more experienced users, as well as their newly acquired pharmacological knowledge, to acquire necessary drug use skills and rationalizations. As long as it was done in moderation, they could access other pharmacists' cache of drugs or even use in the presence of others. The key was to disguise their drug use levels as unchanging and occasional in nature. On a cognitive level, exposure to fellow drug users with relatively similar habits afforded these individuals continued normative reinforcement and rationalizations. Clearly, this early drug use served to satisfy a sense of inquisitiveness or adventure that existed in the neophyte pharmacists. In this regard, the recreational abusers started out their deviant careers as a classic example of what Best and Luckenbill would call "peers" who engage in (social) deviant exchanges and are driven by adventurous motives.

As the frequency and intensity of their prescription drug abuse increased, however, these individuals became fearful that their fellow pharmacists might report them to authorities. Drug use that was originally viewed as tolerable among nonusers and normal among fellow users advanced to the level that any rational observer would view as excessive and dangerous. This realization along with a progressive level of habituation resulted in a shift from "peer"-type relations to more "collegial" relations.

"Colleagues" are said to be significantly different from loners and peers. These individuals act principally on their own, but in an environment where there are fellow deviants present. Best and Luckenbill (1994) point to "pool hustlers and computer hackers" as classic examples of this category of deviants. While, like the loners, there is a private quality to their deviant actions (i.e., individual deviance), these individuals are afforded the opportunity to observe or interact with fellow deviants as a way of refining and advancing their deviant techniques and justifications. The authors contend that the loose social organization of their rule-breaking behavior exposes members of the colleague category to a deviant subculture that affords them subtle but important normative direction and reinforcement for their behaviors (i.e., behavioral, cognitive, and ideological guidance). They posit that these individuals are driven by adventurous, reward-based motives.

Best and Luckenbill (1994) contend that colleague-type deviants engage in their aberrant behaviors within a common social environment but do not involve themselves in collective deviant acts. Fearful of detection and the resultant negative stigma, recreational abusers reported that they commonly tried to disguise increased drug theft and usage from their fellow pharmacists. While they curbed their collective crime and deviance, recreational abusers were still aware of drug-using pharmacists who shared their passion for the drugs and relied on this small circle for behavioral and motivational reinforcement. This shift generally occurred late in pharmacy school or during one's earliest work experiences. In other words, we observed a pronounced shift in pharmacists' criminal/deviant careers as they move from experimentation to habituation. Referring to Best and Luckenbill's (1994) model, it can be said that the individual evolves from peer-like conditions to a colleague-based mode of interaction. The scope of deviant exchanges is tightened and a considerable amount of individual offending emerges. Still, the maturing recreational abuser maintains his/her adventurous motives.

All 23 of the recreational abusers described experiencing an epiphany marking the realization that they were no longer in control of their prescription drug use. In short, as their habituation intensified, their denial systems eventually broke down and they had to come to grips with the fact that their benign recreational drug use had now progressed into full-blown addiction. This realization was generally precipitated by serious drug-related physical manifestations (e.g., bleeding ulcers, overdoses, blackouts) or through an embarrassing social incident whereby their pronounced abuse/addiction came to the attention of others.

At this point, the recreational abusers change from acting like deviant "colleagues" to "loners" (Best & Luckenbill, 1994). The distinguishing characteristic between these two categories is that the latter involves more secretive offending that is reinforced internally instead of externally. When these pharmacists began using exorbitant amounts of prescription drugs on a daily basis, they could no longer look to fellow drug-using pharmacists for behavioral or motivational assistance. They regressed into a pronounced routine of private offending. In effect, they were left to fend for themselves. More adventurous motives were replaced by abject fear, while the individuals desperately sought to stay afloat functionally. During this stage of their criminal/deviant careers, the recreational abusers accepted the problematic nature of their heavy drug use and took it underground to avoid detection and stigma. In effect, these individuals were simply trying to postpone the inevitable crash—desperately trying to escape detection and the loss of their jobs. This survivalist mentality accompanied by secretive drug use behavior was observed in all of the mature therapeutic self-medicators' career trajectories.

CONCLUSIONS

There are several critical points underlying Best and Luckenbill's (1994) depiction of criminal careers. First, the authors stress that we must be aware of structure, process, and social organization when studying deviant behaviors as they emerge and evolve over time. Second, they underscore that we must be sensitive to the interconnections that exist between the deviant actor and the social ecology of the deviant acts. Third, their emphasis on roles, subculture, and the transactional nature of deviant events reinforces the fluid and evolving nature of the cognitive and behavioral aspects of the subject matter. Finally, at the core of their framework is the importance that interactions and the resulting learning play in the social organization of deviants and deviance.

Some of the criminal and deviant behavior that was observed among the respondent pharmacists fits neatly into the Best and Luckenbill (1994) typology. Pharmacists that we classify as therapeutic self-medicators resemble loners with defensive motives who engage in acts of individual offending. However, the criminal/deviant careers of other pharmacists were not so static. Recreational abusers follow an evolving career path whereby they start out as "peers," grow as "colleagues," and then spend their mature years as "loners." Corresponding changes are also observed in the nature of their criminal/deviant transactions and motives. While ideological issues appeared to remain constant throughout, the longer that the habitual drug use continued, the more similar the traits of the recreational abusers and therapeutic self-medicators became. This leads us to conclude that two criminal/deviant trajectories that started out looking quite dissimilar eventually became quite similar. While Best and Luckenbill allow for the possibility of intercategory flexibility, this is the first empirical inquiry to provide systematic and detailed documentation of this type of fluidity. We believe that this discovery represents an important finding of this study, as it provides critical evidence that even the most focused forms of crime and deviance are marked by both typological differentiation and commonality, especially if one examines the offender's entire career.

Our findings lead us to endorse a conceptual middle ground. Namely, it seems most advantageous for scholars to seek out a conceptual space that lies between the abstractions of the abstract conceptual models of criminal careers and the pragmatic findings that are generated by the drug ethnographer. While there is much merit in deductive reasoning efforts such as those of Best and Luckenbill (1994) or Tittle and Paternoster (2000), from time to time we must return to the field and undertake inductively based exercises to reevaluate the posited abstractions. In the present case, this allows us to validate many of the claims set forth by Best and Luckenbill while adding important new insights.

Moreover, we submit that our findings have important public policy relevance, especially for those social control entities that deal with drug-addicted pharmacists. These include drug treatment professionals, private security personnel, and members of the criminal justice system.

As mentioned at the outset of this article, drug treatment professionals have long been aware of the propensity for pharmacists to abuse the drugs that they are entrusted to dispense (Hankes & Bissell, 1992). At present, members of the drug treatment community and state licensure agencies alike generally operate under the assumption that there exist two separate, mutually exclusive types of drug-using pharmacists: those who use for therapeutic reasons and those who use for recreational reasons. While we have been able to confirm this general trend, our data suggest that treatment professionals can benefit from taking a fluid approach to the prescription drug user. It appears that considerable time, effort, and money can be saved by evaluation and treatment modalities that are sensitive to the evolving and overlapping qualities of prescription drug use among pharmacists. Most importantly, our research, which targeted individuals with severe histories of drug abuse, provides a glimmer of hope that focused prevention efforts might well stem early drug use behavior from ever maturing into full-blown addiction.

Pharmacists are a highly sought-after commodity in this country. At the same time that we see a new hospital or retail pharmacy popping up on virtually every street corner, the news reports serious shortages of licensed pharmacists. In light of this supply and demand squeeze, employers have been forced to be less selective about who they hire. The authors' personal conversations with corporate executives from major retail drug chains verify that "zero tolerance" policies have been relaxed, and some companies now hire pharmacists who are known to have had a past drug abuse problem. Increased surveillance and social control will undoubtedly be a byproduct of these liberal personnel decisions, and security personnel must be sensitive to the ever-changing nature of these individuals' criminal careers and thus devise intervention and surveillance programs that are duly flexible.

Nationwide data collection efforts have established that illicit prescription drug use levels are on the rise in the United States (Substance Abuse and Mental Health Services Administration, 1999). Of particular concern are the disturbing increases among young people. With increasing regularity, adolescents are turning away from traditional street drugs and coming to rely more heavily on prescription drugs (i.e., narcotics such as OxyContin or stimulants such as Ritalin or Meridia) to satisfy their recreational drug use urges. This situation has produced a coordinated call to arms in which government agencies such as the National Institute on Drug Abuse (NIDA) have begun to direct research dollars toward understanding the trends. In addition, law enforcement agencies from the Drug Enforcement Administration (DEA) on down to the local sheriff's department have begun to simultaneously step up interdiction efforts. Preliminary findings suggest that unethical or incompetent pharmacists play an important role in the proliferation of these drugs into the hands of street users (National Institute on Drug Abuse, 2001). Moreover, the past year alone has seen the flagship trade journal of the pharmacy industry publish several commentaries on the topic of prescription drug abuse amongst their ranks (Baldwin, 2001; Baldwin & Thibault, 2001; Dabney, 2001). Pressure continues to mount at the state and local levels to address levels of prescription-dispensing errors that endanger the patients and customers that entrust our nation's pharmacists. These trends suggest that it is only a matter of time until regulatory, private security, and criminal justice agents launch a concerted effort to more stringently regulate the pharmacy profession. When such an initiative gets underway, it is critical that the powers that be direct considerable attention toward the types of deviant pharmacists that were interviewed in the present study. In doing so, it is critical that the inquiry consider (1) the evolving nature of the drug abuse that impacts some pharmacists, (2) whether the deviant drug use careers documented in this report coincide with or exacerbate additional forms of professional wrongdoing, and (3) whether the career trajectories outlined in the present study are applicable on a larger scale.

REFERENCES

Adler, P. (1993). *Wheeling and dealing: An ethnography of an upper-level drug dealing and smuggling community.* New York: Columbia University Press.

Baldwin, J. N. (2001). Self-medication by pharmacists: Familiarity breeds attempt? *Journal of the American Pharmaceutical Association, 41*(3), 371.

Baldwin, J. N., & Thibault, E. D. (2001). Substance abuse by pharmacists: Stopping the insanity. *Journal of the American Pharmaceutical Association, 41*(3), 373–375.

Becker, H. S. (1953). Becoming a marijuana user. *American Journal of Sociology, 59,* 235–242.

———. (1963). *Outsiders.* New York: Free Press.

Best, J., & Luckenbill, D. F. (1994). *Organizing deviance.* Englewood Cliffs, NJ: Prentice Hall.

Bissell, L., Haberman, P. W., & Williams, R. L. (1989). Pharmacists recovering from alcohol and other drug addictions: An interview study. *American Pharmacy, NS29*(6), 19–30.

Blackwell, J. S. (1983). Drifting, controlling and overcoming: Opiate users who avoid becoming chronically dependent. *Journal of Drug Issues, 13,* 219–235.

Chi, J. (1983). Impaired pharmacists: More programs move to handle the problem. *Drug Topics, 127*(47), 24–29.

Coombs, R. H. (1981). Drug abuse as career. *Journal of Drug Issues, 11,* 369–387.

Dabney, D. A. (1997). *A sociological examination of illicit prescription drug use among pharmacists.* Unpublished Ph.D. diss., University of Florida, Gainesville, FL.

———. (2001). The onset of prescription drug use among pharmacists. *Journal of the American Pharmaceutical Association, 41*(3), 392–400.

Dabney, D. A., & Hollinger, R. C. (1999). Illicit prescription drug use among pharmacists: Evidence of a paradox of familiarity. *Work & Occupations, 26*(1), 77–106.

Faupel, C. (1987). Heroin use and criminal careers. *Qualitative Sociology, 10*(2), 115–131.

———. (1991). *Shooting dope: Career patterns of hard-core heroin users.* Gainesville: University of Florida Press.

Faupel, C., & Klockars, C. B. (1987). Drug-crime connections: Elaborations from the life histories of hard-core heroin addicts. *Social Problems, 34*(1), 54–68.

Gallegos, K. V., Veit, F. W., Wilson, P. O., Porter, T., & Talbott, G. D. (1988). Substance abuse among health professionals. *Maryland Medical Journal, 37*(3), 191–197.

Greenberg, D. (1996). *Criminal careers,* Vol. 2. Dartmouth University Press.

Hafley, S. R., & Tewksbury, R. (1996). Reefer madness in bluegrass country: Community structure and roles in the rural Kentucky marijuana industry. *Journal of Crime and Justice, 19*(1), 75–94.

Hankes, L., & Bissell, L. (1992). Health professionals. In J. H. Lowinson, P. Ruiz, R. Millman, & J. G. Langrod (Eds.), *Substance abuse: A comprehensive textbook* (2nd ed., pp. 897–908). Baltimore: Williams & Wilkins.

Martin, S. (1993). Pharmacists number more than 190,000 in United States. *American Pharmacy, NS33*(7), 22–23.

McAuliffe, W. E. (1984). Nontherapeutic opiate addiction in health professionals: A new form of impairment. *American Journal of Drug & Alcohol Abuse, 10*(1), 1–22.

McAuliffe, W. E., Santangelo, S. L., Gingras, J., Rohman, M., Sobol, A., & Magnuson, E. (1987). Use and abuse of controlled substances by pharmacists and pharmacy students. *American Journal of Hospital Pharmacy, 44*(2), 311–317.

National Institute on Drug Abuse. (2001). *Prescription drugs abuse and addiction.* Washington, DC: National Institute on Drug Abuse.

Nettler, G. (1982). Lying, cheating and stealing. *Social Forces, 631*(1), 283–295.

Normack, J. W., Eckel, F. M., Pfifferling, J-H., & Cocolas, G. (1985). Impairment risk in North Carolina pharmacists. *American Pharmacy, NS25*(6), 45–48.

Penna, R. P., & Williams, R. L. (1985). *Helping the impaired pharmacist: A handbook for planning and implementing state programs.* Washington, DC: American Pharmaceutical Association.

Quinney, R. (1963). Occupational structure and criminal behavior: Prescription violation by retail pharmacists. *Social Problems, 11,* 179–185.

Rubington, E. (1967). Drug addiction as a deviant career. *International Journal of the Addictions, 2*(1), 3–21.

Sheffield, J. W. (1988). Establishing a rehabilitation program for impaired pharmacists. *American Journal of Hospital Pharmacy, 45*(10), 2092–2098.

Sheffield, J. W., O'Neill, P., & Fisher, C. (1992). Women in recovery: from pain to progress, parts I & II. *Texas Pharmacy, 8*(1), 29–36 and *8*(2), 22–34.

Smith, D. R., & Smith, W. R. (1984). Patterns of delinquent careers: An assessment of three perspectives. *Social Science Research, 13,* 129–158.

Substance Abuse and Mental Health Services Administration. 1999. *National household survey on drug abuse: Population estimates 1999.* Washington, DC: Department of Health and Human Services.

Tittle, C. R., & Paternoster, R. (2000). *Social deviance and crime: An organizational and theoretical approach.* Los Angeles: Roxbury.

Waldorf, D. (1983). Natural recovery from opiate addiction: Some social psychological processes of untreated recovery. *Journal of Drug Issues, 13,* 237–280.

Winick, C. (1961). Physician narcotic addicts. *Social Problems, 9,* 174–186.

Illegal Occupations

In the previous section, we examined crimes committed by persons in the course of their legal occupations. In this section, we consider offenders whose occupations violate formal law. The central activities of such work are illegal, yet they share many commonalities with legal occupations. Most of those who engage in illegal occupations have regular customers, suppliers, and a formal set of roles and activities that do not substantially differ from those of people who perform legal work.

The chapters in this section take a look at drug dealing, smuggling, and prostitution. What is salient about the chapters presented here is how the authors examine criminal enterprises through an occupational lens. That is, they uniquely analyze how offenders give meaning to their criminal enterprises, as one would with a legitimate occupation. We use the term *occupation* here in the sense that these activities involve some effort or exertion of purpose. The series of articles in this section shed light on criminality as an occupation; the organization, structure, profit, or lack thereof; and hidden markets of crime.

In Chapter 14, "The 'Myth of Organization' of International Drug Smugglers," Scott H. Decker and Jana S. Benson provide a rare look into drug smuggling. Based on interviews with a diverse cross-section of offenders, the authors examine the flow of information, networks, and links of a drug-smuggling operation, along with the various work roles that exist internally within the organization. They discover that high-level international drug-smuggling groups are relatively loosely organized networks containing small groups of people who work together and typically do not have knowledge of what takes place throughout the organization. This paints a far different picture than what many criminologists once believed about these organizations. Drug-smuggling organizations have largely been viewed as being structured much like a "corporate organization." The authors underscore the point that drug-smuggling operations, instead of being rationally focused on maximizing profits, tend to be more focused on minimizing the risk of being detected by law enforcement authorities.

In Chapter 15, Scott Jacques and Richard Wright interview 50 unincarcerated drug dealers to explore how the frequency and seriousness of popular justice, affect the price and rate of drugs sales. The authors employ rational choice and opportunity perspectives to explore the connection between informal control and drug trading.

In Chapter 16, Eva Rosen and Sudhir Alladi Venkatesh examine the ways in which sex work has become a solution to the employment needs of the urban poor in a bounded geographic field site located in Chicago. The authors make use of interviews of 38 subjects and over one year of participant observation of Chicago's sex work economy. The authors argue that sex work acts as a short-term solution that "satisfices" the demands of persistent poverty and instability. Moreover, they argue that sex work provides a meaningful option in the quest for a job that provides autonomy and personal fulfillment.

The studies presented in Section VI illustrate that while the activities of the participants are illegal, they tend to see themselves as "business persons" with a product or a service for sale to the public. They have similar goals and are faced with many of the same problems and goals prevalent in legitimate enterprises. We also learn in this section that sex work, to some in Chicago's Southside, offers a rational and viable solution to the problem of income generation. This section is rich with insight into illegal occupations and offers a host of possibilities to inform fundamental criminal justice practice.

CHAPTER 14

The "Myth of Organization" of International Drug Smugglers

Scott H. Decker and Jana S. Benson

Until recently, most criminologists viewed international drug smuggling as a highly structured and organized operation with vertical lines of responsibility and communication. This view was based on old models of organized crime and romanticized versions of the Medellín cartels that operated in Colombia in the 1980s. The amount of money involved in international drug smuggling is enormous, and it is generally assumed that where large sums of money are present, they will be accompanied by a high level of organization. This view of group offending as highly structured is not confined to international drug smugglers. Criminologists have typically overascribed the levels of structure, organization, and rationality of groups of offenders such as gangs, burglars, robbers, and street-level drug sellers. Often this is the case because information about the organization of offending groups comes from law enforcement, which sees only a small fraction of offenders. In other cases, criminologists' interviews are restricted to "kingpins" or supposed leaders in groups, without external validation of their real role in offending.

INTRODUCTION

This chapter examines the nature and extent of organization in international drug-smuggling groups. Based on interviews with 34 convicted international drug smugglers, we find very little formal organization or vertical structure in drug-smuggling groups. Following a description of these offenders, we discuss the literature on the organization of drug smugglers and other active groups of offenders. This discussion focuses on three major categories of organization: structure, interactions, and rationality. Having established a context for our analysis, we then use the words of convicted drug smugglers to illustrate our findings.

Source: Written especially for this volume.

Finally, conclusions are drawn about the sources of the "myth of organization" in international drug smuggling.

The Current Study

The following analysis is based on interviews conducted with 34 individuals held in U.S. federal prisons. A semistructured questionnaire was used to elicit information from individuals who were selected based on their extensive involvement in high-level international drug smuggling. We found 135 of these individuals in federal prisons. Of the 73 individuals approached for participation in the study, 34 agreed. We compared the group who refused participation with the subjects who did take part and found them to be similar in terms of level of involvement in smuggling—specifically, how serious the crime was and their role in the offense. In the end, we assembled a sample of 34 individuals who were heavily involved in drug smuggling. We also gained access to these individuals' federal presentence reports and were able to verify their extensive involvement in drug smuggling.

Table 14.1 presents a summary of key characteristics of the smugglers we interviewed. Of the 34 subjects, the modal category for age at sentencing was 40 to 49 years. Within the sample, 82% reported being between 30 and 59 years old at the time of sentencing. All of the subjects were male. Although almost half of the subjects were U.S. citizens, Cubans and Colombians were also significantly represented in the sample. Twenty-nine individuals, or 85% of the sample, reported being of Hispanic origin. All of the drug smugglers we interviewed operated through the Caribbean, with a majority of the drugs originating in Colombia. Smuggling activity also was described as occurring in the Bahamas, Panama, Cuba, the Dominican Republic, Mexico, Haiti, Peru, Puerto Rico, and Venezuela. The method of smuggling varied, with both private and commercial boats and airplanes being used.

All of the subjects we interviewed were arrested and charged with smuggling large quantities of cocaine. Three individuals also reported smuggling marijuana in connection with the current offense. The mean amount of cocaine with which the subjects were caught was 1,136 kg, or just less than 2,500 pounds. Overall, amounts carried ranged from 15 kg to 5,000 kg. The mean year of arrest was 1993, with reported values ranging from 1988 to 1997. Twenty-two members of the sample were serving a sentence of 20 years or more, with five doing life and six doing a sentence of 30 years or more. Only one subject received a sentence of less than 10 years for his involvement in the smuggling operation.

The individuals interviewed for this study were heavily involved in international drug smuggling. None of the smugglers in the sample were caught on their first act of smuggling. In fact, more than half of the subjects reported having been involved in *at least* 10 prior smuggling operations. These contentions were consistent with the results of their presentence investigations. The smugglers played a variety of roles in the smuggling event for which they were caught, ranging from broker or organizer to transporter or manager. Only one of the individuals

Table 14.1 Characteristics of Smuggler Respondents

ROLE	METHOD	REGION	AGE RANGE	WEIGHT OF DRUGS (KG)	SENTENCE LENGTH (Y)
Recruiter	Private vessel	Colombia/ Bahamas	40–49	480	30
Organizer	Commercial vessel	Colombia	40–49	1,500	27
Manager	Commercial vessel	Colombia	40–49	630	30
Supervisor	Vessel	Colombia	40–49	165	31
Organizer	Commercial vessel	Colombia	40–49	1,500	8
Organizer	Commercial vessel	Bahamas	40–49	3,345.5	17.5
Leader	Private plane/ commercial vessel	Colombia	60–69	500	30.5
Recruiter	Commercial vessel	Colombia	50–59	40	17.5
Broker	Private vessel	Panama	30–39	59	17.5
Leader	Private vessel	Cuba/ Dominican Republic	30–39	515	17.5
Leader	Private vessel	Cuba	40–49	2,350.5	19.5
Organizer	Private vessel	Colombia	30–39	728	27.5
Transporter	Private vessel	Mexico	40–49	5,000	
Captain	Private vessel	Colombia/Haiti	30–39	150+	15
Offloader	Private plane	Colombia	40–49	500	16.25
Organizer	Commercial airplane	Peru	50–59	500	20
Leader	Private vessel	Bahamas/Cuba	40–49	50	10
Manager	Commercial airplane	Venezuela	30–39	605.5	27
Leader	Private vessel	Bahamas	50–59	414	15
Recruiter	Commercial airplane	Colombia	50–59	15–50	22
Leader	Private vessel	Caribbean	50–59	1,450	25.5
Manager	Commercial airplane	Haiti	40–49	2,200	15
Captain/ Investor	Private vessel	Bahamas	70–79	776.3	27.5
Organizer	Commercial vessel	Panama	30–39	800–1,000	18.5
Organizer	Private airplane/private vessel	Bahamas	50–59	488	

could be described as playing a minor role in drug smuggling (offloader), but this individual had an extensive history of involvement in drug smuggling.

We observed diversity in the methods of smuggling used by members of our sample, which included both commercial and private vessels (boats) and private and commercial airplanes. Combinations of vessels and aircrafts were also reported. The most commonly used transportation was private vessels, with 62% of the individuals reporting experience with this method. In short, this high-level group of drug smugglers with extensive experience in smuggling was in a position to know and understand the structure of drug-smuggling organizations.

LITERATURE ON DRUG SMUGGLERS AND OTHER ACTIVE OFFENDERS

The widely held perception about groups of international drug smugglers is that they are highly structured organizations (i.e., cartels). However, some recent literature on drug smugglers and other active offenders suggests that this is not the case. We here incorporate information on active groups of offenders to discount any possible criticisms that might arise about the inclusion in our sample of only convicted offenders. Recent ethnographic research on active offenders such as burglars, robbers, carjackers, and gang members suggests that offenders do not organize themselves very effectively. Our examination of international drug-smuggling groups will concentrate on the following three features of organization: structure, interactions, and rationality.

Structure

One of the most readily identifiable characteristics of a highly organized group is a hierarchical structure. Formal hierarchies have ranked levels of authority that clearly delineate super- and subordinates, with those in superordinate positions being responsible for overseeing those in the lower offices (Weber, 1946). Highly organized groups have a clear chain of command that signifies the downward movement of decision-making power. Such groups also have functions associated with each level of the structure. The organizational structures of these groups tend to be pyramidal or vertical in nature.

In contrast to hierarchical structures, some groups are organized in a less formal manner. Williams (1998) suggests that some drug-smuggling organizations are more accurately described as networks of connected nodes that are linked across and within organizations. There is no definite vertical chain of command, as individual cells can operate independently from the larger organization because of their individual access to information and technology. To a certain degree, this independence isolates various stages of the drug-smuggling process from others.

Recent research on international drug smuggling suggests that many groups are organized as a series of connected nodes. Zaitch (2002) studied drug importation from Colombia to the Netherlands and found little evidence of vertical hierarchies in drug smuggling. Instead, he perceived smuggling operations as flexible networks comprising dynamic groups that could change tactics quickly and were relatively insulated from other groups found earlier or later in the smuggling transaction chain.

A structure of connected nodes rather than a vertical hierarchy is supported by research on a variety of active offenders. In fact, descriptions of human trafficking and smuggling (Zhang, 2007; Zhang, 2008), terrorist groups (9/11 Commission, 2004; Sageman, 2008), and international trafficking of stolen vehicles (Clarke & Brown, 2003) depict such groups as small networks of individuals who lack much in the way of a formal structure. In addition, research on active burglars (Cromwell, Olson, & Avery, 1994; Shover, 1996), robbers (Wright & Decker, 1997), carjackers (Jacobs, Topali, & Wright, 2003), and gang members (Decker, Katz, & Webb, 2007) also conclude [sic] that offenders do not organize themselves in an effective or formal manner.

Interviews with the 34 convicted drug smugglers provided support for the idea that drug-smuggling operations are not well organized. Williams's (1998) concept of connected nodes was illustrated in his interviews with various smugglers, especially those in the role of transporter.

> Transportation is one thing, okay. That office in Colombia is supposed to get the people in Miami to do the smuggling, right? And I was the head, you know, my own group. Got 20 people working for me doing the smuggling, 10 people, whatever, and it was my responsibility. They got nothing to do with that. They just pay me for me to do the job. The other offices, when you get to Miami, I did the smuggling. I brought it already in from the Bahamas, whatever. I get in contact with the people in Miami and give it to them. Then they got it through the names. . . . Call those people and give it to them. Then those people got their own buyers or whatever they do. . . . That would be another whole operation. There would be a whole operation to sell it in. There is another office working in Colombia to deal with the money. (2)
>
> The original owner of the load was somebody in Colombia that I don't know. I know the guy who was, that I went to Colombia with, and he make some arrangements in there. The original owner, I don't know the owner. I never knew the original owner. Never. The owner of the merchandise gave the merchandise to a guy that I knew that I went to Colombia with. Well, the guy I went to Colombia with, he was, he was a fugitive from this country, and I was in charge of, in here, to make all of the arrangements and all of the preparations to everyone get his part, and I get mine. I didn't know the people who were going to drive the boat to Fort Lauderdale. No, I only knew one guy—two guys in this, in this enterprise, and there were about 13 or 14 people in the deal, involved there. (4)
>
> Well, I had a connection in New York at the airport. So, basically, [my friend] would package the drugs in '80 and he had a connection at the airport in '80 as well. Well, as far as I know, some of [the drugs] came from Colombia, but that wasn't my connection, you know. That was the person I was dealing with. My part started when it got to Haiti. . . . I would meet with the guy and we would package everything, do whatever we do so the drugs wouldn't be able to detect by smelling it. . . . Whenever I come back, my guys would get the drugs,

and either he would arrange it with someone to get it through the airport in Haiti, or if he did come in Haiti, I would arrange it. There's a transaction that takes place between Colombia and Haiti that I don't know about. I don't know the Colombians. The only thing I know is that whatever they would give me, it would have 40%. (11)

In addition to illustrating the concept of nodes, the following quote also exemplifies the independent nature of those nodes, similar to what Williams (1998) describes.

The first load they asked me to bring in, I think it was—the exact amount of 383 keys. . . . I had no idea where it was coming from. I had no idea where it was going other than I would get back, the guy would pick it up. I picked it up in the Bahamas and brought it to Jupiter [Florida]. . . . So they recruited me and asked me to pick up the drugs and set up the operation. . . . I had the boat reconfigured. I engineered all the little particulars like they'd call on the phone, the warehouse, and the codes for the beeper and everything. (21)

The smugglers also explained how a load (or shipment) of cocaine would be organized in Colombia for transportation into the United States. Instead of a single company or group of individuals owning the load, as would be the case with a highly organized operation, various independent parties would contribute to the shipment that would eventually be transported:

The way they do it, you have a collector, and it's—and this was interesting because I learned this myself firsthand at the time. A bunch of people will invest in the load. It's like selling shares of stock. This person will put up this amount of money. Another person will put up another amount of money, and they in effect maybe own two or three keys. Then the collector, or whoever, whatever you want to call him, puts all this together, and this joint venture goes on a plane. So a proprietary interest in this was really shared by many. (30)

Weber (1946) describes formal organizations as having a chain of command; however, the current study found drug-smuggling organizations to lack this structural feature. Here, a transporter explains that he did not receive commands from a higher authority about how to operate his stage of the operation:

I'm the transport. I'm the one that tells them this is how we're going to play the game. We're going to do it this way. We're not going to use this. We're going to do this because I'm in charge and I'm aware of surveillance. I know everything— how the government is running things, how things are happening. So I keep constant contact with the office. All the broker does is pick up the drugs and give me the money for my services. And the broker is the one in charge of delivering the money back to Colombia for the load and the profit. (14)

Interviews with the 34 subjects also supported Zaitch's (2002) contention that international drug-smuggling groups have dynamic structures. The adaptable and dynamic nature of these organizations is described by the following individuals as they explain how drug-smuggling groups adapt quickly to changes in personnel or tactics:

When organizing a group of captains and people who could sell these drugs, they were still able to do it once I was caught. They do it with somebody else. They find somebody, they find somebody. (16)

We would constantly change the routes . . . through the Caribbean. You go around through the Peninsula to the west or you go to the east around the Caribbean Basin.

Interactions

Waring (2002) argues that the way groups of co-offenders are organized rarely corresponds to the structure of formal organizations. Her key focus is on behavior within offending networks, not elements of the structure, as a means to avoid a strict focus on hierarchy or structure. This approach is consistent with that championed by Burt (1992), who argues that all social structure is the product of relations between individuals. Accordingly, we will examine the nature of interactions both within and amongst drug-smuggling groups to better understand their organization.

As a consequence of the vertical hierarchy of authority, highly organized groups are characterized by sustained, formal interactions between members. Interactions typically occur between specific individuals as a result of the vertical nature of the chain of command and the highly structured patterns of communication within such groups. In such groups, direct correspondence commonly occurs only between an individual and one other person, his or her immediate supervisor. Organizational communication in such groups rarely involves personal interaction. Instead, information tends to be exchanged through more formal channels, where correspondence can be more easily documented (e.g., written messages or formal meetings).

In contrast to the concept of highly organized offenders, Best and Luckenbill (1994) suggest that deviance and deviants are generally not well organized. They outline a descriptive typology of co-offending groups using the nature of association among individuals involved in offenses together. In our interviews, we found that the associations between offenders were not formal, had short temporal spans, and were specific to individual offenses. We describe such associations as episodic. More recent research on the interactions between drug smugglers is consistent with these findings. In contrast to interactions based on roles or a chain of command, Zaitch (2002) finds that transactions between smugglers are based on kinship, ethnicity, and language.

Our research on international drug-smuggling groups supports the idea that interactions in these groups are not formal, sustained, or based on hierarchical chains of command. Consistent with Best and Luckenbill's (1994) typology of co-offending groups, the smugglers interviewed described their interactions as more episodic than sustained:

I had very few people working with me. In total, about six or eight people. Some of them were part of my crew, and some of them were what we used to [call] independent contractors. If I needed him, I would hire him. If I didn't need him, he would go to somebody else. (5)

> Well, I don't know anything about sale. You know what I mean? . . . The load come from Haiti, but the cocaine was from Colombia. And my job, to take it from Haiti [to] the U.S. I knew the people in Haiti, but it was the first time I work with them. I knew the people in Colombia. I had not worked with them in the past. They get in touch with me because I know somebody from Haiti. I never work with him before in drugs, you know? I know him because I was there before. So he reached me here in Miami. (6)

In a formally organized group, interactions and communication among members is [sic] based on the hierarchy and chain of command. Interviews with the smugglers indicated that this structure was not the way their smuggling activities were organized. In fact, interactions among individuals within and between nodes tended to be based less on hierarchy and structure and more on trust and informal relationships. Consistent with Zaitch (2002), many times this trust was established through nationality or kinship.

> You know, they knew that I been in drug smuggling or anything. I never used a weapon in my life. I had no need for it with the people I was dealing with. They were people that would keep their word, and if I see anybody that I didn't like that would create trouble in the future, I would avoid and try not to do business with. (5)
>
> So I called them and I told them I have an importation from Venezuela and the name of the containers, and they go and pick them up and put them in my warehouse. I don't usually bring drugs. It was my first time. I was chosen because I was trusted. They trusted me because they saw my job, my experience. (18)
>
> So, when I was getting a pair of pants made [in South America], some guys comes and talks to me, and he said, "Listen, how's it going? I see you're from Miami." "Yeah, I'm from Miami." He asked me if I wanted to make some money, and I said sure, that's cool. He goes "Well, next time you're in Miami, call some people and see what we can do." . . . And I said, the hell with it, and I gave him a call. He said, "Well, come on. We're at the club." I come over to a club and he just happened to be in [Miami]. I was in Miami now. I left Colombia and went back to Miami. . . . Three months later, after working for him, he gave me a call and told me to come to Colombia, come back to Colombia and talk to him. I get over there. I see a couple of guys. We talk and hang out, and then they start telling me what's going. (24)

This quotation describes how trust in international drug-smuggling organizations can be established simply through one's nationality. It also illustrates how interactions are less formal and involve more direct communication than in highly organized groups. This latter point is also supported by the account of following smuggler, who describes his contact with the owners of the loads.

> I have to meet the people [whose drugs I am delivering]. I have to meet them. Because they give me the contract, you understand me? I mean, the owner of the boat and the merchandise, you know. The owners. All the time, owners, not representatives. (6)

Rationality

In addition to the structure and nature of interactions, we can examine the rationality of offending groups to better understand their organization. We refer to the rationality of an organization as the degree to which the organization is structured to achieve specific goals. In other words, a rationally organized group has a structure and operating procedures that are based on logical reasoning, not chance or other untested criteria.

Cressey (1972) uses the core concept of rationality to describe the extent and nature of organization within offending groups, particularly organized crime. Role specialization and coordination are key concepts by which he describes variation in the degree of organization among offending groups. He notes that well-organized groups are those that are most rationally arranged in the pursuit of efficiency and maximized profits. Therefore, according to Cressey, well-organized groups are very rational because they display high levels of specialization (division of labor based on qualifications) and coordination of activities (interdependence) in an attempt to maximize profits efficiently.

Applying the concept of rationality to offending groups, Donald and Wilson (2000) studied the organization of ram raiders, or individuals who engage in a pattern of smash, grab, and flee at jewelry stores. They found that these groups exhibited generalized roles (no specialization), had low levels of interdependence, and lacked a rational foundation for their structure. Warr (2002) examined active groups of offenders and found them to display little evidence of rational planning or calculation. Some research on gang organization also suggests that these offenders do not organize themselves rationally (Decker & Van Winkle, 1996).

Based on the interviews in the current study, it was clear that drug-smuggling groups foster little specialization or coordination of activities. The following quote shows how the lack of coordination between the nodes of the operation does not cause the entire operation to fail:

> I had a freighter, I knew the owner of the land strip in Guajira. Sometimes they had the loads waiting there for two or three weeks and no one would show up to pick it up. So this guy would call me to ask if I pick it up; I said yes, and the other people would call me. Sometimes they would ask me, for instance, to drop the merchandise in the Bahamas, and I would do it. But I never met those guys. The other guy, the broker, would do everything. He didn't work for anybody. He worked on commission and he trusted me. (17)

Although these groups did not appear to be rationally organized to efficiently maximize profits, reports from the smugglers suggested they might be rationally organized around another goal: managing risk. In his examination of drug-smuggling networks, Williams (1998) notes that while their organization is not highly formal, it does provide the group with various means of self-protection. For example, the lack of a formal structure allows drug-smuggling groups the ability to adapt quickly to changes in law enforcement and therefore minimize the risk of detection. The following subjects describe how smuggling operations in their groups were not based on maximizing profits but instead on minimizing the risk of detection by law enforcement. As such, they were flexible and able to change methods, drugs, and routes.

> Never smuggled heroin, no. I was offered it, but [the boats] weren't ready for the loads at the time, but if we would have, probably I would have done it, because it was a big profit of margin there. There was a big margin there. Smaller amount, and it was about three times the profit that you would get from coke. (5)
>
> We started tightening up right after the war on drugs. Surveillance really picked up. So, I mean, the big plane was out of the question. . . . It was getting more difficult. You know, the boats, my cigarette boats, were like, you know, law enforcement already knew. I mean, a 37-foot Midnight Express with four engines in the back, they knew what the boat was for. So, you know, my operation was getting obsolete already. . . . We did [an air drop] right here in the Bahamas. It was in '89 or '90. I picked up maybe 150 keys and brought it into the Florida Keys, and after that, we waited a while and then we started changing things over here. We started air dropping right in the middle of the Gulf of Mexico. All the way from Colombia to the Gulf of Mexico. . . . [I moved] from marijuana to cocaine, from the late '80s. Right after I moved to Georgia and I came back, I'd say I came back smuggling cocaine because, you know, surveillance was heavier, and I didn't want to work bulky material. I wanted to work something that was, there was plenty of money in it and something that I can get in and out and, you know, do my deliveries fast, didn't have to use a lot of people. You know, a lot more people were cooperating with the government, and you didn't know who was who. So you wanted a small group. You wanted real trusting friends. (14)
>
> A lot of people in smuggling are in more places than one. In other words, they not only do it in boats. They do it—now with Mexico in the business, they're doing vehicles. They're doing airplanes. (29)

As noted earlier, trust and kinship are key characteristics of the interactions between drug smugglers. The previous quote reinforces this point. Many subjects described how a structure of isolated nodes acts to protect individuals from detection when others involved in the operation are apprehended, thus suggesting that the rational foundation of these groups' organization is based on reducing risk.

> Never been stopped by law enforcement. Like I said, you know, they don't catch very much unless somebody tells them, and usually if you find out, when you interview people in prison, most of their cases or their indictments is dry. I mean, what I mean, they didn't catch the drugs. It was just a conspiracy unless somebody talked about. I'm sure you have found that out. They catch very little drugs coming through. I mean, they catch some, but very little overall. It's more dangerous after you have it here in the United States, distribution [more dangerous] than actually bringing it in. (3)
>
> Never been arrested before this. It's been close, but no cigar. The guys who were bringing the marijuana, they were caught, but I wasn't. At the time they

didn't talk. When they saw me. . . . Well, they really didn't know me that well. I'm sure that they cooperated right away when they got caught, but they didn't know me that well. And I was, you know, when you work with a lot of people, you got to protect yourself. You can't, you know, you can't like, "Well, I live here. I live here. This is my last name." So [I gave them] no personal information at all.

We contend that international drug-smuggling groups are rationally organized around reducing risk, *not* increasing profit. This contention is supported when one examines the persistence of these smugglers' offending. Whereas a group that is based on maximizing profit would have high levels of persistence (continued activity over periods of time), the drug smugglers we interviewed reported low levels of persistence in their groups as a result of an effort to reduce risk of detection.

> For a load of marijuana [I would make] $50,000 or $60,000. If I was single at that time, [money would last] about three, four months. Party every day, you know. And that's when I look for another trip that someone needs done. [I would] get the money and party, and when the money starts to run out, I have 20 trips [offered] already. When my money starts to run out, have offers and just take one. . . . I think I had offers from people because of both connections and I was successful. Because everybody knows me, you know? (6)
>
> Well, I knew [how] the government and law enforcement worked and how they set their surveillance, how they would do their interdictions, and I always I'd be a step ahead of them. My technology was always a step ahead of them. So I knew it was impossible for them to catch me. . . . I would have taken more chances because I know I would have kept doing loads, but the more you did it, that would increase your chance of being caught. You typically wait between loads—if I saw things good, it would be two weeks. And if [I] saw things bad, a month or two. (14)

Although Warr (2002) proposes that groups of offenders show little evidence of rational planning, this was not the case with the smugglers we interviewed. Although it is true that little planning or organization was done around the goal of maximizing profits, many subjects described their group taking advanced and deliberate measures to minimize the risk of detection. The following quote from an organizer illustrates how many groups are not searching for the most efficient means of smuggling cocaine into the United States. Instead, they consider techniques that are less likely to be subject to law enforcement detection, not produce the most profit possible.

> I started meeting people, and you know, you learn. When I started doing my own stuff, I would get everybody in a room, the guys that was supposed to be involved in it, and in the planning of the project, how we're going to do it. . . . I always figure that if all of them would come to the same conclusion that this is the best way to do it, then the police and the DEA, too, would think this was the best way to do it. So to me, the best way was to go all different [techniques]. (1)

DISCUSSION AND CONCLUSIONS

Much prior research and many law enforcement descriptions overascribe the level of organization among groups of offenders. One good example is the description of the organizational structure of active gang members. Most gangs appear to be considerably less well organized than public or law enforcement conceptions of them. Similarly, descriptions of active burglars, armed robbers, and street-level drug sellers generally depict individuals who live somewhat disorganized, and even chaotic, lives. Very little structure is found in the offending activities of these individuals, and their behavior does not reflect a high degree of rationality. There is reason to suspect, however, that high-level international drug smuggling groups might have more formal structures, that their interactions would be more rule directed, and that their behavior—as both individuals and groups—would be more rational. After all, the large sums of money involved in such activities, coupled with the apparent sophistication necessary to successfully smuggle drugs and the age of the individuals involved, would lead one to expect that such groups would be highly organized. Our analysis of interviews with 34 high-level drug smugglers suggests quite a different picture.

A corporate organizational structure suggests a pyramid with a leader on the top who passes on orders to a group of subordinates, who in turn pass on orders to their subordinates. From this perspective, organizational communication is structured by role and rank within an organization. High-level international drug smugglers outline a very different picture of their activities. Their drug-smuggling groups resemble a series of loosely coupled nodes, small groups of individuals who work together largely unaware of who and what takes place at other steps in their "organization." Many of the individuals we interviewed did not know anyone outside of their immediate group and were recruited based on informal relationships, kinship, or ethnicity rather than the possession of a specific skill. Instead of being rationally focused on maximizing profits, such groups focused on minimizing risk of detection and apprehension. We believe that this is a key to understanding how these groups' activities are organized.

It is important to have a fuller understanding of groups of offenders, whether those offenders are terrorist groups, gangs, burglars, or international drug smugglers. Such an understanding aids our ability to better understand their goals, structure, interactions, and rationality. Equally important, such an understanding can more fully inform policies designed to minimize the harm caused by drug importation, gang activity, or burglary. As with many offending groups, the information provided directly from offenders—in their own words—provides an important counterbalance to information gleaned from a single source of official information.

REFERENCES

9/11 Commission. (2004). *Final report of the National Commission on Terrorist Attacks upon the United States*. New York: Norton.

Best, J., & Luckenbill, D. (1994). *Organizing deviance*. Englewood Cliffs, NJ: Prentice Hall.

Burt, R. (1992). *Structural holes*. Cambridge, MA: Harvard University Press.

Clarke, R. V., & Brown, R. (2003). International trafficking in stolen vehicles. In M. Tonry, ed., *Crime and justice: A review of research* (vol. 30). Chicago: University of Chicago Press, pp. 197–228.

Cressey, D. (1972). *Criminal organization: Its elementary forms*. New York: Harper & Row.

Cromwell, P., Olson, J., & Avary, D. (1994). *Breaking and entering*. Thousand Oaks, CA: Sage.

Decker, S. H., Katz, C., & Webb, V. (2007). Understanding the black box of gang organization: Implications for involvement in violent crime, drug sales and violent victimization. *Crime & Delinquency, 54*(1), 153–172.

Decker, S. H., & Van Winkle, B. (1996). *Life in the gang: families, friends, and violence*. Cambridge, UK: Cambridge University Press.

Donald, I., & Wilson, A. (2000). Ram raiding: Criminals working in groups. In D. Canter & L. Alison, eds., *The social psychology of crime*. Burlington, VT: Ashgate, pp. 191–246.

Jacobs, B., Topali, V., & Wright, R. (2003). Carjacking, streetlife and offender motivation. *British Journal of Criminology, 43*, 673–688.

Sageman, M. (2008). *Leaderless jihad: Terror networks in the twenty-first century*. Philadelphia: University of Pennsylvania Press.

Shover, N. (1996). *Great pretenders: Pursuits and careers of persistent thieves*. Boulder, CO: Westview Press.

Waring, E. (2002). Co-offending as a network form of social organization. In E. Waring & D. Weisburd, eds., *Crime and social organization*. New Brunswick, NJ: Transaction, pp. 31–48.

Warr, M. (2002). *Companions in crime: The social aspects of criminal conduct*. New York: Cambridge.

Weber, M. (1946). Bureaucracy. In H. H. Gerth & C. W. Mills, eds., *Max Weber: Essays in sociology*. New York: Oxford University Press. pp. 47–56.

Williams, P. (1998). The nature of drug-trafficking networks. *Current History, 97*, 154–159.

Wright, R., & Decker, S. H. (1997). *Armed robbers in action: Stickups and street culture*. Boston: Northeastern University Press.

Zaitch, D. (2002). *Trafficking cocaine: Colombian drug entrepreneurs in the Netherlands*. The Hague, Netherlands: Kluwer.

Zhang, S. X. (2007). *Smuggling and trafficking in human beings: All roads lead to America*. Westport, CT: Praeger.

Zhang, S. X. (2008). *Chinese human smuggling organizations*. Stanford, CA: Stanford University Press.

CHAPTER 15

Informal Control and Illicit Drug Trade

Scott Jacques and Richard T. Wright

Antidrug legislation and enforcement are meant to reduce the trade in illegal drugs by increasing their price. Yet the unintended consequence is an increase in informal control, including retaliation, negotiation, avoidance, and toleration, among drug users and dealers. Little existing theory or research has explored the connections between informal control and drug trading. This article uses the rational choice and opportunity perspectives to explore how and why the frequency and seriousness of popular justice—as a whole or for each form—affect the price and rate of drug sales. The proposed theory is grounded on and illustrated with qualitative data obtained from drug dealers. This article concludes by discussing the scholarly and policy implications.

INTRODUCTION

Legislation and law enforcement are the most widely discussed methods of deterring the illegal drug trade (Moskos, 2008; NRC, 2001, 2010). Theory suggests that as penalties are increased, become more certain, or are enforced more quickly, then the size and scope of drug markets should be reduced. This theory is a staple of local, national, and international efforts to control the trading of illicit drugs (MacCoun and Reuter, 2001; Zimring and Hawkins, 1992). Yet control in the drug underworld is not restricted to formal intervention. To handle and manage conflict, drug market participants exercise informal social control. There are various kinds of "popular justice" (Black, 1998; Cooney, 2009). Illicit drug markets are notorious for retaliation, but other—more peaceful—forms of conflict management also exist therein, including negotiation, avoidance, and toleration (Jacques and Wright, 2008a; Taylor, 2007).

Source: Jacques, S., & Wright, R. T. (2011). Informal control and illicit drug trade. *Criminology*, *49*(3), 729–765.

Although drug law and enforcement are meant to reduce the trade in illegal drugs, the unintended consequence is a reduction in formal mediation among drug traders—i.e., buyers and sellers. Whereas law-abiding citizens can make a report to police or file a lawsuit, criminals have fewer formal means of extracting justice from victimizers (e.g., robbers and defrauders) and of settling market-based conflicts (e.g., over territory and price). In turn, the absence of formal dispute resolution causes pronounced increases in informal control. Not only does retaliation become more likely (Black, 1998; Goldstein, 1985; Jacobs and Wright, 2006), but so too do less aggressive forms of conflict management (Jacques and Wright, 2008a).

The past 25 years have witnessed an exponential growth in knowledge about the effect of law on drug trading and informal control, especially retaliation. *Yet far less is known about how the various forms of informal control affect drug trade.* Put differently, there is sparse information on how the price and frequency of drug sales are affected by the rate and seriousness of retaliation, negotiation, avoidance, and toleration used by drug traders. It important to follow this line of inquiry because it may be that the *unintended* consequence of prohibiting drug trading—namely increasing informal control—is reducing *or* increasing the rate of drug trading and increasing *or* decreasing the price.

This article aims to use the rationality and opportunity perspectives to explore and theorize the influence of various forms of informal control among drug traders. We begin by defining and discussing drug trade, formal control of the drug trade, and informal control of the drug trade; in doing so, we briefly review existing theory and research on the connections between these behaviors. After describing the method and data used in the article, namely qualitative descriptions provided by drug dealers, we examine how each form of informal control affects drug trade. We conclude by discussing the implications of the theory and the findings for future work and policy.

DRUG TRADING AND SOCIAL CONTROL

Criminologists have provided a substantial amount of theory and research on the role of legislation and law enforcement in altering the rate and price of drug sales. In addition, the field has increasingly explored the effect of formal control on its informal counterpart, especially retaliation. After reviewing the work on these connections, we suggest an area of study that is less developed, namely, the effect of informal control on the rate and price of drug sales.

Drug Trade

A trade (i.e., sale or deal) is a reciprocal giving and taking of resources between actors. Drugs may be traded for money, objects, or services. Drug selling is concerned with trading drugs for resources, and drug buying is concerned with trading resources for drugs. For any given exchange, the quantity of resources given in return for a particular type (e.g., marijuana or cocaine) and quantity (e.g., 1 gram or 1 pound) of drugs is the price. In determining the price for a given sale, the numerator will always reflect the quantity of a drug traded, but the denominator in the equation—the resource(s) traded for a drug—can take various forms. A resource is anything that can be traded for a drug. Resources are conceptually divisible according to whether they are money—a medium of exchange—or an object or service that may be bartered, such as weapons, sex, or drugs (see, e.g., Denton, 2001; Ratner, 1993).

Studies of drug markets typically focus on variability in the rate and price of drug sales. Although there is a degree of stability, these two aspects of drug trade are known to differ according to the type of drug, its purity/strength, and the amount being traded. Variation in the rate and price also depends on such things as the area, time, and characteristics of traders. For instance, 7 grams of high-grade marijuana may cost $85 to $100 in some parts of the United States (Jacques and Wright, 2008a), whereas a gram of low-grade marijuana sells for less than $5 (Sifaneck et al., 2007). The effect of place-based differences may be seen, for example, when considering the price of small quantities of heroin: The cost may be as little as £5 in the United Kingdom (Lupton et al., 2002), $50 in Australia (Coomber and Maher, 2006), or up to $130 in America (Hoffer, 2006). The era also matters; the price of heroin and cocaine decreased by almost fourfold between 1980 and 1995 (MacCoun and Reuter, 2001: 31).

Formal Control of the Drug Trade

Formal social control refers to any governmental action that defines or responds to deviance (Black, 1976); this is also known as formal justice. It includes every act of the legal system, from legislation; to criminal investigations; to the arrest of suspects, their prosecution in court, the judge or jury's verdict of guilt, and punishment, which may include obligated community service or treatment, fines, asset forfeiture, probation, imprisonment, or even death. Considered in this way, formal justice becomes a quantitative variable. It increases with every additional act of legislation, investigation, arrest, prosecution, or punishment (Cooney, 2009).

As a quantitative variable, it is possible to measure the amount of law that defines and reacts to the drug trade. The different levels of law—both its rate and magnitude—may be measured and compared across times, places, situations, demographic groups (e.g., male vs. female), drug markets (e.g., marijuana vs. cocaine), or roles therein (e.g., dealer vs. user). Over time, for instance, data show that in 2009 there were approximately 30,000 arrests by the U.S. Drug Enforcement Administration (DEA, 2010), but 10 years prior, there were more than 40,000 arrests. Between regions of the United States, the South has almost 350,000 people on probation for drug offenses, which is about five times the number of drug probationers in the West (Glaze and Bonczar, 2009). Or consider how imprisonment varies across the offender's role in the market: Based on data from a 1997 study, Sevigny and Caulkins (2004) show that most incarcerated drug dealers are mid-level rather than retail-level or "kingpins."

The Effect of Formal Control on the Drug Trade

As noted, antidrug legislation and law enforcement are the most pronounced features of local, national, and international approaches for reducing drug trading (MacCoun and Reuter, 2001; NRC, 2001). This approach accepts the premise that reducing drug-related harms entails the costs of law enforcement, such as police and prisons (Zimring and Hawkins, 1992: 7). Rational choice theory and present-d ay government policies and practices assert that greater, more certain, and quicker arrests, prosecutions, convictions, and formal punishments (e.g., fines and prison) increase the price of drugs and thereby reduce the rate of drug trading (see Bentham, 1988 [1789]).

Longitudinal and cross-national evidence, however, seem to suggest that the validity of this theory, policy, and practice is questionable (Bushway and Reuter, 2011; Caulkins and Reuter, 2010). In the United States, the price trends for cocaine, heroin, and marijuana are largely unaffected over time by the level of law enforcement (MacCoun and Reuter, 2001: 31). Between nations, research also shows that the prevalence of drug use is not significantly reduced by criminalization or higher levels of enforcement (MacCoun and Reuter, 1997; Reinarman, Cohen, and Kaal, 2004). At present, the debate continues over whether punitive acts by governments toward drug-involved persons are positive or negative or significant and substantive.

Informal Control Among Drug Traders

Informal social control, or popular justice, is conflict management absent the government. Instead, it is performed by "the people," not politicians or law enforcement officials (Cooney, 2009). Such behavior includes several actions (Black, 1998). Toleration is doing nothing about deviance. Avoidance is curtailing interaction with the deviants. Negotiation involves disputants talking out a conflict, whereas informal mediation involves a neutral third party resolving the dispute, both of which sometimes result in compensation. Retaliation is unilateral self-help accomplished through theft, fraud, vandalism, or violence. These forms of informal control may be conceptualized as an ordinal variable: Toleration is the least severe form of popular justice; avoidance is more severe, but not as severe as negotiation, which is less severe than retaliation (Cooney, 2009).

Thought of in this way, it is possible to measure the amount of informal control that defines and reacts to deviance in the drug trade, such as victimizations involving fraud (e.g., fake drugs or money), theft (e.g., burglary), violence (e.g., robbery), or market-related disputes (e.g., over territory) that occur against and among drug traders. As is true with drug sales and formal control, the rate and severity of popular justice varies as a whole and between its different forms. In other words, informal control is more common among some situations, people, places, or drug markets than others. Similarly, the different kinds of informal control—such as retaliation or avoidance—also vary in their prevalence and severity. For example, drug markets located in urban, lower-class neighborhoods are known to be rife with violent retaliation (Jacobs and Wright, 2006), but this form of control seems to be less common among suburban drug traders who prefer to handle conflicts through toleration or avoidance (Jacques and Wright, 2008b).

The Effect of Formal Control on Conflict Management Among Drug Traders

Broadly speaking, two types of conflict exist among drug traders: victimization- and market-related disputes. Victimization-related conflict involves a person committing an offense against another person. Market-related disputes involve two or more people engaged in a conflict over price, territory, or market share. These conflicts may be managed formally or informally. Formal mediation is when the government intervenes, whereas informal control is when the victim or disputants handle the problem without government help.

A great deal of theory and empirical evidence supports the notion that illicit drug market-related victimizations and conflicts are unlikely to be handled with formal mediation (see, e.g., Goldstein, 1985; Jacques and Wright, 2008a). This is true for at least three reasons related to the formal control—specifically the illegality—of such markets. For one, criminals typically do not report their victimization to police for fear of revealing their own offending to the government and subsequently being punished for it. Two, in the underworld, fair prices cannot be set or monitored by the government, "[c]ontracts cannot be enforced through written documents and the legal system," and "[t]erritories cannot be allocated through bidding for desirable locations" (Reuter, 2010: 275). Third, even when drug market conflicts do come to the attention of government agents, they are taken less seriously by police, prosecuted less forcefully, and punished less harshly (Black, 1976, 1998; Klinger, 1997; Moskos, 2008; Stanko, 1981/2). In short, making a market illegal (i.e., formally controlling it) means conflicts related to it are rarely formally mediated.

Because drug market conflicts are unlikely to be handled with government mediation, the role of informal control becomes more pronounced (see Black, 1976, 1983). Although several forms of informal control may be employed to handle such conflicts (Black, 1998; Cooney, 2009; Jacques and Wright, 2008a), the extant research is focused disproportionately on popular justice meted out via retaliation (Goldstein, 1985; Jacobs and Wright, 2008a). Retaliation, or vengeance, is informal control achieved through violence, fraud, theft, or vandalism (see Jacques, 2010). It is rational to the degree that it provides victims with a way to punish and deter offenses. Quantitative and qualitative research clearly shows that retaliation is common and serious among drug traders (see, e.g., Goldstein, 1985; Goldstein et al., 1997; Jacobs, 2000; Levitt and Venkatesh, 2000; Moskos, 2008; Reuter, 2010).

Recent research on informal control in drug markets has increasingly turned its attention to more peaceful approaches such as toleration, avoidance, and negotiation (Jacques and Wright, 2008a; Taylor, 2007). Although qualitatively different from vengeance, these less aggressive types of informal conflict management have benefits for victims seeking justice. Toleration is useful because it may allow dealers to resume business rather than expend time and energy searching for their victimizer (Topalli, Wright, and Fornango, 2002). Avoidance of prior offenders helps victims insulate themselves from further problems (Denton, 2001). Negotiation may provide a path to compensation (Hoffer, 2006). We see, then, that there are several ways in which victims may respond to their drug market-related conflicts.

To summarize, the unintended consequence of criminalizing drugs and enforcing laws against them is an increase in informal control among drug traders resulting from a reduction in the likelihood of their conflicts being mediated by the government.

The Effect of Informal Control on Drug Trade

The current state of knowledge about drug markets suggests that more antidrug legislation and law enforcement 1) have ambiguous effects on the price or rate of drug sales but 2) almost surely increase the rate and seriousness of informal control, including not only violent retaliation but also less forceful forms. Although theory and research on these two topics are increasingly nuanced, what lags far behind is theoretical or empirical information about the effect of informal control on drug sales. In other words, *how, why, and to what degree does the rate and seriousness of popular justice—as a whole or for each form—affect the price and rate of drug sales?* By determining the effect of informal control on drug trade, we will gain a deeper understanding of formal control's net effect on the illicit drug trade.

To our knowledge, only three prior studies have explicitly examined this research question (Caulkins, Reuter, and Taylor, 2006; Levitt and Venkatesh, 2000; Topalli, Wright, and Fornango, 2002). This work focuses on retaliation's effect on drug trade and says little about the influence of other forms of informal control—negotiation, avoidance, and toleration. Our goal is to examine the effect of each form of informal control on drug trade. Before doing so, however, it is important to describe our orienting paradigms—namely, rational choice and opportunity theories, and the data used throughout—qualitative descriptions obtained from drug dealers.

THE RATIONAL CHOICE AND OPPORTUNITY PERSPECTIVES

This article's theoretical orientation is anchored in two paradigms: rational choice and opportunity (Cornish and Clarke, 1986; Felson, 1998).

Rational Choice

The rationality perspective explains any particular action as the outcome of the actor's decision that its perceived overall utility—meaning the sum of benefits minus the costs—is greatest relative to other actions (Cornish and Clarke, 1986; Jacobs, 2010). As relates to crime and control, they should increase as they become more beneficial or less costly. This calculation involves consideration of alternative lines of action, such as engaging in different crimes, exercising other forms of social control, or refraining from these behaviors.

Bentham (1988 [1789]: 24) thought of benefits and costs as pleasures and pains, which are two sorts of sanctions. Altogether, four kinds of sanctions exist: political, popular, physical, and religious. The two sanctions at the heart of this article are political and popular. The former refers to pleasures and pains meted out by government officials, whereas the latter comes from persons in the community (Bentham, 1988 [1789]: 25). In other words, political sanctions are formal control; popular sanctions are informal control. Punishments are painful sanctions (Bentham, 1988 [1789]: 26). The death penalty is an example of a political punishment, whereas retaliatory murder is an example of a popular punishment. Punishments are a way to reduce the costs to or increase the benefits for the controller/punisher by increasing costs for the person controlled/punished.

To obtain the greatest benefits/pleasures and lowest costs/pains, individuals (e.g., a police officer, drug dealer, or buyer) and groups (e.g., governments or gangs) play a "strategic game" of offending and sanctioning with and against each other (Goffman, 1969, 1974; Schelling, 1960). For instance, people might engage in illegal drug trading to obtain the pleasures of money or intoxication, but—to reduce the potential costs of these behaviors for society—police may arrest, prosecute, and fine or imprison these offenders (i.e., apply political punishment). Alternatively, a drug buyer may refrain from paying a drug seller what is owed to obtain the benefit of intoxication without incurring the financial pains, but—to redress this injustice and deter future problems—the victimized dealer may retaliate against, negotiate with, or afterward avoid the offender (i.e., apply popular punishment). What must always be kept in mind, however, is that punishing others may not be worth the price; i.e., the costs may be greater than the benefits. In such cases, toleration is the more rational response.

In short, the rational choice perspective views offenses and punishments as interactive calculations grounded in the motive of maximizing the overall utility of action. Thus, offenders' and control agents' behavior is determined through a decision process whereby the utility of conceivable actions are assessed and then the most beneficial and least costly option is enacted.

Opportunity

The key insight of the opportunity perspective is that certain minimal elements are necessary for any given behavior to occur (Cohen and Felson, 1979; Cohen, Kluegel, and Land, 1981: 508–9; Sparks, 1982: 29–30). Put more plainly, even when a person wants to act in a certain way, he or she may not have the opportunity to do so. As relates to victimization, for example, a robber cannot steal cash from a victim if that person does not have any cash. Or, as relates to social control, a victim cannot retaliate if unable to locate the offender (see Jacobs and Wright, 2006; Jacques, 2010). Thus, crime and control are not constants; they vary across situations—meaning specific times and places—depending on not only the motives of people but also on the opportunities available to them. Situations differ in their ripeness for crime, conflict, and control (Felson and Clarke, 1998).

The opportunity and rationality perspectives are considered theoretical siblings; without the other, each perspective loses power to make accurate predictions (Felson and Clarke, 1998). The opportunity theory of crime proposed by Cohen and Felson (1979; also see Felson, 1998) suggests that crime requires three minimal elements: a motivated offender, a suitable target, and a capable guardian, or control agent. The more valuable the target or the less capable the control agent, then the more likely is crime to occur because it is more rational.

This article is focused on the social control of wrongdoers, defined as either victimizers or someone with whom there is a market-based dispute (i.e., a disputant). Therefore, we partially depart from Cohen and Felson's (1979) idea of targets and guardians. For this article, targets are both items of value that may be stolen (e.g., drugs, money, or territory) and the wrongdoers that people are seeking to control (e.g., retaliate against, negotiate with, or avoid). The notion of guardians is replaced with the idea of controllers. There are agents of formal (e.g., police) or informal (e.g., retaliators, negotiators, and avoiders) control who engage in deterrence or retribution; control agents may be victims, disputants, or partisans (e.g., friends or family members) who act on their behalf.

In short, targets attract victimization and control, but controllers deter and punish victimization and conflict. Whether various forms of victimization, disputing, or control occur depends on 1) their utility and 2) the opportunity to engage in them.

Summary and Looking Forward

To summarize, governmental efforts to control drug markets and academic efforts to understand them have relied heavily on rational choice and opportunity theories of crime and control. They suggest that given the opportunity, people engage in whichever line of action has the most utility. Victimizing, disputing, and controlling have benefits and costs, and they require specific minimal elements to occur. In the following discussion, we draw on these theoretical lenses to develop a theory of how rationality and opportunity associated with informal conflict management techniques—retaliation, negotiation, avoidance, and toleration—affect the price of drugs and their rate of trading.

WHAT IS THE EFFECT OF INFORMAL CONTROL ON DRUG TRADE?

As noted, formal control of the illicit drug trade is intended to reduce its rate by increasing the price. An unintended consequence of doing so, however, is it increases informal control among traders. This raises the question: What is the effect of informal control on drug trade? To address this question, we will work from four key theoretical premises grounded in the rationality and opportunity perspectives.

(1) *Rationality affects informal social control.* Exercising control may come with costs to the controller. The kind and size of the cost depends on the nature of the form being considered (e.g., retaliation vs. avoidance) and the amount exercised (e.g., more or less retaliation). However, exercising control may have utility for the controller depending on the degree of retributive benefits and/or deterred conflict. Whether a controller exercises a particular form and amount of informal control is a decision determined by weighing its relative utility against the alternatives. *The form and amount of control enacted should be the one with the perceived greatest overall utility for the controller.*

(2) *Informal social control affects the price and rate of drug trading.* Related to the above is that a controller's decision to use a particular form and amount of control is affected by its anticipated effect on drug trade. Each form and amount of control may increase or decrease the price or frequency of exchange, which, in turn, entails benefits and costs for the controller. Holding constant other benefits and costs, *the form and amount of control enacted should be the one perceived to maximize the profits from drug trading for the controller.*

(3) *Opportunity affects informal social control.* With the possible exception of toleration, each form of control requires certain minimal elements, or opportunities, to occur. The elements required depend on the nature of the form being considered. *Unless the necessary conditions for a specific form of control converge in time and space, that form of control is not possible.*

(4) *Informal social control affects the opportunity for drug trading.* Each form and amount of informal social control restricts and presents distinct opportunities that inhibit or facilitate drug trading. The kind of opportunities restricted or presented depends on the nature of the form being considered. *The necessary conditions for a specific form of control may facilitate or inhibit drug trading between the controller and the wrongdoer.*

In the discussion that follows, we explore these theoretical possibilities by examining the experiences of drug dealers. The data from our own study will be supplemented with similar data obtained by other researchers; this is done to add empirical variety and theoretical generalizability. We start with the most severe form of popular justice, namely retaliation, and move toward less severe forms: negotiation, avoidance, and toleration.

The Effect of Retaliation on Drug Trade

Retaliation is conflict management involving aggression, fraud, theft, or destruction (Black, 1983). At least four kinds of retaliation exist (Jacques, 2010). Violent retaliation uses threats and aggression, such as robbery or murder. Fraudulent retaliation is vengeance obtained by engaging in unfair trade. Stealth retaliation refers to cases where the wrongdoer's property is covertly stolen; burglary is an example. And, destructive retaliation is the damaging or destroying of property as "payback"; some cases of vandalism fit this category. These four types of retaliation differ in the amount of violence involved (by definition, it is none except for cases of violent retaliation) and the amount of resources stolen or damaged.

Victimization, Retaliation, Rationality, and the Effect on Drug Trade

The value of retaliation resides in its ability to punish victimizers and prevent subsequent victimization (Topalli, Wright, and Fornango, 2002). In terms of utility, there are two fundamental aspects of this type of informal control: retribution and deterrence. The former is focused on increasing benefits, whereas the latter is intended to reduce future costs. Retribution focuses on regaining respect and, in some cases, regaining stolen wealth. Deterrence is largely concerned with avoiding disrespect, injury, and theft.

Prior research demonstrates that an enhanced fear of victimization resulting from recently being victimized may serve as a factor leading criminals to desistance (Decker and Lauritsen, 2002). In effect, dealers learn that the potential pains of drug trade—including anger, injury, and theft—are not outweighed by the pleasures (Jacques and Wright, 2008b: 1027–8). But if retaliation is capable of punishing and deterring further victimization, then termination is not necessary and the pleasure of crime can continue unfettered. For this reason, enacting vengeance may increase traders' long-term viability and thereby increase the number of trades they engage in over their criminal career. For example, a drug dealer from St. Louis, Stub, noted the long-term consequences of not retaliating:

INTERVIEWER: So what did you do [after this happened]?

STUB: After that I got out [of the hospital], recuperated, and got back out [dealing drugs].

INTERVIEWER: What about this guy [that robbed you] though?

STUB: He got his . . . In so many details, he got his, he's no longer.

INTERVIEWER: He's no longer?

STUB: In existence.

when asked why he reacted as he did, this urban dealer explained:

STUB: See, you have to realize if I didn't get back at him you . . . could say [Stub's] a punk. Everybody can go take [Stub's] shit. So if he [gets] hurt, everybody knows who hurt him. They might not know exactly, but they have an idea. See, the thing is, if somebody robbed you and you in the dope game, you don't want to be robbed first off cause see then . . . I got the fucking city saying you can rob him. So if you handle your business, you ain't got to even worry about it cause they gonna say that time so-and-so robbed [Stub] and shit, [the robber] came up missing. So that gonna give them the fear right there not to fuck with you . . . That's very important if you gonna live that lifestyle. You need to let it be known you ain't gonna take no shit, you know what I'm saying? Fuck no, you'd be out of business . . . cause you would have people, little kids, coming up trying to rob you [thinking] he ain't gonna do nothing, he's a punk. (Topalli, Wright, and Fornango, 2002: 342–3)

To the extent retaliation deters the costs of victimization, then drug trade may last longer (i.e., occur more often) because its costs are reduced; yet the benefits remain the same or are enhanced. The flip side to this argument is that refraining from retaliation may, in the end, push the drug trader toward the end of that career—"you'd be out of business."

Market-Based Disputes, Retaliation, Rationality, and the Effect on Drug Trade

Retaliation may also have an effect on the price of drugs and, in turn, the rate of trade. Caulkins, Reuter, and Taylor (2006: 1–2) argue that the "nastiest dealers"— meaning the most violent ones—have a continuous cost advantage over their competitors. In effect, being nasty reduces the price of drugs, which earns them more customers and profit in the long run (i.e., a higher rate of sales). In theory, this reduction in price results from the ability "to secure advantageous physical locations from which to base their operations; these locations provide added protection from detection from law enforcement and thus lower costs of operation." Stated differently, when dealers use violence to obtain the best territory, they reduce the costs of law enforcement and this reduces the price for drugs offered to customers.

This notion is based on the standard economic premise that higher business-related risks, such as the likelihood of formal punishment, lead to higher prices. Thus, when a dealer uses violence to secure safer territory from which to sell drugs, the risks of selling are reduced and so the price of drugs should drop accordingly. And because dealers who sell for a lower price should attract more customers, their rate of trade should also increase if they manage to secure a safer area from which to sell. In essence, the argument proposed by Caulkins, Reuter, and Taylor (2006) suggests that retaliation may increase the rate of drug trading and reduce the price to the extent it provides dealers with a competitive advantage (see also Levitt and Venkatesh, 2000: 780).

This theory is especially interesting because it adds new insights into the victimization-centered theory proposed by Topalli, Wright, and Fornango (2002). If lesser risks for dealers lead to lower prices provided by them, then it stands to reason that when dealers deter victimization via retaliation, a similar reduction in price should occur. Retaliators thus may extend their involvement in drug dealing by gaining a market advantage from selling at a lower price than competitors who strike back less often or seriously.

Retaliation, Opportunity, and the Effect on Drug Trade

Retaliation is affected by opportunity, and the threat and act of retaliation affects the opportunity for drug trading. This issue involves a set of complex interactions. Consider a string of victimizations reported by a lower-class dealer known as East-Side Pimp:

> INTERVIEWER: [D]id any of your customers like steal from you . . .?
>
> EAST-SIDE PIMP: Oh I got ganked [i.e., stolen from], got ganked by some motherfucker. This dude, motherfucker didn't have no money. They got food stamps. You know you get the food stamps and they cancel the card

on your motherfucking ass and you don't see them for four or five months and then they return. By that time you got over it and you don't want to fuck the bastards back. When they come to you they got some money and you've forgotten all about what they owe you, so yeah.

INTERVIEWER: So is this some person in particular that does this to you?

EAST-SIDE PIMP: Yeah, a lot of motherfuckers that have done that to me with the food stamps, that's how they get you. They got the card, and you get the card and it's got so and so amount of money on it, and they get home and cancel the fucker and then they get another card and they do another motherfucker like that. And then when they do it to you, you don't see them.

INTERVIEWER: So have you ever done anything in retaliation to that? Like have you ever been threatened anyone or fucked anyone up?

EAST-SIDE PIMP: There's one broad [i.e., female] and I was aware of this cause I really needed it at the time, so I was pissed. She was dirty to me, and I ran up on her ass in my apartment, just to snipe shit out of her motherfucking ass, but that was it.

INTERVIEWER: What do you mean, "snipe the shit out of her"?

EAST-SIDE PIMP: I gave her $225 worth of fucking pain, fucking me out of those food stamps. I just smacked the shit out of her . . . And I felt better . . .

INTERVIEWER: Do you still sell to her?

EAST-SIDE PIMP: Yeah. This shit is a motherfucker.

INTERVIEWER: So she came back to you to buy from you and all that?

EAST-SIDE PIMP: But I won't fuck with her on a food stamp level, but yeah she got the money then I'll deal with her. And of course I cheat her.

INTERVIEWER: How do you do that?

EAST-SIDE PIMP: I give her less than what she pays for.

This account offers a few noteworthy insights. The opening lines demonstrate that retaliation is not always possible. Even though East-Side Pimp wanted to get even with the food stamp defrauders, this could not be done because they stayed away from him for "four or five months." These wrongdoers reduced the probability of retaliation against them by reducing one of the minimal elements required to strike back: contact between them and the dealer.

So by controlling the opportunity for retaliation, these wrongdoers were reducing the possibility of vengeance. But in doing so, they also were restricting the rate of drug sales that could occur. Put plainly, retaliation takes interaction, but so too does drug trading. When interaction is avoided as a way of managing retaliation, this inherently requires drug trading to be avoided as well—at least until the dealer has "forgotten all about" what is owed. We see, then, that although retaliation may decrease the price of sales and increase the frequency of trade (Caulkins, Reuter, and Taylor, 2006; Topalli, Wright, and Fornango, 2002), it may also have the inadvertent effect of scaring away customers and thereby reducing trade (see Levitt and Venkatesh, 2000: 758, 777). The chance of being punished for wrongdoing by an aggressive trader or getting caught in the crossfire of a market-based dispute is a risk that some people are unwilling to take.

The account also makes it evident that retaliation can be accomplished through fraud instead of through violence (Jacques, 2010). To a degree, the female food stamp defrauder was probably deterred from cheating East-Side Pimp again after he punished her with violence. The retributive satisfaction is clear when he says, "I felt better" afterwards. Nevertheless, East-Side Pimp continued to retaliate by ripping off the defrauder in later sales, a bit of tit-for-tat. As relates to the focus of this article, this retributive defrauding is interesting; in effect it raises the price of drugs because the customer is "give[n] less than what she pays for." In essence, then, the price of drugs has been increased as an act of retaliation, which added to the dealer's profits. This experience shows that retribution is especially beneficial when the payback involves stealing the wrongdoer's resources, which occurs in cases of retaliatory fraud, robbery, and theft.

In regard to opportunity theory, the very nature of fraudulent retaliation requires the wrongdoer and controller to engage in trade and to have agreed on terms of exchange (Jacques, 2010). Had the victimizer avoided East-Side Pimp— or at least curtailed future trades with him—then fraudulent retaliation could not have occurred.

At the same time, this discussion of retaliation leads to another opportunity- and rationality-based implication for drug trade. Retaliation takes time and effort, which are costs to the retaliator. This is especially true in cases of delayed, deferred, or calculated retaliation in which the offender must be identified, tracked down, or lured into a vulnerable situation (see Jacobs and Wright, 2006). Those who prey on drug dealers know this and employ a variety of techniques to manage the threat of retaliation, all of which have the effect of increasing the effort required to strike back at them (see Jacobs, Topalli, and Wright, 2000). Drug dealers who seek vengeance, therefore, do so at the cost of reduced drug sales, at least in the short term. The factors outlined earlier suggest that—for reasons related to rationality and opportunity—handling conflict with retaliation may decrease the rate of exchange. Fraudulent retaliation is perhaps an exception to this, as a minimal element for it is continued trade between the wrongdoer and the controller; however, the higher price paid by the wrongdoer may eventually lead this person away from engaging in trade with the retaliator.

Summary

Informal control premised on *lex talionis* aims both to reduce costs and to increase benefits. Punishing and deterring victimization or rivals is a way to reduce the costs of conflict in the long run, and, in turn, increase benefits not only through continued trade but also by gaining market advantage and greater profits. An added benefit from retaliation is obtained when the vengeance involves taking the wealth of the wrongdoer via violence (e.g., robbery), fraud, or stealth (e.g., burglary). For any particular seller, however, retaliation may backfire if scaring away potential victimizers and disputants comes at the cost of deterring potential trade partners. In addition, what must always be kept in mind is that retaliation takes time and thereby reduces opportunity for selling, except for fraudulent retaliation that, by its very nature, requires trade to occur and results in higher costs for the wrongdoer as part of the punishment.

The Effect of Negotiation on Drug Trade

Not all drug market disputes are managed through retaliation. Some disputants "talk out" the problem among themselves. Negotiation is management of conflict through a joint decision by the offender and the victim (Black, 1998: 83). This form of popular justice is measurable by the degree of convergence between disputants' ideas about what is right and wrong— including how to solve the dispute and move forward.

Negotiated conflict resolution may involve compensation, meaning the payment of wealth such as money or drugs, to right a wrong (Cooney, 2009). "Compensatory social control involves the payment of a debt from offender to their victims . . . Offenders are obligated to compensate victims for damage or other harm that they have suffered. Once restitution has been provided, the matter is settled" (Horwitz, 1990: 47).

Victimization, Negotiation, and the Effect on Drug Trade

Negotiation is beneficial to controllers to the extent it results in compensation from victimizers, who may perceive it as rational to pay up to avoid the costs of retaliation or to maintain a beneficial business relationship. A middle-class dealer, William, offended his supplier by failing to pay him for some drugs. The resulting conflict illustrates the effects of rationality and opportunity on negotiation. Although compensation has monetary benefits, obtaining them may require interaction between the victim and the offender and continued drug trading, which itself increases the profits of negotiation.

> INTERVIEWER: Did you ever get threatened while you were dealing?
> WILLIAM: No . . . One time when I first started dealing . . ., I bought a 20 pack [of ecstasy] and I had sold it for a decent amount of money. And we [—my friend and I—] went out, and I figured I still had ten left to sell and that would make my money back and I could still pay him back, so we went out and blew the money, you know, and I still had these ten. Well, me and my friends went back to his house, me and three friends, me and my three friends. We went back there and we took off the next day. [The supplier had] fronted it to me 'cause I wanted to get on my feet and I was like, [but I had to call him and say,] "I haven't got the money, you'll have to front me some more to get it." And I thought he was going to beat the hell out of me. This is the guy I got the rolls from.
> INTERVIEWER: What did he say to you?

WILLIAM: He was like, "Oh you need some more, let's sit down and talk about this." And I'm like, "Holy Shit!" I thought he was going to beat the fuck out of me. It would have been an even fight, . . . [but] I want to get stuff from him again so I'm gonna have to let him win! I mean I need him! So I went back to him and sat down and he was like, "All right," 'cause he knew I ate them too, "I don't want you to sell anything less than $20, here's a ten pack."

INTERVIEWER: What do you mean? . . .

WILLIAM: No rolls for less than 20. Let's see, I had bought the 20 pack for $280 . . . So he was like, "Here is a ten pack and I don't want you to sell any less than $20, and I want at least $200."

INTERVIEWER: So did you sell them for more?

WILLIAM: I had to sell them for more than $200 . . . [He said,] "I want you to come back with more than $200. I'll give you a price break since you're getting back up. So I'll give them to you for $12 apiece, so I had $120 worth of product and I had to come back with 200 so I'd knocked out 80 of my debt. And I came back two hours later with like 240 so I'd knocked out $120 of my debt, 160 to go. I did the same thing again and made it up to 160 bucks and that's when he bumped up my price back to $15. He had done the $12 apiece to help me out.

William's account demonstrates that rationality influences negotiation. Related to this is the fact that negotiation affects the benefits of drug trade, which is affected by its price and rate of occurrence. His conflict is somewhat complex in terms of how it was resolved, but it might be best summarized as follows: This dealer was fronted drugs but was not able to repay the debt when the time came. He knew he was in trouble with his supplier and even suspected the guy "was going to beat the fuck out of" him. Rather than retaliate, however, the supplier negotiated an agreement with William. The original debt was $280 (for 20 ecstasy pills priced at $14 each). To help William get "back up," the supplier gave him "a price break" by lowering the price per pill to $12. (Whether this is truly a price break is questionable because the supplier told William to "come back with more than $200" [$20 per pill sold], which is more profit per pill for the supplier than originally required.)

This business arrangement effectively allowed William to "knock . . . out 80 of [his] debt" and, as well, for the supplier to obtain the money he was owed. William did what was required and, in time, fully repaid his debt. After William's bad credit had been made good, he and his supplier began a more mutually beneficial partnership by continuing business with each other. In the short run, William's punishment involved paying a higher price for ecstasy and making less profit. Although not discussed in the quote, William and this supplier did continue to do business with each other for many more months—this was a long-term benefit of negotiation for both of the disputants. The supplier had someone to sell to and profit from, and William had a supplier to front him drugs that he could then turn into profit by selling them to users. Also, the supplier obtained short-term benefits from negotiation by gaining compensation for the delayed payment.

It is obvious that William was intent on remaining in this business relationship and willing to do almost anything to make restitution. He was even willing to lose a fight, saying: "I want to get stuff from him again so I'm gonna have to let him win! I mean I need him!" William had made a rational decision: He was willing to endure the pain of violence because he believed it was outweighed by the pleasures of profits from continued drug selling. We see, then, that the negotiation surrounding William's dispute had several effects on the price and rate of drug trading: in the short run, the controller (the supplier) increased the price per pill paid by the defrauder (William), and in the long run, both were allowed to continue or perhaps even increase their rate of drug trading.

This example of drug market conflict also sheds light on how opportunity shapes informal social control and drug trade. Negotiation requires being together and talking things out. After learning that William did not have his money, the supplier said, "Let's sit down and talk about this." The supplier could have ignored the infraction or ended the relationship, but instead he decided that the best way to proceed was to maintain contact and keep the lines of communication open. Similarly, William could have avoided the supplier, either out of fear of being beaten or out of disregard for his debt. In the end, however, both of them decided to "sit down and talk . . . things out."

Their negotiated agreement, moreover, required them to continue trading drugs with each other and, for William, with customers. In other words, fulfilling their joint agreement on how to resolve the dispute made it necessary for the supplier to front ecstasy to William, for him to sell drugs to people, and for William to pay back the supplier. The nature of negotiation, at least in this case, is that drug trade was an absolutely essential minimal element of exercising control and settling the conflict.

Market-Based Disputes, Negotiation, and the Effect on Drug Trade

Market-based disputes are handled with negotiation as well. Consider the case that follows, which again involves William, the same middle-class dealer who did not pay back his ecstasy supplier on time and was forced to pay compensation. This conflict was with a separate supplier in the business of pharmaceuticals. William deemed this person a wrongdoer for not adequately dividing up the stock for sale. For this reason, he negotiated a compromise with the supplier:

> WILLIAM: I had a dispute with one of my suppliers because the guy I got the Valiums from, I had got rid of about 5,000 in 2 days for him, and the next shipment came in at 10,000 and he gave me 5,000 and somebody else 5,000. I said "He's gonna take a week and a half to two weeks to do it, so at least give me 2,500 out of his." He was like, "No, he'll do that 5,000 in about three days." I was like, "Come on, I need some and the next shipment

doesn't come in for two weeks." I'm like, "I need some now." And so he went to this guy, call him Johnny. He went to Johnny and asked how many he had left and Johnny had about 3,500, and he was like, "Well I want 17." He said, "17 of them?" He said, "No, 1,700." He said, "Why?" He said "'Cause the other guy's already sold his 5,000." . . . So he gave him the 1,700, and that was what pissed me off was that he wouldn't get them all.

In this example, the likely result of negotiation is the facilitation of illicit pharmaceutical sales, with the more successful dealer receiving additional stock from one who could not move the product as quickly. This negotiation benefited William by allowing him to increase his trade.

SUMMARY

In sum, negotiation is a form of conflict management focused on benefits. Benefits may come from compensation or from continued drug trading between controller and wrongdoer. When people are motivated to maintain their business ties, then negotiation is especially likely. Like retaliation, however, negotiation requires time and effort, which may reduce the opportunity for trading with other persons.

The Effect of Avoidance on Drug Trade

Disputants are not always able or willing to negotiate or retaliate. Avoidance is popular justice involving the "curtailment of interaction with a person whose behavior is offensive" (Baumgartner, 1988: 11; Black, 1998: 79–83). Avoidance is measurable in time and pervasiveness. It can be everlasting or momentary and can encompass only one aspect of social interaction or all parts of life (Jacques and Wright, 2008a).

Avoidance is rational because it reduces the opportunity for victimization- and market-based disputes. Curtailing interaction clearly is an effective way of minimizing conflict. For better or worse, however, the nature of this form of control inhibits drug trading between the controller and the wrongdoer or that person's associates (in cases where collective avoidance is being exercised). Whether avoidance occurs, then, depends on if the perceived pain associated with potential future victimization (or disputes) outweighs the perceived pleasures of drug trade.

Market-Based Disputes, Avoidance, and the Effect on Drug Trade

Avoidance is a strategy for resolving market-based disputes, such as those regarding prices and territory. Consider the case of lower-class dealer $50-Holler, who cut off customers who were unable to pay the going price for drugs. For $50-Holler, an added benefit of avoidance—or really a reduced cost—was that it allowed him to refrain from retaliation:

> $50-HOLLER: I had to cut off these three customers last week. One dude got mad 'cause I told him that I ain't messing him with no more, ain't dealing with him no more.

INTERVIEWER: And why did you do that?

$50-HOLLER: 'Cause he came back and said he was short. He never had all the money, but he wanted the product, so I told him I'm cutting him short. "Go find someone else to get your shit from. I can't deal with your shit no more." He's like, "Come on man, please." But I'm like, "No man, get the fuck off. If you don't then I'm gonna beat your ass." . . . I had to turn a woman away. She offered me sex for it. I told her I don't want sex; I want money. She's like, "Please, I'll let you fuck me. I'll let you fuck my daughter." I said, "You let me fuck your daughter? Your daughter's 10 years old!" That really turned me off man. I told her, "I can't do that. If you don't go then I'll hurt you."

Sometimes people will use avoidance to prevent the escalation or continuation of disputes and to reduce the potential for retaliatory victimization. An interesting example of this comes from Smooth, a lower-class dealer:

INTERVIEWER: Have you ever had any problems with other dealers like when they get on your turf or they try to get you out of their space or anything like that? . . .

SMOOTH: It only happened to me one time when I first started off in the neighborhood. I was really young and sometimes I had more crack than a grownup had and they'd get mad and say, "Look at that!" They'd see me making some money, and they'd be like, "You can't sell, you ain't from around here," all that bullshit. Then I'd have to just lie low and go somewhere else or just do what I gotta do to get my money. Just hop in the car and ride; go downtown somewhere to sell it.

In this market-based conflict, Smooth had at least two conceivable courses of action: benefit from continuing to sell in the disputed territory but run the risk of being retaliated against for doing so or give in to the demands of his competitors, reduce his rate of trade in that territory, and set up shop somewhere else. Rather than fight a turf battle, Smooth reacted to this dispute through flight. In doing so, he saved himself and others from potential violence.

Victimization, Avoidance, and the Effect on Drug Trade

Avoidance also is used to handle conflicts springing from victimization. As noted, a cost of avoidance is that it reduces the opportunity for trade and the pleasures associated with it. Yet for this same reason, avoidance is a rational strategy for deterring victimization and for managing potential problems. Hoffer's (2006: 76) study of heroin sellers provides an example:

I noticed that Kurt [a seller] forgave lots of the money he could have insisted on collecting [from indebted customers]. Why? Extending credit and forgiving debts were reinforcements Kurt used for customers who were honest with him. Kurt immediately collected debts in full from customers who disrespected his rules. The ultimate punishment was not violence, but cutting the customer off so that they would no longer be able to buy heroin from Kurt. Enforcing the rules was easy for Kurt: all the customers knew the rules and how each rule related to the network's protection and safety. Breaking them was the customer's fault, and if they were cut off by Kurt, this action was justified.

It is evident from this example that avoidance is a conflict management strategy that deters victimization, albeit at the cost of reduced drug trading. Avoidance is used not only to deter victimization but also to handle transgressions that *already* have occurred. Many drug-dealing networks rely on "weak ties" (Granovetter, 1973) to bring drug-involved persons willing to make a transaction into contact with one another. Such ties often are precarious. Christopher, a middle-class drug dealer interviewed for our study, discussed his reaction to being swindled in a fraudulent trade: "A few days after the jacking, I felt like something had gotten around and now I was somebody that people could take advantage of. So, pretty much, at that point I stopped dealing with anybody in that crew [of people associated with the predator]. I don't remember dealing with anybody [again] who I thought would be part of them." In effect, being victimized in a fraudulent trade caused Christopher to avoid not only the offender but also all of his known or presumed associates, eliminating an unknown number of "could-have-been" future trades in the process. This response had the dual effect of lowering the chance of victimization and the frequency of drug trading.

Summary

In short, avoidance is rational in that it reduces the costs of conflict, but in doing so, it inhibits the opportunity for drug trading. Thus, avoidance's emphasis is on minimizing costs rather than on maximizing benefits. A caveat here is that—unlike retaliation and negotiation—avoidance typically takes little or no time and effort and this may increase the rate of trade. In addition, avoidance may actually reduce the price of drug sales by reducing the conflict costs of selling.

The Effect of Toleration on Drug Trade

Social control, formal or informal, is not an inevitable result of deviance. A ubiquitous alternative is toleration, defined as the absence of social control where it might otherwise have existed. "Although arguably not a form of conflict management at all, toleration is sometimes consciously advocated or adopted as the most effective response to deviant behavior, disagreement, or disruption" (Black, 1998: 88). Toleration is a quantitative variable "measurable by comparing what might otherwise occur under the same circumstances" (Black, 1998: 88).

Toleration may seem counterintuitive given the typical perception of drug markets as contexts rife with retaliation (Jacobs, 1999, 2000; Jacobs and Wright, 2006). Yet, in practice, toleration seems to be widespread in such markets. For instance, May and Hough (2001: 150) concluded that drug debtors often expect toleration from unpaid creditors: "In most cases there was an element of trust between buyer and seller—buyers could rely on the quality and size of their deal, and just under three quarters . . . received credit from their dealer. For those who received credit, three-quarters believed that *nothing* would happen if they could not repay the debt" (our emphasis).

Toleration, Rationality, and the Effect on Drug Trade

Toleration is valuable to disputants because it maintains the *status quo*. Toleration takes no time or effort, nor is it illegal. Therefore, disputants may prefer to do nothing rather than exercise more costly forms of informal control. Tolerating a grievance may allow for the reparation of formerly beneficial partnerships and thereby facilitate drug trading. There is a hint of this in a story told by Shot Caller, a lower-class dealer, who had grown weary of being retaliated against by a supplier he had offended:

> SHOT CALLER: I don't even lie; I disappeared all fucked up [when I got fronted one time and didn't pay it back]. You know [the supplier] was calling me and I wasn't answering the phone. Finally at the same spot where I met him, in the club, we bumped heads so he got his two little bodyguards onto me. They keep guns . . . I'm like, "Ah, here I go," but he said to me, "You spend too much money with me to be fucking with me like that, everything was so damn good, so what do you think I should do to you?" "Me? Shit!" So he gave me another chance, so I mean we laughed over it, got drunk over it. I was still sweating and nervous cause, "You a killer, you play it off, like it's all good." You know, I could be walking about that club and BOOM! You know he's bad as a doughnut, but he let me go cause I [bought] hundreds of pounds with him through the years. Fifteen years is a long time to be dealing with one person.

Drug traders will sometimes refrain from retaliation and other forms of popular justice for fear of subsequent retaliation, which may entail the cost of injury or theft. This is especially true for victimizers perceived to be unstable as a result of their drug problems. A middle-class seller, Dave, describes this chain of events:

> DAVE: I went over to an apartment complex, and he was with me and I dropped him off at the apartment complex where he knew about five or six other people who lived in that area, and as soon as he went up into the stairs he just didn't come out for like 30 minutes, and you just kinda figure it out—he's not coming back . . . I knew that there were other people that he knew that lived in the apartment complex that I didn't know, but it just kinda sucks because I thought I knew him; he always treated me nice in high school, he'd always invite us to parties and shit, he was a kid that was like a couple years older than us that was always cool. [Eventually] I talked to him up where I go to college. He just told me a bunch of crap like he was on a bunch of hardcore drugs, he just needed the money. It's gonna be tough getting it from him because he doesn't have that money.

INTERVIEWER: How much money was that?

DAVE: $1,000. He'd probably rather die than give me that money . . . He's just a psycho case who does way too much crack [cocaine] and stuff like that, so it just wasn't worth it.

As noted, a reputation for retaliation may deter potential trade partners. After all, who would want to do business with a vengeance-prone dealer? Tolerant persons are the best to do business with for the very reason that they are unlikely to apply control. A dealer interviewed by Topalli, Wright, and Fornango (2002: 348) said it best: "that shit's bad for business" (cf. Paoli, Greenfield, and Reuter, 2009: 207).

There is clearly a rational component to toleration, and this raises the question: How great are the benefits of retaliation, negotiation, and avoidance? The seriousness of the dispute has a part to play in determining the best course of action. As Smooth, a lower-class dealer, explained:

SMOOTH: Last time I gave credit I gave it to a dude, he wasn't one of my friends, he was an associate. He asked me if he could hold a sack, I let him hold it and I never got my money back.

INTERVIEWER: Like how much worth?

SMOOTH: I don't know, a 1.2—a gram and 2 tenths.

INTERVIEWER: And you never saw it back?

SMOOTH: No.

INTERVIEWER: Did you ever see him again?

SMOOTH: No.

INTERVIEWER: Did you go looking for him?

SMOOTH: No.

INTERVIEWER: No, you didn't care?

SMOOTH: No, $10 ain't gonna matter.

Toleration, Opportunity, and the Effect on Drug Trade

Toleration is less costly than retaliation or negotiation because the time and effort costs are nil. Yet unlike avoidance, the benefit of toleration is that it does not reduce the opportunity for trade. Although toleration may be a sign of weakness and susceptibility to predation, it does allow the buying and selling of drugs to continue. Drug traders realize this and often tolerate victimization as a result. In their study of drug market robbery and retaliation, Topalli, Wright, and Fornango (2002: 346) found the following:

A number of drug dealer/victims indicated that, in the absence of direct retaliation, the only way to recover from a robbery was simply to go back out and resume selling. For example, one seller who had been robbed three times by his own customers, stated, "I can always get $50. I just said fuck it. I said I ain't tripping off that . . . I'm gonna make that back anyway." These individuals not only were unwilling to suffer the potentially serious consequences of retaliating (i.e., counter-retaliation or arrest and incarceration), they also considered retaliation an inefficient use of time better spent hustling.

Victimizers seem to be aware that toleration is—at least for some drug traders and in some situations—a more rational response than applying social control. A study of drug *robbers* concluded that many of them did not worry about retaliation, believing that dealers are more concerned about making money than they are about getting back at the person who robbed them: "Time spent seeking retaliation can be better spent making money, and for many [dealers who are robbed], the opportunity cost of lost sales may be too high to justify the effort. As Blackwell put it, 'I don't think I'm . . . gonna get retaliated back on by them [drug dealers] 'cause they want to go back on the corner and sell drugs'" (Jacobs, Topalli, and Wright, 2000: 178).

Summary
At the heart of toleration is a willingness to proceed with life as is or to return to what it was. Ironically, toleration suggests that doing nothing affects drug trade. If we hold constant the possibility that toleration invites conflict, it seems that this form of informal control increases drug trading for reasons related to rationality and opportunity: It allows former business partnerships to continue; it does not scare away and might even attract trade partners; and it does not take any time or effort. What is more, toleration eliminates costs to controllers that may come from retaliation by wrongdoers who were themselves retaliated against, avoided by, or made to pay compensation. As regards price, because tolerating is the absence of action, the best guess is that it has no influence on price other than to maintain it at the present level; however, it may indirectly alter drug trade by inviting victimization or reducing counter-retaliation.

DISCUSSION AND CONCLUSION

It is commonly accepted that criminalizing a market reduces access to law among sellers and buyers and thereby encourages informal responses to victimization- and market-based disputes (Black, 1976, 1983; Jacobs and Wright, 2006; Reuter, 2010). If that is true, we hypothesize that formal control affects drug markets via an indirect effect on informal control. Taken together, the data presented here demonstrate that the different forms of informal control—retaliation, negotiation, avoidance, and toleration—all may affect the rate and price of drug trading in various ways. These effects are the product of both rationality and opportunity: 1) The form and amount of control enacted should be the one with the perceived greatest overall utility for the controller, which is determined in part by the effect on subsequent drug trading; and what must be kept in mind is that 2) the available options for control may be limited because each form requires minimal elements to occur and may require or inhibit drug trading between the controller and the wrongdoer.

Although this theory is seemingly straightforward, in reality, the effect of informal control—as a whole or for each form—on drug trade is complex. *Retaliation* has the most complex effect on drug trade. On the one hand, it has retributive and deterrent effects; retribution allows the controller to obtain respect or take the wrongdoer's wealth. Deterrence prevents future victimization and disputes and, in doing so, may increase the number of trades made over the course of a criminal career and reduce the price. On the other hand, a reputation for retaliation may conceivably scare away traders or take time away from making sales, which would reduce the rate of trade. *Negotiated compensation* has short-term costs for wrongdoers and benefits for controllers, but this type of informal control may benefit both parties in the long run by allowing trade to continue; like retaliation, however, time and effort spent on negotiation may reduce the opportunity for and, in turn, the amount of drug trading. *Avoidance* necessarily reduces trade between the controller and the wrongdoer, but unlike retaliation and negotiation, it may provide more time to trade with persons not being controlled; it also is plausible that avoidance reduces the price of drugs by lowering the probability of conflict and the costs associated with it. The nature of *toleration* suggests it should increase the rate of trade and either decrease the price or have no effect on it because it requires no time, effort, or minimal elements to occur; yet it might alter drug trade by inviting victimization or preventing counter-retaliation.

Policy Implication

The theoretical and empirical endeavor proposed in this article is important for reasons that extend beyond academia. Legislation and law enforcement are widely used tools to control drug markets (NRC, 2001; Zimring and Hawkins, 1992). Unfortunately, these efforts seem to have little effect on the price of drugs or on the amounts sold (MacCoun and Reuter, 2001). Perhaps even worse, what drug law *does* seem to do is deny drug market participants access to formal means of dispute resolution and thereby encourage participation in popular justice (Moskos, 2008).

Although these patterns increasingly are being recognized, practically no research has explored their interconnectedness (but see Caulkins, Reuter, and Taylor, 2006; Levitt and Venkatesh, 2000; Topalli, Wright, and Fornango, 2002). We simply do not know how, why, and to what degree the various forms of informal control affect the size and scope of illicit drug trade. Perhaps informal control significantly and substantially increases drug trading by reducing the price. Or maybe the opposite is true. Or maybe there is no effect at all. Or maybe it depends on the form of informal control and the context under consideration. Understanding such matters is crucial to the formulation of a rational and effective drug control policy. For this reason, we urge future research to develop this line of inquiry further, which will shed light on how the unintended consequence of drug law, a rise in a rise in popular justice—may be causing the intended or opposite effect, be it a net reduction or a net increase in drug trading.

REFERENCES

Baumgartner, M. P. 1988. *The Moral Order of a Suburb*. New York: Oxford University Press.

Bentham, Jeremy. 1988 [1789]. *The Principles and Morals of Legislation*. Amherst, NY: Prometheus Books.

Black, Donald. 1976. *The Behavior of Law*. New York: Academic Press.

Black, Donald. 1983. Crime as social control. *American Sociological Review*, 48:34–45.

Black, Donald. 1998. *The Social Structure of Right and Wrong*, rev. ed. San Diego, CA: Academic Press.

Bushway, Shawn D., and Peter Reuter. 2011. Deterrence, economics, and the context of drug markets. *Criminology & Public Policy*, 10:183–94.

Caulkins, Jonathan, and Peter Reuter. 2010. How drug enforcement affects prices. In *Crime and Justice: A Review of Research*, vol. 39, ed. Michael Tonry. Chicago, IL: University of Chicago Press.

Caulkins, Jonathan, Peter Reuter, and Lowell Taylor. 2006. Can supply restrictions lower price: Illegal drugs, violence and positional advantage. *Contributions to Economic Analysis and Policy* 5(Article 3).

Cohen, Lawrence E., and Marcus Felson. 1979. Social change and crime rate trends: A routine activity approach. *American Sociological Review*, 44:588–608.

Cohen, Lawrence E., James R. Kluegel, and Kenneth C. Land. 1981. Social inequality and predatory criminal victimization: An exposition and test of a formal theory. *American Sociological Review*, 46:505–24.

Coomber, Ross, and Lisa Maher. 2006. Street-level drug market activity in Sydney's primary heroin markets: Organization, adulteration practices, pricing, marketing and violence. *Journal of Drug Issues*, 36:719–53.

Cooney, Mark. 2009. *Is Killing Wrong? A Study in Pure Sociology*. Charlottesville: University of Virginia Press.

Cornish, Derek B., and Ronald V. Clarke, eds. 1986. *The Reasoning Criminal*. New York: Springer.

Decker, Scott H., and Margaret Townsend Chapman. 2008. *Drug Smugglers on Drug Smuggling: Lessons from the Inside*. Philadelphia, PA: Temple University Press.

Decker, Scott H., and Janet L. Lauritsen. 2002. Leaving the gang. In *Gangs in America III*, ed. C. Ronald Huff. Thousand Oaks, CA: Sage.

Denton, Barbara. 2001. *Dealing: Women in the Drug Economy*. Sydney, Australia: University of New South Wales Press.

Drug Enforcement Administration. 2010. *Compendium of Federal Justice Statistics, 2003*. http://www.justice.gov/dea/statistics.html.

Eck, John E. 1995. A general model of the geography of illicit retail marketplaces. In *Crime and Place*, eds. John E. Eck and David L. Weisburd. Monsey, NY: Criminal Justice Press.

Felson, Marcus. 1998. *Crime and Everyday Life*, 2nd ed. Thousand Oaks, CA: Pine Forge Press.

Felson, Marcus, and Ronald V. Clarke. 1998. *Opportunity Makes the Thief*. Crime Prevention and Detection Series, Paper 98. London, U.K.: Home Office.

Glaze, Lauren E., and Thomas P. Bonczar. 2009. *Probation and Parole in the United States, 2008*. Washington, DC: U.S. Department of Justice. http://bjs.ojp.usdoj.gov/content/pub/pdf/ppus08.pdf.

Goffman, Erving. 1969. *Strategic Interaction.* Philadelphia: University of Pennsylvania Press.

Goffman, Erving. 1974. *Frame Analysis: An Essay on the Organization of Experience.* Boston, MA: Northeastern University Press.

Goldstein, Paul J. 1985. The drugs/violence nexus: A tripartite conceptual framework. *Journal of Drug Issues,* 15:493–506.

Goldstein, Paul J., Henry H. Brownstein, Patrick J. Ryan, and Patricia Bellucci. 1997. Crack and homicide in New York City: A case study in the epidemiology of violence. In *Crack in America: Demon Drugs and Social Justice,* eds. Craig Reinarman and Harry G. Levine. Los Angeles: University of California Press.

Granovetter, Mark. 1973. The strength of weak ties. *American Journal of Sociology,* 78:1360–80.

Hoffer, Lee D. 2006. *Junkie Business: The Evolution and Operation of a Heroin Dealing Network.* Belmont, CA: Wadsworth.

Horwitz, Allan V. 1990. *The Logic of Social Control.* New York: Plenum Press.

Jacobs, Bruce A. 1999. *Dealing Crack.* Boston, MA: Northeastern University Press.

Jacobs, Bruce A. 2000. *Robbing Drug Dealers.* New York: Aldine de Gruyter.

Jacobs, Bruce A. 2010. Deterrence and deterrability. *Criminology,* 48:417–41.

Jacobs, Bruce A., Volkan Topalli, and Richard Wright. 2000. Managing retaliation: Drug robbery and informal sanction threats. *Criminology,* 38:171–98.

Jacobs, Bruce A., and Richard Wright. 2006. *Street Justice: Retaliation in the Criminal Underworld.* New York: Cambridge University Press.

Jacques, Scott. 2010. The necessary conditions for retaliation: Toward a theory of nonviolent and violent forms in drug markets. *Justice Quarterly,* 27:186–205.

Jacques, Scott, and Richard Wright. 2008a. The relevance of peace to studies of drug market violence. *Criminology,* 46:221–53.

Jacques, Scott, and Richard Wright. 2008b. The victimization–termination link. *Criminology,* 46:1009–38.

Jacques, Scott, and Richard Wright. 2010. Drug law and violent retaliation. In *Criminology and Public Policy: Putting Theory to Work,* 2nd ed., eds. Hugh Barlow and Scott H. Decker. Philadelphia, PA: Temple University Press.

King, Gary, Robert O. Keohane, and Sidney Verba. 1994. *Designing Social Inquiry: Scientific Inference in Qualitative Research.* Princeton, NJ: Princeton University Press.

Klinger, David A. 1997. Negotiating order in patrol work: An ecological theory of police response to deviance. *Criminology,* 35:277–306.

Laub, John H., and Robert J. Sampson. 2003. *Shared Beginnings, Divergent Lives: Delinquent Boys to Age 70.* Cambridge, MA: Harvard University Press.

Levitt, Steven D., and Sudhir A. Venkatesh. 2000. An economic analysis of a drug-selling gang's finances. *Quarterly Journal of Economics,* 115:755–89.

Lupton, Ruth, Andrew Wilson, Tiggey May, Hamish Warburton, and Paul J. Turnbull. 2002. *A Rock and a Hard Place: Drug Markets in Deprived Neighborhoods.* London, U.K.: Home Office.

MacCoun, Robert J., and Peter Reuter. 1997. Interpreting Dutch cannabis policy: Reasoning by analogy in the legalization debate. *Science,* 278:47–52.

MacCoun, Robert J., and Peter Reuter. 2001. *Drug War Heresies: Learning from Other Vices, Times, and Places.* New York: Cambridge University Press.

May, Tiggy, and Mike Hough. 2001. Illegal dealings: The impact of low-level police enforcement on drug markets. *European Journal on Criminal Policy and Research,* 9:137–62.

Moskos, Peter. 2008. *Cop in the Hood: My Year Policing Baltimore's Eastern District.* Princeton, NJ: Princeton University Press.

National Research Council (NRC). 2001. *Informing America's Policy on Illegal Drugs: What We Don't Know Keeps Hurting Us,* ed. Charles F. Manski, John V. Pepper, and Carol V. Petrie. Washington, DC: National Academies Press.

National Research Council (NRC). 2010. *Understanding the Demand for Illegal Drugs,* ed. Peter Reuter. Washington, DC: National Academies Press.

Paoli, Letizia, Victoria A. Greenfield, and Peter Reuter. 2009. *The World Heroin Market: Can Supply Be Cut?* New York: Oxford University Press.

Ratner, Mitchell S., ed. 1993. *Crack Pipe as Pimp: An Ethnographic Investigation of Sefor Crack Exchanges.* Lexington, MA: Lexington Books.

Reinarman, Craig, Peter D. A. Cohen, and Hendrien L. Kaal. 2004. The limited relevance of drug policy: Cannabis in Amsterdam and in San Francisco. *American Journal of Public Health,* 94:836–42.

Reuter, Peter. 2010. Systemic violence in drug markets. *Crime, Law and Social Change,* 52:275–89.

Reynald, Danielle. 2009. Guardianship in action: Developing a new tool for measurement. *Crime Prevention and Community Safety: An International Journal,* 11:1–20.

Rosenfeld, Richard, Bruce A. Jacobs, and Richard Wright. 2003. Snitching and the code of the street. *British Journal of Criminology,* 43:291–309.

Schelling, Thomas C. 1960. *The Strategy of Conflict.* Cambridge, MA: Harvard University Press.

Sevigny, Eric, and John P. Caulkins. 2004. Kingpins or mules: An analysis of drug offenders incarcerated in federal and state prisons. *Criminology & Public Policy,* 3:101–35.

Shadish, William R., Thomas D. Cook, and Donald T. Campbell. 2002. *Experimental and Quasi-Experimental Designs for Generalized Causal Inference.* Boston, MA: Houghton Mifflin.

Sifaneck, Stephen J., Geoffrey L. Ream, Bruce D. Johnson, and Eloise Dunlap. 2007. Retail marijuana purchases in designer and commercial markets in New York City: Sales units, weights, and prices per gram. *Drug and Alcohol Dependence,* 90(Suppl 1): S40–51.

Sparks, Richard F. 1982. *Research on Victims of Crime: Accomplishments, Issues, and New Directions.* Rockville, MD: National Institute of Mental Health.

Stanko, Elizabeth Anne. 1981–1982. The impact of victim assessment on prosecutors' screening decisions: The case of the New York county district attorney's office. *Law & Society Review,* 16:225–40.

Taylor, Angela P. 2007. *How Drug Dealers Settle Disputes: Violent and Nonviolent Outcomes.* Monsey, NY: Criminal Justice Press.

Topalli, Volkan. 2005. When being good is bad: An expansion of neutralization theory. *Criminology,* 43:797–836.

Topalli, Volkan, Richard Wright, and Robert Fornango. 2002. Drug dealers, robbery and retaliation: Vulnerability, deterrence and the contagion of violence. *British Journal of Criminology,* 42:337–51.

Wright, Richard, Scott H. Decker, Allison Redfern, and Dietrich Smith. 1992. A snowball's chance in hell: Doing fieldwork with active residential burglaries. *Journal of Research in Crime and Delinquency,* 29:148–61.

Zimring, Franklin E., and Gordon Hawkins. 1992. *The Search for Rational Drug Control.* New York: Cambridge University Press.

CHAPTER 16

A Perversion of Choice: Sex Work Offers Just Enough in Chicago's Urban Ghetto

Eva Rosen and Sudhir Alladi Venkatesh

Based on their interviews and participant observation of Chicago's sex work economy, the authors of this study argue that sex work is one part of an overall low-wage, off-the-books economy of resource exchange among individuals in a bounded geographic setting. To an outsider, the decision to be a sex worker seems irrational, but the authors argue that specific localized conditions invert this decision and render it entirely rational. For the men and women in the study, sex work acts as a short-term solution that "satisfices" the demands of persistent poverty and instability, and it provides a meaningful option in the quest for a job that provides autonomy and personal fulfillment.

This article examines the ways in which sex work has become a solution to the employment needs of the urban poor. We argue that sex work is a constituent part of an overall low-wage economy. Individual decisions to participate in sex work are framed in relation to other economic opportunities—including legal and off-the-books work. The data for the study is based on in-depth interviews and participant observation of Chicago's sex work economy over a year-long period.

What makes someone turn to sex work? To an outsider, the decision to be a sex worker in the ghetto may seem irrational, particularly given the nature of the work, the risks and stigma associated with it, and the low rate of remuneration (Murphy and Venkatesh 2006; Venkatesh 2006; Miller 1986). We suggest that in specific social contexts of limited labor market opportunities, this decision can

Source: Adapted from Rosen, E., & Venkatesh, S. A. (2008). A "perversion" of choice: Sex work offers just enough in Chicago's urban ghetto. *Journal of Contemporary Ethnography,* 37(4), 417–41.

be rational. For the men and women in our study, sex work offers a viable solution to the problem of income generation. Many view this segment of the underground economy as both a survival mechanism and as preferable relative to other available opportunities to earn income.

Our inquiry into sex work proceeds from the vantage point of low-wage labor. We do not see sex work as only a social problem that begs enforcement, policy, advocacy, and so on. Sex workers in the ghetto are certainly in need of assistance—many are impoverished, homeless, drug addicted, and involved in other dangerous activities. The challenge, however, is to see sex workers as more than simply victims—an outcome of the social problems approach. Our aim is to document the ways in which sex workers' choices are framed by a context of opportunities for earnings and self-efficacious behavior.

The women and men we studied have not been not forced into sex work, at least not overtly, and they do not have pimps. And, over the course of a month or year, they will move back and forth from sex work to other employment. We seek to understand the factors that push them into sex work. The men and women explained to us that sex work offers *just enough* money, stability, autonomy, and professional satisfaction. In other words, it meets a basic level of satisfaction of needs.

In the struggle to make ends meet, compromises must be made; sex work—although risky in many ways—is an attractive option because it allows sex workers to provide for themselves and their families in a situation of limited resources and job opportunities. We will argue that the sex work offers just enough money and flexibility to make the job worthwhile, and just enough autonomy and professional satisfaction to make it more attractive than other options.

THE PERVERSION OF CHOICE

In this section, we explore how the choice of sex work becomes a viable option in this community. We highlight three main factors: the structural factor of a tight job market, particularly for poor inner-city African Americans; the community context which legitimizes the decision to turn to sex work; and most importantly, the ways in which sex work emerges as a *better* option relative to others available, satisficing the needs of the sex workers by providing them with *just enough*.

Our notion of decision-making, which we call the *just enough* explanation, attempts to place agency at the center. When outside factors come into play—such as limited resources, education, information, or limited time—pure rationality is not possible, and so individuals make decisions using "bounded rationality," producing quick solutions in the immediate, local environment that enables them to solve a problem or choose among alternatives, even though the solution or choice is not necessarily optimal or desirable in the abstract. The solution or choice, to utilize the active phrasing, "satisfices." With this idea of bounded rationality, we argue that the men and women in our sample turn to sex work as a means of satisficing the problems and challenges posed by their

position in the labor market. Sex work offers *just enough* to meet their requirements for a job; it offers them some money, some stability, a certain amount of
autonomy, and even some sense of self-worth.

Jobs in the Ghetto

In his book, *When Work Disappears,* William Julius Wilson discusses the disappearance of employment opportunities for poor Black men and women in the
inner city. The disappearance of work in many inner-city neighborhoods is in
part related to the nationwide decline in the fortunes of low-skilled workers.
Changes in the class, racial, and demographic composition of inner-city neighborhoods contributed to the high percentage of jobless adults who continue to
live there. Wilson paints a picture of "the new urban poverty" (Wilson 1996, 19)
referring to poor segregated neighborhoods where the majority of working-aged
individuals are unemployed or are not part of the formal labor force. He emphasizes social psychological factors in addition to the cultural and social structural
factors in explaining the current situation of inner-city joblessness and poverty.
"The problems reported by the residents of poor Chicago neighborhoods are not
a consequence of poverty alone. Something far more devastating has happened
that can only be attributed to the emergence of concentrated and persistent joblessness and its crippling effects on neighborhoods, families, and individuals"
(Wilson 1996, 17).

The testimonies of the men and women in our sample confirm their exclusion
from the mainstream job market. Ricky, a thirty-two-year-old man, states: "If I
could do it differently I would have finished school, gone on to more school, probably gone on to college. Without an education I can't really do nothing. If I could
have a job in the office, but make the same money, I'd take the job." Many of the
sex workers in our study have concrete ideas about what kind of job they would
want if they had the opportunity. In response to the question, "If you could stop
[sex work] right now what would you do?" Sherry says, "I would start my own hair
business." "What's keeping you from getting a job in the hair business?" "I haven't
been to school. I have an ID problem. I don't have ID. You need ID to get ID. What
kind of fucked-up shit is that." Tracy says, "I have felonies and it's hard for me to
find work. If I get my background expunged then maybe I can find work."

Where jobs are not readily available, Wilson suggests that the urban poor
become used to unemployment, such that joblessness becomes a mindset (see
Wilson 1996, 52–53). People no longer have much hope when they look for work
in venues where they, their parents, and their peers have been rejected so many
times. They stop looking altogether—a common state for the men and women in
our sample, many of whom state that they will experience weeks or months without actively searching for work.

Community Context Legitimizes Sex Work

The personal accounts of the sex workers in our sample indicate the importance
of peer influence on their own individual choice. That is, when the time comes for

them to start earning money, they look at role models and peers to see what their options are. Here are two statements below; the first is from Tracy, a forty-six-year-old woman who has two grown children and has lived with her fiancé for seventeen years, whom she met first as a client. The second is from Amber, a twenty-one-year-old woman who used to work at McDonald's, and plans to stop doing sex work when she has a husband and children.

> TRACY: I had friends. I saw them doing it. Also, I have people in my family who did it so hustling has been around me. People in my family did it, I just never did. I had aunts who did it. They never talked about it to me directly, but I heard them talking about it. They know that I do it. My kids know. It's not hard to talk about. They know they have to eat, they know I gotta put food on the table.
>
> AMBER: I started when I was seventeen. I wasn't nervous or anything, I just wanted the money. I'm a strong person. The job didn't intimidate me, I was just doing it for the money. I saw what everyone else was doing, and I thought that I needed money. So I started.

These two women told us that they realized sex work was an option at a young age, and they were constantly encountering other women who viewed hustling on the streets as an acceptable way to make ends meet. The result was that sex work seemed feasible as an employment choice. Furthermore, many women and men in our sample stated that before they began doing sex work, they were propositioned by passersby on the street. This repeated propositioning eventually led them to consider the trade. For example, Jo, a thirty-four-year-old woman with three children at home, recounts what led to her first experience doing sex work:

> I'm walking down the street one day, you know, smoking . . . and a car pulled over, and I'm like, damn, you know, for sensual, for, you know [sex]. . . .
>
> Do you think it often happens that way?
>
> I'm not gonna say a hundred percent, but I believe it's a lot of times when females be walking down the street when they first get started. . . .

It is interesting to note that the men and women in our sample do not often express being in dire situations when they began sex work. Sherry, a forty-four-year-old woman who does not have children, explains how she entered the trade:

> I've been doing it all my life. It first started on my twenty-first birthday. I just tried it. I was just curious. You know if I'm curious about something I'll try it out. I was just curious. The first time it was nothing. I didn't know what I was looking for. I wasn't nervous. I don't know if I liked it, I didn't know what to look for. On my twenty-second birthday I tried it again.

Sherry and Priscilla did not engage in sex work out of desperation, which is in sharp contrast to conventional academic and popular wisdom. Sherry needed money—not unusual for young persons—which pushed her to look for work. Sex work was among the options readily available to her in the community. She knew of many others around her who sold sexual services. In this way, sex work became a plausible option. Nearly all of the men and women in the sample point out similar circumstances in their personal histories.

Sex Work Satisfices: Job Flexibility and Autonomy

For some, sex work is a *better* option than others that are available. It is useful to briefly consider one of the other readily available occupations open to men and women in this community, namely the fast food industry. Newman's work on low-income New Yorkers sheds light on the job situation for men and women in the inner city. She discusses the stigma attached to the fast-food industry, and argues that: "Even though we honor the gainfully employed over the unemployed, all jobs are not created equal. Fast food jobs, in particular, are notoriously stigmatized and denigrated" (Newman 1999, 89). The men and women in our sample confirmed that the nature of fast food work renders it highly distasteful. Ricky described his experience at the fast-food restaurant.

> I tried working at Popeye's, it was difficult. Because I was a man they expected me to do all this stuff. . . . The money wasn't even that good. I worked there for four months. I don't like people being in charge of me. That's what I like about this job, I'm in charge of myself, nobody is my boss. If I want to take a day off, I can, I can take a day off. I don't need to call anybody or anything like that. When you know the money is good you work [doing sex work], at Popeye's I was making minimum wage.

Ricky suggests that minimum wage was simply not sufficient to justify the work that he was doing at Popeye's. Tom, a thirty-six-year-old father of eight, also explains that his old job waiting tables "was pretty frustrating, I had to deal with big crowds of people who were rude."

The men and women in our sample tend to live at a basic level of sustenance. When asked what the primary benefit one can derive from sex work is, the answer most often given was "the money." The workers in our sample reported earning somewhere between ten and fifty dollars per client (for about thirty minutes with the customer), the majority earned in the twenty to thirty dollar range. If they see about ten clients a week on average, they can earn about two hundred to three hundred dollars a week. From a middle-class standard, this is not a substantial amount of money. However, this amount must be compared to other viable employment opportunities for low-income workers. For example, these wages from sex work are substantially higher (per hour) than a formal low-wage job such as McDonald's—and to earn at this rate, the men and women work far fewer hours. They are earning just enough to support themselves, the same amount of money as they would in a formal job. But combined with the flexibility that sex work allows them, sex work satisfies their practical need for income in a way that a formal job would not.

The flexibility that sex work offers is important for the urban poor because they may not have a permanent residence and their households are constantly under economic pressure. Therefore they look for work that allows for the erratic and unstable nature of their daily lives. In fact, for many it was the flexibility of sex work that propelled them into the trade. Ricky explains:

> I was about fifteen when I started hustling. I've been doing this continuously since I started. I started hustling on the street. . . . When I first started it was once in a while. When I got older, and I started needing stuff, I knew this was the quickest way I could get it. So it became like a regular routine, it became a job. It started feeling like that not after long. I was making money, I was saving money, paying bills. I left school in my senior year cause I was making so much money. I'd go to school, do my work, then go out and hustle.

Certainly, given that the men and women in the sample are predominantly poor, there is an aspect of desperation and survival that color their work choices. However, we have found that men and women say that sex work is the preferred low-income employment option—one that sustains them while offering them flexibility to develop other parts of their life.

This level of flexibility also means that there is time for other commitments and obligations. In our sample, the women in particular have children or relatives to care for in addition to partners and spouses who move in and out of their apartments. About 64 percent of the sex workers in our sample have children. In many cases, the children live with the parent, but sometimes the children live with a grandparent, or have been placed in foster homes by the state. For some men and women, sex work allows a parent to vacillate between working and free time, affording them the flexibility to go visit their children at a relative's house for periods of time. Also, there are often extended family members who move in and out of the homes of the subjects, and who experience their own ups and downs in the job market. Therefore, the number of people who live with a sex worker and for whom she is responsible—both financially and otherwise—is constantly in flux. Many say that because of these added responsibilities, it is not feasible to be working a regular, full-time shift. For example, Barbara, a thirty-eight-year-old mother of eight, explained that she used to work at McDonald's, but was fired because she often had to stay home and care for her children.

Many sex workers take advantage of the flexibility of sex work by combining it with other jobs—either in the formal market, or other forms of hustling. Sherry explains how sex work is intertwined with other kinds of work to provide a flexible solution for income.

> SHERRY: See, I'm an outgoing person. I'm a people person. As far as hustling, see, when I go do house cleaning that's a way of hustling. . . . See I'm a hustler and a helper. So if I can help people I like that. But also, I like to have a job where I can get something out of it. I'm an excellent housekeeper and sometimes housekeeping and hustling, the two mix.
>
> INTERVIEWER: Do you have any regulars?

SHERRY: I have a few, not many. Let me tell you this. Sometimes I do, sometimes I don't do it. To tell you the truth, it's not like I'm out there every day
all the time.

For Sherry, sex work can be used to make ends meet as necessary. From her perspective, it is a practical solution.

The perception of job autonomy contributes to the feeling that sex work is a
better option. At numerous points in the encounter sex workers exercise choice in
terms of when and where a trick occurs, for how much, and under what conditions. This kind of highly bounded self-efficacy leads to a sense of autonomy and
feelings of pride. Karen says, "I like it. I do it because I feel free. It depends on the
day and what I feel like doing." They also can decide which clients they will take,
and which they will refuse. If they don't like the look of someone, if they think the
person might not have the money to pay them, or if simply if the person smells
bad or gives them a bad feeling, they do not have to accept the offer. Robin says,

> I'm not afraid of my neighborhood. But you know, whatever happens is going to
> happen. You can't trust everybody. You always have to have your guard up. I
> make my choice about whether or not to go with somebody based on how they
> look, how they dress, how they smell, how they talk to me. If the respect isn't
> there, I'll say, "I'll see you later."

Robin frames her decision making in terms of preserving her self-respect. She
sets limits about what she will do with a client and where she will go. She says: "I
can't take the risk of working in a car, I still have a little respect. If he wants something he has to realize that I want something too, we have to meet halfway." This
aspect of control is extremely important in giving the sex workers a sense of autonomy. Although there may be other factors that have a role in whether or not
they take a client, they can and do exercise choice in clients. Laura explains how
she maintains her control through a sense of professionalism:

> I know what I want and I won't sell it for nothing less—it's the way you act, the
> way you carry yourself—you know all the men can walk in and they know you
> demand more money—the way you look, your appearance and everything, be-
> cause I don't know where it says that you have to be a filthy bug to be a working
> girl, that's not true. I brush my teeth every day, I shower, I do my hair, I stay
> clean, and it's okay, a lot of people, you know, certain individuals I don't date
> because, you know, they don't look right. You know, and I can be sick as hell and
> need some money, but you know, hey, that's where I draw the line. All money
> ain't good money.

Laura draws clear lines in the way that she offers her services; her ability to do
this contributes to her positive feelings about her work.

Men in particular seem to have a great deal of choice. Some of the men in our
sample saw both male and female clients, while others saw either only female or
only male clients. James, a fifty-seven-year-old man who sees only female clients,
professed very specific preferences and criteria for his clients. "I've been approached many times by male clients . . . but I just don't get down like that." Here,

again, we see disdain for the way that other sex workers operate, and pride in his own choices. "If you don't have boundaries, you don't have nothin'." For example, James chose not to accept female clients who were overweight. He says,

> I don't date fat women, I don't date big women. I don't. I like small women. Cause I don't wanna be hasslin' with all that and I don't care how much money you got I just ain't doin' it, and a lot of times I be approached by big women and I'm like damn. I can't do it . . . it's just how I am, I'm real with myself, so if I'm real with myself it, it ain't happenin'.

For James, "keeping it real" with himself (staying true to his personal preferences and principles) was a matter of self-respect. And if he is with a client who makes him uncomfortable, he removes himself from the situation:

> I don't get down like that. I have had people that transform on me, become a whole 'nother species of people, I be like damn, you didn't tell me you was like this. And so I'm gonna get the hell away from you cause, this is getting outta whack and in order to keep respect of myself and you, I'm gonna leave. And the best thing I can do is I'm gonna go.

Sex workers in our sample also controlled the acts they would perform with a client. Some preferred oral sex to penetration, while other preferred the opposite. Some preferred as little contact as possible, while others had few limitations. Jo explains what she would not do with a client:

> I don't have sex with guys, I give 'em head, but sex is something that I cherish so I don't have sex so much with these guys, know what I'm sayin, I turn sex down a lot, so I don't care how much money they got, because, I dunno, it's something about my body, it just means something to me . . .

In this way, Jo separates her work with clients from the sexual experiences in her personal life. Similarly, Sherry sets her own limits:

> I prefer doing stuff with feet, you know there're a lot of people out there who are into that kind of stuff. But as far as that goes I prefer posing, where there's no touching. No contact. I prefer that. Those are the kind of people I mostly deal with, people who just want me to pose. If they try to touch me, shoot, I'll leave. I'll do what I want to do, they can't pressure me into doing stuff like that.

Sherry and other sex workers suggest that in almost all cases, their clients accept the limits that are set.

In most cases, the sex workers in our sample negotiated their own wages with clients. When asked: "How do you determine what you charge them?" Jim responded: "I do it based on what we're going to do. I tell him what I charge for whatever he wants." Sherry says, "I [decide the prices]. If they don't like it— tough." Many sex workers also explained that they even charged on a sliding scale. Sherry explains: "But see it depends on how much each girl [sex worker] wants. I charge ten to fifteen dollars, whatever they have on them. If I think they have a lot of money I charge more. I don't really care whether or not they have a lot of money."

Although we have found that the main incentive for engaging in sex work is the perception of job autonomy, it is important to remember that it is just that, a perception. Although sex workers pride themselves in the range of choices that they have in terms of who they take as clients, what acts they perform and what boundaries they set, and their ability to negotiate payment, these negotiations take place within a set of circumstances that constrain their choices. Stated differently, they have autonomy over their work conditions, but it is quite limited. They can decide which client to take, they can decide where to go with the client, they can decide when they want to work; but, only to the extent there actually is variation in the choices *and* that the sex worker does not need money immediately. The choice is limited by many outside factors that dictate the extent to which the sex worker is truly capable of making an informed decision. These factors include the specific power relations between the sex worker and his or her client—determined by race, gender, socioeconomic background—and the fact that one party is using her body to perform a work-related task during the exchange. We can see that agency is therefore contingent, as it is negotiated according to the desires, intentions, and power of each interacting individual (Sanchez 1997, 545; Goffman 1967). These constraints do not render sex workers' choices and perceptions of autonomy irrelevant, but they do circumscribe them. They have just enough choice to make sex work a better job than the alternative. Just because it is *better* than the alternative doesn't mean it is *good* in itself, it merely satisfices.

Drug Use and Abuse

The issue of drug use further complicates motivations for women and men who engage in sex work. Sex workers like to control their use of drugs. Many of the men and women in our sample are what we would call "functional users"; that is, they use drugs for recreational purposes, while maintaining control over their lives and stability for their families. When asked, "Do you have a problem with drugs that plays a role in your sex work?" Tracy, a forty-six-year-old woman who started doing sex work when she was seventeen to support herself and her child, replied, "No. Sometimes I use drugs. I use drugs, drugs don't use me." Others separate their drug use from their professional activities. According to Sherry: "I think it's better to not be high [on the job] . . ."

Some of the subjects in our study made the choice not to use drugs at all. James chooses not to do drugs and explains that he doesn't like the way people around him act when they are high:

> I don't like to go through the scratch part, I ain't with that shit. I seen some of these girls, they do heroin . . . they scratch sores on them . . . I don't like getting stuck . . . The people that smoke this shit [crack] are transformers . . . that's what they become. Cocaine is the one . . . (mumbled). If you tell yourself you do stupid shit, stupid shit is what you do . . . People pop rocks through walls, and they go hidin' behind you puttin' a knife . . . and that's they sick ass that tell 'em to do that . . . and I see this a lot and I be talking to these people that do it and alright just don't do that shit in my face.

Although James looks down on those who do drugs, he is a heavy drinker. For him, drug and alcohol use are different: he feels that one can retain control over one's body while drinking, but not while high.

In contrast, many of the sex workers in our sample feel that they need to be high to do the work. Jim, a twenty-six-year-old man who sees both male and female clients, explains, "At the time [while working] I think about my addiction. If I was sober I'd be thinking about the consequences of what I'm doing. I can't be in that mode though. I have to be high to do it." For Jim, being high allows him to disengage from a practice that he otherwise finds unpleasant. Robin, a thirty-two-year-old woman who takes pride in "making ends meet" and not accepting money from the government, explains:

> I got one main guy. He gives me money to support my drug habit. It's not really like a relationship. I appreciate the things he does for me, but I'm not in love with him. He's got some issues. If I wasn't high I would not fuck with him. He's verbally abusive. But he gives me some money.

She says she sometimes puts up with abuse because she is high and cannot make proper judgments.

Men and women are also quick to point out that sex work can act as a Band-Aid, facilitating self-destructive behavior like drug addiction. Sex work is not a guaranteed, regular source of income, and it is not a labor option that enables sex workers to develop human capital. Unlike other kinds of underground income— e.g., making clothes or food and selling under the table—sex work is not viewed as possessing transferable skills. Few say that they learned how to become better businesspersons by participating in the sex-work trade.

Drug use also impedes the sex worker from seeking, and holding on to, jobs. When asked, "What keeps you from going back?" Valerie responds, "I just have to make my mind up to do it. I need to be more focused on what I do. I've just gotta get away from drugs." Valerie implies in this statement that the first step for her is getting off drugs, and the second is quitting sex work. When asked, "What's the worst part about the job?" Valerie answers in a way that echoes others in the sample: "I'm getting high all the time. All this time I'm getting high. I can't get away from it. I have to be high to be with a guy." At the same time though, as we mentioned above, many find the drugs necessary to bear the emotional costs of sex work. If the drugs are necessary to withstand sex work, and there is a need to sell sex to pay for the drugs, we can identify a self-perpetuating cycle. In Robert's words: "this business is addictive."

A unique characteristic of sex work—as opposed to jobs that require regular hours or high levels of concentration—is that it allows the men and women to earn an income while being users, as they are often unable to hold a steady job because of their habit. Money from sex work allows them to consume narcotics, with enough left over to continue paying rent and supporting their families. It also allows workers to use drugs on the job. In this way it is clear that sex work can act as a Band Aid, enabling men and women to sustain their drug addiction and keeping them in unstable circumstances. Here, the idea of *just enough* represents the delicate balance between sex work, drugs, and satisfaction, and the contradiction that sex work sustains and is sustained by drug use.

THE TENSION BETWEEN CHOICE AND EXPLOITATION

A final way in which sex work satisfices is in affording some sense of self-worth. Here, too, there is a tension between certain underlying feelings of exploitation and the simultaneous fulfillment that arises because one is developing close relationships with clients and providing them with a service. For sex workers, there is a tension between perceptions of being exploited and the feeling of fulfillment. Many sex workers in our sample report feelings of exploitation and degradation, as well as dissatisfaction with their situation. The nature of sex work—that is, using one's body—is not to be ignored. Many sex workers do express that this is difficult for them. Angie, a fifty-six-year-old woman who has two grown children, has been a sex worker since age eighteen, and says:

> Giving up my body is the hardest part of this work. But you know, I just gotta grit my teeth and clench my fists. At my age it's difficult. I'm doing a lot less of it. The only reason I do is the money, it has nothing to do with any type of satisfaction. . . . The worst job I've had is working on the streets, ain't nothing can catch that.

Many of the sex workers in our sample would like to be doing different work. Leslie is a thirty-seven-year-old woman who is planning to stop sex work when she moves out of state in a few months. She says "I don't fuck for a living"—she sees it as a temporary solution only. She says:

> The hardest thing is that I know I'm better than this, I know that I can do better, but based on the situation I'm in I gotta do what I gotta do. If I had another way, I'd do it. But right now it's the only thing I got. There isn't anything good about this, I never feel good about it. It doesn't make me happy. If I could something that was better for me I'd job to it.

Leslie is unhappy for two reasons. When she says, "I know I better than this," she is expressing that fact that she does not see the work as morally valuable. But she is also unhappy on a more individual level. She feels that she personally could do better, and that a different job would help her do this.

Despite these negative feelings about sex work, many women and men (sometimes even the same ones who expressed certain feelings of exploitation) identified a certain satisfaction in the work. Audrey is forty-five and has been a sex worker for twenty-five years. She has three kids, and sometimes feels uncomfortable about "catering to a specific person's wants," but she concentrates on sex work as a job and a means of earning money. She says:

> Prostitution is the best and worst job I've ever did. The money is great, the money is the best part. But the worst thing is the stuff they make you do. You

have to put yourself in degrading circumstances that just make you feel degraded.

At the same time she remarks:

> I would say that the money is good and that you're providing a service for somebody, you know they say prostitution is the oldest profession in the world—it came before the butcher, the baker, and the candlestick maker. It's just something that I got to do.

Many felt good about the personal service that they were providing to their clients. These positive feelings are often reflected in the terms that the sex workers used to describe their clients. For example, James refers to them not as "clients," "tricks," "customers," or even "friends" the way many of his peers do, but as "lovers." He professes,

> Love is the greatest gift God ever gave a human. Unconditional love. Now, you should be paid for it, because it's a big difference between fuckin', screwin', and making love. I don't fuck and I don't screw. Everything I do is with passion.

Since most of the workers in our sample dealt primarily with "regular" clients, they came to develop congenial relationships with them. When asked what advantages there were to sex work, Tony explained that "you meet interesting people," and he forged important and valuable "social connections" with his clients. He also explained that grateful clients often cared for him in return. He believed that there was mutual respect, such that the regular clients saw him as more than a street hustler, that "some don't care about the sex" as much as they do about the personal connection. These relationships become a source of satisfaction for the sex workers.

CONCLUSION: JUST ENOUGH

This article has examined the structure of the contemporary urban sex work trade from the vantage point of those toiling day to day. In economically depressed neighborhoods, sex work can turn out to be one of the few available means of subsistence—it is, for better or worse, steady work. We began the article by challenging the conventional picture often painted of sex workers, namely that they are primarily victims and otherwise passive agents who generally do not make active choices to better their lives. We find that sex workers are indeed saddled by impoverishment and limited socioeconomic opportunity, but they are also quite active in making decisions about their future. The men and women in our sample certainly do not describe the sale of sexual services as their overall employment preference. Instead, they enter (and return to) sex work by weighing other options for income generation—legal and illegal. In the inner city, sex work can emerge as a preferable labor market choice when menial low-wage work or other more dangerous forms of underground material gain are the options. And the decision to pursue sex work—whether to begin participating or return to the trade—quickly becomes a plausible means of solving pressing economic demands. As such, it may be viewed as a rational decision given their context of social mobility opportunities.

We have drawn on the concept of "satisficing" to suggest that the choices individuals make exhibit rational dimensions, while being constrained. True, sex work fulfills certain needs—monetary and emotional—but the concept of "satisficing" also helps us understand that women and men's needs are only nominally fulfilled via sex work. Sex workers on the street never make enough money or attain enough security to move on with their lives in less dangerous, and more mainstream, economic arenas. They are trapped in worlds of low-wage work. Nevertheless, individuals are attuned to some of the tangible benefits of sex work, such as flexibility and untaxed cash. Notably, the perceptions of job autonomy in sex work are without parallel in other available low-wage professions. The stability is a ruse, if one takes a long-term perspective. That is, the work offers men and women just enough to deter them from seeking another—perhaps less risky—job. The money is just enough to sustain a drug habit; some are able to functionally use while others spiral into instability. There is just enough room for choice to make them feel autonomous, while still being objectively rather constrained. In other words, although sex work is a better option, it is not necessarily a good option.

REFERENCES

Bagley, C. 1997. Child sex rings: Marginal, deprived and exploited children. In *Children, sex and social policy: Humanistic solutions for problems of child sexual abuse.* Brookfield: Avebury.

Barrett, D. 1998. Young people and prostitution: Perpetrators in our midst. *International Review of Law, Computers & Technology,* 12 (3): 475–86.

Barry, K. 1979. *Female sexual slavery.* New York: New York University Press.

———. 1995. *The prostitution of sexuality.* New York: New York University Press.

Bell, H., and C. Todd. 1998. Juvenile prostitution in a midsize city. *Journal of Offender Rehabilitation,* 27 (3/4): 93–105.

Bell, L., ed. 1987. *Good girls/bad girls: Feminists and sex trade workers fact to face.* Seattle: The Seal Press.

Bernstein, E. 1999. What's wrong with prostitution? What's right with prostitution? Comparing markets in female sexual labor. *Hasting's Women's Law Journal,* 10: 91–117.

———. 2001. The meaning of purchase. *Ethnography,* 2 (3): 389–452.

Brock, D. R. 1998. *Making work, making trouble: Prostitution as a social problem.* Toronto: University of Toronto Press.

Brown, M. 1978. Teenage prostitution. *Adolescence,* 14: 665–80.

Chapkis, W. 1997. *Live sex acts: Women performing erotic labor.* Routledge: New York.

Dalder, A. L. 2004. *Lifting the ban on brothels.* The Hague: Netherlands Ministry of Justice.

Decker, J. 1979. *Prostitution: Regulation and control.* Littleton, CO: Rothman.

Delacoste, F., and P. Alexander. 1998. *Sex work: Writings by women in the industry,* 2nd ed. San Francisco: Cleis Press.

Dworkin, A. 1981. *Pornography: Men possessing women.* New York: Putnam.

Elias, J., L. Vern, V. Bullough, V. Elias, and G. Brewer, eds. 1998. *Prostitution: On whores, hustlers, and johns.* New York: Prometheus Books.

Edin, K., and L. Lein. 1997. *Making ends meet: How single mothers survive welfare and low-wage work.* New York: Russell Sage Foundation Publications.

Farley, M. 2004. Bad for the body, bad for the heart: Prostitution harms women even if legalized or decriminalized. *Violence Against Women,* 10: 1087–125.

Giobbe, E. 1991. Prostitution: Buying the right to rape. In *Rape and sexual assault III: A research handbook,* edited by A. Burgess. New York: Garland Press.

Goffman, Erving. 1967. *Interaction ritual.* New York: Pantheon.

Halldorson, J. L. 1998. Voices from the shadows: Canadian children and youth speak out about their lives as street sex trade workers. *Out From the Shadows: International Summit of Sexually Exploited Youth Project.* Canada: National Summary.

Hwang, S. 2004. Juveniles' motivations for remaining in prostitution. *Psychology of Women Quarterly,* 28 (2): 136.

Inciardi, J. 1984. Little girls and sex: A glimpse at the world of the "Baby Pro." *Deviant Behaviour,* 5: 77–8.

———. 1995. Crack, crack house, sex, and HIV risk. *Archives of Sexual Behavior,* 24 (3): 249–69.

James, J., and J. Meyerding. 1977. Early sexual experience and prostitution. *American Journal of Psychiatry,* 134: 1.

Jeffrey, L. A., and G. MacDonald. 2006. "It's the money, Honey": The economy of sex work in the Maritimes. *Canadian Review of Sociology and Anthropology,* 43 (3): 313.

Jeffreys, S. 1997. *The idea of prostitution.* North Melbourne, Australia: Spinifex.

Klinger, K. 2003. Prostitution, humanism and a woman's choice. *The Humanist,* 63: 1.

Kurtz, S., H. Surratt, J. Inciardi, and M. Kiley. 2004. Sex work and "date" violence. *Violence Against Women,* 10 (4): 357–85.

Laner, M. R. 1974. Prostitution as an illegal vocation: A sociological overview. In *Deviant behavior: Occupational and organizational bases,* edited by C. Bryant, 177–205. Chicago: Rand McNally.

Leigh, C., ed. 1994. In defense of prostitution: Prostitutes debate their "choice" of profession. *Gauntlet,* 1 (7).

MacKinnon, C. 1989. *Toward a feminist theory of the state.* Cambridge, MA: Harvard University Press.

Maher, L., and K. Daly. 1996. Women in the street-level drug economy. *Criminology,* 34 (4): 465–91.

McClintock, A. 1992. Screwing the system: Sexwork, race, and the law. *Boundary,* 2 (19): 70–95.

McIntyre, S. 1999. The youngest profession—the oldest oppression: A study of sex work. In *child sexual abuse and adult offender new theory and research,* edited by C. Bagley and K. Mallick. London: Ashgate.

Miller, E., and K. Romenesko. 1989. The second step in double jeopardy: Appropriating the labor of female street hustlers. *Crime and Delinquency,* 35 (1): 109–35.

Miller, E. M. 1986. *Street woman.* Philadelphia: Temple University Press.

Monto, M. 2004. Female prostitution, customers, and violence. *Violence Against Women,* 10: 160–8.

Murphy, A., and S. Venkatesh. 2006. Vice careers: The changing contours of sex work in New York City. *Qualitative Sociology,* 29: 129–54.

Nagle, J. 1997. *Whores and other feminists*. New York: Routledge.

Nandon, S. M., C. Koverola, and E. H. Schludermann. 1998. Antecedents to prostitution: Childhood victimization. *Journal of Interpersonal Violence*, 13: 206–21.

Newman, K. S. 1999. *No shame in my game: The working poor in the inner city*. Westminster, MD: Alfred A. Knopf Incorporated.

Pavetti, L. 1993. *The dynamics of welfare and work: Exploring the process by which women work their way off welfare*. The Malcolm Weiner Center for Social Policy, The Kennedy School of Government, Harvard University, Dissertation Series #D-93-1.

Pheterson, G. 1993. The whore stigma: Female dishonor and male unworthiness. *Social Text*, 37: 39–64.

———., ed. 1989. *A vindication of the rights of whores*. Seattle: The Seal Press.

Potterat, J. J., R. B. Rothenberg, S. Q. Muth, W. W. Darrow, and L. Phillips-Plummer. 1998. Pathways to prostitution: The chronology of sexual and drug abuse milestones. *Journal of Sex Research*, 35: 333–40.

Raphael, J., and D. L. Shapiro. 2004. *Sisters speak out: the lives and needs of prostituted women in Chicago*. Chicago: Center for Impact Research.

Raymond, J. 1998. Prostitution as violence against women: NGO stonewalling in Beijing and elsewhere. *Women's Studies International Forum*, 21: 1–9.

Sanchez, L. 1997. Boundaries of legitimacy: Sex, violence, citizenship, and community in a local sexual economy. *Law and Social Inquiry*, 22: 543–80.

Satz, D. 1995. Markets in women's sexual labor. *Ethics*, 106 (1): 63–85.

Scott, M. 2001. *Street prostitution*. Washington, DC: U.S. Department of Justice.

Silbert, M., and A. Pines. 1982. Entrance into prostitution. *Youth and Society*, 13: 471–500.

Simon, Herbert. 1976. *Administrative behavior*, 3rd ed. New York: The Free Press.

Simons, R., and L. Whitbeck. 1991. Sexual abuse as a precursor to prostitution and victimization among adolescent and adult homeless women. *Journal of Family Issues*, 12: 361–79.

St. James, M. and P. Alexander. 1993. In *Making it work: Prostitutes' rights movement in perspective*, edited by V. Jenness. Piscataway, NJ: Aldine Transaction.

Sycamore, M. B. 2000. *Tricks and treats: Sex workers write about their clients*. New York: Harrington Park Press.

Venkatesh, S. A. 2006. *Off the books: The underground economy of the urban poor*. Cambridge, MA: Harvard University Press.

Weitzer, R. 2005. New directions in research on prostitution. *Crime, Law, and Social Change*, 43: 211–35.

Wilson, W. J. 1996. *When work disappears*. New York: Vintage Books.

Zatz, N. 1997. Sex work/sex act: Law labor and desire in construction of prostitution. *Signs*, 22 (2): 277–308.

SECTION VII

Gangs and Crime

This section examines gangs and crime. Gangs are not a new phenomenon in the United States. They have been around since the early 1800s, when gangs such as the Forty Thieves, Bowery Boys, Dead Rabbits, Roach Guards, and the like battled to gain control of their territories in New York City (Etter, 2012). Despite the long prevalence of gangs in the United States, these groups are still not well understood. Gangs are known to use violent tactics to intimidate and protect their turf/neighborhoods, to control trade such as illegal drugs, to commit acts as revenge, and to control others. In recent years, the criminal justice system and academic researchers have demonstrated a renewed interest in gangs as these groups have increased sharply in both numbers and violence. The National Youth Gang Center (2015) estimates that there are over 850,000 gang members in the United States today, which represents an increase over recent years. Gangs are dispersed across the United States but tend to be more concentrated in larger cities.

Unlike the turf-oriented gangs of the 1950s and 1960s, the gangs of today are heavily involved in a variety of criminal activities, including drug trafficking. Some experts have described modern street gangs as the new urban tribes because they combine themselves into self-administered structures to help them conduct their criminal enterprises and avoid the police (Etter, 1998). Many gangs have adopted a pseudo-warrior culture to facilitate their criminality. In many cases, gang membership is determined along racial or ethnic lines. Some gangs operating in the United States view themselves as race warriors, street warriors, or road warriors (Etter, 2012).

This section contributes to our understanding of gangs. In Chapter 17, "Gang-Related Gun Violence: Socialization, Identity, and Self," Paul B. Stretesky and Mark R. Pogrebin examine how gang socialization leads to gun violence, as well as the role that guns play in protection efforts and "impression management"— that is, the ways they serve to project and protect a tough gang reputation. The researchers discover that gangs serve as agents of socialization that assist in shaping their members' sense of self and identity. The authors argue that guns are far more important to the daily lives and identities of gang members than most policymakers might imagine, because they help project a reputation and create respect. The authors argue that if gang culture could be changed through the re-socialization of gang members, gun-related gang violence might significantly decrease. These findings suggest strategies for reduction in gun violence.

In recent years, female gang activity has increased considerably. Where women once served primarily in adjunct roles, mixed-gender gangs have become more common. In Chapter 18, "Gender and Victimization Risk Among Young Women in Gangs," Jody Miller draws from interviews of 20 female gang members to examine gender and victimization in gangs. She discovers that female gang members experience considerable levels of victimization not only at the hands of their gang peers, but also from other gangs. The author points out that joining a gang often involves submission to victimization at the hands of other members, and that gang activities thereafter place female gang members at risk for further victimization.

In Chapter 19, "Voices from the Barrio: Chicano/a Gangs, Families, and Communities," Marjorie S. Zatz and Edwardo L. Portillos look at the relationships among gang members, their families, and other residents of poor Chicano and Mexican barrios in Phoenix. The authors interviewed 33 youth gang members and 20 adult neighborhood leaders and youth service providers. Zatz and Portillos conclude that listening to the multiple voices of community members allows for a multifaceted understanding of the complexities and contradictions of gang life, both for the youths and for the larger community. The authors draw on a community ecology approach to help explain the tensions that develop, especially when community members vary in their desires and abilities to control gang-related activities. They discuss ways in which gender, age, education, traditionalism, and level of acculturation can help explain variation in the type and strength of private, parochial, and public social control within a community.

REFERENCES

Etter, G. (1998). Common characteristics of gangs: Examining the cultures of the new urban tribes. *Journal of Gang Research, 5*(2), 19–33.

Etter, G. (2012). Gang investigation. In M. L. Birzer & C. Roberson, eds., *Introduction to criminal investigation.* Boca Raton, FL: CRC, pp. 313–34.

National Gang Center. *National Youth Gang Survey Analysis.* Retrieved October 25, 2015, from http://www.nationalgangcenter.gov/Survey-Analysis

CHAPTER 17

Gang-Related Gun Violence: Socialization, Identity, and Self

Paul B. Stretesky and Mark R. Pogrebin

To examine how violent norms are transmitted in street gangs and to examine socialization as a mechanism between gang membership and violence, the authors interviewed 22 Colorado inmates convicted of gang-related gun violence. These data were obtained from a subset of respondents in a larger study of gun violence (see Chapter 11 in this volume). The median age of the respondents was 25 years, although they were much younger at the time of the offense for which they were incarcerated. At the time of the interviews, the respondents had been incarcerated an average of 4.7 years. Thirteen of the subjects were African American, five were white, three were Hispanic, and one was Asian. All had been convicted of violent gun-related crimes, including murder, manslaughter, robbery, and kidnapping. All but one was male. The researchers found that gangs are important agents of socialization that help shape a gang member's sense of self and identity. In addition, inmates reported that whereas guns offered them protection, they were also important tools of impression management that helped to project and protect a tough reputation. The findings provide greater insight into the way gang socialization leads to gun-related violence and has implications for policies aimed at reducing that violence.

INTRODUCTION

This study considers how gangs promote violence and gun use. We argue that socialization is important because it helps to shape a gang member's identity and sense of self. Moreover, guns often help gang members project their violent identities. As Kubrin (2005, p. 363) argues, "The gun becomes a symbol of power

Source: Adapted from Stratesky, P. B., & Pogrebin, M. R. (2007). Gang-related gun violence: Socialization, identity and self. *Journal of Contemporary Ethnography, 36*(1), 85–114. © Sage Publications, 2007.

and a remedy for disputes." We examine the issue of gang socialization, self, and identity formation using data derived from face-to-face qualitative interviews with a sample of gang members who have been incarcerated in Colorado prisons for gun-related violent crimes. Our findings, although unique, emphasize what previous studies have found—that most gangs are organized by norms that support the use of violence to settle disputes, achieve group goals, recruit members, and defend identity.

Before our analysis of gang members, we briefly review the literature on the relationship between gangs, crime, guns, and violence. In that review, we emphasize the importance of socialization and the impact of gangs on identity and self. We explain how guns help gang members shape and convey their identity. Finally, in our discussion, we relate our findings to the relative efficacy of different intervention strategies that are focused on reducing gang violence.

GANGS AND VIOLENCE

Research suggests that gang members are more likely than nongang members to engage in crime—especially violent crime (Gordon et al., 2004). According to Thornberry et al. (1993, p. 75), the relationship between gang affiliation and violence "is remarkably robust, being reported in virtually all American studies of gang behavior regardless of when, where, or how the data were collected." Whereas the relationship between gangs and violence is pervasive, "little is known about the causal mechanisms that bring it about" (Thornberry et al., 1993, p. 76). Do gangs attract individuals who are predisposed to violence or do they create violent individuals? The debate in the literature about these explanations of gang violence is rather extensive.

Thornberry et al. (1993) point out that there are three perspectives that inform the debate concerning the relationship between gangs and violence. First, the selection perspective argues that gang members are individuals who are delinquent and violent before joining the gang. Thus, gang members are individuals who are likely to engage in violent and deviant behavior even if they are not gang members (Gerrard, 1964; Yablonsky, 1962). From this perspective, what makes gang members more criminal than nongang members is that criminal individuals have self-selected or been recruited into gangs. The second perspective is known as the social facilitation perspective. This perspective argues that gang members are no different from nongang members until they enter the gang. Therefore, the gang serves a normative function. In short, the gang is the source of delinquent behavior because new gang members are socialized into the norms and values of gang life, which provides the necessary social setting for crime and violence to flourish. The enhancement perspective is the third explanation for the relationship between gang and crime (Thornberry et al., 1993). The enhancement perspective proposes that new gang members are recruited from a pool of individuals who show propensity to engage in crime and violence, but their level of violence intensifies once they enter the gang because the gang provides a structure that encourages crime and violence (see also Decker & Van Winkle, 1996).

According to McCorkle and Miethe (2002, p. 111), the second and third explanations for gang-related crime are the most popular explanations in the literature because both perspectives rely on the assumption that social disorganization increases socialization into the gang subculture, which produces crime. Recent criminological research suggests that the enhancement perspective is the most likely explanation for the association between gang involvement and criminal behavior. For instance, Gordon et al. (2004) discovered that individuals who join gangs are, in general, more delinquent than their peers *before* they join the gang. However, Gordon et al. also found that violent behavior among individuals who join a gang significantly increases *after* they become gang members. Although the work by Gordon et al. provides some answers concerning the potential causal mechanisms of gang violence, it still leaves open the question about why gang members increase their violent behavior after they join a gang. It is for that reason that we focus our research on the concept of socialization as a mechanism that leads to gang-related gun violence.

GANG SOCIALIZATION

Research on gang socialization—the process of learning the appropriate values and norms of the gang culture to which one belongs—suggests that group processes are highly important (Miller & Brunson, 2000; Sirpal, 1997; Vigil, 1988;). In addition, Moore (1991) believes that many city gangs have become quasi-institutionalized. In these cities, gangs have played a major role in ordering individuals' lives at the same time that other important social institutions such as schools and families play less of a normative role (see also Bjerregaard & Lizotte, 1995; Blumstein, 1995; Bowker & Klein, 1983; Vigil 1988). Vigil (1988, p. 63) has found that gangs help to socialize "members to internalize and adhere to alternative norms and modes of behavior and play a significant role in helping . . . youth acquire a sense of importance, self-esteem, and identity." One way to attain status is to develop a reputation for being violent (Anderson, 1999). This reputation for violence, however, is likely to develop (at least to some degree) after an individual joins a gang.

The reasons individuals join gangs are diverse (Decker & Van Winkle, 1996). According to Decker and Van Winkle (1996), the most important instrumental reason for joining a gang is protection. In addition to instrumental concerns, a large portion of all gang members indicate that their gang fulfills a variety of more typical adolescent needs—especially companionship and support, which tend to be more expressive in nature. That is, the gang is a primary group. The idea that the gang is a primary group into which individuals are socialized is not new. For instance, long ago Thrasher (1927, p. 230) pointed out,

> [The gang] offers the underprivileged boy probably his best opportunity to acquire status and hence it plays an essential part in the development of his

personality. In striving to realize the role he hopes to take he may assume a tough pose, commit feats of daring or vandalism, or become a criminal.

Thus, gang violence may often be viewed as expressive in nature. The value of masculinity as a form of expression plays an important role in gang socialization (Miller & Decker, 2001). Oliver (1994) argues that gang violence is often a method of expressing one's masculinity when opportunities to pursue conventional roles are denied. Acts of manhood, note Decker and Van Winkle (1996, p. 186), are "important values of [a member's] world and their psyches—to be upheld even at the cost of their own or others' lives." Katz (1988) also believes violence plays an important and acceptable role in the subculture of people living in socially isolated environments and economically deprived areas because violence provides a means for a member to demonstrate his toughness, and displays of violent retaliation establish socialization within the gang.

According to Short and Strodtbeck (1965; see also Howell, 1998), a good portion of all gang violence can be attributed to threats to one's status within the gang. Gang membership, then, helps to create within-group identity that defines how group members perceive people outside their formal organizational structure. By way of altercasting (i.e., the use of tactics to create identities and roles for others), gangs cast nonmembers into situated roles and identities that are to the gang's advantage (Weinstein & Deutschberger, 1963). Altercasting, then, is an aggressive tactic that gangs often use to justify their perception of other gangs as potentially threatening rivals, and it is used to rationalize the use of physical violence against other gangs. If the objective of a gang is to be perceived by the community, rival gangs, law enforcement officials, and others in a particular way, then their collective group and individual identities will be situated in these defining situations. Even though there is a good deal of research examining the important relationship between violence and status within the gang as it relates to socialization, little is known about the specific ways that status impacts gang violence.

Socialization into the gang is bound up in issues of identity and self. Identity, according to Stone (1962), is the perceived social location of the person. Image, status, and a host of other factors that affect identity are mostly created by group perceptions of who we are and how we define ourselves. "People see themselves from the standpoints of their group and appropriate action in relation to those groups becomes a source of pride" (Shibutani, 1961, p. 436). Berger (1963, p. 92) notes that "identities are socially bestowed, socially maintained, and socially transformed."

Moore (1978, p. 60) has suggested that "the gang represents a means to what is an expressive, rather than an instrumental, goal: the acting out of a male role of competence and of 'being in command' of things." The findings of Decker and Van Winkle (1996) and Moore suggest that although instrumental reasons for joining a gang are important, once a member joins a gang they largely see the gang as an important primary group that is central to their lives and heavily influences their identity and personality. Because this is a primary group, the approval of gang peers is highly important. It is this expressive reason for remaining in a gang that may help to explain gang crime and violence, especially as it relates to socialization. Hughes and Short (2005) provide insight into the area of identity and gang violence. Specifically, they find that when a gang member's identity is challenged, violence is often a result—especially if the challenger is a stranger. If a gang member does not comply with gang role expectations when they are challenged, the result may be a loss of respect. It is important to project a violent reputation to command respect and deter future assaults. Walking away from conflict is risky to one's health (Anderson, 1999). Gang members must by necessity make efforts to show a continued commitment to role expectations to the group (Lindesmith & Strauss, 1968). From this perspective, it appears that character traits that are a consequence of being socialized into street gangs may result in youthful acts of violence through transformations in identity (Vigil, 1996).

Initiation rights are one important aspect of identity formation (Hewitt, 1988; Vigil, 1996). Initiation rites that new gang members are obligated to go through demonstrate commitment to the gang and attest to an individual's desire to gain official membership in the organization. Hewitt (1988) argues that these types of acts help create a "situated self," where a person's self can be defined and shaped by particular situations. Thus, notions of identity formation are highly consistent with notions of gang violence as a function of social facilitation and enhancement perspectives in that they explain why gang members may increase their levels of crime and violence once they join the gang. Moreover, research suggests that the more significant the relationship to a gang is, the more committed an individual is to a gang identity (Callero, 1985; Stryker & Serpe, 1982). In short, gangs provide a reference group for expected role behavior and shape a member's identity and sense of self (Callero, 1985). The greater the commitment a person has to a gang identity, the more frequently that person will perform in ways that enact that identity, ways that include acts of violence (Stryker & Serpe, 1982).

Guns also play an important role in many gangs and are often reported to be owned for instrumental reasons (Decker & Van Winkle, 1996). Gang members who perceive a threat from rival gangs are believed to carry guns to protect themselves and their neighborhoods (Decker & Van Winkle, 1996; Horowitz, 1983; Lizotte et al., 1994; Wright & Rossi, 1986). Gang membership "strongly and significantly increases the likelihood of carrying a gun" (Thornberry et al., 2003, p. 131). However, the reason that gang members carry guns is still unclear. It is likely that in addition to instrumental reasons for carrying a gun, gang members carry guns for expressive reasons (Sheley & Wright, 1995). That is, guns provide gang members with a sense of power, which may be extremely important in identity formation. Guns help gang members project a tough image. Thornberry et al. (2003, p. 125) report that gang members who carry guns may feel "emboldened to initiate criminal acts that they may otherwise avoid."

Sociologists have long recognized that symbols are important indicators of identity. This is especially true of gangs (Decker & Van Winkle, 1996; Vigil, 2003). Gang members often display symbols of gang membership, and this is part of being socialized into the role of a gang member:

> Wearing gang clothes, flashing gang signs, and affecting other outward signs of gang behavior are also ways to become encapsulated in the role of gang member, especially through the perceptions of others, who, when they see the external symbols of membership respond as if the person was a member. (Decker & Van Winkle, 1996, p. 75)

Bjerregaard and Lizotte (1995, p. 42) argue that it is plausible that "juveniles are socialized into the gun culture by virtue of their gang membership and activity."

Although there is some indication that gang members are more likely to own guns than nongang members prior to joining a gang, gang membership also clearly appears to increase the prevalence of gun ownership. Bjerregaard and Lizotte (1995) believe that future research needs to focus on why gang membership encourages gun ownership. In this vein, Sanders's (1994) research on drive-by shootings provides some insight into why gang membership may encourage gun ownership. Drawing on Goffman's (1961) notion of realized resources, Sanders argues that gangs are organizations that provide the necessary context for drive-bys. Sanders is clear when he states that guns and cars are the least important resource in producing drive-bys. However, it is also true that guns are necessary for drive-bys to occur and as such are an important part of gang culture to the extent that drive-bys help gang members "build an identity as having heart" (Sanders, 1994, p. 204). Thus, notions of character and identity provide a way to look at drive-by shootings as a product of the gang structure, where guns are important instruments in building identity. Given the importance of guns to a gang member's identity, it is interesting to note that little research exists that examines the relationship between guns and gangs in terms of identity formation.

FINDINGS

We divide our findings into four sections. First, we focus on our subjects' socialization into the gang and the impact that socialization has on their self and identity. Second, we explore the importance of gang commitment as reinforcing a gang member's self and identity. Third, we focus on masculinity as a central value among gang members. During our discussions of masculinity, gang members often referred to notions of respect and reputation. Reputation is a way that gang members can project their image of masculinity to others. Respect was often referenced when their masculine identity was challenged. Finally, we focus on the importance of guns as instruments central to the lives of our gang members in the sense that they help project and protect masculine identities.

Gang Socialization, Self, and Identity

Goffman (1959) argues that as individuals, we are often "taken in by our own act" and therefore begin to feel like the person we are portraying. Baumeister and Tice (1984) describe this process as one where initial behaviors are internalized so that they become part of a person's self-perception. Once initial behaviors are internalized, the individual continues to behave in ways consistent with his or her self-perception. Related to the current study, the socialization process of becoming a gang member required a change in the subject's self-perception. That is, who did our gang members become as compared with who they once were? Social interaction is highly important in the process of socialization because it helps create one's identity and sense of self, as Holstein and Gubrium (2003, p. 119 [emphasis added]) point out:

> As personal as they seem, ourselves and identities are extremely social. They are hallmarks of our inner lives, *yet they take shape in relation to others: We establish who and what we are through social interaction.* In some respects, selves and identities are two sides of the same coin. Selves are the subjects we take ourselves to be; identities are the shared labels we give to these selves. We come to know ourselves in terms of the categories that are socially available to us.

Most inmates we interviewed appeared to indicate that their socialization into the gang began at a relatively young age:

> At about 15, I started getting affiliated with the Crips. I knew all these guys, grew up with them and they were there. . . . I mean, it was like an influence at that age. I met this dude named Benzo from Los Angeles at that time. He was a Crip, and he showed me a big wad of money. He said, "Hey man, you want some of this?" "Like yeah! Goddamn straight. You know I want some of that." He showed me how to sell crack, and so at 15, I went from being scared of the police and respecting them to hustling and selling crack. Now I'm affiliated with the Crips; I mean it was just unbelievable.

Another inmate tells of his orientation in becoming a member of a gang. He points out the glamour he associated with membership at a very impressionable age:

> I started gangbanging when I was 10. I got into a gang when I was 13. I started just hanging around them, just basically idolizing them. I was basically looking for a role model for my generation and ethnic background; the main focus for us is the popularity that they got. That's who the kids looked up to. They had status, better clothes, better lifestyle.

One of our black study participants residing with his father in a predominantly white, suburban community felt estranged from the minority friends he had in his former neighborhood. He discussed his need to be among his former peers and voluntarily moved back to his old neighborhood:

> A lot of the people that lived where my father was staying were predominantly white. I mean, not to say I didn't get along with white kids, but, you know, it was just two different backgrounds and things of that nature.

His racial and socioeconomic identification in the white community, where he resided with his father, offered little opportunity for him to fit in. When he returned to the city, he became involved with a gang quite rapidly:

> I started getting charged with assaults. Gang rivalry, you know, fighting, just being in a gang.

Because he was better educated and did not use street vernacular as his peers did, our participant claims he had to continually prove his racial proclivity to his peers:

> Other kids would call me "whitewash" because I spoke proper English. Basically, I wanted to be somebody, so I started hanging around with gang bangers. I was planning on being the best gang member I can be or the best kind of criminal I can be or something like that.

Consistent with Goffman's (1959) observations, once our subjects became active gang members, their transformation of identity was complete. That is, consistent with the notion of social facilitation and enhancement perspectives (Thornberry et al., 1993), the self-perceptions and identity of the subjects in our study appear to have changed from what they were before joining the gang. Shibutani (1961, p. 523) explains such changes by claiming that a person's self-perception is caused by a psychological reorientation in which an individual visualizes his world and who he thinks he is in a different light. He retains many of his idiosyncrasies, but develops a new set of values and different criteria of judgment.

Violent behavior appeared to play an important role in this transformation of identity and self. Most gang members noted that they engaged in violent behavior more frequently once they joined the gang.

> At an early age, it was encouraged that I showed my loyalty and do a drive-by ... anybody they [gangster disciples] deemed to be a rival of the gang. I was going on 14. At first, I was scared to, and then they sent me out with one person and I seen him do it. I saw him shoot the guy.... So, in the middle of a gang fight I get pulled aside and get handed a pistol, and he said, "It's your turn to prove yourself." So I turned around and shot and hit one of the guys [rival gang members]. After that, it just got more easier. I did more and more. I had no concern for anybody.

A further illustration of situated identity and transformation of self is related by another inmate, who expresses the person he became through the use of violence and gun possession. Retrospectively, he indicates disbelief in what he had become.

> As a gang banger, you have no remorse, so basically, they're natural-born killers. They are killers from the start. When I first shot my gun for the first time at somebody, I felt bad. It was like, I can't believe I did this. But I looked at my friend, and he didn't care at all. Most gang bangers can't have a conscience. You can't have remorse. You can't have any values. Otherwise, you are gonna end up retiring as a gang banger at a young age.

The situations an individual finds oneself in, in this case collective gang violence, together with becoming a person who is willing to use violence to maintain membership in the gang, is indicative of a transformed identity. Strauss (1962) claims that when a person's identity is transformed, they are seen by others as being different than they were before. The individual's prior identity is retrospectively reevaluated in comparison with the present definition of a gang member. Such a transformation was part of the processional change in identity that our prisoners/gang members experienced.

Commitment to the Gang

> As a creature of ideas, man's main concern is to maintain a
> tentative hold on these idealized conceptions of himself, to
> legitimate his role identities.
> —MCCALL & SIMMONS, 1966, p. 71

Commitment to the gang also serves individual needs for its members. We found that gang identification and loyalty to the group was a high priority for our subjects. This loyalty to the gang was extreme. Our subjects reported that they were willing to risk being killed and were committed to taking the life of a rival gang member if the situation called for such action. That is, gang membership helped our subjects nourish their identity and at the same time provided group maintenance (Kanter, 1972). As Kanter (1972) points out, the group is an extension of the individual and the individual is an extension of the group. This notion of sacrifice for the group by proving one's gang identification is expressed by an inmate who perceives his loyalty in the following terms:

> What I might do for my friends [gang peers] you might not do. You've got people out there taking bullets for their friends and killing people. But I'm sure not one of you would be willing to go to that extreme. These are just the thinking patterns we had growing up where I did.

Another inmate tells us about his high degree of identity for his gang:

> If you're not a gang member, you're not on my level. . . . Most of my life revolves around gangs and gang violence. I don't know anything else but gang violence. I was born into it, so it's my life.

The notion of the gang as the most important primary group in a member's life was consistently expressed by our study subjects. Our subjects often stated that they were willing to kill or be killed for the gang in order to sustain their self-perception as a loyal gang member. This extreme degree of group affiliation is similar to that of armed services activities during wartime. The platoon, or in this case, the local gang, is worth dying for. In this sense, the notion of the gang as a protector was an important part of gang life. All members were expected to be committed enough to aid their peers should the need arise. The following gang member points to the important role his gang played for him in providing physical safety as well as an assurance of understanding:

> That's how it is in the hood, selling dope, gangbangin', everybody wants a piece of you. All the rival gang members, all the cops, everybody. The only ones on your side are the gang members you hang with.

For this particular member, his gang peers are the only people he perceives will aid him from threatening others. The world appears full of conflicting situations, and although his gang affiliation is largely responsible for all the groups that are out to harm him in some way, he nevertheless believes his fellow gang members are the only persons on whom he can depend.

Violence against rival gangs was a general subject that the majority of the inmates interviewed discussed freely. However, only a few of our study participants focused on this subject compared with the less violence-prone gang-affiliated inmates. The violent gang members perceived other gangs as ongoing enemies who constantly presented a threat to their safety. As our literature review suggests, there is some debate about whether gang members would be violent without belonging to a gang, or if formal membership in the group provided them with the opportunity to act out this way. However, we find clarity in the inmate accounts that a gang member's identity provided the context necessary to resort to violence when confronted with conflicting events, as the following inmate notes:

> I have hate toward the Crips gang members and have always had hate toward them 'cuz of what they did to my homeboys. . . . I never look back. I do my thing. I always carry a gun no matter what. I am a gang member, man! There are a lot of gang members out to get me for what I done. I shot over 40 people at least. That's what I do.

This perception of being a person who is comfortable with violence and the perception of himself as an enforcer type characterizes the above inmate's role within his gang. Turner (1978) suggests that roles consistent with an individual's self-concept are played more frequently and with a higher degree of participation than roles that are not in keeping with that individual's self-concept. Our study subject in this situation fits Turner's explanation of role identity nicely. His hatred for rival gangs and his willingness to retaliate most likely led to his incarceration for attempted murder.

Masculinity, Reputation, and Respect

For those gang members we interviewed, socialization into the gang and commitment to the gang appear to be central to the notion of masculinity. That is, all gang members we interviewed spoke of the importance of masculinity and how it was projected (though the creation of a reputation) and protected (through demands for respect). The notion of masculinity was constantly invoked in relation to self and identity. In short, masculinity is used to communicate to others what the gang represents, and it is used to send an important signal to others who may wish to challenge a gang's collective identity. A gang member's masculine reputation precedes him or her, so to speak. On an individual level, similar attributes apply as well.

> Whatever an individual does and however he appears, he knowingly and unknowingly makes information available concerning the attributes that might be imputed to him and hence the categories in which he might be placed. . . .

The physical milieu itself conveys implications concerning the identity of those who are in it. (Goffman, 1961, p. 102)

According to Sherif and Wilson (1953), people's ego attitudes define and regulate their behavior toward various other groups and are formed in concert with the values and norms of that person's reference group. They formulate an important part of their self-identity and their sense of group identification. For our gang member study population, the attributes that the gang valued consisted of factors that projected a street image that was necessary to sustain. It was a survival strategy.

Masculinity

"Every man [in a gang] is treated as a man until proven different. We see you as a man before anything." This comment by a gang member infers that masculinity is a highly valued attribute in his gang. The idea of manhood and its personal meanings for each interviewed prisoner was a subject consistently repeated by all participants. It usually was brought up in the context of physical violence, often describing situations where one had to face danger as a result of another's threatening behavior or testing of one's willingness to use physical force when insulted by someone outside of the group.

> Even if you weren't in one [gang], you got people that are going to push the issue. We decide what we want to do; I ain't no punk, I ain't no busta. But it comes down to pride. It's foolish pride, but a man is going to be a man, and a boy knows he's going to come into his manhood by standing his ground.

Establishing a reputation coincides with becoming a man, entering the realm of violence, being a stand-up guy who is willing to prove his courage as a true gang member. This strong association between a willingness to perpetrate violence on a considered rival, or anyone for that matter, was a theme that defined a member's manhood. After eight years in the gang, the following participant was owed money for selling someone dope. After a few weeks of being put off by the debtor, he had to take some action to appease his gang peers who were pressuring him to retaliate.

> I joined the gang when I was 11 years old. So now that I'm in the gang for eight years, people are asking, "What are you going to do? You got to make a name for yourself." So we went over there [victim's residence], and they were all standing outside, and I just shot him. Everybody was happy for me, like "Yeah, you shot him, you're cool," and this and that.

A sense of bravado, when displayed, played a utilitarian role in conflicting situations where a gang member attempts to get others to comply with his demands by instilling fear instead of actually utilizing violent means. Having some prior knowledge of the threatening gang member's reputation is helpful in preventing a physical encounter, which is always risky for both parties involved. Again, the importance of firearms in this situation is critical.

> The intimidation factor with a gun is amazing. Everybody knows what a gun can do. If you have a certain type of personality, that only increases their fear of

you. When it came to certain individuals who I felt were a threat, I would lift my
shirt up so they would know I had one on me.

In this case, the showing of his firearm served the purpose of avoiding any altercation that could have led to injury or even worse. Carrying a gun and displaying
it proved to be an intimidating, preventative factor for this gang member. The
opposite behavior is noted in the following example of extreme bravado, where
aggressive behavior is desired and a clear distinction (based on bravery) between
drive-by shootings and face-to-face shootings is clear.

If someone is getting shot in a drive-by and someone else gets hit, it is an accident. You know, I never do drive-bys. I walk up to them and shoot. I ain't trying
to get anyone else shot to take care of business.

A final example of masculinity and bravado, as perceived by this particular study
participant, illustrates his commitment to being a stand-up guy, a person who
will face the consequences of gang activity. The situation he discussed had to do
with his current incarceration. Here he explains how he adhered to the gang
value of not being a snitch and refused to provide information about rival gang
members' involvement in two homicides to the police, which could have helped
in his prosecution for murder.

I know what I did [gang war murder], you know what I mean? I'm not gonna
take the easy way out [snitch on rival gangs for two homicides]. I know what I
did. I'm facing my responsibility.

An interesting note in this scenario has to do with the above inmate's continued
loyalty to the values of his gang when he was outside of prison. His information
on the rival gang's homicides most likely could have had the criminal charges
against him reduced, and subsequently, he would have received a lesser prison
sentence. We are taking into consideration that the inmate's cultural code is similar if not the same as the gang code, and our study participant was simply adher-
ing to the same value system.

The image of toughness fits well under masculinity and bravado as an attribute positively perceived by gang members we interviewed. Its importance lies in
projecting an image via reputation that conveys a definition of who the collective
group is and what physical force they are willing to use when necessary. A clear
explanation of this attribute is related by the following subject.

Everybody wants to fight for the power, for the next man to fear him. It's all
about actually killing the motherfuckers and how many motherfuckers you can
kill. Drive-by shootings is old school.

The implication here is that having a collective reputation for being powerful
motivates this prisoner. He notes that the tough image of shooting someone you
are after instead of hiding behind the random shooting characterized by drive-
bys projects an image of toughness and power.

There are others who prefer to define their toughness in terms of physical fighting without the use of any weapons—though it was often noted that it was too difficult to maintain a tough reputation under such conditions. For instance, the predicament the following gang member found himself in is one where rival gangs used guns and other lethal instruments, and as a result of this, his reputation as an effective street fighter proved to be of little value. In short, his toughness and fighting skills were obsolete in life-threatening encounters.

> Like my case, I'm a fighter. I don't like using guns. The only reason I bought a gun was because every time I got out of the car to fight, I'd have my ribs broken, the back of my head almost crushed with a baseball bat. I was tired of getting jumped. I couldn't get a fair fight. Nobody wanted to fight me because I had a bad reputation. Then I decided, why even fight? Everybody else was pulling guns. It's either get out of the car and get killed or kill them.

The fact that this prisoner had good fighting skills ironically forced him to carry a gun. The rules of gang fighting found him outnumbered and unarmed, placing him in a very vulnerable position to defend himself. The proliferation of firearms among urban street gangs is well documented by Blumstein (1995) and others. Lethal weapons, mainly firearms, drastically changed the defining characteristics of gang warfare in the late 1980s and 1990s, when most of our study subjects were active gang members in the community.

Reputation

On a collective group level, developing and maintaining the gang's reputation of being a dangerous group to deal with, especially from other groups or individuals who posed a threat to their drug operations, was important. The following inmate points out the necessity of communicating the gang's willingness to use violent retaliation against rivals. Guns often played an important role in the development and maintenance of reputation, though they were rarely utilized in conflicting situations:

> We had guns to fend off jackers, but we never had to use them, 'cause people knew we were straps. People knew our clique, they are not going to be stupid. We've gotten into a few arguments, but it never came to a gun battle. Even when we were gangbangin', we didn't use guns, we only fought off the Bloods.

In addition to a collective reputation, the group serves the identifying needs of its individual members (Kanter, 1972). Our study participants related their need to draw upon the reputation of the gang to help them develop their own reputation, which gave them a sense of fulfillment. People want to present others with cues that will enhance desired typifications of who they are. They desire to present who they are in ways that will cause those they interact with to adhere to their situated claims (Hewitt & Stokes, 1975). The following participant discusses the way gang affiliation enhanced his reputation as a dangerous individual, a person not to be tested by others.

> There are people that know me; even ones that are contemplating robbing me know of me from the gang experience. They know if you try and rob me [of drugs and money], more than likely you gonna get killed. I was gonna protect what was mine. I'll die trying.

Another study subject perceives gang membership differently. He attained a reputation through gang activity, and guns clearly played an important role in that process.

> Fear and desire to have a reputation on the streets made me do it. When I got into the streets, I saw the glamour of it. I wanted a reputation there. What better way to get a reputation than to pick up a pistol? I've shot several people.

Although each prisoner/gang member interviewed expressed a desire to be known in the community for some particular attribute, there were some gang members who simply wanted to be known, sort of achieving celebrity status.

> You basically want people to know your name. It's kind of like politicians, like that, you wanna be known. In my generation, you want somebody to say, "I know him, he used to hang around with us."

Respect

One constantly associates the subject of disrespect in gang vernacular with retaliatory violence. Interactions with rivals stemming from an affront to one's self-image often became the excuse to use a gun to redeem one's reputational identity. Strauss (1969) argues that anger and withdrawal occur when a person is confronted with a possible loss of face. For our subjects, this anger was apparent when rivals challenged their self-identity (i.e., when our subjects were disrespected).

According to the gang members we talked to, disrespect, or rejection of self-professed identity claims by others, often was the cause of violence. Violence is even more likely to be the result of disrespect when no retaliatory action may lead to a loss of face. The following inmate relates his view on this subject in general terms.

> Violence starts to escalate once you start to disrespect me. Once you start to second guess my manhood, I'll fuck you up. You start coming at me with threats, then I feel offended. Once I feel offended, I react violently. That's how I was taught to react.

The interface of their manhood being threatened seems to be directly associated with Strauss's (1962) concept of identity denial by an accusing other. This threat to one's masculinity by not recognizing another's status claims is apparently an extremely serious breach of gang etiquette.

> When someone disrespects me, they are putting my manhood in jeopardy. They are saying my words are shit, or putting my family in danger. . . . Most of the time, I do it [use violence] to make people feel the pain or hurt that I feel. I don't know no other way to do it, as far as expressing myself any other way.

Hickman and Kuhn (1956) point out that the self anchors people in every situation they are involved in. Unlike other objects, they claim that the self is present in all interactions and serves as the basis from which we all make judgments and plans of reaction toward others who are part of a given situation. When being confronted by gang rivals who have been perceived as insulting an opposing gang member, the definition of street norms calls for an exaggerated response. That is, the disrespectful words must be countered with serious physical force to justify the disrespected individual's maintenance of self (or manhood). A prime example of feeling disrespected is discussed in terms of territory and the unwritten rules of the street by one gang member who told us of an encounter with a rival gang who disrespected him to the point that he felt he was left with no other alternative choice of action but to shoot them.

> So, as we were fighting, they started saying that this was their neighborhood and started throwing their gang signs. To me, to let somebody do that to me is disrespect. So I told them where I was from.

A little while later the gang members in question showed up in our study subject's neighborhood and shot at him as he was walking with his two small children to a convenience store to get ice cream. He continues to recite the tale:

> I was just so mad and angry for somebody to disrespect me like that and shoot. We got a rule on the street. There is rules. You don't shoot at anybody if there is kids. That's one of the main rules of the street. They broke the rules. To me that was telling me that they didn't have no respect for me or my kids. So, that's how I lost it and shot them. I was so disrespected that I didn't know how to handle it.

The notion of disrespect is analogous to an attack on the self. Because many of the inmates in our sample reported that masculinity is an important attribute of the self, they believed any disrespect was a direct threat to their masculinity. For those brought up in impoverished high-crime communities, as these study population participants were, there are limited alternatives to such conflicting situations (Anderson, 1999). Retaliation to redeem one's self-identity in terms of his internalized concept of manhood precludes a violent reaction to all actions of insult. To gang members caught in those confrontational encounters, there is a very limited course of action, that of perpetrating violence toward those who would threaten their self-concept of who they believe they are.

Gangs and Guns

The perceived necessity by gang participants to carry handguns became a reality for our study group. They collectively expressed the danger of their life on the street, whether it was selling narcotics, committing a robbery, being a provocateur against rivals, or being the recipient of violent retaliation on the part of perceived enemies. They viewed their world as fraught with potential danger; thus the need for the possession of guns. It is necessary, then, to take the person's definition of the situation into account in explaining their unlawful conduct

(Hewitt, 1988). Often, the interviewed prisoners emphasized the importance of the gun as an attribute that communicated their masculinity in some situations but was protection in others. Quite often, both definitions of the situation existed simultaneously.

Our analysis of the interview data dichotomized those gun-using encounters as expressions of either power or protection, based on each participant's perceived definition of the situation.

Carrying a firearm elicits various feelings of power.

> When I have a gun, I feel like I'm on top of it, like I'm Superman or something. You got to let them know.

Another participant explains that the larger the gun, the more powerful he felt:

> I was 15 at that point in time, and I had a fascination with guns. It was like the more powerful impact the gun had, the more fascinated I got and the more I wanted it.

The actual use of a firearm is described in a situation that most lethally expressed the power of guns in an attempt to injure those belonging to rival gangs. In this situation, our subject points out that they were not trying to injure or kill anyone for personal reasons but rather to display a sense of willingness to commit a lethal act for purposes of dominance.

> When I was younger, we used to do drive-bys. It didn't matter who you were. We didn't go after a specific person. We went after a specific group. Whoever is standing at a particular house or wherever you may be, and you're grouped up and have the wrong color on; just because you were in a rival gang. You didn't have to do anything to us to come get you, it was a spontaneous reaction.

When not being involved in collective gang violence, individual members find themselves being involved in gun-use situations as instigators when confronting rivals on one's own.

> My cousin told me if you pull it you better use it. So you gotta boost yourself. When the time came, I was just shooting.

Our findings showed that in the vast majority of gang member–related shootings, most of these violent gun-using situations involved individuals as opposed to large numbers of gangs confronting each other with firearms. Yet, we were told that in gang representation, either on an individual basis or in a small group, whether it be in a protective or retaliatory mode, gang members needed to display a power position to those confronting them to maintain their reputations, and guns were important in that respect.

The issues surrounding gun possession often have to do with interpersonal conflict as opposed to collective gang situations. The fear of being physically harmed within their residential environment, coupled with the relative ease with which a person can attain a firearm, has resulted in a proliferation of weapons in the community. Growing up in such high-crime neighborhoods and then joining a gang can shape a minority teen's perceptions of his or her social world.

> There's a lot of brutality, there is a lot of murder around us. There is a lot of violence, period. There are enemies and all. A lot of pressure, you know. If you're not going to do this, then they're going to do it to you. I'd rather get caught with a gun than without.

The perceived fear for potential harm caused this female gang member to carry a gun with her outside her home. When she expresses the violence that is prevalent in her environment, she is also telling us how random threats can often occur and sees the necessity to harm rivals before they harm her.

Individually or collectively, rival gang members constantly pose a physical threat according to the next inmate. He also discusses the need for protection and how drug sales caused him to be a target for those who would try and rob him.

> I carried a gun because I knew what I was doing, especially since I was in a gang. Other gangs are gonna try and come after us. So I used it [gun] against those gangs and to make sure that my investments in the drugs was protected. I don't want nobody to take money from me.

Finally, one study subject relates the need to carry a gun all the time to protect his jewelry, which he openly displays as a symbol of his monetary success through the use of illegal means.

> I basically carried a gun for protection. Just like you have a best friend. You and your best friend go everywhere. I got over $10,000 of jewelry on me. People see all this jewelry and may try and beat me up. There may be two or three and just myself.

For our prisoner/gang member study population, the descriptive attributes they related all played an important role in shaping their individual gang identity. The roles they learned to play through their processional development into bona fide gang participants were accomplished by group socialization. Their acting upon those perceived valued attributes resulted in their transformed identity. Once the socializing process is complete, the novice gang member has to sustain his reputation and status personally as well as collectively with the formal group.

> An individual who implicitly or explicitly signifies that he has certain social characteristics ought in fact to be what he claims he is. In consequence, when an individual projects a definition of the situation and thereby makes an implicit or explicit claim to be a person of a particular kind, he automatically exerts a moral demand upon others, obliging them to value and treat him in the manner that persons of his kind have a right to expect. (Goffman, 1959, pp. 1–5)

For Goffman, the claims (attributes) our sample of gang members desired to convey to others of just who they perceived themselves to be directly affected their sense of self.

DISCUSSION AND CONCLUSION

Gangs not only fulfill specific needs for individuals that other groups in disadvantaged neighborhoods may fail to provide, but as our interviews suggest, they are also important primary groups into which individuals become socialized. It is not surprising, then, that self-concept and identity are closely tied to gang membership. Guns are also important in this regard. We propose that for the gang members in our sample, gang-related gun violence can be understood in terms of self and identity that are created through the process of socialization and are heavily rooted in notions of masculinity. Thus, our analysis provides insight into the way gang socialization can produce violence—especially gun-related violence.

We find that related to the issue of gun violence, the possession and use of guns among gang members is relatively important because, in addition to protecting gang members, guns are tools that aid in identity formation and impression management. As many of our subject narratives suggest, guns were often connected in some way to masculine attributes. Gang members reported to us that they could often use guns to project their reputation or reclaim respect. We believe that the consequences of our findings regarding gang violence and guns are important for public policy for three reasons.

First, because our sample only consisted of those gang members who committed the most severe forms of violence (i.e., they were incarcerated for relatively long periods of time for their gun-related violence), there may be some interest in targeting individuals like the ones in our sample early in their criminal careers to "diminish the pool of chronic gang offenders" (Piehl, Kennedy, & Braga, 2000, p. 100). We believe this may be one potential method for reducing gang-related violence because the gang members in our sample often had extensive violent histories. Moreover, in studies of gang violence, researchers have generally found that a small number of offenders commit most of the crime. For instance, Kennedy, Piehl, and Braga (1996) found that less than 1% of Boston's youth were responsible for nearly 60% of the city's homicides. Thus, identifying the rather small pool of chronic gang members may be a useful approach to reducing gang violence because they are the ones engaged in most of the violence. This approach, however, is somewhat problematic because identifying chronic offenders is both difficult and controversial (Walker, 1998). Moreover, Spergel and Curry (1990), who studied the effectiveness of various gang-related intervention strategies, argue that law enforcement efforts seem to be one of the least effective methods for reducing gang-related problems.

Second, our research suggests that policies aimed at reducing gang violence should take gang socialization into account. Simply reducing gun availability through law enforcement crackdowns on violent gang members is probably not sufficient (see Piehl, Kennedy, & Braga, 2000). In addition, our interviews suggest that guns are probably far more important to the daily lives and identities of gang members than most policymakers might imagine, precisely because they help project a reputation and create respect. Thus, it might be pointed out that if gang culture could be changed through the resocialization of gang members, gun-related gang violence might significantly decrease. Indeed, studies of gun initiatives such as the Boston Gun Project suggest that gang violence is reduced when gang culture is changed. As Piehl, Kennedy, and Braga (2000, p. 100) point out, one reason homicides in Boston decreased as a result of the Boston Gun Project was because that initiative focused on "establishing and/or reinforcing nonviolent norms by increasing peer support for eschewing violence, by improving young people's handling of potentially violent situations."

Overall, however, the strategy of focusing on gang socialization, however, falls most closely in line with social intervention perspectives that have not proved to be highly successful in various situations (Shelden, Tracy, & Brown, 2001). In short, altering the values of gang members to make gang-related violence less likely may not be the most promising approach to reducing gang violence. As Klein (1995, p. 147) recently noted, "Gangs are by-products of their communities: They cannot long be controlled by attacks on symptoms alone; the community structure and capacity must also be targeted." Whether gang violence can be reduced by the resocialization of gang members appears to remain open to debate, but it is clearly one avenue of intervention that requires further attention in the research.

Third, it is not clear from our research whether simply eliminating or reducing access to guns can reduce gun-related gang violence. For example, studies like the Youth Firearms Violence Initiative conducted by the U.S. Department of Justice's Office of Community Oriented Policing Services does suggest that gun violence can be reduced by focusing, at least in part, on reducing access to guns (Dunworth, 2000). However, that study also indicates that once these projects focusing on access to guns end, gang violence increases to previous levels. Moreover, our interviews suggest that there is little reason to believe that gang members would be any less likely to look to gangs as a source of status and protection and may use other weapons—though arguably less lethal than guns—to aid in transformations of identity and preserve a sense of self. Thus, although reduction strategies may prevent gang-related violence in the short term, there is little evidence that this intervention strategy will have long-term effects because it does not adequately deal with gang culture and processes of gang socialization.

Overall, our findings suggest that gang socialization produces gang-related gun violence through changes to identity and self. Although the problems of gang-related violence appear to play out at the micro level, the solutions to these problems do not appear to be overwhelmingly situated at this level. Instead, we believe that intervention efforts must reside at the macro level and impact socialization processes at the micro level. We agree with Short (1997, p. 181) that "absent change in macro level forces associated with [gang violence], vulnerable individuals will continue to be produced" (see also Shelden, Tracy, & Brown, 2001). Thus, it may be more fruitful to focus on intervention efforts aimed at improving the economic and social environments that create gangs.

REFERENCES

Anderson, E. (1999). *Code of the street: Decency, violence, and the moral life of the inner city*. New York: W. W. Norton.

Baumeister, R., & Tice, D. (1984). Role of self-presentation and choice in cognitive dissonance under forced compliance. *Journal of Personality and Social Psychology, 46*, 5–13.

Berger, P. (1963). *Invitation to sociology: A humanistic perspective*. Garden City, NY: Doubleday.

Bjerregaard, B., & Lizotte, A. (1995). Gun ownership and gang membership. *Journal of Criminal Law and Criminology, 86*, 37–58.

Blumstein, A. (1995). Violence by young people: Why the deadly nexus? *National Institute of Justice Journal, 229*, 2–9.

Bowker, L., & Klein, M. (1983). The etiology of female juvenile delinquency and gang membership: A test of psychological and social structural explanations. *Adolescence, 18*, 739–751.

Callero, P. (1985). Role identity salience. *Social Psychology Quarterly, 48*, 203–215.

Decker, S., & Van Winkle, B. (1996). *Life in the gang: Family, friends, and violence*. New York: Cambridge University Press.

Dunworth, T. (2000). *National evaluation of youth firearms violence initiative. Research in brief*. Washington, DC: U.S. Department of Justice, Office of Justice Programs, National Institute of Justice.

Gerrard, N. (1964). The core member of the gang. *British Journal of Criminology, 4*, 361–371.

Goffman, E. (1959). *The presentation of self in everyday life*. Garden City, NY: Doubleday.

———. (1961). *Encounters: Two studies in the sociology of interaction*. Indianapolis, IN: Bobbs-Merrill.

Gordon, R., Lahey, B., Kawai, K., Loeber, R., Stouthamer-Loeber, M., & Farrington, D. (2004). Antisocial behavior and youth gang membership: Selection and socialization. *Criminology, 42*, 55–88.

Hewitt, J. (1988). *Self and society*. Boston: Allyn & Bacon.

Hewitt, J., & Stokes, R. (1975). Disclaimers. *American Sociological Review, 40*, 1–11.

Hickman, C. A., & Kuhn, M. (1956). *Individuals, groups, and economic behavior*. New York: Dryden.

Holstein, J., & Gubrium, J. (2003). *Inner lives and social worlds*. New York: Oxford University Press.

Horowitz, R. (1983). *Honor and the American dream*. New Brunswick, NJ: Rutgers University Press.

Howell, J. (1998). Youth gangs: An overview. *Juvenile Justice Bulletin*, August. Washington, DC: U.S. Department of Justice, Office of Juvenile Justice and Delinquency Prevention.

Hughes, L., & Short, J. (2005). Disputes involving youth street gang members: Micro-social contexts. *Criminology, 43*, 43–76.

Kanter, R. (1972). *Commitment and community: Communes and utopias in sociological perspective*. Cambridge, MA: Harvard University Press.

Katz, J. (1988). *Seductions of crime: Moral and sensual attractions in doing evil*. New York: Basic.

Kennedy, D., Piehl, A. M., & Braga, A. (1996). *Youth gun violence in Boston: Gun markets, serious youth offenders, and a use-reduction strategy. Research in brief*. Washington, DC: U.S. Department of Justice, Office of Justice Programs, National Institute of Justice.

Klein, M. (1995). *The American street gang*. New York: Oxford University Press.

Kubrin, C. (2005). Gangstas, thugs, and hustlas: Identity and the code of the street in rap music. *Social Problems, 52*, 360–378.

Lindesmith, A., & Strauss, A. (1968). *Social psychology*. New York: Holt, Rinehart and Winston.

Lizotte, A., Tesoriero, J., Thomberry, T., & Krohn, M. (1994). Patterns of adolescent firearms ownership and use. *Justice Quarterly, 11*, 51–74.

McCall, G., & Simmons, J. (1966). *Identities and interactions: An examination of human associations in everyday life*. New York: Free Press.

McCorkle, R., & Miethe, T. (2002). *Panic: The social construction of the street gang problem*. Upper Saddle River, NJ: Prentice Hall.

Miller, J., & Brunson, R. (2000). Gender dynamics in youth gangs: A comparison of males' and females' accounts. *Justice Quarterly, 17*, 419–448.

Miller, J., & Decker, S. (2001). Young women and gang violence: Gender, street offender, and violent victimization in gangs. *Justice Quarterly, 18*, 115–140.

Moore, J. (1978). *Homeboys: Gangs, drugs, and prison in the barrios of Los Angeles*. Philadelphia: Temple University Press.

———. (1991). *Going down to the barrio: Homeboys and homegirls in change*. Philadelphia: Temple University Press.

Oliver, W. (1994). *The violent world of black men*. New York: Lexington.

Piehl, A. M., Kennedy, D., & Braga, A. (2000). Problem solving and youth violence: An evaluation of the Boston gun project. *American Law and Economics Review, 2*, 58–106.

Sanders, W. (1994). *Gang-bangs and drive-bys: Grounded culture and juvenile gang violence*. New York: Walter de Gruyter.

Shelden, R., Tracy, S., & Brown, W. (2001). *Youth gangs in American society*. Belmont, CA: Wadsworth.

Sheley, J., & Wright, J. (1995). *In the line of fire: Youth, guns and violence in America*. New York: Aldine de Gruyter.

Sherif, M., & Wilson, M. (1953). *Group relations at the crossroads*. New York: Harper.

Shibutani, T. (1961). *Society and personality: An interactionist approach to social psychology*. Englewood Cliffs, NJ: Prentice Hall.

Short, J. (1997). *Poverty, ethnicity, and violent crime*. Boulder, CO: Westview.

Short, J., & Strodtbeck, F. (1965). *Group processes and gang delinquency*. Chicago: University of Chicago Press.

Sirpal, S. K. (1997). Causes of gang participation and strategies for prevention in gang members' own words. *Journal of Gang Research, 4*, 13–22.

Spergel, I., & Curry, G. D. (1990). Strategies and perceived agency effectiveness in dealing with the youth gang problem. In C. R. Huff (Ed.), *Gangs in America* (pp. 288–309). Newbury Park, CA: Sage.

Stone, G. (1962). Appearance and self. In A. Rose (Ed.), *Human behavior and social processes* (pp. 86–118). Boston: Houghton Mifflin.

Strauss, A. (1962). Transformations of identity. In A. Rose (Ed.), *Human behavior and social processes: An interactional approach* (pp. 63–85). Boston: Houghton Mifflin.

———. (1969). *Mirrors and masks: The search for identity*. New York: Macmillan.

Stryker, S., & Serpe, R. (1982). Commitment, identity salience and role behavior. In W. Ikes & E. Knowles (Eds.), *Personality, roles and social behavior* (pp. 199–218). New York: Springer-Verlag.

Thornberry, T., Krohn, M., Lizotte, A., & Chard-Wierschem, D. (1993). The role of juvenile gangs in facilitating delinquent behavior. *Journal of Research in Crime and Delinquency, 30,* 75–85.

Thornberry, T., Krohn, M., Lizotte, A., Smith, C., & Tobin, K. (2003). *Gangs and delinquency in developmental perspective.* Cambridge, UK: Cambridge University Press.

Thrasher, F. (1927). *The gang.* Chicago: University of Chicago Press.

Turner, R. (1978). The role and the person. *American Journal of Sociology, 84,* 1–23.

Vigil, J. (1988). *Barrio gangs.* Austin: University of Texas Press.

———. (1996). Street baptism: Chicago gang initiation. *Human Organization, 55,* 149–153.

———. (2003). Urban violence and street gangs. *Annual Review of Anthropology, 32,* 225–242.

Walker, S. (1998). *Sense and nonsense about crime and drugs.* Belmont, CA: Wadsworth.

Weinstein, E., & Deutschberger, P. (1963). Some dimensions of altercasting. *Sociometry, 26,* 454–466.

Wright, J., & Rossi, P. (1986). *Armed and considered dangerous: A survey of felons and their firearms.* New York: Aldine de Gruyter.

Yablonsky, L. (1962). *The violent gang.* New York: Macmillan.

CHAPTER 18

Gender and Victimization Risk Among Young Women in Gangs

Jody Miller

This selection examines how gendered situational dynamics shape gang violence, including participation in violent offending and experiences of violent victimization. Although there are numerous studies of gangs and gang-involved individuals, few have explored the concept of victimization of gang members. The author found that young women, even regular offenders, highlight the significance of gender in shaping and limiting their involvement in serious violence. Based on interviews with 20 female gang members in Columbus, Ohio, Miller found that being a member increases one's risk of assaults and other physical victimization, and that these risks are greater for females than for males. She suggests that the act of joining a gang often involves submission to victimization at the hands of other members of the gang, and that gang activities thereafter place these individuals at risk for further victimization.

GIRLS, GANGS, AND CRIME

Until recently . . . little attention was paid to young women's participation in serious and violent gang-related crime. Most traditional gang research emphasized the auxiliary and peripheral nature of girls' gang involvement and often resulted in an almost exclusive emphasis on girls' sexuality and sexual activities with male gang members, downplaying their participation in delinquency (for critiques of gender bias in gender research, see Campbell, 1984; Campbell, 1990; Taylor, 1993).

However, recent estimates of female gang involvement have caused researchers to pay greater attention to gang girls' activities. This evidence suggests that

Source: From Miller, J. (1998). Gender and victimization: Risk among young women in gangs. *Journal of Research in Crime & Delinquency, 35,* 429–453. Copyright © 1998. Reprinted with permission from Sage Publications, Inc.

young women approximate anywhere from 10% to 38% of gang members (Campbell, 1984; Chesney-Lind, 1993; Esbensen, 1996; Fagan, 1990; Moore, 1991), that female gang participation may be increasing (Fagan, 1996; Spergel & Curry, 1993; Taylor, 1990), and that in some urban areas, upward of one-fifth of girls report gang affiliations (Bjerregaard & Smith, 1993; Winfree et al., 1992). As female gang members have become recognized as a group worthy of criminologists' attention, we have garnered new information regarding their involvement in delinquency in general, and violence in particular.

Few would dispute that when it comes to serious delinquency, male gang members are involved more frequently than their female counterparts. However, this evidence does suggest that young women in gangs are more involved in serious criminal activities than was previously believed and also tend to be more involved than nongang youths—male or female. As such, they likely are exposed to greater victimization risk than nongang youths as well.

In addition, given the social contexts described above, it is reasonable to assume that young women's victimization risk within gangs is also shaped by gender. Gang activities (such as fighting for status and retaliation) create a particular set of factors that increase gang members' victimization risk and repeat victimization risk. Constructions of gender identity may shape these risks in particular ways for girls. For instance, young women's adoption of masculine attributes may provide a means of participating and gaining status within gangs but may also lead to increased risk of victimization as a result of deeper immersion in delinquent activities. On the other hand, experiences of victimization may contribute to girls' denigration and thus increase their risk for repeat victimization through gendered responses and labeling—for example, when sexual victimization leads to perceptions of sexual availability or when victimization leads an individual to be viewed as weak. In addition, femaleness is an individual attribute that has the capacity to mark young women as "safe" crime victims (e.g., easy targets) or, conversely, to deem them "off limits." My goal here is to examine the gendered nature of violence within gangs, with a specific focus on how gender shapes young women's victimization risk.

METHODOLOGY

Data presented in this article come from survey and semistructured in-depth interviews with 20 female members of mixed-gender gangs in Columbus, Ohio. The interviewees ranged in age from 12 to 17 years; just over three-quarters were African American or multiracial (16 of 20), and the rest (four of 20) were white.

Girls who admitted gang involvement during the survey participated in a follow-up interview to talk in more depth about their gangs and gang activities. The goal of the in-depth interview was to gain a greater understanding of the nature and meanings of gang life from the point of view of its female members.

The in-depth interviews were open-ended and all but one were audiotaped. They were structured around several groupings of questions. We began by discussing girls' entry into their gangs—when and how they became involved, and what other things were going on in their lives at the time. Then we discussed the structure of the gang—its history, size, leadership, and organization, and their place in the group. The next series of questions concerned gender within the gang; for example, how girls get involved, what activities they engage in and whether these are the same as the young men's activities, and what kind of males and females have the most influence in the gang and why. The next series of questions explored gang involvement more generally—what being in the gang means, what kinds of things they do together, and so on. Then, I asked how safe or dangerous they feel gang membership is and how they deal with risk. I concluded by asking them to speculate about why people their age join gangs, what things they like, what they dislike and have learned by being in the gang, and what they like best about themselves. This basic guideline was followed for each interview subject, although when additional topics arose in the context of the interview we often deviated from the interview guide to pursue them. Throughout the interviews, issues related to violence emerged; these issues form the core of the discussion that follows.

SETTING

The young women I interviewed described their gangs in ways that are very much in keeping with these findings. All 20 are members of Folks, Crips, or Bloods sets. All but three described gangs with fewer than 30 members, and most reported relatively narrow age ranges between members. Half were in gangs with members who were 21 or over, but almost without exception, their gangs were made up primarily of teenagers, with either one adult who was considered the OG ("Original Gangster," leader) or just a handful of young adults. The majority (14 of 20) reported that their gangs did not include members under the age of 13.

Although the gangs these young women were members of were composed of both female and male members, they varied in their gender composition, with the vast majority being predominantly male. Six girls reported that girls were one-fifth or fewer of the members of their gang; eight were in gangs in which girls were between a quarter and a third of the overall membership; four said girls were between 44% and 50% of the members; and one girl reported that her gang was two-thirds female and one-third male. Overall, girls were typically a minority within these groups numerically, with 11 girls reporting that there were five or fewer girls in their set.

This structure—male-dominated, integrated, mixed-gender gangs—likely shapes gender dynamics in particular ways. Much past gang research has assumed that female members of gangs are in auxiliary subgroups of male gangs, but there is increasing evidence—including from the young women I spoke with—that many gangs can be characterized as integrated, mixed-gender groups.

GENDER, GANGS, AND VIOLENCE

Gangs as Protection and Risk

An irony of gang involvement is that although many members suggest one thing they get out of the gang is a sense of protection (see Decker, 1996; Joe & Chesney-Lind, 1995; Lauderback, Hansen, & Waldorf, 1992), gang membership itself means exposure to victimization risk and even a willingness to be victimized. These contradictions are apparent when girls talk about what they get out of the gang, and what being in the gang means in terms of other members' expectations of their behavior. In general, a number of girls suggested that being a gang member is a source of protection around the neighborhood. Erica, a 17-year-old African American, explained, "It's like people look at us and that's exactly what they think, there's a gang, and they respect us for that. They won't bother us. . . . It's like you put that intimidation in somebody." Likewise, Lisa, a 14-year-old white girl, described being in the gang as empowering: "You just feel like, oh my God, you know, they got my back. I don't need to worry about it." Given the violence endemic in many inner-city communities, these beliefs are understandable, and to a certain extent, accurate.

In addition, some young women articulated a specifically gendered sense of protection that they felt as a result of being a member of a group that was predominantly male. Gangs operate within larger social milieus that are characterized by gender inequality and sexual exploitation. Being in a gang with young men means at least the semblance of protection from, and retaliation against, predatory men in the social environment. Heather, a 15-year-old white girl, noted, "You feel more secure when, you know, a guy's around protectin' you, you know, than you would a girl." She explained that as a gang member, because "you get protected by guys . . . not as many people mess with you." Other young women concurred and also described that male gang members could retaliate against specific acts of violence against girls in the gang. Nikkie, a 13-year-old African American girl, had a friend who was raped by a rival gang member, and she said, "It was a Crab [Crip] that raped my girl in Miller Ales, and um, they was ready to kill him." Keisha, an African American 14-year-old, explained, "If I got beat up by a guy, all I gotta do is go tell one of the niggers, you know what I'm sayin'? Or one of the guys, they'd take care of it."

At the same time, members recognized that they may be targets of rival gang members and were expected to "be down" for their gang at those times even when it meant being physically hurt. In addition, initiation rites and internal rules were structured in ways that required individuals to submit to, and be exposed to, violence. For example, young women's descriptions of the qualities they valued in members revealed the extent to which exposure to violence was an expected element of gang involvement. Potential members, they explained, should be tough, able to fight and to engage in criminal activities, and also should be loyal to the group and willing to put themselves at risk for it. Erica explained that they didn't want "punks" in her gang: "When you join something like that, you might as well expect that there's gonna be fights. . . . And, if you're a punk, or if you're scared of stuff like that, then don't join." Likewise, the following dialogue with Cathy, a white 16-year-old, reveals similar themes. I asked her what her gang expected out of members, and she responded, "To be true to our gang and to have our backs." When I asked her to elaborate, she explained:

> CATHY: Like, uh, if you say you're a Blood, you be a Blood. You wear your rag even when you're by yourself. You know, don't let anybody intimidate you and be like, "Take that rag off." You know, "You better get with our set." Or something like that.
>
> JM: Ok. Anything else that being true to the set means?
>
> CATHY: Um. Yeah, I mean, just, just, you know, I mean it's, you got a whole bunch of people comin' up in your face, and if you're by yourself they ask you what's your claimin', you tell 'em. Don't say nothin'.
>
> JM: Even if it means getting beat up or something?
>
> CATHY: Mmhmm.

One measure of these qualities came through the initiation process, which involved the individual submitting to victimization at the hands of the gang's members. Typically this entailed either taking a fixed number of "blows" to the head and/or chest or being "beaten in" by members for a given duration (e.g., 60 seconds). Heather described the initiation as an important event for determining whether someone would make a good member:

> When you get beat in, if you don't fight back and if you just, like, stop and you start cryin' or somethin', or beggin' 'em to stop and stuff like that, then they ain't gonna, they'll just stop and they'll say that you're not gang material because you gotta be hard, gotta be able to fight, take punches.

In addition to the initiation and threats from rival gangs, members were expected to adhere to the gang's internal rules (which included such things as not fighting with one another, being "true" to the gang, respecting the leader, not spreading gang business outside the gang, and not dating members of rival gangs). Breaking the rules was grounds for physical punishment, either in the form of a spontaneous assault or a formal "violation," which involved taking a specified number of blows to the head. For example, Keisha reported that she talked back to the leader of her set and "got slapped pretty hard" for doing so. Likewise, Veronica, an African American 15-year-old, described her leader as "crazy, but we gotta listen to 'im. He's just the type that if you don't listen to 'im, he gonna blow your head off. He's just crazy."

It is clear that regardless of members' perceptions of the gang as a form of "protection," being a gang member also involves a willingness to open oneself up to the possibility of victimization. Gang victimization is governed by rules and expectations, however, and thus does not involve the random vulnerability that being out on the streets without a gang might entail in high-crime neighborhoods. Because of its structured nature, this victimization risk may be perceived as more palatable by gang members. For young women in particular, the gendered nature of the streets may make the empowerment available through gang involvement an appealing alternative to the individualized vulnerability they otherwise would face. However, as the next sections highlight, girls' victimization risks continue to be shaped by gender, even within their gangs, because these groups are structured around gender hierarchies as well.

Gender and Status, Crime and Victimization

Status hierarchies within Columbus gangs, like elsewhere, were male dominated (Bowker, Gross, & Klein, 1980; Campbell, 1990). Again, it is important to highlight that the structure of the gangs these young women belonged to—that is, male-dominated, integrated, mixed-gender gangs—likely shaped the particular ways in which gender dynamics played themselves out. Autonomous female gangs, as well as gangs in which girls are in auxiliary subgroups, may be shaped by different gender relations, as well as differences in orientations toward status and criminal involvement.

All the young women reported having established leaders in their gang, and this leadership was almost exclusively male. Although LaShawna, a 17-year-old African American, reported being the leader of her set (which had a membership that is two-thirds girls, many of whom resided in the same residential facility as her), all the other girls in mixed-gender gangs reported that their OG was male. In fact, a number of young women stated explicitly that only male gang members could be leaders. Leadership qualities, and qualities attributed to high-status members of the gangs—being tough, able to fight, and willing to "do dirt" (e.g., commit crime, engage in violence) for the gang—were perceived as characteristically masculine. Keisha noted, "The guys, they just harder." She explained, "Guys is more rougher. We have our G's back, but it ain't gonna be like the guys, they just don't give a fuck. They gonna shoot you in a minute."

For the most part, status in the gang was related to traits such as the willingness to use serious violence and commit dangerous crimes, and, though not exclusively, these traits were viewed primarily as qualities more likely and more intensely located among male gang members.

Because these respected traits were characterized specifically as masculine, young women actually may have had greater flexibility in their gang involvement than young men. Young women had fewer expectations placed on them—by both their male and female peers—in regard to involvement in criminal activities such as fighting, using weapons, and committing other crimes. This tended to decrease girls' exposure to victimization risk compared to male members, because they were able to avoid activities likely to place them in danger. Girls could gain status in the gang by being particularly hard and true to the set. Heather, for example, described the most influential girl in her set as "the hardest girl, the one that don't take no crap, will stand up to anybody." Likewise, Diane, a white 15-year-old, described a highly respected female member in her set as follows:

People look up to Janeen just 'cause she's so crazy. People just look up to her 'cause she don't care about nothin'. She don't even care about makin' money. Her, her thing is, "Oh, you're a Slob [Blood]? You're a Slob? You talkin' to me? You talkie' shit to me?" Pow, pow! And that's it. That's it.

However, young women also had a second route to status that was less available to young men. This came via their connections—as sisters, girlfriends, cousins—to influential, high-status young men. In Veronica's set, for example, the girl with the most power was the OG's "sister or his cousin, one of 'em." His girlfriend also had status, although Veronica noted that "most of us just look up to our OG." Monica, a 16-year-old African American, and Tamika, a 15-year-old African American, both had older brothers in their gangs, and both reported getting respect, recognition, and protection because of this connection. This route to status and the masculinization of high-status traits functioned to maintain gender inequality within gangs, but they also could put young women at less risk of victimization than young men. This was both because young women were perceived as less threatening and thus were less likely to be targeted by rivals, and because they were not expected to prove themselves in the ways that young men were, thus decreasing their participation in those delinquent activities likely to increase exposure to violence. Thus, gender inequality could have a protective edge for young women.

Young men's perceptions of girls as lesser members typically functioned to keep girls from being targets of serious violence at the hands of rival young men, who instead left routine confrontations with rival female gang members to the girls in their own gang. Diane said that young men in her gang "don't wanna waste their time hittin' on some little girls. They're gonna go get their little cats [females] to go get 'em." Lisa remarked,

> Girls don't face as much violence as [guys]. They see a girl, they say, "We'll just smack her and send her on." They see a guy—'cause guys are like a lot more into it than girls are, I've noticed that—and they like, "Well, we'll shoot him."

In addition, the girls I interviewed suggested that, in comparison with young men, young women were less likely to resort to serious violence, such as that involving a weapon, when confronting rivals. Thus, when girls' routine confrontations were more likely to be female on female than male on female, girls' risk of serious victimization was lessened further.

Also, because participation in serious and violent crime was defined primarily as a masculine endeavor, young women could use gender as a means of avoiding participation in those aspects of gang life they found risky, threatening, or morally troubling. Of the young women I interviewed, about one-fifth were involved in serious gang violence: a few had been involved in aggravated assaults on rival gang members, and one admitted to having killed a rival gang member, but they were by far the exception. Most girls tended not to be involved in serious gang crime, and some reported that they chose to exclude themselves because they felt ambivalent about this aspect of gang life. Angie, an African American 15-year-old, explained,

> I don't get involved like that, be out there goin' and just beat up people like that or go stealin', things like that. That's not me. The boys, mostly the boys do all that, the girls we just sit back and chill, you know.

Likewise, Diane noted,

> For maybe a drive-by, they might wanna have a bunch of dudes. They might not put the females in that. Maybe the females might be weak inside, not strong enough to do something like that, just on the insides. . . . If a female wants to go forward and doin' that, and she wants to risk her whole life for doin' that, then she can. But the majority of the time, that job is given to a man.

Diane was not just alluding to the idea that young men were stronger than young women. She also inferred that young women were able to get out of committing serious crime, more so than young men, because a girl shouldn't have to "risk her whole life" for the gang. In accepting that young men were more central members of the gang, young women could more easily participate in gangs without putting themselves in jeopardy—they could engage in the more routine, everyday activities of the gang, like hanging out, listening to music, and smoking bud (marijuana). These male-dominated, mixed-gender gangs thus appeared to provide young women with flexibility in their involvement in gang activities. As a result, it is likely that their risk of victimization at the hands of rivals was less than that of young men in gangs who were engaged in greater amounts of crime.

Girls' Devaluation and Victimization

In addition to girls choosing not to participate in serious gang crimes, they also faced exclusion at the hands of young men or the gang as a whole (see also Bowker, Gross, & Klein, 1980). In particular, the two types of crime mentioned most frequently as "off-limits" for girls were drug sales and drive-by shootings. LaShawna explained, "We don't really let our females [sell drugs] unless they really wanna and they know how to do it and not to get caught and everything." Veronica described a drive-by that her gang participated in and said, "They wouldn't let us [females] go. But we wanted to go, but they wouldn't let us." Often, the exclusion was couched in terms of protection. When I asked Veronica why the girls couldn't go, she said, "So we won't go to jail if they was to get caught. Or if one of 'em was to get shot, they wouldn't want it to happen to us." Likewise, Sonita, a 13-year-old African American, noted, "If they gonna do somethin' bad and they think one of the females gonna get hurt, they don't let 'em do it with them. . . . Like if they involved with shooting or whatever, [girls] can't go."

Although girls' exclusion from some gang crime may be framed as protective (and may reduce their victimization risk vis-a-vis rival gangs), it also served to perpetuate the devaluation of female members as less significant to the gang—not as tough, true, or "down" for the gang as male members. When LaShawna said her gang blocked girls' involvement in serious crime, I pointed out that she was actively involved herself. She explained, "Yeah, I do a lot of stuff 'cause I'm tough. I likes, I likes messin' with boys. I fight boys. Girls ain't nothin' to me." Similarly, Tamika said, "Girls, they little peons."

Some young women found the perception of them as weak a frustrating one. Brandi, an African American 13-year-old, explained, "Sometimes I dislike that the boys, sometimes, always gotta take charge and they think sometimes, that the girls don't know how to take charge 'cause we're like girls, we're females, and like that." And Chantell, an African American 14-year-old, noted that rival gang members "think that you're more of a punk." Beliefs that girls were weaker than boys meant that young women had a harder time proving that they were serious about their commitment to the gang. Diane explained,

> A female has to show that she's tough. A guy can just, you can just look at him. But a female, she's gotta show. She's gotta go out and do some dirt. She's gotta go whip some girl's ass, shoot somebody, rob somebody or something. To show that she is tough.

In terms of gender-specific victimization risk, the devaluation of young women suggests several things. It could lead to the mistreatment and victimization of girls by members of their own gang when they didn't have specific male protection (i.e., a brother, boyfriend) in the gang or when they weren't able to stand up for themselves to male members. This was exacerbated by activities that led young women to be viewed as sexually available. In addition, because young women typically were not seen as a threat by young men, when they did pose one, they could be punished even more harshly than young men, not only for having challenged a rival gang or gang member, but also for having overstepped "appropriate" gender boundaries.

Monica had status and respect in her gang both because she had proven herself through fights and criminal activities and because her older brothers were members of her set. She contrasted her own treatment with that of other young women in the gang:

> They just be puttin' the other girls off. Like Andrea, man. Oh my God, they dog Andrea so bad. They like, "Bitch, go to the store." She like, "All right, I be right back." She will go to the store and go and get them whatever they want and come back with it. If she don't get it right, they be like, "Why you do that, bitch?" I mean, and one dude even smacked her. And, I mean, and, I don't, I told my brother once. I was like, "Man, it ain't even like that. If you ever see someone tryin' to disrespect me like that or hit me, if you do not hit them or at least say somethin' to them. . . . " So my brothers, they kinda watch out for me.

However, Monica put the responsibility for Andrea's treatment squarely on the young woman: "I put that on her. They ain't gotta do her like that, but she don't gotta let them do her like that either." Andrea was seen as "weak" because she did not stand up to the male members in the gang; thus, her mistreatment was framed as partially deserved because she did not exhibit the valued traits of toughness and willingness to fight that would allow her to defend herself.

An additional but related problem was when the devaluation of young women within gangs was sexual in nature. Girls, but not boys, could be initiated into the gang by being "sexed in"—having sexual relations with multiple male members of the gang. Other members viewed the young women initiated in this way as sexually available and promiscuous, thus increasing their subsequent mistreatment. In addition, the stigma could extend to female members in general, creating a sexual devaluation that all girls had to contend with. The dynamics of "sexing in" as a form of gang initiation placed young women in a position that increased their risk of ongoing mistreatment at the hands of their gang peers. According to Keisha,

> If you get sexed in, you have no respect. That means you gotta go ho'in' for 'em; when they say you give 'em the pussy, you gotta give it to 'em. If you don't, you gonna get your ass beat. I ain't down for that.

One girl in her set was sexed in and Keisha said the girl "just do everything they tell her to do, like a dummy." Nikkie reported that two girls who were sexed into her set eventually quit hanging around with the gang because they were harassed so much. In fact, Veronica said the young men in her set purposely tricked girls into believing they were being sexed into the gang and targeted girls they did not like:

> If some girls wanted to get in, if they don't like the girl, they have sex with 'em. They run trains on 'em or either have the girl suck their thang. And then they used to, the girls used to think they was in. So then the girls used to just come try to hang around us and all this little bull, just 'cause, 'cause they thinkin' they in.

Young women who were sexed into the gang were viewed as sexually promiscuous, weak, and not "true" members. They were subject to revictimization and mistreatment, and were viewed as deserving of abuse by other members, both male and female. Veronica continued, "They [girls who are sexed in] gotta do whatever, whatever the boys tell 'em to do when they want 'em to do it, right then and there, in front of whoever. And, I think, that's just sick. That's nasty, that's dumb." Keisha concurred, "She brought that on herself, by bein' the fact, bein' sexed in." There was evidence, however, that girls could overcome the stigma of having been sexed in through their subsequent behavior, by challenging members that disrespect them and being willing to fight. Tamika described a girl in her set who was sexed in, and stigmatized as a result, but successfully fought to rebuild her reputation:

> Some people, at first, they call her "little ho" and all that. But then, now she startin' to get bold. . . . Like, like, they be like, "Ooh, look at the little ho. She flicked me and my boy." She be like, "Man, forget y'all. Man, what? What?" She be ready to squat [fight] with 'em. I be like, "Ah, look at her!" Uh huh. . . . At first we looked at her like, "Ooh, man, she a ho, man." But now we look at her like she just our kickin'-it partner. You know, however she got in, that's her business.

The fact that there was such an option as "sexing in" served to keep girls disempowered, because they always faced the question of how they got in and of whether they were "true" members. In addition, it contributed to a milieu in which young women's sexuality was seen as exploitable. This may help explain why young women were so harshly judgmental of those girls who were sexed in. Young women who were privy to male gang members' conversations reported that male members routinely disrespect girls in the gang by disparaging them sexually. Monica explained,

> I mean the guys, they have their little comments about 'em [girls in the gang], because I hear more because my brothers are all up there with the guys and everything, and I hear more just sittin' around, just listenin'. And they'll have their little jokes about "Well, ha, I had her," and then everybody else will jump in and say, "Well, I had her, too." And then they'll laugh about it.

In general, because gender constructions defined young women as weaker than young men, young women were often seen as lesser members of the gang. In addition to the mistreatment these perceptions entailed, young women also faced particularly harsh sanctions for crossing gender boundaries—causing harm to rival male members when they had been viewed as nonthreatening. One young woman participated in the assault of a rival female gang member who had set up a member of the girl's gang. She explained, "The female was supposingly goin' out with one of ours, went back and told a bunch of [rivals] what was goin' on and got the [rivals] to jump my boy. And he ended up in the hospital." The story she told was unique but nonetheless significant for what it indicates about the gendered nature of gang violence and victimization. Several young men in her set saw the girl walking down the street, kidnapped her, then brought her to a member's house. The young woman I interviewed, along with several other girls in her set, viciously beat the girl, and then, to their surprise, the young men took over the beating, ripped off the girl's clothes, brutally gang-raped her, then dumped her in a park. The interviewee noted, "I don't know what happened to her. Maybe she died. Maybe, maybe someone came and helped her. I mean, I don't know." The experience scared the young woman who told me about it. She explained,

> I don't never want anythin' like that to happen to me. And I pray to God that it doesn't. 'Cause God said that whatever you sow you're gonna reap. And like, you know, beatin' a girl up and then sittin' there watchin' somethin' like that happen, well, Jesus that could come back on me. I mean, I felt, I really did feel sorry for her, even though my boy was in the hospital and was really hurt. I mean, we coulda just shot her. You know, and it coulda been just over. We coulda just taken her life. But they went farther than that.

This young woman described the gang rape she witnessed as "the most brutal thing I've ever seen in my life." While the gang rape itself was an unusual event, it remained a specifically gendered act that could take place precisely because young women were not perceived as equals. Had the victim been an "equal," the attack would have remained a physical one. As the interviewee herself noted, "We coulda just shot her." Instead, the young men who gang-raped the girl were not just enacting revenge on a rival but on a young woman who had dared to treat a young man in this way. The issue is not the question of which is worse—to be shot and killed, or gang-raped and left for dead. Rather, this particular act sheds light on how gender may function to structure victimization risk within gangs.

DISCUSSION

Gender dynamics in mixed-gender gangs are complex and thus may have multiple and contradictory effects on young women's risk of victimization and repeat victimization. My findings suggest that participation in the delinquent lifestyles associated with gangs clearly places young women at risk for victimization. The act of joining a gang involves the initiate's submission to victimization at the hands of her gang peers. In addition, the rules governing gang members' activities place them in situations in which they are vulnerable to assaults that are specifically gang-related. Many acts of violence that girls described would not have occurred had they not been in gangs.

It seems, though, that young women in gangs believed they have traded unknown risks for known ones—that victimization at the hands of friends, or at least under specified conditions, was an alternative preferable to the potential of random, unknown victimization by strangers. Moreover, the gang offered both a semblance of protection from others on the streets, especially young men, and a means of achieving retaliation when victimization did occur.

Lauritsen and Davis Quinet (1995) suggest that both individual-specific heterogeneity (unchanging attributes of individuals that contribute to a propensity for victimization, such as physical size or temperament) and state-dependent factors (factors that can alter individuals' victimization risks over time, such as labeling or behavior changes that are a consequence of victimization) are related to youths' victimization and repeat victimization risk. My findings here suggest that, within gangs, gender can function in both capacities to shape girls' risks of victimization.

Girls' gender, as an individual attribute, can function to lessen their exposure to victimization risk by defining them as inappropriate targets of rival male gang members' assaults. The young women I interviewed repeatedly commented that young men were typically not as violent in their routine confrontations with rival young women as with rival young men. On the other hand, when young women are targets of serious assault, they may face brutality that is particularly harsh and sexual in nature because they are female—thus, particular types of assault, such as rape, are deemed more appropriate when young women are the victims.

Gender can also function as a state-dependent factor, because constructions of gender and the enactment of gender identities are fluid. On the one hand, young women can call upon gender as a means of avoiding exposure to activities they find risky, threatening, or morally troubling. Doing so does not expose them to the sanctions likely faced by male gang members who attempt to avoid participation in violence. Although these choices may insulate young women from the risk of assault at the hands of rival gang members, perceptions of female gang members—and of women in general—as weak may contribute to more routinized victimization at the hands of the male members of their gangs. Moreover, sexual exploitation in the form of "sexing in" as an initiation ritual may define young women as sexually available, contributing to a likelihood of repeat victimization unless the young woman can stand up for herself and fight to gain other members' respect.

Finally, given constructions of gender that define young women as nonthreatening, when young women do pose a threat to male gang members, the sanctions they face may be particularly harsh because they not only have caused harm to rival gang members but also have crossed appropriate gender boundaries in doing so. In sum, my findings suggest that gender may function to insulate young women from some types of physical assault and lessen their exposure to risks from rival gang members, but may also make them vulnerable to particular types of violence, including routine victimization by their male peers, sexual exploitation, and sexual assault.

REFERENCES

Bjerregaard, B., & Smith, C. (1993). Gender differences in gang participation, delinquency, and substance use. *Journal of Quantitative Criminology, 4*, 329–355.

Bowker, L. H., Gross, H. S., & Klein, M. W. (1980). Female participation in delinquent gang activities. *Adolescence, 15*, 509–519.

Campbell, A. (1984). *The girls in the gang.* New York: Basil Blackwell.

———. (1990). Female participation in gangs. In C. R. Huff (Ed.), *Gangs in America* (pp. 163–182). Beverly Hills, CA: Sage.

Chesney-Lind, M. (1993). Girls, gangs and violence: Anatomy of a backlash. *Humanity & Society, 17,* 321–344.

Decker, S. H. (1996). Collective and normative features of gang violence. *Justice Quarterly, 13,* 243–264.

Esbensen, F.-A. (1996). Comments presented at the National Institute of Justice/Office of Juvenile Justice and Delinquency Prevention Cluster Meetings, June, Dallas, TX.

Fagan, J., & Pabon E. (1990). Contributions to delinquency and substance abuse to school dropout among inner-city youth. *Youth and Society, 21*(3), 306–354.

——— (1996). Gangs, drugs, and neighborhood change. In C. R. Hulf (Ed.), *Gangs in America,* 2nd ed. (pp. 39–74). Thousand Oaks, CA: Sage Publications.

Joe, K. A., & Chesney-Lind, M. (1995). Just every mother's angel: An analysis of gender and ethnic variations in youth gang membership. *Gender & Society, 9,* 408–430.

Lauderback, D., Hansen, J., & Waldorf, D. (1992). "Sisters are doin' it for themselves": A black female gang in San Francisco. *Gang Journal, 1*(1), 57–70.

Lauritsen, J. L., & Davis Quinet, K. F. (1995). Repeat victimization among adolescents and young adults. *Journal of Quantitative Criminology, 1,* 143–166.

Moore, J. (1991). *Going down to the barrio: Home-boys and homegirls in change.* Philadelphia: Temple University Press.

Perkins, D. B., & Taylor, (1996). Ecological assessments of community disorder: Their relationship to fear of crime and theoretical implications. *American Journal of Community Psychology, 24*(1), 63–107.

Spergel, I. A., & Curry, G. D. (1993). The National Youth Gang Survey: A research and development process. In A. P. Goldstein & C. R. Huff (Eds.), *The gang intervention handbook* (pp. 359–400). Champaign, IL: Research Press.

Taylor, C. (1990). *Dangerous society.* East Lansing, MI: Michigan State University Press.

Winfree, L. T., Jr., Fuller, K., Vigil, T., & Mays, G. L. (1992). The definition and measurement of "gang status": Policy implications for juvenile justice. *Juvenile and Family Court Journal, 43,* 29–37.

CHAPTER 19

Voices from the Barrio: Chicano/a Gangs, Families, and Communities

Marjorie S. Zatz and Edwardo L. Portillos

The authors interviewed 33 youth gang members and 20 adult neighborhood leaders and youth service providers to explore the complicated relationships among gang members, their families, and other residents of poor Chicano/a and Mexicano/a barrios in Phoenix. Listening to the multiple voices of community members allows for a multifaceted understanding of the complexities and contradictions of gang life, both for the youths and for the larger community. The researchers use a community ecology approach to help explain the tensions that develop, especially when community members vary in their desires and abilities to control gang-related activities. The authors point to some of the ways in which gender, age, education, traditionalism, and level of acculturation may help explain variation in the type and strength of private, parochial, and public social control within a community.

Criminologists have long been fascinated with the problems posed by youth gangs. In recent years, community ecology approaches to gangrelated crime and social control have become popular. One strand of research has focused on macrosocial patterns of crime and inequality among the urban underclass (e.g., Sampson and Laub, 1993; Sampson and Wilson, 1996; Wilson, 1987). A second strand has examined the "dual frustrations" facing inner-city parents who fear both gang- and drugrelated crime *and* police harassment of young men of color (Meares, 1997:140; see also Anderson, 1990; Madriz, 1997). These concerns converge in research that examines the connections between and among the structural causes and community-level effects of economic deprivation, institutional and personal networks within a community, the capacity of local networks to

Sources: Adapted from Zatz, M. S., & Portillos, E. L. (2000). Voices from the barrio: Chicano/a gangs, families, and communities. *Criminology, 38*(2), 369–402. Used with permission of publisher.

garner human and economic resources from outside the community, and gang-related crime (Anderson, 1990; Bursik and Grasmick, 1993a,b; Hagedorn, 1998; Moore, 1991; Spergel, 1986; Sullivan, 1989). Bursik and Grasmick (1993a) take this approach the farthest theoretically, incorporating Hunter's (1985) three tiers of local community social control into a reformulation of Shaw and McKay's (1942) social disorganization framework. Their theory of community relations recognizes the relevance of long-term economic deprivation and institutional racism for community-based social control at the private, parochial, and public levels.

Bursik and Grasmick suggest that traditional social disorganization theory, sometimes in combination with subcultural theories, placed an emphasis on the private level of systemic control, as reflected in family and friendship dynamics. In underclass neighborhoods characterized by stable, high levels of delinquency, however, parochial (e.g., churches and schools) and public (e.g., police) forms of social control become more apparent. A few researchers, most notably Hagedorn (1998) and Decker and Van Winkle (1996), have applied Bursik and Grasmick's theory to inner-city gang research. Yet, these studies have been limited to Midwestern cities. We also draw on this theory of community social control, but focus our research in a Chicano/a and Mexicano/a community in the Southwest.[1] As we will demonstrate, our research site reflects a pocket of poverty in the midst of an almost unprecedented economic boom. Also, the community is close to the Mexican border, allowing perhaps for a greater range of traditionalism than might be found in Midwestern cities.

Informed by the gang studies noted above and by other scholarship on the urban poor (e.g., Hernandez, 1990; Moore and Pinderhughes, 1993; Wilson, 1996), we see gang members as integral parts of their communities, engaging in some actions that hurt the community and in some that help it. At the same time, we are particularly attentive to the ways in which gender, age, educational status, and degree of traditionalism differentiate the adults' perceptions of the gangs and choice of private, parochial, or public forms of social control.

THEORETICAL FRAMEWORK: A SYSTEMIC APPROACH TO NEIGHBORHOOD AND GANG DYNAMICS

Most gang research in the United States has been grounded in social disorganization theory, subcultural theories, or, most recently, economic marginalization theories derived from Wilson's (1987) work on the underclass. Bursik and Grasmick (1993a) offer a theoretical framework that combines key elements of Shaw and McKay's (1942) social disorganization theory with recent work on gangs in underclass communities. The central problem with social disorganization theory for gang research, they suggest, is that it overemphasizes family dynamics, focusing on individualized resources and constraints to the exclusion of larger structural concerns. Accordingly, social disorganization approaches cannot adequately account for ongoing patterns of gang behavior in stable neighborhoods where families may live in the same houses or on the same block for many years, often spanning several generations. The gangs in these neighborhoods are often multi-generational, with several members of the extended family belonging to the gang in each generation.

Although initially subcultural theories became popular because of the inability of traditional social disorganization approaches to explain these multigenerational gangs, Moore (1978, 1985, 1991, 1998), Vigil (1988), Hagedorn (1991, 1998), and Sullivan (1989), among others, have offered an alternative explanation that refocuses attention at structural factors, including, especially, the economic marginalization of underclass communities. These scholars point to the crucial importance of whether, and to what extent, residents of poor but stable neighborhoods have access to public resources. Bursik and Grasmick (1993a) weave these concerns into a larger, more encompassing framework that examines access to private, public, and parochial resources. Drawing from Hunter's (1985) typology of local community social control, they suggest that these three dimensions operate simultaneously and that gang activity is most likely to emerge "in areas in which the networks of parochial and public control cannot effectively provide services to the neighborhood" (Bursik and Grasmick, 1993a:141).

Private social control refers to the influences and actions of family and close friends, which could be the nuclear family, the extended family, or the interwoven networks of family and friends that characterize stable barrio communities. Through the family's actions supporting or disdaining particular behaviors, social control is exerted. Parochial social control reflects "the effects of the broader local interpersonal network and the interlocking of local institutions, such as stores, schools, churches and voluntary organizations" (Bursik and Grasmick, 1993a:17). Control is exerted through residents supervising activities within the neighborhood and the integration of local institutions into many aspects of everyday life. Individuals and neighborhoods will vary in the extent to which they can harness parochial forms of social control. For example, monolingual Spanish-speaking parents may encounter difficulties and be easily intimidated when they try to communicate with their children's teachers or school authorities. Public social control, in turn, focuses "on the ability of the community to secure public goods and services that are allocated by agencies located outside the neighborhood" (Bursik and Grasmick, 1993a:17). As Moore and Hagedorn have noted most pointedly, poor barrio communities often do not have access to or alliances with key urban institutions. For instance, although many barrio residents must interact regularly with health care, education, welfare, criminal justice, and immigration authorities, they do so from a position of little or no individual or institutional power. The absence of people who might serve as power brokers, interceding between community residents and institutional authorities, means that residents of economically marginal communities cannot effectively use public systemic control. One example that surfaced often in our interviews was access to police. Although many residents perceived the police to be omnipresent, the same residents complained that the police did not respond quickly when they called for help.

Combining these three forms of social control into a fully systemic model enables a more complete understanding of gang–community dynamics. Following Bursik and Grasmick (1993a), we apply this model to Chicano/a and Mexicano/a gangs in Phoenix. We draw from interviews with gang youths and with adults active in the communities to explore how they perceive gang–neighborhood dynamics. One of the unique contributions of our research to this theoretical agenda is our recognition that access to parochial and public resources is very much gendered. Moreover, as we shall show, recent immigrants and parents with more traditional Mexicano beliefs and values may be more intimidated by key societal institutions and by their children. Thus, we suggest that gender and traditionalism cross-cut age, educational level, and income to influence the extent to which individual parents and neighborhoods can draw on private, parochial, and public social control.

ADULT PERSPECTIVES ON GANGS
AND THE COMMUNITY

The adults expressed a wide range of views, from seeing gangs as a normal part of adolescence to viewing them as social parasites that must be routed from the neighborhoods. This contrast is not surprising, given the heterogeneity of life experiences among barrio residents. Jankowski (1991), Moore (1991), Hagedorn (1998), Decker and Van Winkle (1996), Sullivan (1989), Padilla (1993), and Venkatesh (1996) also report contradictory or ambivalent stances toward gangs in the communities they studied. In the discussion that follows, we attempt to tease out these different perspectives and to account for some of the divergent opinions.

Gangs, the Neighborhood, and the Local Economy

According to a neighborhood specialist for the city, the major problems that surfaced in a survey of South Phoenix residents were crime, homes and landscaping not being well maintained, graffiti, and a shortage of streetlights, followed by the lack of recreational opportunities for young people. Similarly, community leaders repeatedly voiced the fear that graffiti, combined with the threat of drugs and violence, contributes to urban decay by making the neighborhood less attractive to businesses.[2] Yet, gang activity is only one factor affecting the local economy and can as easily be seen as an outcome of economic dislocation as its cause. The weak linkages to centers of economic and political power, in turn, reduce residents' abilities to exercise public systemic control very effectively (Bursik and Grasmick, 1993a:146; Moore, 1985; Moore and Pinderhughes, 1993). It is in precisely such contexts that Bursik and Grasmick suggest gang activity is most likely to develop.

One of the most important and visible forms of public social control is the police. Although a substantial portion of the community is very willing to work with local police in at least some limited ways to eradicate gangs and crime, another portion sees the police, courts, and similar institutions as unable or unwilling to adequately protect them. Tensions between Latino community members and the police have historically been high, the result of years of institutionalized racism in police and court processing (Escobar, 1999; Mirande, 1987; National Minority Advisory Council on Criminal Justice, 1980; U.S. Commission on Civil Rights, 1970; Vigil, 1988). Allegations of police use of excessive force often lie at the heart of these strained relations. In Phoenix, community anger with the police has centered around the violent deaths of three young men: Rudy Buchanan, Jr., Edward Mallet, and Julio Valerio. Buchanan was African American and Latino. A member of the Crips gang who had reputedly threatened that he was going to kill a police officer, Buchanan was shot at 89 times in January of 1995, with 30 bullets entering his body. His family was awarded $570,000 in a settlement with the City of Phoenix in March 1998. Edward Mallet was a 25-year-old African-American double amputee who died in 1994 after being placed in a neck hold by police officers. In March 1998, a jury awarded Mallet's parents $45 million, finding that the police used excessive force that resulted in his death. The city later settled with Mallet's family, paying about $5 million. Finally, 16-year-old Julio Valeria's case is still pending. He was holding a butcher knife when he was pepper sprayed and then shot at 25 times in 1996 by police (Fiscus and Leonard, 1999).

Access to public social control goes beyond policing to encompass the range of agencies and actors who can provide public goods and services. The South Phoenix community did not perceive itself as well situated with regard to such access. Respondents criticized state and local politicians and other city officials for reducing the community's resource base and for placing it low on the priority list for revitalization, and businesses for taking money from the community but not investing in it. . . .

Some neighborhood residents work directly with the youths to curtail gang activities. Exercising both private and parochial social control, some residents tutor neighborhood teens with their studies and help them to find jobs; other residents work with voluntary organizations and local churches, organizing block watches to prevent violence, burglaries, graffiti, and drug sales in the neighborhood. . . .

In the past, our respondents noted, "Mexican gangs were tied closely to the community. This has changed." Today, gangs "rob people of their sense of security. They barricade themselves in their homes because they feel so vulnerable." Another adult respondent told us:

> If a gang is neighborhood based, they protect their neighborhoods and one another, and to the extent they can, their families and the families of other gang members. But that doesn't always work.

These quotes reinforce one of the central contradictions inherent in neighborhood gangs. The youths see themselves as protectors of their communities and the police as abusive interlopers, regardless of whether this imagery appears exaggerated to outsiders. The protection gangs' offer may be reduced today to simply making sure that competing gangs do not gain a foothold in the neighborhood, but the youths are adamant that protection of the community is still one of their primary responsibilities. In this sense, they are an integral component of parochial social control. Nevertheless, gangs also wreak havoc in their communities, both by their actions and by the lure they present to rival gangs. In particular, neighborhood residents are at greater risk of injury today than they were a generation ago because of the increase in drive-by shootings. A youth service provider expressed the views of many adults:

> A lot of innocent people get hurt in drive-bys. They're just there in the wrong place at the wrong time and get killed or shot when they don't have anything to do with the problem.

Similarly, a Chicano social worker commented:

> Neighbors feel they can't go out at night, can't sit on the porch. There's violence and crime. Many gang members may hang out in the neighborhood and not be involved in violence, but they're targets. Somebody will drive by and verbally abuse them, throw things in their yard, or shoot them.

Thus, two different, though interrelated, perspectives surface within the community. Some residents blame the gangs, seeing "the stigma of having gang problems" as contributing to businesses and middle-class families leaving the neighborhood. Other residents focus on the city's and the media's willingness to ignore economic problems in parts of town where poor people of color live. When city officials and reporters do pay attention to the area, they focus only on the negative aspects of life there, without doing much to improve the infrastructure. To better understand these varied perspectives, we looked for structural patterns in the data. As we will demonstrate, much of the variation can be explained by gender, age, number of generations in the United States, educational level, traditionalism, and the extent to which the person's family is gang identified.

The Men's Voices

We asked all of the adult respondents to tell us not only their own opinions about the relationships among gang kids, their families, and the community, but also how they thought other adults in the community perceived these issues. We expected men and women to differ somewhat in their views, consistent with the extant literature on fear of crime and neighborhood-based crime control efforts (Bursik and Grasmick, 1993a:91; Madriz, 1997; Skogan and Maxfield, 1981). Considering first how men in South Phoenix viewed gangs, the neighborhood activists and service providers saw men's opinions as determined primarily by whether they are gang identified. For example, one woman observed

> Fathers don't have a big problem with gangs. They were involved in one way or another when they were younger. They always had a homie-type camaraderie.

Other respondents tied acceptance of gangs to prison life, and pointed to the difficulty of private, familial social control of youths with incarcerated parents. From this perspective,

> [some men] are accepting of [gangs] and are in prison gangs themselves. We have a gang problem because the adult male population is in prison, so the kids are in street gangs.

Regardless of whether they ever formally joined gangs themselves, adults whose families belong to multigenerational gangs appear to be more accepting of their children's involvement in them, may gain prestige from their children's acts, and see the gang as a barrio institution through which cultural norms of personal and family honor are played out. This finding is consistent with similar research in other cities (Harris, 1994; Horowitz, 1983; Horowitz and Schwartz, 1974; Moore, 1978, 1991; Padilla, 1993; Vigil, 1988). A neighborhood specialist for the city said:

> It's multigenerational. The grandfather may have been in a gang. Grandfathers of 40 could still have ties with the gang. You could have a great-grandfather with ties to old gangs!

As they get older, the men ease out of gang life. Yet, as a Latina director of a youth service center commented:

> The oldsters, old gangsters, sit back and watch what's happening. They are very aware. They are learning they have to pull away if they want to live, but those are strong friendships that last forever.

An African-American male police officer expressed a similar opinion:

> In areas with multi-generational gangs, it is difficult for older males to understand why society comes down so hard on the young ones. The degree of criminal activity has not hit them upside the head until they lose a loved one to a shooting. . . . If the men get a reality slap, they see the differences over time. Or they'll say to the kids, 'Why don't you have a gang like we had? We had a good gang.'

Yet, some differences of opinion surface among the men. The neighborhood specialist quoted above continued

> Some men view the gangs with disdain, seeing them as a blight on the community and a threat to community life, and others feel it provides a sense of fraternity, an opportunity to become involved with others who think and act like they'd like to; it provides them with an outlet.

An African-American woman working closely with neighborhood residents drew similar distinctions:

> Some of them are from multigenerational gang families. The parents are hardcore members supportive of the life, and they're raising their kids in it. Others are very hardcore in opposition to it, saying to make prisons tougher. They are harder, more judgmental, saying, "if you do the crime, do the time." . . . They say,

"I'm gonna stop it by buying a .45 and blowing away the first motherfucker who comes in my door."

Thus, for some adult men in the community, gangs are perfectly normal, acceptable parts of life. They take pride in their children following in their footsteps. Other adult men abhor today's gangs. Key factors accounting for these differences of opinion include the extent to which the men hold traditional Mexican values, the length of time spent in the United States and educational achievements. . . .

According to the adults we interviewed, men born in Mexico generally hold the most traditional values and tend to disapprove of the gang life. Yet, they are stymied by their inability to control their children or grandchildren, and if public resources exist that they might employ to better control the youths, these immigrant men do not know how to access them. They are also uncomfortable requesting help from parish priests, school teachers, or social workers. The women, as we shall see, are somewhat more willing to reach out for these parochial forms of social control.

A middle-aged woman directing a neighborhood association providing educational and employment-related services and training for youths noted, "Grandfathers disapprove, see them as lazy and shiftless." A Puerto Rican social worker stated similarly:

A grandfather will say, "I worked in the fields, why can't you?" Kids killing one another is not readily understood by the more traditional older generation.

Yet, another man working closely with boys in the neighborhood said

For the *abuelos* (grandfathers), they have a firm grasp of life, they've lived through many tragedies so they appreciate life and the foolish wasting of it in gangs.

Our data indicate that substantial changes have occurred over time in the perceived extent to which gangs protected the larger community, the dangers to gang members and others in the community posed by today's more lethal weapons, and, generally, the respect with which gang members were and are held by others in the community. We were told:

The general consensus is gangs are negative. This is especially from grandparents who are used to gangs, from the Zoot Suits. They were respected, they were not a danger to the community. They say, "I don't understand these punks, why are they doing these things, not taking care of us, of the neighbors. They talk all the time about being part of the neighborhood but they don't take care of us."

INTERVIEWER: What about the fathers?

When I was a kid we had gangs, but we never used guns. We used chains. When we had a problem and fought, it was one-on-one, or a gang on a gang, but never three, five, six to one. That sounds cowardly to them [the fathers]. This generation gap is a problem. The kids say, "Your way wasn't better, it didn't work. I have more money than you, so how can you tell me it's not right, that your way is better?" This is a big issue. They make money! And they [fathers] can't make money in society.

Another local social worker also reminisced about the "old days" when he was involved in gangs:

> In the past, we weren't out to kill each other. Maybe there'd be fist fights or knives, but we weren't out to kill each other. Guns and drugs are the problem, and they're easily bought on the streets.

Thus, educational level, age, and the recency of their family's immigration to the United States structure barrio men's views about gangs and the range of resources they see as available to them. Grandfathers and fathers who immigrated to the United States may be leery of public forms of social control, such as the police and the juvenile justice system, and more hesitant than their wives to call on the Catholic Church for aid. They rely most heavily on the extended family to control youths, often unsuccessfully. In contrast, men raised in the gang life and still tied to it are more accepting of their children's involvement. Finally, the men raised in the barrio but now successful in local businesses and social services (e.g., probation, clinical psychology) have greater access to political and economic brokers in the metropolitan area and, perhaps for this reason, are more willing to rely on public as well as parochial and private forms of social control. Our data suggest that less variation exists within women's perspectives, with the key distinguishing factor being whether they were raised in a traditional Mexican family, either in the United States or in Mexico.

The Women's Voices

The consensus among our adult respondents was that most women disapprove of gangs. A Puerto Rican male working with families of gang members had the impression that "nine out of ten mothers despise gangs." Some of the women were members themselves when they were younger and may remain at least peripherally involved, but as they become mothers many grow increasingly fearful that their children could die in a gang-related shooting.

Gendered cultural expectations of child-rearing responsibilities appear to have contributed to mothers becoming more active than fathers in opposing gang activities. Also, many of the barrio's adult men are incarcerated, or for other reasons do not interact much with their children. Neighborhood leaders, both male and female, commented that it is primarily the women who come forward to work with them. One neighborhood activist said:

> [The women] are pretty fed up with it . . . 60% of those who come to community meetings are female. They are very vocal, fed up, afraid to lose their children. Some have already lost their children, or their nephews and nieces, at the hands of guns. They want to bring the neighborhood back under control.

Some of these mothers take a very strong line and "won't let daughters date boys who look like *cholos*." Neighborhood women are also well represented at funerals. A parish priest with the dubious honor of burying the neighborhood's children told us, "At wakes you will see 400 kids, 50 mothers, and maybe 10 fathers." Mothers Against Gangs, a grassroots organization begun by a mother after her 16-year-old son died in a gang shooting, is a prime example of women organizing to reduce gang violence. Again, we see a link between private and parochial forms of social control. When parents and grandparents are not able to control the youths, they often turn to community organizations, such as Mothers Against Gangs (see, similarly, Fremon, 1995). Moreover, we see that these examples of private and parochial social control are very much gendered.

Mothers and grandmothers raised with traditional values were less likely to be out on the streets and so did not themselves live the gang life. These traditional women often do not know what to do about their children's involvement with gangs. As an activist knowledgeable about gangs said of the mothers who moved here from Mexico:

> [They] feel helpless. It's something new for them. Many of them have problems with language. The kids speak English better than they [the mothers] do and better than they speak Spanish, so the parents can't communicate with the kids. It's not like in Mexico, where the *abuelos* can say and do things. Here, it depends on the parents.

Similarly, a Chicano social worker stated that for mothers,

> The general feeling is powerlessness. They have to care for them and love them and wish they weren't involved. They may feel guilty. It must be their fault, what did they do wrong . . . it is very painful if the girls are in gangs.

The sense of individual, rather than societal, responsibility for gang violence was stressed by many of our respondents. Specifically, they suggested that young mothers often have inadequate parenting skills. A probation officer raised in the barrio commented

> These kids intimidated their parents way before this. The hardline mothers and grandmothers who really push their kids to stay out [of gangs] are winning the battle. Those who are afraid, and they're mostly the 18–20-year-olds, are afraid because they didn't put their foot down enough. It comes down to parenting skills, taking a hard line.

Social workers and neighborhood activists suggest that some mothers are unwilling to believe that their children are involved in gangs, even when signs are all around them. We were told that traditional women, in particular,

> [see gangs as] a danger to the family unit. They don't want their kids involved in it, are very protective. But they also may have blinders when it comes to their own kids, saying, "My kid isn't into that" when he is.

A South Phoenix parish priest related a story about a mother who wanted her son to be buried in a red shirt and the pallbearers to wear red, claiming it was always her son's favorite color. Another mother insisted that her son was not involved with gangs, until the priest turned to the young man and asked him to explain the significance of his red shoelaces to his mother.

In conclusion, then, our data suggest that whether and when adults rely on private, parochial, or public forms of social control depends on their access to economic and political resources and their position within the family and neighborhood power structures. One of our contributions to this literature is to show that this access may also be gendered, with women evidencing more indicators of powerlessness, such as not speaking English, and less experience dealing with businesses, courts, and the like. These women are most likely to advocate for a mix of parochial and public social control. They fear for their children's lives, but they tend to be among the most intimidated by their sons and daughters. Many of these women have organized within their communities and work with the police to at least a limited extent, hoping that these efforts will help to keep their children alive. This combination of private, parochial, and public social control is the premise of groups such as Mothers Against Gangs. In contrast, women who were in gangs as teenagers and who maintained that identity are generally the most accepting, and perhaps the least fearful, of gang violence and the least willing to let the police into their communities. Even these women, however, express fears of losing their children to gang violence and may draw on parochial forms of social control within the community.

The perceptions held by adult service providers and residents may be plagued by faulty, perhaps romanticized, recollections of what gangs were like in earlier generations. Also, many of the adults we interviewed had vested interests in the gang problem. Reliance solely on their perceptions ignores how young people see their own lives and the relationship between their gangs and other community members. Consistent with our emphasis on multiple standpoints, we turn now to the thoughts and concerns of the youths.

YOUTH PERSPECTIVES ON GANGS AND THE COMMUNITY

Historically, gangs have been important neighborhood institutions offering disenchanted, disadvantaged youths a means of coping with the isolation, alienation, and poverty they experience every day (Decker and Van Winkle, 1996; Hagedorn, 1991, 1998; Horowitz, 1983; Jackson, 1991; Joe and Chesney-Lind, 1995; Moore, 1978, 1985, 1991; Padilla, 1993; Sullivan, 1989; Vigil, 1988). Yet, gangs are dynamic, responding to transformations in the larger social order. Sometimes, changes in the social and economic structures also cause cracks in what we call the gang–family–barrio equality. It is not so unusual today to find families living in two different neighborhoods and, thus, often participating in two or more gangs. When this situation occurs, fissures appear in the cement bonding the community's social structure together.

Gangs as Neighborhood Institutions

Regardless of what other neighborhood residents may think of them, the youths identify strongly with their neighborhoods, consider themselves to be integral parts of their barrios, and view their gangs as neighborhood institutions. They see themselves as protectors of their neighborhoods, at least against intrusion by rival gangs. A few youths take pride in their care of elderly residents. However, most youths acknowledge that they do not contribute much to their neighborhoods, excluding community service stipulated as part of their probation or parole agreements.[3] For example, one youth stated:

> We spray-paint the walls and stuff like that, stealing cars, shooting people when we do drive-bys and stuff like that.

Moreover, some youths recognize that innocent bystanders are occasionally shot in drive-bys or other revenge killings

> People are getting smoked every day and you don't even hear about it on the news, only if it is crazy and shit.

Chicano/a gangs often take the name of their barrio as their gang name. With few exceptions, the youths must live in the neighborhood and be of Mexican origin to become a member of the neighborhood gang.[4] These membership requirements hold whether the youth is "born into" the gang or "jumped" in. Some, particularly the young women, are simply "born" into the gang because they live in the neighborhood. They do not need any more formal initiation rites: It is their neighborhood, so it is their gang. If they want to be taken seriously as a gang member, though, being "born in" is not enough. The youths—male and female—must endure a serious beating by a group of their homeboys or homegirls (Portillos, 1999).

Beyond feeling ties to the physical boundaries of the barrio, the youths feel strong emotional ties because neighbors are often family members. If we contextualize the term "family" more broadly to include the nuclear family, the extended family, and the fictive family (*compadres* and *comadres*), gang–family ties become even stronger. All of the youths in our sample claimed that at least one other family member was involved in gangs. For example, a youth informed us

> I got two aunts that were in a gang, my dad was in a gang, my grandpa was in a gang, and I got a lot of cousins in gangs. Most of them are in my barrio but some of them aren't.

Siblings, cousins, and family friends so close as to be considered cousins are frequently members of the same gang, resulting in what often appears to be a gang–family–barrio equality. Although these overlapping social relationships have characterized Chicano/a gangs in the past (Moore, 1991; Vigil, 1988; Zatz, 1987), and in large part continue to define them today, we find that geographic dispersion has altered the tight bonds among the gang, the family, and the barrio.

COMMUNITIES IN TURMOIL:
FAMILY FIGHTING FAMILY

Family mobility was another issue that came up frequently in our interviews and provides insights into some of the ways in which public social control and, to a lesser extent, parochial control shape and constrain private forms of social control. Sometimes, families moved because of divorce or job opportunities elsewhere in the valley. Other times, they moved because the parents were so fearful of gang activity in the neighborhood. Children also went to live with grandparents or aunts when their parents were incarcerated. Finally, teenagers unable to get along with their parents sometimes moved in with relatives. An unfortunate and ironic side effect of this mobility is that it may lead to gang rivalries cross-cutting families. That is, if gang warfare erupts between these different neighborhoods, families may literally be caught in the cross-fire. This phenomenon of family fighting family is anathema to more traditional Chicanos/as and Mexicanos/as, challenging existing notions of private, familial social control.[5] A 15-year-old female commented that more than 50 members of her extended family are or were in gangs:

> We can't have family reunions or anything because they are always fighting, like my *tios* (uncles) fight. At the funerals they fight, or at the park, or at a picnic when we get together, they just fight. So sometimes the family don't get together, only for funerals, that's the only time.

Similarly, a 16-year-old male reported that his dad was mad because

> I am from westside; they are from eastside. See, I was supposed to be from eastside, but I didn't want to be from there. He don't want me to be his son because I'm not from eastside.

For the family that is split across two feuding gangs, cycles of revenge killings are particularly devastating. A 17-year-old male described the conflicts within his family:

> And it's crazy because we are like from different gangs, only me and my cousin are from the same gang. Like my brother, I always disrespect him because he's from Camelback and shit, they did a drive-by on my house and shit, and then he called me. I was like, "Fuck you, motherfucker, fuck your barrio and shit," and he was like, "Don't disrespect," and I was like, "Fuck you." That's the only thing bad about it if you decide to join the wrong gang.[6]

Similarly, a young Mexicano-Indian clarified his relationship with his uncles:

> They are from different gangs, though . . . but I don't care about them because they be trying to shoot at us all the time. My own uncle shot at me, one of them tried to kill me already, but that's alright.

He explained further that although most members of his family, including brothers, sisters, aunts, uncles, his dad, his mom, his grandfather, and numerous cousins were in the same gang, a few claimed different neighborhoods. He noted rather matter-of-factly:

> I got about two uncles in a gang. I had four of them, but one is dead. My uncles killed him for some reason, I don't know, different barrio maybe.

When family feuds become entwined with gang rivalries, it is clear that the private system of social control has broken down. Family and friendship dynamic are no longer able to keep peace within a community. Under these conditions, parochial and public forms of social control typically come into play.

NOT TO DIE FOR

Gang members are supposed to be willing to do anything for their homeboys and homegirls, even to die for them. The importance of demonstrating one's "heart," or willingness to be "down" for the gang, is the major reason for jumping in new members and the basis for extolling acts of bravery and craziness (*locura*) by gang members (Portillos et al., 1996). To assess the relative importance of gangs and families as predominant institutions in the youths' lives, Decker and Van Winkle (1996) explicitly asked gang members to choose between their family or the gang. The overwhelming majority, 89%, of the youths chose their families. As Decker and Van Winkle explain their finding, "For most gang members, the gang was a place to find protection, companionship and understanding. Their family, however, represented something deeper, a commitment that most saw as transcending life in the gang" (1996:251). As we have shown, often gang members *are* family members.

Given the assumed importance of gangs and historically close ties among the gang, the family, and the barrio, one of our most interesting findings was that more than half of the youths would *not* willingly die for all of their homeboys and homegirls. About a third were willing to die for specific individuals who were in their gang, but not for everyone. Another third straightforwardly stated that they would not willingly die for their gangs. The reason, they said, was "because I know they wouldn't die for me, they ain't that stupid."

In response to the direct query, "For whom would you willingly die?" all of the youths claimed that they would die for their families. When probed, they named their mothers, their children, their siblings, maybe an aunt or grandmother, and specific friends and relatives. Some of these family members belonged to the gang, but others did not. The distinction between someone who is simply a member of one's gang and someone who is family (including fictive kin) was clarified for us by a 16-year-old male who, a few days previously, had been struck by a bullet that, had he not gotten in the way, would have hit a friend's grandmother. He said, "I will die for my *true* homeboy; he would die for me."

We suggest that affirming one's willingness to die for a friend takes on new meaning when easy access to guns makes death a real possibility. When asked about the bad parts of gang life, "death" was typically the first factor named by both the gang members and adults. Probing indicated that the youths have a very real sense that they could die if they remain in *la vida loca*. In earlier generations of gangs, when death was not so common a feature, it may have been far easier to claim, with plenty of bravado, that one would die for one's gang.

The responses to our question reinforce the gendered nature of gang life. Even though female gang members prided themselves on their fighting skills, none of the young women declared a willingness to die for her gang. A few confessed that they might have done so when they were younger, but their tone suggested that this was a phase they had outgrown. These gendered responses are consistent with the general findings in the literature of lower rates of violence and lesser acceptance of violence among females than males (Chesney-Lind and Sheldon, 1998; Curry, 1998; Joe and Chesney-Lind, 1995), but they may also reflect the greater relevance of the family and private social control for young women than for young men.

It is difficult to determine at this point whether we are simply seeing an aging or maturation effect, in which as youths become older and perhaps leave the gang life behind, they see the gang in less romantic terms. They may be maturing into a more adult way of taking care of the barrio, which as we have maintained *is* their extended family, or we may be seeing evidence of a crack in the gang–family–barrio equality.

Of particular interest to our thesis, we suggest that the apparent contradiction between intrafamily fighting and a willingness to die only for one's family may be explained by a more careful analysis of variation in the forms that private social control may take. That is, family fighting family suggests a *reduction* in the amount of private social control, but when youths report that they would die for their families, but not for their gangs (excepting gang members who are family or close family friends), this indicates that the family remains a potent force in their lives. Thus, we do not see a complete breakdown in private social control, but rather what appear to be some changes in the form that private social control takes as we move from more traditional families to more acculturated families. When we add economic stresses and political disenfranchisement, we also see few opportunities for courting public social control on the community's terms. In the section that follows, we return to our earlier theme of economic and political dislocations and what these imply for local youths.

GANGS, MULTIPLE MARGINALITIES, AND URBAN DISLOCATIONS

The final theme that emerged from interviews with the youths brings us back to Vigil's concept of multiple marginalities and urban dislocations. The immediate world within which these youths live is marked by poverty, racial discrimination, cultural misunderstandings, and gendered expectations. As one young man stated, "We are a bunch of project kids, always on the move."

All of the youths in our sample were either kicked out or dropped out of school, and many had not completed ninth grade. This lack of education makes it exceedingly difficult to leave their marginal positions in the inner city and the gang life in their neighborhoods behind (see, similarly, Anderson, 1990; Padilla, 1993; Spergel, 1986). They spoke at length about problems they faced in school. For example:

> I use to go to Lincoln Middle School. The teachers, fuckin' white teachers. The gym teacher, you know just because I was messin' around, threw me up against the locker and I reported him. And nobody said shit about it. I told them, "fuck that, I ain't coming to this school no more" and they didn't even call the damn police. When they did call the police, they said they were going to take me to jail. So I just took off, I was like what the fuck, the motherfucker, he was the one pushing me.

It is interesting to note that the only times when the youths spoke about what we might call parochial and public forms of social control, it was to complain about them. As the above quote indicates, teachers were not viewed as a resource by most of these youths, but rather as authority figures who reinforced their daily experiences of racism, marginality, and alienation. Moreover, their sense was that the police regularly sided with the teachers, rather than protecting the youths against what they perceived to be assaults and other forms of aggression on the part of the teachers.

The teens we interviewed are cognizant of the barriers confronting them. They recognize that their criminal and academic records make it almost impossible for them to move up the socioeconomic ladder. Yet, they still hold very mainstream aspirations. They see themselves as settling down to life with a steady partner or spouse and children, and they hope to be able to find a decent job. They want to become jet pilots, police officers, and firefighters, and they aim someday to purchase their own homes. For example, a young man expressed high hopes for his future but recognized the sad reality of life in the barrio:

> I want to become an Air Force pilot, that wouldn't be a bad thing to be. The only fucked-up thing is that I can't become a pilot because I have already been convicted of a felony in adult court.

Thus, although these youths may aspire to very mainstream futures, they recognize that poor schooling, inadequate job training, felony records, and racial/ethnic discrimination limit their potential for success.

CONCLUSIONS

In closing, we must stress that ours is an exploratory study, and our conclusions are based on only 53 interviews. Also, we did not set out to test Bursik and Grasmick's thesis; thus, our study does not constitute a full test of their model. We found, however, that attention to private, parochial, and public social control helped us to better understand the complexities of the relationship between gang members and other community residents.

We urge further research examining the perspectives of adults living and working with the youths. They know a lot about the youths' lives. Some adults are very sad and jaded, having watched their own children die in gang-related incidents. Other adults remain hopeful of making small changes in their worlds, with or without the help of police, business leaders, or politicians. Many adults are themselves former gang members and can shed light on historical shifts in the relationship between the gang, the family, and the neighborhood. Their insights, we suggest, should be incorporated into future studies of neighborhood-based gangs.

In conclusion, our study contributes to the growing body of research on gangs as situated socially and politically within poor urban communities of color. Like many other gang researchers (e.g., Curry and Decker, 1998; Curry and Spergel, 1988; Decker and Van Winkle, 1996; Hagedorn, 1991, 1998; Horowitz, 1983, 1987; Jankowski, 1991; Joe and Chesney-Lind, 1995; Klein, 1995; Moore, 1978, 1985, 1991; Padilla, 1993; Vigil, 1988), we assert that the social, economic, and political contexts within which gang life is set help to explain the complex and often contentious relations among gang members, their families, and the larger communities of which they form a part.

The gang was, and is, composed of brothers, sisters, cousins, and neighbors. The gang gives them a sense of community, a place where they belong. Kicked out of school, assumed to be troublemakers, looking tough and feeling scared, these young people are well aware that their options in life are very much constrained by poverty, racial discrimination, cultural stereotyping, and inadequate education.

Within this context, we suggest that Bursik and Grasmick's (1993a) theory of neighborhood dynamics helps explain the complex and often contradictory relations among the gang, the family, and the barrio. Their attention to private, parochial, and public levels of community-based social control are evident in the barrio we studied, and they point further to the difficulties facing community residents when they try to garner political and economic resources from outside their communities. It is, perhaps, to these political and economic linkages and disconnections that gang researchers and others concerned with crime in poor urban communities should look next.

NOTES

1. For purposes of this paper, Chicano/a refers to men (Chicano) and women (Chicana) of Mexican descent living in the United States. Mexicano/a refers to men (Mexicano) and women (Mexicana) who were born in Mexico. While the Mexicano and Mexicana youths must be living in the United States to become part of our sample, they may or may not be U.S. citizens or permanent residents.

2. Neighborhood vehemence against gangs defacing the community was highlighted in October of 1995, while we were conducting our field work. More than 40 angry residents appeared at a juvenile court hearing, hoping to convince the judge that two

16-year-olds should be prosecuted in adult court. The youths had gone on a rampage, spray-painting 32 houses and some cars (Whiting, 1995).

3. Members of the gangs we studied sell drugs, steal cars, and commit other crimes as both individual and gang-related activities. Unlike the gangs discussed by Padilla (1993) and Jankowski (1991), however, these gangs are not organized as criminal enterprises.

4. The major exception is a predominantly Mexicano gang that accepts some white youths as members.

5. The theme of inter-gang conflicts within families arose during the course of our interviews with the youths. Because interviews with adults were taking place at the same time, we were not able to systematically ask the adults for their perceptions of how extensive this problem had become. We did, however, ask samples of probation officers and juvenile court judges whom we later interviewed for a related project to discuss this issue, and we incorporate their views here.

6. Pseudonyms are used in place of individual and gang names throughout this analysis. Street names have also been changed so as not to identify particular neighborhoods.

REFERENCES

Anderson, E. (1990). *Street wise.* Chicago, IL: University of Chicago Press.

Bursik, R. J., Jr., & Grasmick, H. G. (1993a). *Neighborhoods and crime: The dimensions of effective community control.* New York: Lexington.

———. (1993b). Economic deprivation and neighborhood crime rates, 1960–1980. *Law and Society Review, 27*(2), 263–283.

Chesney-Lind, M., & Sheldon, R. G. (1998). *Girls, delinquency, and juvenile justice* (2nd ed.). Belmont, CA: Wadsworth.

Curry, G. D. (1998). Female gang involvement. *Journal of Research in Crime and Delinquency, 35*(1), 100–118.

Curry, G. D., & Decker, S. H. (1998). *Confronting gangs: Crime and community.* Los Angeles: Roxbury.

Curry, G. D., & Spergel, I. A. (1988). Gang homicide, delinquency, and community. *Criminology, 26,* 381–405.

Decker, S. H., & Van Winkle, B. (1996). *Life in the gang: Family, friends, and violence.* New York: Cambridge University Press.

Escobar, E. J. (1999). *Race, police, and the making of a political identity: Mexican Americans and the Los Angeles Police Department, 1900–1945.* Berkeley: University of California Press.

Fremon, C. (1995). *Father Greg and the homeboys.* New York: Hyperion.

Hagedorn, J. M. (1991). Gangs, neighborhoods, and public policy. *Social Policy, 38*(4), 529–542.

———. (1998). *People and folks: Gangs, crime and the underclass in a Rustbelt city* (2nd ed.). Chicago: Lake View.

Harris, M. G. (1994). Cholas, Mexican-American girls, and gangs. *Sex Roles, 30*(3/4), 289–301.

Hernández, J. (1990). Latino alternatives to the underclass concept. *Latino Studies Journal, 1,* 95–105.

Horowitz, R. (1983). *Honor and the American dream.* New Brunswick, NJ: Rutgers University Press.

———. (1987). Community tolerance of gang violence. *Social Problems, 34,* 437–450.

Horowitz, R., & Schwartz, G. (1974). Honor, normative ambiguity and gang violence. *American Sociological Review, 39,* 238–251.

Hunter, A. J. (1985). Private, parochial and public school orders: The problem of crime and incivility in urban communities. In G. D. Suttles & M. N. Zald (Eds.), *The challenge of social control: Citizenship and institution building in modern society.* Norwood, NJ: Ablex.

Jackson, P. I. (1991). Crime, youth gangs and urban transition: The social dislocations of postindustrial economic development. *Justice Quarterly, 8,* 379–98.

Jankowski, M. S. (1991). *Islands in the street: Gangs and American urban society.* Berkeley: University of California Press.

Joe, K., & Chesney-Lind, M. (1995). Just every mother's angel: An analysis of gender and ethnic variation in youth gang membership. *Gender and Society, 9,* 408–40.

Klein, M. W. (1995). *The American street gang: Its nature, prevalence and control.* Oxford: Oxford University Press.

Madriz, E. (1997). *Nothing bad happens to good girls: Fear of crime in women's lives.* Berkeley: University of California Press.

Meares, T. L. (1997). Charting race and class differences in attitudes toward drug legalization and law enforcement: Lessons for federal criminal law. *Buffalo Criminal Law Review, 1,* 137–74.

Mirandé, A. (1987). *Gringo justice.* South Bend, IN: Notre Dame Press.

Moore, J. W. (1978). *Homeboys: Gangs, drugs, and prison in the barrios of Los Angeles.* Philadelphia: Temple University Press.

———. (1985). Isolation and stigmatization in the development of an underclass: The case of Chicano gangs in East Los Angeles. *Social Problems, 33,* 1–10.

———. (1991). *Going down to the barrio: Homeboys and homegirls in change.* Philadelphia: Temple University Press.

———. (1998). Gangs and the underclass: A comparative perspective. In J. Hagedorn (Ed.), *People and folks* (2nd ed.). Chicago: Lake View.

Moore, J. W., & Pinderhughes, R. (Eds). (1993). *In the barrios: Latinos and the underclass debate.* New York: Russell Sage.

National Minority Advisory Council on Criminal Justice. (1980). *The inequality of justice.* Washington, DC: U.S. Department of Justice.

Padilla, F. (1993). *The gang as an American enterprise.* New Brunswick, NJ: Rutgers University Press.

Portillos, E. L. (1999) Women, men and gangs: The social construction of gender in the barrio. In M. Lind & J. Hagedorn (eds.), *Female gangs in America: Girls, gangs and gender.* Chicago: Lake View Press.

Portillos, E. L., Jurik, N. C., & Zatz, M. S. (1996). Machismo and Chicano/a gangs: Symbolic resistance or oppression. *Free Inquiry in Creative Sociology, 24*(2), 175–83.

Sampson, R. J., & Laub, J. H. (1993). Structural variations in juvenile court processing: Inequality, the underclass, and social control. *Law and Society Review, 27*(2), 285–311.

Sampson, R. J., & Wilson, W. J. (1996). Toward a theory of race, crime and urban inequality. In J. Hagan & R. D. Peterson (Eds.), *Crime and inequality.* Stanford: Stanford University Press.

Shaw, C. R., & McKay, H. D. (1942). *Juvenile delinquency and urban areas.* Chicago: University of Chicago Press.

Skogan, W. G., & Maxfield, M. G. (1981). *Coping with crime: Individual and neighborhood reactions*. Beverly Hills, CA: Sage.

Spergel, I. A. (1986). The violent gang problem in Chicago: A local community approach. *Social Service Review, 60*, 94–131.

Sullivan, M. (1989). *"Getting paid": Youth crime and work in the inner city*. Ithaca, NY: Cornell University Press.

U.S. Commission on Civil Rights. (1970). *Mexican Americans and the administration of justice in the Southwest*. Washington, DC: U.S. Government Printing Office.

Venkatesh, S. A. (1996). The gang in the community. In R. C. Huff (Ed.), *Gangs in America* (2nd ed.). Beverly Hills, CA: Sage.

Vigil, J. D. (1988). *Barrio gangs: Street life and identity in southern California*. Austin: University of Texas Press.

Whiting, B. (1995). Adult justice sought for two teenage taggers. *Arizona Republic*, pp. B1-B6.

Wilson, W. J. (1987). *The truly disadvantaged*. Chicago: University of Chicago Press.

———. (1996). *When work disappears: The world of the new urban poor*. New York: Random House.

Zatz, M. S. (1987). Chicano youth gangs and crime: The creation of a moral people. *Contemporary Crises, 11*, 129–58.

SECTION VIII

Drugs and Crime

One of the most enduring controversies in criminology is that surrounding the relationship between drugs and crime. Although no one disputes the correlation between drugs and crime, the issue of causation is controversial. Do drugs cause crime, or are they related in some other manner? For some time, the drugs–crime hypothesis has captured the attention of criminologists. There are some data indicating that offenders who commit property crimes (burglary and theft) are more likely to commit these crimes in order to get money to buy drugs. The Bureau of Justice Statistics (BJS) reports that about a quarter of convicted property offenders incarcerated in local jails committed their crimes to get money for drugs, compared to only 5% of violent and public order offenders. The BJS also reports that the pattern among state prisoners is very similar (Mumola & Karberg, 2004). Drug dependence among offenders is also alarmingly high. One BJS survey found that 53% of federal inmates and 45% of federal inmates met the criteria for, respectively, drug dependence and abuse (Guerino, Harrison, & Sabol, 2011).

The chapters in this section examine the issue from the perspectives of those who use and sell drugs. These articles illuminate how illicit drug offenders construct and give meaning to their involvement with drugs and its accompanying lifestyle.

In Chapter 20, Wilson R. Palacios and Melissa E. Fenwick provide a vivid narrative of what it's like to participate in the Ecstasy culture. During a 15-month participant-observation study, the authors attended dozens of all-night (and sometimes several days in length) "clublike" parties, observing and asking questions of participants. Their article provides a plethora of thick, rich descriptions of how individuals experience Ecstasy, from the method of ingestion and euphoric effects to the eventual coming down. The chapter serves as an introduction to a continuing study, one of the first of its kind examining contemporary Ecstasy culture in America.

In Chapter 21, "'Cooks Are Like Gods': Hierarchies in Methamphetamine-Producing Groups," Robert Jenkot takes a behind-the-scenes look at female methamphetamine users, dealers, and producers. The author interviewed

31 incarcerated women about their experiences with methamphetamine. He focused on the experiences of methamphetamine producers, or "cooks" as they are referred to in the illicit trade. This study offers insight into the hierarchies of the methamphetamine trade.

REFERENCES

Guerino, P., Harrison, P. M., & Sabol, W. J. (2011). *Prisoners in 2010* (NCJ 236096). Washington, DC: U.S. Department of Justice, Bureau of Justice Statistics.

Mumola, C. J., & Karberg, J. C. (2004). *Drug use and dependence, state and federal prisoners, 2004* (NCJ 213530). Washington, DC: United States Department of Justice, Bureau of Justice Statistics.

CHAPTER 20

"E" Is for Ecstasy: A Participant-Observation Study of Ecstasy Use

Wilson R. Palacios and Melissa E. Fenwick

The authors offer an insider's view of the Ecstasy culture in south Florida (Tampa). During a 15-month participant-observation study, they attended dozens of all-night (and sometimes several days in length) "clublike" parties, observing and asking questions of participants. Attending the nightclubs and parties where Ecstasy was freely available, the researchers were able to allay suspicion by presenting themselves as a couple interested in the music underground. In some cases, they advised the others that they were researchers; in other cases, they did not, preferring to observe incognito. This chapter is a brief introduction to a continuing study, one of the first of its kind examining contemporary Ecstasy culture in America.

INTRODUCTION

In *Writing on Drugs,* Sadie Plant argues that "every drug has its own character, its own unique claim to fame" (1999, p. 4). This is certainly true in the case of Ecstasy (MDMA). In 1986, Jerome Beck wrote that

> MDMA has been thrust upon the public awareness as a largely unknown drug which to some is a medical miracle and to others a social devil. . . . There have been the born-again protagonists who say that once you have tried it you will see the light and will defend it against any attack, and there have been the staunch antagonists who say this is nothing but LSD revisited and it will certainly destroy our youth. (p. 305)

Beck's statements have proven to be as relevant today as they were 25 years ago, accurately characterizing the current media blitz surrounding the drug MDMA/

Source: Written especially for this volume. This project was supported by funds from USF Research & Creative Scholarship Grant #12-21-926RO.

Ecstasy. On July 1, 1985, at the behest of the U.S. Drug Enforcement Administration, MDMA/Ecstasy was temporarily placed in Schedule I of the Controlled Substance Act (CSA) and permanently placed on November 13, 1986. Although it may seem easy to understand the DEA's objectives in banning MDMA/Ecstasy, their actions inadvertently paved the way for the development of a large, international underground manufacturing and distribution network worth millions of dollars and, to a greater extent, a larger hidden population of users.

Law enforcement officials and politicians have led this new charge against MDMA/Ecstasy and its users. Newspaper headlines such as "Drug's Night Club Pull Seems Hard to Curb" (*Boston Globe*), "Raving and Behaving: The Reputation of the High-Energy, All-Night Dance Parties Outpaces the Reality" (*Buffalo News*), and "Deputies: Ecstasy Overdose Killed Teen" (*St. Petersburg Times*) have been used to usher in a new "war on drugs," which, like our previous efforts with crack cocaine, stands to dramatically increase jail and prison populations and challenge our taken-for-granted notions concerning civil liberties.

Despite attention from the criminal justice system, Ecstasy use and abuse has received minimal coverage from the social scientific community, in particular the field of criminology. Much of what we think we know about patterns of use and abuse concerning this drug stems largely from existing self-report surveys, such as Monitoring the Future, drug surveillance systems such as Drug Abuse Warning Network, and the Arrestee Drug Abuse Monitoring program. Until now, there has been little in the way of active ethnographic fieldwork in this country concerning MDMA/Ecstasy use and its culture.

This chapter is derived from an ongoing, two-year ethnographic study concerning the use of "club drugs" (e.g., MDMA/Ecstasy, ketamine/Special K, GHB, and nitrates) and club culture in Florida. The research focuses on the emotional state of individuals who ingest MDMA/Ecstasy, the local market for such drugs, and the vernacular of this drug culture.

The drug, formally named 3, 4-methylenedioxymethamphetamine (MDMA), is commonly referred to on the street as Ecstasy (Cohen, 1998). Although other names such as Adam, the Love Drug, Mickey, X, Raven, and M&M's are used to refer to MDMA, the term *Ecstasy* is the most recognizable. In the Hillsborough and Pinellas County area, the terms *bean*(s) and *rolls* are used interchangeably to refer to Ecstasy. When asked about the origin of these terms, interviewees told us that Ecstasy pills are called *beans* because they "look like little lima beans" and *rolls* because of the way they make you feel.

Ecstasy tablets are sold on the street under names pressed in distinctive designer logos on one side of the pill. For example, in the field we came across Ecstasy pills sold under such names as Mitsubishi, Smurfs, Calvin Kleins, Nikes, Anchors, Rolls Royce (RR), Starburst, Pink Hearts, Double Stack Crowns, Navigator, KnockOuts, Blue Gene, and Red Gene. Many of the Ecstasy pills we encountered in the field were of various colors, although white was the most common. Moreover, we quickly learned that the popularity of these pills was solely dependent on word-of-mouth marketing from the individual consumer level. Ecstasy represents a marketing bonanza because of its ability to induce an intense physiologically and psychologically euphoric state without the stigma associated with drugs like crack cocaine or heroin. In addition, it is a drug that many feel they can realistically walk away from or "schedule" into their lives on an as-needed basis. The following comments typify this attitude:

> It's not like doing crack or smack [heroin]. . . . You don't hit a pipe or needle. . . .
> I wouldn't do that 'cause my friends would be like. . . . Hey, crack monster . . . or
> crack freak . . . and that's not cool. . . . Think about it . . . it's a little pill which
> takes you for a ride and then it's over. . . . You don't feign [crave] for it. . . . You
> can do it every weekend or once a month or once or twice a year . . . just depends
> on what you've got going in your life and the people around you. (Jason, a single
> white male, 20 years of age)
>
> When I was in college I would roll [use Ecstasy] every weekend except for
> midterms and finals . . . but since I've been out I haven't rolled in the last two
> years. . . . I'm not saying that I won't . . . but I've just been busy with work, and
> since I work for the system [referring to the criminal justice system] I know they
> drug test. . . . If I will do it again I'll just plan for it. . . . It stays in your system
> from two to five days. (Mark, a single white male, 29 years of age)

The intense physiological (amphetamine-like) rush from Ecstasy is referred to as *blowing up* or *rolling*. This experience varies across individuals. However, the overwhelming sensation of a heightened emotional and physical state was a commonly reported characteristic. The following comments typify this recurring theme:

> When you're blowing up it is like your fucking skin is going to come undone. Just
> imagine an orgasm, but 20 or 50 times better and intense. That's the lure of X.
> (Jerry, a single white male, 25 years of age)
>
> I felt like I was coming undone from the inside. You can feel every inch of
> your skin, even the tiny little hairs on your arms and legs . . . feels that good.
> (Amy, single white female, 19 years of age)

Valter and Arrizabalaga (1998, p. 13) argue that "the world-wide and still increasing use and abuse of MDMA (Ecstasy) is due to its euphoriant properties and capacity to enhance communication and contact with other people." Actually, because of this last property, Ecstasy is really a member of a small class of compounds called *entactogens* or *empathogens* (which means creating contact or empathy) and therefore should not be classified as a "hallucinogenic-amphetamine" drug (see Cohen, 1998). This feeling of connecting with other people is what makes Ecstasy such a psychological draw for most people, including our participants:

> I know I could go to [local nightclub] and after I eat my pill I won't care what
> people think of me. . . . I won't care if they think I'm fat, too skinny, or if I am
> wearing the wrong shoes. . . . I just don't care because it becomes about meeting
> people and just meeting different kinds of people. (Betty, a single white female,
> 25 years of age, mother of two)

It's about having a good time. . . . I even don't have to worry about guys trying to hook up [reference to sex] with me. . . . If guys are rolling, you know they are not looking at you that way . . . at least not when they are rolling . . . maybe later on the comedown [referring to the end of the night], but not during. (Carrie, a white Latina female, 21 years of age)

BLOWING UP

Our participants gauged the strength and purity of a pill according to the intensity of their *blowing up* or *rolling* experience. Some acute reactions experienced by our participants during the blowing up or rolling stage were bruxism (teeth grinding), trismus (jaw clenching), uncontrollable fidgeting of extremities, rapid eye movements, and a heightened sensitivity to all external stimuli (touch, lights, sounds, etc.). To tap into these varied experiences, we asked the following: "How do you know you are/were blowing up?" These are some of the responses we received:

It usually wouldn't come on until after 30 or 40 minutes, but when it did, you would just feel this overwhelming sensation of all your emotions being flooded [released] throughout your body. I would say after 45 minutes into it I would feel my eyes twitch, and I would have this need to just massage everything and anything around me. One night I was massaging my arms so hard without realizing it or feeling any pain that the next day I woke up and had broken my skin. I was in pain the next morning, but I did not remember feeling any pain when I was doing this. . . . It just feel so good. (Tim, a white Latino male, 27 years of age, married)

You can't help being or wanting to be touched. . . . I've seen men touching each other without all the worry about people thinking they were gay or anything. . . . You know you're rolling when somebody comes up to you and begins massaging your neck, shoulders, or back. . . . It feels just so good that one time I had my girlfriend massage my lower back so hard that she made me pee in my pants—now that was a good bean. . . . You can't know what I'm talking about unless you've been there. (Stacie, a white single female, 18 years of age)

The first time I rolled I didn't feel a thing. . . . I was pissed because I spent some money and everyone around me was rolling their asses off and I was the only one in the group sitting there like a dumb fuck . . . but the second time I rolled . . . that's when I can tell you that I honestly blow up. . . . I first noticed it because of the lights. . . . Everything was clearer and brighter. . . . I would see the bright colors from the corner of my eyes and then my feet started swaying to the music. . . . I looked at my feet and it was like they weren't even mine. . . . I kept wanting to get up and just walk around and talk to people. . . . I didn't care what people thought of [me] . . . I just wanted to be around people. (Lady X, a single white female, 23 years of age)

I really don't like anything speedy. . . . My father died of a heart attack at a young age. . . . I don't think I have a heart condition, but I just don't want anything speeding my heart. . . . I usually like the ones that are not speedy. . . . I like for it [Ecstasy] to come on slow and gradually over the night. . . . I want it to last.

. . . I'm not one for dancing or stuff like that, I just want to sit there and take it all in. (Jane, a single white female, 27 years of age)

Side Effects

Of all of the possible acute reactions—papillary dilation, headache, hypertension, nausea, tachycardia, blurred vision, hypertonicity, and tremors—that Ecstasy induces, jaw clenching and teeth grinding (trismus and bruxism) were among the side effects most cited by our participants:

> You must always have something to chew on or you'll end up loosening your teeth. (Mary, a single white female, 21 years of age; using Ecstasy for two years)
> The only thing I hate about rolling is how your jaw feels the next morning. You just can't help chewing gum, but you can chew the same piece of gum all night long and not realize it. . . . You can keep chewing because you need something in your mouth, but you don't realize how much pain your jaw is going to be [in] the next day. There have been times when I couldn't even open my mouth for one or two days after rolling. . . . It's a good thing I didn't want to eat. (Ms. S, a single Latina female, 18 years of age)
> The next day I noticed a lot of sores in my mouth . . . probably from my teeth grinding down on my gums. . . . The inside of my mouth hurts for about two or three days after. (Joe, a single white female, 21 years of age)

A number of our participants used candy such as Gummy Bears, Starbursts, Jolly Ranchers, and BlowPops to help mitigate the unpleasantness of their jaw muscles clenching. Actually, any form of hard candy or chewing gum can work as long as it keeps the user from grinding his or her teeth and straining the jaw muscles:

> I've worn away all of my back teeth and I have four sores in my mouth from just grinding the inside of my teeth. I chipped my front teeth one night after dropping [ingesting] five beans. . . . I was blowing up hard. . . . I felt my eyes roll towards the back of my head. I also bit my lip because I didn't realize I was biting down on it until I went to the bathroom at this club and looked in the mirror and noticed a little bit of blood from my upper lip. . . . No biggie, but it scares the shit out of you looking in the mirror and seeing blood. (Ms. G, a single Latina female, 29 years of age)
> A BlowPop or a piece of gum never tasted so fucking good as when you are rolling . . . but it helps not lose your teeth, because with a good bean, your teeth will chatter. (Greg, a single white male, 24 years of age)

BUYING ECSTASY

Ecstasy's street price makes it attractive and affordable. Currently, in the Tampa area, the price ranges from $10 to $20 per pill, with an average cost of $15. Factors that determine the price of a pill are market availability and whether or not one is known to the dealers. Market availability is just that—supply and demand. When a large number of pills are on the market, prices are lower. As might be expected, prices are usually higher for strangers than for those people known to the dealer. Prices at nightclubs are also more expensive than prices at other locations. We asked one dealer who we had met during a rolling party whether he overcharged people at nightclubs. He offered the following view:

> If I don't know the person, I will, and definitely if it's in a club. . . . It's the price of doing business in a club. . . . I have to worry about the bouncers [security personnel], off-duty undercover cops, and narcs [people working for the police] . . . just too much hassle. But I'm going to make my money. . . . People just have to pay. . . . If I know you, I'll cut you a break, but not by much. . . . I really just don't like dealing in clubs.

Our participants preferred to buy and take Ecstasy before arriving at their destinations as a way of minimizing the risk of detection from law enforcement. The following statements are typical:

> I always buy a few days before I know I am going out. That way I don't get caught up with people saying that they can or can't get it [Ecstasy] and then having to go to the club and buying something from I don't know who . . . a narc or undercover, and paying something crazy like $20. (Vanessa, a 20-something Latina female)
>
> We would always drop [take Ecstasy] at our apartment and then go to the clubs. . . . We knew that we would be at the clubs like in 20 minutes, so we knew that our rolls wouldn't kick in yet or they would start to kick in just as we were in line to get into the clubs. . . . That's how we'd do it. . . . We would never have anything on us . . . just in case they would search you at the door. (Jimmy, a white male, 19 years of age)

Onset of Effects

The average user begins to feel the effects from one Ecstasy pill in about 30 to 45 minutes. The overall effects of Ecstasy, or an "E trip," as it is commonly known, can last from four to six hours. Time periods are contingent on what and how recently people have eaten, a person's physiology, and whether the pill has adulterants. In recent years, the media and some ill-informed law enforcement officials have alleged that Ecstasy pills contain substances like rat poison and crushed glass, as well as other illegal drugs such as cocaine, heroin, and LSD. However, others have shown (see Beck & Rosenbaum, 1994; Cohen, 1998; Saunders & Doblin, 1996) that these allegations are more myth than reality.

According to DanceSafe, a harm-reduction organization, recent adulterant screening efforts have revealed the presence of such drugs as dextromethorphan, phenylpropanolamine, ephedrine, pseudoephedrine, glyceryl guaiacolate, other amphetamine-like substances (e.g., MDA, MDEA, DOM, 2-CB, and DOT), caffeine, and ketamine, with only trace amounts of such substances as heroin and LSD (DanceSafe, 2001). It is believed that underground manufacturers in clandestine laboratories add many of these substances purely as a cost-saving method, although some of these ingredients do increase the risk for negative reactions, including overdose.

The fact that they could be ingesting a host of other substances in addition to MDMA did not appear to concern our subjects greatly. Our participants took Ecstasy one of three ways: (1) orally, (2) snorting, or (3) "parachuting"/"packing." Some participants elected to use either one or a combination of all three methods during the evening, depending on when they wanted to feel the effects of the pill. With oral ingestion, initial effects were usually felt within 30 to 40 minutes. Snorting produced effects within 10 to 15 minutes, while parachuting or packing produced effects within 5 minutes.

"Parachuting" Ecstasy involves inserting the pill into the anus, like a suppository. Parachuters believe that this method allows the pill to be absorbed faster and the effects felt in a shorter time. The process of parachuting is described in the following field note excerpt:

> The time was 6:15 a.m. and we had just left an after-hours club where we had spent the last three hours with a group of people we met up with at another club earlier in the evening. In leaving this after-hours club we all got into our cars and headed for a gas station nearby. I asked David, a white male about 29 years of age, what we were looking to get at this gas station. He answered, "I need to refuel. I need to stop and get some Red Bull before we continue or I'm not going to make it." The gas station was less than 10 city blocks from the after-hours club, and we were there within 10 minutes. All three cars pulled into the gas station, and most of the passengers got out of their cars.
>
> In total there were five cars and 10 people all together. One of the drivers, Jake, a Latino male in his early twenties, pulled his red Honda Civic to a gas pump, got out, inserted a credit card, and began to pump gas. I waited outside the car I was riding in for the rest of the group. I noticed that most were in line inside the gas station with items in their hands. Since it was early in the morning on a Sunday and no one was around, I decide to go inside just to be with the folks. In walking into the gas station I noticed that most had either Red Bull, Gatorade, or PowerAde sport drinks in their hands. Two individuals had two bottles of water, Evian, in their hands. I noticed that Fred, a white male in his late twenties was walking towards the back of the gas station.
>
> Soon there was Henry, a white male in his early thirties, following behind him. I think Mary, a Latina female about 20 years of age, noticed I was looking at them, and, in a very low whisper, said, "They going to the bathroom to shoot." I asked, "To shoot what?" She replied, "They still have some beans left," and that's all she said. Now, I knew that shooting beans did not mean using a needle, since I have not seen anyone use this method for taking Ecstasy. So I thought she was referring to "parachuting," but I was not sure. It is a term I had heard before, but I had never seen anyone actually do it. I could not help it, but curiosity got the better of me, and so I headed for the bathroom, and just as I got to the door, Fred looked at me and said, "Hey, professor, do you want to see something?" I replied, "What?" Henry replied, "Come see."
>
> There we were . . . in the men's bathroom, three males, and I could not help think that under other circumstances, this scene would represent something altogether different. However, there we were. I stood directly in front of the door, and Fred, while reaching for his right pants pocket, said, "I know you've

heard about 'parachuting.'" I replied, "Yeah . . . but I think I know what it is." Fred's reply was, "Well, here you go . . . " As he said this, he pulled out three beans from a small baggie. . . . They were white in color, and I knew they were known as RR or Rolls Royce, because that was what the group had been taking for most of the night. As he produced the beans and threw the baggie on the floor, Henry walked over to a bathroom stall and tore off a piece of toilet paper, probably about less than one inch in length. He walks over to the faucet and just wets the piece of paper with a small amount of water. Fred then walks over and places the three beans into the center of the paper. Henry begins to fold the paper over the pills and forms a nice little wad of paper with its end twisted. He licks the twisted ends and I asked, "Why are you doing that?" His response, "To make sure that it's all nice and tight and that it doesn't come undone when it goes in." As he says this, Fred walks over to a bathroom stall, unzips his pants and lets his pants come down to his thigh area. Henry walks over to him and says, "Are you ready?" Fred's response: "Go ahead." Fred bends only halfway, and Henry takes that wad of paper with the twisted ends and begins to insert it anally into Fred. There I am watching this, and all I could say, "Why can't you do it yourself, Fred?" Fred stands up, and as he zips up his pants he turns around and says, "I just don't like putting anything into me." Henry adds, "I do myself all the time, and I do my girl this way." In almost a comic relief tone, Fred adds, "Now that's 'parachuting,' professor." My only response: "No confusing that one . . . that's 'parachuting.'"

Coming Down

Toward the end of the blowing up stage of an E trip, people respond in many different ways. Some just want to engage in a free-flowing conversation about their lives and their own personal anxieties and fears. Some just want to sit outside to watch the sunrise and feel the cool morning breeze brushing up against their skin. A few have some difficulty accepting that their experience is about to end and therefore consume marijuana as a method for "kicking it back in":

> I always like to have some kind [of] bud [high-quality marijuana] on me to smoke towards the end. . . . [It] takes the edge off and kicks my roll back in. . . . It won't be as intense, but you do feel it somewhat. . . . [It] just relaxes me and give me a smoother roll at the end. (Diego, a white male Latino in his early 20s)

Some also consume drugs like Valium and Xanax as a way of coping with the edginess they felt from Ecstasy:

> The morning after I take a Xane bar [referring to Xanax], then I'm OK . . . I can go to sleep. . . . If I don't, my fucking mind is not going to stop talking to me. . . . It's like you want to go to sleep because you know you're tired but your mind won't let you go. . . . A Xane bar or some Valium would do the trick. (Keith, a white male in his early 30s)

For some of our participants, the day or days after their use of Ecstasy consisted of moderate to intense fatigue. In communicating the nature of this psychological and physical exhaustion, they used the term *ate-up*. For most, this ate-up feeling was characterized as a loss of appetite, mental exhaustion, some nausea, intense thirst, and body aches. Although these symptoms sound remarkably similar to those experienced in a hangover, many of our participants did not see such similarities:

> The only thing I hate about E is how I feel the next day. . . . I just can't do any-thing. . . . I mean, I sleep all day, so I waste an entire day and then I get up and just want to lay in my bed. . . . I can't think, and if I do, I can't get the music or people out of my head. I really don't want to eat anything, but I force myself to eat something. . . . I'm not hungry, but I just force myself. (Christine, a white female in her 20s)
>
> I just can't do anything the next day . . . all I want to is sleep. . . . I love to take a shower when I get home because it feels good, but then I just head for my bed. . . . I get no headaches or feel like throwing up, but I just don't want any-thing. (Mike, a white male in his early 20s)
>
> I really don't feel ate-up the next day. . . . I sleep for about six or eight hours and get up. . . . I eat a little something and then I just sit around, turn the TV on, but I really don't watch it. . . . I just want to sit there and think. . . . My legs hurt a bit, but that's from the dancing. . . . If that's ate-up, then maybe, yeah, but nothing like what my friends feel. (Judy, a white female in her late 20s)
>
> For me, the worst is about three days after I rolled. I just feel down . . . can't start or really finish anything. . . . I just want to lay in my bed and do absolutely nothing. . . . I stop and think that I won't ever do that again [use Ecstasy], but then I remember I had a good time on it, and, well . . . you know. (Sue, a white female in her late teens)

Such aftereffects are mitigated by the person's physiology, health status prior to use, frequency of use, concurrent drug use (e.g., LSD, cocaine, heroin, or alcohol), and the type and amount of Ecstasy pills consumed. As a result, the ate-up experience is never the same for any one individual.

CONCLUSION

Philippe Bourgois (1999, p. 215) argues, "A major task of participant-observers is to put themselves in the shoes of the people they study in order to see local realities through local eyes." As participant-observers, we have presented a local picture of Ecstasy use among a diverse network of individuals. There is no denying that for our participants, taking Ecstasy—despite all the known risks—is pleasurable. A "local reality" is that Ecstasy is relatively affordable, does not have the same stigma associated with other illegal drugs, and is very much a part of the local youth culture (individuals between the ages of 18 and 35). Because this is an ongoing ethnographic study, there are many areas that we have not yet studied. We wanted to present a "local portrait" of Ecstasy use. We only hope that we remained true to our participants in setting out to accomplish this goal.

REFERENCES

Beck, J. (1986). MDMA: The popularization and resultant implications of a recently controlled psychoactive substance. *Contemporary Drug Problems, 13,* 305–13.

Beck, J., & Rosenbaum, M. (1994). *Pursuit of ecstasy: The MDMA experience.* New York: State University of New York Press.

Boston Globe. (n.d.). "Drug's Night Club Pull Seems Hard to Curb."

Bourgois, P. (1999). Theory, method, and power in drug and HIV-prevention research: A participant-observer's critique. *Substance Use & Misuse, 34,* 2155–72.

Buffalo News. (2000, September 8). "Raving and Behaving: The Reputation of the High-Energy, All-Night Dance Parties Outpaces the Reality," p. G 20.

Chen, R. S. (1998). *The love drug: Marching to the beat of Ecstasy.* New York: Haworth.

DanceSafe. (2001). Retrieved August 2001 from http://www.dancesafe.org/labtesting/.

Plant, S. (1999). *Writing on drugs.* New York: Farrar, Straus and Giroux.

Saunders, N., & Doblin, R. (1996). *Ecstasy: Dance, trance and transformation.* Oakland, CA: Quick American Achieves.

St. Petersburg Times. (n.d.). "Deputies: Ecstasy Overdose Killed Teen."

Valter, K., & Arrizabalaga, P. (1998). *Designer drugs directory.* New York: Elsevier.

CHAPTER 21

"Cooks Are Like Gods": Hierarchies in Methamphetamine-Producing Groups

Robert Jenkot

This article uses findings from a qualitative study of female methamphetamine users, dealers, and producers in Missouri and Arkansas. The authors interviewed 31 incarcerated women to explore their experiences with methamphetamine, focusing on 18 methamphetamine producers ("cooks"). This study provides insights into the hierarchies within methamphetamine-producing groups, moving from "simple users" at the bottom, to "dope ho's," "shoppers," "gas men/juicers," and "cooks" at the top. Understanding this hierarchy can help us understand how new members are added to the group, existing members leave, and new groups form from the existing group. The researchers also examine in-group mobility with regard to group solidarity and reintegration after confinement and discuss the interaction between status and gender within the methamphetamine-producing group.

In 1965 members of the Hell's Angels Motorcycle Club found that they could produce the synthetic drug methamphetamine; their efforts provide the first documented clandestine methamphetamine production (Lavigne 1996a,b). The "discovery" of clandestine methamphetamine production roughly coincided with legislation to control its illicit use (Young et al. 1977). Since the 1970s, we have seen an increase in the domestic clandestine production of methamphetamine and a proportionate rise in known methamphetamine use through the 1990s (DEA 2000). Little is known about the social relations within the groups that produce methamphetamine. Even less is known about women's social position within these groups.

Source: Adapted from Jenkot, R. (2008). "Cooks Are Like Gods:" Hierarchies in methamphetamine groups. *Deviant Behavior, 29*(8), 667–89.

The present study, part of a larger study of women involved with methamphetamine use, sales, and production, seeks to inform our understanding of the social relations within these groups. This study in particular uncovers the types of hierarchies present within methamphetamine-producing groups. Understanding the types of hierarchies that exist within these groups can shed light on how members of a methamphetamine-producing group function over time as new members arrive, members leave, or new groups are formed. Further, because the sample is exclusively female, some findings will also illuminate how gendered relations are affected by the hierarchies present in methamphetamine-producing groups.

LITERATURE REVIEW

Studies of domestic methamphetamine use, sales, and production have uncovered four unique characteristics when international smuggling is omitted. First, methamphetamine production is dominated by white Anglo-Americans (Riley 2000; Pennell et al. 1999). Secondly, white women's use of methamphetamine is often on par with men's use patterns (Riley 2000). Third, much of the methamphetamine supply is due to domestic production (DEA 2000). Fourth, small, tight-knit groups of economically marginalized people perform much of the domestic production of methamphetamine (Lavigne 1996a,b).

Beyond the generalizations noted, determining who is producing methamphetamine is not as clear as who uses the drug. The ADAM (Arrestee Drug Abuse Monitoring) project, as well as associated federally funded projects, has little if any mention of who is involved with methamphetamine production (Meth et al. 2001; Pennell et al. 1999; Riley 1999a,b, 2000). Research on women involved with methamphetamine production is limited to non-academic reports (Kurtis 1997). Although the gendered relationships that exist within these groups have not been explored, it is clear that women are taking part in the production process. The production of illicit drugs goes beyond the expected behavior of women who take part in deviant activities. In effect, women have limitations on their behavior in both licit and illicit groups (Denton and O'Malley 1999). However, there is a distinct lack of research detailing women's involvement with the production of drugs. It is here that I believe that this research can begin to fill that gap in the literature.

Comparing methamphetamine production to the manufacture of other drugs is troublesome. Although cocaine is a drug with similar psychopharmacological effects, it is usually produced in clandestine laboratories in South America. Crack cocaine is easily produced locally and by a single individual (Bourgois 1996). The result is that hierarchies have not been explored within crack cocaine manufacturing: the literature on crack cocaine focuses on the sale of the drug and the subsequent hierarchies that exist within the distribution networks (see Schatzberg and Kelly 1997).

Another drug that is readily "manufactured" domestically is marijuana. Much research exists on the topic but is often relegated to social relations outside of the producing group or apart from the producer. For example, Hafley and Tewksbury (1995, 1996) consider the social relationships between the marijuana growers and the communities in which they exist. Weisheit (1990, 1991) approaches the idea of hierarchies in marijuana cultivation, but his research subjects reflect more on their personal accomplishments and rewards from the behavior. In short, he finds that growers self-rank themselves based on the quality and/or potency of the marijuana they cultivate (Weisheit 1991). Also, Weisheit's research shows that much marijuana cultivation is performed by individuals and not groups (1990, 1991).

The differences between methamphetamine production compared to crack cocaine and marijuana include: only the production of methamphetamine can result in fire and explosions, the chemicals necessary for methamphetamine production are controlled, and the production of methamphetamine takes greater specialized knowledge than either of the other drugs' production. The production of methamphetamine is a multistage process where specialized knowledge, risky tasks, and time-consuming processes are necessary. In fact, the production of methamphetamine can easily necessitate a division of labor. Unlike the domestic production of crack cocaine and marijuana, methamphetamine production could—and does—benefit from group involvement.

Adding gender into the phenomena of methamphetamine production supports much recent research that illustrates women's involvement in criminal behavior. Until the 1980s, women were often depicted as secondary to males with regard to their criminality. Female offenders have historically been considered status offenders and non-violent (e.g., runaways) or took part in very gender-specific crimes (e.g., prostitution) (Schur 1984). Recently we have seen women taking greater part in crimes of all sorts. There are rising numbers of women being arrested and convicted for drug and drug-related offenses as well as violent offenses. Women's prison facilities are getting more crowded. Also we have seen the emergence of "girl gangs" that are involved in violence and drugs. But what are the effects within single- and/or mixed-sex groups taking part in criminal behavior?

Warr (2002) provides a concise means of understanding the interaction between social learning and peer pressure. Using three key issues, solidarity within the peer group can be established and maintained. These three issues are loyalty, status, and fear of ridicule (Warr 2002). Although maintaining loyalty to fellow group members is clear, Warr provides mechanisms for the establishment of statuses. The more experienced, loyal, and skilled the group member is at either leadership or deviant techniques, the higher the status of that group member. Aiding the division of group members within a hierarchy is the use of ridicule to maintain group cohesion and norms. Using Warr's concepts we can see that within criminal groups hierarchies can be established and maintained.

Through interviews with women who have been charged with drug-related offenses, a recurring theme of status within their peer group was evident. This study seeks to uncover what statuses are present in methamphetamine-producing groups. Further, how do group members maintain these statuses? By identifying what statuses exist within the groups, we can better understand the mechanisms that provide for new members to enter the group and mobility within the group.

METHODS

The data for this study was obtained through in-depth surveys with 31 women incarcerated in county jails in Missouri and Arkansas. Using current lists provided by each facility, every female inmate charged with drug-related offenses (i.e., possession, intent to deliver, maintaining a drug premises) was contacted personally and requested to take part in the study. Two women refused to take part in the study. Each participant selected a pseudonym to allow for confidentiality. Each interview lasted at least one hour, to a maximum of three hours. . . .

DEMOGRAPHICS OF THE SAMPLE

The average age of the sample was 36 years old, with a range of 18 to 48 years old. One woman was 18 years old. Seven women were between 21 and 29 years old, 12 women were between 30 and 39 years old, and 11 women were between 40 and 49 years old. The sample consisted of 28 white women, 1 African-American woman, and 2 Hispanic women. The majority of the sample, 19 women, were single at the time of their interview; 4 women were married, 4 women were separated, and 4 women were divorced. Of the 31 women involved in this study, 18 stated that they had "cooked" methamphetamine; the same 18 reported that they had sold or traded methamphetamine for money or other items of value. All 31 women reported that they had used methamphetamine at least one time.

Every woman interviewed was employed prior to incarceration; however, their employment status varied considerably. Fifteen women had regular legitimate occupations (e.g., restaurant managers, retail clerks, and fast food cooks), 11 women were employed in seasonal or family-operated businesses (e.g., drywall installers, roofing companies, and house painters), and the remaining 5 women drifted between low-level minimum wage jobs and/or maintained illegitimate occupations (e.g., methamphetamine production, prostitution). With regard to educational attainment, 26 women had a high school diploma or a GED and the remaining 5 women possessed an Associate's degree, bachelor's degree, or some form of post-secondary education (e.g., Med-Tech training, paramedic training).

The combination of educational attainment and occupation can be considered hallmarks of class standing. The women in this sample can be considered largely lower- to working-class individuals. Many, if not most, had illegitimate income in addition to income derived from their occupations (e.g., illicit drug sales and/or prostitution). The result is that many reported indicators of wealth (e.g., multiple new automobiles, high-grade stereo equipment, and cash on hand), yet none of the participants reported assets that are normally associated with the wealthy (e.g., real estate, stocks).

The demographic data provided can be used to illustrate that a typical participant in this study would be a single white woman in her mid-thirties employed in either a service sector job or manual labor position. She would also hold a high school diploma and live comfortably, but financially would have little to no net worth. She would also be a regular methamphetamine user who occasionally sells the drug, and is capable of producing the drug.

FINDINGS

The hierarchy within methamphetamine-producing groups focuses on maintaining a supply of the drug. From the participants' comments, every action is connected with the production process or used to rank the people present. Of the 18 participants who had experience as a cook, they all related that a similar hierarchy was present in their group. The responses from these women varied in detail. Annie relates the hierarchy present in her group in great detail from highest status to lowest: Cook, Gas Man/Juicer, shopper, Dope Ho, and lastly the "simple user." Because Annie's experiences with a methamphetamine-producing group were related in the greatest detail, her comments comprise the bulk of the narrative regarding statuses within these groups.

The Methamphetamine Cook

Annie (a 32-year-old white woman) is 5'2" tall, blonde, currently separated from her second husband, and she has 3 children. She appears to be in good health and claims that the jail food has "bulked" her up. Annie has a long sentence yet appears in good humor. Her good humor was evidenced by the pseudonym she chose. She said that Annie was short for anhydrous ammonia, a key ingredient to the production of methamphetamine. She has earned a college degree and worked as a Registered Nurse and has had paramedic training. Her second husband began sexually molesting her oldest child from her first marriage; she subsequently separated from him. She stated that the stress of the abuse of her child combined with being alone caused her to gain weight. Her weight ballooned to 285 pounds. Annie stated that her existing stress was compounded by her own self-image as being "fat." It is at this point that she contacted an old friend from high school. The old friend and Annie used to use drugs together during high school. It was this old friend who first offered Annie methamphetamine as a means to control her weight and feel better. She initially began to use methamphetamine to escape from her feelings of powerlessness regarding her second husband's sexual abuse of her oldest daughter. As she said, "I had to just [long pause] get my mind off that shit; meth'll do that for ya for sure." A bounty hunter captured Annie; she had multiple outstanding warrants for drugs. Upon her arrival at the jail, she was in possession of both methamphetamine and marijuana.

All 18 women stated that the cook holds the highest position of privilege and prestige within the group. Annie explains:

> If you are a cook you are all set. I mean, like, you could have anything you wanted. You want other drugs? You got 'em. You want a stereo? You got it. It might be hot, but you got it. Everyone in every group I saw was like tuned-in to the cook. [What do you mean, "tuned-in"?] Well, like the cook is the top dog. Without the cook you'd have to go buy meth on your own—or schmooze [persuade] it outta somebody else.

Reinforcing her experience with methamphetamine-producing groups, Annie clarifies the position of cooks:

> Anyway, at the top of the group was the cook. There might be like two or three cooks in a group like mine, we had, wait, let's see, 5 people who could cook decent dope. Cooks are like gods. I mean, everyone does whatever they can to keep the cook happy. Food, stereos, supplies, sex, whatever they want, they got.

Annie's recollection of methamphetamine cooks as "top dog" constructs the position of methamphetamine cook as a goal for non-cooks. Attaining this position includes a constant supply of methamphetamine, deference from others, and the ability to have anything you want. This power can be considered economic in nature, with methamphetamine being the currency.

Group members had to learn that the cook was the most valued member of the group. Although learning this may appear to be simple, learning who holds the greatest power within the group aids in the neophyte understanding the entire structure of the group. As Annie's comments continue, we see how members of the group relegate value and status to its members relative to their behavior within the group.

The Gas Man/Juicer

Annie also provides another position in the hierarchy of methamphetamine-producing groups:

> Above the Shoppers were the Gas Men or Juicers. [What is a Juicer or Gas Man?] These are the guys—usually guys—that would go get the anhydrous ammonia. It was a real ordeal trying to get anhydrous, if ya fucked up you'd blow up or get burned by the anhydrous. A couple of weeks back I was driving on 55 [Interstate 55] and I saw this car burning on the side of the road and you could smell the, well, it smells special, that smell of anhydrous. They fucked up.

Second only to the cook, whose behavior is very risky and highly valued by the group, being a Gas Man is much more risky. A Shopper (discussed later) can succeed in her or his role by legitimately buying the necessary items while a gas man cannot. Gas men run the risk of arrest but also run the risk of injury and death.

The increased risk Gas Men face is due to the need for anhydrous ammonia. Anhydrous ammonia (a key precursor chemical in the production of some forms of methamphetamine) is a "dry" form of household ammonia that is in a gaseous state and when it comes into contact with air, it chemically tries to bond with the water molecules present in the air (Falkenthal 1997; Hargreaves 2000). If it comes into contact with human skin, it leaches out the water in the skin, resulting in a chemical burn (Falkenthal 1997; Hargreaves 2000). If inhaled, the anhydrous ammonia will leach out the water in the mouth, sinuses, throat, and lungs, resulting in internal chemical burns (Falkenthal 1997; Hargreaves 2000). Additionally, anhydrous ammonia is explosive (Falkenthal 1997; Hargreaves 2000). With this in mind, Gas Men are at substantially higher risk than any other group member who does not handle the substance. The higher risk accords them more status and privilege within the group.

Whereas 17 women noted the status of Gas Man or Juicer from their experiences, 1 woman was involved with a group that did not use anhydrous ammonia. Elizabeth detailed her assistance in the production process: "They needed red phosphorus to cook with, so I would get it for 'em." Elizabeth (a 45-year-old white woman) is 5'7" tall, blonde, divorced, and she has 2 children. She stated that she was bipolar and had only received one of her two daily injections to control her condition. As a result she was pacing in the small interview visitor's room. Although she was very pleasant and talkative, she was apparently agitated, or on edge. She had a high school diploma and worked (until recently) at her husband's restaurant. Elizabeth claimed that her husband was the son of the local mafia boss. As her marriage began to dissolve, largely due to her husband's use of crack cocaine, she stated that her husband had hired a "hit-man" to kill her and that her husband had tried to kill her with a kitchen knife as well. She began using methamphetamine when friends offered it to her husband, as she said, "When in Rome." She was arrested after a traffic stop resulted in the police finding methamphetamine in her purse. She is unable to pay her bond because none of her friends will accept a collect call from jail, and she is too afraid of her husband to call him. As a result, she is just waiting for her case to come to court.

Regardless of the method of producing methamphetamine used, the person who supplied the integral ingredient held a higher status. Again, status in the group is connected with the risk taken by the group member. With regard to the hierarchy Annie detailed, Elizabeth would hold a status about equal with a Shopper and below a Gas Man. Elizabeth explains:

INTERVIEWER: Did you buy it [red phosphorus], or what?
ELIZABETH: Well, I used to think that you bought like a can of it but all you gotta do is scrape off the striker part of book of matches. [You mean the match heads? The top end that you light with?] Oh no! On the actual book, the little strip that you use to light the match. That is where the red phosphorus is. All you gotta do is scrape it away. Takes forever, but you gotta do it just so. I mean if you dig too deep you get paper, but you want all the red phosphorus. So ya gotta do it just so and I was good at it. So I'd lend a hand doing it. I'd sit there for hours scraping away with a knife.

We'd have piles of matchbooks but no way to light them! [laughs] [So, you'd watch them cook and just scrape away huh?] Yeah, separating those pills takes a while. So we'd bullshit as I would scrape and then by the time they were ready for the red phosphorus I'd be about done. Course if I wasn't done they'd have to wait for me. Shit I remember once I showed up and there was this asshole scraping matchbooks, I was kinda pissed cuz he was like taking my job ya know. Then Joe [a pseudonym] told him to stop and for me to take over.

Elizabeth's status was reaffirmed when the "temp scraper" was pushed aside by the cook so that she could resume her "job." In order for Elizabeth to perform her task within the production process, she had to learn the techniques specific to the task. How did she come to know that the red phosphorus was contained in the striker of the matchbook and not the match head? She learned this from an existing "scraper."

The Shopper

There are other levels of power and status within these groups, as Annie explains:

Now above the users and Dope Ho's were the people that would actually help out. First ya got the Shoppers. [What did the Shoppers do?] They would go get anything. I mean anything. They'd get the supplies to cook with: pills, buckets, lithium, tubing, whatever. Shit, I remember this one cook's car broke down and she asked for a Thunderbird. So this Shopper I know goes out and steals one— bingo! The cook is happy again. The best Shoppers were the ones who would really put their ass on the line. The ones that used like real money to buy pills were still good and all, but the ones that would hold up a store and take all their pills—now that was great. You still had your cash, and the pills. So I guess there is levels within the levels of power there.

The establishment of a specialized role in the methamphetamine-producing group to obtain the goods requested by the cook reaffirms the formal social structure within the group. In their quest to obtain the requested goods any means were acceptable, even theft. In fact, Annie states that the more risk the Shopper takes, the greater she or he is valued. What is important to note is that Shoppers are integral to the production process within the group.

Brandy (a 42-year-old white woman) is 5'5" tall with dark brown hair; her skin appears to be blotchy, red, and irritated. She is single and has a 19-year-old son. She considers herself to be a functioning addict. She will use a class of drugs (e.g., stimulants or depressants) for a time, then switch to another class of drugs. Much of her drug use parallels what she can obtain via theft and fraud. She has an off-putting personality and is not very talkative. When she responds to a question it is usually a one-word response. Further probing gains little additional information. She is currently in jail for cooking methamphetamine in her house.

Brandy could produce methamphetamine on her own, but often chose to be an assistant. As she stated, "I would shop a lot, you know go get the pills. Truck stops are great for that, plus you get to go on a nice drive!" Additionally, she would ". . . just lend a hand here or there." Each of the 18 women spoke of their group having at least one shopper; some groups had up to four shoppers. As they described the behaviors of these group members, they echoed Annie's comments. If members of the group wanted anything, especially the cook, the shopper was the person slated to obtain it.

The Dope Ho

Although "simple users" may be at the bottom of the methamphetamine group hierarchy, another status, Dope Ho, is only slightly above them. Most of the participants knew Dope Ho's (15 of the 18 participants); the remaining 3 had heard of men and women trading sex for drugs but had never personally experienced the phenomena. Annie explains the in-group social position of Dope Ho's:

> Along with users are Dope Ho's. Now Dope Ho's are not a problem really. They are around just to trade a blow or a lay for some meth. They are ALWAYS there. Like I said, they are not a problem like the users but they really don't do anything to help out. Dope Ho's are like baggage, they are there taking up space. Now some guy cooking meth would like to have 'em. [Why would guy cooks like them?] OH! Well, the Dope Ho's take care of the cook, with sex. They are not there for everyone to fuck, just the cook. So, like guys are right, they always wanna get laid so the Dope Ho's handle that. You know, there might be a few Dope Ho's at a time. It's funny, it's like the cook has a choice who he's gonna bang, "No, not her, not her, yeah I'll bang her today!" That sort of thing.

Positions similar to that of a Dope Ho are not unique among drug-using groups. We know about people trading sex for crack cocaine, even for a hit of that drug (Ratner 1993; Maher 1997). However, with regard to crack cocaine, many of these women are prostitutes who trade sex with "Johns" for the drug that they hold (Ratner 1993; Maher 1997). As Annie reports, Dope Ho's are accepted members of the group unlike the "simple users." Dope Ho's function to keep the cook happy (sexually), which aids in the production process. The fascinating thing about the presence of Dope Ho's is how this (usually) heterosexual relationship interacts with other heterosexual relationships.

> INTERVIEWER: What about a wife or girlfriend? Wouldn't they get mad? Or were the wives and girlfriends of these guys the Dope Ho's?
> ANNIE: Nah, they were nobody's girlfriend or wife, just Ho's. Nobody really cared about them either, they were just always there. They were cool and all, just kinda looked down at, I mean, shit, you know, they were tradin' a blowjob for a buzz—not a bag of Dope, just a buzz. Kinda sad now that I think of it.
> INTERVIEWER: Were there guys as Dope Ho's too?

ANNIE: Yeah, I saw a few and heard of more. But, you know how girls are, they can get laid anytime they want and they don't have to give meth away to get laid! Guys will jump on anything, anytime—"sex? I'll do it!"—so why have the burden of carrying someone else's habit just to get laid. Still, some chicks would have some around but it was not like normal to see Guy-Ho's.

Annie's comments regarding the relationship between Dope Ho's and men are important. As Annie said, "nobody really cared about them," indicating that Dope Ho's hold a certain status within the group. They occupy a low-status position in which they are marginalized to such a degree that wives and girlfriends apparently do not consider them threats to their monogamous relationship with the male cooks.

To hear Annie talk about Dope Ho's, her inflection is important; these people are looked down on. However, the status of Dope Ho can be considered slightly higher than that of the "pain in the ass" user.

The Users of Methamphetamine

Every woman involved in this project agreed that the position that lacks any prestige is that of the simple user. Annie provides a very clear image of the user:

At the bottom were the users. These were the people that just wanted to buy meth, if ya think of the most strung out, tweeked freaks, that is the user. They are not really in the group. I mean, we all know them, but they are more of a pain in the ass. They always show up at the worst times. They show up when the batch [of methamphetamine] ain't done yet. They show up when you wanna sleep. They show up, well just like a pain in the ass, there is no good time.

The presence of users in a group creates the issue of risk and trust as being at odds with each other. Members of the group know the users or else they would not be allowed to socialize with the group. However, these people also pose a risk if they are undercover police officers or user-informers. Users are a burden to the group.

Users vs. Simple Users

It is important to differentiate between the types of methamphetamine users: users and "simple users." All of the participants in this study had used methamphetamine at some point in their lives. Most of the methamphetamine cooks (16 of the 18 cooks) were also current methamphetamine users. However, those women who took part, in whatever way, in the production process held a status above the "simple user." The "simple user" only uses the drug. The methamphetamine user is part of the group; the "simple user" is a "pain in the ass," meaning not part of the group.

As Annie (and others) relate, there is a distinct hierarchy within methamphetamine-using groups. Status within these groups is related to the activity regarding the methamphetamine production process. The greater the involvement and/or risk with the production process, the higher the status. Other participants in this study provided information on the process of upward mobility in the group as well as some variations of the statuses in these groups.

In-Group Mobility and Status Variations

There is a process involved in the production of methamphetamine. This process includes multiple people performing specific tasks. The performance of these tasks relates to the performance of social roles in the group. Brandy stated that she was able to cook, purchase the pills used as the base for the drug, and help out where needed. Other tasks that need to be completed in order for the methamphetamine production to be successful include: obtaining key precursor chemicals (P2P, red phosphorus, or anhydrous ammonia), obtaining the other items and compounds used in the production process (containers, lithium, hydrochloric acid, and hot plates), and the actual production of methamphetamine. These associations form a peer group for Brandy where she would ". . . shop a lot." Her performance at this task was positive for the group and she was not stopped from doing it. Because she was able to cook methamphetamine as well, she was able—and allowed—to perform other functions.

The key point to understand is that these groups grow and splinter into networks that maintain some degree of association with each other. In these groups, gender differences fade as the actor rises in status within the group. Once the status of cook has been achieved, the drive for quality drugs equalizes the gender disparity evident at lower levels of these methamphetamine production groups.

Annie knew how to cook and did so frequently. However, she would also take part in schemes to obtain anhydrous ammonia, illustrating her mobility within her group. She has earned the highest status, but was able to choose to work at a lower status. For example, Annie stated:

> Me and another girl would get all dolled up and go to farmers' houses. We'd knock on the door, wiggle, wink, giggle and shit. Then just ask if we could have some anhydrous. That always worked. [*So would you be treated as a Juicer when you did that?*] Fuck no! [laughs] Shit once you can cook you are golden, you know. I was just helpin' out. Now the guy we was with, he was the Juicer. [What about the woman you went with?] Well, actually she was a Dope Ho. But she was cool.

Status can be earned by working with other members of the group and learning by their example. However, a formal learning process also takes place within methamphetamine-using groups. Cammy (a 42-year-old white woman) is 5'3" tall with brown hair and lives in a suburban area. She is fairly thin, but not as thin as some of the women in this study. Cammy appeared to be depressed and sad about her current situation. She was willing to take part in the interview, yet would often reply with one-word answers and little more when prodded. She did not want to say if she had any children, but she was separated from her husband. Her arrest occurred at a methamphetamine lab raided by the police. She possessed marijuana. Cammy illustrates how she learned to cook within the structure of the methamphetamine-producing group when she states:

> I was livin' with this cook right. We was jus' like in the same house, not fuckin' or nothin'. OK, so I know how to cook but not real good. I asks this guy, don't wanna say his name, if he can teach my boyfriend to cook right. So he's like, "cool," right. OK, so he's showin' my man how to cook and I am learnin' too right. OK, so like now we both are cooks and we get our own thing goin' and we cook like crazy! It was cool.

Cammy, due to her status with her house-mate and as a cook, was able to bring her non-cooking boyfriend up in status. Once she and her boyfriend were both cooks, their position within their group was solidified; however, shortly afterward they left this group to form their own group. In their new group they were able to complete all of the functions necessary to produce methamphetamine. Cammy's experiences provide us with a way that methamphetamine groups spread. As the unique knowledge is disseminated so too do the groups that hold this knowledge spread. It should be clear that these groups will be connected in a network of multiple cells of methamphetamine production.

The goal for these groups is the production of methamphetamine, not its sale. The various members of the group operate within a hierarchy where a neophyte can be upwardly mobile within the group, roles are defined, and power and prestige are linked to the status one holds. Interestingly, because the goal is paramount, in these groups they are more willing to dispose of social constructs valid in the dominant culture in order to further their goal. As a result, women who move up in the hierarchy of the production process are not stigmatized for the roles they play. Instead, women appear to become, or perceive themselves to be, the equals of their male counterparts.

Gender and Status in Methamphetamine-Producing Groups

Producing methamphetamine is rather easy even though it involves a number of processes and chemicals that can be hard to obtain. Annie and Brandy illustrated that their ability to change the role they played within the group is tied to their ability to cook methamphetamine themselves. This reflects the status that a methamphetamine cook holds within her group. Brandy can decide to cook one day and go for a drive the next day to obtain other material for the production of methamphetamine. Annie would cook methamphetamine, or choose to assist in obtaining anhydrous ammonia. Holding the status of a cook can be equated with the freedom to play the role of their own choosing, not to be relegated to a subordinate role defined by others within her group.

In every case, the women reported that they were able to complete the entire production process themselves. Their choice to simply "assist" was personal: every woman interviewed stated that she never felt that she was pressured to stand aside. Bea (a 41-year-old Hispanic woman), a homemaker in a suburban community who has a GED, is 5'3" tall with long blonde hair and she is apparently healthy. Although some people appear to be younger than their actual age, Bea is the opposite; she appears to be much older than she actually is. Bea is married; her husband was also in the jail for unrelated charges. She has no children, but would have liked to have had some. Bea has been a methamphetamine user since the 1970s. She was very willing to discuss every aspect of her involvement with methamphetamine. At times her explanations sounded almost canned, as if she had been telling people about her experiences for years. Bea was arrested for possession of methamphetamine during the course of a traffic stop.

As Bea stated, "Shit, all we wanted was meth. You cook, I cook, who cares so long as it's good! I been cooking for what now [long pause] 20 years? Yeah, been about 20 years of cookin'. I am cool with the guys that cook, and they are cool with me."

Bea's statement identifies that the goal of these groups was methamphetamine, not money, nor material goods, nor quibbling over traditional gender expectations. However, as Bea stated, the higher the quality of the methamphetamine, the more desirable it is. This is an important point as it relates to gendered relationships within the hierarchy of methamphetamine-producing groups. This perceived equality intimates that methamphetamine cooks hold a status that transcends constructed gender statuses evident among female users. The master status for female methamphetamine cooks appears to change from "female" to "methamphetamine cook" due to the group's focus on the production of the drug.

The finding that female cooks can hold power over other group members is contrary to traditional gender expectations. Considering this finding we must recall that the goal of the group is acquiring more methamphetamine. The group members are not trying to replicate the dominant cultural view of women, nor are they overtly trying to maintain male dominance in the methamphetamine subculture; all they want is more methamphetamine. Realizing that the group's goal is task-oriented, it makes sense that the group members would not care who produces—so long as the drug is being produced and a supply of methamphetamine is maintained.

These findings support Warr's (2002) research on peer pressure. The presence of a hierarchy (statuses) aids in the maintenance of loyalty and solidarity among group members. Marginal, unneeded, or unwanted persons are derided for their behavior (the "pain in the ass user"). Importantly, Warr's work is centered on the theoretical premise of social learning and Sutherland's differential association; aspects of such learning can be seen in the methamphetamine-producing group.

Although gendered behavior appears to fade away at the upper levels of methamphetamine-producing groups, female cooks are still willing to use gendered expectations to achieve their ends. For example, Annie relates two other events that occurred with some regularity:

> Well, if you cook in the woods, like way out, we always had a guy and a girl cookin'. That way if ya hear someone walkin' up ya just start rollin' in the leaves

> kissin'. Shit we got by a bunch of Park Rangers that way. They smell the cook right, they find us makin' out and they freakin' apologize—can ya believe that! We get all huffy right, then we just leave . . . never got busted that way, never.

This recollection is one strategy to disguise their illegal activity. Often methamphetamine production takes place on public lands; the cook[s] will remain nearby, but not necessarily at the production site (Falkenthal, 1997; Hargreaves, 2000). During his investigation, the Park Ranger comes upon a couple kissing and apologizes for interrupting a behavior that has been constructed as "normal." Interestingly, Annie and her friend showed that they understood the social construction of gender. They used expected gender roles to hide the fact that they were actually producing methamphetamine. The reaction by the Park Ranger reinforced their idea that their use of constructed gender roles was accurate. However, there are other means employed to disguise illegal activities that take place in public places. Annie continues:

> Another thing we'd do, and it is kinda funny too, while the guys would be gettin' anhydrous I'd hang by the car with the hood up like somethin's wrong. If anybody stop, I just say that my boyfriend would be back soon with a wrecker. Plus that way I was a lookout too. Any cop roll up, I just ask for help and I'll be damned if the car don't start! [laughs] I drive off and then circle back in a bit and pick up the boys. [laughs] Funny huh?

In the second instance, Annie used the traditional gendered idea of a "damsel in distress." Relying on widely held constructions of gender Annie had been able to avoid arrest. Throughout these two recollections, Annie and her group knowingly used gendered behavior to dispel any thoughts that deviant activity was taking place.

CONCLUSION

The roles that the women in this study play within their methamphetamine-producing groups are varied. The findings show that some statuses are more highly valued by the group, whereas others are not. The value placed on certain statuses indicates the presence of a hierarchy.

It should also be noted that illicit drug sales was not incorporated in the hierarchy of a methamphetamine-producing group Annie (or any other participant) detailed. At no time did Annie or any other participant provide a rank or status for a dealer of methamphetamine or any other drug. However, it is telling that members of these groups did trade and sell methamphetamine yet do not fit the ideal type of drug dealers.

The statuses that these women hold in their methamphetamine-producing groups range from "simple user" to cook. Introduction into the group would begin at the user level. The low status of the neophyte must be negotiated to obtain higher status. The neophyte would not simply obtain high status (e.g., a Juicer) until she or he had shed the label of "pain in the ass" user. Group members in the upper echelon could easily take part in behavior that was "below" them without losing status. The rationale for this mobility is that the goal of the group was preeminent: the production of more methamphetamine.

The consensus among the participants is that the status associated with being a methamphetamine cook carries with it power and prestige within the group. It is expected that group members would seek to achieve this status. The data does not provide any intimation regarding persons holding a status that is disagreeable to them (for example, a Shopper who disliked holding that position). We can assume that the ready supply of methamphetamine would ameliorate any discontent as the group members could use the drug free of charge.

Central to understanding methamphetamine-producing groups is the realization that they are organized to produce the drug they use. By producing their own supply of methamphetamine, they eliminate the need for a dealer (middleman), save money, decrease their risk of arrest, and are assured of the quality of the drug they will use. To facilitate that goal, these groups have developed a hierarchy to achieve their aim.

Understanding the statuses and relationships within methamphetamine-producing groups illustrates the difficulties encountered by women as they leave jail or prison. Successful reintegration can be hampered by the loss of power and status they once enjoyed in methamphetamine-producing networks. This loss is exacerbated by the unwelcome realization that they are viewed as just another drug user. Although that label is accurate in societal terms, the women are reduced to what they once despised—"pain in the ass users." Thus, imprisonment results in a crisis of self-identity as well as the loss of power and status in a former social network.

Providing drug treatment, diversionary programs, or other social services to these women should include an acknowledgment of the statuses that these women have held. Beyond a general idea of reintegration, these women will face their crisis of self-identity in any conforming group they would join. Having once been the "top dog," finding themselves as anything less is another hurdle for the recovering drug user to overcome.

REFERENCES

Bourgois, Philippe. 1996. *In Search of Respect: Selling Crack in El Barrio.* Cambridge, MA: Cambridge University Press.

DEA. 2000. *United States Drug Enforcement Administration Internet Site.* Available at (www.usdoj.gov/dea).

Denton, Barbara and Pat O'Malley. 1999. "Gender, Trust, and Business: Women Drug Dealers in the Illicit Economy." *The British Journal of Criminology* 39:513–530.

Falkenthal, Greg. 1997. "Clan Labs: A Modern Problem." *Fire Engineering* 150(9):41.

Hafley, Sandra R. and Richard Tewksbury. 1996. "Reefer Madness in Bluegrass Country: Community Structure and Roles in the Rural Kentucky Marijuana Industry." *Journal of Crime and Justice* 19(1):75–94.

———. 1995. "The Rural Kentucky Marijuana Industry: Organization and Community Involvement." *Deviant Behavior* 16(3):201–221.

Hargreaves, Guy. 2000. "Clandestine Drug Labs." *FBI Law Enforcement Bulletin* 69(4):1–7.

Kurtis, Bill. 1997. *Investigative Reports: Meth's Deadly High.* [Video]The Arts and Entertainment Television Networks.

Lavigne, Yves. 1996a. *Hell's Angels: "Three Can Keep a Secret If Two Are Dead."* Secaucus, NJ: Carol Publishing Group.

———. 1996b. *Hell's Angels: Into the Abyss.* New York: Harper Collins.

Maher, Lisa. 1997. *Sexed Work: Gender, Race, and Resistance in a Brooklyn Drug Market.* New York: Oxford.

Meth, Marcia, Rebecca Chalmers, and Gail Bassin. 2001. *Pulse Check: Trends in Drug Abuse Mid-Year 2001.* Washington, DC: Office of National Drug Control Policy.

Pennell, Susan, Joe Ellett, Cynthia Rienick, and Jackie Grimes. 1999. *Meth Matters: Report on Methamphetamine Users in Five Western Cities.* Washington, DC: U.S. Government Printing Office.

Ratner, Mitchell S. 1993. "Sex, Drugs, and Public Policy: Studying and Understanding the Sex-for-Crack Phenomenon." Pp. 1–36. In *Crack Pipe for Pimp: An Ethnographic Investigation of Sex-for-Crack Exchanges,* edited by M. S. Ratner. New York: Lexington.

Riley, Jack. 2000. *1999 Annual Report on Drug Use Among Adult and Juvenile Arrestees.* Washington, DC: U.S. Government Printing Office.

———. 1999a. *1998 Annual Report on Drug Use Among Adult and Juvenile Arrestees.* Washington, DC: U.S. Government Printing Office.

———. 1999b. *Research Report: 1998 Annual Report on Methamphetamine Use Among Arrestees.* Washington, DC: National Institute of Justice.

Schatzberg, Rufus and Robert J. Kelley. 1997. *African-American Organized Crime: A Social History.* Piscataway, NJ: Rutgers University Press.

Schur, Edwin M. 1984. *Labeling Women Deviant: Gender, Stigma, and Social Control.* New York: McGraw Hill.

Warr, Mark. 2002. *Companions in Crime: The Social Aspects of Criminal Conduct.* New York: Cambridge University Press.

Weisheit, Ralph A. 1991. "The Intangible Rewards From Crime: The Case of Marijuana Cultivation." *Crime and Delinquency* 37(4):506–527.

———. 1990. "Domestic Marijuana Growers: Mainstreaming Deviance." *Deviant Behavior* 11(2):107–129.

Young, Lawrence A., Linda G. Young, Marjorie M. Klein, Donald M. Klein, and Dorianne Beyer. 1977. *Recreational Drugs.* New York: Berkley Books.

SECTION IX

Quitting Crime

Section IX examines the issue of desistance from crime. What factors make offenders stop engaging in crime? Do criminals continue their careers over a lifetime? Do they desist at some point or begin to engage in less serious offenses? What motivates these changes in criminal activity?

There is a vast literature devoted to attempting to understand why individuals engage in criminality, but far fewer studies are devoted to investigating the issue of desistance—quitting or reducing involvement in criminal activities. Generally, what we do know about desistence is that the majority of offenders will desist from criminality as they get older.

The two articles in this section contribute to the body of literature that focuses on criminal desistance. These articles provide rich insight into desistance from the perspective of a group of former offenders. What is unique about these two articles is that both describe a process that offenders go through in the period leading up to desistance. Whether this process stems from a reexamination or change of the criminal calculus or the experience of hitting rock bottom, it inevitably occurs.

In Chapter 22, "Getting Out of the Life: Crime Desistance by Female Street Offenders," Ira Sommers, Deborah R. Baskin, and Jeffrey Fagan examine the role of life events and the relationship of cognitions and life situations to the desistance process. The authors conducted 30 life-course interviews with 30 female offenders who had desisted from criminality. The women were selected based on two criteria: they all had at least one past arrest for a violent street crime, and they all had desisted from crime for at least two years prior to the study. Participants' decision to desist from crime was a result of hitting bottom—that is, reaching a point at which criminality seemed senseless. Once they reached this point, they worked to "clarify and strengthen their nondeviant identities." The authors readily point out that data findings are the result of retrospective information from offenders who had not offended for two years and as such cannot state with certainty whether desistance from crime is permanent. However, this study is salient inasmuch as it sheds light on the long and painful process that female offenders undergo before they quit crime.

In Chapter 23, "The Victimization–Termination Link," Scott Jacques and Richard Wright explore the role of one kind of negative event, victimization, as a positive turning point toward the termination of a negative trajectory, illicit drug dealing. The stories of drug dealers reveal that victimizations can mark turning points toward the end of criminal careers. They use life-course theoretical perspective in explaining a promising theory of how criminals may desist from criminality. Jacques and Wright illustrate their theory of a victimization–termination link through in-depth interviews with young middle-class drug dealers.

CHAPTER 22

Getting Out of the Life: Crime Desistence by Female Street Offenders

Ira Sommers, Deborah R. Baskin, and Jeffrey Fagan

This chapter considers the role of life events and the relationship of cognitions and life situations to the desistance process. The authors explore whether men and women differ in the processes and events that bring them to the decision to give up crime. They interviewed 30 women who had at least one official arrest for a violent street crime and had desisted from crime for at least two years prior to the study. Life history interviews were conducted by the first two authors. Each interview lasted approximately two hours. The subjects had engaged in a wide range of criminal activities. Eighty-seven percent were addicted to crack, 63 percent had been involved in robberies, 60 percent had committed burglaries, 94 percent had sold drugs, and 47 percent had at some time been involved in prostitution. The authors found that the reasons for desistance from crime were remarkably similar to those found for men. Like the male subjects in Shover's (1985) study, these women had begun to take the threat of incarceration seriously and attempted to reestablish links with conventional society while severing relationships with the deviant subculture.

Studies over the past decade have provided a great deal of information about the criminal careers of male offenders. (See Blumstein et al. 1986 and Weiner and Wolfgang 1989 for reviews.) Unfortunately, much less is known about the initiation, escalation, and termination of criminal careers by female offenders. The general tendency to exclude female offenders from research on crime and delinquency may be due, at least in part, to the lower frequency and comparatively less serious nature of offending among women. Recent trends and studies, however, suggest that the omission of women may seriously bias both research and theory on crime.

Source: Sommers, I., Baskin, D. R., & Fagan, J. (1994). Getting out of the life: Desistance by female street offenders. *Deviant Behavior, 15*(2), 125–49. Reprinted with permission.

Although a growing body of work on female crime has emerged within the last few years, much of this research continues to focus on what Daly and Chesney-Lind (1988) called generalizability and gender-ratio problems. The former concerns the degree to which traditional (i.e., male) theories of deviance and crime apply to women, and the latter focuses on what explains gender differences in rates and types of criminal activity. Although this article also examines women in crime, questions of inter- and intragender variability in crime are not specifically addressed. Instead, the aim of the paper is to describe the pathways out of deviance for a sample of women who have significantly invested themselves in criminal social worlds. To what extent are the social and psychological processes of stopping criminal behavior similar for men and women? Do the behavioral antecedents of such processes vary by gender? These questions remained unexplored.

Specifically, two main issues are addressed in this paper: (1) the role of life events in triggering the cessation process, and (2) the relationship between cognitive and life situation changes in the desistance process. First, the crime desistance literature is reviewed briefly. Second, the broader deviance literature is drawn upon to construct a social-psychological model of cessation. Then the model is evaluated using life history data from a sample of female offenders convicted of serious street crimes.

THE DESISTANCE PROCESS

The common themes in the literature on exiting deviant careers offer useful perspectives for developing a theory of cessation. The decision to stop deviant behavior appears to be preceded by a variety of factors, most of which are negative social sanctions or consequences. Health problems, difficulties with the law or with maintaining a current lifestyle, threats of other social sanctions from family or close relations, and a general rejection of the social world in which the behaviors thrive are often antecedents of the decision to quit. For some, religious conversions or immersion into alternative sociocultural settings with powerful norms (e.g., treatment ideology) provide paths for cessation (Mulvey and LaRosa 1986; Stall and Biernacki 1986).

A model for understanding desistance from crime is presented below. Three stages characterize the cessation process: building resolve or discovering motivation to stop (i.e., socially disjunctive experiences), making and publicly disclosing the decision to stop, and maintaining the new behaviors and integrating into new social networks (Stall and Biernacki 1986; Mulvey and Aber 1988). These phases . . . describe three ideal-typical phases of desistance: "turning points" where offenders begin consciously to experience negative effects (socially disjunctive experiences); "active quitting" where they take steps to exit crime (public pronouncement); and "maintaining cessation" (identity transformation):

Stage 1: Catalysts for change

Socially disjunctive experiences
- Hitting rock bottom
- Fear of death
- Tiredness
- Illness

Delayed deterrence
- Increased probability of punishment
- Increased difficulty in doing time
- Increased severity of sanctions
- Increasing fear

Assessment
- Reappraisal of life and goals
- Psychic change

Decision
- Decision to quit and/or initial attempts at desistance
- Continuing possibility of criminal participation

Stage 2: Discontinuance
- Public pronouncement of decision to end criminal participation
- Claim to a new social identity

Stage 3: Maintenance of the decision to stop
- Ability to successfully renegotiate identity
- Support of significant others
- Integration into new social networks
- Ties to conventional roles
- Stabilization of new social identity

Stage 1: Catalysts for Change

When external conditions change and reduce the rewards of deviant behavior, motivation may build to end criminal involvement. That process, and the resulting decision, seem to be associated with two related conditions: a series of negative, aversive, unpleasant experiences with criminal behavior, or corollary situations where the positive rewards, status, or gratification from crime are reduced. Shover and Thompson's (1992) research suggests that the probability of desistance from criminal participation increases as expectations for achieving rewards (e.g., friends, money, autonomy) via crime decrease and that changes in expectations are age-related. Shover (1983) contended that the daily routines of managing criminal involvement become tiring and burdensome to aging offenders. Consequently, the allure of crime diminishes as offenders get older. Aging may also increase the perceived formal risk of criminal participation. Cusson and Pinsonneault (1986, 76) posited that "with age, criminals raise their estimates of the certainty of punishment." Fear of reimprisonment, fear of longer sentences, and the increasing difficulty of "doing time" have often been reported by investigators who have explored desistance.

Stage 2: Discontinuance

The second stage of the model begins with the public announcement that the offender has decided to end her criminal participation. Such an announcement forces the start of a process of renegotiation of the offender's social identity (Stall and Biernacki 1986). After this announcement, the offender must not only cope with the instrumental aspects (e.g., financial) of her life but must also begin to redefine important emotional and social relationships that are influenced by or predicated upon criminal behavior.

Leaving a deviant subculture is difficult. Biernacki (1986) noted the exclusiveness of the social involvements maintained by former addicts during initial stages of abstinence. With social embedment comes the gratification of social acceptance and identity. The decision to end a behavior that is socially determined and supported implies withdrawal of the social gratification it brings. Thus, the more deeply embedded in a criminal social context, the more dependent the offender is on that social world for her primary sources of approval and social definition.

The responses by social control agents, family members, and peer supporters to further criminal participation are critical to shaping the outcome of discontinuance. New social and emotional worlds to replace the old ones may strengthen the decision to stop. Adler (1992) found that outside associations and involvements provide a critical bridge back into society for dealers who have decided to leave the drug subculture. With discontinuance comes the difficult work of identity transformations (Biernacki 1986) and establishing new social definitions of behavior and relationships to reinforce them.

Stage 3: Maintenance

Following the initial stages of discontinuance, strategies to avoid a return to crime build on the strategies first used to break from a lengthy pattern of criminal participation: further integration into a noncriminal identity and social world and maintenance of this new identity. Maintenance depends in part on replacing deviant networks of peers and associates with supports that both censure criminal participation and approve of new nondeviant beliefs. Treatment interventions (e.g., drug treatment, social service programs) are important sources of alternative social supports to maintain a noncriminal lifestyle. In other words, maintenance depends on immersion into a social world where criminal behavior meets immediately with strong formal and informal sanctions.

Despite efforts to maintain noncriminal involvement, desistance is likely to be episodic, with occasional relapses interspersed with lengthening of lulls in criminal activity. Le Blanc and Frechette (1989) proposed the possibility that criminal activity slows down before coming to an end and that this slowing-down process becomes apparent in three ways: deceleration, specialization, and reaching a ceiling. Thus, before stopping criminal activity, the offender gradually acts out less frequently, limits the variety of crimes more and more, and ceases increasing the seriousness of criminal involvement.

Age is a critical variable in desistance research, regardless of whether it is associated with maturation or similar developmental concepts. Cessation is part of a social-psychological transformation for the offender. A strategy to stabilize the transition to a noncriminal lifestyle requires active use of supports to maintain the norms that have been substituted for the forces that supported criminal behavior in the past.

FINDINGS

Resolving to Stop

Despite its initial excitement and allure, the life of a street criminal is a hard one. A host of severe personal problems plague most street offenders and normally become progressively worse as their careers continue. In the present study, the women's lives were dominated by a powerful, often incapacitating, need for drugs. Consequently, economic problems were the most frequent complaint voiced by the respondents. Savings were quickly exhausted, and the culture of addiction justified virtually any means to get money to support their habits. For the majority of the women, the problem of maintaining an addiction took precedence over other interests and participation in other social worlds.

People the respondents associated with, their primary reference group, were involved in illicit behaviors. Over time, the women in the study became further enmeshed in deviance and further alienated, both socially and psychologically, from conventional life. The women's lives became bereft of conventional involvements, obligations, and responsibilities. The excitement at the lifestyle that may have characterized their early criminal career phase gave way to a much more grave daily existence.

Thus, the women in our study could not and did not simply cease their deviant acts by "drifting" (Matza 1964) back toward conventional norms, values, and lifestyles. Unlike many of Waldorf's (1983) heroin addicts who drifted away from heroin without conscious effort, all of the women in our study made a conscious decision to stop. In short, Matza's concept of drift did not provide a useful framework for understanding our respondents' exit from crime.

The following accounts illustrate the uncertainty and vulnerability of street life for the women in our sample. Denise, a 33-year-old black woman, has participated in a wide range of street crimes including burglary, robbery, assault, and drug dealing. She began dealing drugs when she was 14 and was herself using cocaine on a regular basis by age 19.

> I was in a lot of fights: So I had fights over, uh, drugs, or, you know, just manipulation. There's a lot of manipulation in that life. Everybody's tryin' to get over.

Everybody will stab you in your back, you know. Nobody gives a fuck about the next person, you know. It's just when you want it, you want it. You know, when you want that drug, you know, you want that drug. There's a lot of lyin', a lot of manipulation. It's, it's, it's crazy!

Gazella, a 38-year-old Hispanic woman, had been involved in crime for 22 years when we interviewed her.

I'm 38 years old. I ain't no young woman no more, man. Drugs have changed, lifestyles have changed. Kids are killing you now for turf. Yeah, turf, and I was destroyin' myself. I was miserable. I was . . . I was gettin' high all the time to stay up to keep the business going, and it was really nobody I could trust.

Additional illustrations of the exigencies of street life are provided by April and Stephanie. April is a 25-year-old black woman who had been involved in crime since she was 11.

I wasn't eating. Sometimes I wouldn't eat for two or three days. And I would . . . a lot of times I wouldn't have the time, or I wouldn't want to spend the money to eat—I've got to use it to get high.

Stephanie, a 27-year-old black woman, had used and sold crack for 5 years when we interviewed her.

I knew that, uh, I was gonna get killed out here. I wasn't havin' no respect for myself. No one else was respecting me. Every relationship I got into, as long as I did drugs, it was gonna be constant disrespect involved, and it come . . . to the point of me gettin' killed.

When the spiral down finally reached its lowest point, the women were overwhelmed by a sense of personal despair. In reporting the early stages of this period of despair, the respondents consistently voiced two themes: the futility of their lives and their isolation.

Barbara, a 31-year-old black woman, began using crack when she was 23. By age 25, Barbara had lost her job at the Board of Education and was involved in burglary and robbery. Her account is typical of the despair the women in our sample eventually experienced.

The fact that my family didn't trust me anymore, and the way that my daughter was looking at me, and, uh, my mother wouldn't let me in her house any more, and I was sleepin' on the trains. And I was sleepin' on the beaches in the summertime. And I was really frightened. I was real scared of the fact that I had to sleep on the train. And, uh, I had to wash up in the Port Authority.

The spiral down for Gazella also resulted in her living on the streets.

I didn't have a place to live. My kids had been taken away from me. You know, constantly being harassed like 3 days out of the week by the Tactical Narcotics Team [police]. I didn't want to be bothered with people. I was gettin' tired of the lyin', schemin', you know, stayin' in abandoned buildings.

Alicia, a 29-year-old Hispanic woman, became involved in street violence at age 12. She commented on the personal isolation that was a consequence of her involvement in crime:

> When I started getting involved in crime, you know, and drugs, the friends that I had, even my family, I stayed away from them, you know. You know how you look bad and you feel bad, and you just don't want those people to see you like you are. So I avoided seeing them.

For some, the emotional depth of the rock bottom crisis was felt as a sense of mortification. The women felt as if they had nowhere to turn to salvage a sense of well-being or self-worth. Suicide was considered a better alternative than remaining in such an undesirable social and psychological state. Denise is one example:

> I ran into a girl who I went to school with that works on Wall Street. And I compared her life to mine and it was like miserable. And I just wanted out. I wanted a new life. I was tired, I was run down, looking bad. I got out by smashing myself through a sixth-floor window. Then I went to the psychiatric ward and I met this real nice doctor, and we talked every day. She fought to keep me in the hospital because she felt I wouldn't survive. She believed in me. And she talked me into going into a drug program.

Marginalization from family, friends, children, and work—in short, the loss of traditional life structures—left the women vulnerable to chaotic street conditions. After initially being overwhelmed by despair, the women began to question and reevaluate basic assumptions about their identities and their social construction of the world. Like Shover's (1983) male property offenders, the women also began to view the criminal justice system as "an imposing accumulation of aggravations and deprivations" (212). They grew tired of the street experiences and the problems and consequences of criminal involvement.

Many of the women acknowledged that, with age, it is more difficult to do time and that the fear of incurring a long prison sentence the next time influenced their decision to stop.

Cusson and Pinsonneault (1986) made the same observation with male robbers. Gazella, April, and Denise, quoted earlier, recall:

> First of all, when I was in prison I was like, I was so humiliated. At my age [38] I was really kind of embarrassed, but I knew that was the lifestyle that I was leadin'. And people I used to talk to would tell me, well, you could do this, and you don't have to get busted. But then I started thinking why are all these people here. So it doesn't, you know, really work. So I came home, and I did go back to selling again, but you know I knew I was on probation. And I didn't want to do no more time. (Gazella)
>
> Jail, being in jail. The environment, having my freedom taken away. I saw myself keep repeating the same pattern, and I didn't want to do that. Uh, I had missed my daughter. See, being in jail that long period of time, I was able to detox. And when I detoxed, I kind of like had a clear sense of thinking, and that's when I came to the realization that, uh, this is not working for me. (April)

> I saw the person that I was dealing with—my partner—I saw her go upstate to Bedford for 2 to 4 years. I didn't want to deal with it. I didn't want to go. Bedford is a prison, women's prison. And I couldn't see myself givin' up 2 years of my life for something that I knew I could change in another way. (Denise)

As can be seen from the above, the influence of punishment on these women was due to their belief that if they continued to be involved in crime, they would be apprehended, convicted, and incarcerated.

For many of the women, it was the stresses of street life and the fear of dying on the streets that motivated their decision to quit the criminal life. Darlene, a 25-year-old black woman, recalled the stress associated with the latter stage of her career selling drugs:

> The simple fact is that I really, I thought that I would die out there. I thought that someone would kill me out there and I would be killed; I had a fear of being on the front page one day and being in the newspaper dying. I wanted to live, and I didn't just want to exist.

Sonya, a 27-year-old Hispanic woman, provided an account of what daily life was like on the streets:

> You get tired of bein' tired, you know. I got tired of hustlin', you know. I got tired of livin' the way I was livin', you know. Due to your body, your body, mentally, emotionally, you know. Everybody's tryin' to get over. Everybody will stab you in your back. Nobody gives a fuck about the next person. And I used to have people talkin' to me, "You know, you're not a bad-lookin' girl. You know, why you don't get yourself together."

Perhaps even more important, the women felt that they had wasted time. They became acutely aware of time as a diminishing resource (Shover 1983). They reported that they saw themselves going nowhere. They had arrived at a point where crime seemed senseless, and their lives had reached a dead end. Implicit in this assessment was the belief that gaining a longer-range perspective on one's life was a first step in changing. Such deliberations develop as a result of "socially disjunctive experiences" that cause the offender to experience social stress, feelings of alienation, and dissatisfaction with her present identity (Ray 1961).

Breaking Away from the Life

Forming a commitment to change is only the first step toward the termination of a criminal career. The offender enters a period that has been characterized as a "running struggle" with problems of social identity (Ray 1961, 136). Successful desisters must work to clarify and strengthen their nondeviant identity and redefine their street experience in terms more compatible with a conventional lifestyle. The second stage of the desistance process begins with the public announcement or "certification" (Meisenhelder 1977, 329) that the offender has decided to end her deviant behavior. After this announcement, the offender must begin to redefine economic, social, and emotional relationships that were based on a deviant street subculture.

The time following the announcement was generally a period of ambivalence and crisis for the study participants, because so much of their lives revolved around street life and because they had, at best, weak associations with the conventional world. Many of the women remembered the uncertainty they felt and the social dilemmas they faced after they decided to stop their involvement in crime.

> I went and looked up my friends and to see what was doing, and my girlfriend Mia was like, she was gettin' paid. And I was livin' on a $60 stipend. And I wasn't with it. Mia was good to me, she always kept money in my pocket when I came home. I would walk into her closet and change into clothes that I'm more accustomed to. She started calling me Pen again. She stopped calling me Denise. And I would ride with her knowing that she had a gun or a package in the car. But I wouldn't touch nothin'. But that was my rationale. As long as I don't fuck with nothin'. Yeah, she was like I can give you a grand and get you started. I said I know you can, but I can't. She said I can give you a grand, and she kept telling me that over and over; and I wasn't that far from taking the grand and getting started again. (Denise)
>
> After I decided to change, I went to a party with my friend. And people was around me and they was drinkin' and stuff, and I didn't want to drink. I don't have the urge of drinking. If anything, it would be smokin' crack. And when I left the party, I felt like I was missing something—like something was missing. And it was the fact that I wasn't gettin' high. But I know the consequences of it. If I take a drink, I'm gonna smoke crack. If I, uh, sniff some blow, I'm gonna smoke crack. I might do some things like rob a store or something stupid and go to jail. So I don't want to put myself in that position. (Barbara)

At this stage of their transition, the women had to decide how to establish and maintain conventional relationships and what to do with themselves and their lives. Few of the women had maintained good relationships with people who were not involved in crime and drugs. Given this situation, the women had to seek alternatives to their present situation.

The large majority of study participants were aided in their social reintegration by outside help. These respondents sought formal treatment of some kind, typically residential drug treatment, to provide structure, social support, and a pathway to behavioral change. The women perceived clearly the need to remove themselves from the "scene" to meet new friends, and to begin the process of identity reformation. The following account by Alicia typifies the importance of a "geographic" cure:

> I love to get high, you know, and I love the way crack makes me feel. I knew that I needed long-term, I knew that I needed to go somewhere. All away from everything, and I just needed to away get from everything. And I couldn't deal with responsibility at all. And, uh, I was just so ashamed of the way that I had, you know, became and the person that I became that I just wanted to start over again.

Social avoidance strategies were common to all attempts at stopping. When the women removed themselves from their old world and old locations, involvement in crime and drugs was more difficult.

> Yeah, I go home, but I don't, I don't socialize with the people. I don't even speak to anybody really. I go and I come. I don't go to the areas that I used to be in. I don't go there anymore. I don't walk down the same blocks I used to walk down. I always take different locations. (April)

> I miss the fast money; otherwise, I don't miss my old life. I get support from my positive friends, and in the program. I talk about how I felt being around my old associates, seeing them, you know, going back to my old neighborhood. It's hard to deal with, I have to push away. (Denise)

Maintaining a Conventional Life

Desisters have little chance of staying out of the life for an extended period of time if they stay in the social world of crime and addiction. They must rebuild and maintain a network of primary relations who accept and support their nondeviant identity if they are to be successful (the third stage of this model). This is no easy task, since in most cases the desisters have alienated their old nondeviant primary relations.

To a great extent, the women in this study most resemble religious converts in their attempts to establish and maintain support networks that validate their new sense of self. Treatment programs not only provide a ready-made primary group for desisters, but also a well-established pervasive identity (Travisano 1970), that of ex-con and/or ex-addict, that informs the women's view of themselves in a variety of interactions. Reminders of "spoiled identities" (Goffman 1963) such as criminal, "con," and "junkie" serve as a constant reference point for new experiences and keep salient the ideology of conventional living (Faupel 1991). Perhaps most important, these programs provide the women with an alternative basis for life structure—one that is devoid of crime, drugs, and other subcultural elements.

The successful treatment program, however, is one that ultimately facilitates dissociation from the program and promotes independent living. Dissociation from programs to participate in conventional living requires association, or reintegration, with conventional society. Friends and educational and occupational roles helped study participants reaffirm their noncriminal identities and bond themselves to conventional lifestyles. Barbara described the assistance she receives from friends and treatment groups:

> A bunch of friends that always confronts me on what I'm doin' and where I'm goin', and they just want the best for me. And none of them use drugs. I go to a lot like outside support groups, you know. They help me have more confidence in myself. I have new friends now. Some of them are in treatment. Some have always been straight. They know. You know, they glad, you know, when I see them.

In the course of experiencing relationships with conventional others and participating in conventional roles, the women developed a strong social-psychological commitment not to return to crime and drug use. These commitments most often revolved around renewed affiliations with their children, relationships with new friends, and the acquisition of educational and vocational skills. The social relationships, interests, and investments that develop in the course of desistance reflect the gradual emergence of new identities. Such stakes in conventional identity form the social-psychological context within which control and desistance are possible (Waldorf et al. 1991).

In short, the women in the study developed a stake in their new lives that was incompatible with street life. This new stake served as a wedge to help maintain the separation of the women from the world of the streets (Biernacki 1986). The desire to maintain one's sense of self was an important incentive for avoiding return to crime.

> I like the fact that I have my respect back. I like the fact that, uh, my daughter trusts me again. And my mother don't mind leavin' me in the house, and she don't have to worry that when she come in her TV might be gone. (Alicia)
>
> I have new friends. I have my children back in my life. I have my education. It keeps me straight. I can't forget where I came from because I get scared to go back. I don't want to hurt nobody. I just want to live a normal life. (Barbara)

Janelle, a 22-year-old black woman, started dealing drugs and carrying a .38-caliber gun when she was 15. She described the ongoing tension between staying straight and returning to her old social world:

> It's hard, it's hard stayin' on the right track. But letting myself know that I'm worth more. I don't have to go in a store today and steal anything. I don't deserve that. I don't deserve to make myself feel really bad. Then once again I would be steppin' back and feel that this is all I can do.

Overall, the success of identity transformations hinges on the women's abilities to establish and maintain commitments and involvements in conventional aspects of life. As the women began to feel accepted and trusted within some conventional social circles, their determination to exit from crime was strengthened, as were their social and personal identities as noncriminals.

DISCUSSION

The primary purpose of this study was to describe—from the offenders' perspective—how women embedded in criminal street subcultures could end their deviance. Desistance appears to be a process as complex and lengthy as that of initial involvement. It was interesting to find that some of the key concepts in initiation of deviance—social bond, differential association, deterrence, age— were important in our analysis. We saw the aging offender take the threat of punishment seriously, reestablish links with conventional society, and sever association with subcultural street elements.

Our research supports Adler's (1992) finding that shame plays a limited role in the decision to return to conventional life for individuals who are entrenched in deviant subcultures. Rather, they exit deviance because they have evolved through the typical phases of their deviant careers.

In the present study, we found that the decision to give up crime was triggered by a shock of some sort (i.e., a socially disjunctive experience), by a delayed deterrence process, or both. The women then entered a period of crisis. Anxious and dissatisfied, they took stock of their lives and criminal activity. They arrived at a point where their way of life seemed senseless. Having made this assessment, the women then worked to clarify and strengthen their nondeviant identities. This phase began with the reevaluation of life goals and the public announcement of their decision to end involvement in crime. Once the decision to quit was made, the women turned to relationships that had not been ruined by their deviance, or they created new relationships. The final stage, maintaining cessation, involved integration into a nondeviant lifestyle. This meant restructuring the entire pattern of their lives (i.e., primary relationships, daily routines, social situations). For most women, treatment groups provided the continuing support needed to maintain a nondeviant status.

The change processes and turning points described by the women in the present research were quite similar to those reported by men in previous studies (Shover 1983, 1985; Cusson and Pinsonneault 1986). Collectively, these findings suggest that desistance is a pragmatically constructed project of action created by the individual within a given social context. Turning points occur as "part of a process over time and not as a dramatic lasting change that takes place at any one time" (Pickles and Rutter 1991, 134). Thus, the return to conventional life occurs more because of "push" than "pull" factors (Adler 1992), because the career of involvement in crime moves offenders beyond the point at which they find it enjoyable to the point at which it is debilitating and anxiety-provoking.

Considering the narrow confines of our empirical data, it is hardly necessary to point out the limits of generalizability. Our analysis refers to the woman deeply involved in crime and immersed in a street subculture who finds the strength and resources to change her way of life. The fact that all the women in this study experienced a long period of personal deterioration and a "rock bottom" experience before they were able to exit crime does not justify a conclusion that this process occurs with all offenders. Undoubtedly, there are other scenarios (e.g., the occasional offender who drifts in and out of crime, the offender who stops when criminal involvement conflicts with commitments to conventional life, the battered woman who kills) in which the question of desistance does not arise. Hence, there is a need to conceptualize and measure the objective and subjective elements of change among various male and female offender subgroups. Furthermore, the evidence presented here does not warrant the conclusion that none of the women ever renewed their involvement in crime. Because the study materials consist of retrospective information, with all its attendant problems, we cannot state with certainty whether desistance from crime is permanent. Still, it is also clear that these women broke their pattern of involvement in crime for substantial lengths of time and have substantially changed their lives.

REFERENCES

Adler, Patricia. 1992. "The 'Post' Phase of Deviant Careers: Reintegrating Traffickers." *Deviant Behavior* 13: 103–126.

Anglin, Douglas, and George Speckhart. 1988. "Narcotics Use and Crime: Multisample, Multimethod Analysis." *Criminology* 26: 197–234.

Biernacki, Patrick A. 1986. *Pathways from Heroin Addiction: Recovery Without Treatment.* Philadelphia: Temple University Press.

Biernacki, Patrick A., and Dan Waldorf. 1981. "Snowball Sampling: Problems Techniques of Chain Referral Sampling." *Sociological Methods and Research* 10: 141–163.

Blumstein, Alfred, Jacqueline Cohen, Jeffrey A. Roth, and Christy A. Visher. 1986. *Careers and Career Criminals.* Washington, DC: National Academy Press.

Collins, J., R. Hubbard, and J. V. Rachal. 1985. "Expensive Drug Use and Income: A Test of Explanatory Hypotheses." *Criminology* 23: 743–764.

Cusson, Maurice, and Pierre Pinsonneault. 1986. "The Decision to Give Up Crime." In *The Reasoning Criminal: Rational Choice Perspectives on Offending,* edited by Derek Cornish and Ronald Clarke. New York: Springer-Verlag.

Daly, Kathy, and Meda Chesney-Lind. 1988. "Feminism and Criminology." *Justice Quarterly* 5: 101–143.

Faupel, Charles. 1991. *Shooting Dope: Career Patterns of Hard-Core Heroin Users.* Gainesville: University of Florida Press.

Goffman, Erving. 1963. *Stigma: Notes on the Management of Spoiled Identity.* Englewood Cliffs, NJ: Prentice-Hall.

Hirschi, Travis, and H. C. Selvin. 1967. *Delinquency Research: An Appraisal of Analytic Methods.* New York: Free Press.

Le Blanc, Marc, and M. Frechette. 1989. *Male Criminal Activity from Childhood Through Youth: Multilevel and Developmental Perspective.* New York: Springer-Verlag.

Matza, David. 1964. *Delinquency and Drift.* New York: Wiley.

Meisenhelder, Thomas. 1977. "An Exploratory Study of Exiting from Criminal Careers." *Criminology* 15: 319–334.

Mulvey, Edward P., and John F. LaRosa. 1986. "Delinquency Cessation and Adolescent Development: Preliminary Data." *American Journal of Orthopsychiatry* 56: 212–224.

Petersilia, Joan, Peter Greenwood, and Marvin Lavin. 1978. *Criminal Careers of Habitual Felons.* Washington, DC: Law Enforcement Assistance Administration, U.S. Department of Justice.

Peterson, M., and H. Braiker. 1980. *Doing Crime: A Survey of California Prison Inmates.* Santa Monica, CA: Rand.

Pickles, Andrew, and Michael Rutter. 1991. "Statistical and Conceptual Models of 'Turning Points' in Developmental Processes." In *Problems and Methods in Longitudinal Research: Stability and Change,* edited by D. Magnusson, L. Bergman, G. Rudinger, and B. Torestad (pp. 110–136). New York: Cambridge University Press.

Ray, Marsh. 1961. "The Cycle of Abstinence and Relapse Among Heroin Addicts." *Social Problems* 9: 132–140.

Shover, Neil. 1983. "The Latter Stages of Ordinary Property Offenders' Careers." *Social Problems* 31: 208–218.

———. 1985. *Aging Criminals.* Newbury Park, CA: Sage.

Shover, Neil, and Carol Thompson. 1992. "Age, Differential Expectations, and Crime Desistance." *Criminology* 30: 89–104.

Stall, Ron, and Patrick Biernacki. 1986. "Spontaneous Remission from the Problematic Use of Substances: An Inductive Model Derived from a Comparative Analysis of the Alcohol, Opiate, Tobacco, and Food/Obesity Literatures." *International Journal of the Addictions* 2: 1–23.

Travisano, R. 1970. "Alteration and Conversion as Qualitatively Different Transformations." In *Social Psychology Through Symbolic Interaction,* edited by G. Stone and H. Farberman (pp. 594–605). Boston: Ginn-Blaisdell.

Waldorf, Dan. 1983. "Natural Recovery from Opiate Addiction: Some Social Psychological Processes of Untreated Recovery." *Journal of Drug Issues* 13: 237–280.

Waldorf, Dan, Craig Reinerman, and Sheila Murphy. 1991. *Cocaine Changes.* Philadelphia: Temple University Press.

Weiner, Neil, and Marvin E. Wolfgang. 1989. *Violent Crime, Violent Criminals.* Newbury Park, CA: Sage.

Weis, Joseph G. 1989. "Family Violence Research Methodology and Design." In *Family Violence,* edited by Lloyd Ohlin and Michael Tonry (pp. 117–162). Chicago: University of Chicago Press.

CHAPTER 23

The Victimization–Termination Link
Scott Jacques and Richard T. Wright

The life histories of drug dealers suggest that victimizations sometimes mark turning points toward the end of criminal careers, which is a criminologically important but neglected empirical connection that the authors of this chapter label the "victimization–termination link." According to this theory, when serious victimizations occur in the context of crime, a break from the customary provides an opportune situation for adaptation, and when victims have social bonds and agency, when they define the event as the result of their own criminal involvement, and when they find other adaptations unattractive, they are likely to adapt by terminating crime. The authors illustrate this desistance process with qualitative data obtained through interviews with young, middle-class drug dealers and conclude by exploring promising avenues for future work.

To date, life-course criminology has focused primarily on the ways in which positive life events (e.g., marriage or gaining employment) can serve as positive turning points toward the termination of law-breaking and the ways in which negative life events (e.g., imprisonment, divorce, or losing employment) can serve as negative turning points that lead to or exacerbate criminal behavior (Laub and Sampson, 2003; Sampson and Laub, 1993, 1997). Less empirical or theoretical attention has been paid to the ways in which *negative* life events, under certain circumstances, can serve as *positive* turning points toward the termination of crime (for empirical examples, see Bennett, 1986: 93; Cusson and Pinsonneault, 1986: 73–5; Decker and Lauritsen, 2002; Haggard, Gumpert, and Grann, 2001: 1055–6; Laub and Sampson, 2003: 139; Sampson and Laub, 1993: 223–4, 230–1; Sutherland, 1937: 183–91).

Illicit drug dealers often experience victimization—a negative event—because they have little access to formal mediation and so are rational targets for predators such as robbers and burglars (Jacobs, 2000; Wright and Decker, 1994,

Source: Adapted from Jacques, S., & Wright, R. T. (2008). The victimization–termination link. *Criminology*, *46*(4), 1009–38.

1997). Such victimizations can be contagious to the extent that they provoke re-taliation (Jacobs and Wright, 2006). Retaliation is relatively common in illicit drug markets because criminal-victims are unlikely to contact the police or file a lawsuit in court (Black, 1983; Goldstein et al., 1997; Jacobs, 2000; Topalli, Wright, and Fornango, 2002). Nevertheless, the empirical fact remains that *victimizations do not always lead to retaliation* (Jacques and Wright, 2008a). Instead, some drug dealers respond to victimization by ending their own illicit entrepreneurial career.

This article contributes to criminology and life-course theory by exploring and explicating the role of one kind of negative event, victimization, as a positive turning point toward the termination of a negative trajectory, illicit drug dealing. The stories of drug dealers reveal that victimizations can mark turning points toward the end of criminal careers, a criminologically important but neglected empirical connection we term the "victimization–termination link." We suggest a theory of this link that uses the logic of the life-course perspective (Elder, 1985) and Laub and Sampson's (2003) age-graded theory of social control: When seri-ous victimizations occur in the context of crime, a break from the customary provides an opportune situation for adaptation, and when victims have social bonds and agency, when they define the event as the result of their own criminal involvement, and when they find other adaptations unattractive, criminal-victims are likely to adapt by terminating crime.[1] We illustrate our theory of the victimization–termination link with qualitative data obtained through in-depth interviews with young, middle-class drug dealers recruited from the suburbs of Atlanta, Georgia.

We begin by briefly summarizing our theoretical lens (Elder, 1985; Laub and Sampson, 2003). We then explicate the use of life-course concepts and theory for making sense of the empirical connection between victimization and termina-tion. After outlining our research method, we draw on qualitative data obtained from young, middle-class drug dealers to illustrate the theory. We conclude by discussing the implications of our findings for future work in criminology. The primary goal of this article is to stimulate theorizing and testing aimed at verify-ing, explaining, or discrediting the empirical connection between victimization and termination.

LIFE-COURSE CRIMINOLOGY

The life-course perspective is arguably "the pre-eminent theoretical orientation in the study of lives" (Elder, Johnson, and Crosnoe, 2003: 3). The "pioneering study" (Elder, 1985: 24) of the life-course perspective is Thomas and Znaniecki's (1918–1920) *The Polish Peasant in Europe and America*. Since publication of that study, and especially in recent decades, the life-course paradigm has been applied to many forms of behavior (see Mortimer and Shanahan, 2003) and has been particularly fruitful in understanding onset, persistence, and desistance in crime (see, e.g., Laub and Sampson, 2003; Moffitt, 1993, 2006; Sampson and Laub, 1993).

Three key concepts in the life-course perspective are *trajectories, transitions,* and *turning points* (Elder, 1985). Any given life moves through various trajectories—"pathways or lines of development" (Laub, Sampson, and Sweeten, 2006: 314), and these may differ in direction, degree, and rate of change (Elder, 1985: 31). A person, for instance, may be on a more or less positive trajectory—such as having employment and a stable family life—or be on a more or less negative trajectory—such as engaging in criminal activity on a daily basis. Trajectories represent long-term patterns in life, whereas the notion of transitions refers to the "short-term events embedded in trajectories" (Laub, Sampson, and Sweeten, 2006: 314). Transitions, like trajectories, can be positive or negative; positive transitions, for example, include becoming married or employed, and negative ones include divorce, being fired, or being arrested. Transitions are important to understanding trajectories because "[s]ome events are important turning points in life—they redirect paths" (Elder, 1985: 35). "A major concept in [the life-course perspective] is the dynamic process whereby the interlocking nature of trajectories and transitions generates *turning points* or a change in life course" (Laub and Sampson, 1993: 304). In other words, some life events—negative or positive—mark an important change in the direction of a life trajectory.

"Adaptation to life events is crucial because the same event . . . followed by different adaptations can lead to different trajectories" (Laub and Sampson, 1993: 304). An important adaptation in understanding criminal trajectories, transitions, and turning points is the termination of crime that results from the process of desistance. The conceptual difference between termination and desistance is subtle but important: Termination is the point at which one stops criminal activity, whereas desistance is the causal process that supports the termination of offending. Although it is difficult to ascertain when the process of desistance begins, it is apparent that it continues after the termination of offending. That is, the process of desistance maintains the continued state of non-offending. Thus both termination and the process of desistance need to be considered in understanding cessation from offending. By using different terms for these distinct phenomena, we separate termination (the outcome) from the dynamics underlying the process of desistance (the cause), which have been confounded in the literature to date. The termination of offending is characterized by the absence of continued offending (a nonevent). . . . Desistance, by contrast, evolves over time in a process (Laub and Sampson, 2003: 21–2; also see Laub and Sampson, 2001).

Laub and Sampson's (2003) revised, age-graded theory of social control attempts to make sense of why some persons desist from crime and others persist in their criminal careers. According to that theory, the three causal influences on desistance and the resulting termination of crime are social bonds, routine activities, and human agency.[2] Simply put, Laub and Sampson's theory predicts that criminal involvement varies inversely with the strength/quantity of social bonds, structured routine activities, and human agency—"purposeful execution of choice and individual will" (Sampson and Laub, 2005: 176). Thus, termination of crime should result from events and transitions that increase social bonds, structured activities, and human agency; conversely, criminal activity should increase as a person loses social bonds, structured activities, and human agency. In sum, differences in social bonds, routine activities, and human agency are the factors that produce variable adaptations to life events and transitions, which, in turn, alter life trajectories. (For a review of the empirical validity of the theory, see Laub, Sampson, and Sweeten, 2006: 324–7.)

THEORIZING THE VICTIMIZATION–TERMINATION LINK

Existing social bonds, routine activities, and human agency may not always be powerful enough to prevent the onset or result in the termination of crime (Laub and Sampson, 2003; Sampson and Laub, 1993). Control theories seek to explain why people do not commit crime (see, among many others, Gottfredson and Hirschi, 1990; Hirschi, 1969; Laub and Sampson, 2003). The experiences of some middle-class drug dealers suggest that victimizations experienced in the context of drug dealing can be turning points toward termination—a life trajectory with more control.

We suggest the following line of reasoning: "Opportune situations for modifications or a change in course are those which represent a break from the customary, a disturbance of habit in which customary behavior can no longer be maintained" (Elder, 1985: 42). For drug dealers who are victimized in the course of their work, a "break from the customary"— being in control of drugs—is experienced, and this may lead to "a disturbance of habit in which a customary behavior can no longer be maintained," namely drug dealing. "[A]daptations to crisis situations are ways of dealing with resources and options in order to achieve control" (1985: 42). An adaptation that may flow from personal victimization (a negative event) suffered while engaging in drug dealing (a negative trajectory) is the termination of drug dealing (a positive turning point and transition). By terminating (controlling) one's drug dealing, the probability of victimization is reduced (the crime of others is controlled), and the life course experiences a turning point toward a more positive trajectory.

According to Elder, the outcome of turning points cannot be appraised without taking into account four sets of variables: "(1) the nature of the event or transition, its severity, duration, and so on; (2) the resources, beliefs, and experiences people bring to the situation; (3) how the situation or event is defined; and (4) resulting lines of adaptation as chosen from available alternatives" (1985: 35). We suggest that termination is an adaptation that follows severe victimizations of drug dealers (first variable) with social bonds and agency (second variable) who define their victimizations as the result of their own criminal involvement (third variable) and find other adaptations, such as retaliation, to be unattractive (fourth variable).

In sum, then, given the existence of social bonds and human agency (Laub and Sampson, 2003), serious victimizations that drug dealers define as the outcome of their own law-breaking can increase the probability of termination. Although victimization is a negative event, *if the experience occurs while participating in crime,* then it may serve as a turning point toward the termination of offending because termination is an adaptation that allows persons to gain control over their lives and to reduce the probability of future victimization. In this respect, negative life events can be positive turning points that mark a transition to a new life trajectory with more control.

After reviewing our research method, this article draws on the experiences of young, middle-class drug dealers to illustrate the theoretical process described above. To be clear, the objective here is not to test our theory but rather to demonstrate that dealers themselves associate social bonds, agency, and victimization with their termination and, therefore, that the victimization–termination link seems to be a fruitful line of inquiry for future criminological work.

METHODOLOGY

This article relies on the in-depth analysis of interviews with two drug sellers, Pete and Christian, drawn from a larger study of drug dealers in Atlanta and St. Louis (for details, see Jacques and Wright, 2008a: 224–5, 2008b). Pete and Christian both are white. At the time of the interview, both were in their early 20s, enrolled in college, and had never been arrested. According to the Census Bureau, the town in which Pete and Christian went to high school is about 90 percent white, 90 percent of adults have a high-school degree or higher, and the median household income is almost $70,000.[3]

EVIDENCE FOR A VICTIMIZATION–TERMINATION LINK

We suggest above that victimizations that occur in the context of crime provide drug dealers with an opportune situation for adaptation and that the adaptation of termination follows from 1) severe victimizations of drug dealers, 2) who have social bonds and agency, 3) who define the victimizations as the result of their own crime, and 4) who find alternative adaptations, such as violent retaliation, to be unattractive. In this way, a negative life event, victimization, can be a positive turning point that marks a transition toward a life trajectory with more control and less crime.

Social Bonds + Victimization → Termination

"In its most general sense, 'social control' refers to the regulation of human behavior" (Sampson, 1986: 276). As observed in the work of Hirschi (1969) and Sampson and Laub (1993), the control tradition in criminology is especially concerned with persons' "bonds to family, school, and community, which affect or embody the social controls that account for the costs of delinquency" (Kornhauser, 1978: 25). Crime can be contained through internal (self-invoked) or external (other-invoked) controls and direct (purposeful) or indirect (by-product) actions (1978: 24). This article is interested in how direct internal controls and direct external controls serve as mechanisms that intertwine with victimization to lead to termination.

"Direct internal controls are manifested in guilt and shame, the products of effective socialization, which varies across persons and over the lifetime of a person. . . . Direct external controls are the products of scrutiny, supervision, and surveillance, designed to preclude, deter, or detect deviance" (Kornhauser, 1978: 24). When a person experiences direct internal control or is subject to direct external control, the social bond of the person is strengthened. If a dealer's victimization leads to shame or regret or promotes greater levels of supervision and intervention by family, then that victimization has interacted with social control and strengthened the social bond. If a dealer's bond before victimization is "strong" but not "strong enough" to control crime, then the strengthening of the bond that follows victimization may result in the termination of drug dealing.

Pete's story is illustrative of how victimization can interact with direct internal controls, namely shame, and direct external controls, namely supervision and punishment applied by family. Before termination, of course, comes onset, and Pete's termination can be better understood by knowing the conditions surrounding the onset of his drug dealing career:

> PETE: The first time I bought an ounce [28 grams of marijuana], I bought it for 350 bucks and sold all of it but an eighth [3.5 grams, typically worth $50 at the retail level].
> INTERVIEWER: Why did you decide to get an ounce and sell it like you did?
> PETE: So I didn't have to pay for the weed I wanted to smoke . . .
> INTERVIEWER: So take me along this time line of selling.
> PETE: Once I bought one for $350, and then the next time I bought an ounce for like $325; I got it cheaper. And, actually, I made like 50 bucks and got to keep a sixteenth [1.75 grams] of it for free [to smoke]. And then I started trying to make profit, and profit, and profit. I'd buy an ounce—try to make a little more money, buy an ounce—try to make a little more money. And then eventually when I had enough money, I started buying two ounces, and then more and more, gradually and gradually . . . . When I started it was for free drugs, and then as I went along it was like, "Wow, the more I buy, the cheaper I get it, and the more I sell, the more money I can make and the more I can smoke."
> INTERVIEWER: How old were you at this point?
> PETE: 17, a senior in high school.

The drug-dealing life was "good" to Pete, but, as they say, all good things must come to an end. Having sold marijuana for almost 6 months, the desistance process for Pete began on the night he was "set up" and violently victimized in the parking lot of a neighborhood pool:

PETE: I was looking for a QP [quarter pound], and most of my regular guys [suppliers] didn't have it. I got a call from a kid that I thought was my friend, and he told me he could get it for me: "I hear you're looking for some weed, and I can get you a QP." I said, "Yeah." He was like, "Well come pick me up, and we'll go get it." So I went and picked him up, met these people. . . . They said, "You got the money?" I said, "Yeah, I got the money." They were like, "Okay, let me see it, and I'll go get it." I was like, "I don't think so. I'll come with you, or you can go and get it and come back." So I got out of the car [and then] got hit in the side of the face. . . . I acted as though I was knocked out and lay on the ground face down. I had the money in my jacket pocket . . . and I felt somebody drag me and roll me over to try and get the money, and when they did that, I grabbed them, pulled them down, got up, and got in my jeep and drove off.

INTERVIEWER: Really?

PETE: Yeah.

INTERVIEWER: How did you pull him down?

PETE: Just grabbed his shirt and pulled him.

INTERVIEWER: OK.

PETE: They were wearing masks.

INTERVIEWER: How many were there?

PETE: Two of them.

INTERVIEWER: Where did you meet them up at?

PETE: We met at a neighborhood pool.

INTERVIEWER: So once it was done, you just left, you said?

PETE: Yeah.

INTERVIEWER: And what did you do? What were you thinking to yourself?

PETE: "Shit, that sucks."

INTERVIEWER: Were you hurt?

PETE: I didn't have any broken bones or anything. I think I dislocated one joint, but that's about it. And I was beat up, dude. I was black and blue all over.

INTERVIEWER: What did you decide to do? Like, what were you going through in your head? Were you thinking about trying to get back at these guys? Did you know who it was?

PETE: I dunno, man. I really can't even tell you what I was thinking when it happened. I was thinking . . . well, I didn't even realize I was getting jumped until I got hit in the face about three times. First time I got hit, it made me like dazed, you know. Then I was like, "Shit, shit, they're trying to steal my money." . . . I got out and started driving off, [and] I was like, "What the fuck? What the hell? What the hell's going on?" And I was at a party at one of my friend's houses just before. Not a party, but we just had a little get-together, so I went back over there, went to his house, [and] got in the shower 'cause I was bleeding everywhere. And, yeah, then we were trying to find out who did it.

INTERVIEWER: What do you mean, "We were trying to find out who did it?" How did you do that?

PETE: Me and my friends.

INTERVIEWER: And how did you go about trying to find out who did it?

PETE: We called the kid that set me up, and he lied and said . . . you know, he bullshit us and said, "Oh, I got hit in the face, too. I don't know what happened. Blah-blah-blah." . . . He said, "Dude, I don't know what happened, man, because I got hit in the face, too, 'cause the guy's not really my good friend. The guy's not really my good friend. I just kind of know him a little bit. Blah-blah-blah. I can't believe they did that to us." I'm like, "All right, man." I sort of believed him at first 'cause I didn't think he would do something like that to me, but he did. . . . I was like, "Well, alright, but I'm gonna find out who did this." Basically, . . . I didn't really care. . . . I didn't know if these guys were trying to kill me or what, you know. I was just glad that I was fucking alive 'cause I had bigger things on my mind.

Receiving a black eye and almost losing more than $1,000 in cash were not, according to Pete, the only, or even the worst, negative events he experienced that week—a week that marked a turning point toward a more conventional trajectory. As evidenced in the story below, a victimization experienced in the context of drug dealing can be a turning point toward termination by contributing to the production of direct internal controls, such as regret, guilt, and shame, and direct external controls, such as supervision and shaming by family members.

PETE: I had to go to my grandfather's funeral the next day, in front of all my family, beat the fuck up because I was trying to sell weed. . . . That's the thing in my life that I regret most in my life ever, having my whole entire family having to see me all beat up because I was selling weed.

INTERVIEWER: Did they know that?

PETE: They knew.

INTERVIEWER: How did they know?

PETE: I told them someone tried to steal my car and blah-blah-blah. I told them a bullshit story, but everyone knew.

INTERVIEWER: Who did you tell a bullshit story to?

PETE: My whole family, my parents, everybody. My parents didn't buy it. Everyone else was like, "Oh, really, that's awful!" But I know everyone in my family, and they knew I was bullshitting to them.

INTERVIEWER: So you never told your parents what happened?

PETE: Eventually, I told my parents what really happened.

INTERVIEWER: How long did it take you to tell them?

PETE: About a week after that happened. . . . Christmas Eve. . . .

INTERVIEWER: And what brought that on?

PETE: My mom asked me if I was selling drugs because she knew nobody was going to steal my fucking car. . . . She said, "I know you're selling weed." I was like, "Why?" She said, "Because of this," and she showed me . . . $1,000 I had and just a stash of cash [I had] in my room.

INTERVIEWER: So what did you say?

PETE: I was like, "Damn." I got mad at first and said, "No, I've just been saving up money" and just kept trying to lie.

INTERVIEWER: Why did you do that?

PETE: 'Cause I didn't want my parents to think that I was selling drugs.

INTERVIEWER: Why not?

PETE: Because I didn't want them to be disappointed in me.

INTERVIEWER: Why would they be disappointed in you if you were selling drugs?

PETE: . . . it's just the concept of "He's a drug dealer," you know. All these. Women say, "Oh, he's a drug dealer, he's a drug dealer, scum of the earth," like that's the fucking title given to drug dealers, and I didn't want to be that, and I didn't want anybody to know that's what I was.

INTERVIEWER: And yet you still sold drugs?

PETE: Yes, because I didn't think that I was [a bad person]. I still don't think I was, for selling weed. . . . I wasn't a bad person. Yeah, I sold drugs that were illegal—I mean, I don't think they should be illegal, but that's not what it's about. I dunno, I just don't think I fit the description of what everyone thinks a drug dealer is—what everybody makes out a drug dealer to be.

INTERVIEWER: Which is what?

PETE: Like a violent person who steals, fucking has guns, is sketched out, all tripped out on drugs and all, [and] has no self-control.

INTERVIEWER: Oh, OK. So did you quit dealing then? When did you quit dealing?

PETE: I quit like 2 weeks after I had that confrontation with my mom.

INTERVIEWER: So you got jumped and you quit dealing?

PETE: No, I got jumped, and then I kept trying to buy the weed, and then I found the weed, and then my mom was like, "Yeah, you're selling, blah-blah-blah," and I sold the rest of the weed I had.

INTERVIEWER: Which was how much?

PETE: Like a QP. I bought a QP and sold it in ounces, and then I had that confrontation with my mom, on Christmas Eve. I was down and felt like shit. My parents knew that I was selling weed, and my parents thought that I was a bad person because of it. . . . My dad said I was an idiot. . . . He just talked down to me like I wasn't a person, you know, like I was a fucking dog or something. For about a week, 2 weeks, I felt like shit. . . .

INTERVIEWER: And what about your mom?

PETE: My mom was like, "I can't believe this has happened, but it's alright. I still love you." . . . She said I was lucky they didn't kill me. Mom was just scared.

INTERVIEWER: And she told you that or you just felt that?

PETE: She told me that.

INTERVIEWER: OK, and do you have any other family members like brothers or sisters?

PETE: Yeah.

INTERVIEWER: What do you have?

PETE: I have two sisters and a brother. . . .

INTERVIEWER: And what did they say about it?

PETE: They said that I'm stupid.

Pete was victimized in an act of violent predation, and although this act did not result in immediate termination, the incident did spur the desistance process that resulted in termination. The victimization led Pete to experience greater levels of social control, and so his bond was strengthened. When Pete's extended family saw his black eye at the funeral and consoled him, Pete experienced internal direct control, namely, regret and shame (see Kornhauser, 1978: 25). Pete said, "That's the thing in my life that I regret most in my life ever, having my whole entire family having to see me *all beat up because I was selling weed*" (emphasis added). Shame and regret related to victimization and drug dealing strengthen the social bond and thereby reduce the probability of future drug dealing.

The victimization also led Pete to experience greater levels of direct external control, such as "scrutiny . . . and surveillance" (Kornhauser, 1978: 25). Pete's parents were suspicious that their son was involved in crime because victimization is a rare event in their community. For that reason, Pete's mom engaged in surveillance by going into his room and searching for evidence of deviance, which resulted in her finding more than $1,000 in cash. After finding the suspected drug money, Pete's mother and father scrutinized and shamed their child (Braithwaite, 1989; Sampson and Laub, 1993: 68). Pete's father told him he was an "idiot" and treated him as if he "wasn't a person" and like "a fucking dog or something"; his siblings simply told him that he was "stupid." Pete's mother, however, applied social control through expressions of caring and concern. The direct external control applied to Pete by his family resulted in greater levels of internal direct control, as he felt "down" and "like shit" for a couple weeks after the victimization and confrontation with his family. Direct external control and direct internal control strengthen the bond, and Pete's victimization led him to experience greater levels of control on both fronts, thereby becoming more tied to society.

Although social bonds are an important ingredient in the termination equation, some lives, such as Pete's, require the addition of another ingredient that serves to "kick start" social control and strengthen social bonds. Victimization, at least in the life of Pete, was that ingredient—it enhanced social control and, in turn, social bonds. Pete's victimization resulted in him experiencing regret and shame and being subjected to greater levels of surveillance and scrutiny by his family. Victimization, a negative event in Pete's life, provided an opportune situation for a positive adaptation and change in his life—the termination of drug dealing. Victimization and social bonds interacted in a way that produced Pete's desistance from drug dealing and the termination of that activity. Without social bonds, the victimization may have not been followed by termination. Without victimization, Pete's dealing career may have continued longer than it did.

Agency + Victimization → Termination

Agency is another mechanism that interacts with victimization to produce termination. Nagin (2007: 262) defines agency as "a decision-making process, however crude or faulty, that reflects the benefits, costs, and risks of alternative courses of action." Elder, Johnson, and Crosnoe (2003: 11) think of agency as the process through which "[i]ndividuals construct their own life course through the choices and actions they take within the opportunities and constraints of history and social circumstance." To be clear, "the concept of human agency cannot be understood simply as a proxy for motivation. Rather, the concept of agency has the element of projective or transformative action within structural constraints" (Laub, Sampson, and Sweeten, 2006: 323). When a dealer is victimized, there is reason to reweigh the costs and benefits of dealing, owing not only to the chance of future victimizations but also to one's stake in conformity and to the potential penalties attached to breaking the law.

The interplay of drug dealing, agency, victimization, and termination is evidenced in the life of Christian. Christian's drug-using career began in the ninth grade with a hit of marijuana. His marijuana-dealing career began after completing high school:

> [I] started talking to this kid on my [sports] team, and we decided, me and my friend, that we'd go in together with our graduation money and buy some quantity [of marijuana] and we'd start selling, right when we graduated from high school.... [W]e graduated from high school and ... what we did is we went and bought a scale [and] bought an ounce for like [$]325, maybe we bought 2 ounces, but I think we bought one.... We worked together ... and ... it went well.

All was well, at least for a while. Eventually, however, Christian became the victim of a fraudulent trade—one without violence but with misinformation between traders (Jacques and Wright, 2008a). The following quote illustrates the relationship among victimization, agency, and termination:

> INTERVIEWER: Was there any one factor that led you to quitting?
> CHRISTIAN: Well, I remember, we [my family] go to [place name] for vacation because that's where we're from. And I remember being in the ... airport about to come back, and I had been gone for like 10 days ... and didn't bring my cell phone with me or anything, but I remember sitting in the airplane ... and I remember thinking to myself, "When I go back, do I want to keep doing this?" 'cause I knew I was 18 and that if I got caught I was fucked.
> INTERVIEWER: So you managed to get some time away from it?

CHRISTIAN: Basically, yeah, 10 days away from it and just thought it out. . . . I basically decided that when I got back that I needed a change. . . . I was going to stop dealing. And the other thing is, I knew I was coming to [college]. Like I remember thinking to myself that I'm going to [college], and I'm not going to make enough money [dealing drugs] to make it worth basically fucking up your life and not being able to go to [college]. 'Cause it was basically like I was on the right track, and I was done with high school, and it was finally time for me to go off and make something of myself. And I just knew that if I was going to continue to deal, I was going to put that at a heavy risk, and it just wasn't worth it. I mean having the money was nice, but the rest of my life wasn't worth the money. . .

INTERVIEWER: So there was no incident that made you quit?

CHRISTIAN: Well, I remember before I left [for vacation], this is like a week or 2 before I left, I . . . got jacked. . . . [W]hat happened was I was working out at the [gym], and some guy called me up and asked me if I'd meet his friend, and I was like, "Yeah, tell him to meet me outside the [gym] in like an hour." And I talked to this guy who came up to meet me, and it's a public space or whatever so I'm not really concerned about him jumping me or whatever, and he doesn't know where my stuff is anyways. So he's like, "I want a quarter," and I was like, "Alright, let's do it." And he was like, "No, follow me to my house 'cause I don't want to do it here." And I was like, "No, I'm pretty sure we can do it right here. What's the big deal? Break that money out, I'll give you the stuff, and it's over." And he's like, "No, no, I don't want to do that," and I continued the conversation with him, and I don't know why. And he starts telling me he had just got out of jail, and he doesn't want to get caught or anything. And I look in his front seat, and there's a bat and a fucking crowbar. And I look at this, and I say to him, "Why do you have a bat and a crowbar?" And he doesn't really give me an answer, so I kinda knew what was up, but I didn't want to believe that this kid actually intended to whatever. So I continued this conversation with him for like 20 minutes, and I don't know if it's 'cause I actually enjoyed a conversation that was this retarded because the conversation was going nowhere. And so finally, I was like, "Whatever, I'm gone, give me a call later or something." And so he calls me back like hours later looking for a half ounce, and I should have known when he upped the weight that this is definitely not right, but we decided to meet at [a local business]. . . . I still remember the ride over there and where we met, and the whole ride I was like, "Why the fuck am I doing this? I'm about to get robbed. Why the fuck am I doing this?" . . . so, whatever, I meet him, and, this is one of the most embarrassing stories I have, I knew he was going to rob me. It's like I just let it happen. I have no idea why. But he opens the door, and I was like, "You the weed." [He] runs off, and, sure enough, I open it up and there's $18. . . . my loss on it was $142 or something, if I remember correctly.

A full appraisal of any turning point requires consideration not only of the "resulting line of adaptation," which in Christian's case is ultimately termination, but also the "available alternatives" (Elder, 1985: 35), such as the escalation of crime through violent retaliation. Christian's immediate reaction to his victimization, coupled with his thoughts about his propensity to engage in violence, shed light on why vengeance did not take place and, thus, why termination was a more likely adaptation:

> [S]o I was like, "He can have it 'cause it's not worth getting shot," 'cause this is somebody I didn't know, and he had just gotten out of jail, and he had a crowbar and a bat. So . . . at this point, it's like, "It's not worth getting shot." . . . I'll pay somebody $150 not to shoot me. . . . I've never been in a fight. Like I've always thought, like I remember being 8 years old and thinking, "If I get in a fight I'm kinda screwed 'cause I don't want to hurt somebody." Like I can't imagine punching somebody in the face and hurting them, and I've always been like that. So it's like the idea of physical violence as retribution has never been something I wanted [to do], particularly when I'm not going to get my money back.

Christian's drug dealing trajectory took the following path: He began his marijuana-selling career after completing his high-school career and concluded it before beginning his college career. According to Christian, the termination of dealing flowed from two key events in his life: his victimization in a fraudulent trade in which he lost almost $150 worth of marijuana and his choice to make something of himself and discontinue dealing.

Christian was victimized in a fraud. Just before being victimized, Christian recognized that he had lost control and said to himself, "Why the fuck am I doing this? I'm about to get robbed. Why am I doing this?'" Christian could not find the strength to stop himself from doing a drug deal that he predicted would result in his own victimization. After being victimized, he could have tried to find the offender and exact vengeance, but Christian did not want to take the chance of getting shot. What is more, "physical violence as retribution has never been something [he] wanted" to partake in, and so he did not find the adaptation of retaliation to be an attractive option. Although victimization did not result in Christian instantly terminating his illicit activity, the desistance process was set in motion because he started to reevaluate the benefits and costs of dealing in relation to alternative lines of action available to him.

The victimization and subsequent vacation provided Christian with an opportune situation to reflect on his current and potential future life trajectories. Christian made a decision while on the plane "that reflects the benefits, costs, and risks of alternative courses of action" (Nagin, 2007: 262). Christian considered that he was 18 years of age and thus no longer a minor, that he was going to college soon, that the profit of dealing was not large enough to offset the risks, and that it was time for him to go and make something of himself. In the end, Christian decided that dealing was too hazardous and that termination was the best course of action.

In sum, the two most important factors that, in Christian's mind, facilitated his termination of drug dealing were being victimized in a fraudulent trade and his *choice* to make something of himself and avoid the negative consequences of acting criminally. Without agency, the victimization may not have been followed by termination. Without victimization, Christian's dealing career may have continued longer than it did.

IMPLICATIONS FOR CRIMINOLOGY

Examining the qualitative and quantitative aspects of any given transitional event alongside the sociological and psychological conditions surrounding the affected person enhances our understanding of how and why various adaptations lead to new life trajectories (Elder, 1985: 35). What the qualitative data outlined above suggest is that—when coupled with social bonds and agency (Laub and Sampson, 2003)—victimizations that occur in the context of illicit activities may mark turning points toward a life trajectory with less crime. Termination of drug dealing is an adaptation to victimization to the extent that it allows drug sellers to gain more control over their resources, health, and reputation by reducing the probability of future victimization (controlling the crime of others). So what are the implications of this possibility for the future of criminology? We suggest that theoretical specification and formal testing are important avenues for future work.

Theoretical Specification

Appraising and explaining the outcome of any given turning point requires consideration of four sets of variables: "(1) the nature of the event or transition, its severity, duration, and so on; (2) the resources, beliefs, and experiences people bring to the situation; (3) how the situation or event is defined; and (4) resulting lines of adaptation as chosen from available alternatives" (Elder, 1985: 35). In this section, we suggest possible ways in which theorists may want to specify how conditions relevant to the above variables affect the victimization–termination link.

Because "the nature of the event or transition, its severity, duration, and so on" (1985: 35) affects turning points, theorists should explicate how qualitative and quantitative variability in victimization influence termination. Quantitatively, the theory presented above states that the more serious the victimization, as measured by money, drugs, or violence, the more likely is termination to occur. What we do not know is whether violence or the loss of resources (money or drugs) has a larger effect on the termination of crime. Is money less important than health, or vice versa, in determining life trajectories? As relates to the "nature" (quality) of victimization, our theoretical principle is restricted to the influence of victimizations that occur in the context of crime rather than applying to all victimizations across time and place. But what follows from victimizations that do not occur in the context of crime? Also related to the quality of victimizations is whether they are predatory or retaliatory in nature (Cooney and Phillips, 2002; Jacques and Wright, 2008a). Are predatory victimizations more or less likely than retaliatory ones to result in termination?

As relates to the "resources, beliefs, and experiences" brought by the dealer to the victimization situation, this article has argued that dealers with social bonds and agency are especially likely to terminate drug selling after being victimized. Important questions left unanswered are as follows: Are some social bonds more important than others in contributing to the victimization–termination link? Do social bonds and agency both need to be present to produce termination after victimization, or is one alone sufficient? The nature of our data precluded exploring the effect of routine activities on crime (Cohen and Felson, 1979), which is a component of the revised, age-graded theory of social control (Laub and Sampson, 2003), and so future work should develop the theoretical implications of routine activities theory for making sense of the victimization–termination link.

The definition of an event influences its effect on the trajectory of a life. For a victimization to lead to termination, the dealer must define it as a product of her or his own criminal behavior. Otherwise, no logical link is found, in the dealer's mind, between selling and being a victim, and thus no impetus is felt by the dealer to choose a different path or feel shame and embarrassment for being victimized. Similarly, if an agent of social control, such as a parent, does not identify a drug-related victimization as the outcome of the victim's own law-breaking, then social control will not occur, social bonds will not be strengthened, and the likelihood of termination will not be enhanced. Future work should delve deeper into how variability in definitions of victimizations affects termination. For instance, it seems to us that the world of middle-class dealers is in many respects different from the one inhabited by lower-class, urban drug dealers (see, e.g., Jacobs, 1999), who often live in neighborhoods where victimization is a way of life regardless of your criminal involvements and where legitimate opportunities for success are limited (see Wilson, 1987, 1996; Wright and Decker, 1994, 1997). Do offenders who live in crime-saturated communities less often define their victimizations as the result of their own criminal involvement? If so, does this reduce the likelihood of termination after victimization occurring in the context of crime?

Also important to understanding the victimization–termination link is generating information bearing on the causes of alternative adaptations and, in turn, how those adaptations affect life trajectories. "[A]daptations to crisis situations are ways of dealing with resources and options in order to achieve control" (Elder, 1985: 42), and "[a]daptation to life events is crucial because the same event or transition followed by different adaptations can lead to different trajectories" (Laub and Sampson, 1993: 304). Besides termination, another adaptation to victimization is retaliation, which achieves control both by providing victims with retribution and by deterring future victimizations (Topalli, Wright, and Fornango, 2002). To the degree that dealers find retaliation to be an unattractive adaptation, then termination will occur, and vice versa. Although drug dealers are mostly thought of as violent people, we believe that some drug dealers simply do not have a "cognitive landscape" (Sampson and Wilson, 1995) conducive to retaliation. A cognitive landscape refers to "ecologically structured norms . . . regarding appropriate standards and expectations of conduct" (1995: 46). The middle-class dealers we have interviewed did not grow up in neighborhoods with broken windows, nor did they see bullet-filled bodies on street corners; instead what they saw everywhere were well-kept homes, pharmacies, restaurants, grocery stores, and other staples of suburban life. In the streets, the smallest conflict may lead to retaliation (see Anderson, 1999; Cooney, 1998), but in the suburbs, conflict usually leads to avoidance or toleration (see Baumgartner, 1988). Whereas lower-class persons from urban areas may witness serious acts of violence and suffering on a regular basis, most middle-class "kids" are entirely insulated from violence, and so they develop a cognitive landscape devoid of violence and permeated with peaceful forms of conflict management. When middle-class dealers are victimized, their nonviolent cognitive landscape inhibits them from enacting physical vengeance, and therefore, termination (and other adaptations) becomes more likely to occur. The cognitive landscape theory is but one approach to understanding alternative adaptations; theorists should develop other explanations of alternative adaptations and explain how those alternatives affect change and continuity in life trajectories.

Alternative Theories

Regardless of whether the mixing of social bonds, agency, and victimization affect the likelihood of termination, it may be useful to develop alternative explanations of the victimization–termination link. Five alternative theories of crime that seem to hold promise for explaining the victimization–termination link are deterrence theory (see, e.g., Beccaria, 1995 [1764]; Bentham, 1988 [1789]), social learning theory (see, e.g., Akers and Jensen, 2006; Moffitt, 1993), identity theory (see, e.g., Giordano, Cernkovich, and Rudolph, 2002; Maruna, 2001), reintegrative shaming theory (Braithwaite, 1989), and strain theory (see, e.g., Agnew, 1992; Merton, 1938). A theory that does not seem to hold much promise for explaining the victimization–termination link is self-control theory (Gottfredson and Hirschi, 1990). We explore the implications of these theories for understanding the victimization–termination link, in turn.

Deterrence theory argues that as sanctions associated with behavior increase, the prevalence of that behavior decreases, all else equal (Blumstein et al., 1986; Cook, 1980; Nagin, 1998; Paternoster, 1987; Pratt et al., 2006; Zimring and Hawkins, 1973). "Political sanctions" and "popular sanctions" (Bentham, 1988 [1789]: 24–5) have both been found to reduce crime (Cook, 1980; Nagin, 1998), but "physical sanctions" also influence criminal careers, at least in theory.

> Physical sanctions are . . . those consequences of behavior that follow automatically from it. . . . It turns out many criminal or deviant acts are sufficiently risky or inherently difficult that they are, at least to some extent, naturally limited. . . .

Such consequences of course tend to deter people from committing the acts in question. For example, intravenous drug use apparently produces great pleasure, but it also carries with it a large increase in the risk of accident, infection, permanent physiological damage, and death. (Gottfredson and Hirschi, 1990:6)

The idea that illicit drug dealing has inherent risks above and beyond those associated with "everyday" life is far from new (e.g., Goldstein et al., 1997; Levitt and Venkatesh, 2000; Reuter, MacCoun, and Murphy, 1990). These risks are sometimes related to conflicts over right and wrong, but the risks can also be physical (not moralistic) (see, e.g., Jacobs, 2000; Wright and Decker, 1994, 1997). If a drug dealer is victimized for reasons unrelated to social control, then that dealer has suffered a physical sanction or "predatory victimization" (see Jacques and Wright, 2008a). What this all suggests is that deterrence theorists and researchers may want to explicate how variability in victimization, both physical (predatory) and popular (moralistic), affects the costs, benefits, and prevalence of drug selling.[4]

Social learning theory explains behavior as the outcome of differential associations, definitions, imitation, and differential reinforcement (Akers and Jensen, 2006). As relates specifically to drug dealing, this theoretical perspective suggests that persons who use drugs and/or know drug dealers (differential association) and hold positive attitudes toward drug-related behavior (definitions) will learn how to deal drugs and then begin dealing themselves (imitation), and the costs and benefits of that behavior will determine persistence and desistance (differential reinforcement). Social learning theory would explain the empirical connection between victimization and termination as the consequence of differential reinforcement, or the sum of rewards and punishments that follow from a behavior. "Whether individuals will refrain from, or commit, a crime at any given time (and whether they will continue, or desist, from doing so in the future) depends on the balance of past, present, and anticipated future rewards and punishments for their actions" (Akers and Jensen, 2006: 39–40). Victimization, in the language of social learning theory, is a "punishment," and so, in theory, it reduces the probability of whatever behavior or context it is associated with in the mind of the victim. Whether victimization is followed by termination or persistence depends not only on the costs of the victimization but also on past learning experiences and structural constraints. Social learning theorists should stipulate the various hypotheses that emanate from this theoretical lens for explaining the victimization–termination link.

A less positivistic approach to understanding the victimization–termination link is identity theory (see, e.g., Giordano, Cernkovich, and Rudolph, 2002; Maruna, 2001). Building on labeling theory, phenomenology, and symbolic interactionism (see, e.g., Blumer, 1969; Lofland, 1969), this perspective asserts "that human life is essentially and fundamentally narrated and that understanding human interaction, therefore, requires some understanding of these stories" (Crewe and Maruna, 2006: 109). The focus of identity theory is how people tell the story of their own lives, how stories are made sense of, how stories are affected by structural constraints, and the effect of persons' stories on their subsequent behavior. Identity theorists may suggest that victimizations in the context of drug dealing facilitate cognitive transformations and narrative reconstructions. After victimization, dealers may begin to wonder: "Who am I, a drug dealer or a good kid? Can I be both at the same time? Should I continue selling drugs, or is it time for me to go off and make something of myself?" In this way, victimizations may lead to cognitive transformations and narrative reconstructions that produce identity change and the termination of drug dealing. To the degree that identity theorists take up the challenge of producing their own theory of the victimization–termination link, criminology will benefit.

Braithwaite's (1989: 102) theory of reiterative shaming argues that interdependency and communitarianism increase the likelihood that individuals will be susceptible to shaming, and when the shaming is reintegrative, as compared with stigmatizing, the chance of future crime is reduced because "disapproval is dispensed without eliciting a rejection of the disapprovers, so that the potentialities for future disapproval are not dismantled." Reintegrative shaming theorists typically have examined how the discovery and pronouncement of crime by the government leads to shaming situations and reintegration into the community. Differently, the story of Pete—the dealer who was robbed and then confronted by his family—shows that victimization can lead to shame and reintegration if it reveals the criminal behavior of the victim, and then the family or larger community responds with disapproval but also with "words or gestures of forgiveness" (1989: 100). Recall what Pete's mother said to her son after finding out about his drug-dealing career: "I can't believe this has happened, but it's alright, I still love you." Theorists working in the reintegrative shaming tradition may want to outline the implications of victimization for shame and its effect on subsequent crimes.

At first glance, Agnew's (1992, 2006) strain theory does not seem capable of explaining the victimization–termination link. According to strain theory, "a range of strains or stressors increase[s] the likelihood of crime. . . . These strains may involve the inability to achieve positively-valued goals . . . , the loss of positively-valued stimuli . . . , and the presentation of negatively-valued or aversive stimuli. These strains make people feel bad and they may cope through crime" (Agnew, 2006: 101). Any given victimization of a drug dealer can involve the application of negatively valued stimuli (pain or suffering) and the loss of positively valued stimuli (drugs or money) and may stop the dealer from achieving positively valued goals (buying something or getting high). The logic of this theory suggests that victimizations should result in more strain and, for that reason, more crime, such as violent retaliation or "working more hours" to make up for the loss (for empirical examples, see Topalli, Wright, and Fornango, 2002). However, Agnew (1992: 69) is careful to specify that under certain conditions strain will not lead to crime: "Behavioral coping may assume several forms. . . . Individuals . . . may seek to . . . *terminate* or *escape* from negative stimuli." Agnew notes that this prosocial coping strategy is more or less likely to occur under several psychological and social circumstances (1992: 71–4; for a test, see Broidy, 2001). Strain theorists should focus their attention on specifying the conditions conducive to "escape" from victimization through termination.

In contrast to the theories discussed, Gottfredson and Hirschi's (1990) self-control theory seems unable to explain the victimization–termination link. Self-control theory asserts that low self-control is the cause of crime and that self-control is invariant across the life course. The theory also posits that events analogous to crime, such as being victimized, are the outcome of low self-control. If self-control is invariant across time and is the cause of crime and victimization, then it logically follows that there can be no victimization–termination link because victimization cannot increase self-control and, thus, cannot lead to termination.[5] In short, the logic of self-control theory suggests that victimization has no influence on crime other than, perhaps, an incapacitative one.

Formal Testing

The foregoing discussion suggests that the theory we explicate in this article (also see Elder, 1985; Laub and Sampson, 2003), deterrence theory (Nagin, 1998; Paternoster, 1987), learning theory (Akers and Jensen, 2006; Moffitt, 1993, 2006), identity theory (Giordano, Cernkovich, and Rudolph, 2002; Maruna, 2001), reintegrative shaming theory (Braithwaite, 1989), and strain theory (Agnew, 1992, 2006) may "make sense" of the victimization–termination link, whereas self-control theory (Gottfredson and Hirschi, 1990) cannot. The incongruence of theories' predictions about the victimization–termination link is valuable to criminology because it provides an opportunity for evaluating which theory is "better" than the others: If victimization does not affect crime at all, then self-control theory gains credibility; if victimization produces termination under the conditions specified in this article or by deterrence, learning, identity, reintegrative shaming, or stain theories, then they gain credibility, and the assertions of self-control theory perhaps become more questionable.

Qualitative data are valuable in prompting new lines of theorizing, but quantitative data and statistical analyses are necessary to put hypotheses to the test. Unfortunately, data suitable for testing theories of the victimization–termination link are extremely limited (Lauritsen and Laub, 2007). Before researchers can test the effect of victimization on termination and the mechanisms that result in that empirical relationship (or inhibit it from occurring), it will be necessary to collect longitudinal data on social bonds and agency, costs and benefits of drug dealing, shaming in communities, strains experienced by dealers, and dealers' self-control. Given the existence of such data, it will then be possible—and we believe worthwhile—for researchers to use statistical analyses to determine whether, to what degree, and under what circumstances victimization has a significant and substantive effect on the termination of drug dealing and other forms of law-breaking.

NOTES

1. As we note toward the end of this article, the proposed theory is not necessarily the explanation of the victimization–termination link but is rather one of many theoretical options for making sense of the relationship.

2. A fourth factor in desistance and persistence in crime is "random developmental noise," which "conceives of development as the constant interaction between individuals and their environment, coupled with the factor of chance" (Laub, Sampson, and Sweeten, 2006: 323).

3. To protect the confidentiality of participants, we cannot reveal the name of the town. Accordingly, we have not provided a full reference for the source information on the town's statistics.

4. Among others, questions that could be addressed are as follows: 1) Does an increase in the objective severity and certainty (S&C) of victimization reduce drug dealing? 2) Does an increase in the objective S&C of victimization increase the perceived S&C of victimization? 3) Does an increase in the perceived S&C of victimization reduce drug selling? 4) Do the general (vicarious) and specific (personal) effects (Paternoster and Piquero, 1995; Stafford and Warr, 1993) of victimization differ, and if so, how? 5) Do victims experience a "resetting effect" (Pogarsky and Piquero, 2003), and how does this affect termination? And 6) What are the effects of political and popular sanctions on the S&C of victimization, and vice versa?

   Also note that the effect of of victimization on criminals is important for calculating the "costs" of victimization to society. As mentioned by Cohen, Miller, and Rossman: "it is possible that intentional injury will result in offsetting social benefits. For example, suppose a career criminal is robbed at gunpoint and fatally shot. The social cost of this murder might be partially offset by the reduced cost of other future crimes the victim was likely to commit." (1994, p. 75). The above insight suggests that "social benefits" flow from victimization of criminals to the degree that those events lead to the termination of crime.

5. Given that injury from the victimization does not physically incapacitate the criminal and thereby reduce opportunity.

REFERENCES

Agnew, Robert A. 1992. Foundation for a general strain theory of crime and delinquency. *Criminology* 30:47–87.

Agnew, Robert A. 2006. General strain theory: Current status and directions for future research. In *Taking Stock: The Status of Criminological Theory*, eds. Francis T. Cullen, John Paul Wright, and Kristie R. Blevins. New Brunswick, NJ: Transaction Publishers.

Akers, Ronald L., and Gary F. Jensen. 2006. The empirical status of social learning theory. In *Taking Stock: The Status of Criminological Theory*, eds. Francis T. Cullen, John Paul Wright, and Kristie R. Blevins. New Brunswick, NJ: Transaction Publishers.

Anderson, Elijah. 1999. *Code of the Street: Decency, Violence, and the Moral Life of the Inner City*. New York: W.W. Norton.

Baumgartner, Mary Pat. 1988. *The Moral Order of a Suburb*. New York: Oxford University Press.

Beccaria, Cesare. 1995 [1764]. *On Crimes and Punishments and Other Writings*. New York: Cambridge University Press.

Bennett, Trevor. 1986. A decision-making approach to opioid addiction. In *The Reasoning Criminal: Rational Choice Perspectives on Offending*, eds. Derek B. Cornish and Ronald V. Clarke. New York: Springer-Verlag.

Bentham, Jeremy. 1988 [1789]. *The Principles of Morals and Legislation*. Amherst, NY: Prometheus Books.

Black, Donald. 1983. Crime as social control. *American Sociological Review* 48:34–45.

Blumer, Herbert. 1969. *Symbolic Interactionism: Perspective and Method*. Englewood Cliffs, NJ: Prentice Hall.

Blumstein, Alfred, Jacqueline Cohen, Jeffrey A. Roth, and Christy A. Visher (Eds.). 1986. *Criminal Careers and Career Criminals*. Washington, DC: National Academy Press.

Braithwaite, John. 1989. *Crime, Shame and Reintegration*. New York: Cambridge University Press.

Broidy, Lisa M. 2001. A test of general strain theory. *Criminology* 39:9–36.

Cohen, Lawrence E., and Marcus Felson. 1979. Social change and crime rate trends: A routine activity approach. *American Sociological Review* 44:588–608.

Cohen, Mark A., Ted R. Miller, and Shelli B. Rossman. 1994. The costs and consequences of violent behavior in the United States. In *Understanding and Preventing Violence: Consequences and Control*, vol. 4, eds. Albert J. Reiss and Jeffrey A. Roth. Washington, DC: National Academy Press.

Cook, Philip. 1980. Research in criminal deterrence: Laying the groundwork for the second decade. In *Crime and Justice: A Review of Research*, vol. 2, eds. Norval Morris and Michael H. Tonry. Chicago, IL: University of Chicago Press.

Cooney, Mark. 1998. *Warriors and Peacemakers: How Third Parties Shape Violence*. New York: New York University Press.

Cooney, Mark, and Scott Phillips. 2002. Typologizing violence: A Blackian perspective. *International Journal of Sociology and Social Policy* 22:75–108.

Crewe, Ben, and Shadd Maruna. 2006. Self-narratives and ethnographic fieldwork. In *The Sage Handbook of Fieldwork*, eds. Dick Hobbs and Richard Wright. Thousand Oaks, CA: Sage.

Cusson, Maurice, and Pierre Pinsonneault. 1986. The decision to give up crime. In *The Reasoning Criminal: Rational Choice Perspectives on Offending*, eds. Derek B. Cornish and Ronald V. Clarke. New York: Springer-Verlag.

Decker, Scott H., and Janet L. Lauritsen. 2002. Leaving the gang. In *Gangs in America III*, ed. C. Ronald Huff. Thousand Oaks, CA: Sage.

Elder, Glen H., Jr. 1985. Perspectives on the life course. In *Life Course Dynamics*, ed. Glen H. Elder, Jr. Ithaca, NY: Cornell University Press.

Elder, Glen H., Jr., Monica Kirkpatrick Johnson, and Robert Crosnoe. 2003. The emergence and development of life course theory. In *Handbook of the Life Course*, eds. Jeylan T. Mortimer and Michael J. Shanahan. New York: Kluwer.

Giordano, Peggy C., Stephen A. Cernkovich, and Jennifer L. Rudolph. 2002. Gender, crime, and desistance: Toward a theory of cognitive transformation. *American Journal of Sociology* 107:990–1064.

Giordano, Peggy C., Ryan D. Schroeder, and Stephen A. Cernkovich. 2007. Emotions and crime over the life course: A neo-Meadian perspective on criminal continuity and change. *American Journal of Sociology* 112:1603–61.

Goldstein, Paul J., Henry H. Brownstein, Patrick J. Ryan, and Patricia A. Bellucci. 1997. Crack and homicide in New York City: A case study in the epidemiology of violence. In *Crack in America: Demon Drugs and Social Justice,* eds. Craig Reinarman and Harry G. Levine. Los Angeles: University of California Press.

Gottfredson, Michael R., and Travis Hirschi. 1990. *A General Theory of Crime.* Stanford, CA: Stanford University Press.

Haggård, Ulrika, Clara H. Gumpert, and Martin Grann. 2001. Against all odds: A qualitative follow-up of high-risk violent offenders who were not reconvicted. *Journal of Interpersonal Violence* 16:1048–65.

Hirschi, Travis. 1969. *Causes of Delinquency.* Berkeley: University of California Press.

Jacobs, Bruce A. 1999. *Dealing Crack.* Boston, MA: Northeastern University Press.

Jacobs, Bruce A. 2000. *Robbing Drug Dealers.* New York: Aldine de Gruyter.

Jacobs, Bruce A., and Richard Wright. 2006. *Street Justice: Retaliation in the Criminal Underworld.* New York: Cambridge University Press.

Jacques, Scott, and Richard Wright. 2008a. The relevance of peace to studies of drug market violence. *Criminology* 46:221–54.

Jacques, Scott, and Richard Wright. 2008b. Intimacy with outlaws: The role of relational distance in recruiting, paying, and interviewing underworld research participants. *Journal of Research in Crime and Delinquency* 45:22–38.

Kornhauser, Ruth Rosner. 1978. *Social Sources of Delinquency.* Chicago, IL: University of Chicago Press.

Laub, John H., and Robert J. Sampson. 1993. Turning points in the life course: Why change matters to the study of crime. *Criminology* 31:301–25.

Laub, John H., and Robert J. Sampson. 2001. Understanding desistance from crime. In *Crime and Justice: A Review of Research,* vol. 28, ed. Michael H. Tonry. Chicago, IL: University of Chicago Press.

Laub, John H., and Robert J. Sampson. 2003. *Shared Beginnings, Divergent Lives: Delinquent Boys to Age 70.* Cambridge, MA: Harvard University Press.

Laub, John H., Robert J. Sampson, and Gary A. Sweeten. 2006. Assessing Sampson and Laub's life-course theory of crime. In *Taking Stock: The Status of Criminological Theory,* vol. 15, *Advances in Criminological Theory,* eds. Francis T. Cullen, John Paul Wright, and Kristie R. Blevins. New Brunswick, NJ: Transaction.

Lauritsen, Janet L., and John H. Laub. 2007. Understanding the link between victimization and offending: New reflections on an old idea. In *Crime Prevention Studies,* vol. 22, eds. Mike Hough and Mike Maxfield. Monsey, NY: Criminal Justice Press.

Levitt, Steven, and Sudhir Alladi Venkatesh. 2000. An economic analysis of a drug-selling gang's finances. *Quarterly Journal of Economics* 115:755–89.

Lofland, John. 1969. *Deviance and Identity.* Englewood Cliffs, NJ: Prentice-Hall.

Maruna, Shadd. 2001. *Making Good: How Ex-Convicts Reform and Rebuild their Lives.* Washington, DC: American Psychological Association.

Merton, Robert K. 1938. Social structure and anomie. *American Sociological Review* 3:672–82.

Moffitt, Terrie E. 1993. "Life-course-persistent" and "adolescence-limited" antisocial behavior: A developmental taxonomy. *Psychological Review* 100:674–701.

Moffitt, Terrie E. 2006. A review of research on the taxonomy of life- course persistent versus adolescence-limited antisocial behavior. In *Taking Stock: The Status of Criminological Theory,* vol. 15, eds. Francis T. Cullen, John Paul Wright, and Kristie R. Blevins. New Brunswick, NJ: Transaction.

Mortimer, Jeylan T., and Michael J. Shanahan (eds). 2003. *Handbook of the Life Course.* New York: Kluwer.

Nagin, Daniel S. 1998. Criminal deterrence research at the outset of the twenty-first century. In *Crime and Justice: A Review of Research,* vol. 23, ed. Michael H. Tonry. Chicago, IL: University of Chicago Press.

Nagin, Daniel S. 2007. Moving choice to center stage in criminological research and theory. *Criminology* 45:259–72.

Paternoster, Raymond. 1987. The deterrent effect of the perceived certainty and severity of punishment: A review of the evidence and issues. *Justice Quarterly* 4:173–217.

Paternoster, Raymond, and Alex R. Piquero. 1995. Reconceptualizing deterrence: An empirical test of personal and vicarious experiences. *Journal of Research in Crime and Delinquency* 32:251–86.

Piquero, Alex R., David P. Farrington, and Alfred Blumstein. 2003. The criminal career paradigm. In *Crime and Justice: A Review of Research,* vol. 30, ed. Michael H. Tonry. Chicago, IL: University of Chicago Press.

Pogarsky, Greg, and Alex R. Piquero. 2003. Can punishment encourage offending? Investigating the "resetting" effect. *Journal of Research in Crime and Delinquency* 40:95–120.

Pratt, Travis C., Francis T. Cullen, Kristie R. Blevins, Leah E. Daigle, and Tamara D. Madensen. 2006. The empirical status of deterrence theory: A meta-analysis. In *Taking Stock: The Status of Criminological Theory,* vol. 15, *Advances in Criminological Theory,* eds. Francis T. Cullen, John Paul Wright, and Kristie R. Blevins. New Brunswick, NJ: Transaction.

Reuter, Peter, Robert MacCoun, and Patrick Murphy. 1990. *Money from Crime: A Study of the Economics of Drug Dealing in Washington, D.C.* Santa Monica, CA: RAND Corporation.

Sampson, Robert J. 1986. Crime in cities: The effects of formal and informal social control. In *Crime and Justice: Communities and Crime,* vol. 8, eds. Albert J. Reiss, Jr., and Michael H. Tonry. Chicago, IL: University of Chicago Press.

Sampson, Robert J., and John H. Laub. 1993. *Crime in the Making: Pathways and Turning Points Through Life.* Cambridge, MA: Harvard University Press.

Sampson, Robert J., and John H. Laub. 1997. A life-course theory of cumulative disadvantage and the stability of delinquency. In *Developmental Theories of Crime and Delinquency,* vol. 7, ed. Terence P. Thornberry. New Brunswick, NJ: Transaction.

Sampson, Robert J., and John H. Laub. 2005. A general age-graded theory of crime: Lessons learned and the future of life-course criminology. In *Integrated Developmental & Life-Course Theories of Offending,* ed. David P. Farrington. New Brunswick, NJ: Transaction.

Sampson, Robert J., and William J. Wilson. 1995. Toward a theory of race, crime, and urban inequality. In *Crime and Inequality,* eds. John Hagan and Ruth Peterson. Stanford, CA: Stanford University Press.

Shaw, Clifford R. 1930. *The Jack-Roller: A Delinquent Boy's Own Story.* Chicago, IL: University of Chicago Press.

Shaw, Clifford R. 1931. *The Natural History of a Delinquent Career.* Chicago, IL: University of Chicago Press.

Shaw, Clifford R. 1938. *Brothers in Crime.* Chicago, IL: University of Chicago Press.

Shover, Neal. 1996. *Great Pretenders: Pursuits and Careers of Persistent Thieves.* Boulder, CO: Westview.

Stafford, Mark C., and Mark Warr. 1993. A reconceptualization of general and specific deterrence. *Journal of Research in Crime and Delinquency* 30:123–35.

Sutherland, Edwin H. 1937. *The Professional Thief.* Chicago, IL: University of Chicago Press.

Thomas, William I., and Florian Znaniecki. 1918–1920. *The Polish Peasant in Europe and America,* vols. 1–5. New York: Knopf.

Topalli, Volkan, Richard Wright, and Robert Fornango. 2002. Drug dealers, robbery and retaliation: Vulnerability, deterrence and the contagion of violence. *British Journal of Criminology* 42:337–51.

Wilson, William J. 1987. *The Truly Disadvantaged: The Inner City, the Underclass, and Public Policy.* Chicago, IL: University of Chicago Press.

Wilson, William J. 1996. *When Work Disappears: The World of the New Urban Poor.* New York: Vintage.

Wright, Richard, and Scott Decker. 1994. *Burglars on the Job.* Boston, MA: Northeastern University Press.

Wright, Richard, and Scott Decker. 1997. *Armed Robbers in Action.* Boston, MA: Northeastern University Press.

Zimring, Franklin E., and Gordon J. Hawkins. 1973. *Deterrence: The Legal Threat in Crime Control.* Chicago, IL: University of Chicago Press.